The Canadian Hidden Job Market Directory

Canada's Best Directory
For Finding The Unadvertised Jobs

7th Edition

SENTOR MEDIA INC.

Toronto, Ontario

Published By:
Sentor Media Inc.
388 Richmond Street West, Suite 1120
Toronto, Ontario
M5V 3P1
Tel: 416-971-5090
Fax: 416-971-5857
E-mail: info@sentormedia.com
Internet: www.sentormedia.com
Bookstore: www.careerbookstore.ca

Kevin Makra, Publisher
Tristan Block, Editor
Natalie Hosmer, Editor

Cover Design: Craig Francis Design

Printed in Canada by Printcrafters

Library and Archives Canada Cataloguing in Publication

The Canadian hidden job market directory.

"Canada's best directory for finding unadvertised jobs."
Annual.
7th ed.-
Continues: Canadian job directory, ISSN 1491-2821.
ISSN 1719-2218
ISBN 978-1-896324-32-6 (7th edition)

1. Job hunting--Canada--Directories.
2. Job hunting--Canada--Information resources.

HF5382.75.C3C36   331.12'802571   C2006-901478-7

Table of Contents

Tired of searching for a job?

Find all the career information you need in one convenient place.

careerBOOKSTORE.ca
great books, better prices.

**With hundreds of books at your fingertips,
your job search just got easier.**

we have what you are looking for at CareerBookstore.ca

Introduction

Up to 80% of all jobs are found through the hidden job market!

Welcome to our 7th edition of **The Canadian Hidden Job Market Directory** (previously known as The Canadian Job Directory). This practical book shows you how to find jobs *before* they are advertised. Imagine being the first one there when new opportunities appear. No crowds of other applicants ahead of you; just the job, the employer – and you! That's the power of the hidden job market.

Want to learn its secrets? We have just what you need inside, where you'll discover the following:

- how to network and tap into the hidden job market like a pro
- information on nearly 1,000 potential employers
- profiles of recruiting agencies across Canada
- industry and professional associations for networking
- career resources on the Internet to boost your marketability
- trade directories with valuable industry and employer information
- sector councils for a wide variety of industries

Find out why you should look beyond the classified ads and online job banks – where the competition is fierce. You have a much better chance of finding work by networking into the hidden job market as well. It's all about knowing how to be in the right place at the right time; face-to-face with decision makers at the companies you've always wanted to work for.

Use proven methods that career experts have been sharing with their clients for years. You will vastly expand your contact network, gain helpful insights into your field, and access leads you may never hear about otherwise. Plus, you can shorten your job search by uncovering more, and better, opportunities.

We hope that you will have a look at Sentor Media Inc.'s other books as well:

For Job Seekers and Career Changers:

- **Get Wired, You're Hired!**—The best-selling Canadian Internet Job Search Guide

For Student and Recent Grad Job Hunters:

- **Hire Power – The Ultimate Canada Student Employment Guide**, for landing that vital first job
- **The Canadian Summer Job Directory**, designed especially for students

For Students still in School:

- **Guide to Professional Programs in Canada**, exclusively for university students
- Ten Way's to Straight A's, our guide to studying and succeeding in school

Information on these titles (and many more useful career books) can be found at careerbookstore.ca

---

Good luck in your job search!

How To Use This Book

The Canadian Hidden Job Market Directory helps you uncover employment opportunities that haven't been advertised yet. Use this book to round out your overall work search; one that includes answering job ads, working with recruiters, sending out targeted mailings to potential employers, posting your resumé strategically and networking to find unpublished positions.

Apply each section in this book to its best advantage. Employers, recruiters, industry and professional associations, career resources on the Internet, trade directories and sector councils are all avenues that can open doors to opportunities you might not find elsewhere. Leverage them all to boost your efforts!

> The address indicated within each company and recruiter profile is generally the firm's head office, unless otherwise specified. Although only one address appears, this does not mean that individuals should not apply elsewhere. To get the most out of your job search, individuals are encouraged to check for, and apply to, local branches or regional offices.

Part I: FINDING THE HIDDEN JOBS

What exactly is the hidden job market? How do you network to reveal unpublished opportunities? Read this section for details on "warm" marketing, "cold" marketing, and which should be used when. For instance, networking is *not* about calling everyone you know and asking them for a job. You will also learn:

- the best ways to leverage, and expand, your contact base
- three types of networking: for information, for contacts, and for meetings with hiring managers
- how to turn cold calling into targeted messaging
- where to post and distribute your resumé for maximum effect and minimal security risk
- how to work with recruiters and which types you should be contacting

Learn the steps career professionals share with their clients to open doors at employers in your target market.

Part II: DIRECTORIES OF RESOURCES

We have provided you with a number of directories in this book that list resources according to specific categories. Skim each one to start with and choose the sections that will further your job search most.

Firms & Organizations

Nearly 1,000 major employers are listed alphabetically here within their industry sectors. Each profile contains the organization's name, address, telephone and fax numbers, a brief description of what they do, and their Internet address. But don't stop there! By conducting research on many more companies, and clearly understanding your career field, you'll have a far greater chance of finding success in the job market See our Directory section, "Career Resources on the Internet" for research tools.

Reminder: The companies listed here do not necessarily have current job openings. This is a directory of selected major employers across the country, not a listing of jobs available at present. Also, change is constant in the world of work so be sure to stay up to date. For instance, if you plan on applying for a job at a specific employer, call their switchboard or review their website for contact information and related details.

Recruiters

Recruiters are arranged alphabetically by the region of their head office. Their profiles contain the name of the recruiting firm, address, telephone and fax numbers, plus e-mail and Internet addresses, if available. Note that recruiters (also known as employment agencies, personnel firms and headhunters) may have access to some jobs that are not published elsewhere. Although they account, on average, for fewer than 15% of all the jobs available, they are a necessary part of your work search.

Industry and Professional Associations

Industry and professional associations are listed alphabetically within their specific sectors. Each of their profiles contains the association's name, address, telephone and fax numbers, and contact name(s). Their e-mail and Internet addresses are also provided, if applicable. These associations are great places to network with people in your field, learn about trends and new developments, and find out about trade shows/conferences/exhibits you could attend.

Career Resources on the Internet

Career resources on the Internet are listed alphabetically by category. Each career site profile includes the site's name, Internet address, and a brief description of the site's function and benefits. Contact information regarding the site is also included where possible. We've provided the best starting points, career planning and exploration, education, volunteering and employment-related research resources to get you on your way.

Trade Directories

Trade and business directories are listed alphabetically. Each listing contains the name of the directory, a brief description of its contents, and contact information on the publishers of the book. The great thing about trade directories is that they point you to dozens, if not hundreds, of potential employers in your industry and region. By obtaining detailed information on a company's annual sales, number of employees, key products and services, etc., you can match them to your work preferences.

Sector Councils

An alphabetical listing of some of the more prominent sector councils in Canada, which are organizations that bring together representatives from business, labour, education, and other professional groups in order to address industry-wide issues. They are sources of information on the industries, companies and organizations you might want to work in.

Our publications are always a "work-in-progress." Any feedback or suggestions you have to improve this book is always appreciated. If you are an organization or firm that would like to be included in an upcoming edition, please do not hesitate to contact us.

In addition, please note that while we have worked hard to make this book as accurate as possible, keep in mind that inevitably some of the information will have changed. This is especially true regarding telephone/fax numbers and specific web page addresses. We would appreciate receiving information on any corrections or omissions you find.

PART I

FINDING THE HIDDEN JOBS

Finding The Hidden Jobs

By now you have probably heard many times that up to 80% of all available jobs are not advertised. These openings make up what is commonly known as the "hidden job market," which consists of positions that become available without being widely published. These types of situations are all around us. For example, someone may quit their job unannounced, leaving an immediate opening. Or else a company might secure a major new client and suddenly need to hire quickly. These types of examples form the hidden job market – positions that are filled by, or created for, candidates who come to the employer's attention through employee recommendation, referrals from trusted associates, recruiters, direct inquiries, and the networking efforts of a job seeker.

Looking for work in the classifieds or career section of your local newspaper, scouring the online job banks, and applying to positions posted on the websites of employers are common ways of trying to land an advertised job. However, when responding to one of these "want ads," you're typically competing with hundreds, or possibly thousands of other applicants for the same position. Employers can afford to be picky, and your chances of getting noticed by them are usually quite slim. That's why including a hidden job market search is so much more effective than if all you did was spend your days answering ads. You will be contending with fewer applicants, and you will give employers the opportunity to meet you face-to-face so that they get to know you more informally than in a standard job interview. Tapping into this hidden market is your best-odds approach for securing meaningful employment in today's competitive economy. There are a number of ways to find work that has not been publicized.

METHODS OF TAPPING INTO THE HIDDEN JOB MARKET

Regardless of how you approach it, your search for work is an exercise in marketing yourself. So there are two basic paths in terms of job hunting for positions that are unpublished. One is called **Cold Marketing**, which simply means that the employers you apply to do not know you previously, and thus you are "going in cold." The other type is called **Warm Marketing**. As its name implies, here your path has been paved for you by someone who knows the employer beforehand. As a result, you receive a "warm welcome" instead of a cooler reception.

Cold Marketing is all about getting your resumé in front of people who can hire you. Warm Marketing is all about getting you in front of people who can hire you at the places you'd like to work for. What follows is a quick review of the tactics you can use in each approach.

1. TECHNIQUES TO USE FOR "COLD" MARKETING

One of the appeals of Cold Marketing is that it is relatively easy to do. After all, sending out unsolicited resumés and working with recruiters who have access to jobs in your field is fairly uncomplicated. The problem is that most job seekers focus the bulk of their efforts in precisely these two areas – either because it's all they've ever learned to do, or because it feels fairly comfortable. That's why you end up competing with countless others. In spite of this, there is value in applying some of your valuable time to these methods.

Applying to Firms & Organizations, No Job Advertised

The single most popular strategy used in a hidden market job search is to send out resumés with cover letters (either electronically or by post) to as many potential employers as you can, even though you don't know whether they are hiring or not at the time of application. This is a very low yield tactic: on average, maybe 5% of available work is found this way. When it does succeed, it's usually because some firms are always on the lookout for qualified candidates, while others may happen to have a posting that suits you right about the time your application arrives.

The **Firms & Organizations** section of this book lists a cross-section of major companies across the country. Although it is not clear whether they will be hiring in the near future or not, remember that this is why they call it a "hidden" job market. However, don't bother blindly applying to every employer listed (known as "mass mailing") or you'll end up with a stack of rejection letters and an e-mail inbox filled with "thanks, but no thanks" messages. Instead, apply to companies that most interest you, and to those that fit your career plans. Use a targeted system: do research on the employer (learn more about this in our **Trade Directories Index**); find out the names, titles and spelling of the people who do the hiring; customize your letter to the employer and position you are applying for; and after you send in your submission follow up with a phone call a week or so later to ask if they've received your material, and would they like to meet with you face-to-face to further discuss the opportunity.

The flip side of applying directly to employers is to post your resumé on websites where employers go to search for candidates. This is another of the so-called "passive job search" techniques: rather than actively pursuing firms you have targeted, you're advertising your availability to a wide audience and hoping at least one will take the bait. Not surprisingly, this method also accounts for only 5% or so of all the jobs that are open. The most popular online resumé banks in Canada are Workopolis.com, Monster.ca, Working.com and JobBoom.com (which is mainly Québec but expanding fast). See our **Career Resources on the Internet Index** for related sites and more.

Recruiters

On average, about 15% of all new jobs are found through recruiters. This can fluctuate dramatically depending on your industry, position level, occupation, location and salary. At certain pay scales, as with administrative assistants and accounting clerks, the 'temporary personnel agencies' account for a large share of all placements. People in the performing arts, scientists and tradespeople, however, are largely left to their own devices.

Turn to our **Recruiters Index** for a representative list of employment agencies across the country. Before you do, have a look at the following articles on how to deal effectively with recruiters, written by our executive editor, Mark Swartz. They first appeared in his Toronto Star column and reveal some ins and outs you might want know about.

Part One: What You Need To Know About Recruiters

Pop quiz: What's the difference between recruiting, placement and executive search? If you're like most folks, you might think these terms are interchangeable. But when you're hooking up with a headhunter, it pays to know exactly what type to seek out.

Search firms are an important piece of a wide-ranging job hunt. All told, they give you access to maybe 10 – 20% of all available positions. In general there are three types of firms to be aware of. Roughly speaking, they're split in terms of the salary levels they deal with.

Employment / Temp Agencies and Personnel Firms

This is the entry-level portion of the spectrum. Names like Kelly Services, Drake, Ajilon Pinstripe (owned by Addeco), Manpower and Randstad come to mind. These companies specialize in filling positions in the under $50,000's range. Administrative assistants, customer service representatives and data entry clerks are typical assignments.

Firms like the ones just mentioned often, though not exclusively, place candidates as "temps." You're sent to an employer for a fixed term, say three weeks to three months or so. During this time you get paid an hourly fee by the placement agency, not the employer. The agency earns its money by charging the employer for your time—up to double what you end up receiving.

Temp positions can sometimes turn into longer term or even permanent roles. You should speak to the agency about its policies, and your goals, before accepting a temp assignment. This way there'll be no confusion about how to manage the arrangement.

Recruiting Firms

Moving up a notch on the ladder brings us to recruiters, also known as placement consultants and search groups. If you're pulling down from the mid $50,000's up to $100,000, this is who you would approach. There are hundreds of search companies to choose from. Some are specialists. Others are generalists.

The way to start finding the right ones for you is to use a directory (such as the one in this book). Your local library should have a copy of The Directory of Canadian Recruiters, from Continental Records Company (**www.directoryofrecruiters.com**). You can also try searching **www.employmentagencies.ca**. Yet another route is to visit one of the big job banks, like Monster or Workopolis, find the jobs you'd like to apply for, and note the agencies who may have posted those positions.

Locating a recruiter is the easy part. Getting one to give you the time of day is like getting a minority government to work harmoniously. They are notorious for ignoring your calls, e-mails or rocks with messages hurled through windows. It's because of how they work:

they're accountable to the employers that pay them—not to you (if a recruiter ever asks you for payment, run for the hills, but not before reporting them to the Better Business Bureau). They can only place people for job orders they've manage to scrounge. And they only look at resumés that closely match existing assignments.

How then to grab the attention of a busy recruiter? You can start by sending in your resumé to firms that have postings in your field. Try calling first to get the name and e-mail address of the person on the gigs you're applying to. Then attach your perfected, third party reviewed resumé to a brief e-mail describing your background and interest in the position. Follow up within three business days with a polite phone call—"Just checking to see if you've received my application. I realize you're busy but have you had a chance to review it yet? I'd like to discuss opportunities with you further."

A more effective approach is to get someone the recruiter knows to refer you in to them (a Warm Marketing technique). Nothing beats starting your cover letter along the lines of "You may remember Cheryl, who you placed last year at my company. She says you really helped her out and recommended I speak to you directly." Unless of course you've hired people yourself and have good contacts with search firms.

One note of caution: find out from the start if the recruiter is working on "contingency" or "retainer." A retainer search means the recruiter is likely the exclusive agent for this particular job. Contingency means a whole bunch of firms will probably compete to fill the position. If you're working with multiple agencies, make sure you insist each one notifies you before you allow them to send out your resumé. The last thing you want is for your application to end up on some H.R. manager's desk three or four times, all from different search firms. It could put you out of the running if there's potential for dispute over who got there first.

Executive Search

This is the stratosphere of recruiting. Senior executives and highly paid professionals are welcome at such headhunters as Caldwell Partners International, Heidrick & Struggle and Korn/Ferry. Usually Directors and V.P.'s are the starting point, right up to CEO's. It's an exclusive group. Yet even at this level the odds of getting your calls returned are daunting. Best bet is to network your way in via other players. Otherwise, make yourself a known quantity by getting published in trade magazines, speaking at industry conferences, or getting quoted by the media.

Regardless of the type of search firm you go after, there are certain rules of the game. For instance, always treat the recruiter like they're the employer – because they're your gateway to the true decision makers. Be on your best game with them whether e-mailing, speaking by phone or meeting face-to-face. Also, if you agree to go on an interview, even if your heart's not in it, prepare to shine. Otherwise you make your recruiter (and yourself, of course) look less than professional. Then try getting them to send you out ever again.

A few more hints: Don't be belligerent or bossy with recruiters. They usually have plenty of other candidates to choose from. Respond to their messages promptly. Be polite and enthusiastic. And if you really want to get on their good side, give them the names of other strong candidates you know who are looking for a new job. The bottom line is that search firms should be used strategically in your job hunt. If you treat them right and they send you on appropriate interviews, you've broadened your chances for success. You also have the right to walk if you're being treated unfairly. The end game is for both of you to come out happy: you with a great new position, them with bucks in their pockets. Just remember it's up to you, not them, to make sure things proceed apace.

Part Two: Games Recruiters Play—And How to Win Them

You're sitting nervously in the reception area of a company you've spent hours researching, in preparation for today's interview. Hands shaking slightly you barely notice the magazine you're thumbing through. Now it's show time. Only the session doesn't go as planned. The job they're describing is far too junior for you, not at all like your recruiter described. So what's going on here?

In the world of headhunting, it might be a simple miscommunication, or else a tactic known as the old "bait and switch." The recruiter you're working with may have knowingly sent you on a job interview you're overqualified for—in the hopes you're desperate enough to take it. If you do, the employer can win (they get a better employee than they bargained for), and the recruiter scores (they get paid for placing you). But you end up with less money and a lesser title than you might have earned elsewhere, plus a position that might bore you to tears within six months.

If this doesn't strike you as fair, that's because it isn't. Not that job seekers are always forthright in their dealings with recruiters. Headhunters I've spoken to complain about candidates (job seekers) who lie through their teeth, don't show up as promised at interviews, show up but are embarrassingly unprepared, or gratefully accept a job then fail to appear their first day because they've found something else behind the recruiter's back.

Spotting The Games Recruiters Play

Like any industry, recruiting has many highly ethical players and a host of barracudas. Knowing how to spot when you're being manipulated saves you time and frustration. Here are some of the main ways less trustworthy recruiters jerk people around.

The "Oreo Cookie" Maneuver. In this little scam, you get sent to a job interview, although the recruiter knows you'll never get the offer here. Then he sends in a top notch candidate who knocks the employer's socks off. Following that, he sends another job seeker in who, like you, isn't a perfect fit for this specific assignment. You've both been served up as the outer crust surrounding a creamy, delicious centre. Guess who gets left on the shelf.

"Gone Fishing." Ever responded to one of those "blind ads" in the paper? That's where the job sounds great but there's zero info about who the company is. Likely as not, this ad may have been posted by a recruiter looking to fill their database with potential candidates. They're happy to get your resumé along with the hundreds of others they'll

likely receive. Then they can call employers and boast about all the great candidates they have. Mind you, if they do find a job for you this way, you end up better off. But wouldn't you rather have control over who gets your resumé and where it ends up?

"Under Pressure." I once found myself using a notoriously unprincipled recruiter back in my corporate marketing days. I'd heard stories about him but figured I could deal with whatever he threw my way. Anyway, after one of the job interviews he'd arranged for me, he called me to ask how it went. On a Friday night at 10:30 p.m.. Then again early Saturday morning. That afternoon and evening too. Sunday morning again, to see if I'd made my mind up yet. Two more times that day to harangue me and threaten that if I didn't take the job he'd blacklist me from all of his employers. Then a Monday morning wake up and make up call: "You're terrific, Mark. I guarantee you'll love this job. Your wife will love you more for taking it." Adoration aside, I turned the offer down because it definitely wasn't right for me. Funny thing is a while back this same guy left a voicemail for me, out of the blue, after a fifteen year absence. Probably still hoping I'll accept the job he'd been pushing!

"Hold The Mayo." A recruiter acts as a gatekeeper. They get paid by the employer and may have little loyalty to you. So you might get held back from certain opportunities without ever knowing it. For instance, a headhunter might believe you'd be a great fit for job A. He feels you could easily do job B as well, even though it's not quite what you're hoping for. The recruiter has another candidate who'd be great at job A too, but wouldn't match the company culture at job B. So the other candidate is sent on the interview and snags job A. All you're ever told about is job B, which you end up taking because really, it's not so bad, and after all you've been looking for months now and the kids are fed up having to eat Kraft dinner every night. Meanwhile the recruiter gets two separate commissions and is celebrating with champagne at the local upscale diner.

Managing the Recruiter

Fortunately there are ways to stay on top of recruiters and reduce the chances of getting exploited. Like insisting that your approval is necessary before your resumé is sent anywhere. Refusing to go on interviews if you know that the company or position is very likely not to be a fit. Limiting your applications to blind ads. And approaching as many employers as you can on your own, thus reducing your reliance on middlemen. If you're being harassed or pressured, you can hang up or leave the recruiter's office. Follow up with a warning that you'll use another agency if this persists. Tell the recruiter you'll spread the word to every single one of your friends and colleagues about their abusiveness. And report especially offensive or illegal behaviour to your local Consumer and Commercial Relations Ministry and Better Business Bureau.

Bare in mind that not all recruiters are bad. In fact, many have built a reputation for honesty and fairness. The idea is to find ones you feel reasonably comfortable with. Inquire around and have friends or colleagues refer you to the better firms. Ask headhunters for references (they'll be requesting yours soon enough). And walk away from a bad situation, because there are many headhunters to choose from. If you do find a good one, reward them with honesty, enthusiasm and referrals. And stay in touch over the years. Because a recruiter who's your ally might be just the edge you need to land

Industry Associations

Few people appreciate just how much an industry association in your chosen field can help you connect with the hidden job market. Industry and professional groups (also known collectively as trade associations) are set up to advance a specific industry or profession and can provide a wealth of information to the job seeker. When you become a member of one of these groups, or go to their meetings, they can often provide industry and company literature, let you know who the decision makers are in the industry, and give great insight into how things really operate and who the key players are.

Many associations provide seminars, and have guest speakers who are influential in the industry. They may also sponsor trade shows, conferences and exhibits you can attend to gather insights and meet potential employers who are displaying their goods and services. The most important advantage of industry associations is that they provide a built-in way for you to network with key individuals. Remember, networking leads to opportunities. It is not a short term process, but it's a great way of marketing yourself. You'll learn more about this when you get to "Warm Marketing," below. In the meantime, visit our section on **Industry Associations** for a sampling of organizations that may be relevant to you.

Career Sites On The Internet

While the Internet is used for many purposes in today's information age, its vast opportunities have brought the job search to a new advanced level. Job seekers can now gather company information cheaply, contact employers quickly, and apply to firms online. As boundaries for the new labour market are expanding and becoming international in scope, the Internet is bringing job seekers and employers together in more and more ways.

In order to compete with others in the job market, it's crucial that you incorporate the Internet as part of your 'hidden job' strategy. There are many sites for career planning and exploration, education and employment-related research. You may even be interested in participating in various job newsgroups (discussion groups) online. Whatever you do, take advantage of this wide reaching medium. Our book, "Get Wired, You're Hired!" goes into great depth on how to get the most from job hunting via the Internet.

Trade Directories

There are many different trade and business directories that can vastly expand your job search. They contain detailed company information, along with industry related facts and data. Be sure to use these directories when researching potential employers. They're a wonderful way to add to your target list of employer you would like to work for. Make sure to search according to your work preferences, such as how far the company is from your home, whether it's a large or small firm, how long it's been in business, who the parent company is, and other such factors. Also, if you know the name of a firm in a particular industry, you can find that company's SIC (Standard Industrial Code), then search for many of its competitors – increasing your hidden job possibilities!

2. TECHNIQUE TO USE FOR "WARM" MARKETING: NETWORKING

For most readers, networking is the most important tactic you will use in searching for employment. Knowing how to do so effectively will shorten your job search and provide you with information, leads, and opportunities others won't have access to.

What Exactly Is Networking?

There are many misconceptions surrounding the concept of networking. Did you know, for instance, that there are three distinct types? Or that there are certain protocols to be followed if you hope to overcome resistance? The following information guides you through some of the fundamentals on how to use your contacts to lead you to job opportunities.

To better grasp the true nature of networking, it is helpful to start with what it is not. When most people think of networking, they envision picking up the phone, calling everyone they know, announcing they're out of work, and asking their contacts if they know of any job leads. This is not the right way to network.

Networking is NOT:

- Calling the people you know and simply asking for work.
- Speaking only to the people in your immediate circle.
- Making cold calls to strangers.

At its most fundamental level, networking is drawing on your system of existing contacts (that is, the people you already know), gaining what you can from each one, and then selectively getting referred to the people they know - hoping that at each point along the way you will be helped in some manner to ultimately meet with hiring managers and decision makers at employers you'd like to work for.

The Three Types of Networking

Not all networking is the same. There are three fundamental types, and each one should be used to accomplish specific goals, as follows.

Goal A: To connect with people you know and increase your circle of contacts

Type of Networking: Contact mining

The term "contact mining" refers to getting in touch with people you already know. These could be friends, family, former colleagues, supervisors, suppliers, members of your social clubs or religious organizations, etc. The common factor is that you already have some sort of relationship with each of these individuals.

You approach them first because there is likely a bond of trust and familiarity between you. People who know you and like you are far more inclined to help you than are complete strangers. Maybe a friend of yours knows about an opening they're about to announce at his or her place of work. Or perhaps your insurance broker or cousin-in-law can refer you to someone they know who can assist you in some way, either by providing information, news of openings, or by referring you to other people that they know.

The Canadian Hidden Job Market Directory

This is what makes networking so powerful. Instead of making cold calls to strangers, you end up getting in touch with people you know directly, or with those your existing contacts have referred you to. The reason that the new people will agree to speak to you (or preferably meet with you face-to-face), is because your contact is essentially vouching for you.

Goal B: Learning about an industry or profession

Type of Networking: Information meetings

In this sort of networking you are not yet seeking a job. It's before that, where you are going out to meet people solely to gain knowledge. For instance, you might get in touch with a person who knows all about the key trends in your industry. Or, you may reach someone else who is familiar with the major players in your field, and can share this knowledge with you to help focus your search. Information networking is used extensively when making a career change. It is also a way to meet people who can tell you what it's really like to work in the industry or profession you're considering. And you don't have to be nervous because there isn't pressure to get hired.

Goal C: Meeting people who can hire you, or else refer you to others who can

Type of Networking: Pre-employment meetings

This mode is all about getting hired. You go out to meet a variety of people with the expectation that one of them will actually have work for you at some point, or can at least refer you to others who do. You don't actually state this directly though, or else you may close the door before you have a chance to meet the person. Instead you ask the contact for advice, and try to meet with them face-to-face so that they can get to know you better.

Employment networking can be further broken down into two specific types: *general networking*, where you try to meet as many new people as possible in order to expand your network; and *targeted networking*, where you attempt to get referred to decision makers at employers you have targeted – in particular the ones that closely match your work preferences.

The Process of Networking, Step-By-Step

Regardless of which type of networking you're ready for, you should start by doing a bit of strategic planning. That's because, as with any other process, there are progressive steps to achieve your goals. Here, quickly, are the primary stages in planning your networking campaign:

1. Create a comprehensive contact list.
2. Sort the list according to how people can help you.
3. Decide on whom to contact first.
4. Put together a brief script before you make your first round of calls.
5. Make your calls and set up appointments.
6. Prepare for your phone calls or face-to-face meetings.
7. Follow up professionally.

1. Create a comprehensive contact list.

Begin by writing down the names of all the people you can think of (family, friends, former colleagues and bosses, suppliers who've done work for you, professionals such as lawyers, doctors, bankers, etc.). Keep in mind that the people you already know have contact networks of their own, and that this is what you're eventually aiming to tap into.

2. Sort the list according to how people can help you.

Once you've put together a list of all the relevant people you know, it's time to think about how each one might help you. Generally, there are three categories of assistance that a contact can provide:

- *Information*

Does your colleague from your previous job know how much people in competing companies earn? Can that person you met at your social club fill you in on what's happening in your industry? If so, get in touch with them.

- *Employment Leads*

    Some of your contacts might be able to direct you to other people they know who are in the midst of hiring, or who know of others who are.

- *Referrals to Hiring Managers/Decision Makers at Employers You Have Targeted.*

    At some point, it will be time to focus your networking. Once you have a broad base of contacts, the next stage is asking for referrals directly to the decision makers at the companies you'd like to work for. Although you will have to work hard to establish these connections, they are your best hope for finding work before it's advertised.

For each of your contacts, identify the ways in which he or she can be of assistance to you. This enables you to be clear and focused, and will help each contact to address your need most effectively.

3. Decide on who to contact first.

If you're new to networking, or if you're not feeling that sure of yourself just yet, then it may be best to begin with a few of the people you know and trust the most. This way you minimize the risk if you make mistakes, and you can feel more comfortable in your efforts. Sometimes it helps to call up a friend or family member first and explain to them honestly what your situation is. When asking them for assistance, let them know that you've chosen them first because you are hoping to get some practice at networking. This often relieves the tension, and your contact may be more inclined to support you in a variety of ways.

4. Put together a script before you make your first round of calls.

The first few times that you call people to practice networking, it is likely you will be somewhat nervous. After all, this is unfamiliar territory for you. Many people find that preparing the outline of a script enables them to focus on what they have to say, rather than on how they may be feeling. Doing so also provides you with a mini-agenda for your call. This increases your chances of covering all the important points you are hoping to talk about.

The script can be point form, and include such elements as why you are calling, who referred you (if this applies), why you've chosen this particular contact to speak to at this time, how you think they can help you, and anything else you want to add. Keep it brief and upbeat.

5. Make your calls and set up appointments

When you begin to make your networking approaches, either by phone, letter or e-mail, bear in mind that you will want to keep track of your contact information. This way you will stay organized and increase your efficiency.

At the beginning, when you contact friends, family and other people you feel comfortable with, it's fine to use the phone or e-mail as your primary communication tool. Once you move beyond this initial comfort zone - for example, to people you haven't seen for a while, and to people your existing contacts refer you to - it becomes increasingly important to strive for a face-to-face meeting. This is because the person you want to meet does not know you yet. Letting them see you and learn more about you creates a stronger impression.

A sample telephone script for generating meetings is provided further on in this section.

6. Prepare for your phone calls and face-to-face meetings

Try not to speak to new people until you have taken time to prepare. You'll want to know a bit about their background, so that you have a sense of how they might be of help. It is also useful to do some research about the field, industry and company they represent. This way you will be more knowledgeable and better prepared; two traits that will impress your contact.

A sample agenda for a networking meeting is presented further on.

7. Following up professionally

Since people are doing you a favor by giving you their time, information and/or leads, you should treat them accordingly. Here are some things you can do to make sure you follow up properly:

- Send a thank you note, either by mail or e-mail, within five business days of your conversation or meeting with a networking contact.

A sample Thank You note is shown below.

- Fulfill any promises or commitments you have made, such as sending a resumé or addressing any unanswered questions.

- If your contact has referred you to someone they know, keep this contact in the loop as to how this new connection is going.

- Provide something useful to the person you've met, if possible, such as an article that might appeal to their interests, or the name of someone you know who might be of help to them.

- Update your database records to reflect the activities you are undertaking with each contact.

Wrapping It Up

So does networking sound like a lot of work? To do it right, it definitely takes time, effort and organization. Fortunately, it typically exposes you to all sorts of hidden opportunities that you might never come across otherwise. Moreover, you will learn a great deal about your industry and profession, as well as the people in it.

The end goal is to be in the right place at the right time. The best way to do this is to be top of mind with decision makers when it comes time to hiring. Being out there and active is your key to getting considered for employment – before the jobs go public!

Sample Phone Call For Generating Networking Meetings

Making networking arrangements by phone can be fast and efficient. Many of the people you call will be happy to help you, but they may not have much time. Therefore it's important to make your point briefly and succinctly.

As described earlier, you may find it helpful to write out a script ahead of time, but try to memorize rather than read it. Calling someone you don't know can be stressful. If you are uncomfortable doing this, practice with a friend and get feedback on your presentation. When you're well prepared, these calls become increasingly easier. You have nothing to lose by calling - if you don't try, you'll never find out if there was good information or a job lead at the other end. If you do call, you may be successful.

Example

Use the sample below as a guide for making a networking phone call:

You: "Hello, Keisha, my name is James Roberts. Ruth Chang suggested I speak to you about the medical supply industry. She says that you're something of an expert in the field."

Keisha: "Oh really, that's very nice of her. How is Ruth?"

You: "She seems to be doing well. We met last week for lunch and she insisted that I call you."

Keisha: "So how can I help you?"

You: "Well, most recently I was a financial analyst with Kodak for three years. Since their merger, I've been exploring other options in finance and accounting. I've always been interested in medical supplies because of the emphasis on improving people's health.

What I'd hope to do is meet with you one day this week for about 20 minutes, just to get some advice you may have to offer. Would Thursday morning be convenient?"

Keisha: "Actually, Thursday's no good for me. How's next Tuesday at 8:30 a.m. sharp. Things are kind of hectic these days and that's pretty well my only opening."

You: "That would be fine, Keisha. I would really like to meet with you and I'd be happy to be flexible. Shall we meet at your office?"

Keisha: "Yes, that would be fine."

You: "Thanks so much, Keisha. Can I give you my contact information just in case you need to reach me beforehand?..."

Note: after the call, make sure to note the meeting time and place in your diary or journal. If you are unsure of the exact location, call the switchboard and ask for directions.

Sample Agenda For Networking Session

Background

Now that you're calling and writing the people on your master contact list, you're beginning to line up some appointments. But what do you talk about when you actually meet with your contact? Networking is not just idle chitchat. If you don't know exactly what you're meeting about, you risk alienating your contact. You asked for the meeting, so it's your agenda. It's your responsibility to have comments and questions to direct the conversation. Help the other person help you by gently steering the meeting in the direction of your objectives.

Your goals in networking generally will be to publicize your availability, to get advice and information about trends in your industry and occupation of interest, to learn of potential job leads, and to get referred in to see other helpful people – including employers who are hiring.

Mini-Agenda

1. *Build rapport.* To accomplish the aims cited above, you must first make an effort to get to know your contacts (if you don't already), and give them an opportunity to get to know you. Build rapport. People help other people that they like, people they trust, people who belong to a group they belong to, or people with whom they feel some connection. Take advantage of whatever you have in common with each other.

   Begin by thanking your contact for meeting you. Reinforce that you are not here for a job, and will appreciate any information, such as specific industry trends, etc.

   Most people will sense, consciously or unconsciously, the attitude that you bring with you. If you simply use people as stepping stones to get what you want, it will be difficult to hide that. On the other hand, if you approach networking as a way of building and maintaining relationships for their own sake, people will feel good about you and will be more eager to help out.

2. *Give your networking contact a chance to talk about themselves.* People enjoy talking about themselves and their work. Ask questions that elicit information about how they got into their line of work, how their business is doing now, how they like their work, and how they see someone like you fitting into their industry or a workplace similar to their own.

3. *Tell accomplishment stories.* The information you want others to have about you should be presented in the form of short, interesting stories about your accomplishments, both in and out of the workplace. Consult your resumé to develop your stories. Practice telling them beforehand. Describe the situation, the actions you took, and the results. Keep your stories short. Avoid dominating the conversation and try for a comfortable balance between speaking about yourself and letting the other person talk as well.

4. *Pose questions you've prepared in advance.* Your questions should be designed to accomplish two purposes: a) to get information that will be helpful to you, and b), to give some indication that you are well informed about your contact's industry or company.

5. *Gather names.* Finally, ask for names of other people you can talk to who will broaden the scope of your research. Many of your contacts will introduce you or refer you to other people. Add these names to you master contact list. Follow up on these new contacts as appropriate.

Increasing the Effectiveness of Your Meetings

As with any other business meeting, you should always try to be enthusiastic and professional. Here are some additional tips:

- *Be on time.* Don't stay longer than the amount of time you requested and agreed on for the meeting. This shows respect for the other person and is a fundamental principle of business courtesy.

- *Don't put them on the spot.* Networking etiquette requires that you not ask people directly for a job. It's fine to tell everyone that you're engaged in the job search process, however. You are letting them know that you are available, you are gathering information, and you are seeking referrals to other people you might talk to who might help with your job search process. If they are impressed with you and have – or know of – openings that might suit you, they will share this information with you.

  Asking someone directly for a job often proves counterproductive. If they do not have a job to give you, there's a risk of making the other person feel awkward or guilty. They may subsequently avoid you. It is easier and more gracious to ask for information and referrals than to ask for a job.

- *When to meet.* If you're not employed and not a full-time student, just about any time that is convenient for your contact ought to be fine for you as well. Set up the appointment when your contact is available.

- *Where to meet.* Whenever possible, meet your contacts at their place of business. There are several reasons why this works in your favour. For one thing, you have a chance to get a feel for their work environment. Also, when your contacts are on their own turf, they are likely to feel more relaxed; they may think better and come up with more ideas. Another reason is that your contacts will not have to travel to meet with you, and you are more likely to get more of their time. Another big advantage is that you may be introduced to your contact's colleagues who work down the hall. Finally, and most importantly, when you meet with your contacts in their offices, they will probably have their contact database at hand, increasing the odds that some of those critical contacts will be provided to you.

- You may be tempted to invite your contact to meet over lunch. This is an option, but it can get expensive. When you are job hunting, your contacts often will offer to pick up the tab. When you are the one who does the inviting, however, business etiquette dictates that you pay. Another alternative is to invite your contacts to meet over a cup of coffee. The best choice, as mentioned above, will almost always be to meet your contacts at their workplaces. If they invite you to lunch, you can say that you'd like to have a chance to see their office or plant, and you'd be glad to take a rain check for lunch. Once you are employed, consider taking them to lunch as a way of thanking them and maintaining the relationship.

- *Dress for success.* Make sure that you wear appropriate clothing to your interviews and that you are well-groomed for the occasion.

Follow Up Letter For Networking Meetings

After meeting with a networking contact, it is excellent form to send a thank you note (via e-mail or post) as a way of acknowledging the contact's consideration. It also gives you a chance to remind your contact of your strengths and goals.

Your Name

Corebond Packaging Ltd.   Date
C/O Sharleen Mitel
Manager, Policies and Procedures
(Company's full address here)

Dear Sharleen,

It was a genuine pleasure to meet with you last Thursday to talk about the industrial packaging industry. Your insights were extremely valuable and I appreciate the time you spent talking with me.

You mentioned that I should consider getting in contact with Nabil Mustafa, and Carol Ellerwhip. I would like to let you know that I have had a chance to get in touch with Nabil, and he and I will be meeting next week. I will let you know how our session turns out.

In the interim, kindly keep me in mind if any opportunities arise or if there are any other contacts you believe would be beneficial for me to meet with. I am very interested in securing employment in quality control within the packaging and container field.

Thank you for your efforts on my behalf, Sharleen. Best of luck in your endeavours.

Sincerely,

(Your Name)

Your Address, City, Province, Postal Code
Your Phone Number and E-mail

PART II

DIRECTORIES OF RESOURCES

Firms & Organizations

Firms & Organizations

It has been said many times that over 80% of jobs available today are not advertised in newspapers, but rather found in the hidden job market. For this reason, it is important to conduct a thorough search on as many companies as possible in the industry you wish to enter.

This section contains hundreds of profiles on firms and organizations across the country, organized by industry sector. These companies may or may not be hiring in the near future. Their inclusion in this book is simply to give job seekers a starting point to obtain a bit of background on some of the most popular firms in the country. Use these company profiles to complement other job search strategies. Additional information on firms and organizations can be found in the Trade Directories section of the book.

INDUSTRY SECTORS

- Accounting & Legal
- Aerospace & High Technology
- Biotechnology & Pharmaceuticals
- Business Services
- Consumer Manufacturing
- Diversified
- Educational Institutions
- Energy
- Engineering & Architectural
- Entertainment & Leisure
- Financial Institutions
- Food Manufacturers & Wholesalers
- Government
- Hospitality
- Hospitals & Medical
- Industrial Manufacturing
- Insurance
- Investment
- Management & Consulting
- Oil & Mining
- Printing, Publishing & Forestry
- Retail
- Social Services
- Telecommunications & Media
- Transportation

Accounting & Legal

BDO DUNWOODY • 33rd Floor, Royal Bank Plaza, P.O. Box 32 • Toronto, ON • M5J 2J8 • Tel: 416-865-0200 • Fax: 416-865-0887 • Contact: Human Resources • E-mail: toronto@bdo. ca • Internet: www.bdo.ca • BDO Dunwoody is a major accounting firm offering a wide range of accounting, auditing and bookkeeping services to individuals, businesses and other groups. Operating across Canada, the firm provides specific services including taxation, insolvency, bankruptcy, mergers and acquisitions, and litigation support.

BLANEY MCMURTY LLP • 2 Queen Street East, Suite 1500 • Toronto, ON • M5C 3G5 • Tel: 416-593-1221 • Fax: 416-593-5437 • Internet: www.blaney.com • Blaney McMurty is a full service law firm with over 100 lawyers, secretaries and support staff. Blaney McMurtry LLP provides a full spectrum of legal services, assisting clients to overcome challenges and seize opportunities by combining in-depth industry knowledge and creative legal expertise. Blaney McMurtry reaches across borders for assistance in representing clients' interests anywhere in the world. As part of the TAGLaw network, they have access to the resources and expertise of leading lawyers in every province of Canada, as well as in major centres throughout the United States, and globally.

BRATTY & PARTNERS LLP • 7501 Keele Street, Suite 200 • Vaughan, ON • L4K 1Y2 • Tel: 905-760-2600 • Fax: 905-760-2900 • Contact: Human Resources • Internet: www.bratty.com • In more than forty years of practice, Bratty and Partners, LLP has earned its reputation as a leader in real estate and land development law. Their success is evident in the long working relationships they enjoy with many of their clients. Bratty and Partners, LLP is a dynamic, mid-sized firm large enough to offer their clients a broad range of expertise, yet small enough to remain responsive to their concerns.

CASSELS BROCK • 40 King Street West, Suite 2100 • Toronto, ON • M5H 3C2 • Tel: 416-869-5300 • Fax: 416-360-8877 • Contact: Manager, Human Resources • Internet: www.casselsbrock. com • Cassels Brock has been providing legal services to Canadian and international clients for more than 115 years. It is a full service law firm with more than 180 lawyers, including a team that practices in French. Cassels Brock is dedicated to supplying high quality, timely and innovative legal services.

MCINNES COOPER • 1300-1969 Upper Water Street, Furdy's Wharf II, P.O. BOX 730 • Halifax, NS • B3J 2V1 • Tel: 902-425-6500 • Fax: 902 425 4197 • Internet: www.mcinnescooper.com • McInnes Cooper is a law firm with a total of 300 employees, partners and associates. Support staff positions within the company are most likely to be that of legal secretary. However, the firm sometimes hires for some accounting, administrative and computer positions.

MEYERS NORRIS PENNY & CO. • 1401 Princess Avenue • Brandon, MB • R7A 7L7 • Tel: 204-727-0661 • Fax: 204-726-1543 • Contact: Mr. Jeff Cristall, CA, CBV Recruitment Coordinator • E-mail: Jeff.Cristall@mnp.ca • Internet: www.mnp.ca • Since the 1940s, Meyers Norris Penny LLP has helped individuals and businesses in Western Canada get results. In the beginning, they provided advice and services in the tradition of a full-service accounting firm. Today, however, MNP offers a diverse suite of services to meet the ever-changing needs of individuals and businesses. Their advisory services, which go well beyond traditional accounting services, include corporate finance, human resource consulting, business and strategic planning, succession planning, valuations support, self-employment training and agricultural advisory consulting. With more than 1200 team members and 43 full-time and 29 part-time offices in urban and rural locations across Western Canada, MNP has the people and the services to make a difference for their clients.

MINTZ & PARTNERS • 200 - 1 Concorde Gate, Suite 200 • Toronto, ON • M3C 4G4 • Tel: 416-391-2900 • Fax: 416-391-2748 • Contact: Ms. Nancy Stallone, HR Manager • E-mail: hr@mintzca.com • Internet: www.mintzca.com • Mintz & Partners is a leading provider of innovative business solutions to entrepreneurial business. Their business areas include: Assurance and Advisory Services, Taxation, Corporate Recovery and Insolvency, Business Valuation and Litigation, Forensic Accounting, Arbitration and Mediation, Corporate Finance, Information Technology and Business Processes Consulting, Human Resources Consulting, Health Care and Professional Practice Services, Real Estate Consultation, Small Business Consulting, and Hospitality Consulting.

PRICEWATERHOUSECOOPERS • Royal Trust Tower, TD Centre, P.O. Box 82 • Toronto, ON • M5K 1G8 • Tel: 416-863-1133 • Fax: 416-365-8178 • Contact: Human Resources • Internet: www.pwc.com • For more than 97 years PricewaterhouseCoopers has provided industry-focused assurance, advisory and tax services for public, private and government clients in four areas: corporate accountability, risk management, structuring and mergers and acquisitions, and performance and process improvement. In Canada, PricewaterhouseCoopers has more than 4,200 partners and staff in 24 locations from St. John's, Newfoundland to Vancouver, British Columbia.

Aerospace & High Technology

ADVANTECH AMT INC. • 657 Orly Avenue • Dorval, QC • H9P 1G1 • Tel: 514-420-0045 • Fax: 514-420-0073 • Contact: Ms. Gabrielle Neben, Human Resources Manager • E-mail: gabrielle. neben@advantechAMT.com • Internet: www.advantechAMT.com • Advantech AMT™ is a world leading designer and manufacturer of satellite and wireless telecommunications products. With facilities in the USA, Europe and Canada, as well as local representatives worldwide, Advantech has become a global one-stop shop for most communication needs. Advantech designs and manufactures Solid State Power Amplifiers (10 Watts to 4000 Watts), Block-up Converters, Transceivers, Booster Amplifiers, Converters, Modems, Data Broadcast Receivers, Satellite Terminals and Antenna Control systems. For Wireless applications in L and S-Bands, Advantech AMT provides Base Station products including Converters, Amplifiers, Repeaters and LNA's for indoor or tower mounted outdoor use.

AGFA GROUP • 455 Phillip Street • Waterloo, ON • N2L 3X2 • Tel: 519-746-2900 • Fax: 519-746-3745 • Contact: Human Resources • Internet: www.agfa.com • The Agfa Group ranks among the world's leading imaging companies. Agfa develops, produces and markets analog and digital systems, primarily for the graphics industry, healthcare, non-destructive testing, micrographics, motion picture film and consumer imaging and photography markets. Agfa employs more than 21,000 people in 40 countries, and has 120 agents throughout the world.

ALCATEL CANADA INC. • 2425 Matheson Blvd. East • Mississauga, ON • L4W 5K4 • Tel: 905-238-5214 • Fax: 905-238-0581 • Contact: Mr. Thomas Ediq, Human Resources, Senior Vice President • Internet: www.alcatel.ca • Alcatel provides end-to-end communications solutions, enabling carriers, service providers and enterprises to deliver content to any type of user, anywhere in the world. Leveraging its long-term leadership in telecommunications network equipment as well as its expertise in applications and network services, Alcatel enables its customers to focus on optimizing their service offerings and revenue streams.

AML WIRELESS SYSTEMS INC. • 260 Saulteaux Crescent • Winnipeg, MB • R3J 3T2 • Tel: 204-949-2411 • Fax: 204-889-1268 • Contact: Human Resources • E-mail: careers@amlwireless. com • Internet: www.amlwireless.com • AML Wireless Networks designs, manufactures, markets, installs and services state of the art broadband RF signal transmission systems to provide solutions to video, voice or data distribution requirements. Since 1969 AML has been a world leading supplier of these types of systems with applications in CATV, SMATV, MMDS, security, traffic control, education and other wireless applications.

AUTODATA SOLUTIONS COMPANY • 345 Saskatoon Street • London, ON • N5W 4R4 • Tel: 519-451-2323 • Fax: 519-451-6615 • Contact: Ms. Sairoz Kovacs, Human Resources • E-mail: sairoz.kovacs@autodata.net • Internet: www.autodata.net • Autodata Solutions, Inc. is one of North America's leading automotive software and data providers and has focused on the automotive industry for over 17 years. Founded in 1990, Autodata provides automotive content, research, and technology implementation services to most of the auto manufacturers who distribute vehicles in North America, helping them develop, market and sell their products more effectively and profitably.

BECKMAN COULTER CANADA INC. • 6755 Mississauga Road, Suite 600 • Mississauga, ON • L5N 7Y2 • Tel: 905-819-1234 • Fax: 905-819-1485 • Contact: Human Resources • Internet: www.beckmancoulter.com • Beckman Coulter, Inc. is a leading provider of instrument systems and complementary products that simplify and automate laboratory processes. From integrated laboratory automation solutions to centrifuges and blood analyzers to diagnostic rapid-test kits, the company's products are used throughout the world in all phases of the battle against disease. Beckman Coulter has offices in 130 countries around the world.

BOMBARDIER AEROSPACE • 123 Garratt Blvd. • Downsview, ON • M3K 1Y5 • Tel: 416-633-7310 • Fax: 416-375-4519 • Contact: Human Resources • E-mail: humanresources@dehavilland.ca • Internet: www.bombardier.com • Bombardier Aerospace is a part of Bombardier Inc., a world leader in recreational products, rail transportation equipment and aerospace. Today, they are the world's third largest manufacturer of civil aircraft. They focus on the design, manufacture, sale and support of regional and amphibious aircraft and business jets, as well as airframe components. Bombardier Aerospace combines the resources of four leading aircraft manufacturers: Canadair and de Havilland in Canada, Learjet in the United States and Shorts in the United Kingdom.

BRISTOL AEROSPACE LIMITED • 660 Berry Street, P.O. Box 874 • Winnipeg, MB • R3C 2S4 • Tel: 204-775-8331 • Fax: 204-775-7494 • Contact: Human Resources Department • E-mail: balhrs@bristol.ca • Internet: www.bristol.ca • Bristol Aerospace Limited is a Magellan Aerospace Company that operates from three facilities in Winnipeg, Manitoba. Bristol has over 70 years of history in the aviation and aerospace industry and a reputation for manufacturing quality products defect free and in conformance with customer requirements.

CANON CANADA INC. • 6390 Dixie Road • Mississauga, ON • L5T 1P7 • Tel: 905-795-2111 • Fax: 905-795-2130 • Contact: Human Resources • Internet: www.canon.ca • Canon Canada, established in 1973, is a highly respected Canadian market leader in business and consumer imaging equipment and information systems. They have 93,000 employees.

CARTE INTERNATIONAL INC. • 1995 Logan Avenue • Winnipeg, MB • R2R 0H8 • Tel: 204-633-7220 • Fax: 204-694-0614 • Contact: Mr. Harvey Schmidt, Human Resources • Internet: www.carte.ca • Carte International Inc. is a privately owned company with over 27 years experience suppling and manufacturing liquid filled transformers for Electrical Utilities, Electrical Distributors, and large Industrial customers. Carte specializes in both standard and custom-made transformers.

Seek a Job You Love
There are far too many people today working at a job they dislike simply to earn a paycheque. Do what you love and the paycheque will follow. In the long run, you will be a much happier individual.

CELESTICA INTERNATIONAL INC. • 12 Concord Place, 5th Floor • Toronto, ON • M3C 3R8 • Tel: 416-448-5800 • Fax: 416-448-4699 • Contact: Corporate Human Resources • E-mail: apply_toronto@celestica.com • Internet: www.celestica.com • Celestica is a world leader in the delivery of innovative electronics manufacturing services with operations in Asia, Europe and the Americas. The Celestica site in Toronto, is the original and flagship site of the company, specializing in Electronic Manufacturing Services, Printed Circuit Assembly, system assembly, test and design.

CGI • 1130 Sherbrooke Street West, 5th Floor • Montréal, QC • H3A 2M8 • Tel: 514-841-3200 • Fax: 514-841-3299 • Contact: HR Coordinator • Internet: www.cgi.ca • CGI is the largest independent information technology (IT) services firm in Canada. For more than 30 years, CGI has worked with clients in a wide range of industries to help them optimize their business performance and produce value-driven results. Its clients benefit from CGI's experience in systems integration, consulting, managed IT services, and business process services.

COE MANUFACTURING • 150 - 15100 River Road • Richmond, BC • V6V 3B2 • Tel: 604-276-1722 • Fax: 604-276-2160 • Contact: Human Resources • Internet: www.coemfg.com • "Product Innovation and Service Excellence" is what makes COE a global industry leader today. Employing the latest technology, talents of their design teams and experience gained through long-standing relationships with their customers, they continue to develop the high-performance, quality-rich solutions that the wood industries have come to depend on to meet ever-changing needs. COE is the "single supplier solution" for Veneer Systems, Sawmill Systems, Planermill Systems, Scanning and Optimization Technology, Panel and Plywood Press Systems, Dry Kilns, Engineered Wood Systems, LVL Systems, and Excellence in Customer Support, Service and Training.

COGNOS INCORPORATED • 3755 Riverside Drive, P.O. Box 9707, Station T • Ottawa, ON • K1G 4K9 • Tel: 613-738-1440 • Fax: 613-738-0002 • Contact: Human Resources • E-mail: student.recruiter2@cognos.com • Internet: www.cognos.com • Founded in 1969, Cognos is the world leader in business intelligence (BI) and performance planning software for the enterprise. Cognos' solutions support companies in all the key management activities including planning, budgeting, measuring and monitoring performance, reporting and analysis.

COM DEV INTERNATIONAL • 155 Sheldon Drive • Cambridge, ON • N1R 7H6 • Tel: 519-622-2300 • Fax: 519-622-1691 • E-mail: spacetech.resumes@comdev.ca • Internet: www.comdev.ca • In business for 30 years, COM DEV, based in Cambridge, Ontario is the largest Canadian-based designer and manufacturer of space hardware subsystems. COM DEV, with facilities in Canada and the United Kingdom, manufactures advanced products and subsystems that are sold to major satellite prime contractors for use in communications, space science, remote sensing and military satellites.

COMTRONIC COMPUTER INC. • 3950 rue Griffith • Saint-Laurent, QC • H4T 1A7 • Tel: 519-731-1223 • Fax: 519-731-1667 • Contact: Human Resources Manager • E-mail: ccmd@contronic.ca • Internet: www.comtronic.ca • Comtronic, established in 1987, has grown to be one of Canada's leading computer distributors. Comtronic is a privately held national distributor of brand name and OEM computer systems, peripherals, key components with full integration services and technical support. Comtronic is Canada's largest Acer and AOpen distribution. Comtronic's offices are located in Thornhill, Montreal, Calgary, Ottawa, Dartmouth and Vancouver.

CORADIANT INC. • 1100 Rene-Levesque Blvd West • Montreal, QC • H3B 4N4 • Tel: 514-908-6300 • Fax: 514-908-6333 • Contact: Mr. Michael Chuli, President and Chief Executive Officer • E-mail: careers@coradiant.com • Internet: www.coradiant.com • Founded in 1997, Cordiant has worked on production-grade web applications in some of the most demanding network environments in the world. Cordiant's management teams brings together years of experience in performance engineering web infrastructure, network security and enterprise-class systems management.

CORECO INC. • 7075 Place Robert-Joncas, Suite 142 • St-Laurent, QC • H4M 2Z2 • Tel: 514-333-1301 • Fax: 514-333-1388 • Contact: HR Administrator • E-mail: hrc@corecoimaging.com • Internet: www.corecoimaging.com • Established in 1979, Coreco Imaging is a world leader in the design, development and marketing of computer vision products and the treatment of video images by computers. Coreco Imaging machine vision components and systems allow customers to acquire, display, process, and compress images with unprecedented power, speed, and performance. Their customers are equipment manufacturers who use their products to improve quality control, productivity and competitiveness.

COREL CORPORATION • 1600 Carling Avenue • Ottawa, ON • K1Z 8R7 • Tel: 1-800-772-6735 • Internet: www.corel.com • Corel Corporation is an internationally recognized developer of award-winning graphics and business productivity applications. Development of market-leading products such as CorelDRAW line of graphics applications and the Corel WordPerfect Suite of business tools is continually evolving to meet the demands of the corporate, retail and academic markets. They employ approximately 950 individuals.

DELL CANADA • 155 Gordon Baker Road, Suite 501 • Toronto, ON • M2H 3N5 • Tel: 416-758-2100 • Fax: 416-758-2302 • Contact: Human Resources Department • Internet: www.dell.ca • Dell Canada, one of Canada's fastest growing vendors of PCs, notebooks, workstations and enterprise products, is a premier supplier to major Canadian corporations, educational institutions and governments, as well as small and medium businesses and customers. Dell Canada employs over 460 people in its North York, Ontario headquarters and sales offices in Halifax, Montreal, Ottawa and Vancouver.

DEVELCON ELECTRONICS LTD. • 155 Champagne Drive, Suite 7 • Toronto, ON • M3J 2C6 • Tel: 416-385-1390 • Fax: 416-385-1610 • Contact: Human Resources • E-mail: info@develcon.com • Internet: www.develcon.com • Develcon Electronics is a Canadian developer and marketer of local and remote LAN access products. Founded in 1974 to address the need for remote computer access, they now operate offices throughout Canada, and in the United States, Europe and South-East Asia. Their products are sold and supported in 55 countries through over 500 local distributors and resellers.

ELECTRONICS ARTS (CANADA) INC. • 4330 Sanderson Way • Burnaby, BC • V5C 4X1 • Tel: 604-456-3600 • Fax: 604-412-8350 • Contact: Human Resources Department • Internet: http://eacanada.ea.com/ • EA is home to the finest game development talent in the world. Their studio locations include EA Redwood Shores, EA Los Angeles, Bioware, and Pandemic in the United States; Criterion Games in the UK; DICE in Sweden; and EA Black Box (Burnaby, BC) and EA Montréal in Canada; to name just a few. Their development teams are backed by a world-class publishing organization that distributes EA games to more than 75 countries. Being a large global company with multiple office locations around the world allows them to provide their staff with great opportunities for career growth company-wide and worldwide.

EMJ DATA SYSTEMS LTD. • 107 Woodlawn Road West • Guelph, ON • N1H 1B4 • Tel: 519-837-2444 • Fax: 519-821-6708 • Contact: Ms. Sarah Oliver, Benefit Administrator • E-mail: jobs@emj.ca • Internet: www.emj.ca • EMJ Data Systems Ltd., headquartered in Guelph, Ontario, is distributor of computer products and peripherals, specializing in niche-market products for Apple, bar coding/auto-ID/point-of-sale, build-to-order, digital video, networking and security applications. EMJ has Canadian branch offices in Richmond (BC), Montreal and Guelph.

EPSON CANADA LIMITED • 3771 Victoria Park Avenue • Scarborough, ON • M1W 3Z5 • Tel: 416-498-9955 • Fax: 416-498-4574 • Contact: HR Department • E-mail: recruiting@eea.epson.com • Internet: www.epson.com • Epson Canada Limited is a manufacturer and distributor of high quality printers, as well as high tech OEM equipment. The company employs approximately 300 individuals.

ESPIAL GROUP INCORPORATED • 200 Elgin Street, Suite 900 • Ottawa, ON • K2P 1L5 • Tel: 613-230-4770 • Fax: 613-230-8498 • Contact: Human Resources • E-mail: hr@espial.com • Internet: www.espial.com • With more than 90 device design wins with companies such as Intel, Motorola, On Command, Philips, Sony and Samsung, Espial has deployed proven solutions for devices relying on Internet technology. Espial software allows customers to create services, deliver devices, manage infrastructure while building revenue in a cost effective manner. Espial technology applies universally across sectors such as TV, wireless, automotive and other connected devices. Visit www.espial.com.

FISHER SCIENTIFIC LIMITED • 112 Colonnade Road • Nepean, ON • K2E 7L6 • Tel: 613-226-3273 • Fax: 613-226-7658 • Contact: Human Resources • E-mail: help@fishersci.ca • Internet: www.fishersci.ca • Fisher Scientific is a major provider of instruments, equipment and other products to the Canadian scientific community. They provide more than 250,000 products and services to research centres, health care, educational and industrial customers nationwide. Fisher serves scientists engaged in biomedical, biotechnology, pharmaceutical, chemical and other fields of research and development. They are also a supplier to clinical laboratories, hospitals, health care alliances, environmental testing centers, quality-control laboratories and many other customers.

FROGWARE INC. • 30 Duncan Street, Suite 101 • Toronto, ON • M5V 2C3 • Tel: 416-216-4700 • Fax: 416-216-4666 • Contact: Ms. Kerry Bader, Office Manager, Operations • Internet: www.frogware.com • frogware develops custom software solutions used in many different markets, from finance, to publishing, to furniture, to automobile manufacturing. Visit their website for more information.

GOODRICH LANDING GEAR • 1400 South Service Road West • Oakville, ON • L6L 5Y7 • Tel: 905-827-7777 • Fax: 905-825-1583 • Contact: Ms. Stacey Dow, Human Resources • E-mail: staceydow@goodrich.com • Internet: www.goodrich.com • Goodrich Landing Gear is a global leader in the design, manufacture and testing of integrated, state-of-the-art landing gear and flight control systems. The company employs more than 600 individuals at its Oakville location.

HB STUDIOS MULTIMEDIA LTD. • P.O. Box 725 • Lunenburg, NS • B0J 2C0 • Fax: 902-634-3647 • E-mail: jobs@hb-studios.com • Internet: www.hb-studios.com • Founded in 2000 in Lunenburg, Nova Scotia, HB Studios is an electronic entertainment company specializing in creating computer and console video games. HB studios currently employs over 120 individuals.

IBM CANADA LTD. • 3600 Steeles Avenue East • Markham, ON • L3R 9Z7 • Tel: 905-316-2000 • Contact: Human Resources Employment • Internet: www.ibm.com/careers • IBM is the world's leading provider of advanced information technology products, services and solutions with over 20,000 employees working throughout Canada. IBM Canada operates a semiconductor manufacturing facility in Bromont Quebec, two world-class software development laboratories in Markham, Ontario and Ottawa, three e-business Innovation Centres in Toronto, Edmonton and Vancouver, and the largest ibm.com sales centre in the world in Toronto, Ontario. IBM Canada hires university graduates from across Canada into a variety of entry-level positions. Your undergraduate or graduate degree in Business, Computer Science or Engineering, along with your strong academic standing, demonstrated extra-curricular activities and related summer, co-op or internship experience will be the type of assets that we are looking for in our new employees. All of our new graduate positions are posted on-line at ibm.com/careers. Please select Canada from the country selection lists to be considered for employment with IBM Canada. To be considered for new graduate positions at IBM, you will need to apply on-line to each country that you are legally able to permanently work in upon graduation.

INFORMATION GATEWAY SERVICES • 240 Sparks Street • Ottawa, ON • K1P 1A1 • Tel: 800-268-3715 • Fax: 613-233-2266 • E-mail: employ@igs.net • Internet: www.renc.igs.net • Information Gateway Services (IGS) is an Internet Service Provider which operates in 18 locations across Canada. IGS Offers a range of services for both private individuals and corporate or business customers, including Highspeed DSL, Dial-up, Wireless, web hosting, mail hosting, and website development.

INTELCAN TECHNOSYSTEMS INC. • 69 Auriga Drive • Ottawa, ON • K2E 7Z2 • Tel: 613-228-1150 • Fax: 613-228-1149 • E-mail: hr@intelcan.com • Internet: www.intelcan.com • Intelcan is a global leader in the provision of Air Traffic Management (ATM) systems for civilian and military applications. Since 1973, Intelcan has delivered flexible, custom-designed solutions based on the latest technology to customers in over 60 countries around the world. They supply Communications, Navigation, Surveillance and Air Traffic Management systems on a complete turnkey basis, backed by their extensive experience in System Engineering, Airport Infrastructure and Telecommunications.

JDS UNIPHASE CORPORATION • 61 Bill Leathem Drive • Ottawa, ON • K2J 0P7 • Tel: 613-843-3000 • Fax: 613-843-2800 • Contact: Human Resources • E-mail: ca.resume@jdsu.com • Internet: www.jdsunph.com • JDS Uniphase is a high technology company that designs, develops, manufactures, and distributes a comprehensive range of products for the growing fiberoptic communications market. These products are deployed by system manufacturers worldwide to develop advanced optical networks for the telecommunications and cable television industries.

KODAK CANADA INC. • 6 Monogram Place • Toronto, ON • M9R 0A1 • Tel: 416-766-8233 • Fax: 416-766-5814 • Contact: Kraft Canada Talent Management Team • E-mail: hrs@kodak.com • Internet: www.kodak.ca • Kodak's mission is to empower customers to create, share and use pictures to the greatest extent possible. Kodak Canada Inc. was founded in 1899, almost a decade after the incorporation of its parent company, Rochester-NY-based Eastman Kodak Company.

KONICA MINOLTA BUSINESS SOLUTIONS (CANADA) LTD. • 369 Britannia Road East • Mississauga, ON • L4Z 2H5 • Fax: 905-890-0497 • Contact: Human Resources • E-mail: careers@ph.konicaminolta.ca • Internet: www.konicaminolta.ca • Leading the world in document imaging innovation, Konica Minolta Business Solutions (Canada) Ltd., a division of Konica Minolta Holdings, Inc., is one of the foremost providers of systems and solutions for document creation, production and distribution. They deliver a complete line of black & white and full-color printers, copiers, facsimile machines and multifunctional document systems, as well as the support services and the software solutions that bring it all together. Konica Minolta Business Solutions delivers the most technologically advanced products, the most comprehensive support and the best solutions for your document processes.

Have a Professional Resumé
Nothing puts your resumé more quickly at the bottom of an employer's pile – or worse, in their garbage can – than a handwritten or illegible resumé. Your resumé must be in a concise and easy-to-read format.

KONTRON CANADA • 616 Curé-Boivin • Boisbriand, QC • J7G 2A7 • Tel: 450-437-5682 • Fax: 450-437-8053 • Contact: Ms. Annie-Lyne Côté, Senior Specialist, Human Resources • E-mail: cv@ca.kontron.com • Internet: www.kontron.com • Kontron Canada is a member of Kontron Group, one of the world's largest suppliers of embedded computer technology. They have a diversified customer base covering virtually all industries. Kontron's ability to service global customers in markets that move at light speed is strengthened through business groups and facilities across Asia, Canada, Europe and the United States. Combining the strengths and means of a multinational corporation with the flexibility and human touch of a family business makes them successful.

MACDONALD DETTWILER AND ASSOCIATES LTD. • 13800 Commerce Parkway • Richmond, BC • V6V 2J3 • Tel: 604-278-3411 • Fax: 604-278-1837 • Contact: Recruiting Office • E-mail: info@mda.ca • Internet: www.mda.ca • MacDonald, Dettwiler and Associates Ltd. (MDA) provides customers around the world with essential information solutions used for decision making. Operating through two groups-INFORMATION PRODUCTS and INFORMATION SYSTEMS-MDA is active in data collection, information extraction, and information distribution. They operate internationally and employ over 2,600 people.

MATROX ELECTRONIC SYSTEMS LTD. • 1055, boul. St-Régis • Dorval, QC • H9P 2T4 • Tel: 514-822-6000 • Fax: 514-822-6274 • Contact: Mr. Patrick Chayer, Human Resources • E-mail: personnel@matrox.com • Internet: www.matrox.com • Over the years, Matrox has earned its reputation as industry leader and innovator in today's most state-of-the-art technologies, designing software and hardware solutions in the fields of Graphics, Video editing and Image processing. Privately held, the company employs over 900 people worldwide at its headquarters in Montreal, as well as in international offices in the United Kingdom, Ireland, Germany, and China.

MAYA HEAT TRANSER TECHNOLOGIES LTD. • 4999 St. Catherine Street West, Suite 400 • Montreal, QC • H3Z 1T3 • Tel: 514-369-5706 • Fax: 514-369-4200 • E-mail: jobs@mayahtt.com • Internet: www.mayahtt.com • Founded in 1982, MAYA (MAYA Heat Transfer Technologies Ltd.) is a leading supplier of advanced thermal and fluid flow analysis software, structural analysis software, and related training and consulting services in mechanical engineering.

MITEL NETWORKS CORPORATION • 350 Legget Drive, P.O. Box 13089 • Kanata, ON • K2K 2W7 • Tel: 613-592-2122 • Fax: 613-592-4784 • Contact: Human Resources • Internet: www.mitel.com • Mitel Networks Corporation is a leading global provider of enterprise and small business communications solutions and services. The company focuses on blending powerful infrastructure with an intuitive human interface to deliver the benefits of voice, video and data convergence to the user.

MORTICE KERN SYSTEMS INC.(MKS) • 410 Albert Street • Waterloo, ON • N2L 3V3 • Tel: 519-884-2251 • Fax: 519-884-8861 • Contact: Human Resources • E-mail: info@mks.com • Internet: www.mks.com • MKS is the preeminent provider of enterprise technology management solutions for the global 1000. Their solutions let companies manage the technology governing the enterprise by enabling all of the key steps in the technology lifecycle, from requirements capture and business process design to global development team collaboration, to metrics management and reporting to complete auditing of software and system change in support of IT governance initiatives. MKS solutions are distinguished for their speed of implementation and low total cost of ownership.

MOSAID TECHNOLOGIES INC. • 11 Hines Road • Kanata, ON • K2K 2X1 • Tel: 613-599-9539 • Fax: 613-591-8148 • Contact: Human Resources • E-mail: communications@mosaid.com • Internet: www.mosaid.com • MOSAID is a global leader in semiconductor memory, serving its customers with innovative design, test and intellectual property products and services.

MOTOROLA CANADA LTD. • 8133 Warden Avenue • Markham, ON • L6G 1B3 • Tel: 905-948-5489 • Fax: 905-948-5259 • Internet: http://motorolacareers.com • Motorola is a global leader in providing integrated communications solutions and embedded electronic solutions. Their Intelligence EverywhereTM solutions include: software-enhanced wireless telephone and messaging, two-way radio products and systems, as well as networking and Internet-access products, for consumers, network operators, and commercial, government and industrial customers; end-to-end systems for the delivery of interactive digital video, voice and high-speed data solutions for broadband operators; embedded semiconductor solutions for customers in wireless communications, networking nad transportation markets; integrated electronic systems for automotive, Telematics, industrial, telecommunications, computing and portable energy sytems markets.

M-TECH INFORMATION TECHNOLOGY, INC. • 500, 1401 - 1st Street SE • Calgary, AB • T2G 2J3 • Tel: 403-233-0740 • Fax: 403-233-0725 • Contact: Human Resources • Internet: http://mtechit.com • M-Tech is a leading provider of identity management solutions. M-Tech's solutions offer comprehensive password management, user provisioning and access management capabilities that provide organizations with improved security, increased productivity and effective policy compliance management.

NETRON INC. • P.O. Box 73570, 509 Street Clair Avenue West • Toronto, ON • M6C 1C0 • Tel: 416-636-8333 • Fax: 416-636-4847 • Contact: Human Resources • E-mail: hr@netron.com • Internet: www.netron.com • Netron is a computer service, product and consulting organization specializing in products and services for the information technology industry.

NORTHSTAR AEROSPACE • 695 Bishop Street North • Cambridge, ON • N3H 4V2 • Tel: 519-653-5774 • Fax: 519-653-7190 • Contact: Human Resources • E-mail: infocambridge@ northstar-aerospace.com • Internet: www.nsaero.com • Northstar Aerospace is a Toronto Stock Exchange listed corporation with aerospace operations in Canada and the United States. It manufactures flight critical parts for military aircraft applications and non-flight critical parts for commercial aircraft. The Company specializes in technically complex machined components. The company's aerospace operations began in 1984 and is now one of the most profitable aerospace companies in North America.

OPTIMAL GROUP INC. • 2 Place Alexis Nihon, 3500 de Maisonneuve West, Suite 800 • Montreal, QC • H3Z 3C1 • Contact: Human Resources • E-mail: personnel@optimalgrp.com • Internet: www.optimalgrp.com • Optimal Group is a leading payments and services company. They operate their payment-processing business and our services business through our wholly owned subsidiaries, Optimal Payments and Optimal Services Group.

ORACLE CORP. CANADA INC. • 110 Matheson Blvd. West, Suite 100 • Mississauga, ON • L5R 3P4 • Tel: 905-890-8100 • Fax: 905-890-1207 • Contact: Human Resources • E-mail: marketinfo@ca.oracle.com • Internet: www.oracle.ca • Since 1977, Oracle has provided technology, applications, and services that bring companies the most up-to-date and accurate information possible. They know that the right information leads to good decisions and good decisions lead to successful businesses.

POWER MEASUREMENT LTD. • 2195 Keating Cross Road • Saanichton, BC • V8M 2A5 • Tel: 250-652-7100 • Fax: 250-652-0411 • Contact: Human Resources • E-mail: careers@pwrm.com • Internet: www.pml.com • Power Measurement is an energy information technology company founded on innovation and a global leader in enterprise energy management systems. Our products and services help energy suppliers and consumers take control of the cost and quality of energy.

POWERTECH LABS INC. • 12388 88th Avenue • Surrey, BC • V3W 7R7 • Tel: 604-590-7500 • Fax: 604-590-5347 • Contact: Human Resources • E-mail: info@powertechlabs.com • Internet: www.powertechlabs.com • Powertech solves technical problems with power equipment and systems throughout their life cycle, from the design stage through service life, to disposal and re-use. Many technical issues are complex, requiring knowledge across several disciplines for complete assessment and remediation. In a single facility Powertech offers electrical, chemical, environmental, gas technologies, mechanical, metallurgical, materials, civil and structural engineering expertise gained over years of research and testing.

PRATT & WHITNEY CANADA INC. • 1000 route Marie-Victorin • Longueuil, QC • J4G 1A1 • Tel: 450-677-9411 • Fax: 450-647-3620 • Contact: Human Resources • E-mail: human. resources@pwc.ca • Internet: www.pwc.ca • Pratt & Whitney Canada is engaged in the design, development, and manufacture of gas turbine engines for air, sea and land applications. The company is a wholly owned subsidiary of United Technologies Corporation of the United States.

PSION TEKLOGIX INC. • 2100 Meadowvale Blvd. • Mississauga, ON • L5N 7J9 • Tel: 905-813-9900 • Fax: 905-812-6300 • Contact: Human Resources • Internet: www.psionteklogix.com • Psion Teklogix Inc. is a global provider of solutions that enable enterprises to mobilize their business applications. Psion Teklogix provides customers with fully integrated mobile computing solutions that include rugged hardware, secure wireless networks, robust software, professional services and exceptional support programs.

RAYTHEON SYSTEMS CANADA LTD. • 1640-360 Albert Street • Ottawa, ON • K1R 7X7 • Tel: 613-233-4121 • Internet: www.raytheon.ca • Raytheon Systems Canada Ltd. is modernizing Canada's air traffic control business by developing the industry's safest and most advanced automated systems. They are part of Raytheon Systems Company, a global leader in defence electronics and complex integrated information systems. Their Richmond facility employs more than 300 individuals.

SASKATCHEWAN RESEARCH COUNCIL, THE • 125 - 15 Innovation Blvd. • Saskatoon, SK • S7N 2X8 • Tel: 306-933-5400 • Fax: 306-933-7446 • Contact: Ms. Lynne Gorgchuck, Human Resources Specialist • E-mail: humanresources@src.sk.ca • Internet: www.src.sk.ca • SRC is Saskatchewan's leading provider of applied R&D and technology commercialization. They take the leading-edge knowledge developed in Saskatchewan and sell it to the world and, at the same time, bring the best knowledge the work has to offer and apply it to the unique Saskatchewan situations. RC was established in 1947 to advance the development of the province in the physical sciences. Today, the company has evolved to become a market driven corporation, selling services and products to companies in Saskatchewan and around the world. The corporation has more than 300 staff.

SCHLUMBERGER INFORMATION SOLUTIONS CALGARY TECHNOLOGY CENTRE • 525 - 3rd Avenue S.W. • Calgary, AB • T2P 0G4 • Tel: 403-509-4000 • Fax: 403-509-4021 • Contact: Human Resources • Internet: www.sis.slb.com • Schlumberger Information Solutions Calgary Technology Centre develops and markets Windows™ application software for the upstream energy industry. The Merak value and risk extensive suite of integrated tools assists in the evaluation of exploration risk, production forecasts, economic projections, investment viability, and production operations. Features include mapping, portfolio optimization, budgeting, regime specific financial projections, reserves and production data management.

SED SYSTEMS • 18 Innovation Blvd., P.O. Box 1464 • Saskatoon, SK • S7K 3P7 • Tel: 306-931-3425 • Fax: 306-933-1486 • Contact: Human Resources • Internet: www.sedsystems.ca • Since 1965, SED has been supplying innovative ground systems and services to major satellite manufacturers and operators around the world. Their systems, now operating on six continents, use the latest in hardware and software technologies to: test satellites before they are launched and after they are in orbit, control and monitor remote sensing and communications satellites, and link satellite and terrestrial communications networks to provide mobile voice and data communications, digital radio via satellite, and access to the Internet.

SIEMENS ELECTRIC LTD. • 1450 Appleby Line • Burlington, ON • L7L 6X7 • Tel: 905+315-6868 • Contact: Human Resources • Internet: www.siemens.ca • Siemens leads the pursuit of technological innovation for health care, information & communications, energy & power, industry & automation, transportation, and lighting. Worldwide, this fascination with innovation devotes approximately $2 million in research & development every business hour of every business day. It is little wonder Siemens is recognized internationally as a relentless pioneer of innovation. As a subsidiary of Siemens AG, Siemens in Canada draws on the global network of innovation to provide global solutions at a local level. As an active member of the business community, they develop solutions for the entire country and export Canadian-made products around the world.

SIERRA SYSTEMS GROUP INC. • 1177 West Hastings Street, Suite 2500 • Vancouver, BC • V6E 2K3 • Tel: 604-688-1371 • Fax: 604-688-6482 • Contact: Human Resources • Internet: www.sierrasystems.com • The driving force behind Sierra Systems since opening their first office in 1966, is improving their clients' business through technology. Today, they have more than 1,000 employees in 18 locations across the United States and Canada, with seven specialty practices and an extensive list of prominent organizations they proudly call their clients.

SOFTIMAGE CO. • 3510 St-Laurent Blvd. • Montreal, QC • H2X 2V2 • Tel: 514-845-1636 • Fax: 514-845-5676 • Contact: Human Resources • E-mail: resume@softimage.com • Internet: www.softimage.com • Softimage is an industry leader in 3D animation, 2D cel animation, compositing and special effects software, designed to address the demands of the film and commercial/broadcast and games/interactive industries. SOFTIMAGE|XSI software, an integral player in Avid's Make, Manage and Move Media™ strategy, is the flagship product offering from Softimage. It is the industry's first 3D nonlinear production environment providing animators and digital artists the freedom to make professional animation, visual effects and games - from major motion pictures, to cartoons and commercials, to animated content for video games and Web sites. Softimage is proud to count amongst its customers: Ubisoft, Capcom, Konami, SONY, Valve, Pandemic, Taito, Sega, Atari, Omation Studios, R!OT, The Mill, Stan Winston Studios, Pixel Liberation Front, Blue Sky Studios, Hybride, Janimation, Quiet Man, PSYOP, Cinepix and Nerd Corps. For more information about Softimage visit www.softimage.com.

SOLUTIONINC LIMITED • 5692 Bloomfield Street • Halifax, NS • B3K 1T2 • Tel: 902-420-0077 • Fax: 902-420-0233 • Contact: Human Resources • E-mail: jobs@solutioninc.com • Internet: www.solutioninc.com • SolutionInc Limited is a leading supplier of Internet (IP) provisioning, authentication, and billing software. Its award winning software SolutionIP enables organizations and Internet service providers to offer secure wired, wireless and Wi-Fi hotspot high speed Internet. SolutionIP makes Internet access easy. Around the world, thousands of customers daily use SolutionIP to run VPN's, send and receive email and securely access Internet based applications in places like hotels, convention centers, libraries and universities.

SPAR AEROSPACE LIMITED • 7785 Tranmere Drive • Mississauga, ON • L5S 1W5 • Tel: 905-673-6000 • Fax: 905-671-5802 • Contact: Human Resources • E-mail: SparEast.hr@L-3com.com • Internet: www.spar.ca • Spar began as the Special Products and Applied Research division of the deHavilland Canada aircraft company. This division was heavily involved in the Avro Arrow project, which was cancelled by the Diefenbaker Government in 1959. A management buyout took place in 1967 and the newly formed company was publicly listed on the Toronto Stock Exchange in 1968. In 2001, Spar was bought by L-3 Communications Corporation, a New York City-based merchant supplier of communications and aerospace equipment.

SPEEDWARE CORP. INC. • 6380 Cote de Liesse • Saint-Laurent, QC • H4T 1E3 • Tel: 514-747-7007 • Fax: 514-747-3380 • Contact: Human Resources • Internet: www.speedware.com • Founded in 1976, Speedware Corporation is a leading provider of enterprise software solutions serving a variety of vertical markets. Our suite of products includes enterprise resource planning (ERP) applications for distributors, business intelligence solutions, productivity tools, and a wide range of complementary professional services.

SYMANTEC CORPORATION • 3381 Steeles Avenue East, 4th Floor • Toronto, ON • M2H 3S7 • Tel: 416-774-0000 • Contact: Human Resources • Internet: www.symantec.ca • Symantec is the global leader in information security providing a broad range of software, appliances and services designed to help individuals, small and mid-sized businesses, and large enterprises secure and manage their IT infrastructure. Symantec's Norton brand of products is the worldwide leader in consumer security and problem-solving solutions. Headquartered in Cupertino, California, Symantec has operations in 40 countries.

TALEO CORPORATION • 330, rue St-Vallier Est, bureau 400 • Quebec, QC • G1K 9C5 • Tel: 418-524-5665 • Fax: 418-524-8899 • Contact: Human Resources • E-mail: hr-canada@taleo.com • Internet: www.taleo.com • Taleo Corporation (formely Recruitsoft, Inc.) develops web-based employee recruitment and staffing management software for large employers.

TELVENT CANADA LTD. • 10333 Southport Road S.W. • Calgary, AB • T2W 3X6 • Tel: 403-253-8848 • Fax: 403-259-2926 • Contact: Human Resources • Internet: www.telvent.com • Telvent, Abengoa's Information Technology subsidiary, specializes in IT solutions with high technological added value for specific industrial sectors such as Energy, Environment, Traffic, Transport, Telecom and Public Administration. Telvent is a leading supplier to these industries in Spain, North America, Latin America and Asia.

THALES SYSTEMS CANADA • 1 Chrysalis Way • Ottawa, ON • K2G 6P9 • Tel: 613-723-7000 • Fax: 613-723-5600 • Contact: Mr. Don Bolduc Manager, Human Resources • E-mail: don.bolduc@ca.thalesgroup.com • Internet: www.thales-systems.ca • Located in Ottawa, Ontario, and with offices in Kingston, Ontario and Quebec City, Quebec, Thales Systems Canada, a division of Thales Canada Inc., is one of four Thales companies in Canada (over $170 million revenue and over 260 employees), is a Turnkey Systems Integration company that delivers complex mission system and sensor communication systems, and C4ISR systems for military and civil applications. The company also develops and maintains real-time software for surveillance systems (radar, electro-optical), for radio communication systems (message handling / processing, ARQ, HF email, and system control and monitoring), and for tactical command and control systems. In 50 countries, their 62,000 employees are dedicated to creating a safer future, worldwide.

Be Innovative in Your Job Search
Stand yourself out from others in the job search. Take out a classified ad in your local paper, or have business cards made up that list your credentials. Creative thinking will help you to get noticed!

TOP PRODUCERS SYSTEMS INC. • 10651 Shellbridge Way, Suite 155 • Richmond, BC • V6X 2W8 • Tel: 604-270-8819 • Fax: 604-270-8218 • Contact: Human Resources • E-mail: careers@ topproducer.com • Internet: www.topproducer.com • Top Producer Systems was founded in 1982, and since the early 90's, has been the #1-selling provider of leads management and marketing software for real estate professionals. Our internet compatible suite of products, feature extensive contact management, mass e-mailing, scheduling, prospecting, CMA, presentation, mobile data synchronization and web-based real estate marketing tools.

TOSHIBA OF CANADA LTD. • 191 McNabb Street • Markham, ON • L3R 8H2 • Tel: 905-470-3500 • Fax: 905-470-3509 • Contact: Human Resources • E-mail: resumes@toshiba.ca • Internet: www.toshiba.ca • Toshiba of Canada is a leading manufacturer and distributor of mobile computer systems; home entertainment products, including televisions, DVD players, and VCRs; office products, including photocopiers, facsimiles, multimedia projectors, and business telephone systems; and medical diagnostic imaging equipment. In Canada, they rank in the top three in the high technology, office products, and electronics markets in which they compete.

TRIUMF • 4004 Wesbrook Mall • Vancouver, BC • V6T 2A3 • Tel: 604-222-1047 • Fax: 604-222-1074 • Contact: Human Resources • Internet: www.triumf.ca • Triumf is a world-class subatomic physics research laboratory located on the campus of the University of British Columbia, a twenty-minute drive from downtown Vancouver. Triumf is one of three subatomic research facilities in the world that specialize in producing extremely intense beams of particles. The heart of the facility is the world's biggest cyclotron, which is used to accelerate 1000 trillion particles each second! A cyclotron is a special type of particle accelerator that accelerates particles as they follow a spiral path through it.

TROJAN TECHNOLOGIES INC. • 3020 Gore Road • London, ON • N5V 4T7 • Tel: 519-457-3400 • Fax: 519-457-3030 • Contact: Ms. Sandi Parachuk HR Specialist • Internet: www. trojanuv.com • Trojan designs, manufactures and sells UV systems for municipal wastewater and drinking water facilities, as well as for the industrial, commerical and residential markets. The company also provides UV treatment for the removal of toxic chemicals from water.

TUCOWS INC. • 96 Mowat Avenue • Toronto, ON • M6K 3M1 • Tel: 416-531-0123 • Fax: 416-535-5584 • Contact: Human Resources • Internet: www.tucows.com • Tucows is an internet services company that provides back office solutions and wholesale internet services to a global network of more than 6,000 web hosting companies, internet service providers (ISPs) and other service providers worldwide. As the largest ICANN accredited wholesale domain registrar, Tucows offers a suite of complementary internet services including: domain name registration and management, digital certificates, email services and website publishing tools. Tucows back office solutions, including the Platypus Billing System and customer relationship management solutions, enable service providers to automate and enhance their service offerings. Our company is in the business of managing data and simplifying complex business processes for this large and expanding network of service providers, who, in turn, provide e-business products and services to their customers - an estimated 40-million end-users worldwide. These end-users, primarily small and medium-sized enterprises (SMEs) and individuals, represent one of the fastest growing segments of the Internet economy.

UNISYS CANADA INC. • 2001 Sheppard Avenue East • Toronto, ON • M2J 4Z7 • Tel: 416-495-0515 • Fax: 416-495-4495 • Contact: Human Resources • Internet: www.unisys.com • Unisys is a worldwide information technology services and solutions company. Their people combine expertise in systems integration, outsourcing, infrastructure, server technology and consulting with precision thinking and relentless execution to help clients, in more than 100 countries, quickly and efficiently achieve competitive advantage. They employ 37,000 people.

VOLT HUMAN RESOURCES • 10 Kelfield Street, Suite 100 • Toronto, ON • M9W 5A2 • Tel: 877-287-6139 • Fax: 416-306-1449 • Contact: Human Resources • E-mail: torontotechjobs@volt.com • Internet: www.volt.com • Volt Human Resources provides professional, scientific and technical/IT workers for more than 60 of the largest firms within North America, including Hewlett-Packard, Eli Lilly, Boeing, Rockwell and Microsoft.

WEBCANADA • 120 Carlton Street, Suite 308 • Toronto, ON • M5A 4K2 • Tel: 416-977-4411 • Fax: 416-977-4434 • Contact: Human Resources • E-mail: hr@webcanada.com • Internet: www.webcanada.com • Since 1995, WebCanada has been building efficient, interactive web sites and providing a wide range of Internet and multimedia-related services. Their corporate and government clients throughout North America include Air Canada, Airline Training Council, Canadian Foundation for Economic Education, GENESIS Travel Distribution System, Ontario Ministry of Environment and Energy, and Molson Breweries.

WESTPORT INNOVATIONS INC. • 1750 West 75th Avenue, Suite 101 • Vancouver, BC • V6P 6G2 • Tel: 604-718-2000 • Fax: 604-718-2001 • Contact: Human Resources • E-mail: careers@westport.com • Internet: www.westport.com • Westport Innovations is dedicated to leading the shift of the international commercial engine industry from oil-based to gaseous fuels. They develop technologies that allow diesel engines to operate on alternative fuels such as natural gas, propane and hydrogen. Their market is anything that requires a diesel engine from transportation and industrial applications to power generation.

XWAVE SOLUTIONS • 1550 Enterprise Road, Suite 120 • Mississauga, ON • L4W 4P4 • Tel: 905-670-1225 • Fax: 905-670-1344 • Internet: www.xwave.com • xwave, an Aliant company, delivers complete IT services to clients in three areas: integration, infrastructure and fulfillment solutions. These areas offer clients, in key sectors where xwave has extensive experience, a broader delivery capability to plan, design, build and operate IT solutions that span both corporate and operational systems, and to fulfill the equipment and infrastructure upon which they are built. With more than $300 million in revenues and 2,300 people, xwave is one of the largest IT companies in Canada, with offices in St. John's, Halifax, Moncton, Saint John, Fredericton, Montreal, Ottawa, Toronto, Calgary, Edmonton and Dallas.

YFACTOR • 133 Richmond Street West, Suite 202 • Toronto, ON • M5H 2L3 • Tel: 416-977-9724 • Fax: 416-642-1959 • E-mail: careers@yfactor.com • Internet: www.yfactor.com • YFactor Inc. was established in 1997. Recognizing the necessity to provide a high calibre of interactive communication for the corporate environment is the main purpose of YFactor. With services ranging from internet/intranet development, to corporate communications and spatial graphics, they are focused on providing corporations and government with fresh ideas, communication strategy, expertise in technology and large project management.

Biotechnology & Pharmaceuticals

ACCUCAPS INDUSTRIES LIMITED • 2125 Ambassador Drive • Windsor, ON • N9C 3R5 • Tel: 519-969-5404 • Fax: 519-250-3321 • Contact: Human Resources • E-mail: info@accucaps.com • Internet: www.accucaps.com • Accucaps is a full-service contract manufacturer that supplies softgel capsules to a variety of industries, including pharmaceutical, health and nutritional, and bath and beauty customers.

ALLIED RESEARCH INTERNATIONAL INC. • 4520 Dixie Road • Mississauga, ON • L4W 1N2 • Tel: 905-238-0599 • Fax: 905-238-0682 • Contact: Human Resources • E-mail: careers@allied-research.com • Internet: www.allied-research.com • Allied Research International Inc. (formerly known as Allied Clinical Research) is a dynamic group of scientific and medical professionals dedicated to the advancement of clinical research. For over ten years, Allied Research International

(ARI) has been providing services to Pharmaceutical and Biotechnology industries. These services range from conducting complex single site Phase I / Bioequivalence /Bioavailability (BE/BA) studies or early Phase II studies, to being a site in multi-center Phase II and III studies.

APOTEX FERMENTATION INC. • 50 Surfield Blvd. • Winnipeg, MB • R3Y 1G4 • Tel: 204-989-6830 • Fax: 204-989-9160 • Contact: Human Resources • E-mail: hr@apoferm.mb.ca • Internet: http://apoferm.com/ • Apotex Fermentation Inc. (AFI) is a member of the Apotex Pharmaceutical Group of Companies which includes Apotex Inc., the largest Canadian-owned pharmaceutical firm. AFI is an advanced technology company utilizing state-of-the-art techniques for search and discovery, strain selection and improvement, and bioprocess scale-up. AFI employees are highly qualified and trained in sophisticated chemical, biological and pharmaceutical technologies.

ASTRAZENECA • 1004 Middlegate Road • Mississauga, ON • L4Y 1M4 • Tel: 905-277-7111 • Fax: 905-270-3248 • Contact: Human Resources Department • Internet: www.astrazeneca. ca • AstraZeneca is one of the largest pharmaceutical companies in the world. Their innovative and extensive product portfolio spans six therapeutic areas: cardiovascular, gastrointestinal, oncology, respiratory, neuroscience and infection. AstraZeneca employs more than 64,000 people in 150 countries.

BAYER INC. • 77 Belfield Road • Etobicoke, ON • M9W 1G6 • Tel: 416-248-0771 • Fax: 416-248-5373• Contact: Human Resources • Internet: www.bayer.ca • A research-based, highly diversified company with businesses in specialty chemicals, polymers and life sciences, Bayer Inc. is one of Canada's leading companies. Canadian Bayer facilities include the Toronto headquarters, offices in Ottawa and Calgary, as well as a manufacturing facility in Sarnia, Ontario. Bayer Inc. has approximately 930 employees across Canada.

BIOVAIL CORPORATION • 7150 Mississauga Road • Mississauga, ON • L5N 8M5 • Tel: 905-286-3000 • Fax: 905-286-3050 • Contact: Human Resources • Internet: www.biovail.com • Biovail Corporation is a full-service pharmaceutical company, engaged in the formulation, clinical testing, registration, manufacturing, sale and promotion of pharmaceutical products by utilizing advanced oral controlled-release and FlashDose® technologies. Biovail's primary business strategy is to support the commercialization of its product development pipeline by expanding its sales and marketing presence in the United States and Canada. The Company intends to complement its product pipeline by acquiring established pharmaceutical products and in-licensing products in the early stages of development from third parties.

CANADA SAFEWAY PHARMACY • 14360 Yellowhead Trail • Edmonton, AB • T5L 3C5 • Tel: 780-439-4337 • Fax: 780-439-4227 • Contact: Mr. Farzin Rawji, Pharmacy Recruitment Coordinator • E-mail: farzin.rawji@safeway.com • Internet: www.safewaypharmacy.ca • Canada Safeway is one of Canada's most respected food and drug retailers. Their company operates over 180 full service pharmacy departments across Canada. They offer a dynamic working environment. One that encourages excellence and achievement. A place of challenges, opportunities and rewards. A place where continued personal and professional growth is encouraged and supported. It's an environment ideally suited for patient-focused energetic individuals who work within a team environment.

 Career Tip

Put Yourself in an Employer's Shoes
If you were looking to hire, what strengths and qualities would you look for in a candidate? What characteristics would lead you to choose one applicant over another? These are the same traits that you should market to employers.

CHROMATOGRAPHIC SPECIALTIES INC. • P.O. Bag 1150, 300 Laurier Blvd. • Brockville, ON • K6V 5W1 • Tel: 613-342-4678 • Fax: 613-342-1144 • Contact: Mr. Ken Jordan, Sales and Technical Marketing Manager • E-mail: sales@chromspec.com • Internet: www.chromspec.com • Chromatographic Specialties is a laboratory supply company to the Canadian marketplace, specializing in chromatography and sample preparation solutions.

ELI LILLY CANADA INC. • 3650 Danforth Avenue • Scarborough, ON • M1N 2E8 • Tel: 416-694-3221 • Contact: Human Resources • Internet: www.lilly.ca • Eli Lilly Canada is a brand name pharmaceutical company specializing in products related to diabetes, infectious diseases, cancer, the central nervous system and gastrointestinal diseases. The company's current research is focused on osteoporosis, the cardiovascular system, the central nervous system, anti-infectives and oncology. Eli Lilly employs more than 41,000 people worldwide and markets its medicines in 143 countries.

GLAXOSMITHKLINE • 7333 Mississauga Road • Mississauga, ON • L5N 6L4 • Tel: 905-819-3000 • Fax: 905-819-3099 • Contact: Human Resources • Internet: www.gsk.ca • GlaxoSmithKline Inc. (GSK) is a world leading research-based pharmaceutical company with a powerful combination of skills and resources that provides a platform for delivering strong growth in today's rapidly changing healthcare environment. Their mission is to improve the quality of human life by enabling people to do more, feel better and live longer. More than 1,800 people are employed by GSK.

HEMOSOL INC. • 2585 Meadowpine Blvd. • Mississauga, ON • L5N 8H9 • Tel: 905-286-6200 • Fax: 905-286-6300 • Contact: Manager, Human Resources • E-mail: hr@hemosol.com • Internet: www.hemosol.com • Hemosol is a biopharmaceutical company focused on the development and manufacturing of biologics, particularly blood-related proteins. Hemosol's expertise in the bioconjugation of proteins is also being used in the development of products directed at anti-viral and anti-cancer therapeutics.

HOFFMANN-LA ROCHE LIMITED • 2455 Meadowpine Blvd. • Mississauga, ON • L5N 6L7 • Tel: 905-542-5555 • Fax: 905-542-7130 • Contact: Human Resources Dept. • Internet: www.rochecanada.com • Hoffmann-La Roche Limited is one of the world's leading health care companies. In 2004, the company made the list of the Top 50 Best Companies to Work for in Canada, selected by the Globe and Mail's Report on Business Magazine. Hoffmann-Roche was voted as the fifth best company to work for. In Canada, Roche has always been guided by a commitment to research and development, pursuing innovative approaches in its search for superior healthcare products through its diagnostic and pharmaceuticals divisions. Celebrating more than 70 years of business in Canada, Roche employs almost 700 people across the country, with two head offices, one for its pharmaceutical division in Mississauga, Ontario, and one for its diagnostic division in Laval, Quebec.

INTEGRATED RESEARCH INC. • 1351 Sunnybrooke Boulevard • Montreal, QC • H9B 3K9 • Tel: 514-683-1909 • Fax: 514-683-0121 • Contact: Ms. Cynthia Hansen, Manager, Human Resources • E-mail: hr@iricanada.com • Internet: www.iricanada.com • Integrated Research Inc. is a Canadian contract research organization providing clinical research management services and expert assistance to pharmaceutical and biotechnology firms worldwide in the development of their therapeutic agents. Our comprehensive services include study site and data management along with regulatory and statistical support that extends from Phase I to Post-Marketing Surveillance research programs.

IOGEN CORPORATION • 310 Hunt Club Road East • Ottawa, ON • K1V 1C1 • Tel: 613-733-9830 • Fax: 613-733-0781 • Contact: Ms. Cathy Kirkham, Human Resources • E-mail: careers@iogen.ca • Internet: www.iogen.ca • Iogen Corporation is the leading biotechnology firm specializing in bioethanol, a clean fuel that has no CO_2 emissions and can be used in cars today. The company's proprietary enzyme technology for producing bioethanol offers a low cost, consumer friendly way to reduce fossil fuel use and CO_2 emissions in the transportation industry.

ISOTECHNIKA INC. • 5120 - 75th Street• Edmonton, AB • T6E 6W2 • Tel: 780-487-1600 • Fax: 780-484-4105 • Contact: Human Resources • E-mail: hr@isotechnika.com • Internet: www. isotechnika.com • Founded in 1993 by Dr. Robert Foster, Isotechnika Inc. is an international biopharmaceutical company headquartered in Edmonton, Alberta. Drawing upon our in-house expertise led by Dr. Randall Yatscoff in medicinal chemistry and immunology, we are focused on the discovery and development of novel immunosuppressive therapeutics that are safer than currently available treatments. Our entrepreneurial management and world-class team of scientists are building a pipeline of immunosuppressive drug candidates for use in the prevention of organ rejection in transplantation and in the treatment of auto-immune diseases. Isotechnika looks to become the leader in development of immunosuppressant therapies.

PATHEON INC. • 7070 Mississauga Road, Suite 350 • Mississauga, ON • L5N 7J8 • Tel: 905-821-4001 • Fax: 905-812-2121• Contact: Human Resources • E-mail: tro.hr@patheon. com • Internet: www.patheon.com • Patheon is a leading global provider of outsourced drug development and manufacturing services to pharmaceutical and biotechnology companies. With eleven facilities and more than 4700 employees in North America and Europe, Patheon has the capacity, expertise and global reach to meet the growing needs of the international pharmaceutical industry. They serve more than 100 pharmaceutical and biotechnology client companies, including 15 of the world's 20 largest pharmaceutical companies.

RAYLO CHEMICALS INC. • 8045 Argyll Road NW • Edmonton, AB • T6C 4A9 • Tel: 403-472-6439 • Fax: 403-468-4784 • Contact: Human Resources • Raylo Chemicals Inc., a Laporte Fine Chemicals company located in Edmonton, is one of the Canadian leaders in developing and manufacturing pharmaceutical activities in intermediates under cGMP. They employ approximately 200 individuals.

SCP SCIENCE • 21800 Clark Graham • Baie D'Urfé, QC • H9X 4B6 • Tel: 514-457-0701 • Fax: 514-457-4499 • Contact: Human Resources • E-mail: mbox@scpscience.com • Internet: www. scpscience.com • SCP Science is a market leader in the manufacturing of sample preparation products and standards for analytical chemistry laboratories. They distribute exclusive analytical chemistry instrumentation throughout Canada, for well-known manufacturers. Operating since 1980, they have expanded to a new integrated facility located in the Baie D'Urfé Industrial Park on the West Island of Montreal.

Business Services

1-800-GOT-JUNK? • 200-1523 West 3rd Avenue • Vancouver, BC • V6J 1J8 • Tel: 1-800-GOT-JUNK• Contact: Human Resources • Internet: www.1800gotjunk.com • The company concept is simple for 1-800-GOT JUNK? Not everyone has a truck or the time to take their junk to the dump. Since everyone has junk there is a universal need for junk removal. The company has established its North American presence with one name and one phone number: 1-800-GOT-JUNK? Individuals can apply online.

APEX LAND CORP. • 1710 14th Avenue NW, Suite 300 • Calgary, AB • T2N 1M5 • Tel: 403-264-3232 • Fax: 403-263-0502 • Contact: Human Resources • E-mail: info@apexland.com • Internet: www.apexland.com • For over a decade, APEX has been a leading Calgary based real estate development company operating within select Canadian and United States market segments. Apex operates four divisions: Land Development, Multi Family Development, Single

Family Home Construction and Senior Retirement Residences. APEX's land development division acquires, develops and sells land for the construction of single and multi-family housing.

ARBOR CARE TREE SERVICE LTD. • 10100 114th Avenue SE • Calgary, AB • T3S 0A5 • Tel: 403-273-6378 • Fax: 403-272-1536 • E-mail: trees@arborcare.com • Internet: www.arborcare. com • ArborCARE Tree Service Ltd. is a Canadian company, based in Calgary and Edmonton, Alberta, Canada. ArborCARE provides guaranteed service to residential, commercial, municipal and utility customers. You can depend on ArborCARE's ISA Certified Arborists to provide you with timely, courteous and knowledgeable service. ArborCARE has been incorporated since 1983.

ARCTIC CO-OPERATIVES LIMITED • 1645 Inkster Blvd. • Winnipeg, MB • R2X 2W7 • Tel: 204-697-1625 • Fax: 204-697-1880 • Contact: Human Resources • E-mail: HumanResources@ ArcticCo-op.com • Internet: www.arcticco-op.com • Arctic Co-operatives Limited is a service federation that is owned and controlled by 35 community-based Co-operative business enterprises that are located in Nunavut, Northwest Territories, and northern Manitoba. Arctic Co-operatives Limited coordinates the resources, consolidates the purchasing power and provides operational and technical support to the community based Co-operatives to enable them to provide a wide range of services to their local member owners in an economical manner.

ARMOR PERSONNEL • 8 Nelson Street West, Suite 104A • Brampton, ON • L6X 4J2 • Tel: 905-454-3333 • Fax: 905-459-0132 • Contact: Professional Recruitment Services • E-mail: brampton@armorpersonnel.com • Internet: www.armorpersonnel.com • Armor Personnel is a professional employment organization specializing in recruitment services and job placements for permanent, temporary, and contract positions at no charge to applicants.

BELL & HOWELL LTD. • 5650 Yonge Street, Suite 1802 • Toronto, ON • M2M 4G3 • Tel: 800-889-6245 • Fax: 416-228-2438 • Contact: Ms. Linda Wisson, Human Resources Manager • Internet: www.bowebellhowell.ca • Bell & Howell offers a range of solutions for the document finishing and conversion industry, including state-of-the-art hardware, leading-edge software and unparalleled customer service.

BROOKFIELD PROPERTIES CORPORATION • Brookfield Place, 181 Bay Street, Suite 300 • Toronto, ON • M5J 2T3 • Tel: 416-363-9491 • Fax: 416-365-9642 • Contact: Human Resources Department • E-mail: jobs@brookfieldproperties.com • Internet: www.brookfield.ca • Brookfield Properties Corporation owns and manages a portfolio of premier North American office properties and also develops master-planned residential communities.

CANPAR TRANSPORT L.P. • 1290 Central Parkway West, Suite 500 • Mississauga, ON • L5C 4R9 • Tel: 905-276-3700 • Fax: 905-897-3630 • Contact: Human Resources • Internet: www. canpar.com • Canpar Transport L.P. is one of Canada's leading small parcel delivery companies with over sixty terminals coast to coast. Founded in 1976, their expertise as a parcel delivery specialist comes down to their people. The 1,700 members of the Canpar team are dedicated to building solid working relationships with their customers as part of their overriding commitment to service.

CBV COLLECTIONS SERVICES LTD. • 1200-100 Sheppard Avenue East • Toronto, ON • M2N 6N5 • Tel: 416-482-9323 • Fax: 416-482-9359 • Contact: Mr. Michael Entwistle, Branch Manager • E-mail: mentwistle@cbvcollections.com • Internet: www.cbvcollections.com • CBV Collections Services Ltd. Is a third party debt collector. They perform collections of overdue accounts over telephone.

CERIDIAN CANADA • 125 Garry Street • Winnipeg, MB • R3C 3P2 • Tel: 204-947-9400 • Fax: 204-975-5700 • Contact: Human Resources • Internet: www.ceridian.ca • Ceridian Canada is a leading provider of comprehensive human resource solutions to over 40,000 Canadian businesses of all sizes and in various industries. Ceridian enables companies to be free to succeed in their core business through its innovative human resource solutions for HRMS, payroll, tax filing, time and attendance, benefits administration and organizational and employee effectiveness services.

ENTERPRISE RENT-A-CAR • 554 Pembina Highway • Winnipeg, MB • R3T 6A5 • Tel: 204-478-7800 • Fax: 204-478-8118 • Contact: Ms. Leanne Bonnar, Recruiting Supervisor • E-mail: leanne.bonnar@erac.com • Internet: www.enterprise.com/careers • Enterprise is the largest car rental company in North America and arguably the world. They are a $7.4 billion company with more than 735,000 vehicles in our rental and leasing fleet, more than 57,000 employees and over 6,000 locations in the U.S., Canada, Germany, the United Kingdom and Ireland.

FEDEX • 5985 Explorer Drive • Mississauga, ON • L4W 5K6 • Tel: 905-212-5000 • Fax: 905-212-5678 • Contact: Human Resources • Internet: www.fedex.com • FedEx Express is involved in the courier business, shipping packages and goods of all sizes across the country. The firm has an employee base of over 4,000 individuals.

FLINT ENERGY SERVICES LTD. • 300 - 5th Avenue S.W., Suite 700 • Calgary, AB • T2P 3C4 • Tel: 403-218-7100 • Fax: 403-215-5445 • Contact: Human Resources • E-mail: hr@flint-energy.com • Internet: www.flint-energy.com • Flint Energy Services Ltd. is one of Canada's largest integrated downstream oilfield services, industrial construction and fabrication components. Flint Energy Services was formed in 1999 as a result of the purchase or merger with five of Canada's premier oilfield service and construction companies including Flint Canada Inc., Reid's Construction Group, Braidnor Construction, HMW Construction, and Titan Electric and Controls.

GENERATION 5 MATHEMATICAL TECHNOLOGIES INC. • 515 Consumers Road • Toronto, ON • M2J 4Z2 • Tel: 416-441-6800 • Fax: 416-441-2771 • Contact: Human Resources • E-mail: info@generation5.net • Internet: www.generation5.net • Generation 5 produces mathematical software specifically for business applications and have developed the most geographically refined predictive modelling tool currently available in Canada and the largest micro marketing database in North America.

INNOVATIVE RESPONSE MARKETING INC. • 2825 Argentia Road, Unit 4 • Mississauga, ON • L5N 8G6 • Tel: 905-826-1411 • Fax: 905-826-1450 • Contact: Ms. Linda Campbell, Vice-President • E-mail: lcampbell@inno-mktg.com • Internet: www.inno-mktg.com • Innovative Response Marketing is a direct marketing agency offering direct mail, printing and fulfillment services to a wide range of clients. Please visit their website for more company information.

INTERCON SECURITY LTD. • 40 Sheppard Avenue West • Toronto, ON • M2N 6K9 • Tel: 416-229-6811 • Fax: 416-229-1207 • Contact: Mr. Bryan Kelly, Recruiting Manager • E-mail: bryan_kelly@interconsecurity.com • Internet: www.interconsecurity.com • Intercon Security provides security personnel and systems to individuals, businesses, and other enterprises across Canada and internationally. Offering detective and protective services, Intercon Security employs over 2200 individuals across the country and another 270 personnel work for the company worldwide. Individuals interested in working for Intercon, can call the Career Line at 416-229-6949.

Looking For a Job is Hard Work
Understand from the beginning that looking for employment is a full-time job in itself. It requires a tremendous amount of dedication, hard work and patience. Be prepared to stay the course!

KABA ILCO INC. • 7301 Décarie • Montréal, QC • H4P 2G7 • Tel: 514-735-5411 • Fax: 514-735-5732 • Contact: Human Resources • E-mail: cv@kaba-ilco.com • Internet: www.kaba-ilco.com • Kaba Ilco is a global provider of access control solutions for business, government, military, education and the lodging industry, worldwide. Kaba Ilco employs more than 9000 people located in 60 countries.

KRUG INC. • 421 Manitou Drive • Kitchener, ON • N2C 1L5 • Tel: 519-748-5100 • Fax: 519-748-5177 • Contact: Human Resources • E-mail: jobs@krug.ca • Internet: www.krug.ca • Krug Inc. is a leading manufacturer of high end business furniture including casegoods, seating and conference tables. The company's head office is in Kitchener, Ontario.

LAMBERT SOMEC INC. • 1505 rue des Tanneurs • Québec City, QC • G1N 4S7 • Tel: 418-687-1640 • Fax: 418-688-7577 • Contact: Director HR • E-mail: lamsoadm@lambertsomec.com • Internet: www.lambertsomec.com • Founded in 1961, Lambert Somec, is considered one of the leading electromechanical construction companies in the province of Quebec. It has participated in numerous major projects around the world in the industrial, commercial and institutional sectors.

LEVEL A INC. • 277 George Street North, Suite 212 • Peterborough, ON • K9H 3G9 • Tel: 705-749-1919 • Fax: 705-749-5494 • Contact: Ms. Kathy Pyle, President • E-mail: submitresume@levela.net • Internet: www.levela.net • Level A Inc. is a full-service personnel agency that specializes in qualifying and placing talented individuals with experience in general office, clerical and data entry work, intermediate to senior administration, financial, technical areas such as IT and AutoCAD and key management/executive search and placement. Any employment opportunities are dependant on their clients' requirements. They fill their employment needs as they arise. Depending on the position to be filled, the client may require a level of practical job experience in addition to the educational requirements needed.

LOSS PREVENTION GROUP INC. • Unit K, 2151 Portage Avenue • Winnipeg, MB • R3J 0L4 • Tel: 204-487-0487 • Contact: Human Resources • E-mail: rickgreen@losspreventiongroup.com • Internet: www.losspreventiongroup.com • Since 1989 the Loss Prevention Group Inc. has provided Canada's retail, hospitality and manufacturing sectors with comprehensive loss prevention and profit retention services that include consulting, training services, in-house and industry seminars.

LYRECO OFFICE PRODUCTS • 7303 Warden Avenue, Suite 200 • Markham, ON • L3R 5Y6 • Tel: 905-968-1320 • Contact: Human Resources •E-mail: contact.canada@lyreco.com • Internet: www.lyreco.ca • Lyreco Office Products is involved in the distribution of stationary products to various businesses. In Canada, Lyreco has a sales force of 175 highly trained professionals. Our team of over 500 employees services all markets in Canada, coast to coast.

M. MCGRATH CANADA LIMITED • 111A Rideau Street • Ottawa, ON • K1N 5X1 • Tel: 613-241-8420 • Fax: 613-241-1653 • E-mail: collections@mcgrathcanada.com • Internet: www.mcgrathcanada.com • M. McGrath Canada Limited, founded in 1953, is an International Collection, Credit Management and Credit Consultant agency. It is one of the largest independent agents in Canada.

MARKETLINC • 100 - 201 21st Street East • Saskatoon, SK • S7K 0B8 • Tel: 306-956-7000 • Fax: 306-668-5812 • Contact: Ms. Jennifer James, Employee Development Services • E-mail: jjames@marketlinc.com • Internet: www.marketlinc.com • MarketLinc is a sales and marketing firm that helps high-tech organizations unlock the potential of their markets through our proprietary methodology of Prospect Relationship Management (PRM). We deliver sales for organizations, knowledge about their prospects and customers and insight into their marketplace. We have developed a proprietary methodology called Prospect Relationship Management (PRM) that enables us to complete on an international level and deliver complex sales and marketing solutions. We work with four of the world's ten largest software companies; Microsoft, Business Objects (formerly Crystal Decisions), Network Associates Inc. (McAfee.com), and BMC Software.

MARKS SUPPLY INC. • 300 Arnold Street • Kitchener, ON • N2H 6E9 • Tel: 519-578-5761 • Fax: 519-743-2364 • Contact: Human Resources • E-mail: hr@markssupply.net • Internet: www. markssupply.net • We are a plumbing and HVAC distributor with 7 locations in Ontario. We are located in Kitchener, Guelph, Brantford, Burlington, Niagara Falls, London and Windsor.

MAXXAM ANALYTICS INC. • 6740 Campobello Road • Mississauga, ON • L5N 2L8 • Tel: 905-817-5700 • Fax: 905-817-5777 • Contact: Mr. Randall Helander, V.P. Human Resources • E-mail: hr@on.maxxam.ca • Internet: www.maxxam.ca • Maxxam Analytics Inc. is one of the largest, multi-disciplinary, independent analytical service companies in Canada. Maxxam conducts over 8 million tests annually in the environmental, industrial, pharmaceutical and food industries. The company operates modern laboratory facilities in 11 Canadian cities and employs more than 700 highly trained people.

MULTI-LANGUAGES • 80 Corporate Drive, Suite 305 • Scarborough, ON • M1H 3G5 • Tel: 416-296-0842 • Fax: 416-296-0859 • Contact: Human Resources • E-mail: translations@multi-languages.com • Internet: www.multi-languages.com • Multi-Languages is a language service company that provides translations, interpretation and typesetting in virtually every language in the world. They have a team of highly professional translators with many years of experience in the most varied fields of translation and interpretation. They employ approximately 1,500 freelance translators.

NBS CARD SOLUTIONS GROUP • 703 Evans Avenue, Suite 400 • Toronto, ON • M9C 5E9 • Tel: 416-621-1911 • Fax: 416-621-8875 • Contact: Human Resources • E-mail: careers@ nbstech.com • Internet: www.nbstech.com • NBS Technologies Inc. is a leading provider of card personalization, payment solutions, and commerce gateway transaction services for financial institutions, governments, and corporations worldwide.

NCR CANADA LTD. • 580 Weber Street North • Waterloo, ON • N2J 4G5 • Tel: 519-884-1710 • Fax: 519-884-0610 • Contact: Human Resources • Internet: www.ncr.com • NCR Waterloo designs, develops, manufactures and markets to customers around the globe, payment processing solutions such as large-scale item and image processing systems. They also produce a family of Automated Teller Machines (ATMs) for customers in the NAFTA region. They employ 32,500 associates in 130 countries.

NEWS MARKETING CANADA • 6 - 2400 Skymark Avenue • Mississauga, ON • L4W 5L3 • Tel: 905-602-6397 • Fax: 905-602-8823 • Contact: Human Resources • Internet: www. newsmarketing.ca • News Marketing Canada is a unit of the international division of News America Marketing and part of the News Corporation Company. Affiliated with diverse news, entertainment and media properties the News Corporation Company is parent company to Twentieth Century Fox, HarperCollins Publishers, British Sky Broadcasting, and Fox Broadcasting, among others. News Marketing Canada offers expert guidance in all areas of promotional planning, execution and analysis.

PALADIN SECURITY & INVESTIGATIONS LIMITED • The Canon Building, 4664 Lougheed Highway, Suite 295 • Burnaby, BC • V5C 5T5 • Tel: 604-677-8700 • Fax: 604-677-8701 • Contact: Human Resources • E-mail: vancouverinfo@paladinsecurity.com • Internet: www. paladinsecurity.com • Paladin Security and Investigations is a detective agency and offers protective services to individuals and businesses in British Columbia. Established in 1976, the detective agency has an employee base of approximately 300 individuals.

PAVCO • 777 Pacific Boulevard • Vancouver, BC • V6B 4Y8 • Tel: 604-482-2200 • Fax: 604-681-9017 • Contact: Human Resources • Internet: www.bcpavco.com • PavCo is a Crown Corporation of the Province of British Columbia, Ministry of Small Business and Economic Development, the Honourable John Les, Minister Responsible. PavCo has developed an excellent track record in facility management that includes professional expertise in marketing, human resources and event coordination. This experience and knowledge comes from the successful operation of four diverse public facilities, together hosting over 365 events annually.

PITNEY BOWES OF CANADA LTD. • 5500 Explorer Drive • Mississauga, ON • L4W 5C7 • Tel: 905-219-3000 • Fax: 905-219-3826 • Contact: Human Resources • Internet: www.pitneybowes. ca • Pitney Bowes Canada is a subsidiary of Pitney Bowes Inc., located in Stamford, Connecticut. With more than 1550 Canadian employees, working in more than 20 branches in major city centres across the country, Pitney Bowes Canada offers an exceptional range of products and an unparalleled level of customer service.

PUROLATOR COURIER LTD. • 11 Morse Street, 2nd Floor • Toronto, ON • M4M 2P7 • Tel: 416-461-9031 • Fax: 416-461-3994 • Contact: Ms. Debbie Kamino, Employment Equity & Recruitment Consultant • E-mail: careers@purolator.com • Internet: www.purolator.com • As Canada's leading overnight courier company, Purolator Courier Ltd. Is committed to making shipping the easiest part of the day for its customers. From automated solutions to around-the-clock pick and delivery, Purolator provides its customers with the services and customized solutions required to get their shipments across town or around the world.

REPLICON INC. • 910 - 7th Avenue SW, Suite 800 • Calgary, AB • T2P 3N8 • Tel: 403-262-6519 • Fax: 403-233-8046 • Contact: Human Resources • E-mail: careers@replicon.com • Internet: www.replicon.com • Founded in 1996, Replicon is the world leader in web-based time and expense management solutions, and the innovator in productivity software. Replicon has grown its total user base to more than 750,000 users in 42 countries today.

REVENUE PROPERTIES COMPANY LIMITED • 55 City Centre Drive, Suite 800 • Mississauga, ON • L5B 1M3 • Tel: 905-281-3800 • Fax: 905-281-1800 • Contact: Human Resources • Internet: www.revprop.com • Revenue Properties Company Limited (the "Company" or "RPC") is a Toronto based corporation engaged in the real estate industry. RPC develops, owns and manages both retail and residential properties. Its primary emphasis is on the acquisition, development and management of income-producing properties. Revenue Properties' objective is to realize continued growth in these areas, and to achieve substantial capital appreciation through careful management of its investment portfolio.

REYNOLDS AND REYNOLDS (CANADA) LIMITED • 3 Robert Speck Parkway, Suite 700 • Mississauga, ON • L4Z 2G5 • Tel: 877-4REYNOLDS • Fax: 905-267-6101 • Contact: Human Resources • Internet: www.reyrey.ca • Reynolds is the leading provider of integrated solutions that help automotive retailers grow, manage change and improve their profitability. We enable car companies and automotive retailers to work together to build the lifetime value of their customers. Today Renyoulds is a billion-dollar company with over 70 years of experience in the automotive retailing industry and operations in 20 countries.

SC INFRASTRUCTURE INC. • 1177 - 11th Avenue SW, 7th Floor • Calgary, AB • T2R 1K9 • Tel: 403-244-9090 • Fax: 403-206-7508 • Contact: Human Resources • E-mail: admin@groupsci. com • Internet: www.groupsci.com • SC Infrastructure recently completed construction of the Confederation bridge. The company is an infrastructure construction and management construction company.

SOMERVILLE MERCHANDISING LTD. • 5760 Finch Avenue East • Toronto, ON • M1B 5J9 • Tel: 905-754-7228 • Fax: 905-754-9574 • Contact: Ms. Paola Muzyka, Human Resources • E-mail: pmuzyka@somerville.ca • Internet: www.somerville.ca • Somerville Merchandising is a custom design and manufacturer of permanent displays and signage.

Consumer Manufacturing

ALBERTO CULVER CANADA INC. • 506 Kipling Avenue • Toronto, ON • M8Z 5E2 • Tel: 416-251-3741 • Fax: 416-251-3062 • Contact: Human Resources • The Alberto-Culver Company grew from a single product in 1955 to a multi-billion dollar corporate good citizen today. Headquartered in Melrose Park, Illinois, the Alberto-Culver Company launched its Canadian operation in 1961. Alberto-Culver, throughout its history, has demonstrated every year its ability to sustain and build powerful brand names and business categories. The company's original and flagship product, Alberto VO5 hairdressing, is still, by far, the market leader in its category after more than 45 years on the retailers' shelves.

ALCAN ALUMINIUM LIMITED • 1188 Sherbrooke Street West • Montréal, QC • H3A 3G2 • Tel: 514-848-8000 • Fax: 514-848-8162 • Contact: Human Resources • E-mail: info@alcan. com • Internet: www.alcan.com • Alcan is a strong force in the global aluminum and packaging industries. A look at the world of Alcan reveals a company with a global reach and exceptional promise for future growth. With approximately 88,000 employees in more than 60 countries, Alcan has leading positions in raw materials, primary metals, fabricated products and packaging. These include products and systems for the automotive and mass transportation markets, aluminum sheet for beverage cans, as well as flexible and specialty packaging for the food, pharmaceutical and personal care industries worldwide.

ALLCOLOUR PAINT LIMITED • 1257 Speers Road • Oakville, ON • L6L 2X5 • Tel: 905-827-4173 • Fax: 905-827-6487 • Contact: Human Resources • Internet: www.allcolour.com • Allcolour Paint Limited is a leading Canadian manufacturer of quality industrial coatings. Founded in 1964, Allcolour has gained recognition through its dedication to leading edge technology and relentless customer service. Allcolour also demonstrates customer commitment through its continuous improvement program through which it manufactures under ISO9002 standards.

AMRAM'S DISTRIBUTING LTD. • 18 Parkshore Drive • Brampton, ON • L6T 5M1 • Tel: 905-789-1880 • Fax: 905-789-1889 • Contact: Ms. Susan Nowocin, Human Resources • E-mail: nrivkin@pathcom.com • Amram Distributing is a wholesaler and distributor of giftware and toys. They have a sales force of 60 people across Canada, and a Canadian head office in Etobicoke.

AURUM CERAMIC DENTAL LABORATORIES LTD. • 115 17 Avenue SW • Calgary, AB • T2S 0A1 • Tel: 403-228-5120 • Fax: 1-800-747-1233 • Contact: Human Resources Department • E-mail: cathyb@aurumgroup.com • Internet: www.aurumgroup.com • Aurum Ceramic Dental Laboratories is the largest crown and bridge lab in Canada. With locations across Canada, Aurum's Group of Companies is a leading supplier of all aspects of esthetic and restorative dentistry. An on-going education program keeps them on the cutting edge of dental techniques and technology, in order to provide the best in materials and craftsmanship.

BASF CANADA INC. • 100 Milverton Drive, 5th Floor • Mississauga, ON • L5R 4H1 • Tel: 289-360-1300 • Fax: 289-360-6000 • Contact: Human Resources • Internet: www.basf.ca • BASF Canada manufactures and markets a broad range of chemicals, fibres, polymers, agricultural products, coatings, colourants, and a wide variety of consumer products. BASF Canada Inc. has approximately 975 employees. Their head office and one of our plant sites are located in Toronto. Other production sites include Arnprior, Windsor, Georgetown and Cornwall, Ontario; Abbotsford, British Columbia; and Blackie, Alberta.

BIC INC. • 155 Oakdale Road • North York, ON • M3N 1W2 • Tel: 416-742-9173 • Fax: 416-741-4965 • Contact: Human Resources • E-mail: HumanResourcesww@bicworld.com • Internet: www.bicworld.com • Bic Inc. is involved in the manufacturing of writing instruments, lighters, and shavers.

CANADIAN THERMOS PRODUCTS INC. • 370 King Street West, Suite 302 • Toronto, ON • M5V 1J9 • Tel: 416-757-6231 • Fax: 416-757-6230 • Contact: Human Resources • Internet: www.thermos.com • Canadian Thermos Products Inc. is involved in the plastics/insulated products manufacturing business. They produce hard and soft coolers and lunch kits, and other useful products.

CASCO INC. • 405 The West Mall, Suite 600 • Etobicoke, ON • M9C 0A1 • Tel: 416-620-2300 • Fax: 416-620-4488 • Internet: www.casco.ca • Canada Starch Operating Company Inc./ Casco Inc. is a wholly-owned subsidiary of Corn Products International, Inc. Through continuous growth, they have remained Canada's largest corn wet milling operation. They have led the corn wet milling industry in pioneering new products, technologies, and manufacturing processes.

CLUB MONACO CORP. • 157 Bloor Street West • Toronto, ON • M5S 1P7 • Tel: 416-591-8837 • Internet: www.clubmonaco.com • Club Monaco is the international retail brand known for great modern style for both men and women. Classics are given a modern take through great design and a current sensibility. For nearly two decades, Club Monaco has been editing the trends in men's and women's fashion. The company's design aesthetic has brought the brand to the forefront of fashion, grabbing the attention of fashion editors and trendsetters around the world. Club Monaco provides style essentials for the modern wardrobe - updated classics that last forever but also have the feeling of the moment. At Caban, you'll find everything for your home. From dining, and bathing to outdoor entertaining. Caban offers a complete shopping experience by mixing fashion and interior design in a unique shopping environment. The result is a modern, edited collection of product that reflects good design, quality and value. The address provided is for their International Office.

COLGATE-PALMOLIVE CANADA INC. • 895 Don Mills Road, 6th Floor • Toronto, ON • M3C 1W3 • Tel: 416-421-6000 • Fax: 416-421-0286 • Contact: Human Resources Department • Internet: www.colgate.ca • Colgate-Palmolive Canada markets and manufactures consumer products for both personal and household care. They market and create everything from toothpaste and toothbrushes, to bar soap, household cleaners, laundry detergent, and even pet food.

DUPONT CANADA INC. • P.O. Box 2200 Streetsville • Mississauga, ON • L5M 2H3 • Tel: 905-821-3300 • Fax: 905-821-5110 • Contact: Staffing Team • Internet: www.dupont.ca • The origins of Dupont Canada, whose new legal name is E. I. du Pont Canada Company, dates back to 1877. Dupot is a diversified science company, headquartered in Mississauga and serving customers across Canada and in more than 40 other countries. The company offers a wide rage of products and services to markets including agriculture, nutrition, electronics, communications, safety and protection.

DYNASTY FURNITURE MANUFACTURING LTD. • 3344 - 54 Avenue SE • Calgary, AB • T2C 0A8 • Tel: 800-567-8872 • Fax: 888-329-7632 • Contact: Human Resources • Internet: www. dynastyf.com • Dynasty Furniture is one of North America's leading upholstery manufacturers. Since its start in 1979, Dynasty Furniture has broadened its focus to include Europe, Asia, and Africa. Almost all of their manufacturing operations are computerized from new product development to cutting, sewing, woodworking, and upholstery.

FEDERATED CO-OPERATIVES LIMITED • Box 1050, 401 - 22nd Street East • Saskatoon, SK • S7K 0H2 • Tel: 306-244-3311 • Fax: 306-244-3403 • Contact: Retail Recruitment • Email: hr@fcl.ca • Internet: www.fcl.ca • More approximately 275 retail co-operatives serve an estimated 1,000,000 individual co-op members from Thunder Bay in northwest Ontario to the Queen Charlotte Islands on British Columbia's West Coast, and from the U.S. border to the Arctic Circle. Retail co-operatives are united as the Co-operative Retail System through their central wholesale organization, Federated Co-operatives Limited.

GIENOW BUILDING PRODUCTS LTD. • 7140 40th Street SE • Calgary, AB • T2C 2B6 • Tel: 403-203-8200 • Fax: 403-230-9309• Contact: Human Resources • Internet: www.gienow.com• They are Western Canada's leading manufacturer of custom made windows and doors with its main manufacturing facility located in Calgary. They currently employ over 750 staff with locations across Alberta, British Columbia, and into Saskatchewan.

GROUP DYNAMITE INC.• 5592, Ferrier Street • Mount-Royal, QC • H4P 1M2 • Tel: 514-773-3962 • Fax: 514-773-3663 • Contact: Ms. Cleo Hamet, Manager, Staffing and Talent Management • E-mail: chamet@dynamite.ca • Internet: www.dynamite.ca • Groupe Dynamite Inc. is a very successful, dynamic, Canadian-owned retailer of fashionable woman's apparel. They employ over 3000 in over 200 stores across Canada and operate under the Dynamite, Garage and Chado brands.

HERBS FOR HURTS INC. • Box 35084, Sarcee RPO • Calgary, AB • T3E 7C7 • Tel: 403-242-6860 • Fax: 403-246-6814 • Contact: President • E-mail: herbsforhurts@booboobears.com • Internet: www.booboobears.com • Herbs for Hurts Inc. markets and manufactures alternative health products for children. Their main product is a boo boo bear (a warm/cool herbal pack).

I P L PLASTICS LTD. • 140 Commerciale Street • Saint-Damien, QC • G0R 2Y0 • Tel: 418-789-2880 • Fax: 418-789-3153 • Contact: Human Resources • E-mail: infoipl@ipl-plastics.com • Internet: www.ipl-plastics.com • IPL Inc. is a leading North American producer of molded plastic products for various industrial sectors. Founded in 1939, the Company employs more than 1000 people and manufactures and markets over 400 products. IPL designs and produces packaging containers and crates for the agrifood, chemical, forest products, petrochemical construction and integrated waste management industries. It also provides high-tech custom molding services for the automotive, transport, maple syrup, telecommunication and defense industries.

IMPERIAL TOBACCO CANADA LIMITED • 3711 St-Antoine Street • Montreal, QC • H4C 3P6 • Tel: 514-932-6161 • Fax: 514-932-3993 • Internet: www.imperialtobaccocanada.com • Imperial Tobacco is Canada's major tobacco company with more than two thirds of the tailor-made cigarette market. Their head office is in Montreal. They operate one cigarette manufacturing plant in Guelph and three tobacco processing plants in Aylmer, Ontario. Sales offices are situated in Laval, Toronto and Calgary. They employ some 1,200 people across Canada.

INTERFOREST LTD. • P.O. Box 170 • Durham, ON • N0G 1R0 • Tel: 519-369-3310 • Fax: 519-369-3316 • Contact: Human Resources • E-mail: careers@interforest.com • Internet: www.interforest.com • Interforest Ltd. is the premier wood veneer producer in North America. Their products are used by furniture manufacturers and architectural designers. They employ 1,000 people in North America at six facilities.

Start Your Job Search Early

Placing time restrictions on your job search will only lead to added stress and, ultimately, disappointing choices. Start your job search early and follow an organized plan of attack.

INTERTAPE POLYMER GROUP INC. • 9999 Cavendish Blvd., 2nd Floor • Ville St. Laurent, QC • H4M 2X5 • Tel: 514-731-7591 • Fax: 514-731-5039 • Contact: Ressources humaines • E-mail: info@itape.com • Internet: www.intertapepolymer.com • Intertape Polymer Group Inc., a publicly owned company, is headquartered in Montreal, Canada, with 15 facilities throughout North America and Europe. The IPG team spans the globe to provide strong support through a dedicated network of local representatives. With a unique and broad range of products and industry expertise, IPG brings innovative packaging solutions to customers worldwide.

JOHN DEERE LIMITED • P.O. Box 1000 • Grimsby, ON • L3M 4H5 • Fax: 905-945-7740 • Contact: Human Resources Specialist • E-mail: grimsbyhumanresources@johndeere.com • Internet: www.deere.com • John Deere is a leading manufacturer and wholesaler of agricultural, construction and forestry, and commercial and consumer products.

JOSTENS CANADA LTD. • 1051 King Edward Street • Winnipeg, MB • R3H 0R4 • Tel: 204-633-9233 • Fax: 204-633-9150 • Contact: Human Resources Specialist • E-mail: hrtechsupport@jostens.com • Internet: www.jostens.com • Founded in 1897 in Owatonna, Minnesota, Jostens Inc. is internationally recognized as a leading provider of high quality school photographs, yearbooks, class and championship rings, scholastic awards, diplomas and graduation announcements. Jostens Canada was formed in 1968 to meet the specific needs of the Canadian educational community. The company's products include yearbooks, class rings, graduation products, school photography, achievement awards and products for athletic champions and their fans.

KIMBERLY-CLARK INC. • 50 Burnhamthorpe Road West • Mississauga, ON • L5B 3Y5 • Tel: 905-277-6500 • Fax: 905-277-6508 • Internet: www.kimberly-clark.com • Kimberly-Clark Inc. manufactures a range of products including diapers, baby wipes, training pants, feminine products, facial tissue, bathroom tissue and napkins. Kimberly-Clark also produces tissue and non-woven products for the industrial service and health care markets.

LEGO CANADA INC. • 45 Mural Street, Unit 7 • Richmond Hill, ON • L4B 1J4 • Tel: 877-518-5346 • Fax: 905-886 3093 • Contact: HR Manager • E-mail: jobs@lego.com • Internet: www.lego.com • Lego Canada is a distributor of construction toys for children. The company employs about 100 individuals.

LENBROOK INDUSTRIES LIMITED • 633 Granite Court • Pickering, ON • L1W 3K1• Tel: 905-831-6555 • Fax: 905-831-6936 • Contact: Human Resources Department • E-mail: humanresources@lenbrook.com • Internet: www.lenbrook.com • Lenbrook Canada is one of the country's leading independent specialty electronics import and marketing organizations. Lenbrook acts as the Canadian «marketing arm» for some of the world's finest manufacturers. It gives the manufacturer complete market service at a fraction of the cost of opening their own subsidiary. It brings immediate and highly visible market presence to these manufacturers and their product.

LIFETOUCH CANADA INC. • 1395 Inkster Blvd. • Winnipeg, MB • R2X 1P6 • Tel: 204-633-1395 • Fax: 204-694-5226 • Contact: Human Resources • Internet: www.lifetouch.ca • • Lifetouch Canada is a photofinishing company that produces school, grad and professional photographs. Their head office is in Winnipeg, Manitoba.

MAAX INC. • 600 Cameron Road • Ste-Marie, QC • G6E 1B2 • Tel: 888-957-7816 • Fax: 800-201-9308 • Contact: Human Resources • E-mail: job@maax.com • Internet: www.maax.com • MAAX is a North American leader in baths, kitchens and spas with a strong history of innovation, style and exceptional products. MAAX currently employs more than 2000 employees in 16 plants throughout North America and Europe.

MACRODYNE TECHNOLOGIES • 311 Connie Crescent • Concord, ON • L4K 5R2 • Tel: 905-669-2253 • Fax: 905-669-0936 • Contact: Ms. Marie Knott, Human Resources • E-mail: mknott@ macrodynepress.com • Internet: www.macrodynepress.com • Macrodyne Technologies is a hydraulic press manufacturer that sells, custom designs and manufactures custom presses.

MCKENZIE SEEDS • 30 - 9th Street, Suite 100 • Brandon, MB • R7A 6E1 • Tel: 204-571-7500 • Fax: 204-728-8671 • Contact: Human Resources • E-mail: customerservice@mckenzieseeds. com • Internet: www.mckenzieseeds.com • McKenzie Seeds is Canada's largest seed packaging company. Flower and vegetable seeds of all varieties are available. Customization of seed packaging is available for activities such as promotion and fund raising.

MITSUBISHI ELECTRIC SALES CANADA • 4299 14th Avenue • Markham, ON • L3R 0J2 • Tel: 905-475-7728 • Fax: 905-475-7861 • Contact: Human Resources • E-mail: careers@ mitsubishielectric.ca • Internet: www.mitsubishielectric.ca • Mitsubishi Electric Sales Canada Inc., established in 1979 as a subsidiary of the Mitsubishi Electric Corporation of Japan, markets an extensive line of consumer, commercial and industrial electronics products including semiconductor devices, automotive equipment, cellular phones, heating and air conditioning systems, projectors, printers, security recorders, large scale video displays for stadiums and arenas, thermal imagers, and product certification services.

MUSTANG SURVIVAL CORP. • 3810 Jacombs Road • Richmond, BC • V6V 1Y6 • Tel: 604-270-8631 • Fax: 604-214-0489 • Contact: Human Resources • E-mail: humanresources@ mustangsurvival.com • Internet: www.mustangsurvival.com • For more than 30 years, Mustang Survival has been committed to providing life support solutions for people exposed to the most hazardous environment. Through constant innovation and the application of new technologies and processes we have become established as a leading supplier of protective garments to the most demanding users, from weekend sailors and powerboaters to jet fighter pilots and even NASA astronauts.

NIKE CANADA LTD. • 175 Commerce Valley Drive West, Unit 500 • Thornhill, ON • L3T 7P6 • Tel: 905-764-0400 • Fax: 905-764-1266 • Contact: Human Resources • Internet: www.nike.ca • Nike Canada is a global entity that manufactures sport and athletic apparel, equipment and footwear.

NYGARD INTERNATIONAL LTD. • One Niagara Street • Toronto, ON • M5V 1C2 • Tel: 416-598-6900 • Fax: 416-979-0506 • Contact: Human Resources • E-mail: employ@nygard.com • Internet: www.nygard.com • Nygård International was founded by Peter J. Nygård in 1973 and has grown to become one of the most successful apparel manufacturers in North America. It has grown to be the number one sportswear manufacturer in Canada and number three in North America. The company expanded into the United States in1978. As a result of its increasingly diverse business activities, in 1987 Nygård opened the company's International Sales and Marketing Headquarters in Toronto. Nygård has five product lines, each targeting women over twenty five years of age. Nygård employs approximately 2,600 people worldwide.

PHILLIPS & TEMPRO INDUSTRIES LTD. • 100 Paquin Road • Winnipeg, MB • R2J 3V4 • Tel: 204-667-2260 • Fax: 204- 667-2041 • Contact: Human Resources • Internet: www. phillipsandtemro.com • Phillips & Tempro Industries is a manufacturer of automobile cold weather starting aids for the automotive, heavy duty and industrial industries.

PROFESSIONAL PHARMACEUTICAL CORPORATION • 9200 Côte de Liesse • Lachine, QC • H8T 1A1 • Tel: 514-631-7710 • Fax: 514-631-2867 • Contact: Human Resources • Internet: www.marcelle.com • Professional Pharmaceutical Corporation is a leading Canadian cosmetics manufacturer employing over 250 employees. They are a dynamic company enjoying steady growth and success, and are seeking an energetic professional to join their team.

ROTHMANS, BENSON AND HEDGES INC. • 1500 Don Mills Road • Toronto, ON • M3B 3L1 • Tel: 416-449-5525 • Fax: 416-449-9601 • Contact: Human Resources • Internet: www. rothmansinc.ca • Rothmans Inc. is the only Canadian owned, publicly traded tobacco company. Rothmans participates in the Canadian tobacco products industry through its 60% ownership interest in Rothmans, Benson & Hedges Inc. The remaining 40% of RBH is owned by an affiliate of Altria Group, Inc. (formerly Philip Morris Companies Inc.). Rothmans Inc. has been a part of the Canadian tobacco industry for the past 100 years. One of their predecessor companies Rock City Tobacco Co., located in Quebec City, began operations in 1899. There are more than 750 employees that make up RBH's head office staff, its marketing department, sales force and manufacturing employees.

ROYAL PHILIPS ELECTRONICS • 281 Hillmount Road • Markham, ON • L6C 2S3 • Tel: 905-201-4100 • Fax: 905-887-4241 • Contact: Human Resources • Internet: www.philips.com • Philips has been inventing and marketing innovative products for over a hundred years, and has been a leading brand in Canada since 1934. Throughout Canada and globally, Philips stands for innovative ideas, quality manufacturing and an ongoing commitment to customer satisfaction. Today, Philips Canada is a leading brand in lighting, personal and small kitchen appliances, medical systems for diagnosis and therapy, consumer electronics, colour monitors, LCD projectors, institutional televisions, speech processing systems, and electronics components. From our new high-tech Canadian headquarters in Markham, Ontario, our national network of sales and service centres employs more than 500 Canadians, and supports millions of Philips customers.

RUBBERMAID CANADA INC. • 2562 Stanfield Road • Mississauga, ON • L4Y 1S5 • Tel: 905-279-1010 • Fax: 905-279-5254 • Contact: Human Resources • Internet: www.rubbermaid. com • Beginning with its first patent for a rubber dustpan in 1933, Rubbermaid creates and manufactures innovative things that organize our lives. As the trendsetter in the housewares industry for innovation and product design, Rubbermaid categories span home storage and garage organization, food storage and laundry, bath and cleaning, closet organization and refuse removal.

SHARP ELECTRONICS OF CANADA LTD. • 335 Britannia Road East • Mississauga, ON • L4Z 1W9 • Tel: 905-890-2100 • Fax: 905-568-7141 • Contact: Human Resources • Internet: www.sharp.ca • Since their founding in 1912, Sharp Corporation has continuously opened up new areas of industry with its original products, from the "Ever-Sharp" mechanical pencils from which the company name was derived, to the commercialization of the first Japanese-made radios and televisions, the world's first LCD electronic calculators, and a host of other products incorporating our state-of-the-art LCD technology. These products have contributed to the improvement of human living and the advancement of society as a whole.

SHERMAG INC. • 2171 King Street West • Sherbrooke, QC • J1J 2G1 • Tel: 819-566-1515 • Fax: 819-566-7323 • Contact: Human Resources • Internet: www.shermag.com • Shermag is a leader in the production and distribution of high-quality residential furniture. The company enjoys an enviable reputation in the North American market and figures prominently in the design of contemporary-style furniture. Shermag's facilities include a network of medium-size factories equipped with state-of-the-art technology.

SILVER JEANS • 555 Logan Avenue • Winnipeg, MB • R3A 0S4 • Tel: 204-788-4249 • Fax: 204-772-6929 • Contact: Human Resources • Internet: www.silverjeans.com • Silver Jeans is a 100% Canadian owned and operated company, privately held and managed. They proudly manufacture almost all of their products in Canada. This ensures the quality they require in every clothing item they make. At Silver, they promote a corporate philosophy that has less to do with balance sheets and more to do with how to be the best company they can be. Implicit in that philosophy is the belief that their 1,200 employees are their greatest asset.

SONY OF CANADA LTD. • 115 Gordon Baker Road • Toronto, ON • M2H 3R6 • Tel: 416-499-1414 • Fax: 416-497-1774 • Internet: www.sony.ca • Sony is Canada's leading provider of electronic and computer solutions for consumers and business. For almost 50 years, Sony of Canada Ltd. has demonstrated an ability to capture people's imaginations and enhance their lives. Today, Sony is a corporation with convergence at its very heart, well positioned for the future to bring numerous benefits to consumers by combining hardware, software, content and services. A national bilingual organization, Sony of Canada Ltd. has offices located in Vancouver, BC, Whitby, ON, Toronto, ON (Head Office), and Montreal, PQ. A subsidiary of Sony Corp. of Japan, Sony of Canada Ltd. is a sales and marketing organization. Sony employs approximately 1100 employees across Canada. The company is divided into two major sales and marketing groups: Wholesale and Retail. The Wholesale group is responsible for marketing and sales of Sony products to consumers through a dealer network, and to professionals through multiple direct sales channels; the Retail group operates over 70 consumer electronics Sony stores and is responsible for direct merchandising and sales of Sony and third party consumer electronic products to the Canadian retail public.

SRI HOMES INC. • 9500 Jim Bailey Road • Kelowna, BC • V4V 1S5 • Tel: 250-766-0588 • Fax: 250-762-0599 • Contact: Human Resources • E-mail: careers@srihomes.com • Internet: www. srihomes.com • SRI Homes Inc. supplies its customers with the highest quality, as well as the most affordable homes and commercial structures from Ontario to British Columbia, from North Dakota to Alaska, from the Northwest Territories to Nunavut and beyond!

STERLING MARKING PRODUCTS INC. • 349 Ridout Street • London, ON • N6A 2N8 • Tel: 519-434-5785 • Fax: 519-434-9516 • Contact: Human Resources • Internet: www.sterling.ca • Sterling Marking Products is a stamp and signage manufacturer that produces pre-inked and rubber stamps, indoor and outdoor signs, name badges and desk plates, and printing of box dies. They employe 197 people.

TIGER BRAND KNITTING COMPANY LIMITED • P.O. Box 188, 96 Grand Avenue South • Cambridge, ON • N1R 5S9 • Tel: 519-624-7800 • Fax: 519-621-2695 • Contact: Human Resources • Internet: www.tigerbrand.com • Tiger Brand Knitting Company is a manufacturer of cotton leisure-wear garments. The firm employs about 270 people.

TOWN SHOES LIMITED • Toronto Eaton Centre • 44 Kodiak Crescent • Downsview, ON • M3J 3G5 • Tel: 416-638-5011 • Fax: 416-638-3847 • Contact: Human Resources • E-mail: superstars@townshoes.com • Internet: www.townshoes.com • Town Shoes is a leading retailer of fashion footwear and accessories. They have two retail divisions, Town Shoes (high fashion ladies footwear and accessories) and The Shoe Company (fashion footwear and accessories for the whole family). They have numerous Town Shoe and Shoe Company stores. They are rapidly expanding across Canada, and offer great career opportunities. They have an excellent salary and benefits package, which includes a staff discount and other incentives! Their structured training programs provide a solid learning environment, which will help accelerate your career development. Their rapid growth coupled with their unparalled commitment to promoting from within, provides excellent opportunities for advancement.

UPLIFT TECHNOLOGIES INC. • 19-10 Morris Drive • Dartmouth, NS • B3B 1K8 • Tel: 902-422-0804 • Fax: 902-422-0798 • Contact: Human Resources • E-mail: info@up-lift.com • Internet: www.up-lift.com • Uplift Technologies manufactures and distributes home medical equipment products. Uplift Technologies Inc. is committed to providing innovative healthcare technology to enhance personal well being. Working together as a team, they strive to meet or exceed customer expectations of quality and value through dedicated service and support.

VECTOR CANADA • 102-4014 Macleod Trail South • Calgary, AB • T2G 2R7 • Tel: 403-243-6635 • Contact: Human Resources • Internet: www.workforstudents.com • Vector is a customer sales and service company. Their representatives work one on one with customers to demonstrate a product. The appointments are pre-set, no door to door, or telemarketing. Their reps are paid per appointment.

WATERGROUP • 580 Park Street • Regina, SK • S4N 5A9 • Tel: 306-761-3247 • Fax: 306-721-0088 • Contact: Human Resources • Internet: www.usfilter.com • Around the world, industries, institutions, and municipalities turn to USFilter -- a Siemens business -- for all their water and wastewater treatment needs. They are a world leader in products, systems, and services for water and wastewater treatment and employ over 200 people across North America.

WEST COAST APPAREL • 611 Alexander Street • Vancouver, BC • V6A 1E1 • Tel: 604-251-8600 • Fax: 604-251-8602 • Contact: Human Resources • Jax is a marketer of women's apparel, sold in fine stores across Canada and the USA.

Diversified

GENERAL ELECTRIC CANADA INC. • 2300 Meadowvale Blvd. • Mississauga, ON • L5N 5P9 • Tel: 905-858-5100 • Fax: 419-858-5641 • Contact: Human Resources • Internet: www.ge.com • General Electric Canada is a diversified technology, manufacturing and services company that offers many different consumer products. General Electric itself operates in more than 100 countries around the world, including 250 manufacturing plants in 26 different nations. GE employs 300,000 people worldwide. General Electric Canada employs 6,100 people.

I M P GROUP INTERNATIONAL INC. • 2651 Joseph Howe Drive • Halifax, NS • B3L 4T1 • Tel: 902-453-2400 • Fax: 902-455-6931 • Contact: HR Generalist • E-mail: hr@impgroup.com • Internet: www.impgroup.com • I.M.P. Group International Inc. is a diversified Halifax-based, privately-owned company engaged internationally in aerospace, aviation, industrial, marine, medical, and hotel industries. I.M.P. employs 3,500 people worldwide.

J.D. IRVING LIMITED • 300 Union Street, P.O. Box 5777 • Saint John, NB • E2L 4M3 • Tel: 506-632-7777 • Fax: 506-648-2205 • Contact: Human Resources Division • E-mail: resumes@jdirving.com. • Internet: www.jdirving.com • J.D. Irving, Limited is a family-owned enterprise with over 100 years of involvement in the business community. They produce a full and wide range of forest products including kraft pulp, newsprint, tissue and corrugating medium. The company owns and operates sawmills in New Brunswick, Nova Scotia, Maine and Quebec.

JAMES RICHARDSON INTERNATIONAL LIMITED • 2800 One Lombard Place • Winnipeg, MB • R3B 0X8 • Tel: 204-934-5961 • Fax: 204-942-4161 • Contact: Human Resources • E-mail: jrihr@jri.ca • Internet: www.jri.ca • James Richardson International is the largest subsidiary of James Richardson & Sons, Limited, a privately owned corporation that has been family controlled for five generations. For nearly 150 years, the Richardson name has been synonymous with the international grain industry. Today, JRI's agrifood operations extend from coast to coast and beyond, positioning JRI as one of Canada's leading agribusinesses. With a world of expertise in merchandising, logistics and market planning, JRI offers growers a proven link to the dynamic world of grain marketing. From seed to sea, JRI can provide the resources that producers need to grow and thrive in today's demanding marketplace.

Understand Labour Market Trends
The labour market is changing rapidly! By learning about and understanding key labour market trends, you will be better equipped to carry out your job search as well as uncover hidden opportunities.

JIM PATTISON GROUP • 1067 West Cordova Street, Suite 1800 • Vancouver, BC • V6C 1C7 • Tel: 604-688-6764 • Fax: 604-687-2601 • Contact: Human Resources • Internet: www. jimpattison.com • The Jim Pattison Group is a diversified organization with consumer oriented lines of business that include food, broadcasting, packaging, transportation and financial services. There are approximately 26,000 individuals employed in various disciplines within the company.

MALTAIS GEOMATICS INC. • 17011 - 105 Avenue • Edmonton, AB • T5S 1M5 • Tel: 780-483-2015 • Fax: 780-484-1360 • Contact: Mr. Irwin Maltais, President and General Manager • E-mail: careers@maltaisgeomatics.com • Internet: www.maltaisgeomatics.com • Maltais Geomatics Inc. (MGI) employs approximately 80 professional and technical staff, and offers a wide range of geomatics services to a large client base. Our Survey Engineering Group has been delivering survey engineering and land surveying services in western and northern Canada for more than 25 years under the leadership of Professional Engineers and commissioned Alberta Land Surveyors and Canada Lands Surveyors. Our Spatial Technology Group provides sophisticated geo-spatial information services, including enterprise-wide and web-based Geographic Information Systems (GIS), together with a wide variety of data and imagery services, tools, and products.

Educational Institutions

ACADIA UNIVERSITY • 21 Horton Avenue • Wolfville, NS • B4P 2R6•Tel: 902-585-2201 • Contact: Human Resources • Internet: www.acadiau.ca • Considered one of the leading undergraduate universities in Canada, Acadia offers students a unique opportunity to experience an environment which combines outstanding academic programs with a diversity of extracurricular activities. The university has over 200 degree combinations from the Faculty of Arts, Pure and Professional Studies, Management and Education, and Theology. On 250 acres, Acadia University has a full time student population of 3,700 individuals from 35 countries. Founded in 1838, the university has a distinctive list of noted alumni.

BAYVIEW TUTORIAL INSTITUTE / FREEMONT ACADEMY • 240 Duncan Mill Road, Suite 303 • Toronto, ON • M3B 1Z4•Tel: 416-385-2888 • Fax: 416-385-2909•Contact: Human Resources•Internet: www.freemontacademy.com • Freemont Academy is a small, private, alternative high school certified by the Ministry of Education. Bayview Tutorial is an established educational centre offering elementary and secondary private tutoring in all academic subjects.

CHAMPION TUTORS • 117 Hawksbury Close NW • Calgary, AB • T3G 3E3 • Tel: 403-547-8674 • Contact: Mr. Lorne Jones, Owner • E-mail: lornejones@championtutors.com • Internet: www.championtutors.com • Champion Tutors offers one-to-one tutoring in all grades and subjects, all in the comfort and safety of your home, anywhere in Canada. No resumes or phone calls please.

BLUEWATER DISTRICT SCHOOL BOARD • 351 1st Avenue North, P.O. Box 190 • Chesley, ON • N0G 1L0 • Tel: 519-363-2014 • Fax: 519-370-2909 • Internet: www.bwdsb.on.ca • The Bruce County Board of Education and The Grey County Board of Education amalgamated on January 1, 1998 to form the new Bluewater District School Board. The new District Board now oversees the programs in 48 elementary schools, 11 secondary schools and an outdoor education facility.

GRANT MACEWAN COLLEGE • City Centre Campus, 7-105 10700 - 104 Avenue • Edmonton, AB • T5J 4S2 • Tel: 780-497-5439 • Fax: 780-497-5430 • Contact: Brian Pearson, Associate Director, Human Resources • E-mail: careers@macewan.ca • Internet: www.gmcc.ab.ca • Within the «Spirit of MacEwan», Grant MacEwan College is a learning organization that has its aim to optimize human potential as an investment in prosperity. They are an open, flexible, learning organization focused on the learner and supported by technology, partnerships, and employee development within a global community.

HOLLAND COLLEGE • 140 Weymouth Street • Charlottetown, PEI • C1A 4Z1 • Tel: 902-566-9636 • Fax: 902-566-9639 • Contact: Ms. Marilyn MacCallum, Human Resources Officer • E-mail: hr@hollandc.pe.ca • Internet: www.hollandc.pe.ca • Holland College provides a wide range of educational programs, particularly in the fields of applied arts and technology, vocational and adult education. The college offers training at 12 centres on an annual basis and responds to training needs in several communities through eastern and western coordinators.

KEYANO COLLEGE • 8115 Franklin Avenue • Fort McMurray, AB • T9H 2H7 • Tel: 780-791-4800 • Fax: 780-791-1555 • Contact: Ms. Maureen Know, Director, Human Resources • E-mail: maureen.knox@keyano.ca • Internet: www.keyano.ca • Keyano College is an award winning comprehensive communicty college, serving the dynamic learning needs of the people and industry of Fort McMurray and the Municipality of Wood Buffalo. With 3,500 career, apprenticeship and university transfer students and almost 10,000 workplace and community education learners, Keyano is a national leader in industry training and aboriginal education.

PEEL DISTRICT SCHOOL BOARD • 5650 Hurontario Street • Mississauga, ON • L5R 1C6 • Tel: 905-890-1099 • Fax: 905-890-4955 • Contact: Ms. Donna White, Employee Relations Officer • E-mail: donna.white@peelsb.com • Internet: www.peelschools.org • The Peel District School Board is responsible for maintaining quality education in elementary and secondary schools in the Region of Peel. Employing approximately 16,000 staff, the Peel Board oversees 211 schools in the area. The Peel Board has a variety of jobs in addition to teaching positions. Our online application centre known as Virtually in Peel (VIP) for teaching, teaching assistants and secretarial, clerical or library technicians positions is accessed from the Work in Peel section of the board's web site. A listing of other positions (business) can be found on the Job Board which is also located in the Work in Peel section of the Board's website. are posted on the Board's teacher application center known as Virtually in Peel (VIP). VIP can be accessed from the Work in Peel section of the Board's web site at www.peelschools.org. A listing of other current positions (business) can be found on the Job Board which is also located in the Work in Peel section of the Board's web site at www.peelschools.org. Individuals should respond to specific advertising for business positions. Our Recruitment Hotlines are: 905-890-1010, ext. 2457 (or 1-800-668-1146) for teaching positions: 905-890-1010, ext. 3052 (or 1-800-668-1146) for business positions.

RYERSON POLYTECHNIC UNIVERSITY • 350 Victoria Street • Toronto, ON • M5B 2K3 • Tel: 416-979-5076 • Fax: 416-979-5163 • Contact: Human Resources • E-mail: hr@ryerson.ca • Internet: www.ryerson.ca • Ryerson Polytechnic University is a post-secondary undergraduate institution that is career oriented and has degree granting status. In addition to academic courses, Ryerson offers business and industry, hotel administration, journalism, and child care programs.

TORONTO CATHOLIC DISTRICT SCHOOL BOARD • 80 Sheppard Avenue East • Willowdale, ON • M2N 6E8 • Tel: 416-222-8282 • Fax: 416-512-3047 • Contact: Human Resources • E-mail: humanresourcesl@tcdsb.org • Internet: www.tcdsb.org • The Toronto Catholic District School Board teaches more than the basics. Through a Christ-centered vision and in partnership with parents, parishes and the community, they serve students from diverse cultural, linguistic and ethnic backgrounds in Canada's largest and most dynamic city. TCDSB educates more than 95,000 students in 201 elementary and secondary schools.

TORONTO DISTRICT SCHOOL BOARD • 5050 Yonge Street • Toronto, ON • M2N 5N8 • Tel: 416-397-3000 • Fax: 416-397-9969 • Contact: Human Resources • Internet: www.tdsb.on.ca • TDSB schools are at the heart of every community in the City of Toronto. Wherever you are in the city, you'll find a local public school to welcome you. They are Toronto's centres of learning, and they are also centres of activity before and after school. They have 558 schools that deliver quality education to our students. More than 550 schools offer elementary level education (including intermediate) and 102 offer secondary level education.

TORONTO FRENCH SCHOOL, THE • 306 Lawrence Avenue East • Toronto, ON • M4N 1T7 • Tel: 416-484-6533 • Fax: 416-488-3090 • Contact: Human Resources • E-mail: dgagne@ tfs.on.ca • Internet: www.tfs.on.ca • TFS students represent more than 40 nationalities, and while 90% of our students join TFS with little or no background in French, they graduate fully bilingual. In addition to French, students learn at least one other language during their TFS career. More than half of our International Baccalaureate diploma recipients chose to pursue a bilingual IB diploma, strong evidence of the opportunities a TFS education provides.

TORONTO PUBLIC LIBRARY BOARD • 789 Yonge Street • Toronto, ON • M4W 2G8 • Tel: 416-393-7000 • Fax: 416-395-5925 • Contact: Human Resources • E-mail: recruitment@ torontopubliclibrary.ca • Internet: www.torontopubliclibrary.ca • The Toronto Public Library is the largest public library system in Canada, with 98 branches and more than 11 million items to borrow or use in the library.

UNIVERSITY COLLEGE OF CAPE BRETON • P.O. Box 5300, 1250 Grand Lake Road • Sydney, NS • B1P 6L2 • Tel: 902-539-5300 • Fax: 902-562-0119 • E-mail: humanresources@ns.aliantzinc.ca • Internet: www.uccb.ns.ca • University College of Cape Breton is a large educational institution with many programs for both post-secondary students and adults alike. They have an employee base of approximately 400 individuals. There are few opportunities for student employment within their institution. Most opportunities are given to the school's own students.

Energy

ALBERTA ENERGY & UTILITIES BOARD • 640 5th Avenue SW • Calgary, AB • T2P 3G4 • Tel: 403-297-8311 • Fax: 403-297-7336 • Contact: Human Resources • E-mail: Human.Resources@ gov.ab.ca • Internet: www.eub.gov.ab.ca • Alberta Energy & Utilities Board is a provincial regulatory board which oversees the province's energy system.

ATCO ELECTRIC • 10035 - 105th Street NW • Edmonton, AB • T5J 2V6 • Tel: 780-420-7310 • Fax: 780-420-7400 • Contact: Human Resources • Internet: www.atcoelectric.com • For nearly 80 years, Albertans have counted on ATCO Electric for the safe, reliable delivery of electricity to their homes, farms, and businesses. They deliver electric energy to petroleum and forestry companies, farms, towns and cities, reserves and Metis settlements in 245 communities.

BALLARD POWER SYSTEMS INC. • 4343 North Fraser Way • Burnaby, BC • V5J 5J9 • Tel: 604-454-0900 • Fax: 604-412-4700 • Contact: Human Resources • Internet: www.ballard.com • Ballard Power Systems is recognized as the world leader in developing, manufacturing, and marketing zero-emission proton exchange membrane (PEM) fuel cells. Ballard is commercializing fuel cell engines for the transportation market, electric drives for both fuel cell and battery-powered electric vehicles, power electronics and fuel cell systems for both portable and stationary power generation markets.

BC HYDRO • 6911 Southpoint Drive • Burnaby, BC • V3N 4X8 • Tel: 604-528-3020 • Fax: 604-528-3007 • Contact: Human Resource Services • Internet: www.bchydro.bc.ca • BC Hydro is Canada's third largest electric utility and a provincial crown corporation. Their job is to support the economic growth of British Columbia through the efficient supply and distribution of electricity throughout the province. They serve 1.4 million customers in an area containing over 92 per cent of British Columbia's population. BC Hydro offers both men and women a wide variety of exciting careers in many different fields. The corporation employs more than 5,400 individuals.

ENBRIDGE INC. • 3000 Fifth Avenue Place, 425 - 1st Street SW • Calgary, AB • T2P 3L8 • Tel: 403-231-3900 • Fax: 403-231-3920 • Contact: Human Resources Department • E-mail: careers@corp.enbridge.com • Internet: www.enbridge.com • Enbridge Inc. is a leader in energy transportation, distribution and services in Canada and the United States. Enbridge operates the world's longest crude oil and liquids pipeline system, and provides natural gas to 1.5 million customers in Ontario, Quebec, and New York State. The company also has a growing involvement in natural gas transmission, international energy projects, electrical power distribution, and the provision of retail energy products and services. The company employs approximately 4,000 people primarily in Canada, the United States and Latin America.

ENERSOURCE HYDRO MISSISSAUGA • 3240 Mavis Road • Mississauga, ON • L5C 3K1 • Tel: 905-273-9050 • Fax: 905-566-2737 • Contact: Human Resources • E-mail: info@enersource. com • Internet: www.enersource.com • Enersource Hydro Mississauga provides all regulated electricity distribution services to the 170,000 customers in the City of Mississauga. A direct subsidiary of Enersource Corporation, the utility is an incorporated business operating on an independent and commercial basis, and owned 90% by the City of Mississauga and 10% by BPC Energy Corporation, a subsidiary of the Ontario Municipal Employees Retirement System (OMERS).

HUSKY ENERGY INC. • 707 - 8th Avenue SW • Calgary, AB • T2P 3G7 • Tel: 403-298-6111 • Fax: 403-298-7464 • Contact: Human Resources • Internet: www.huskyenergy.ca • Headquartered in Western Canadian Place in Calgary, Alberta, Canada, Husky Energy Inc. employs approximately 4100 people and holds almost $21 billion in quality growth assets. Husky Energy is active in the upstream, midstream and refined products oil and gas business, which allows it to take advantage of the full value chain from production at the wellhead to retail sales. Its midstream and downstream assets stabilize Husky Energy's cash flow and income during times of oil price volatility.

HYDRO ONE INC. • 483 Bay Street, South Tower, 15th Floor • Toronto, ON • M5G 2P5 • Tel: 416-345-5000 • Contact: Human Resources • E-mail: Careers@HydroOne.com • Internet: www. hydroone.com • Hydro One owns and operates Ontario's 28,600km high-voltage transmission system. The system transports electricity to 67 large industrial customers, 55 local distribution companies, and its own low-voltage distribution business. Hydro One's distribution system spans 75 per cent of Ontario. The company employs approximately 4,000 full-time staff across the province.

HYDRO QUÉBEC • 75, boulevard René-Lévesque Ouest • Montréal, QC • H2Z 1A4 • Tel: 514-289-3871 • Fax: 514-289-2530 • Contact: Ressources humaines • E-mail: accueil@hydro.gc.ca • Internet: www.hydroquebec.com • Hydro-Québec's mission is to supply power and to pursue endeavours in energy-related research and promotion, energy conversion and conservation, and any field connected with or related to power or energy. Hydro Québec employs 26,000 individuals.

MANITOBA HYDRO • 820 Taylor Avenue • Winnipeg, MB • R3M 3T1 • Tel: 204-474-3311 • Fax: 204-474-4868 • Contact: Employment Support Services • E-mail: employment@hydro. mb.ca • Internet: www.hydro.mb.ca • Manitoba Hydro is the Province's major energy utility, headquartered in Winnipeg, serving 505,883 electric customers throughout Manitoba and 253,631 gas customers in various communities throughout southern Manitoba. Virtually all electricity generated by the Provincial Crown Corporation is from self-renewing water power. They are the major distributor of natural gas in the province. The Corporation's capital assets-in-service at original cost exceed $10 billion, making it one of the largest energy and natural gas utilities in Canada.

NEW BRUNSWICK POWER CORPORATION • P.O. Box 2000, 239 Gilbert Street • Fredericton, NB • E3B 4X1 • Tel: 506-458-4444 • Fax: 506-458-4000 • Contact: Human Resources • E-mail: employment@nbpower.com • Internet: www.nbpower.com • NB Power is the largest electric utility in Atlantic Canada. They are preparing to meet the electricity demands of New Brunswickers in a deregulated industry. They recently reorganized themselves into separate business units and are continuing to evolve into a more efficient, customer driven company. NB Power employs 2,500 people. •

NEWFOUNDLAND AND LABRADOR HYDRO • Hydro Place • Columbus Drive, P.O. Box 12400 • St. John's, NL • A1B 4K7 • Tel: 709-737-1400 • Fax: 709-737-1800 • Contact: Human Resources • E-mail: hydro@nlh.nf.ca • Internet: www.nlh.nf.ca • Newfoundland and Labrador Hydro is a crown corporation committed to providing cost-effective and reliable energy services to our customers for the benefit of all people of the province. Their skilled and committed employees will use innovative methods and technologies, and will maintain high standards of safety and health, and environmental responsibility.

NOVA SCOTIA POWER CORP. • P.O. Box 910 • Halifax, NS • B3J 2W5 • Tel: 902-428-6494 • Fax: 902-428-6171 • Contact: Human Resources • Internet: www.nspower.ca • Nova Scotia Power Corp. is an electric utility company established to transmit and distribute electricity in Nova Scotia. The company employs over 2,200 individuals.

TALISMAN ENERGY INC. • 888 - 3rd Street S.W., Suite 3400 • Calgary, AB • T2P 5C5 • Tel: 403-237-1234 • Fax: 403-237-1902 • Contact: Human Resources • E-mail: careers-can@talisman-energy.com • Internet: www.talisman-energy.com • Talisman Energy is a large independent oil and gas producer. Based in Canada, they employ 1,758 people in their North American and international operations.

TORONTO HYDRO CORPORATION • 14 Carlton Street • Toronto, ON • M5B 1K5 • Tel: 416-542-8000 • Fax: 416-542-3452 • Contact: Human Resources Department • Internet: www.torontohydro.com • Toronto Hydro Corporation operates four wholly owned affiliates in the electricity distribution, retail energy services, telecommunications and street lighting businesses. They set their sights on four key priorities: successfully meeting the challenges of operating in Ontario's competitive electricity marketplace; continuing the implementation of new management systems across their business; delivering customer service at levels that meet or exceed Ontario Energy Board regulated standards; and continuing to improve the safety of their workplace. Toronto Hydro is an equal opportunity employer.

TRANSALTA • P.O. Box 1900, 110 - 12th Avenue SW • Calgary, AB • T2P 2M1 • Tel: 403-267-7110 • Fax: 403-267-4657 • Contact: Staffing • Internet: www.transalta.com • TransAlta is an international electric energy company with about $6 billion in assets. The company is focused on achieving strong earnings growth and enhancing its competitive edge as a low-cost operator of generation and transmission assets, and a successful developer of gas-fired independent power projects. The company is concentrating its growth in Canada, the United States, Australia and Mexico. They employ 2,679 individuals in Canada.

 Career ✓ Tip

Research Companies Before Applying to Them
Do your homework and research a firm to better understand their needs. If you are unable to find information about a particular employer, write to them and ask to be sent literature, such as an annual report.

Engineering & Architectural

ADI GROUP INC. • 1133 Regent Street, Suite 300 • Fredericton, NB • E3B 3Z2 • Tel: 506-452-9000 • Fax: 506-451-7451 • Contact: Ms. Sharon Wilson, Personnel Services • E-mail: jobs@adi.ca • Internet: www.adi.ca • ADI Group Inc. is comprised of several companies employing more than 200 design professionals, scientists, technicians, managers and support staff. The ADI companies provide consulting services and engineer/architect/procure/construct/finance capabilities for a wide variety of government and industrial clients. ADI Group Inc. operates in over 30 countries around the world and has licensing agreements with companies in India, Israel, Korea, Mexico, Turkey, and United Kingdom.

AMEC INC. • 700 University Avenue, 4th Floor • Toronto, ON • M5G 1X6 • Tel: 416-592-2102 • Contact: Human Resources • Internet: www.amec.com • AMEC is an international project management and services company. AMEC designs, delivers and supports infrastructure assets. Specific services include: project management, environmental and technical consultancy, architectural and engineering design, funding and feasibility studies, planning, procurement, construction and multi-technical services, facilities management, maintenance and decommissioning. With office networks across the Americas, continental Europe and Asia, , they employ 45,000 people in over 40 countries.

AQUATIC SCIENCES INC. • P.O. Box 2205, 250 Martindale Road • St. Catharines, ON • L2R 6P9 • Tel: 905-641-0941 • Fax: 905-641-1825 • E-mail: info@asi-group.com • Internet: www.asi-group.com • The dedicated specialists at ASI Group are international experts on water and wastewater management. Their guiding principle is «one innovative partner, many innovative solutions». ASI Group comprises three closely interrelated divisions: engineering, ecological and marine. This unique blend of expertise delivers complete, cost-effective answers to even the most complex water, and engineering issues. ASI Group was founded in 1987 as Aquatic Sciences Inc. by a small team of technical professionals committed to a better environment. Our company has grown extensively to provide industry and government worldwide with integrated leading edge services; from preliminary environmental impact surveys or needs assessment, through design and construction, and continuing with project management, contract plant operations, inspections and repair. With underwater robotic facilities, ecotoxicity labs, fabrication shops and experienced personnel in-house, we assure clients of rapid response and consistent quality.

ATCO NOISE MANAGEMENT • 1243 McKnight Blvd. NE • Calgary, AB • T2E 5T1 • Tel: 403-292-7804 • Fax: 403-292-7816 • Contact: Human Resources • Internet: www.atconoise.com • ATCO Noise Management is a full service engineering, procurement and construction (EPC) company specializing exclusively in industrial noise control.

BECHTEL CANADA CO. • 1500 University Street, Suite 910 • Montreal, QC • H3A 3S7 • Tel: 416-871-1711 • Fax: 416-871-1392 • Contact: Human Resources • Internet: www.bechtel.com • Founded in 1898, Bechtel is one of the world's premier engineering, construction, and project management companies. Their 42,500 employees are teamed with customers, partners, and suppliers on a wide range of projects in nearly 60 countries.

BOSCH REXROTH CANADA CORP. • 490 Prince Charles Drive South • Welland, ON • L3B 5X7 • Tel: 905-735-0510 • Fax: 905-735-5646 • Contact: Human Resources • E-mail: employment@boschrexroth.ca • Internet: www.boschrexroth.ca • Bosch Rexroth Canada is the Canadian partner company of Bosch Rexroth, the worldwide leader in "Drive and Control". Rexroth provides drive and control solutions in the major technology areas of Industrial Hydraulics, Electric Drives and Controls, Linear Motion and Assembly Technologies, Pneumatics, Service Automation and Mobile Hydraulics.

C B C L LIMITED • 1489 Hollis Street, P.O. Box 606 • Halifax, NS • B3J 2R7 • Tel: 902-421-7241 • Fax: 902-423-3938 • Contact: Human Resources • E-mail: info@cbcl.ca • Internet: www.cbcl. ca • CBCL Limited is a multi-discipline Engineering company providing a wide range of Project Management, Design and Construction Management Services for their clients.

CH2M HILL CANADA LIMITED • 255 Consumers Road • Toronto, ON • M2J 5B6 • Tel: 416-499-9000 • Fax: 416-499-4687 • Contact: Human Resources • E-mail: canadiancareers@ch2m. com • Internet: www.ch2m.com • CH2M Hill Canada Limited (CH2M HILL), one of Canada's largest environmental firms, is an employee-owned, Canadian-controlled private corporation that has been in operation for more than 80 years. With more than 10,000 team members worldwide, and the combined resources of more than 400 employees Canada-wide, CH2M HILL offers a complete range of environmental services and technologies to clients across Canada and in the global market.

COLT ENGINEERING CORPORATION • 8133 Warden Avenue • Markham, ON • L6G 1B3 • Tel: 905-940-4774 • Fax: 905-940-4778 • Contact: Human Resources Department • Internet: www.colteng.com • Since 1973, Colt Engineering Corporation has excelled as a multi-discipline engineering contractor in the design of hydrocarbon process facilities in Canada, the USA and in many regions of the world. Colt specializes in the design of conventional oil and gas production/processing facilities, pipelines, refineries, petrochemical plants, electrical power generation and cogeneration facilities, heavy oil facilities and oil sands plants. Colt has extensive experience in handling, treating and transportation of sour oil and gas production, as well as heavy oil and bitumen production. Colt has particularly strong capabilities in both desert and Arctic climates.

E B A ENGINEERING CONSULTANTS LTD. • 14940 - 123 Avenue • Edmonton, AB • T5V 1B4 • Tel: 780-451-2121 • Fax: 780-454-5688 • Internet: www.eba.ca • E B A Engineering Consultants is a multi-discipline consulting firm that is involved in transportation, geotechnical, geophysical, civil, and environmental engineering. The company employs approximately 400 people.

EARTH TECH CANADA INC. • 105 Commerce Valley Drive West, 7th Floor • Markham, ON • L3T 7W3 • Tel: 905-886-7022 • Fax: 905-886-9494 • Internet: www.earthtech.com • Earth Tech Canada Inc. is one of the largest full service engineering companies in Canada. Earth Tech provides high quality consulting, design, construction, and operations services to meet the environmental and infrastructure needs of industry and government. Earth Tech's Canadian operations encompass over 1,000 professional and support personnel in 18 offices across Canada.

ELLISDON CORPORATION • 89 Queensway Avenue West, Suite 800 • Mississauga, ON • L5B 2V2 • Tel: 905-896-8900 • Fax: 905-896-8911• Internet: www.ellisdon.com • EllisDon Construction is one of the largest General Contractors in Canada and has offices throughout North America. EllisDon specializes in construction in the ICI Sector (Industrial, Commercial, Institutional), and currently employs over 1,300 employees comprising a combination of construction professionals and highly skilled trades people.

GIFFELS ASSOCIATES LIMITED • 30 International Blvd. • Toronto, ON • M9W 5P3 • Tel: 416-675-5950 • Fax: 416-675-4620 • Internet: www.giffels.com • Giffels Associates is an engineering and architectural consulting firm, with 1200 professional staff. Primary activities include project management, design and construction of major industrial, institutional and commercial buildings, as well as highways and bridges. They also offer process engineering, logistics planning and general management consulting services.

GOLDER ASSOCIATES LTD. • 2390 Argentia Road • Mississauga, ON • L5N 5Z7 • Tel: 905-567-4444 • Fax: 905-567-6561 • Internet: www.golder.com • Golder Associates is an international group of consulting companies, specializing in ground engineering and environmental science services. With over 6000 employees in over 150 offices worldwide, they are one of the largest employee-owned engineering and earth science companies in the world.

H.H. ANGUS & ASSOCIATES LTD. • 1127 Leslie Street • Toronto, ON • M3C 2J6 • Tel: 416-443-8200 • Fax: 416-443-8290 • Contact: Human Resources • E-mail: office@hhangus. com • Internet: www.hhangus.com • Established in 1919, H.H. Angus & Associates is a full service engineering company. Services involving project management include planning, design, maintenance and operation planning. Process engineering services include consultation, engineering reports, and feasibility studies. As well they offer environmental services including air quality assessment, recycling plans, property redevelopment, environmental inspections and audits. The company employs 250 individuals, including those within affiliate companies. The firm has offices in Canada, the United States and the United Kingdom.

J. D. BARNES LIMITED • 145 Renfrew Drive, Suite 100 • Markham, ON • L3R 6B3 • Tel: 905-477-3600 • Fax: 905-477-3882 • Internet: www.jdbarnes.com • J.D. Barnes Limited was established in 1960 and since that time has become a leader in Canada's surveying, mapping and land information services industry. The firm presently employs approximately 230 staff members comprised of professional surveyors, engineers, technologists and technicians, systems analysts and programmers as well as support staff.

JACQUES WHITFORD LIMITED • 3 Spectacle Lake Drive • Dartmouth, NS • B3B 1W8 • el: 902-468-7777 • Fax: 902-468-9009 • Internet: www.jacqueswhitford.com • Jacques Whitford is one of Canada's fastest growing multi-disciplinary firms of consulting engineers and environmental scientists. Established in 1972, we are an employee-owned firm with over 1600 staff in offices throughout Canada, the eastern United States and internationally.

KINECTRICS INC. • 800 Kipling Avenue • Toronto, ON • M8Z 6C4 • Tel: 416-207-6000 • Fax: 416-207-5875 • Contact: Human Resources • E-mail: hr@kinectrics.com • Internet: www. kinectrics.com • Kinectrics is an independent company formed to help the North American energy sector improve business performance through science and engineering. They develop and apply new technologies for the energy industry, solving problems at operating plants, improving environmental performance, and assessing or improving the economic performance of different energy technologies.

LAURENTIDE CONTROLS LTD. • 18000 Transcanada Highway • Kirkland, QC • H9J 4A1 • Tel: 514-697-9230 • Fax: 514-697-9335 • Internet: www.laurentidecontrols.com • Laurentide Controls is the Eastern Canada sales office for Emerson Process Management. With over 100 employees based here at their Kirkland main office, they have 4 satellite offices, 2 offshore, 1 in Quebec City and 1 in Chicoutimi.

MARSHALL MACKLIN MONAGHAN LTD. • 80 Commerce Valley Drive East • Thornhill, ON • L3T 7N4 • Tel: 905-882-1100 • Fax: 905-882-0055 • E-mail: hr@mmm.ca • Internet: www.mmm.ca • Established in 1952, Macklin Monaghan Limited offers professional services to private and government clients, across Canada and internationally, with emphasis on consulting engineering, geomatics, planning, program and project management. With offices in Ontario, Alberta and the U.S., the firm's mission is to be a leader in the development, marketing and provision of high quality, comprehensive consulting professional services for industrial, urban, rural and resource development throughout Canada and in selected international locations.

MORRISON HERSHFIELD LIMITED • 235 Yorkland Blvd., Suite 600 • Toronto, ON • M2J 1T1 • Tel: 416-499-3110 • Fax: 416-499-9658 • Contact: Human Resources • E-mail: hr@

morrisonhershfield.com • Internet: www.morrisonhershfield.com • A pre-eminent, North American, employee-owned, consulting engineering firm established in 1946. Morrison Hershfield operates in a variety of disciplines that include building engineering, telecommunications services, municipal engineering, transportation and mechanical/electrical engineering.

NLK CONSULTANTS INC. • 855 Homer Street • Vancouver, BC • V6B 5S2 • Tel: 604-689-0344 • Fax: 604-443-1000 • Contact: Human Resources • NLK is a full service consulting engineering firm serving the pulp and paper industry worldwide. They have developed a full range of high quality services based on their specialized knowledge and understanding of the pulp and paper industry. NLK provides expertise in the two main business areas of engineering and strategic planning/marketing services. In both areas, NLK clients are provided with an experienced industry partner from project conception to completion.

O'CONNOR ASSOCIATES ENVIRONMENTAL INC. • Suite 200, 318 - 11th Avenue SE • Calgary, AB • T2G 0Y2 • Tel: 403-294-4200 • Fax: 403-294-4240 • E-mail: hr@oconnor-associates.com • Internet: www.oconnor-associates.com • O'Connor Associates is a Canadian-owned consulting firm offering professional services in a wide variety of engineering disciplines. The firm has a staff of approximately 145, based in offices in British Columbia, Alberta, Manitoba and Ontario. Since 1979 O'Connor Associates has provided environmental services to major oil, chemical and mining companies, industry operators, transportation companies, developers, property managers, insurers, financial companies, regulatory agencies and all levels of government. Subsurface investigations have been carried out at more than 7000 sites throughout Canada, including industrial plant sites and petroleum facilities such as refineries, bulk plants and service stations.

PCL CONSTRUCTORS INC. • 5410 - 99 Street • Edmonton, AB • T6E 3P4 • Tel: 780-733-5000 • Internet: www.pcl.ca • PCL Constructors Inc. is a contractor founded in 1906 that offers experience, competitive pricing, financial strength, professionalism, integrity and a commitment to projects that are supported by quality and workplace safety initiatives. PCL is one of the largest contracting organizations in North America.

PETER KIEWIT SONS CO. • 8135 Fourth Line North • Milton, ON • L9T 5L8 • Tel: 905-875-2556 • Fax: 905-875-1521 • Internet: www.kiewit.com • Peter Kiewit Sons Co. is a construction company established in Canada since 1941. We have earned a strong reputation of leadership in major civil engineering work throughout the country. The permanent staff in Eastern Canada is comprised of more than two hundred engineers and technicians from local universities. We serve the energy, transportation, mining and the heavy industrial markets. Recent major projects feature the York Rapid Transit project, the Grand-Mere Hydro-electric project, development of Voisey's Bay mine, and design-build modules for the White Rose offshore oil platform. Through rigorous recruiting and training of personnel, and a stimulating employee ownership program, Kiewit provides clients with a dynamic team that delivers projects on time and within budget.

SANDWELL • 885 Dunsmuir Street, Suite 600 • Vancouver, BC • V6C 1N5 • Tel: 604-684-9311 • Fax: 604-688-5913 • Internet: www.sandwell.com • Founded in 1948 in Vancouver, Canada, Sandwell made its name in the international pulp and paper industry. They then merged in 1986 with long-time affiliate Swan Wooster Engineering Co. Ltd. Since its inception in 1925, Swan Wooster had built a world-class reputation in the field of infrastructure development. The merger enabled Sandwell to combine its industrial and infrastructure expertise to provide clients with the integrated "total system" service they require in an era of global trade. As an acknowledged industry leader, Sandwell has been successful in recruiting and retaining the services of a talented, motivated corps of professionals, working out of operations centers in North America and Asia. Their staff of more than 700 includes engineers, project and construction managers, economists, planners and designers, technicians and support staff.

SNC-LAVALIN • 455 Boul. Rene-Levesque Ouest • Montréal, QC • H2Z 1Z3 • Tel: 514-393-1000 • Fax: 514-866-0419 • E-mail: info@snclavalin.com • Internet: www.snclavalin.com • SNC-Lavalin is one of Canada's leading engineering construction companies with worldwide projects. Their sectors of activity include defence, power, environment, infrastructure and facilities management, infrastructure and buildings, mining and metallurgy, pulp and paper, pharmaceuticals and biotechnology, chemicals and petroleum, mass transit systems, and telecommunications. They employ more than 10,000 individuals.

THE FOCUS CORPORATION LTD. • 9925 - 109 Street, Suite 300 • Edmonton, AB • T5K 2J8 •Tel: 780-466-6555 • Fax: 780-466-6175 • E-mail: edmonton@focus.ca • Internet: www.focus.ca • The Focus Corporation is a market leader in quality engineering and geomatics services. Focus is a professional engineering firm in the areas of land development and transportation, as well as surveying within the oil and gas sector.

THE MCELHANNEY GROUP LTD. • 100 - 780 Beatty Street • Vancouver, BC • V6B 2M1 • Tel: 604-683-8521 • Fax: 604-683-4350 • Contact: Human Resources • Internet: www.mcelhanney.com • The McElhanney Group Ltd. is divided into two areas of expertise: consulting and land surveys. McElhanney Consulting Services Ltd. provides consulting engineering, surveying, mapping and planning services in the fields of transportation, structures, land development, drainage, water supply and treatment, sewage treatment and disposal, and resource development. Since 1910, McElhanney Land Surveys Ltd.'s core area of services has been to provide a wide variety of land surveying and mapping to the resource industry. Today, their main commitment is to support the construction of well sites, access roads, pipelines and plant sites.

TROW ASSOCIATES INC. • 1595 Clark Blvd. • Brampton, ON • L6T 4V1 • Tel: 905-793-9800 • Fax: 905-793-0641 • Contact: Human Resources • Internet: www.trow.com • Founded in 1957 and celebrating its 46 year anniversary, Trow Associates Inc. has grown into one of the largest engineering and consulting companies in Canada. With offices across Canada and around the globe, Trow offers clients in both the private and public sectors a full range of services provided by a dedicated team of nearly 700, which includes specialist engineers, project managers and technical experts from more than 24 Canadian and U.S. locations. Selected as a winner of Canada's 50 Best Managed Companies Program for 2001 and a requalifier in 2002, Trow practices in over fifty technical disciplines and specializes in Building, Environment, GeoScience, Infrastructure, and Materials and Quality Management.

URBAN SYSTEMS LTD. • 200 - 286 St. Paul Street West • Kamloops, BC • V2C 6G4 • Tel: 250-374-8311 • Fax: 250-374-5334 • E-mail: careers@urban-systems.com • Internet: www.urban-systems.com • Urban Systems is a consulting firm of engineers, planners, landscape architects, and local government advisors. The company currently has six branches located in Kamloops, Kelowna, Vancouver, Fort St. John, British Columbia, and Edmonton, Calgary, Alberta. There are also satellite offices located in Nelson, British Columbia. Urban Systems has approximately 200 permanent employees, with a temporary staff ranging from 20-30 individuals. Interested candidates should include a cover letter explaining how you feel you can contribute to strengthening the company, and your long term career objectives.

Career Tip

Look Towards Industries with a Future
It is important to think and plan strategically. Be sure to consider a career in an industry with a strong future and where there is good potential for growth. Which industry sectors are more promising than others?

WARDROP ENGINEERING INC. • 400 - 386 Broadway • Winnipeg, MB • R3C 4M8 • Tel: 204-956-0980 • Fax: 204-957-5389 • Contact: Human Resources • Internet: www.wardrop.com • Many of the most recognized companies and organizations in the world have relied on Wardrop since 1955 to help them meet their engineering, environmental, business management, and information technology challenges. Their contributions can be seen as far away as the International Space Station and as close as the workings of the human genome. They have responded to some of the world's most complex challenges - from rom Chernobyl to the World Trade Center disasters. At its core, Wardrop is an integrated group of experts who excel at solving complex problems. They take on the challenges that stand between their clients and their goals, designing and implementing the solutions they require, overcoming barriers and constraints, and delivering value while managing risks.

ZEIDLER ROBERTS PARTNERSHIP ARCHITECTS • 315 Queen Street West • Toronto, ON • M5V 2X2 • Tel: 416-596-8300 • Fax: 416-596-1408 • Contact: Human Resources • E-mail: toronto-info@zeidlerpartnership.com • Internet: www.zrpa.com • Zeidler Roberts Partnership Architects provides engineering, architectural, and surveying services to a wide range of businesses and other enterprises in Ontario. Zeidler Roberts Partnership Architects is located in downtown Toronto and employs 220 staff worldwide.

Entertainment & Leisure

BLUE MOUNTAIN RESORTS LIMITED • R.R. # 3 • Collingwood, ON • L9Y 3Z2 • Tel: 705-445-0231 • Fax: 705-444-1751 • Contact: The Recruiting Department • E-mail: apply@bluemountain.ca • Internet: www.bluemountain.ca • Blue Mountain is Ontario's Largest Mountain Resort, located just 90 minutes north of Toronto and 11 km west of Collingwood. The resort is a four-season recreational and conference facility destination. During the winter season, over 600,000+ visitors travel from Southern Ontario and the surrounding northern US States to enjoy 34 ski/snowboarding trails, 4 terrain parks, serviced by 12 lifts and a Snow Tubing Park. In the summer months, the nationally ranked Monterra Golf course welcomes golfers to enjoy its spectacular layout. Blue Mountain employs 450 full-time year round, 1700 winter and 150 summer seasonal employees.

BLUFFER'S PARK MARINA • 7 Brimley Road South • Scarborough, ON • M1M 3W3 • Tel: 416-266-4556 • Contact: Administration Office • E-mail: admin@bluffsparkmarina.com • Internet: www.bluffsparkmarina.com • Bluffer's Park Marina, at the base of the Scarborough Bluffs is one of Toronto's finest waterfront recreational facilities. This complex, situated in over 400 acres of parkland including public beaches, offers a variety of food services and recreational activities.

CAMP WILVAKEN • P.O. Box 141 • Hudson Heights, QC • J0P 1J0 • Tel: 450-458-5051 • Fax: 450-458-2581 • Contact: Ms. Maya Willis • E-mail: wilvaken@wilvaken.com • Internet: www.wilvaken.com • Wilvaken is a co-ed private bilingual (English/French) camp establised in 1958. Our small camp atmosphere allows the campers and staff to build up a wonderful relationship with all. Must be able to communicate in both languages, love children and the outdoors.

CANADIAN MUSEUM OF CIVILIZATION CORPORATION • 100 Laurier Street, P.O. Box 3100, Station B • Hull, QC • J8X 4H2 • Tel: 1-800-555-5621 • Fax: 819-776-8300 • Contact: Human Resources • E-mail: web@civilization.ca • Internet: www.civilization.ca • The Canadian Museum of Civilization, the Canadian Children's Museum, and the Canadian Postal Museum are located in Gatineau, Quebec, on the banks of the Ottawa River, directly opposite Parliament Hill.

CAPILANO SUSPENSION BRIDGE & PARK • 3735 Capilano Road • North Vancouver, BC • V7R 4J1 • Tel: 604-985-7474 • Fax: 604-985-7479 • Contact: Ms. Julie Moreau, Human Resources Generalist • E-mail: csb_jobs@capbridge.com • Internet: www.capbridge.com • Canada's 2003 Tourism Excellence Award winner, Capilano Suspension Bridge, is breathtakingly suspended 230 feet above 450 feet across Capilano River. Cross over to towering evergreens and serene trails. Get a squirrel's eye view of the forest at Treetops Adventure, seven suspension bridges through the trees. Enjoy colourful gardens, spectacular scenery, fascinating exhibits, majestic totem poles, First Nations artisans, nature walks and seasonal entertainment, only 10 minutes from downtown. The Capilano Group of Companies also owns and operates five retails and two high-end lodges (in the Rockies).

CASA LOMA • 1 Austin Terrace • Toronto, ON • M5R 1X8 • Tel: 416-923-1171 • Fax: 416-923-5734 • Contact: Ms. Maria Pimentel-Cook, Supervisor of Operations • E-mail: info@casaloma.org • Internet: www.casaloma.org • Casa Loma is a well-recognized tourist attraction receiving as many as 350,000 visitors yearly. Once a private home belonging to Sir Henry Pellat, it has been shown on A & E's America's Castles for it's beauty and unique architectural structure. Casa Loma is owned by the City of Toronto and has been operated by the Kiwanis Club of Casa Loma since 1937. The Club uses its share of the proceeds to support a wide variety of charitable projects.

CINEPLEX GALAXY LIMITED PARTNERSHIP • 1303 Yonge Street • Toronto, ON • M4T 2Y9 • Tel: 416-323-6600 • Fax: 416-323-6612 • Contact: Human Resources • E-mail: jobs@cineplexgalaxy.com • Internet: www.cineplex.com • Galaxy Cinemas, Cineplex Odeon Cinemas and the associated brands, are owned and operated by Cineplex Galaxy Limited Partnership (CGLP). CGLP is an all-Canadian cinema exhibitor offering movie-going entertainment, with a wide range of services (Cineplex Arcade) and food items for the movie-goer. Visit their website for more information.

COLUMBIA HOUSE • 5900 Finch Avenue East • Scarborough, ON • M1B 5X7 • Tel: 416-299-9400 • Fax: 416-299-7491 • Contact: Recruitment Manager • Internet: www.columbiahousecanada.com • The Columbia House is a mail order distributor and direct marketer of music CDs, cassettes, videos and DVDs. Columbia House employs over 200 individuals to work in various fields in the mail order business.

DECODE ENTERTAINMENT INC. • 512 King Street East, Suite 104 • Toronto, ON • M5A 1M1 • Tel: 416-363-8034 • Fax: 416-363-8919 • Contact: Human Resources • E-mail: decode@decode-ent.com • Internet: www.decode.tv • Decode Entertainment is a children's television production company.

GROUSE MOUNTAIN RESORTS LTD. • 6400 Nancy Greene Way • North Vancouver, BC • V7R 4K9 • Tel: 604-984-0661 • Contact: Ms. Charmaine Carswell, Human Resources Manager • E-mail: ccarswell@grousemountain.com • Internet: www.grousemountain.com • Grouse Mountain, a spectacular mountaintop of adventure and the peak of Vancouver, is a year-round tourist recreational facility. There is so much to explore - just 15 minutes from Downtown Vancouver. Come and experience a spetacular mountaintop of adventure 365 days of the year at the Peak of Vancouver. During summer, enjoy mountain-biking tours, helicopter tours, tandem paragliding, our World Famous Lumberjack Show, the Grouse Mountain Refuge of Endangered Wildlife, Birds in Flight demonstrations and so much more. In winter, discover a snowy wonderland renowned for skiing, snowboarding, snowshoeing, ice skating and sleigh rides.

HARBOURFRONT CENTRE • 235 Queens Quay West • Toronto, ON • M5J 2G8 • Tel: 416-973-4600 • Fax: 416-973-6055 • Contact: Ms. Brenda Brown, Human Resources • E-mail: jobs@harbourfrontcentre.com • Internet: www.harbourfrontcentre.com • Harbourfront Centre, on Toronto's waterfront, is an innovative non-profit cultural organization which creates, for a diverse public, events and activities of excellence that enliven, educate and entertain. Working in partnership with various communities, Harbourfront Centre nurtures and supports educational and recreational activity as well as contemporary artistic creation through showcasing Canadian and international talent. Our year-round operation offers some 4000 internationally acclaimed events ranging from music, literary and theatrical festivals to children's activities and craft workshops. Harbourfront Centre is one of Toronto's most popular tourist attractions, drawing more than 12 million visitors and contributing over $126 million to the local economy annually. Out of what was once a government crown corporation has grown a non-profit, charitable organization that is one of the most unusual and creative cultural centres in the world.

HIPPODROME DE MONTRÉAL • 7440 boulevard Décarie • Montréal, QC • H4P 2H1 • Tel: 514-739-2741 • Fax: 514-340-2025 • E-mail: rhumaines@attractionshippiques.com • Internet: www.attractionshippiques.ca • Established in 1962, Hippodrome de Montréal is a race track in Quebec. The race track is host to many events in Montreal, and employs more than 500 people in the amusement and recreation industry.

HOCKEY HALL OF FAME • Brofield Place, 30 Yonge Street • Toronto, ON • M5E 1X8 • Tel: 416-360-7765 • Fax: 416-360-1501 • E-mail: jschwartz@hhof.com • Internet: www.hhof.com • The Hockey Hall of Fame was founded in 1943 to establish a memorial to those who have developed Canada's great winter sport - ice hockey. Incorporated in 1983, Hockey Hall of Fame and Museum exists in order to honour and preserve the history of the game of ice hockey and, in particular, those who have made outstanding contributions and achievements in the development of the game.

HORSESHOE RESORT CORPORATION • 1101 Horseshoe Valley Road, Comp. 10 • Barrie, ON • L4M 4Y8 • Tel: 705-835-2790 • Fax: 705-835-6352 • Internet: www.horseshoeresort. com • Horseshoe Resort Corporation is a ski and golf resort with a 102 room hotel. The resort has two sit down restaurants, along with banquet and conference rooms. The resort employs about 250 people.

ONTARIO JOCKEY CLUB, THE • 555 Rexdale Boulevard • Etobice, ON • M9W 7G3 • Tel: 416-213-0685 • Contact: Human Resources • Internet: www.ojc.com • The Ontario Jockey Club, now known as the Woodbine Entertainment Group, is one of the oldest and largest sports organizations in North America. The company owns and operates two racetracks in the province of Ontario: Woodbine Racetrack and Mohawk Raceway. They are the largest horse racing operation in Canada and one of the largest in North America.

PANORAMA MOUNTAIN VILLAGE • P.O. Box 7000 • Panorama, BC • V0A 1T0 • Tel: 250-342-6941 • Contact: Human Resources • E-mail: paninfo@intrawest.com • Internet: www. panoramaresort.com • Panorama Mountain Village is a summer/winter resort offering skiing and snowboarding at Panorama Mountain, golf at Greywolf Golf Course and a variety of accommodation options. Ski-in/ski-out, golf-in/golf-out real estate opportunities are available in the upper and lower villages and along the fairway at Greywolf. They are owned and operated by Intrawest Corporation, the leading developer and operator of village-centered resorts across North America. They employ more than 400 people.

PARAMOUNT CANADA'S WONDERLAND • 9580 Jane Street • Vaughan, ON • L6A 1S6 • Tel: 905-832-7401 • Internet: www.canadaswonderland.com • Paramount Canada's Wonderland is our Nation's premiere theme park that caters to families. They sell fun, excitement, and memorable experiences. They also have group events for schools, companies, and others.

POOL PEOPLE LTD. • 135 Matheson Blvd. East • Mississauga, ON • L4Z 1R2 • Tel: 905-501-7210 • Fax: 905-501-7211 • Contact: Human Resources • Email: info@pplgoup.com • Internet: www.poolpeoplelimited.com • Pool People provides products including pools, spas, saunas, and offers construction, renovation, and repair services. The company is also a major lifeguard employer for various apartment and condominium complexes throughout greater Toronto and its vicinities. Employing over 150 lifeguards, there are many summer and permanent opportunities offered within this organization.

RESORTS OF THE CANADIAN ROCKIES INC. • P.O. Box 555 • Lake Louise, AB • T0L 1E0 • Tel: 403-522-3555, ext 2130 • Contact: Human Resources • E-mail: jobs@skilouise.com • Internet: www.skilouise.com • Canada's largest and most beautiful single ski area features infinite and varied terrain. Located in the heart of historic Banff National Park, Lake Louise is a world class ski-area in a World Heritage site. In the summer they have a sightseeing gondola and educational programs. In the winter they are one of the largest ski resorts in Canada.

RIMROCK RESORT HOTEL • P.O. Box 1110, 300 Mountain Avenue • Banff, AB • T1L 1J2 • Tel: 403-762-3356 • Fax: 403-762-4132 • Contact: Human Resources • Internet: www.rimrockresort. com • Built on the side of Sulphur Mountain, The Rimrock Resort Hotel is nestled high above the picturesque Town of Banff in the heart of the Canadian Rockies. A four diamond resort hotel, The Rimrock has restaurants and many hotel services for the business or leisure traveller. The hotel employs between 300 and 400 individuals, depending on the time of the year.

ROCKSTAR GAMES TORONTO • 2871 Brighton Road • Oakville, ON • L6H 6C9 • Tel: 905-829-2203 • Fax: 905-829-2246 • Contact: Human Resources • E-mail: info@rockstartoronto. com • Internet: www.rockstartoronto.com • Rockstar Games Toronto is a development office for Rockstar Games, the makers of the Grand Theft Auto series, and other game titles.

SCIENCE NORTH • 100 Ramsey Lake Road • Sudbury, ON • P3E 5S9 • Tel: 705-523-4629 • Fax: 705-522-4954 • Contact: Human Resources • Internet: www.sciencenorth.ca • Science North is a science, education and entertainment complex which provides science programs and exhibits to schools and the general public. They offer many special events, have a motion simulator, an Imax theatre, and also operate an off-site Earth Sciences Centre "Dynamic Earth". They create, market and sell multi-media theatres, science products and travelling exhibits to other centres world-wide.

SUN PEAKS RESORT CORPORATION • 1280 Alpine Road • Sun Peaks, BC • V0E 5N0 • Tel: 250-578-7222 • Fax: 250-578-7223 • Contact: Human Resources • E-mail: employment@ sunpeaksresort.com • Internet: www.sunpeaksresort.com • With nearly 4000 acres of terrain to explore and light dry snow, Sun Peaks is all about maximizing your vacation experience. Epic powder days experienced on unbelievable terrain are the ultimate combination. In a matter of minutes, you can sweep down from an open, powder filled bowl into the trees of your choice or the perfectly groomed run that you crave. Variety is the name of the game here. There are 117 runs to choose from, spread over the second largest skiable terrain in B.C. They can take you anywhere from the open glades of Mt. Morrisey to the steep face of Tod Mountain. No matter what level of skier or snowboarder you are, there is a perfect run for you at Sun Peaks Resort.

TICKETMASTER CANADA LTD • 1 Blue Jays Way, Suite 3900 • Toronto, ON • M5V 1J3 • Tel: 416-345-9200 • Fax: 416-341-8765 • Contact: Human Resources • E-mail: resumes@ ticketmaster.ca • Internet: www.ticketmaster.ca • Ticketmaster Canada is involved in the sales of entertainment tickets by phone and in person. The firm employs approximately 350 individuals in total.

TORONTO CRICKET SKATING & CURLING CLUB • 141 Wilson Avenue • Toronto, ON • M5M 3A3 • Tel: 416-487-4581 • Fax: 416-487-7595 • Contact: Cheryl Menezes, Human Resources Manager   E-mail: cmenezes@torcricketclub.org • Internet: www.torontocricketclub.com • Toronto Cricket Skating & Curling is a social activities club in Toronto that offers many types of outdoor activities.

TORONTO ZOO • 361A Old Finch Avenue • Scarborough, ON • M1B 5K7 • Tel: 416-392-5900 • Fax: 416-392-5934 • Contact: Human Resources • E-mail: hr@torontozoo.ca • Internet: www.torontozoo.com • The Toronto Zoo is a zoological park just east of downtown Toronto that displays a large collection of wildlife. The Zoo has over 5,000 animals representing over 460 species. The Toronto Zoo has more than 250 permanent employees. During the summer months, more than 200 seasonal staff are hired to assist with Guest Services, Rides, Custodial, Groundskeeping, Membership and Security & Safety.

WESTBURY NATIONAL SHOW SYSTEMS LTD. • 772 Warden Avenue • Toronto, ON • M1L 4T7 • Tel: 416-752-1371 • Fax: 416-752-1382 • Contact: Ms. Cheryl Harris, Labour Coordinator • E-mail: charris@westbury.com • Internet: www.westbury.com • Westbury National Show Systems Ltd. Is involved in the sales, service, rentals, and installations of audio, lighting, staging, and audio-visuals.

WHISTLER BLACKCOMB MOUNTAIN • 4545 Blackcomb Way • Whistler, BC • V0N 1B4 • Tel: 604-938-7366 • Fax: 604-938-7838 • Internet: www.whistler-blackcomb.com • Whistler Blackcomb Mountain is a four-season mountain resort offering skiing, snowboarding, hiking and mountain biking. They offer guests the best big mountain experience around.

YMCA OF LONDON CAMP QUEEN ELIZABETH • 1424 Clarke Road • London, ON • N5V 5B9 • Tel: 519-455-3135 • Fax: 519-455-2519 • Contact: Adam Jarrett, Director • E-mail: ajarrett@londony.ca • Internet: www.campqueenelizabeth.ca • Camp Queen Elizabeth operates as an Outdoor Centre during the spring and fall, and as a summer camp for July and August. Located on Beausoleil Island in Georgian Bay Island's National Park, CQE serves youths and their families from all over the world.

Financial Institutions

AGRICULTURE FINANCIAL SERVICES CORPORATION • 5718 - 56 Avenue • Lacombe, AB • T4L 1B1 • Tel: 403-782-5200 • Internet: www.afsc.ca • Agriculture Financial Services Corporation (AFSC) is in the business of providing unique financial services to Albertans in various areas, helping to contribute to business development and growth in the province. To remain competitive and relevant to our clients, they continue to create innovative ways to deliver responsible lending, insurance, risk management and safety net products and services.

CANADIAN DEPOSITORY FOR SECURITIES LTD. • 85 Richmond Street West • Toronto, ON • M5H 2C9 • Tel: 416-365-8400 • Fax: 416-365-0842 • Internet: www.cds.ca • The Canadian Depository for Securities (CDS) is Canada's national securities clearing and depository services organization. CDS is owned by major Canadian banks, the members of the Toronto Stock Exchange and the Investment Dealers Association of Canada (IDA). The majority of CDS's owners are also users of CD's clearing and depository services. CDS services are provided by approximately 400 permanent staff. Additional resources are brought in for the delivery of specific developmental projects. Employees include professionals, technical staff, customer service representatives and administrative personnel. Please visit their website for a more complete company description.

CANADIAN WESTERN BANK • 10303 Jasper Avenue, Suite 2300 • Edmonton, AB • T5J 3X6 • Tel: 780-423-8888 • Fax: 780-423-0303 • Contact: Human Resources • E-mail: hr@cwbank.com • Internet: www.cwbcareers.com • Canadian Western Bank meets the needs of Western

Canadians by providing sound financial services, innovative and well priced loan arrangements, and highly competitive rates. As a western-based full service bank, Canadian Western Bank is the smallest of only seven banks chartered to operate as a Schedule I Bank.

CITIBANK CANADA • 123 Front Street, Suite 1700 • Toronto, ON • M5J 2M3 • Tel: 416-947-5500 • Contact: Human Resources • Internet: www.citibank.com/canada • Citibank Canada is the country's second largest foreign owned bank, offering banking services to corporations, government and financial institutions, as well as consumers since 1954. Its team of professionals is made up of over 1000 employees, located in Toronto, Montreal, Vancouver, and Calgary. To view careers available with Citibank Canada visit the Careers web page at http://careers.canada.citibank.com/.

COMMUNITY SAVINGS CREDIT UNION • 13450 - 102nd Avenue, Suite 1600 • Surrey, BC • V3T 5X3 • Tel: 604-654-2000 • Fax: 604-586-5156 • Internet: www.comsavings.com • Community Savings Credit Union is a not-for-profit co-operative that is owned by its members. The credit union offers a wide variety of products and services to its members, from savings and checking accounts to consumer loans and mortgages.

CONEXUS CREDIT UNION • 1960 Albert Street • Regina, SK • S4P 2T4 • Tel: 800-667-7477 • Internet: www.conexuscu.com • Conexus Credit Union is a financial institution in Saskatchewan providing a wide range of services to their membership. The credit union currently has more than 80 locations to serve their membership as well as a number of administrative departments. The company employs over 1000 staff.

CREDIT UNION CENTRAL OF ONTARIO • 2810 Matheson Blvd. East • Mississauga, ON • L4W 4X7 • Tel: 905-238-9400 • Fax: 905-238-8196 • Internet: www.cuco.on.ca • Credit Union Central of Ontario is the provincial financial intermediary and trade association for the Ontario credit union system. Its activities are provincial in scope and aim to achieve greater integration among the various members of the credit union system.

EXPORT DEVELOPMENT CORPORATION • 151 O'Connor Street • Ottawa, ON • K1A 1K3 • Tel: 613-598-2500 • Internet: www.edc.ca • Export Development Corporation (EDC) is a Canadian financial institution devoted exclusively to providing trade finance services in support of Canadian exporters and investors in up to 200 countries. Founded in 1944, EDC is a Crown corporation that operates as a commercial financial institution. They employ approximately 850 individuals.

FARM CREDIT CANADA • 1800 Hamilton Street, P.O. Box 4320 • Regina, SK • S4P 4L3 • Tel: 306-780-8100 • Fax: 306-780-5508 • Contact: Human Resources • E-mail: hr-rh@fcc-fac.ca • Internet: www.fcc-fac.ca • Farm Credit Canada (FCC) is a federal Crown corporation reporting to Parliament through the Minister of Agriculture and Agri-Food. Established in 1959, FCC is Canada's largest agricultural term lender. FCC provides financing to help Canadian farmers and agribusiness operators grow, diversify and prosper. Operating out of 100 offices located primarily in rural areas across Canada, the corporations dedicated employees are passionate about the business of agriculture.

Send Your Resumé to Targeted Employers
You will increase your chances of finding work if you send your resumé to a targeted group of employers. Sending resumés out everywhere without consideration of what a firm is looking for will not benefit you.

HSBC BANK CANADA • 885 West Georgia St. • Vancouver, BC • V6C 3G1 • Tel: 604-525-4722 • Internet: www.hsbc.ca • HSBC Bank Canada is a principal member of the HSBC Group, which has 10,000 offices in 82 countries and territories and is one of the world's largest banking and financial services organizations.

INTERIOR SAVINGS CREDIT UNION • 678 Bernard Avenue, Suite 300 • Kelowna, BC • V1Y 6P3 • Tel: 250–869-8200 • Fax: 250-762-9581 • E-mail: chagel@interiorsavings.com • Internet: www.interiorsavings.com • The Interior Savings Credit Union is a financial services institution located in Kelowna, British Columbia. Their financial services include general insurance, life insurance, trust services and portfolio/wealth management. The credit union employs around 250 individuals.

ISLAND SAVINGS CREDIT UNION • 89 Evans Street • Duncan, BC • V9L 1PS • Tel: 250-746-4171 • Fax: 250-746-4175 • Contact: Human Resources Department • Internet: www.iscu.com • Island Savings Credit Union offers its members a full range of financial and insurance products and services. It is owned and operated by its members. The credit union has nine branches, nine insurance offices, and an administration office. They have a membership close to 40,000 people, and employ about 360 individuals. To correspond with Island Savings Credit Union, individuals should submit their resume and cover letter in person to the HR Manager, at the Human Resources/Administration office at the address above.

MCAP INC. • 200 King Street West, Suite 400 • Toronto, ON • M5H 3T4 • Tel: 416-598-2665 • Fax: 416-598-7837 • Internet: www.mcap.com • The MCAP group of companies is a diverse organization with specialists in many areas including underwriting and mortgage administration, investor relations, information technology, finance, marketing, communication and human resources. They employ more than 500 people across Canada.

NEWFOUNDLAND AND LABRADOR CREDIT UNION • 341 Freshwater Road, 2nd Floor • St. John's, NL • A1B 1C4 • Tel: 709-754-2312 • Fax: 709-754-2390 • Internet: www.nlcu.com • Newfoundland and Labrador Credit Union is involved in the financial services industry providing financial products and services to meet individuals and business needs.

PROGRESSIVE FINANCIAL STRATEGY • 5170 Dixie Road, Suite 205 • Mississauga, ON • L4W 1E3 • Tel: 905-212-9149 • Fax: 905-212-9201 • Contact: Human Resources • E-mail: info@pfs.ca • Internet: www.pfs.ca • Progressive Financial Strategy is a financial planning center. They are an investment fund dealer and independent insurance brer. Their representatives study the market and select the companies whose products and services best suit your financial needs.

PROSPERA CREDIT UNION • 3088 Granville Street • Vancouver, BC • V6H 3J8 • Tel: 604-734-5774 • Fax: 604-739-5522 • Internet: www.prosperacreditunion.ca • Prospera Credit Union is the 4th largest credit union in B.C. with assets of more than $2.2 billion under administration. We have 60,000 members with 16 branches, 10 insurance offices, a call centre, 6 commercial banking centres located from Vancouver to the anagan.

ROYAL CANADIAN MINT • 320 Sussex Drive • Ottawa, ON • K1A 0G8 • Tel: 613-993-8990 • Fax: 613-998-4130 • Contact: Human Resources • Internet: www.mint.ca • The Royal Canadian Mint is a global leader in minting, recognized worldwide for its unsurpassed standards of quality and craftsmanship in the production of both circulation and collector coins, and highly respected as a premier refiner of gold. The Royal Canadian Mint combines modern business practices with decades of experience in coin production to deliver optimal value to customers and shareholders.

VALLEY FIRST CREDIT UNION • 184 Main Street, 3rd Floor • Penticton, BC • V2A 8G7 • Tel: 250-490-2720 • Fax: 250-490-3661 • Contact: Assistant Vice-President, Human Resources

• E-mail: hr@valleyfirst.com • Internet: www.valleyfirst.com • Valley First Financial Group provides Credit Union banking, Insurance and Wealth Management services to communities in the South Central Interior of British Columbia with anagan branches in Penticton, Kelowna, Vernon, Armstrong, Lumby, Peachland and Oliver, a Thompson region branch in Kamloops and Similkameen branches in Keremeos and Princeton.

VANCITY SAVINGS CREDIT UNION • P.O. Box 2120 • Station Terminal • Vancouver, BC • V6B 5R8 • Tel: 604-877-7000 • Fax: 604-877-7639 • Contact: Human Resources • Internet: www.vancity.com • VanCity Credit Union is a democratic, ethical and innovative provider of financial services to its members. Through strong financial performance, we serve as a catalyst for the self-reliance and economic well-being of our membership and community. Founded in 1946 to provide financial services to people from all walks of life, they've grown to become a major financial institution serving the people of British Columbia.

WESTMINSTER SAVINGS CREDIT UNION • 960 Quayside Drive, Unit 108 • New Westminster, BC • V3M 6G2 • Tel: 604-517-0100 • Fax: 604-528-3812 • Internet: www.betterbanking.com • Westminster Savings Credit Union is a local credit union serving the citizens of the lower Mainland. The credit union employs approximately 350 individuals in total.

Food Manufacturers & Wholesalers

BAKEMARK INGREDIENTS LTD. • 2480 Viking Way • Richmond, BC • V6V 1N2 • Tel: 604-303-1700 • Fax: 604-303-1705 • Contact: Human Resources • Internet: www.bakemarkcanada.com • Bakemark Ingredients Ltd. is a full line bakery supplier. They distribute and manufacture ingredients to the bakery sector of the food industry.

BLUE WAVE SEAFOODS INC. • P.O. Box 20, 413 Central Port Mouton Road • Port Mouton, NS • B0T 1T0 • Tel: 902-683-2044 • Fax: 902-683-2366 • Contact: Human Resources • Blue Wave Seafoods is engaged in the business of manufacturing fresh and frozen packaged fish and other seafood products. The company was established in 1991, and currently employs approximately 100 individuals to work in various sectors in the food manufacturing industry.

BROWNING HARVEY LIMITED • P.O. Box 455 • Grand Falls-Windsor, NL • A2A 2J8 • Tel: 709-489-2145 • Fax: 709-489-3181 • Contact: Human Resources • Internet: www.aharvey.com/pepsi • Browning Harvey Limited is a soft drink bottler of major brands such as Pepsi, Cadbury and Schewppes.

CANADA BREAD COMPANY LIMITED • 130 Cawthra Avenue • Toronto, ON • M6N 3C2 • Tel: 416-767-8367 • Fax: 416-767-1896 • Internet: www.mapleleafcareers.com • Canada Bread is a major, public Canadian Corporation and part of the Maple Leaf Foods family of companies. It is Canada's leading producer of fresh and frozen bakery products, fresh pasta and sauces.

CANADA SAFEWAY LIMITED • 1020 64th Avenue NE • Calgary, AB • T2E 7V8 • Tel: 403-730-3500 • Fax: 403-730-3888 • Contact: Employment Office • Internet: www.safeway.com • Canada Safeway is a leading retail supermarket chain in western Canada. It has about 210 stores, located primarily in Alberta, British Columbia, Manitoba, and Saskatchewan. Parent company Safeway is one of the largest supermarket operators in North America. Canada Safeway serves independent grocery stores and institutional customers through three distribution centers; it also has 13 Canadian plants that make or process meat, dairy products, fruits and vegetables, bread, and other foods.

CONNORS BROS., LIMITED • 669 Main Street • Blacks Harbour, NB • E5H 1K1 • Tel: 506-456-1233 • Fax: 506-456-1569 • Contact: Human Resources Manager • E-mail: careers@connors.ca • Internet: www.connors.ca • Connors Bros is an international marketer and manufacturer of quality seafood products.

CO-OP ATLANTIC • 123 Halifax Street, P.O. Box 750 • Moncton, NB • E1C 8N5 • Tel: 506-858-6000 • Fax: 506-858-6473 • Contact: Manager, Personnel Services • E-mail: recruitment@coopatlantic.ca • Internet: www.coopatlantic.ca • Co-op Atlantic is a diverse and innovative business serving 128 member co-operatives throughout Atlantic Canada and the Magdalen Islands, with consolidated sales in excess of $500 million. Co-op Atlantic employs over 600 people. All career opportunities are posted internally first.

EDENVALLEY FARMS • 11 Calkin Drive, Unit 1 • Kentville, NS • B4N 3V7 • Tel: 902-678-8323 • Fax: 902-681-8914 • Contact: Human Resources • E-mail: contactus@edenvalleyfarms.com • Internet: www.edenvalleyfarms.com • EdenValley Farms supplies fresh and frozen chicken, turkey and eggs to its many retail customers throughout Atlantic Canada on a daily basis.

FISHERY PRODUCTS INTERNATIONAL • 70 O'Leary Avenue • St. John's, NL • A1C 5L1 • Tel: 709-570-0354 • Fax: 709-570-0436 • Contact: Human Resources • E-mail: recruitment@fpil.com • Internet: www.fisheryproducts.com • Fishery Products International (FPI) is a global seafood enterprise which produces and markets a full range of seafood products, including shrimp, crab, scallops, cod, sole, redfish, pollock, turbot, and haddock. These products are distributed across a wide network throughout North America, Southeast Asia, South America, and Europe. FPI employs 3,900 people.

GAY LEA FOODS CO-OPERATIVE LTD. • 100 Clayson Road • Toronto, ON • M9M 2G7 • Tel: 416-741-0261 • Fax: 416-741-4086 • Internet: www.gayleafoods.com • For more than forty years Gay Lea Foods Co-operative Limited has been an all-important link between Ontario dairy farm operations and Ontario consumers. Gay Lea products have been familiar to Ontario shoppers for many years. They include butter, aerosol whipped toppings, cottage cheese, sour cream, dips and lactose-reduced products. The majority of Gay Lea retail products are market leaders in their categories.

GEORGE WESTON LTD. • 22 St. Clair Avenue East • Toronto, ON • M4T 2S7 • Tel: 416-922-2500 • Fax: 416-922-4395 • Contact: Human Resources • Internet: www.weston.ca • George Weston Limited ("Weston") is a Canadian public company founded in 1882 and is one of North America's largest food processing and distribution companies. Weston has three reportable operating segments: Weston Foods, Food Distribution and Fisheries. Weston is committed to creating value for its shareholders and to participating along with its more than 155,000 employees in supporting the communities in which it operates.

GOLDEN BOY FOODS INC. • 8820 Northbrook Court • Burnaby, BC • V5J 5J1 • Tel: 604-433-2200 • Fax: 604-433-0051 • Internet: www.goldenboyfoods.com • Golden Boy Foods is a processor of peanut butter, snacking nuts and dried fruit. Our Burnaby Plant hosts 10 loading docks and 105,000 square feet of Warehouse. Golden Boy Foods carries products from countries such as Australia, Brazil, Chile, China, Indonesia, India, Greece, Guatemala, Kenya, Malaysia, Mexico, Philippines, Taiwan, Thailand, Turkey and United States of America.

J.S. REDPATH LIMITED • 710 McKeown Avenue • North Bay, ON • P1B 8K1 • Tel: 705-474-2461 • Fax: 705-474-9109 • Contact: Human Resources • E-mail: careers@jsrl.com • Internet: www.jsredpath.com • J.S. Redpath Limited is the founding member of The Redpath Group providing shaft sinking, mine development, underground construction and contract mining services to the mining and civil construction industries.

KRAFT CANADA INC. • 95 Moatfield Drive • North York, ON • M3B 3L6 • Tel: 416-441-5059 • Fax: 416-441-5328 • Internet: www.kraftcanada.com • Kraft is at the forefront of the food industry in Canada, the U.S., and around the world. With products sold in over 150 countries worldwide, Kraft produces everything from confections, desserts and beverages, to refrigerated products, and coffee and main meal products. In Canada, Kraft has a head office in Don Mills, Ontario, 20 manufacturing facilities and several sales and administration offices across the country. Kraft Canada employs approximately 7100 people.

LASSONDE INDUSTRIES INC. • 170 5e Avenue • Rougemont, QC • J0L 1M0 • Tel: 514-878-1057 • Fax: 450-861-9280 • Contact: Mr. Michel Simard, Ressources humaines • E-mail: info@lassonde.com • Internet: www.lassonde.com • Lassonde Industries Inc. is a Canadian leader in the development, manufacture, and marketing of an innovative and distinctive range of fruit and vegetable juices and drinks. Lassonde also develops and markets certain specialty food products such as canned corn-on-the-cob for foreign markets, fondue bouillons and sauces, meat marinades, barbecue sauces, and baked beans.

MANITOBA AGRICULTURE, FOOD AND RURAL INITATIVES • 401 York Avenue, Suite 803 • Winnipeg, MB • R3C 0P8 • Tel: 204-945-3304 • Fax: 204-948-4735 • Contact: Ms. Angie Kudlak, Human Resources • Internet: www.gov.mb.ca/agriculture • Manitoba Agriculture, Food and Rural Initatives' mission of creating a supportive environment that advances the greater prosperity of our farm families, our partners and rural communities is the foundation of our Destination 2010 strategic plan. Many careers with Manitoba Agriculture and Food begin with a background in science, management, finance and administration, computer technology, research and field operations.

MAPLE LEAF CONSUMER FOODS • P.O. Box 70 • Winnipeg, MB • R3C 2G5 • Tel: 204-235-8259 • Fax: 204-233-5413 • Internet: www.mapleleaf.com • Maple Leaf Foods is the largest company in Canada in the manufacturing and distribution of food products. Its head offices are in Toronto and the company's operations extend across Canada and into the global village. The firm employs over 22,500 people in Canada. Maple Leaf merged with J.M. Schneiders this year. The Winnipeg operation is the hams plant for all of Maple Leaf Foods.

MARK ANTHONY GROUP INC. • 887 Great Northern Way • Vancouver, BC • V5T 4T5 • Tel: 604-263-9994 • Fax: 604-263-9913 • Contact: Human Resources • Internet: www.markanthony.com • Mark Anthony Group is Canada's largest private distributor of alcoholic beverages.

MITCHELL'S GOURMET FOODS INC. • 3003 11th Street West, P.O. Box 850 • Saskatoon, SK • S7K 3V4 • Tel: 306-931-4360 • Fax: 306-931-4296 • Contact: Human Resources • E-mail: apply@mgf.ca • Internet: www.mgf.ca • Mitchell's Gourmet Foods is one of Canada's leading value-added pork processors. Headquartered in Saskatoon, Saskatchewan, they employ more than 1,400 people.

MOOSEHEAD BREWERIES LIMITED • 89 Main Street West • Saint John, NB • E2M 3H2 • Tel: 506-635-4462 • Fax: 506-635-7029 • Internet: www.moosehead.ca • Established through a tradition of excellence in brewing, Moosehead Breweries Limited, located in Saint John, New Brunswick, is Canada's oldest independent brewery. The superior taste of Moosehead beer comes from closely guarded recipes passed down from generation to generation of the Oland family.

NEPTUNE FOOD SUPPLIERS LTD. • 1700 Cliveden Avenue • Delta, BC • V3M 6T2 • Tel: 604-540-3701 • Fax: 604-540-3970 • Contact: Human Resources • E-mail: careers@neptunefoodservice.com • Internet: www.neptunefoodservice.com • Neptune Food Service is a holding company that is engaged in the business of food wholesaling and distribution. There are approximately 375 individuals in total that work in various capacities within the company. The firm's head office is in Delta, British Columbia.

NESTLE CANADA INC. • 25 Sheppard Avenue West, Suite 1700 • Toronto, ON • M2N 6S8 • Tel: 416-512-9000 • Fax: 416-218-2654 • Contact: Human Resources • Internet: www.nestle. ca • Nestlé Canada is engaged in the manufacturing and distribution of food products. From their beginnings more than 135 years ago, Nestlé has contributed to almost all areas of the food and beverage market by creating some of the most powerful and popular brands. From instant coffee, ice cream and packaged meals, to chocolate, infant nutrition products and milk powder, they're always developing something new to ensure that people all over the world will continue to get the very best for years to come.

OLAND BREWERIES LIMITED • 3055 Agricola Street • Halifax, NS • B3K 4G2 • Tel: 902-453-1867 • Fax: 902-453-3847 • Contact: Human Resources • Internet: www.labatt.com • Labatt is truly a national brewer, with operations coast to coast including its brewery in St. John's, Newfoundland employing 110 full time employees. Partner Oland Brewery is based in Halifax, Nova Scotia and brews some of Atlantic Canada's favourites such as Keith's IPA, Oland Export and Oland Schooner, named after the famous sailing vessel the Bluenose II. The Oland Brewery has been operating for over 135 years. First brewed in their Dartmouth home, the Oland's special ales were the beginning of a family tradition that would make the Oland name synonymous with extraordinary beer. The Oland Brewery employs 210 full time employees.

OMSTEAD FOODS LIMITED • P.O. Box 520 • Wheatley, ON • N0P 2P0 • Tel: 519-825-4611 • Fax: 519-825-3828 • Contact: Human Resources • Omstead Foods is a food processing facility. It was founded in 1911 and was a family owned and run company until it was sold to John Labatts Foods in 1984. It was then acquired by the H.J. Heinz Co. in 1991 and is still owned by them today. They produce frozen fruit and vegetables, coated products (onion rings, cheese sticks), and fresh and frozen fish products (predominantly perch, smelt and pickerel).

RICH PRODUCTS OF CANADA LIMITED • 12 Hagey Avenue • Fort Erie, ON • L2A 1W3 • Tel: 905-871-2605 • Contact: Human Resources • Internet: www.richs.com • Rich's is known around the world as the founder of the non-dairy segment of the frozen food industry and a leading supplier and solutions provider to the Food Service, In-Store Bakery and Retail marketplaces. Rich's leading brands include Rich's Whip Topping; On Top; Bettercreme; SeaPak; Farm Rich; Casa DiBertacchi; Byron's Barbecue; Bahama Blast; Jon Donaire and Mother's Kitchen specialty desserts.

SUN RYPE PRODUCTS LTD. • 1165 Ethel Street • Kelowna, BC • V1Y 2W4 • Tel: 250-860-7973 • Fax: 250-762-3611 • Email: hr@sunrype.com • Internet: www.sunrype.com • Sun-Rype Products Ltd. is Western Canada's largest manufacturer and marketer of juice-based beverages and all-natural fruit snacks with sales in excess of $100 million. Sun-Rype is headquartered in Kelowna - a city nestled in the Okanagan Valley, the heart of B.C.'s premier fruit growing district. It is here where the Company operates one of the most sophisticated juice and fruit snack processing plants in North America, and maintains its corporate and registered offices.

THOMAS J. LIPTON • 160 Bloor Street East • Toronto, ON • M4W 3R2 • Tel: 416-964-7255 • Fax: 416-964-0294 • Contact: Human Resources • Internet: www.lipton.ca • Lipton is a food manufacturer of a wide range of consumer products. The company prepares many goods such as dried and dehydrated fruits, vegetables and soup mixes, shortening, table oils, margarine, food preparations, and a wide range of other related products. Employing more than 800 people in the Toronto region, a number of these individuals work for the firm on a part time basis.

Consider Demographics in Choosing Your Career
Demographics play a major role in our economy and in the jobs of the future. Keeping abreast of changing demographic trends (e.g. an aging baby boom population). They will be important when choosing your career.

Government

ALBERTA GAMING & LIQUOR COMMISSION • 50 Corriveau Avenue • St. Albert, AB • T8N 3T5 • Tel: 780-447-8600 • Fax: 780-447-8918 • Contact: Human Resources • Internet: www. aglc.gov.ab.ca • On May 25, 1999, the Alberta Gaming and Liquor Commission (AGLC) became part of the Ministry of Gaming. The AGLC is an agent of the Government of Alberta and consists of a Board and a Corporation. The Corporation acts as the operational arm of the organization, while the Board handles policy and regulatory responsibilities. The AGLC ensures that gaming and liquor activities in Alberta are conducted honestly, openly, and with the highest level of integrity. It also endeavours to maximize the economic benefits of gaming and liquor activities in the province to benefit Albertans.

ATHABASCA, TOWN OF • 4705 49 Avenue • Athabasca, AB • T9S 1B7 • Tel: 780-675-2063 • Fax: 780- 675-4242 • Contact: Mr. Harold Gyte, Human Resources • E-mail: town@town. athabasca.ab.ca • Internet: www.town.athabasca.ab.ca • Between the years 1880 and 1914, Athabasca Landing, as the town was then called, became known as the «Gateway to the North,» a jumping off point for the Peace and Athabasca trading rivers flowing to the Arctic. Today, the Town is the modern gateway to the new north country, its economic prospects, natural resource industries, tourism opportunities, natural beauty, and lifestyle choices.

ATLANTIC LOTTERY CORPORATION INC. • P.O. Box 5500, 922 Main Street • Moncton, NB • E1C 8W6 • Tel: 506-853-5800 • Fax: 506-867-5710 • Contact: Human Resources Advisor • E-mail: resume@alc.ca • Internet: www.alc.ca • Contributing to Atlantic Canada's economy and way of life by generating significant revenues for their shareholders, the four Atlantic provinces, has been Atlantic Lottery Corporation's (ALC) vision since their inception in 1976. All net profits from the sale of ALC products are returned to their shareholders to help fund essential provincial programs and services.

BRANDON, CITY OF • 410 - 9th Street • Brandon, MB • R7A 6A2 • Tel: 204-729-2240 • Fax: 204-729-1904 • Contact: Human Resources • E-mail: employment@brandon.ca • Internet: www.brandon.ca • The City of Brandon is the municipal government that functions to serve the citizens of Brandon, Manitoba. The City of Brandon employs individuals in many different areas of specialization to serve the needs of the community.

BRITISH COLUMBIA ASSESSMENT • 1537 Hillside Avenue • Victoria, BC • V8T 4Y2 • Tel: 250-595-6211 • Fax: 250-595-6222 • Contact: Human Resources • Internet: http://bcassessment. gov.bc.ca • The mission of BC Assessment is to produce uniform property assessments that form the basis for local and provincial taxation while providing information to assist people when making real estate decisions.

CALGARY, CITY OF • P.O. Box 2100, Stn. M • Calgary, AB • T2P 2M5 • Tel: 403-268-2489 • Fax: 403-268-3580 • Contact: Human Resources • Internet: www.calgary.ca • The City of Calgary provides a variety of services to Calgarians. To learn more about their services visit their web site.

CANADIAN COMMERCIAL CORP. • 50 O'Connor Street, 11th Floor • Ottawa, ON • K1A 0S6 • Tel: 613-996-0034 • Fax: 613-995-2121 • Contact: Human Resources • E-mail: hr@ccc.ca • Internet: www.ccc.ca • The Canadian Commercial Corporation (CCC) is a Crown corporation wholly-owned by the Government of Canada and accountable to Parliament through the Minister of International Trade. CCC's broad mandate of assisting in the export of goods and services is delivered through an organization of 95-100 employees based in downtown Ottawa. It is a highly skilled, knowledge-based workforce with particular expertise in international contracting, finance, risk management, negotiation, and business development. Visit our website to find out more about us.

CANADIAN DAIRY COMMISSION • Building 55, NCC Driveway, Central Experimental Farm, 960 Carling Avenue • Ottawa, ON • K1A 0Z2 • Tel: 613-792-2000 • Fax: 613-792-2009 • Contact: Human Resources • E-mail: cdc-ccl@agr.gc.ca • Internet: www.cdc.ca • Created through the Canadian Dairy Commission Act of 1966, the CDC reports to Parliament through the Minister of Agriculture and Agri-Food. Funded by the federal government, producers and the marketplace, the CDC strives to balance and serve the interests of all dairy stakeholders - producers, processors, further processors, consumers and governments.

CONSERVATION HALTON • 2596 Britannia Road West, R.R. 2 • Milton, ON • L9T 2X6 • Tel: 905-336-1158 • Fax: 905-336-7014 • Contact: Human Resources Department • Internet: www. conservationhalton.on.ca • Conservation Halton is a community based environmental agency that protects local ecosystems in partnership with its watershed municipalities. As an agency established under the Conservation Authorities Act of Ontario, Conservation Halton forms a partnership with the Province of Ontario and the Regional Municipalities of Halton, Peel and Hamilton-Wentworth and Puslinch Township.

COQUITLAM, CITY OF • 3000 Guildford Way • Coquitlam, BC • V3B 7N2 • Tel: 604-927-3070 • Fax: 604-927-3075 • Contact: Human Resources Manager • E-mail: careers@coquitlam. ca • Internet: www.coquitlam.ca • Located in the heart of the lower mainland, Coquitlam is a rapidly growing city in British Columbia, with a vibrant and dynamic community. The City of Coquitlam offers a broad range of employment opportunities and employs approximately 900 people across the various departments of the City.

CORNER BROOK, CITY OF • P.O. Box 1080 • Corner Brook, NL • A2H 6E1 • Tel: 709-637-1500 • Fax: 709-637-1625 • Contact: Human Resources • E-mail: hr@cornerbrook.com • Internet: www.cornerbrook.com • The City of Corner Brook is a municipal government in Newfoundland that exists to create and uphold policy and laws in areas that fall under its jurisdiction. Individuals employed with The City of Corner Brook work in various fields in local government. There are about 250 employees working for The City of Corner Brook.

EDMONTON ECONOMIC DEVELOPMENT • 9990 Jasper Avenue, 3rd Floor • Edmonton, AB • T5J 1P7 • Tel: 780-424-9191 • Fax: 780-917-7668 • Contact: Human Resources Department • E-mail: careers@edmonton.com • Internet: www.edmonton.com • Edmonton Economic Development Corporation (EEDC), a not-for-profit company, works to promote the City of Edmonton and its surrounding area for both economic growth and prosperity. Guided by a volunteer, 15-person Board of Directors comprised of Edmonton business leaders, EEDC is responsible for regional economic development, regional tourism marketing, management of the Shaw Conference Centre and management of Edmonton Research Park.

GOVERNMENT OF NEWFOUNDLAND - DEPARTMENT OF FINANCE • P.O. Box 8700 • St. Johns, NL • A1B 4J6 • Contact: Human Resources, Finance Department • E-mail: finance@ gov.nl.ca • Internet: www.gov.nf.ca/fin • The Department of Finance within the Government of Newfoundland is responsible for fiscal and economic policy in the province. The department is particularly responsible for the financial resources used in the generation of revenues for the province. These funds are allocated to several areas including the provincial treasury, the management of the provincial debt, the management of pension funds, the payment of employee benefits, and the consolidated fund services. The Department of Finance employs around 320 individuals.

HALIFAX REGIONAL MUNICIPALITY • P.O. Box 1749 • Halifax, NS • B3J 3A5 • Tel: 902-490-4000 • Contact: Human Resources • Internet: www.halifax.ca • Our Regional Municipality encompasses the former cities of Halifax and Dartmouth, the Town of Bedford and the County of Halifax - an area larger than Prince Edward Island, and home to forty percent of our province's population. Metro Halifax is the commercial, educational, research and technological centre of Atlantic Canada. Six universities, an excellent college system and several leading research institutions, make our citizens the best educated in Canada. We are consistently ranked as one of the best places to do business in North America. We are also home to charming seaside communities, sparkling coves and miles of rugged Atlantic shoreline. We are a safe, clean municipality, offering excellent cuisine, live theatre, a professional symphony, numerous art galleries, museums, and the excitement of city living, the charms of small-town life and the pristine beauty of nature - all in one place.

HALIFAX REGIONAL WATER COMMISSION • 6380 Lady Hammond Road, P.O. Box 8338, Stn. A • Halifax, NS • B3K 5M1 • Tel: 902-490-4820 • Fax: 902-490-4749 • Contact: Human Resources Department • E-mail: humanresources@hrwc. ca • Internet: www.halifax. ca/hrwc • The Halifax Regional Water Commission (HRWC) is the municipal water utility for the Halifax Regional Municipality. It provides potable water and fire protection to the urban core and operates small systems throughout the rural parts of the municipality. The HRWC has an employee base of 180 people.

KELOWNA, CITY OF • 1435 Water Street • Kelowna, BC • V1Y 1J4 • Tel: 604-469-8528 • Contact: Human Resources • Internet: www.kelowna.ca • The City of Kelowna is a municipal government in British Columbia that is responsible for the introduction and creation of policy and laws in matters under its jurisdiction, to guide the growth development and operation of the City, to set budgets and to levy taxes to provide services. The City of Kelowna employs staff to work in various capacities for the betterment of the community.

KITCHENER, CITY OF • Human Resources, 3rd Floor, Ebytown Wing, 200 King Street West • Kitchener, ON • N2G 4G7 • Tel: 519-741-2260 • Fax: 519-741-2400 • Contact: Staffing Coordinator, Human Resources Division • E-mail: humres@kitchener.ca • Internet: www. kitchener.ca • The City of Kitchener is a municipal government responsible for the formation of policy and laws in matters under its jurisdiction. The government employs approximately 2,100 staff.

LEDUC, CITY OF • 1 Alexandra Park • Leduc, AB • T9E 4C4 • Tel: 780-980-7177 • Fax: 780-980-7127 • Contact: Human Resources • E-mail: resume@leduc.ca • Internet: www.leduc.ca • The City of Leduc is a municipal government involved in the formation of policy, laws and service delivery under its jurisdiction.

METRO TORONTO WEST DETENTION CENTRE • 111 Disco Road • Rexdale, ON • M9W 1M3 • Tel: 416-675-1806 • Fax: 416-674-4477 • Contact: Superintendent • The Metro Toronto West Detention Centre is a correctional services facility located in Etobicoke. Operating under the Ontario Ministry of Correctional Services. The Detention Centre employs almost 500 people to work in various sectors.

MINISTRY OF NORTHERN DEVELOPMENT AND MINES • 159 Cedar Street, Suite 702 • Sudbury, ON • P3E 6A5 • Tel: 705-564-7940 • Fax: 705-564-7942 • Contact: Human Resources • Internet: www.mndm.gov.on.ca • The Ministry of Northern Development and Mines is a provincial ministry with a mandate to stimulate the economic and social development of Northern Ontario and to ensure that the special needs of northerners are addressed by the government. The Ministry is also set up to encourage and regulate the orderly development and utilization of the province's mineral resources.

MISSISSAUGA, CITY OF • 300 City Centre Drive, 5th Floor • Mississauga, ON • L5B 3C1 • Tel: 905-896-5035 • Fax: 905-615-4185 • Contact: Human Resources • E-mail: hr.info@ mississauga.ca • Internet: www.city.mississauga.ca • The City of Mississauga is a municipal government responsible for the formation of policy and laws in matters under its jurisdiction. The municipality employs approximately 4,100 people in total. More information can be found on their website.

NIAGARA PARKS COMMISSION, THE • 5881 Dunn Street • Niagara Falls, ON • L2G 2N9 • Tel: 905-353-5418 • Fax: 905-356-9019 • Contact: Human Resources • E-mail: humanres@ niagaraparks.com • Internet: www.niagaraparks.com • The Niagara Parks Commission is a self-financed agency of the Ontario Ministry of Tourism and Recreation. The Niagara Region offers an unparalleled variety of sights and sounds, from the majestic Niagara Falls to world-renowned theatres, festivals and wineries.

NOVA SCOTIA LIQUOR COMMISSION • 93 Chain Lake Drive • Halifax, NS • B3S 1A3 • Tel: 902-450-5822 • Fax: 902-450-6025 • Contact: Vice-President, Human Resources • Internet: www.thenslc.com • Nova Scotia Liquor Corporation regulates the sale of liquor products in retail outlets throughout Nova Scotia. They employ about 900 people in total.

ONTARIO LEGISLATIVE OFFICES • Bell Trinity Square, 483 Bay Street, 10th Floor, South Tower • Toronto, ON • M5G 2C9 • Tel: 416-586-3300 • Fax: 416-586-3400 • Contact: Human Resources • E-mail: careers@ombudsman.on.ca • Internet: www.ombudsman.on.ca • The Office of the Ombudsman was established by the Ontario legislature in 1975. The Ombudsman's job is to investigate complaints about provincial government organizations. When he finds something wrong he can make recommendations to resolve the problem, and if these are not acted upon, he can report the case to the Legislature. The Ombudsman can also help resolve complaints informally. Ontario's Ombudsman is an Officer of the provincial Legislature who is independent of the government and political parties.

PEEL REGIONAL POLICE • 7750 Hurontario Street • Brampton, ON • L6V 3W6 • Tel: 905-453-3311 • Fax: 905-453-4722 • Contact: Recruiting • Internet: www.peelpolice.on.ca • Peel Regional Police is engaged in the provision of municipal police services. The police division has 5 locations in the area and employs over 2,000 individuals to work in various areas of law enforcement.

PRINCE ALBERT, CITY OF • 1084 Central Avenue • Prince Albert, SK • S6V 7P3 • Tel: 306-953-4310 • Fax: 306-953-4313 • Contact: Human Resources • Internet: www.citypa.ca • City of Prince Albert is a municipal government for a city of 35,000 people. They are responsible for the formation of policy and laws in matters under its jurisdiction. The City of Prince Albert only accepts resumes when a position has been advertised. The competition number must be on the cover letter to indicate which position the individual is applying for. If there is more than one competition that the individual is applying for there must be resumes sent for each one. All competitions are advertised on the City's web page.

PRINCE GEORGE, CITY OF • 1100 Patricia Blvd. • Prince George, BC • V2L 3V9 • Tel: 250-561-7600 • Fax: 250-612-5605 • Contact: Human Resources • E-mail: servicecentre@city.pg.bc. ca • Internet: www.city.pg.bc.ca • City of Prince George is a local government for the city. They are responsible for the formation of policy and laws in matters under its jurisdiction. They do not have a holding file for resumes, so please submit only from a posted competition.

PUBLIC UTILITIES OF KINGSTON • 211 Counter Street • Kingston, ON • K7L 4X7 • Tel: 613-546-0000 • Fax: 613-542-1463 • Contact: Human Resources • E-mail: info@utilitieskingston. com • Internet: www.utilitieskingston.com • Utilities Kingston is responsible for supplying, distributing and metering electricity and natural gas in the City Central. Utilities Kingston is also responsible for supplying, distributing and metering water and for collecting, pumping and treating sewage for the entire City of Kingston.

REGIONAL MUNICIPALITY OF NIAGARA • 2201 St. David's Road, P.O. Box 1042 • Thorold, ON • L2V 4T7 • Tel: 905-685-1571 • Fax: 905-687-4977 • Contact: Human Resources • E-mail: jobopening@regional.niagara.on.ca • Internet: www.regional.niagara.on.ca • Regional Municipality of Niagara is a regional government spanning water and sewer works, social and senior services, public health, planning and development, waste management, and transportation.

RICHMOND, CITY OF • 6911 No. 3 Road • Richmond, BC • V6Y 2C1 • Tel: 604-276-4000 • Fax: 604-276-4029 • Contact: Human Resources • Internet: www.richmond.ca • City of Richmond is a municipal government responsible for the formation of policy and laws in matters under its jurisdiction.

SASKATCHEWAN GOVERNMENT INSURANCE • 2260 - 11th Avenue • Regina, SK • S4P 0J9 • Tel: 306-751-3327 • Fax: 306-347-0089 • Contact: Human Resources • E-mail: hrinquiries@ sgi.sk.ca • Internet: www.sgi.sk.ca • SGI was created in 1945 and, over time, has evolved into three distinct operations: the Saskatchewan Auto Fund, the province's compulsory auto insurance program; SGI CANADA, which sells property and casualty insurance products in Saskatchewan; and SGI CANADA Insurance Services Ltd. (SCISL), an expansion company which sells property and casualty insurance products outside the province. SGI currently employs more than 1600 people and works with a network of more than 300 independent insurance brokers in Saskatchewan (and 450 motor licence issuers, most of whom are brokers), as well as numerous brokers outside the province. The corporation operates 20 claims centres and five salvage operations in 13 Saskatchewan communities, and a SCISL branch office in Winnipeg, Manitoba.

SASKATOON, CITY OF • 222 3rd Avenue North • Saskatoon, SK • S7K 0J5 • Tel: 306-975-3200 • Fax: 306-975-7651 • Contact: Human Resources • Internet: www.city.saskatoon.sk.ca • The City of Saskatoon is a municipal government which includes administration, engineering, planning, public works, law, recreation, and protective services in the City of Saskatoon.

SASKPOWER • 2025 Victoria Avenue • Regina, SK • S4P 0S1 • Tel: 306-566-2140 • Fax: 306-566-2087 • Contact: Human Resources • Internet: www.saskpower.com • SaskPower provides value-added electrical energy and related services. They achieve this through employee innovation, a competitive spirit and pursuing opportunity for our customers and shareholders.

SOCIÉTÉ DES ALCOOLS DU QUÉBEC • 905 av de Lorimier • Montréal, QC • H2K 3V9 • Tel: 514-873-2020 • Fax: 514-873-6788 • Contact: Human Resources • E-mail: info@saq.com • Internet: www.saq.com • Société des Alcools du Québec specializes in the sale and distribution of alcohol, wine, and imported beer. The company's head office is in Montréal, Québec. They have an employee base of 4,000 people.

ST. LAWRENCE PARKS COMMISSION • 13740 County Road 2 • Morrisburg, ON • K0C 1X0 • Tel: 613-543-3704 • Fax: 613-543-2847 • Contact: Human Resources • Internet: www.parks. on.ca • The St. Lawrence Parks Commission, an agency of the Ontario Government, manages recreational areas from Kingston to near the Quebec border known as the Parks of the St. Lawrence.

ST. LAWRENCE SEAWAY MANAGEMENT CORPORATION, THE • 202 Pitt Street • Cornwall, ON • K6J 3P7 • Tel: 613-932-5170 • Fax: 613-932-7286 • Contact: Human Resources • Internet: www.careers.seaway.ca • The St. Lawrence Seaway Management Corporation operates a navigable waterway between Montreal, Quebec and Lake Erie. The St. Lawrence Seaway Management Corporation's office is located in Cornwall, Ontario.

SURREY, CITY OF • 14245 56th Avenue • Surrey, BC • V3X 3A2 • Tel: 604-591-4117 • Fax: 604-591-4517 • Contact: Human Resources • E-mail: humanresources@city.surrey.bc.ca • Internet: www.surreycareers.ca • The City of Surrey is a municipal government in British Columbia that is responsible for the creation and introduction of policy and laws in areas under its jurisdiction.

THE CORPORATION OF THE TOWN OF NEW TECUMSETH • Box 910, 10 Wellington Street East • Alliston, ON • L9R 1A1 • Tel: 705-435-6219 • E-mail: careers@town.newtecumseth. on.ca • Internet: www.town.newtecumseth.on.ca • Municipal Government operations including Administration, Public Works, Engineering, Planning and Development, Parks, Recreation and Culture, Finance.

TIMMINS, CITY OF • 220 Algonquin Boulevard East • Timmins, ON • P4N 1B3 • Tel: 705-264-1331 • Fax: 705-360-1392 • Internet: www.city.timmins.on.ca • The City of Timmins is a municipal government responsible for the formation of policy and laws in matters under its jurisdiction. The municipality employs more than 780 people.

TORONTO AND REGION CONSERVATION AUTHORITY • 5 Shoreham Drive • Downsview, ON • M3N 1S4 • Tel: 416-661-6600 • Fax: 416-661-6898 • Contact: Human Resources • E-mail: info@trca.on.ca • Internet: www.trca.on.ca • The Toronto and Region Conservation Authority is a public agency devoted to the protection, enhancement, and public enjoyment of the renewable natural resources within nine watersheds in the Great Lakes Basin.

TORONTO FIRE SERVICES • 4330 Dufferin Street • Toronto, ON • M3H 5R9 • Tel: 416-338-9050 • Fax: 416-338-9494 • Contact: Captain Ron Barrow, Recruitment Officer • E-mail: rbarrow@toronto.ca • Internet: www.toronto.ca/fire • The City of Toronto Fire Services is responsible for the fire safety for the citizens of the City of Toronto. Operating an efficient and effective fire and rescue service, Toronto Fire Services employs over 3,000 dedicated individuals who work in various capacities that include fire suppression and rescue, fire and emergency planning, fire prevention and inspections, training, health and safety and community outreach. The Toronto Fire Services has a job hot line at 392-FIRE (3473).

TORONTO POLICE SERVICE • 40 College Street • Toronto, ON • M5G 2J3 • Tel: 416-808-2222 • Fax: 416-808-7152 • Contact: Ms. Maureen Carey Manager • E-mail: careerstorontopolice. on.ca • Internet: www.torontopolice.on.ca • The Toronto Police Service is dedicated to delivering police services, in partnership with their communities, to keep Toronto the best and safest place to be. Their service is committed to being a world leader in policing through excellence, innovation, continuous learning, quality leadership and management. They are committed to deliver police services which are sensitive to the needs of the community, involving collaborative partnerships and teamwork to overcome all challenges.

TORONTO, CITY OF • 55 John Street, 5th Floor • Toronto, ON • M5V 3C6 • Tel: 416-338-0338 • Fax: 416-338-0685 • Internet: www.toronto.ca • The City of Toronto is the largest city in Canada. They employ approximately 39,000 staff in more than 4,000 types of jobs. These jobs are located in more than 2,670 work locations.

WINDSOR, CITY OF • 350 City Hall Square West • Windsor, ON • N9A 6S1 • Tel: 519-255-2489 • Fax: 519-256-3311 • Contact: Human Resources • E-mail: 311@city.windsor.on.ca • Internet: www.citywindsor.ca • The City of Windsor is a municipal government responsible for the formation of policy and laws in matters under its jurisdiction.

YORK REGIONAL POLICE • 17250 Yonge Street • Newmarket, ON • L3Y 4W5 • Tel: 905-830-0303 • Fax: 905-853-5810 • Contact: Human Resources • E-mail: hr@police.york.on.ca • Internet: www.police.york.on.ca • York Regional Police is engaged in the provision of municipal police services in the Region of York. The police division has 7 locations in the area and employs over 800 individuals to work in various areas of law enforcement.

Hospitality

BEST WESTERN PRIMROSE HOTEL • 111 Carlton Street • Toronto, ON • M5B 2G3 • Tel: 416-977-8000 • Fax: 416-977-6323 • Contact: Human Resources • Internet: www.bestwesternontario.com • The Best Western Primrose Hotel Downtown-Toronto is conveniently situated in the heart of downtown Toronto, opposite to the Maple Leaf Gardens and just steps away from Toronto's primary financial, entertainment and cultural districts. Offering 341 newly renovated guest rooms and suites partrons can choose from double, queen and king-size bedrooms, or suites.

BREWSTER MOUNTAIN LODGE • 208 Caribou Street, P.O. BOX 2286 • Banff, AB • T1L 1C1 • Tel: 403-762-2900 • Fax: 403-760-7505 • Contact: Mr. Mark Hosking, General Manager • E-mail: mhosking@brewsteradventures.com • Internet: www.brewstermountainlodge.com • Brewster Mountain Lodge is a 60 room, 17 suite full service hotel in downtown Banff with a tradition of the Brewster family. They have standard room up to full suites.

BURGER KING RESTAURANTS OF CANADA INC. • 700 - 401 The West Mall • Toronto, ON • M9C 5J4 • Fax: 416-626-6696 • Contact: Human Resources Department • Email: bkjobscanada@whopper.com • Internet: www.burgerking.ca • Burger King Restaurants of Canada is a fast food restaurant with operations throughout the country. With its parent company being Burger King Corp. of the United States.

CAMBRIDGE SUITES • 1583 Brunswick Street • Halifax, NS • B3J 3P5 • Tel: 902-420-05555 • Fax: 902-420-9379 • Contact: Sharon Rutland • E-mail: srutland@cambridgesuiteshotel.com • Internet: www.cambridgesuiteshalifax.com • Cambridge Suites is a large hotel establishment with many outlets throughout the country. The hotel provides a wide range of facilities for dining, conventions, banquets, business meetings, and family vacations. The address above is for their location in Halifax, Nova Scotia.

CAMPUS LIVING CENTRES • 5405 Eglinton Avenue West • Toronto, ON • M9C 5K6 • Tel: 416-620-0635 ext. 8090 • Contact: Human Resources • Internet: www.campuslivingcentres.com • Campus Living Centres operates student residences and conference centres. They manage student life activities and provide hotel-like accommodations during the summer. They are looking for recent university/college graduates with an in the hospitality industry and to join their management team.

CANADIAN ROCKY MOUNTAIN RESORTS • 600 6th Avenue S.W., Suite 900 • Calgary, AB • T2P 0S5 • Contact: Stacey Howard, Director of Human Resources • E-mail: hr@crmr.com • Internet: www.crmr.com • Canadian Rocky Mountain Resorts has three luxurious resort hotels with conference centers located in Banff and Lake Louise Alberta, and at Emerald Lake, near Field BC. Our culinary and wine programs have been recognized as among the best in the world, and have been featured at the James Beard Culinary Arts Foundation, in Wine Spectator, and many quality lifestyle publications and television programs. We cater to travellers from around the world, and our clientele include corporate retreats, conferences, conventions, social gatherings, tour clients and FIT's. We offer high standards of excellence in service, and enjoy a large repeat clientele. Our teams are made up of individuals from across Canada, and include housekeepers, guest service agents and bellmen, servers, event coordinators, maintenence workers, and culinary professionals as well as middle and upper tier managers.

Network as Much as Possible
The saying, "Its not what you know, but who you know" holds a good deal of truth. Talk to friends, relatives, teachers, etc. Get out into your professional and local community and meet people who share similar interests.

COWS INC. • 101 Watts Avenue • Charlottetown, PE • C1E 2B7 • Tel: 902-628-3617 • Fax: 902-566-3407 • E-mail: jobs@cows.ca • Internet: www.cows.ca • Cows Inc. is a Prince Edward Island company specializing in Super Premium Ice Cream and original design T-shirts. While Prince Edward Island remains the home base, COWS now operates ten stores! On the Island there is a COWS store on Queen Street in Charlottetown, as well as seasonal stores at six other locations across the Island. Other COWS locations include Halifax, Nova Scotia, Banff, Alberta, and Whistler, British Columbia.

DELTA TORONTO AIRPORT WEST • 5444 Dixon Road • Toronto, ON • L4W 2L2 • Tel: 905-624-1144 • Fax: 905-624-9477 • Internet: www.deltahotels.com • Located in the northwest corner of the city, The Delta Toronto Airport West Hotel is a full service hotel operated under Delta Hotel & Resorts. It features 297 bedrooms to meet customer demand.

DELTA TORONTO EAST HOTEL • 2035 Kennedy Road North • Scarborough, ON • M1T 3G2 • Tel: 416-299-1500 • Fax: 416-754-6941 • Internet: www.deltahotels.com • Founded in 1962 in Richmond, British Columbia, Delta Hotels has grown from a single 62-room motor inn to become Canada's largest first-class hotel management company. Today, it boasts a diversified portfolio of more than 35 city-centre, airport and resort properties, and distinguishes itself as the brand of choice for discerning owners and guests, as an exemplary employer to 7,500 people and as an active corporate citizen.

DRUXY'S INC. • 1200 Eglinton Avenue East, Suite 802 • Toronto, ON • M3C 1H9 • Tel: 416-385-9500 • Fax: 416-385-9501 • Internet: www.druxys.com • Druxy's Inc., also known as Druxy's Famous Deli Sandwiches, is a retail eatery with locations across the province and throughout the country. Employing more than 300 people, Druxy's Inc. offers a large number of flexible part time positions at the management level. The company looks for hardworking and outgoing individuals rather than any specific academic skills.

EXPLORER HOTEL, THE • 4825 - 49th Avenue • Yellowknife, NT • X1A 2R3 • Tel: 867-873-3531 • Fax: 867-873-2789 • Contact: Human Resources • E-mail: operations@explorerhotel.nt.ca • Internet: www.explorerhotel.ca • The Explorer Hotel is a 128 bedroom, full service luxury hotel located just steps away from the commercial and government centre of Yellowknife. The hotel has eight conference rooms suitable for groups of up to 350 people and offers full conference facilities. There are also five associated meeting and banquet rooms within the hotel.

G.B. CATERING • 102 Lindgren Road West, Unit #1 • Huntsville, ON • P1H 1Y2 • Tel: 705-789-8806 • Fax: 705-789-6582 • Contact: Ms. Jennifer Manuell, Human Resources Manager • E-mail: jennifer@gb.on.ca • Internet: www.gb.on.ca • G.B. Catering has been operating successfully in recreational camps and outdoor centres since 1969. In 2005 we plan to service at least twenty locations across Ontario-requiring the recruitment of about 150 employees. We provide service at a variety of camps, including sports-oriented camps, camps for children with special needs (diabetic, learning disabilities, physical disabilities, etc.), religious camps, a family camp, as well as traditional camps. Feeding numbers vary between 70 and 400 people, depending on the site. G.B.'s recipe for success is based on its unique philosophy of preparing high-quality home-cooked meals and fresh-baked goods, including our trademark home-made breads. We are dedicated to bringing customers the highest possible quality in everything we prepare.

GRANITE CLUB • 2350 Bayview Avenue • Toronto, ON • M2L 1E4 • Tel: 416-510-6668 • Fax: 416-510-6683 • Contact: Human Resources • E-mail: hr@graniteclub.com • Internet: www. graniteclub.com • Established in 1875, Granite Club is one of Canada's premier private family clubs, with valued traditions and prestige. We combine a high standard of social, athletic, dining and banquet facilities with uncompromising service to our 10,000 members.

HOLIDAY INN SELECT TORONTO AIRPORT • 970 Dixon Road • Toronto, ON • M9W 1J9 • Tel: 416-675-7611 • Fax: 416-675-9162 • Contact: Employee Services • E-mail: his-toronto-aprt@ichotelsgroup.com • Internet: www.holiday-inn.com • Conveniently located on Toronto's Westside, the Holiday Inn Select Toronto Airport, is just 5 minutes away from Pearson international Airport, International Centre, and the Toronto Congress Centre. The hotel features 444 guest rooms and many conference facilities.

KFC CANADA • 10 Carlson Court, Suite 300 • Rexdale, ON • M9W 6L2 • Tel: 416-674-0367 • Fax: 416-674-5594 • Contact: Human Resources • Internet: www.kfc.ca • KFC Corporation, based in Louisville, Kentucky, is the world's most popular chicken restaurant chain. It is part of Tricon Global Restaurants, Inc., which is the world's largest restaurant system with nearly 30,000 KFC, Taco Bell and Pizza Hut restaurants in more than 100 countries and territories. Visit the website to view and apply to employment opportunities currently available with KFC.

LICK'S ICE CREAM & BURGER SHOPS INC. • 2034 Queen Street East • Toronto, ON • M4L 1J4 • Tel: 416-362-5425 • Fax: 416-690-0504 • Contact: Human Resources • E-mail: info@lickshomeburgers.com • Internet: www.lickshomeburgers.com • LICK'S is dedicated to enhancing a growing need for a quality product in the fast food industry. Their motto is, "Great Food, Served Fast!" LICK's restaurants create a comfortable, inviting environment that incorporates a friendly family feeling with stye and fun. To be considered for future employment opportunities, fill out the on-line application or visit a Lick's location nearest you.

METRO TORONTO CONVENTION CENTRE • 255 Front Street West • Toronto, ON • M5V 2W6 • Tel: 416-585-8000 • Fax: 416-585-8262 • Internet: www.mtccc.com • The Metro Toronto Convention Centre is a full service facility offering convention and show services to individuals, businesses and other enterprises. In the heart of downtown Toronto, the Convention Centre employs over 1,000 individuals to work at this location. Most of those employed with the Convention Centre work in casual, call-in positions.

MOXIE'S CLASSIC GRILL • 31 Hopewell Way NE • Calgary, AB • T3J 4V7 • Tel: 403-543-2600 • Fax: 403-543-2646 • Internet: www.moxie.ca • At Moxie's Classic Grill we believe it is our culture that separates us from our competitors. This culture is built on the foundation of great people, serving fabulous fresh food in an upbeat, stylish décor. We are fast-paced and action-oriented, moving quickly to seize the leading position as the market changes and as new opportunities become availble. We know that to run the best casual restaurants, we need the best Leaders and Team Members operating each Moxie's Classic Grill. To this end, our goal is to be the employer of choice in the restaurant industry.

OLIVER BONACINI RESTAURANTS • 2433 Yonge Street • Toronto, ON • M4P 2H4 • Tel: 647-288-3867 • Fax: 416-486-7674 • Contact: Ms. Valerie Upfold, HR Manager • E-mail: hr@oliverbonacini.com • Internet: www.oliverbonacini.com • Oliver Bonacini Restaurants own and operate six of Toronto's best restaurants - Canoe, Jump, Auberge du Pommier, Biff's, Square and Oliver & Bonacini Cafe.Grill.

PIZZA PIZZA LTD. • 580 Jarvis Street • Toronto, ON • M4Y 2H9 • Tel: 416-967-1010 • Fax: 416-967-3566 • Contact: Human Resources • E-mail: hire_me@pizzapizza.ca • Internet: www.pizzapizza.ca • Pizza Pizza Limited is Ontario's #1 pizza. Their head office provides support for franchisee and corporate stores throughout Ontario. After more than 35 years in the business, Pizza Pizza continues to be a fast-paced, entrepreneurial corporation, and a leader in its industry. In consumer surveys, Pizza Pizza continually ranks first in terms of quality, service and value. Part of the chain's success stems from its leading-edge marketing programs and technology systems.

RAMADA HOTEL AND CONFERENCE CENTRE • 185 Yorkland Blvd. • Toronto, ON • M2J 4R2 • Tel: 416-493-9000 • Fax: 416-493-5729 • Contact: Human Resources • Internet: www. ramada.ca • The Ramada Hotel and Conference Centre, Toronto-Don Valley, is an area landmark, easily visible and accessible from both the Don Valley Parkway and Highways 401 and 404 "The Cross Roads of Toronto". The hotel features 285 well-appointed guest rooms and Jacuzzi suites, distributed over 10 floors. The hotel is a favorite of both business travelers and families alike.

RICHTREE INC. • Brofield Place, 181 Bay Street, 2nd Floor, Box 867 • Toronto, ON • M5J 2T3 • Tel: 800-695-5771 • Contact: Human Resources • Email: rmhr@richtree.ca • Internet: www. richtree.ca • Richtree is the operator of the Movenpick, Marche and Marchelino Restaurants throught North America and the U.S. They operate a unique market style concept in both Quick and Full Service functions. Offering freshly made international food. There is nothing behind the scenes, our skilled staff, cook "on stage" before the customer proving a unique and memorable experience.

SALISBURY HOUSE OF CANADA LTD. • 5540 Portage Avenue • Winnipeg, MB • R4H 1E8 • Tel: 204-831-5780 • Fax: N/A • Contact: Human Resources • Internet: www.salisburyhouse.ca • Salisbury House of Canada is a local restaurant chain in Winnipeg, Manitoba which houses a central kitchen, warehouse, and their head office. The firm employs approximately 600 people in total.

SANDMAN HOTELS, INNS & SUITES • 1755 West Broadway, Suite 310 • Vancouver, BC • V6J 4S5 • Tel: 604-730-6600 • Fax: 604-730-4645 • Contact: Human Resources • E-mail: careers@sandmanhotels.com • Internet: www.sandmanhotels.com • Sandman Hotels, Inns & Suites is a chain of hotels located across Canada. See their website for additional information.

SHERATON FALLSVIEW HOTEL • 6755 Fallsview Blvd. • Niagara Falls, ON • L2G 3W7 • Tel: 905-374-1077 • Fax: 905-374-6224 • Contact: Human Resources • E-mail: humanresources@ fallsview.com • Internet: www.fallsview.com • Located just 300 yards from the edge of the breathtaking and legendary Niagara Falls, the Four Diamond Sheraton Fallsview Hotel and Conference Centre is Niagara's most prestigious and award-winning hotel. They have 402 guestrooms and many specialty suites and lofts, which offer soothing whirlpool bath, ambient decorative fireplaces, warm contemporary decor and spectacular floor to ceiling windows. This hotel is within walking distance of the Falls and the Niagara Fallsview Casino Resort along with all major attractions including Maid of the Mist Boat Ride, Marineland, The Niagara Parks and Casino Niagara. World class golfing, award winning wineries and outlet shopping are all nearby.

THE BOULEVARD CLUB • 1491 Lakeshore Blvd. West • Toronto, ON • M6B 2J2 • Tel: 416-642-6823 • Fax: 416-538-9411 • E-mail: jobs@clubjobs.ca • Internet: www.boulevardclub.com • The Boulevard Club is a private members club for sports and social activities. We have a need for servers for the summer patio, banquets, bar and cafe.

THE FAIRMONT JASPER PARK LODGE • P.O. Box 40 • Jasper, AB • T0E 1E0 • Tel: 780-852-3301 • Fax: 780-852-4946 • Internet: www.fairmontcareers.com • The Fairmont Jasper Park Lodge is surrounded by snow-capped peaks and sparkling lakes, the Lodge is a 451-room award winning luxury resort nestled in the heart of the Canadian Rockies. Charming cabins and rustic elegance of this magnificent resort make it the embodiment of peace, tranquility and natural beauty. The Fairmont Jasper Park Lodge encompasses the operation of rooms, 10 food and beverage outlets, golf course, riding stables, and recreation facilities including boating, cycling, tennis, skating, skiing, and much more! The Lodge is recognized as one of Canada's premier resorts and has been distinguished by receiving the follwoing awards; Canada Select 4 1/2 star rating, Four Diamond Edith Cavell fine dining room, #1 Golf Resort in Canada as rated by SCOREGolf Magazine and the Meeting & Incentives Pinnacle award to name of few.

THE FAIRMONT ROYAL YORK HOTEL • 100 Front Street West • Toronto, ON • M5J 1E3 • Tel: 416-860-4512 • Fax: 416-860-4560 • Internet: www.fairmontcareers.com • At Fairmont Hotels & Resorts every guest expects us to capture their heart. Every colleague is inspired to create memories. It is not a performance for us, it is a natural way of treating people. Satisfying our guests is important to us, and we extend this policy to our colleagues as well. Through outstanding performance in the areas of recruitment, training, advancement and performance management, Fairmont Hotels & Resorts is considered one of North Americas top rated companies to work for. If creating memories and being part of an exceptional guest experience appeals to you, perhaps you would be interested in joining this outstanding team of hospitality professionals in one of our exceptional locations throughout North America. Individuals who have a strong work history - preferably within the hospitality industry are encouraged to apply.

WATERLOO INN • 475 King Street North • Waterloo, ON • N2J 2Z5 • Tel: 519-884-0220 • Fax: 519-884-0321 • Contact: Ms. Donna Doogan, Human Resources Manager • E-mail: ddoogan@waterlooinn.com • Internet: www.waterlooinn.com • Waterloo Inn is a hotel and restaurant that offers facilities and services for both business and family travellers. The hotel employs approximately 200 individuals.

WENDY'S RESTAURANTS OF CANADA INC. • 240 Wyecroft Road • Oakville, ON • L6K 2G7 • Tel: 905-849-7685 • Contact: Human Resources Department • E-mail: canadian_recruitment@ wendys.com • Internet: www.wendys.ca • Wendy's Restaurants of Canada is engaged in the operation of fast food outlets. A quick service family restaurant chain, Wendy's Restaurants is a division of Wendy's International Inc. in the United States. With outlets throughout Canada, the restaurant employs over 5,700 individuals from coast to coast.

WESTIN BAYSHORE RESORT AND MARINA, THE • 1601 Georgia Street West • Vancouver, BC • V6G 2V4 • Tel: 604-682-3377 • Fax: 604-687-3102 • Contact: Human Resources • E-mail: bayshore@westin.com • Internet: www.westinbayshore.com • The Westin Bayshore Resort and Marina is a luxury hotel in downtown Vancouver. The hotel's goal is to be the best and most sought after hotel in Vancouver by delivering exceptional customer service. Visit their website for specific employment information and current job openings.

WESTIN PRINCE HOTEL, THE • 900 York Mills Road • Toronto, ON • M3B 3H2 • Tel: 416-444-2511 • Fax: 416-444-9597 • Internet: www.westin.com/prince • The Westin Prince Hotel is located in North York. A subsidiary of Prince Hotel Inc. of Japan, the Toronto Prince Hotel has a large number of facilities for business meetings, conventions or family retreats. The hotel employs over 315 individuals including part-timers.

WHITE SPOT LIMITED • 1126 Marine Drive S.E. • Vancouver, BC • V5X 2V7 • Tel: 604-321-6631 • Fax: 604-325-1499 • Contact: Human Resources • Internet: www.whitespot.ca • White Spot is a large food service company consisting of over 60 family style restaurants, some of which are corporately owned and operated, the majority of which are franchise operations. White Spot employs more than 3500 people, making it one of British Columbia's largest employers.

Career ✓ Tip

Proofread All Written Communications
Catch all spelling and mechanical errors before you share them with potential employers. Make sure that all of your written correspondence is professionally produced by a computer or typewriter capable of letter quality printing.

Hospitals & Medical

ABERDEEN HOSPITAL • 835 East River Road • New Glasgow, NS • B2H 3S6 • Tel: 902-752-7600 • Fax: 902-752-6231 • E-mail: dianne.edmond@pcdha.nshealth.ca • Internet: www. aberdeenhospital.com • Established in 1895, Aberdeen Hospital is a government owned health care facility with 104 beds. The hospital provides services in areas including intensive care, medicine and surgery, gynaecology, and paediatrics.

ALBERTA BLUE CROSS • 10009 - 108 Street NW • Edmonton, AB • T5J 3C5 • Tel: 780-498-8000 • Fax: 780-498-4627 • Contact: Human Resources • Internet: www.ab.bluecross.ca • Alberta Blue Cross provides supplementary health and dental benefit programs to meet the health needs of over one million Albertans. They offer benefit plans for individuals and families, seniors, and large and small employers. They also administer health programs for provincial, territorial and federal governments.

ALEXANDRA HOSPITAL • 29 Noxon Street • Ingersoll, ON • N5C 3V6 • Tel: 519-485-1700 • Fax: 519-485-9606 • Contact: Ms. Martha Bancroft, Human Resources • E-mail: martha. bancroft@alexandrahospital.on.ca • Internet: www.alexandrahospital.on.ca • Alexandra Hospital is a fully accredited acute care hospital and a community health centre dedicated to treating illness and promoting and enhancing the health of the residents of Ingersoll and the surrounding area.

ALTONA COMMUNITY MEMORIAL HEALTH CENTRE • 240 - 5th Avenue NE, Box 660 • Altona, MB • R0G 0B0 • Tel: 204-324-6411 • Fax: 204-324-1299 • Contact: Human Resources • The Altona Community Memorial Health Centre was opened in 1995. The juxtaposed long term care home was renovated and additional 40 beds were constructed and opened in the summer of 2000. The acute care ward is an active busy unit. They provide low-risk obstetrical service, general surgery, medical and emergency service.

ATLANTIC BLUE CROSS CARE • 644 Main Street, P.O. Box 220 • Moncton, NB • E1C 8L3 • Tel: 506-853-1811 • Fax: 506-869-9651 • Contact: Human Resources • Internet: www.atl. bluecross.ca • Atlantic Blue Cross Care is a leading provider of personal health benefits coverage. They employ more than 1,400 people in all areas of their business.

BAYCREST CENTRE FOR GERIATRIC CARE • 3560 Bathurst Street • Toronto, ON • M6A 2E1 • Tel: 416-785-2500 • Fax: 416-785-2378 • Contact: Employment Services • Internet: www. baycrest.org • The Baycrest Centre for Geriatric Care is a fully-affiliated teaching organization with the University of Toronto which provides facilities, services and programs to enrich the quality of life of the elderly through the integration of care, research and education. Its divisions include Baycrest Hospital, Jewish Home for the Aged, Baycrest Terrace, Baycrest Centre Foundation and Rotman Research Institute.

BELLEVILLE GENERAL HOSPITAL • 265 Dundas Street East • Belleville, ON • K8N 5A9 • Tel: 613-969-7400 • Fax: 613-968-8234 • Contact: Human Resources • Internet: www.qhc.on.ca • Belleville General currently provides primary and secondary care with a total of 206 beds, and offers a full range of clinical and diagnostic services, including: Cardiology, Intensive Care, Oncology, Orthopaedics and Psychiatry/Mental Health Services.

BETHESDA HOSPITAL • P.O. Box 939 • Steinbach, MB • R0A 2R0 • Tel: 204-326-6411 • Fax: 204-326-6931 • Contact: Human Resources • Bethesda Hospital is a general medical and health care facility that was established in 1937. The hospital provides services in the areas of medicine and surgery, pediatrics, gynecology, and extended care, among others. Bethesda Hospital has about 80 beds in total, and has a staff of approximately 235 individuals.

BLOORVIEW MACMILLAN CHILDREN'S CENTRE • 150 Kilgour Road • Toronto, ON • M4G 1R8 • Tel: 416-425-6220 • Fax: 416-424-3868 • Contact: Human Resources • E-mail: humanresources@bloorview.ca • Internet: www.bloorview.ca • Bloorview MacMillan Children's Centre is dedicated to enabling children and youth with disabilities or special needs to achieve their personal best. Each year, more than 6,500 young people and their families from across Ontario benefit from their outpatient clinics, hospital care, assistive technology services and community outreach activities.

CAMBRIDGE MEMORIAL HOSPITAL • 700 Cornation Blvd. • Cambridge, ON • N1R 3G2 • Tel: 519-621-2330 • Fax: 519-740-4907 • Contact: Human Resource Services Program • E-mail: jobs@cmh.org • Internet: www.cmh.org • Cambridge Memorial Hospital is a 220-bed community hospital serving approximately 120,000 area residents of Cambridge and North Dumfries. They have a health care team of approximately 140 medical staff, 1200 health care professionals and support staff and 270 dedicated Auxiliary volunteers and 70 Teen Volunteers.

CAPITAL HEALTH • Walter C. Mackenzie Health Sciences Centre, 8440 - 112 Street • Edmonton, AB • T6G 2B7 • Tel: 780-407-1000 • Contact: Human Resources • E-mail: careers@cha.ab.ca • Internet: www.capitalhealth.ca • Capital Health is one of the largest and top-rated health systems in Canada, providing communities with information on how to stay healthy and avoid health risks. It services 1.6 million people across central and northern Alberta, providing specialized services such as trauma and burn treatment and organ transplants. They also provide additional services including home care services, outreach programs, mental health services and rehabilitation and prevention programs.

CHILDREN'S HOSPITAL OF EASTERN ONTARIO • 401 Smyth Road • Ottawa, ON • K1H 8L1 • Tel: 613-737-7600 • Fax: 613-738-4233 • Contact: Human Resources Department • E-mail: jobs@cheo.on.ca • Internet: www.cheo.on.ca • The Children's Hospital of Eastern Ontario (CHEO) is a 155 bed pediatric health centre created by the determination of local physicians, elected officials, parents and the community. Founded in 1974, the Children's Hospital of Eastern Ontario was established as a special and distinct hospital to serve the children and youth of Eastern Ontario and Western Quebec. As a teaching hospital, CHEO is affiliated with the Faculty of Medicine at the University of Ottawa. CHEO is also partnered with 17 other hospitals in Eastern Ontario, to provide specialized services, exchange knowledge and share expertise.

CHILLIWACK GENERAL HOSPITAL • Fraser Health Authority, 300 - 10233 152A Street • Surrey, BC • V3R 7P8 • Tel: 604-575-5130 • Fax: 604-587-4666 • Contact: Recruitment Services • Internet: www.fraserhealth.ca • Chilliwack General Hospital is a public health care facility with approximately 120 acute care beds and 300 long term care beds. Established in 1911, the hospital provides services in medicine and surgery, pediatrics, psychiatric care, intensive care, obstetrics, emergency and long term care. The hospital employs approximately 1,000 individuals.

CHINOOK HEALTH REGION • 960 - 19 Street South • Lethbridge, AB • T1J 1W5 • Tel: 403-388-6103 • Fax: 403-388-6011 • Contact: Dean Oikawa, Director Human Resources • E-mail: doikawa@chr.ab.ca • Internet: www.chr.ab.ca • Chinook Health Region is one of 9 regions that provides health care services in the province of Alberta. The health authority is responsible for acute care, long term care, and public health services within its region. It employs a team of more than 3800 full-time, part-time and casual employees.

COMMUNITY CARE ACCESS CENTRE OF WATERLOO REGION • 800 King Street West • Kitchener, ON • N2G 1E8 • Tel: 519-748-2222 • Fax: 519-883-5525 • Contact: Ms. Marjorie Smith, Human Resources • E-mail: hr@ww.ccac-ont.ca • Internet: www.ccac-ont.ca • The Community Care Access Centre of Waterloo Region (CCAC) is a non-profit agency funded by the ministry of health to facilitate the delivery of community health care services through case management and placement coordination services. As the central point of access to information and a broad range of community-based health and support services, the Community Care Access Centre of Waterloo Region assists, directs and supports residents in determining, coordinating and ensuring the provision of services in a variety of settings.

DAVID THOMPSON HEALTH REGION • 5110-49 Avenue • Ponoka, AB • T4J 1R8 • Tel: 403-704-2562 • Fax: 403-704-2580 • Contact: Human Resources • E-mail: recruit@dthr.ab.ca • Internet: www.dthr.ab.ca • Delivery of health services involves physicians, nurses and support staff at hospitals, health centres and care centres as well as in the community. Volunteers, lodge and medical clinic staff, partners, municipalities and the public all play a vital role. Third largest health region by population, the DTHR serves nearly 300,000 residents, covers 60 thousand sq. km of territory and employs over 9,000 staff. There are over 350 practicing physicians in the region.

DEER LODGE CENTRE INC. • 2109 Portage Avenue • Winnipeg, MB • R3J 0L3 • Tel: 204-831-2105 • Fax: 204-896-6509 • E-mail: employ@deerlodge.mb.ca • Internet: www.deerlodge.mb.ca • Deer Lodge Centre is a long term care and rehabilitation facility providing a variety of in-patient, out-patient and outreach programs to the community. Deer Lodge Centre serves adults with complex needs who require rehabilitation and specialized care for long term health concerns. The Deer Lodge Centre provides rehabilitation services, outreach programs in psychogeriatrics, respiratory therapy, the Day Hospital and Adult Day Care for cognitively impaired community clients. For information regarding current job vacancies, call the 24-hour Job Line at 204-831-2995 or call the number listed above.

HEALTH CARE CORPORATION OF ST. JOHN'S • 302 Waterford Bridge Road, South Wing • St. John's, NL • A1E 4J8 • Tel: 709-777-1361 • Fax: 709-777-1303 • Contact: Ms. Kathy Hare, Recruitment Officer • E-mail: employment@hccsj.nl.ca • Internet: www.easternhealth.ca • Health Care Corporation of St. John's is the largest health care organization in Newfoundland and Labrador and is one of the province's largest employers. It provides health care services to the St. John's region with a local population of about 200,000. The Corporation employs about 6,500 staff members, 500 doctors, and 100 volunteers.

HEALTH SCIENCES CENTRE • 820 Sherbrook Street • Winnipeg, MB • R3A 1R9 • Tel: 204-787-3668 • Internet: www.hsc.mb.ca • The five hospitals comprising the Health Sciences Centre occupy 32 acres of land in central Winnipeg. They are one of the largest health care facilities in Canada and the major referral center in Manitoba for complex health problems requiring expert consultation and sophisticated investigation and management. Highly skilled teams of professional staff provide acute care and continuing care to the ill and injured. They accept applications for vacancies only within a prescribed posting timeline.

HÔTEL DIEU DE MONTRÉAL • 3840 rue Saint-Urbain • Montréal, QC • H2W 1T8 • Tel: 514-890-8000 • Contact: Ressources humaines • Hôtel Dieu de Montréal is a public health care facility that provides general medical and surgical services. Established in 1642, the hospital has various departments including medicine and surgery, chronic care, psychiatric services, intensive care, and gynecology. The hospital has 570 beds, and employs 2,800 people. Hôtel Dieu de Montréal is affiliated with The University of Montreal.

HUMBER RIVER REGIONAL HOSPITAL • 2111 Finch Avenue West • Downsview, ON • M3N 1N1 • Tel: 416-747-3774 • Fax: 416-747-3758 • Contact: Recruiter, Human Resources • E-mail: recruitment@hrrh.on.ca • Internet: www.hrrh.on.ca • Humber River Regional Hospital is one of Ontario's largest regional acute health centres, with more than 600 inpatient beds, and serving a region of more than 800,000 residents. With a staff of more than 3,200 and over 700 physicians, the hospital offers services in dialysis, emergency, diagnostics, cardiology, intensive care, paediatrics, ambulatory care, mental health, medicine and surgery.

IWK HEALTH CENTRE • 5850/5980 University Avenue • Halifax, NS • B3K 6R8 • Tel: 902-470-8012 • Fax: 902-470-6612 • E-mail: human.resources@iwk.nshealth.ca • Internet: www.iwk.nshealth.ca • Located in Halifax, Nova Scotia, the IWK Health Centre provides quality care to children, youth, women and families in the three Maritime provinces and beyond. As a tertiary care health centre dedicated to education, research, family centred care and health promotion, the IWK proudly promotes a mission of caring, learning and advocacy. First and foremost, our staff, volunteers and partners are committed to helping children, youth and women in the Maritimes be the healthiest in the world. The IWK has 101 adult beds, 110 for babies and 121 beds for children. They have more than 2,400 staff and over 750 volunteers.

JARLETTE HEALTH SERVICES • 689 Yonge Street • Midland, ON • L4R 2E1 • Tel: 705-526-3807 • Fax: 705-528-0023 • Internet: www.jarlette.com • With over 37 years of experience, Jarlette Health Services cares for more than 1600 residents at 17 retirement and long-term care facilities in Ontario. They seek motivated and experienced professionals.

MISERICORDIA HEALTH CENTRE • 99 Cornish Avenue • Winnipeg, MB • R3C 1A2 • Tel: 204-774-6581 • Fax: 204-783-6052 • Contact: Human Resources • E-mail: employment@miseri.winnipeg.mb.ca • Internet: www.misericordia.mb.ca • Misericordia Health Centre is a Roman Catholic health-care facility located in Winnipeg, Manitoba. Established in 1898, the health centre has general medical and surgical facilities and offers services in various departments.

NOR-MAN REGIONAL HEALTH AUTHORITY • P.O. Box 240 • The Pas, MB • R9A 1K4 • Tel: 204-623-9229 • Fax: 204-623-9263 • E-mail: recruit@normanrha.mb.ca • Internet: www.norman-rha.mb.ca • The NOR-MAN Regional Health Authority is situated in the north-west portion of Manitoba. We are an accredited organization that provides a continuum of health services to approximately 25,000 residents. The region is known for its abundance of beautiful lakes, wildlife, and scenic landscapes. It's a great place to raise a family in communities that are safe, have friendly people, excellent educational facilities, modern health care facilities, and excellent recreational opportunities.

NORTHERN LIGHTS REGIONAL HEALTH CENTRE • 7 Hospital Street • Fort McMurray, AB • T9H 1P2 • Tel: 780-714-5631 • Fax: 780-788-1362 • Contact: Human Resources • E-mail: hr@nlhr.ca • Internet: www.nlhr.ca • Northern Lights Regional Health Authority is one of 16 regional health authorities in Alberta. NLRHS provides a broad spectrum of community based and acute care health services to a growing population with increasingly diverse health needs. They provide over 58,000 residents with secondary health centre services. NLRHS is equipped with 24 hour emergency care, an intensive care unit, full surgical services, a radiology unit and a medical laboratory. They currently operate 92 acute care beds, 30 continuing care beds and one respite bed, for a total of 123. They are the only health centre in the region with a Continuing Care unit located right in the facility.

NORTHUMBERLAND HILLS HOSPITAL • 1000 DePalma Drive • Cobourg, ON • K9A 5W6 • Tel: 905-377-7759 • Fax: 905-372-4243 • E-mail: careers@nhh.ca • Internet: www.nhh.ca • The Northumberland Hills Hospital is a new, state-of-the-art, 137-bed medical facility in Cobourg, Ontario. Opening it's doors in October 2003, the hospital aims to better serve the changing needs of local residents. Northumberland Hills Hospital exists in partnership with community and regional health care professionals to provide effective and compassionate patient-centred care in an environment that promotes the dignity and well-being of everyone.

OVERLANDER EXTENDED CARE HOSPITAL • 953 Southill Street • Kamloops, BC • V2B 7Z9 • Tel: 250-554-2323 • Fax: 250-554-3403 • Contact: Human Resources • Overlander Hospital is a 200 bed geriatric care facility located in Kamloop, British Columbia. They provide numerous extended care services.

PARAMED HOME HEALTH CARE • 3000 Steeles Avenue East, Suite 700 • Markham, ON • L3R 9W2 • Tel: 519-439-2222 • Fax: 510-439-2222 • E-mail: infoparamed@extendicare.com • Internet: www.paramed.ca • ParaMed Home Health Care provides nursing, personal care, meal preparation, light housekeeping, nursing care, respite services and palliative care in the home. They can also provide additional services for family members residind in long term care facilities or provide a break for family members by sitting with loved ones confined to hospital.

PEACE COUNTY HEALTH • 10320 - 99 Street • Grande Prairie, AB • T8V 6J4 • Tel: 780-538-5387 • Fax: 780-538-5455 • Internet: www.pchr.ca • A place where urban and rural meet, Peace Country Health spans over 150,000 square kilometres through rolling foothills, rocky mountains and stunning river valleys. Thirty four hundred people work for Peace Country Health, making it the largest employer north of Edmonton. Based out of facilities in 16 communities, our staff and physicians provide health services to a population of 130,000 people in our region and many more from neighbouring B.C. Peace Country Health is progressive and focused on a collaborative work environment that provides the best possible health care in the best possible work environment.

PRINCE ALBERT PARKLAND HEALTH REGION • 1521-6th Avenue West • Prince Albert, SK • S6V 5K1 • Tel: 306-765-6060 • Fax: 306-765-6431 • E-mail: jobs@paphr.sk.ca • Internet: www.paphr.sk.ca • The Prince Albert Parkland Health Region offers excellent opportunities for fulfilling careers while providing an outstanding quality of life. The region is home to over 80,000 residents, about 40,000 live within the city of Prince Albert. 95 per cent of residents are within 30 minutes of a hospital or long term care facility. The health region is located over the geographic centre of Saskatchewan. The major centre and the only city located in the region's boundaries is Prince Albert. The health region employs over 2,300 health care professionals.

QEII HEALTH SCIENCES CENTRE • 1278 Tower Road • Halifax, NS • B3H 2Y9 • Tel: 902-473-5757 • Fax: 902-473-5757 • Contact: Human Resources • E-mail: human.resources@cdha.nshealth.ca • Internet: www.cdha.nshealth.ca • Located in the heart of Halifax, Nova Scotia, the QEII is the largest adult academic health sciences centre in Atlantic Canada, occupying 10 buildings on two sites. It was created in 1996 with the merger of the Victoria General, Halifax Infirmary, Abbie J. Lane Memorial, Camp Hill Veterans' Memorial, Nova Scotia Rehabilitation Centre and the Nova Scotia Cancer Centre.

REGINA QU'APPELLE HEALTH REGION • 2180 23rd Avenue • Regina, SK • S4S 0A5 • Tel: 306-766-5208 • Fax: 306-766-5147 • Contact: Human Resources • E-mail: jobs@rqhealth.ca • Internet: www.reginahealth.sk.ca • The Regina Qu'Appelle Health Region is the largest health care delivery system in southern Saskatchewan, and one of the most integrated health delivery agencies in the country. Regina Qu'Appelle Health Region offers a full range of hospital, rehabilitation, community and public health, long term care and home care services to meet the needs of more than 245,000 residents living in 120 cities, towns, villages, rural municipalities and 16 First Nation communities within the Region. The Region encompasses the former Regina Health District, Touchwood Qu'Appelle Health District and Pipestone Health District. They employ 8,470 staff and over 450 physicians.

ROBARTS RESEARCH INSTITUTE • 100 Perth Drive, P.O. Box 5015 • London, ON • N6A 5K8 • Tel: 519-663-5777 • Fax: 519-663-3789 • Contact: Lana-Lisa Coombs-Jackman, Human Resources Coordinator • E-mail: lljackman@robarts.ca • Internet: www.robarts.ca • Robarts Research Institute is Canada's only independent medical research centre. Since its inception in 1986, Robarts has focused on conducting interdisciplinary research on the treatment and prevention of disabling diseases of the neurological, cardiovascular and immune systems. Those include heart disease and stroke, diabetes, multiple sclerosis, Lou Gehrig's disease (ALS), Alzheimer's and many forms of cancer.

SCARBOROUGH GENERAL HOSPITAL • 3050 Lawrance Avenue East • Scarborough, ON • M1P 2V5 • Tel: 416-431-8126 • Fax: 416-431-8204 • Contact: Human Resources • E-mail: careers@tsh.to • Internet: www.tsh.to • Scarborough General Hospital is a public hospital established in 1956 to serve the community. In September 1998, the Health Services Restructuring Commission (HSRC) confirmed and endorsed a proposal for the amalgamation of The Salvation Army Scarborough Grace Hospital and Scarborough General Hospital into one corporation. This was consistent with a voluntary plan submitted by both hospitals in July, 1998. Today, the two founding hospitals form a single, unified hospital at two locations: The Scarborough Hospital – Grace Division and The Scarborough Hospital – General Division. Today, The Scarborough Hospital (TSH) is Canada's largest urban community hospital, with approximately 3,700 staff members, more than 700 physicians, and 800 volunteers.

SOUTH EASTMAN HEALTH/SANTÉ SUD-EST • Box 470 • LaBroquerie, MB • R0A 0W0 • Tel: 204-424-5880 • Fax: 204-424-5888 • Contact: Human Resources • E-mail: hr@sehealth.mb.ca • Internet: www.sehealth.mb.ca • South Eastman Health/Santé Sud-Est is the Regional Health Authority responsible for providing health care and services to the 60,000 people who call the south-eastern region of Manitoba home.

ST. JOSEPH'S CARE GROUP • 580 Algoma Street North • Thunder Bay, ON • P7B 5G4 • Tel: 807-343-4311 • Fax: 807-345-8745 • Internet: www.sjcg.net • St. Joseph's Care Group is a Catholic Organization committed to provide compassionate and holistic care and services to the people of Northwestern Ontario. The Care Group includes St. Joseph's Heritage, St. Joseph's Hospital, Lakehead Psychiatric Hospital and Hogarth Riverview Manor. These facilities are owned and operated by the Sisters of St. Joseph of Sault Ste. Marie, sponsored by The Catholic Health Corporation of Ontario (CHCO) and managed by a volunteer Board of Directors. Together, they are committed to providing programs and services in complex care, rehabilitation, long term care, supportive housing and mental health to meet the needs of the people in the Districts of Thunder Bay and Kenora-Rainy River.

ST. MARY'S GENERAL HOSPITAL • 911 Queen's Blvd. • Kitchener, ON • N2M 1B2 • Tel: 519-744-3311 • Fax: 519-749-6426 • Contact: Jack Borman, Director • E-mail: jborman@smgh.ca • Internet: www.smgh.ca • As a 191-bed community hospital, we embrace progress and change while maintaining our commitment to the mission and vision of our founders the Sisters of St. Joseph's. We are located in Kitchener, in the heart of Southwestern Ontario's golden triangle. Our community boasts two of the top universities in the country and an award winning community college. You won't spend time stuck in traffic in our city, but if you care to take in Toronto, Hamilton or London, they are less than 90 minutes away.

ST. MICHAEL'S HOSPITAL, UNIVERSITY OF TORONTO • 30 Bond Street • Toronto, ON • M5B 1W8 • Tel: 416-360-4000 • Internet: www.stmichaelshospital.com • This department of St. Michael's Hospital, University of Toronto, is a research group working in a teaching hospital. Our research programme is focused on cancer.

SUDBURY REGIONAL HOSPITAL • 41 Ramsey Lake Road • Sudbury, ON • P3E 5J1 • Tel: 705-523-7100 • Fax: 705-523-7062 • Contact: Human Resources • E-mail: recruitment@hrsrh.on.ca • Internet: www.hrsrh.on.ca • As a regional resource and referral centre, the HRSRH provides hospital-based acute, transitional, rehabilitation and continuing care for over 600,000 residents across northeastern Ontario. The HRSRH is currently undergoing a major expansion, which will consolidate all hospital-based services across three sites, on one site. Once complete, the new hospital will feature state-of-the-art technology and have 17 surgical operating rooms, 3,000 employees, 800 volunteers, and a medical, dental and midwifery complement of 260. The hospital will also become a teaching facility, affiliated with Laurentian University and Lakehead University, once the new Northern Medical School opens its doors in 2005.

SURREY MEMORIAL HOSPITAL • 13750 96 Avenue • Surrey, BC • V3V 1Z2 • Tel: 604-581-2211 • Fax: 604-588-3382 • Contact: Human Resources • Surrey Memorial Hospital is a public healthcare facility in Surrey that offers acute and long term care. The hospital employs about 2,200 individuals in total.

THE OTTAWA HOSPITAL • 1053 Carling Avenue • Ottawa, ON • K1Y 4E9 • Tel: 613-761-4727 • E-mail: jobs@ottawahospital.on.ca • Internet: www.ottawahospital.on.ca • The Ottawa Hospital is a compassionate provider of patient centred health services with an emphasis on tertiary-level and specialty care. As one of Canada's largest teaching hospitals, and among Ottawa's largest employers, The Ottawa Hospital is a unified, multi-campus organization (Civic, General, Riverside and Rehabilitation Centre) employing over 10,000 health care professionals.

THUNDER BAY REGIONAL HOSPITAL • 980 Oliver Road • Thunder Bay, ON • P7B 6V4 • Tel: 807-684-6218 • Fax: 807-684-5829 • Contact: Human Resources • E-mail: humanresources@tbh.net • Internet: www.tbh.net • Thunder Bay Regional Health Sciences Centre is a state-of-the-art acute care facility serving the healthcare needs of people living in Thunder Bay and Northwestern Ontario. An architectural showpiece situated on a landscaped site of nearly 70 acres, the Regional Health Sciences Centre is a stunning award-winning design that is functionally efficient. There are 375 acute care beds.

TORONTO EAST GENERAL HOSPITAL • 825 Coxwell Avenue • Toronto, ON • M4C 3E7 • Tel: 416-461-8272 • Fax: 416-469-6106 • Contact: Human Resources • E-mail: hr@tegh.on.ca • Internet: www.tegh.on.ca • Toronto East General Hospital (TEGH) is a large urban community teaching hospital, affiliated with the University of Toronto Faculty of Medicine and many other educational institutions, serving a diverse population of half a million people. Annually, the Hospital provides care for over 19,000 inpatients and has close to 60,000 emergency visits and over 175,000 outpatient visits. TEGH has approximately 500 beds comprised of acute care, rehabilitation and complex continuing care beds. TEGH has nearly 2,400 employees and 397 physicians on staff.

TORONTO GENERAL HOSPITAL • 190 Elizabeth Street • Toronto, ON • M5G 2C4 • Tel: 416-340-4141 • Contact: Human Resources • Internet: www.uhn.ca/tgh • Toronto General Hospital (TGH) is one of the city's oldest hospitals, dating back to the War of 1812 where it began as a small shed used for a military hospital. The hospital has numerous medical and surgical program specialties including heart and kidney disease, transplantation, an eating disorders clinic, women's health, nephrology, a HIV clinic and psychiatry as well as a busy Emergency Department that treats more than 30,000 patients each year. TGH is leading the way in cardiac care, organ transplants and the treatment of complex patient needs. Home to three of the University Health Network's (UHN) major program groupings (Heart and Circulation, Transplantation and Advanced Medicine and Surgery), their highly skilled teams and dedicated volunteers are committed to UHN's vision of achieving global impact.

YARMOUTH REGIONAL HOSPITAL • 60 Vancouver Street • Yarmouth, NS • B5A 2P5 • Tel: 902-749-2307 • Fax: 902-742-1475 • Contact: Mr. Kevin Vickery, Human Resources • E-mail: hr@swndha.nshealth.ca • Internet: www.swndha.nshealth.ca • Yarmouth Regional Hospital is a regional medical and surgical health care facility serving the community. The hospital also provides an addiction treatment centre, veterans place, a nursing home, and an adult residential centre. The facility is also recognized as a teaching hospital that is affiliated with the nursing programs offered at Dalhousie University in Nova Scotia.

Maintain the Proper Attitude

Most individuals conduct their job search from a "this-is-what-I-want" perspective. In reality, firms are not interested in what you want, but rather, if you can provide what they want.

Industrial Manufacturing

AAR-KEL MOULDS LTD. • 17 Elm Drive South • Wallaceburg, ON • N8A 5E8 • Tel: 519-627-6078 • Fax: 519-627-5925 • Internet: www.aarkel.com • Aar-Kel Moulds Ltd. Is a leader in the design and manufacturing of plastic moulds and die casting dies. They are a full service supplier to the automotive industry, continuously investigating the tool and die marketplace.

ABC GROUP INC. • 2 Norelco Drive • Toronto, ON • M9L 2X6 • Tel: 416-246-1782 • Fax: 416-246-1997 • Contact: Human Resources • E-mail: hr@abcgrp.com • Internet: www.abcgroupinc.com • The ABC Group of Companies is a Canadian-based international manufacturer and a world leader in plastics processing. Their core business (an automotive Tier 1 supplier) is the design, development and production of plastic automotive systems and components for automotive O.E.M.S. worldwide. The company has over 4500 employees and over 35 facilities worldwide.

ACKLANDS-GRAINGER INC. • 90 West Beaver Creek Road • Richmond Hill, ON • L4B 1E7 • Tel: 905-731-5516 • Fax: 905-731-6053 • Internet: www.acklandsgrainger.com • Founded in 1889, Acklands-Grainger has a long and rich history of distributing products and services to a wide range of Canadian businesses. With headquarters in Richmond Hill, Ontario and over 200 branches from coast to coast, they are Canada's largest distributor of MRO (Maintenance, Repair, Operating) products.

AGF - RAYMOND REBAR INC. • 3419 Hawthorne Road • Ottawa, ON • K1G 4G2 • Tel: 613-736-1500 • Fax: 613-736-0844 • Internet: www.agfraymond.com • AGF - Raymond Rebar is involved in the fabrication and installation of reinforcing steel. The firm employs approximately 150 individuals in total.

AGS AUTOMOTIVE SYSTEMS • 675 Progress Avenue • Scarborough, ON • M1H 2W9 • Tel: 416-438-6650 • Fax: 416-431-8766 • Contact: Human Resources • E-mail: agshr@agsautomotive.com • Internet: www.agsautomotive.com • AGS Automotive Systems is a leader in the automotive stamping business. They provide metal framework systems for major vehicle manufacturers in North America. Over the past 50 years, the company has proudly embraced innovation, quality and tradition as important values in the automotive industry.

AIR LIQUIDE CANADA INC. • 1250 Rene Levesque West, Suite 1700 • Montreal, QC • H3B 5E6 • Tel: 514-933-0303 • Fax: 514-846-7700 • Contact: Human Resources Dept. • E-mail: info.alc@airliquide.com • Internet: www.airliquide.ca • Air Liquide is an international group specialized in industrial and medical gases and related services. Founded in 1902, Air Liquide operates in 72 countries through 125 subsidiaries and employs more than 36,000 people.

ALGOMA STEEL INC. • 105 West Street • Sault Ste. Marie, ON • P6A 5P2 • Tel: 705-945-2351 • Fax: 705-945-2203 • E-mail: careers@algoma.com • Internet: www.algoma.com • Algoma Steel Inc. is an integrated steel producer. With approximately 14% of Canadian raw steel production, Algoma Steel Inc. has been a mainstay of the North American steel industry for more than 100 years.

ALLMAR DISTRIBUTORS LTD. • 287 Riverton Avenue • Winnipeg, MB • R2L 0N2 • Tel: 204-668-1000 • Fax: 204-668-3029 • Contact: Human Resources • E-mail: hr@allmar.com • Internet: www.allmar.com • Allmar is a wholesale distributor of architectural hardware, building materials and lumber across Western Canada. Their sales divisions are guided by industry norms, customer relationships, and product knowledge.

ALUMICOR LIMITED • 33 Racine Road • Toronto, ON • M9W 2Z4 • Tel: 416-745-4222 • Fax: 416-745-7759 • Contact: Human Resources • E-mail: info@alumicor.com • Internet: www.alumicor.net • Alumicor Limited is a Canadian based architectural aluminum company, in business since 1959. A recognized leader in it's field, Alumicor Limited today operates through four efficient manufacturing plants in Canada, a number of sales offices in North America and a number of partnerships around the world.

ANCAST INDUSTRIES LTD. • 1350 Saskatchewan Avenue • Winnipeg, MB • R3E 0L2 • Tel: 204-786-7911 • Fax: 204-786-2548 • Contact: Human Resources • Internet: www.ancast.mb.ca • Ancast utilizes state of the art technology, equipment and processes to stay on the cutting edge of ductile and grey iron custom casting production. Their plant is in Winnipeg.

ANTAMEX INTERNATIONAL INC. • 210 Great Gulf Drive • Concord, ON • L4K 5W1 • Tel: 905-660-4520 • Fax: 905-669-4402 • Contact: Human Resources • E-mail: careers@antamex. com • Internet: www.antamex.com • Antamex International is a designer, manufacturer, and installer of curtainwall. Working in a metal fabrication environment, the firm employs about 120 individuals.

ARMETEC LIMITED • 41 George Street • Guelph, ON • N1H 1S5 • Tel: 519-822-0046 • Fax: 519-822-1160 • Internet: www.armtec.com • Armtec Limited is a manufacturer and distributor of steel and high-density polyethylene construction products for use in infrastructure, mining, forestry, industrial, residential, agricultural and municipal applications.

ATCO FRONTEC CORP. • 300, 909 - 11th Avenue SW • Calgary, AB • T2R 1L8 • Tel: 403-245-7701 • Fax: 403-245-7717 • Internet: www.atcofrontec.com • ATCO Frontec, a wholly owned subsidiary of Canadian Utilities Limited, started as a «greenfields» initiative, whose name stood for Frontier Technologies. The Company was incorporated in 1986 to supply electrical services, technical expertise and logistical support in northern Canada, and has become a world-class facilities management and technical services company. With corporate offices located in Calgary, Alberta and over 25 offices internationally, ATCO Frontec provides a wide range of customizable services to a variety of customers in Canada, the United States, United Kingdom, the Balkans and Greenland. The company's projects, businesses and joint ventures employ about 1600 people.

ATLANTIC PACKAGING PRODUCTS LTD. • 111 Progress Avenue • Scarborough, ON • M1G 2Y9 • Tel: 416-298-8101 • Fax: 416-297-2218 • Internet: www.atlantic.ca • Atlantic Packaging Products Ltd. is a manufacturer of corrugated cardboard. The company employs approximately 2,200 individuals.

ATS AUTOMATION TOOLING SYSTEMS INC. • 250 Royal Oak Road, Box 32100, Preston Centre • Cambridge, ON • N3H 4R6 • Tel: 519-653-6500 • Fax: 519-653-6533 • Contact: Human Resources • Internet: www.atsautomation.com • ATS Automation Tooling Systems is the world's leading industrial automation company with approximately 3600 employees and 24 facilities worldwide dedicated to designing and manufacturing advanced factory automation systems, custom automation equipment, standard automation products and turn-key assembly machinery, as well as high-volume precision components, sub-assemblies, solar cells and solar modules.

BABCOCK AND WILCOX CANADA • 581 Coronation Blvd. • Cambridge, ON • N1R 5V3 • Tel: 519-621-2130 • Fax: 519-622-7352 • Contact: Human Resources • E-mail: resume@ babcock.com • Internet: www.babcock.com/bwc • Babcox & Wilcox Canada, Ltd. is a subsidiary of The Babcock & Wilcox Company, North America's largest manufacturer of steam generation products and services. They have over 130 years as a recognized leader in the steam generation industry, and experience in over 90 countries.

BEHLEN INDUSTRIES • 927 Douglas Street • Brandon, MB • R7A 7B3 • Tel: 204-728-1188 • Fax: 204-725-4932 • E-mail: behlen@behlen.ca • Internet: www.behlen.ca • Behlen Industries manufactures a full line of agricultural and commercial products. They are the largest steel manufacturing company in Canada. They have been awarded one of the 50 Best Managed

Companies in Canada. Their in-house engineering and detailing departments offer traditional pre-engineered building systems as well as customized built structures.

BLUE GIANT EQUIPMENT OF CANADA LTD. • 85 Heart Lake Road South • Brampton, ON • L6W 3K2 • Tel: 905-457-3900 • Fax: 905-457-2313 • Contact: Human Resources • E-mail: hr@BlueGiant.com • Internet: www.bluegiant.com • Blue Giant Equipment of Canada is a manufacturer of material handling equipment.

BOSAL CANADA INC. • 1150 Gardiners Road • Kingston, ON • K7P 1R7 • Tel: 800-267-5644 • Fax: 800-267-5602 • Contact: Human Resources Dept. • Internet: www.bosal.com • Bosal Canada is involved in the manufacture of automotive exhaust systems for the aftermarket and original equipment market. The firm has approximately 150 employees.

BUCKEYE CANADA INC. • 7979 Vantage Way • Delta, BC • V4G 1A6 • Tel: 604-946-0677 • Fax: 604-946-3516 • Contact: Human Resources Dept. • E-mail: info@bkitech.com • Internet: www.bkitech.com • Buckeye Technologies Inc. is a leading producer of value-added cellulose-based specialty products. They have leading positions in many of the high-end niche markets in which we compete. Their expertise in polymer chemistry and fiber science, combined with advanced manufacturing practices, has enabled Buckeye to provide innovative and proprietary products to their customers around the globe.

CANADIAN GENERAL TOWER LIMITED • 52 Middleton Street, P.O. Box 160 • Cambridge, ON • N1R 5T6 • Tel: 519-623-1630 • Fax: 519-740-2977 • Internet: www.cgtower.com • Canadian General Tower is a manufacturer of vinyl coated fabrics, film, and related products for many types of industries across the country. A private company, Canadian General Tower has an employee base of approximately 700 individuals. The company's head office is located in Cambridge, Ontario.

CANCARB LIMITED • 1702 Brier Park Crescent NW, P.O. Box 310 • Medicine Hat, AB • T1C 1T8 • Tel: 403-527-1121 • Fax: 403-529-6093 • Internet: www.cancarb.com • Cancarb Limited is the leading international manufacturer and marketer of medium thermal carbon black with customers on six continents. They use natural gas, the cleanest-burning fossil fuel, to produce seven grades of medium thermal carbon black, including Stainless and Ultra-Pure - all marketed under the trade name of THERMAX.

CANCORE INDUSTRIES INC. • 624 Parkdale Avenue North • Hamilton, ON • L8H 5Z3 • Tel: 905-549-5520 • Fax: 905-549-4254 • Internet: www.cancore.net • Cancore is a manufacturer and distributor of automotive radiators, complete with warehouses and retail service shops that offer complete cooling systems services.

CANWEL BUILDING MATERIALS LTD. • 1510 - 700 West Georgia Street, P.O Box 10034, Pacific Centre • Vancouver, BC • V7Y 1A1 • Tel: 604-432-1400 • Fax: 604-436-6670 • Contact: Ms. Susan Allen, Human Resources Department • E-mail: susan_allen@canwel.com • Internet: www.canwel.com • CanWel Building Materials Ltd. is one of Canada's leading distributors of building materials including commodity, industrial and allied products. CanWel distributes their products across Canada to small independent lumber yards, building material dealers, home improvement chains and the Industrial Products market.

CARBONE OF AMERICA (LCL) LTD. • 496 Evans Avenue • Toronto, ON • M8W 2T7 • Tel: 416-251-2334 • Fax: 416-252-1742 • Contact: Human Resources • E-mail: human.resources@ carbonelorraine.com • Internet: www.carbonebrush.com • Carbone of America provides their customers with a full range of services for maintenance, optimization, and diagnosis of electric machines using carbon brushes. They also produce carbon brushes and brush holders for electric motors and current collectors for all kinds of transport and sliding contacts for cranes and traveling cranes.

CARGILL LIMITED • P.O. Box 5900, 300 - 240 Graham Avenue • Winnipeg, MB • R3C 4C5 • Tel: 204-947-0141 • Fax: 204-947-6444 • Contact: Mr. Vik Kail, Employee Development Manager • E-mail: canadahr@cargill.com • Internet: www.cargill.ca • Cargill Limited is the Canadian subsidiary of Cargill Incorporated, an international corporation and respected world leader in food and agriculture. In Canada, Cargill has over 5,000 employees involved in grain marketing, crop inputs marketing, animal nutrition, canola crushing, fertilizer manufacturing, meat processing, salt, sweeteners, starch, malt barley, gas and power, and chocolate.

CASCADE AEROSPACE INC. • 1337 Townline Road • Abbotsford, BC • V2T 6E1 • Tel: 604-850-7372 • Fax: 604-557-2655 • Internet: www.cascadeaerospace.com • Cascade Aerospace performs maintenance, repair and overhaul of commercial aircraft. For more information, please go to their website.

CHEMQUE, INC. • 266 Humberline Drive • Rexdale, ON • M9W 5X1 • Tel: 416-679-5676 • Fax: 416-679-0511 • E-mail: careers@chemque.com • Internet: www.chemque.com • Chemque Inc. is a manufacturer of specialty high performance polymer-based products directed to a variety of industries including construction, automotive, and telecommunications. Over the past three decades, their customer-oriented service and our ability to respond extremely fast to market needs have allowed us to be recognized for the superior quality of our products and services. Every year our PhD scientist team replaces over 20 percent of our products with improved versions or completely new products.

CHRYSLER CANADA LTD. • P.O. Box 1621 • Windsor, ON • N9A 4H6 • Tel: 519-973-2000 • Fax: 519-561-7043 • Contact: Salary Employment • Internet: www.chryslercanada.ca • Chrysler Canada manufactures and distributes cars, light duty trucks, and component parts in Canada, the United States and abroad. Plants are located in Windsor and Brampton, Ontario, while sales and service depots are located throughout the country. Brand names of the company include Chrysler, Dodge and Jeep. The company employs about 18,000 people in hourly and salary positions.

COGNIS CANADA CORPORATION • 2290 Argentia Road • Mississauga, ON • L5N 6H9 • Tel: 905-542-7550 • Fax: 905-542-7566 • Internet: www.cognis.com • Utilizing its 160 years of experience in oleochemicals, Cognis develops innovative products and solutions for personal care, home care and modern nutrition. It also develops high-performance products for numerous industrial markets in Oleochemicals, Care Chemicals, Nutrition and Health, Functional Products, and Process Chemicals.

COMMUNICATIONS & POWER INDUSTRIES CANADA INC. • 45 River Drive • Georgetown, ON • L7G 2J4 • Tel: 905-877-0161 • Fax: 905-877-5327 • Internet: www.cpii.com/cmp • Communications & Power Industries Canada specializes in producing radio and TV transmitting, signaling and detection equipment, as well as radiographic, fluoroscopic, therapeutic and other x-ray equipment. The company employs over 200 people.

COMPX • 501 Manitou Drive • Kitchener, ON • N2J 1L2 • Tel: 519-748-5060 • Fax: 519-748-4095 • Internet: www.compxnet.com • CompX is a manufacturer of components for the office furniture, computer server and appliance industries. Main products are metal ball bearing drawer slides and ergonomic products including keyboard arms.

COMSTOCK CANADA • 3455 Landmark Road • Burlington, ON • L7M 1T4 • Tel: 905-335-3333 • Fax: 905-335-0304 • Contact: HR Administrator • E-mail: hr@comstockcanada.com • Internet: www.comstockcanada.com • Founded in 1904, Comstock provides a wide variety of specialty contracting services to the Canadian industry. They employ field forces capable of performing mechanical, electrical, millwright and rigging projects ranging in size from small single trade projects to large multi-discipline contracts.

D.A. STUART INC. • 43 Upton Road • Scarborough, ON • M1L 2C1 • Tel: 416-757-3226 • Fax: 416-757-3220 • Internet: www.dastuart.com • D A Stuart is recognized as a worldwide leader in the production of superbly engineered lubricants, additives and in-process and production cleaners. The Company provides speciality materials and services to major markets including the automotive, steel, aluminum, D&I containers, aerospace, metalforming, fabrication and forming industries.

DANA CORPORATION • 5095 South Service Road • Beamsville, ON • L0R 1B0 • Tel: 905-563-4991 • Fax: 905-563-5320 • Contact: Human Resources • Internet: www.dana.com • Founded in 1904, and based in Toledo, Ohio, Dana Corporation is a global leader in the design, engineering, and manufacture of value-added products and systems for automotive, commercial, and off-highway vehicles. Delivering on a century of innovation, the company's continuing operations employ approximately 35,000 people worldwide dedicated to advancing the science of mobility.

DEGUSSA CANADA INC. • 235 Orenda Road • Brampton, ON • L6T 1E6 • Tel: 905-451-3810 • Fax: 905-451-4469 • Contact: Human Resources Department • Internet: www.degussa.ca • Degussa is Germany's third-largest chemical company and is a multinational corporation consistently aligned to high-yield specialty chemistry. It is organized into five main divisions: Construction Chemicals, Fire and Industrial Chemicals, Performance Materials, Coatings and Advanced Fillers, and Specialty Polymers. 47,000 employees all over the world work on innovative products and system solutions, helping to make Degussa a world leader in specialty chemicals. Degussa's Canadian offices are located in Ontario, Quebec and Alberta.

DOFASCO INC. • 1330 Burlington Street East, Box 2460 • Hamilton, ON • L8N 3J5 • Tel: 905-544-3761 • Contact: Human Resources • E-mail: hresources@dofasco.ca • Internet: www.dofasco.ca • Dofasco is a leading North American steel solutions provider. They produce a full range of flat rolled steel for their customers in the Automotive, Energy, Pipe and Tube, Appliance, Container, Construction and Manufacturing, and Steel Distribution Industries. Dofasco's success is the result of strong, enduring relationships built on shared expectations and trust. The strength and success of their relationships with their customers results from their employees consistently working with customers to create innovative and unique solutions to their needs.

EDELSTEIN DIVERSIFIED CO. LTD. • 21 Mount Vernon • Montreal, QC • H8R 1J9 • Tel: 514-489-8689 • Fax: 514-489-9707 • Internet: www.edelstein.com • Edelstein Diversified Company Limited, supplier of the ECHOtape brand, is a leader in specialty pressure sensitive tapes. Our Corporate Headquarters are located in Montreal, Canada. Sales, production and warehousing facilities are maintained and operated in Boston, MA; Chicago, IL; Dallas, TX; and Los Angeles, CA.

EMCO LIMITED • 1108 Dundas Street • London, ON • N5W 3A7 • Tel: 519-453-9600 • Fax: 519-645-2465 • Internet: www.emcoltd.com • EMCO is one of Canada's leading distributors and manufacturers of building materials for the home improvement and building construction markets. Emco's manufactured building materials are primarily distributed in Canada and the United States.

Apply to Small-Sized Firms as Well as Larger Ones
Don't restrict your job search just to the larger, well-known firms. In many cases, it's the smaller companies which are expanding and in need of more employees. For info on smaller firms have a look at business directories.

ENERFLEX SYSTEMS LTD. • 4700 - 47th Street SE • Calgary, AB • T2B 3R1 • Tel: 403-236-6800 • Fax: 403-236-6816 • Contact: Human Resources • E-mail: careers@enerflex.com • Internet: www.enerflex.com • With a track record of more than 25 years, Enerflex has become a leading supplier of products and services to the global oil and gas production industry. Headquartered in Calgary, Alberta, Enerflex has operations in Canada, the United States, the United Kingdom, Germany, the Netherlands, Australia, Pakistan and Indonesia.

FABORY METRICAN INC. • 215 Admiral Blvd. • Mississauga, ON • L5T 2T3 • Tel: 905-565-9700 • Fax: 905-565-8088 • Internet: www.fabory.com • Fabory Metrican Inc. is the Canadian division of international fastener distributor involved in sales, marketing, and distribution to major OEM's and distributors across Canada.

FINNING • 16830 107th Avenue • Edmonton, AB • T5P 4C3 • Tel: 780-930-4800 • Fax: 780-930-4801 • Internet: www.finning.ca • Finning sells, services and finances the full line of Caterpiller and complimentary equipment throughout Western Canada. Headquartered in Edmonton, Alberta, Finning is represented in 57 communities in the western part of the country. They employ approximately 4200 individuals.

FLAKEBOARD COMPANY LIMITED • P.O. Box 490 • St. Stephen, NB • E3L 3A6 • Tel: 506-466-2370 • Fax: 506-466-7113 • Internet: www.flakeboard.com • Flakeboard Company is a major manufacturer of particleboard in New Brunswick. The company also produces painted panels, melamine and fibre board. Flakeboard Company employs approximately 300 individuals to work at its location in St. Stephen, New Brunswick.

FOREMOST INDUSTRIES INC. • 1225 - 64th Avenue NE • Calgary, AB • T2E 8P9 • Tel: 403-295-5800 • Fax: 403-295-5810 • Internet: www.foremost.ca • Foremost Industries Inc. is a manufacturer of large terrain vehicles, drills, parts & tooling for water well, construction, mineral exploration, seismic, oil and gas and geotechnical and environmental applications.

FOSTER WHEELER LIMITED • Box 1, 509 Glendale Avenue • Niagara-on-the-Lake, ON • L0S 1J0 • Tel: 905-688-4587 • Fax: 905-688-4588 • Internet: www.fwc.com • Foster Wheeler is an internationally renowned engineering and construction company providing services and products to a broad range of industries, including upstream oil and gas, LNG, gas-to-liquids, refining, chemical, petrochemical, pharmaceutical, biotechnology, healthcare, and power generation.

GDX AUTOMOTIVE • 100 Kennedy Street, Box 1002 • Welland, ON • L3B 5R9 • Tel: 905-735-5631 • Fax: 905-735-5564 • Contact: HR Specialist • Internet: www.gdxautomotive.com • GDX Automotive, a GenCorp company, is a customer-focused automotive supplier, specializing in isolation of vehicle interior systems from the outside environment. Their dedication to customer support assures that their clients always receive the most innovative, cost-effective solutions available.

GOODYEAR CANADA INC. • 450 Kipling Avenue • Toronto, ON • M8Z 5E1 • Tel: 416-201-4300 • Fax: 416-253-3030 • Internet: www.goodyear.ca • Goodyear Canada is a tire and rubber company engaged in the production and sale of tires and related transportation products. Products include new tires and tubes, retreads, automotive repair services, auto belts and hoses, auto molded parts, and engineered rubber products. Goodyear Canada has operations in Ontario, Quebec, Alberta and store locations across Canada. The company employs over 4,800 people throughout the country.

GROUPE SAVOIE INC. • 251 Route 180 • St. Quentin, NB • E8A 2K9 • Tel: 506-235-2228 • Fax: 506-235-3200 • Contact: Line C. Simon, Human Resources • E-mail: line.simon@groupesavoie.com • Internet: www.groupesavoie.com • Groupe Savoie is a leader in hardwood processing and an important player within the New Brunswick forest industry. The company employs about 400 individuals who work in various sectors in the sawmilling industry.

GUILLEVIN INTERNATIONAL CO. • P.O. Box 626, 1850 Vanier Blvd. • Bathurst, NB • E2A 3Z6 • Tel: 506-546-8220 • Fax: 506-546-8229 • Contact: Human Resources • Internet: www.guillevin.com • Founded in 1906, Guillevin International Co. has grown and secured an enviable position at the forefront of the North American distribution industry. Today, Guillevin International is Canada's second largest wholesale distributor of electrical material and health and safety products, and a major distributor of industrial supplies and equipment. From coast to coast Guillevin employs 1,200 employees in over 100 distribution centres. It distributes over 90,000 products supplied by more than 500 world class manufacturers.

HANSON BRICK • 2170 Torquay Mews • Streetsville, ON • L5N 2M6 • Tel: 905-821-8800 • Fax: 905-821-4554 • Contact: Human Resources • Internet: www.hansonbrick.com • Hanson Brick is North America's largest manufacturer of genuine burned clay brick. In Canada, Hanson Brick has two plants in Ontario and in Quebec. There are approximately 500 individuals employed by Hanson Brick in Canada.

HONDA CANADA INC. • 715 Milner Avenue • Scarborough, ON • M1B 2K8 • Tel: 416-284-8110 • Fax: 416-286-1322 • Contact: Human Resources Officer • Internet: www.honda.ca • Honda Canada is involved in the assembly and distribution of vehicles and the distribution of small engines and parts to dealers throughout Canada. The company is jointly owned by Honda Motor Co. Ltd. of Japan and American Honda Motor Co. Inc. Honda Canada employs 5100 individuals to work in the auto industry.

HONEYWELL LTD. • 155 Gordon Baker Road • Toronto, ON • M2H 3N7 • Tel: 416-502-5305 • Fax: 416-502-5390 • Contact: Human Resources • Internet: www.honeywell.ca • Honeywell develops, manufactures, and markets control automation systems, and products for the home, commercial buildings, industrial processing and aerospace markets. Honeywell in Canada is one of the country's leading control companies. Operating in Canada since 1930, Honeywell employs 2,800 employees in more than 50 locations across Canada.

HUBBELL CANADA INC. • 870 Brock Road South • Pickering, ON • L1W 1Z8 • Tel: 905-839-1138 • Fax: 905-839-9108 • Contact: Human Resources Department • E-mail: hr@hubbell-canada.com • Internet: www.hubbell-canada.com • Hubbell Canada with its head office in Pickering, Ontario, sells, markets, services and distributes wiring, lighting and power systems products to industrial, commercial, utility, contractor, consumer channel, wholesale and institutional accounts.

ICI CANADA INC. • 8200 Keele Street • Concord, ON • L4K 2A5 • Tel: 905-669-1020 • Internet: www.coloryourworld.com • Since 1912, Colour Your World has been helping Canadians paint their homes. Currently headquartered in Concord, Ontario, Colour Your World employs over 1,500 people in its manufacturing, distribution, retail and franchise operations. In 1997, Imperial Chemical Industries (ICI) Canada Inc., purchased Colour Your World.

INDALEX LIMITED • 5675 Kennedy Road • Mississauga, ON • L4Z 2H9 • Tel: 905-890-8821 • Fax: 905-890-8385 • Contact: Human Resources Dept. • Internet: www.indalex.com • Indalex Limited is the Canadian aluminum extrusion company and is part of the Indalex Aluminum Solutions Group, that extends across North America. Their company strives to satisfy their customers through manufacturing of the various products they produce.

INTEGRIS METALS LTD. • 161 The West Mall • Toronto, ON • M9C 4V8 • Tel: 416-622-3100 • Fax: 416-622-5868 • Contact: Human Resources • E-mail: contacts@integrismetals.com • Internet: www.integrismetals.com • Integris Metals is one of the largest, most diverse metal service center organizations in North America. Integris Metals operates three dedicated processing centers and 59 branch locations across the U.S. and Canada, with the heart of company operations being the marketing of a complete line of ferrous and non-ferrous metals, and processing services.

IVACO INC. • 1 Place Alexis Nihon, 3400 de Maisonneuve West, Suite 1501 • Montréal, QC • H3Z 3B8 • Tel: 514-288-4545 • Fax: 514-284-9414 • Contact: Human Resources • Internet: www.ivaco.com • Ivaco is a Canadian corporation and is a leading North American producer of steel, fabricated steel products and other diversified fabricated products. Ivaco has operations in Canada and in the United States. Shares of Ivaco are traded on the Toronto Stock Exchange and The Montreal Exchange (IVA).

JOHNSON CONTROLS GROUP • 7400 Birchmount Road • Markham, ON • L3R 5V4 • Tel: 905-475-7610 • Fax: 905-474-5404 • Contact: Human Resources • Internet: www.johnsoncontrols. com • Johnson Controls is a global leader offering solutions in automotive systems and facilities management and controls.

KAWNEER COMPANY CANADA LIMITED • 1051 Ellesmere Road • Scarborough, ON • M1P 2X1 • Tel: 416-755-7751 • Fax: 416-755-1829 • Contact: Human Resources • Internet: www. kawneer.com • Kawneer Company Canada Limited is a manufacturer of architectural aluminium products including windows, doors, curtain wall, skylights and storefronts for industrial and commercial markets.

KENNAMETAL LTD. • 6497 Edwards Blvd. • Mississauga, ON • L5T 2V2 • Tel: 905-564-4663 • Fax: 905-564-3466 • Contact: Manager, Human Resources • Internet: www.kennametal.com • Kennametal is the market leader in North America in metal-cutting tools and is second in Europe and the world. Kennametal serves a vast array of end markets, including industries such as aerospace, automotive, construction and farm machinery, power generation and transmission equipment, home appliances and oil and gas exploration. Kennametal markets its products and services through a multi-channel network that includes a highly trained and skilled direct sales force, direct marketing, the Internet, integrated supply programs and a network of industrial distributors.

LAVA COMPUTER MFG INC. • 2 Vulcan Street • Toronto, ON • M9W 1L2 • Tel: 416-674-5942 • Fax: 416-674-8262 • Internet: www.lavalink.com • Founded in 1984, the Toronto-based Lava Computer MFG Inc. is a leading manufacturer, designer, and worldwide supplier of high-reliability parallel, serial, USB, and FireWire® I/O devices.

LEICA GEOSYSTEMS CANADA INC. • 513 McNicoll Avenue • Willowdale, ON • M2H 2C9 • Tel: 416-497-2460 • Fax: 416-497-2053 • Internet: www.leica-geosystems.com • Leica Geosystems is a globally-active enterprise with a long tradition. It plays a leading role in the development, production and distribution of state-of-the-art systems for the capture and processing of spatial data for surveying, mapping and positioning. To their customers in the engineering, surveying and construction fields, in industry, in telecommunications and in security technology, they offer innovative total solutions based on leading-edge technology.

LEON'S MANUFACTURING COMPANY INC. • Box 5002, 135 York Road East • Yorkton, SK • S3N 3Z4 • Tel: 306-786-2600 • Fax: 306-782-1884 • Contact: Human Resources • E-mail: sales@leonsmfg.com • Internet: www.leonsmfg.com • Leon's Mfg. Company Inc. is a Canadian company with a history that dates back over forty-five years. From a simple blacksmith and machine shop in the rural community of Bankend, Saskatchewan, the company expanded and grew to its present size. Today, Leon's Mfg. Company Inc. by technical innovation, engineering expertise, and a dedication to product quality and service, has become a leading company of international stature, with factories and warehouses located in Canada and the United States.

LES FORGES DE SOREL INC. • 100 McCarthy • Sorel, QC • J3R 3M8 • Tel: 450-746-4030 • Fax: 450-746-4092 • Contact: Ressources humaines • E-mail: hresource@sorelforge.com • Internet: www.sorelforge.com • Over 55 years of forging experience, coupled with the company's strong commitment to technology has allowed Les Forges de Sorel to become the largest producer of open die forgings in Canada.

LOEWEN WINDOWS • 77 Highway 52 West • Steinbach, MB • R5G 1B2 • Tel: 204-326-6446 • Fax: 204-326-5227 • Internet: www.loewen.com • Loewen has 1500 employees, and creates elegantly wrought windows and doors for homeowners around the globe.

LOVAT INC. • 441 Carlingview Drive • Etobicoke, ON • M9W 5G7 • Tel: 416-675-3293 • Fax: 416-675-6702 • Contact: Human Resources • E-mail: humanresources@lovat.com • Internet: www.lovat.com • For more than a quarter century, LOVAT has specialized in the custom design and manufacture of Tunnel Boring Machines (TBM) utilized in the construction of metro, railway, road, sewer, water main, penstock, mine access and telecable tunnels. Founded in 1972 by Richard Lovat, the company's extensive experience, advanced technology and continued development provide the solutions for any tunnelling challenge on any project.

MACDONALD STEEL LTD. • 200 Avenue Road • Cambridge, ON • N1R 8H5 • Tel: 519-620-0400 • Fax: 519-621-4995 • Contact: Human Resources • E-mail: hr@macdonaldsteel.com • Internet: www.macdonaldsteel.com • MacDonald Steel is one of the worlds leading diversified manufacturing companies. As one of the largest manufacturers of custom metal fabrication, they provide services in profile cutting, welding, machining, complete finishing and assembly. They currently have over 200 employees.

MAGNA INTERNATIONAL INC. • 337 Magna Drive • Aurora, ON • L4G 7K1 • Tel: 416-622-8882 • Fax: 416-622-6882 • E-mail: resumes@hcrpsi.com • Internet: www.magnaint.com • Magna International Inc. is a leading global supplier of technologically-advanced automotive systems, components and complete modules. The company employs approximately 84,000 people at 238 manufacturing divisions and 60 product development and engineering centres throughout North and South America, Mexico, Europe and Asia.

MCKAY-COCKER CONSTRUCTION LIMITED • 215 Traders Blvd. East, Unit 4 • Mississauga, ON • L4Z 3K5 • Tel: 905-890-9193 • Fax: 905-890-4940 • Contact: Office Manager • E-mail: info@mckaycocker.com • Internet: www.mckaycocker.com • McKay-Cocker is a general contractor involved in industrial and commercial building. The company's construction management team has become recognized in the industry for its thorough pre-construction services on all types of projects. Their ability to provide design coordination, budget control and advice on constructability issues has resulted in more and more contracts from successful pre-construction services.

MDS NORDION • 447 March Road • Ottawa, ON • K2K 1X8 • Tel: 613-592-2790 • Fax: 613-592-6937 • Contact: Human Resources • E-mail: careers@mds.nordion.com • Internet: www. mds.nordion.com • MDS Nordion values health and well-being - in fact, they make it their business to care about people, and they are dedicated to preserving their health. Everyday, their technology, products and services touch the lives of thousands of people around the world, and are used daily in hospitals and clinics and by the makers of radiopharmaceuticals and medical devices. MDS Nordion is a world leader in radioisotope technology. The main focus of their business is the use of radiation technologies to prevent, diagnose, and treat disease. Two primary areas make up the business: Nuclear Medicine and Ion Technologies.

MOEN INC. • 2816 Bristol Circle • Oakville, ON • L6H 5S7 • Tel: 905-829-3400 • Fax: 905-829-3500 • Contact: Human Resources • E-mail: moencanada@moen.com • Internet: www.moen. com • Moen Incorporated is one of the world's largest manufacturers of plumbing products. In fact, Moen is the number one brand of faucet in North America. In addition to faucets, Moen is also a major supplier of kitchen sinks and bath accessories.

NATIONAL MANUFACTURING OF CANADA INC. • 711 Ontario Street, P.O. Box 640 • Cobourg, ON • K9A 4L3 • Tel: 905-372-9623 • Fax: 905-372-4368 • Contact: Human Resources • Internet: www.natman.com • From its beginnings at the turn of the century, National Manufacturing Company's success has depended on providing quality products and exceptional services to home and farm improvement retailers. They employ over 1600 people.

NETT TECHNOLOGIES INC. • 2 - 6707 Goreway Drive • Mississauga, ON • L4V 1P7 • Tel: 905-672-5454 • Fax: 905-672-5949 • Contact: Mr. Rick Jones, Human Resources • E-mail: hr@nett.ca • Internet: www.nett.ca • Nett Technologies is an environmental company specializing in exhaust pollution control products for internal combustion engines. We manufacture catalytic converters, catalytic mufflers, diesel particulate filters, and other emission controls for diesel, LPG, natural gas and gasoline engines. Our major markets include materials handling, construction, underground mining, as well as urban buses, municipal trucks, and stationary engine applications.

NISSAN CANADA INC. • 5290 Orbitor Drive • Mississauga, ON • L4W 4Z5 • Tel: 800-387-0122 • Fax: 905-629-6553 • Contact: Human Resources • Internet: www.nissancanada.com • Nissan Canada imports and distributes Nissan cars and light trucks, Infinity luxury vehicles, forklift trucks, outboard motors, and associated parts and accessories. Nissan Canada is a wholly owned subsidiary of Nissan Motor Company of Tokyo. The company employs more than 320 individuals across the country.

NORBORD INDUSTRIES • 1 Toronto Street, Suite 600 • Toronto, ON • M5C 2W4 • Tel: 416-365-0705 • Fax: 416-365-3292 • Contact: Human Resources • E-mail: hr@norbord.com • Internet: www.norbord.com • Norbord Inc. is an international forest products company headquartered in Toronto, Ontario. They employ 2700 people in Canada, the United States and Europe.

NRI INDUSTRIES INC. • 35 Cawthra Avenue • Toronto, ON • M6N 5B3 • Tel: 416-657-1111 • Fax: 416-656-1231 • Contact: Human Resources • E-mail: info@nrtna.com • Internet: www.nrtna.com • NRI Industries was founded in 1927 as the National Rubber Company. NRI currently employs 500 people in Toronto. They are North America's largest fully integrated manufacturer of rubber products.

OETIKER LIMITED • 203 Dufferin Street South • Alliston, ON • L9R 1W7 • Tel: 705-435-4394 • Fax: 705-435-3155 • Contact: Human Resources • E-mail: info@ca.oetiker.com • Internet: www.oetiker.com • Oetiker manufactures precision, stainless steel clamps for automotive and other industrial applications. Oetiker Limited has been recognized for its dedication to quality products and customer service. In addition to customer recognition, Oetiker is registered under the ISO/TS 16949 quality system standard and ISO 14001 environmental standard.

Know What You Want To Do
Knowing which direction you wish your career path to follow is the first step in getting there. Understanding your likes and dislikes and your strengths and weaknesses will be a very important part of this process.

PAPERBOARD INDUSTRIES INTERNATIONAL INC. • 404 Marie-Victorin Boulevard, P.O. Box 30 • Kingsey Falls, QC • J0A 1B0 • Tel: 819-363-5100 • Fax: 819-363-5155 • Contact: Human Resources • E-mail: info@cascades.com • Internet: www.cascades.com • Founded in 1964, Cascades Inc. is a North American leader in the production, converting and marketing of packaging products, fine papers and tissue papers. Internationally, the Cascades Group employs more than 14,000 people and operates in over 100 modern and versatile operating units located in Canada, the United States, France, England, Germany and Sweden.

PETROMONT & CO. LTD. PARTNERSHIP • 2931 Marie-Victorin Boulevard • Varennes, QC • J3X 1P7 • Tel: 514-640-6400 • Fax: 514-650-9017 • Contact: Human Resources • E-mail: rh@ petromont.com • Internet: www.petromont.com • Pétromont is a major petrochemical company with average annual sales of about $500 million. It manufactures high-density polyethylene and basic petrochemicals (olefins) which are sold throughout the world, primarily to North American markets.

POSITRON PUBLIC SAFETY SYSTEMS INC. • 5101 Buchan Street • Montréal, QC • H4P 2R9 • Tel: 514-345-2200 • Fax: 514-345-2271 • Contact: Human Resources • E-mail: hr@positron911. com • Internet: www.positroninc.com • Positron Public Safety Systems, with US headquarters in Atlanta, Georgia, is the leader in fully integrated, end-to-end public safety solutions for call handling and dispatching. Positron has been delivering mission critical applications and developing public safety solutions since 1970.

PPG CANADA INC. • 880 Avonhead Road • Mississauga, ON • L5J 2Z5 • Tel: 905-823-1100 • Internet: www.ppg.com • PPG Canada Inc. is a subsidiary of Pittsburgh-based PPG Industries, Inc. and is one of the world's largest coatings producers and is the world's recognized leader in innovative coatings technology. They provide products to automotive manufacturers and users of automotive refinishes, industrial coatings, packaging coatings, architectural coatings and aerospace coatings.

PRECISION DRILLING CORPORATION • 4200, 150 - 6th Avenue SW • Calgary, AB • T2P 3Y7 • Tel: 403-716-4500 • Fax: 403-264-0251 • Internet: www.precisiondrilling.com • Calgary-based Precision Drilling Corporation is an innovative, performance oriented, integrated oilfield drilling and energy service company. It is the leading provider of drilling services to the Canadian oil and gas industry, and also helps to drill its fair share of oil and gas wells around the world. Precision Drilling Corporation is committed to providing technologically advanced equipment and expertise, a safe operating environment and quality service to the oil and gas and industrial businesses.

PREMIER TECH LTD. • 1, avenue Premier • Rivière-du-Loup, QC • G5R 6C1 • Tel: 418-867-8883 • Fax: 418-862-6642 • E-mail: opportunities@premiertech.com • Internet: www. premiertech.com • For 85 years now, Premier Tech has been building its know-how and reputation on the various technology-oriented opportunities offered by sphagnum peat moss, an abundant natural resource in Canada. Its eleven business units, which operate in five areas - Packaging, Environment, Horticulture, Industrial and Life Sciences - have the mission to become technological and commerical leaders in their respective fields of expertise. Buoyed by a multidisciplinary team of nearly 1,600 people based in Canada, United States, Europe and Asia, Premier Tech is buiding on the development of its personnel, on research, development and innovation, the introduction of value-added products, and proactive management of its business units' manufacturing operations. Its strategic approach is supported by ongoing market development efforts in the Americas, Europe and Asia.

QIT-FER ET TITANE INC. • 1625 route Marie-Victorin • Tracy, QC • J3R 1M6 • Tel: 450-746-3000 • Fax: 450-746-4438 • Contact: Human Resources • Internet: www.qit.com • QIT-Fer et Titane exploits an ilmenite deposit at Lac Tio, near Havre-Saint-Pierre, Quebec, and operates a metallurgical complex in Sorel-Tracy, Quebec, where high-quality titanium dioxide, pig iron and steel are extracted from this ore. Furthermore, Quebec Metal Powders (QMP), a company affiliated with QIT that operates within the metallurgical complex, produces iron and metal powders. QIT employs nearly 2000 people.

RAYMOND INDUSTRIAL EQUIPMENT LTD. • 406 Elgin Street, P.O. Box 1325 • Brantford, ON • N3T 5T6 • Tel: 519-759-0358 • Fax: 519-759-0360 • Internet: www.raymondcorp.com • Raymond Industrial Equipment Ltd. is Canada's leading manufacturer of electric forklifts. Their commitment is to quality and their continuous improvement is demonstrated in their superior product, state-of-the-art facility and advanced manufacturing and business systems.

RAYTON PACKAGING INC. • 1110 - 58th Avenue SE • Calgary, AB • T2H 2C9 • Tel: 403-259-4314 • Fax: 403-253-4681 • Contact: Human Resources • E-mail: hr@rayton.com • Internet: www.rayton.com • We are a 24/7 operation that makes plastic bags. It is a fast paced environment and has plenty of room for advancement.

RECOCHEM INC. • 850 Montée de Liesse • Montréal, QC • H4T 1P4 • Tel: 514-341-3550 • Fax: 514-341-3263 • Contact: Human Resources • E-mail: resumes@recochem.com • Internet: www.recochem.com • Recochem Inc. is a global company, headquartered in Canada that manufactures, packages, and distributes a wide range of chemical products to both retail chains and commercial markets.

RIVERSIDE FABRICATING LTD. • 1556 Matthew Brandy Blvd. • Windsor, ON • N8S 3K6 • Tel: 519-945-2325 • Fax: 519-945-0696 • Contact: Human Resources • Riverside Fabricating Ltd. is a metal finishing company. The firm's head office is in Windsor, Ontario.

ROCKWELL AUTOMATION • 135 Dundas Street • Cambridge, ON • N1R 5X1 • Tel: 519-623-1810 • Fax: 519-623-8930 • Internet: www.automation.rockwell.com • Rockwell Automation is a leading industrial automation company focused to be the most valued global provider of power, control and information solutions. With a focus on automation solutions that help customers meet productivity objectives, the company brings together leading brands in industrial automation, including Dodge® mechanical power transmission products, Reliance Electric™ motors and drives, Allen-Bradley® controls and engineered services and Rockwell Software® factory management software. Global technical and customer service is an integral part of Rockwell Automation, with nearly 5,600 distributors, system integrators and agents serving customers in 80 countries.

ROCTEST LTÉE • 665 Pine Avenue • Saint-Lambert, QC • J4P 2P4 • Tel: 450-465-1113 • Fax: 450-465-1938 • Contact: Human Resources • E-mail: cv@roctest.com • Internet: www.roctest. com • Roctest is a Canadian company founded in 1967, specializing in the manufacturing of high technology monitoring instruments. These instruments are primarily used in major civil engineering works and geotechnical applications. Roctest owns two manufacturing facilities, one located with the head office in Saint Lambert, just outside of Montreal, and one located in Quebec City.

S & C ELECTRIC CANADA LTD. • 90 Belfield Road • Toronto, ON • M9W 1G4 • Tel: 416-249-9171 • Fax: 416-249-6051 • Contact: Human Resources • Internet: www.sandc.com • S&C Electric Company is a global provider of equipment and services for electric power systems. Founded in 1911, the Chicago-based company designs and manufactures switching and protection products for electric power transmission and distribution.

SASKFERCO PRODUCTS INC. • 1874 Scarth Street, Suite 215 • Regina, SK • S4P 4B3 • Tel: 306-525-7600 • Fax: 306-525-2942 • Internet: www.saskferco.com • Saskferco Products Inc., located on the Canadian prairie in Saskatchewan, is one of North America's largest producer of granular urea, anhydrous ammonia, and urea ammonium nitrate. We have established ourselves as one of the top producers in the world.

SCHLUMBERGER CANADA LTD. • 525 - 3rd Avenue S.W. • Calgary, AB • T2P 0G4 • Tel: 403-509-4000 • Fax: 403-509-4021 • Contact: Human Resources • Internet: www.schlumberger.com • Schlumberger Limited is the leading oilfield services company supplying technology, project management and information solutions that optimize performance for customers working in the international oil and gas industry. The company comprises two primary business segments - Schlumberger Oilfield Services and WesternGeco. Reflecting their belief that diversity spurs creativity, collaboration, and understanding of customers' needs, they employ over 80,000 people of more than 140 nationalities working in over 80 countries.

SCHNEIDER ELECTRIC CANADA INC. • 19 Waterman Avenue • Toronto, ON • M4B 1Y2 • Tel: 416-752-8020 • Fax: 416-752-6230 • Internet: www.schneider-electric.ca • Schneider Electric is the world leader in electrical distribution, industrial control and automation products, systems and services, and the only electrical manufacturer dedicated solely to the distribution and control of electricity. They employ 61,500 people in 130 countries.

SEMICONDUCTOR INSIGHTS INC. • 3000 Solandt Road • Kanata, ON • K2K 2X2 • Tel: 613-599-6500 • Fax: 613-599-6501 • E-mail: hr@semiconductor.com • Internet: www.semiconductor.com • Semiconductor Insights provides in-depth technical and patent analyses of integrated circuits and structures. They help technology companies capture new markets and improve products. They help legal professionals capitalize on and protect corporate R&D investment.

SENSTAR-STELLAR CORP. • 119 John Cavanaugh Drive • Carp, ON • K0A 1L0 • Tel: 613-839-5572 • Fax: 613-839-5830 • Contact: Human Resources • E-mail: hr@senstarstellar.com • Internet: www.senstarstellar.com • Senstar-Stellar, a member of the Magal Group, is the world's leading supplier of outdoor perimeter intrusion detection sensors and systems. They specialize in providing early warning of intrusions into secure areas, reducing the risk of theft, vandalism, harm, sabotage, kidnapping and escape. More than 30 years of experience in outdoor sensor development and implementation has provided us with extensive knowledge in the proper design, manufacture, integration and support of high performance outdoor security systems. Senstar-Stellar offers the broadest choice of intrusion detection technology, with the most innovative and cost-effective product range available.

SEPROTECH SYSTEMS INCORPORATED • 2378 Holly Lane • Ottawa, ON • K1V 7P1 • Tel: 613-523-1641 • Fax: 613-731-0851 • Contact: Human Resources • E-mail: contact@seprotech.com • Internet: www.seprotech.com • Seprotech was founded in 1985 with a vision to create a company that could solve many of the world's most difficult environmental problems. Some of the most pressing global environmental issues are around the twin problems of growing water pollution on the one hand coupled with water shortages on the other. They have dedicated all of the efforts of our company on applied water and wastewater solutions.

SHOREWOOD PACKAGING CORP. OF CANADA LTD. • 2220 Midland Avenue, Suite 50 • Scarborough, ON • M1P 3E6 • Tel: 416-940-2400 • Internet: www.shorepak.com • Shorewood Packaging Corporation, a business of International Paper's Consumer Packaging Group, is one of the world's leading manufacturers of premium packaging, with multiple facilities in North America, Europe and Asia. Many of the world's premier consumer products manufacturers depend on Shorewood's innovation, advanced technology, world class quality and service to enhance the image of their brands. Among them are the makers of home entertainment (music, home video, electronic games & multimedia), tobacco, cosmetics, personal care, pharmaceutical & healthcare, candy & confectionery, sporting goods, food & beverage and private label products.

SPECTRA PREMIUM INDUSTRIES • 1421 Ampere Street • Boucherville, QC • J4B 5Z5 • Tel: 450-641-3090 • Fax: 450-641-3866 • Contact: Human Resources • E-mail: rh@spectrapremium. com • Internet: www.spectrapremium.com • Innovative and future-oriented, Spectra Premium Industries (SPI) is the leading worldwide manufacturer of new fuel tanks for the replacement-parts market. In a market previously dominated by recycled parts, SPI offers new fuel tanks, sending units and oil pans that meet or exceed OEM standards. SPI is the Canadian leader in the replacement-radiator, radiator-parts, new-condenser and rebuilt oil-pan markets. SPI products reach consumers through an extensive distribution network that includes all major retail chains and parts distributors, totalling over 200 warehouses and 10,000 points of sale in Canada, the United States and Europe. Based in Boucherville, on the outskirts of Montreal, SPI currently employs approximately 1,580 employees and operates eight plants and 19 distribution centres across Canada, the United States and Europe.

STANDEN'S LIMITED • P.O. Box 67, Station "T", 1222 - 58th Avenue SE • Calgary, AB • T2H 2G7 • Tel: 403-258-7800 • Fax: 403-258-7868 • Contact: Human Resources • E-mail: employment@ standens.com • Internet: www.standens.com • From its inception as an automotive leaf spring manufacturing and repair business in the early 1920's, Standen's has expanded its services through investment in people and leading edge technology. Standen's currently manufactures a wide range of heat treated steel products. Products include leaf springs, air beams, trailer axles, cultivator shanks, stabilizer bars, u-bolts, suspension components, draw bars, and specialty steel products. They employ over 500 dedicated and hard working people.

STEELCRAFT INDUSTRIES LTD. • P.O. Box 339, 904 Downie Road • Stratford, ON • N5A 6T3 • Tel: 519-271-4750 • Fax: 519-272-0911 • Contact: Human Resources • E-mail: ssearle@ clemmersteelcraft.com • Internet: www.steelcraft.on.ca • SteelCraft Industries Limited, through its three sales divisions, designs, engineers and manufactures custom steel components, fabrications, mixers, dispersers, processing equipment, custom tanks and pressure vessels for a broad range of industries.

TCG INTERNATIONAL INC. • 4710 Kingsway, Suite 2800 • Burnaby, BC • V5H 4M2 • Tel: 604-438-1000 • Fax: 604-438-7414 • Contact: Human Resources • E-mail: info@tcgi.com • Internet: www.tcgi.com • TCG International Inc. has its foundation firmly rooted in its North American automotive glass products business. From this base they will expand their organization by acquiring and developing complementary operations to this core business. Their corporate competencies, international reach and competitive strength will add value to these new acquisitions and grow the entire organization incrementally.

TENAQUIP LIMITED • 20701 Chemin Ste-Marie • Ste-Anne-de-Bellevue, QC • H9X 5X5 • Tel: 514-457-7800 • Fax: 514-457-4815 • Contact: Human Resources • E-mail: hr@tenaquip.com • Internet: www.tenaquip.com • Established in 1968, Tenaquip became the first company in Canada to distribute industrial product through a catalogue. 40 years later they continue to be a leader in the Canadian industrial marketplace.

THE GARLAND GROUP • 1177 Kamato Road • Mississauga, ON • L4W 1X4 • Tel: 905-624-0260 • Fax: 905-624-5669 • Contact: Human Resources • E-mail: info@garland-group.com • Internet: www.garland-group.com • The Garland Group is a manufacturer of commercial cooking equipment including ovens and ranges. The company employs approximately 400 individuals. They will exceed the expectations of their global customers and shareholders by providing superior quality, innovative foodservice equipment and service solutions.

THE HARD ROCK GROUP • P.O. Box 220, 198 Welland Street • Port Colborne, ON • L3K 5V8 • Tel: 905-835-8413 • Fax: 905-834-3811 • Contact: Gary Sidlar , Manager QMS and Marketing • E-mail: gsidlar@hardrockgroup.com • Internet: www.hardrockgroup.com • The Hard Rock Group is involved in the paving, construction, structures, concrete repairs on bridges and area maintenance contracts.

THOMAS & BETTS LTÉE • 700 Thomas Ave. • Saint-Jean-sur-Richelieu, QC • J2X 2M9 • Tel: 450-347-5318 • Fax: 450-347-1976 • Contact: Human Resources • Internet: www.tnb-canada. com • Thomas & Betts is a leading designer and manufacturer of connectors and components for electrical and communication markets. Thomas & Betts Canada Ltd. was founded in 1928 to serve the unique requirements of the Canadian market. Today, Thomas & Betts Ltd. has more than 1,800 employees across Canada.

TOYOTA CANADA INC. • 1 Toyota Place • Scarborough, ON • M1H 1H9 • Tel: 416-438-6320 • Fax: 416-431-1871 • Contact: Human Resources • Internet: www.toyota.ca • Toyota Canada Inc. (TCI) is the exclusive Canadian distributor of Toyota and Lexus vehicles, and Toyota lift trucks. Toyota Canada's head office is in Toronto, with regional offices in Vancouver, Calgary, Montreal and Halifax. Toyota parts and accessories are distributed through TCI's Parts Distribution Centres in Toronto and Vancouver.

UNI-SELECT INC. • 170 Industrial Boulevard • Boucherville, QC • J4B 2X3 • Tel: 450-641-2440 • Fax: 450-449-4908 • Contact: Human Resources • E-mail: careers@uni-select.com • Internet: www.uni-select.com • Uni-Select's founders are committed to the establishment of an efficient network where all members have access to the tools necessary for fulfilling their objectives. Day by day, and always true to its commitment, Uni-Select fully supports the real people responsible for its expansion, that is, our important network of business owners. Uni-Select gives them access to benefits associated with a national organization while letting them maintain their independence. Uni-Select's tremendous success lies in the commitment and excellence of its members and their employees. Today, Uni-Select has become the leading network of independently owned auto parts dealers in Canada.

VISTEON CANADA INC. • 360 University Avenue • Belleville, ON • K8N 5S7 • Tel: 623-969-1460 • Fax: 613-969-1399 • Contact: Human Resources • Internet: www.visteon.com • Visteon is a global enterprise with nearly a century of automotive design expertise and over 80 years of experience in accomplished integrated systems. Approximately 40,000 people work in manufacturing, sales and service facilities in 26 countries.

VITERRA • 2625 Victoria Avenue • Regina, SK • S4T 7T9 • Tel: 306-569-4411 • Fax: 306-569-4708 • Internet: www.swp.com • Viterra is Canada's premier agribusiness built on the foundation of Saskatchewan Wheat Pool Inc. and Agricore United. The new company has extensive operations and distribution capabilities across Canada and in the United States and Japan. Viterra is connected to customers at each stage of an integrated pipeline that starts with farmers and extends to destination customers around the world.

VOLKSWAGEN CANADA INC. • 777 Bayly Street West • Ajax, ON • L1S 7G7 • Tel: 905-428-6700 • Fax: 905-428-5898 • Contact: Human Resources • Internet: www.vw.ca • Volkswagen Canada is a major car manufacturer. The majority of the firm's departments are in the U.S., under its American counterpart. Accounting services are carried out in Canada plus parts machinery for Canadian dealers.

VOLVO CARS OF CANADA LTD. • 175 Gordon Baker Road • North York, ON • M2H 2N7 • Tel: 416-493-3700 • Fax: 416-496-0552 • Contact: Jodi Koch, Volvo Human Resources • Tel: jkoch8@volvocars.com • Internet: www.volvocanada.com • Volvo Cars of Canada is an automotive manufacturer in North York, Ontario. The company is fully owned by Volvo Canadian Holdings Ltd., and has an employee base of approximately 70 individuals. Volvo makes cars for both the domestic and foreign markets.

WEGU CANADA INC. • 1707 Harbour Street • Whitby, ON • L1N 9G6 • Tel: 905-668-2359 • Fax: 905-668-2481 • Contact: Human Resources • Internet: www.wegucanada.com • Wegu Canada is a manufacturer of molded rubber and plastic products located in Whitby, Ontario. The company employs approximately 120 individuals in total.

WEIR SERVICES • 2360 Millrace Court • Mississauga, ON • L5N 1W2 • Tel: 905-812-7100 • Fax: 905-812-1749 • Contact: Human Resources • Internet: www.peacock.ca • Weir Services-Peacock is North America's leading source of high performance engineered industrial, instrumentation and process control products, world class pumps and engineering and marine services. Through four operating units Process Equipment, Weir Pumps Canada, Engineering Services and Marine Engineering and 700 employees, they offer value added products and services to the solution seeking market.

WELDCO-BEALES MANUFACTURING INC. • 12155 - 154 Street N.W. • Edmonton, AB • T5V 1J3 • Tel: 780-454-5244 • Fax: 780-455-5676 • Internet: www.weldco-beales.com • Weldco-Beales Manufacturing Inc. has been in operation since 1946. What began as a post-World War II welding and repair shop is now, over 60 years later, a world leader in custom design and manufacturing. Weldco-Beales designs and manufacturers specialized heavy equipment attachments and cranes for the construction, resource, forestry, mining, and road maintenance industries. Weldco-Beales employs over 300 individuals who are recognized experts and service oriented professionals with decades of experience and know-how.

WILSON AUTO ELECTRIC LTD. • 600 Golspie Street • Winnipeg, MB • R2K 2V1 • Tel: 204-667-5535 • Fax: 204-668-0308 • Internet: www.wilsonautoelectric.com • • Wilson Auto Electric Limited is the largest independent North American manufacturer and re-manufacturer of alternators, starters and electrical component parts for the automotive, agricultural, industrial, heavy duty truck, and marine aftermarkets.

WINPAK LTD. • 100 Saulteaux Crescent • Winnipeg, MB • R3J 3T3 • Tel: 204-889-1015 • Fax: 204-888-7806 • E-mail: humanresources@wd.winpak.com • Internet: www.winpak.com • Winpak is part of a global packaging group operating ten production facilities in Canada and the United States. Winpak offers customers global coverage and expertise. The North American business units assist customers throughout the United States, Canada, Latin America and the Pacific Rim countries. Winpak's strategic alliance with Wipak, one of Europe's leading manufacturers of packaging materials, allows global customers to reduce costs, simplify product development and consolidate packaging solutions.

WIRE ROPE INDUSTRIES LTD. • 5501 Trans-Canada Highway • Pointe-Claire, QC • H9R 1B7 • Tel: 514-697-9711 • Fax: 514-697-3534 • Contact: Human Resources • E-mail: mail@wirerope.com • Internet: www.wirerope.com • Wire Rope Industries is the largest manufacturer of high-performance wire rope products in North America. For over 100 years, the company has been a leader in its field. With their knowledge and expertise, they have been able to refine the art of rope making into a science. They provide rope solutions for a wide variety of industrial applications, including general industrial and construction, forestry, mining, oil and gas, fishing and marine, elevator, and utilities industries, as well as for ski lifts, bridges, supported structures and the U.S. Navy.

Career ✔ Tip

The Structure of Work is Changing
Understand how the structure of work is changing. More part-time and contract jobs are being created, while the traditional working hours of 9-5 are no longer considered the norm.

YAMAHA MOTOR CANADA LTD. • 480 Gordon Baker Road • Toronto, ON • M2H 3B4 • Tel: 416-498-1911 • Fax: 416-491-3517 • E-mail: careers@yamaha-motor.ca • Internet: www. yamaha-motor.ca • Yamaha Motor Canada is a wholesale distributor of products made by Yamaha Motor Co. of Japan. Its Canadian operation opened in 1973. The company's products include motorcycles, power products, outboard motors, jet-skis, all-terrain vehicles, and parts and accessories. Today, the company has diversified into many new fields, becoming a comprehensive manufacturer of products ranging from sports and leisure goods to industrial equipment. Yamaha Motor Company employs approximately 180 individuals.

Insurance

ACE INA INSURANCE • 130 King Street West, 12th Floor • Toronto, ON • M5X 1A6 • Tel: 416-368-2911 • Fax: 416-594-2600 • Internet: www.ace-ina-canada.com • ACE INA Insurance and ACE INA Life Insurance are members of the ACE Group of Companies. With offices in over 50 countries, ACE is a leading provider of property and casualty and accident and health products and services.

ALLIANZ CANADA • 130 Adelaide Street West, Suite 1600 • Toronto, ON • M5H 3P5 • Tel: 416-915-4247 • Fax: 416-961-5442 • Contact: Human Resources • E-mail: info@allianz.ca • Internet: www.allianz.com • Founded in 1890, the Allianz Group is one of the leading global services providers in insurance, banking and asset management. With approximately 181,000 employees worldwide the Allianz Group serves more than 80 million customers in about 70 countries.

ALLSTATE INSURANCE CO. OF CANADA • 27 Allstate Parkway, Suite 100 • Markham, ON • L3R 5P8 • Tel: 905-477-6900 • Fax: 905-475-4924 • Contact: Human Resources • E-mail: careers@allstate.ca • Internet: www.allstate.ca • The Allstate Insurance Company of Canada is a member of one of the largest insurance organizations in the world. Allstate has been a provider of property and casualty insurance products in Canada since 1953. They provide Canadians with peace of mind by delivering a full line of auto, home, individual life and financial products through their network of 450 agents and 1,000 employees.

ANTHONY INSURANCE INC. • 35 Blackmarsh Road • St. John's, NL • A1B 3N2 • Tel: 709-758-5500 • Fax: 709-758-5729 • Contact: Human Resources • Anthony Insurance offers personal automobile, home and commercial insurance. They also provide life insurance and many financial products.

ASSUMPTION MUTUAL LIFE INSURANCE • P.O. Box 160, 770 Main Street • Moncton, NB • E1C 8L1 • Tel: 506-853-6040 • Fax: 506-853-5421 • Contact: Human Resources • E-mail: human.resources@assumption.ca • Internet: www.assumption.ca • Assumption Life operates in the area of financial services. Through its team of highly qualified representatives and selected partners, the company offers its clients a comprehensive range of products required for sound financial planning. The goal of Assumption Life is to assist clients in planning for the future, realizing their dreams, and achieving well-deserved peace of mind.

AVIVA CANADA INC. • 2206 Eglinton Avenue East • Scarborough, ON • M1L 4S8 • Tel: 416-288-1800 • Fax: 416-288-9756 • Contact: Human Resources • Internet: www.avivacanada.com • Aviva Canada Inc. is one of the leading property and casualty insurance groups in Canada. In addition to providing home, auto, and commercial insurance, Aviva provides specialty commercial products and construction surety bonding. Aviva Canada is a wholly-owned subsidiary of UK-based Aviva plc, the world's fifth largest insurance group.

AXA INSURANCE (CANADA) • 5700 Yonge Street, Suite 1400 • Toronto, ON • M2M 4K2 • Tel: 416-218-4188 • Fax: 416-218-4174 • Internet: www.axa.ca • AXA is one of the country's leading property/casualty insurers. Through our subsidiaries in Quebec, Ontario, Western Canada and the Atlantic provinces, we offer a wide range of property/casualty and life insurance products and financial services. We do business through brokers from coast to coast.

ECON GROUP INC. • 500 - 1400 Blair Place • Ottawa, ON • K1J 9B8 • Tel: 613-786-2000 • Fax: 613-786-2001 • Contact: Stephanie Farrington, Human Resources • E-mail: stephanie. d.farrington@encon.ca • Internet: www.encon.ca • ENCON Group Inc. is Canada's largest professional liability underwriter and a leading third party administrator, serving clients through its national network of more than 4,000 agents and brokers. The company's Association Business division offers programs designed to meet the specific needs of a broad range of organizations and their members, with products such as life and health, travel, residential and auto insurance.

FM GLOBAL • 165 Commerce Valley Drive West, Suite 500 • Thornhill, ON • L3T 7V8 • Tel: 905-763-5555 • Fax: 905-763-5556 • Internet: www.fmglobal.com • FM Global is the world's largest commercial and industrial property insurance and risk management organization specializing in property protection.

ING CANADA FINANCIAL SERVICES INTERNATIONAL • 700 University Avenue, • Toronto, ON • M5G 0A1 • Tel: 416-341-1464 • Fax: 416-941-5320 • Contact: HR Consultant • E-mail: infoING@INGcanada.com • Internet: www.ingcanada.com • ING companies in Canada are members of the ING Group - one of the world's largest integrated financial services organizations. Together, they form a network of Canadian businesses bringing an expanding range of insurance, financial security and wealth-building solutions to customers across the country.

INSURANCE CORP. OF B.C. • Human Resources Business Operations, 224 - 151 West Esplanade • North Vancouver, BC • V7M 3H9 • Tel: 604-661-2800 • Fax: 604-661-6450 • Contact: Human Resources • Internet: www.icbc.com • The Insurance Corporation of British Columbia is a provincial Crown corporation established in 1973 to provide universal auto insurance to BC motorists. In addition, the Corporation is responsible for driver licensing, vehicle registration and licensing.

JOHNSON INCORPORATED • 95 Elizabeth Avenue, P.O. Box 12049 • St. John's, NL • A1B 1R7 • Tel: 709-737-1500 • Fax: 709-737-1580 • Contact: Supervisor, Human Resources • E-mail: headoffice@johnson.ca • Internet: www.johnson.ca • Johnson Incorporated is a personal insurance and benefits consulting/administration company. The company provides consulting and benefits administration services. The firm operates in Ontario, B.C., Alberta and in the Atlantic Provinces with its head office in Newfoundland. In 1997, The Johnson Corporation, became an autonomous member of Royal & SunAlliance Group of Companies. Established more than 280 years ago, Royal & SunAlliance is the oldest incorporated insurance business in the world, and does business in 130 countries around the globe.

MANITOBA PUBLIC INSURANCE CORPORATION • P.O. Box 6300 • Winnipeg, MB • R3C 4A4 • Tel: 204-985-7000 • Fax: 204-985-3525 • Contact: Human Resources • E-mail: hr@mpi. mb.ca • Internet: www.mpi.mb.ca • Manitoba Public Insurance is a nonprofit Crown Corporation that has provided basic automobile coverage since 1971. Their services are available throughout Manitoba in claim centres and Customer Service centres. A staff of about 1700 makes them one of the largest employers in the province.

PENNCORP LIFE INSURANCE COMPANY • 55 Superior Boulevard • Mississauga, ON • L5T 2X9 • Tel: 800-268-2835 • Fax: 905-795-2316 • Contact: Human Resources • E-mail: jobs@penncorp.ca • Internet: www.penncorp.ca • PennCorp Life is a life insurance company dedicated to providing quality products and personalized service to their policyholders. They are committed to meeting self-employed and seniors' life and health insurance needs.

PILOT INSURANCE COMPANY • 90 Eglinton Avenue West • Toronto, ON • M4R 2E4 • Tel: 416-487-5141 • Fax: 416- 487-6905 • Contact: Human Resources • E-mail: jobs@pilot. ca • Internet: www.pilot.ca • An Ontario-only company with a strong reputation among their customers and industry peers, Pilot has acquired over 440,000 policyholders and one billion dollars in assets, ranking them among the province's largest insurers. They serve policyholders from 23 Claims Branches across Ontario. Their rate of retaining customers exceeds 90%, one of the highest rates in the industry. Pilot also recently ranked first in a Broker satisfaction survey conducted by the Insurance Brokers Association of Ontario (IBAO).

ROYAL & SUNALLIANCE INSURANCE CO. OF CANADA • 10 Wellington Street East, 2nd Floor • Toronto, ON • M5E 1L5 • Tel: 416-366-7511 • Fax: 416-367-9869 • Contact: Human Resources • Internet: www.royalsunalliance.ca • Royal & SunAlliance Canada is part of the Royal & Sun Alliance Insurance Group plc. Dating back to 1710, the Group provides a comprehensive range of insurance and financial services to customers worldwide.

SMARTCOVERAGE INSURANCE AGENCY LTD. • 4510 Rhodes Drive, #400 • Windsor, ON • N8W 5C2 • Tel: 519-974-1641 • Fax: 519-974-7290 • Internet: www.smartcoverageinsurance. ca • SmartCoverage Insurance Agency is a GMAC joint venture company, specializing in automobile insurance.

SSQ LIFE • 2525 Laurier Boulevard, P.O. Box 10500, Stn Sainte-Foy • Sainte-Foy, QC • G1V 4H6 • Tel: 418-651-7000 • Contact: Human Resources • Internet: www.ssq.qc.ca • SSQ Life is a major insurance company in Quebec that provides group insurance specializing in life, disability, accident and sickness insurance, along with pension plans. The insurance company has one sales office in Quebec City, and one in Montreal. SSQ Life has an employee base of more than 1300 individuals.

STATE FARM INSURANCE COMPANIES • 100 Consilium Place, Suite 102 • Scarborough, ON • M1H 3G9 • Tel: 416-290-4100 • Fax: 416-290-4716 • Contact: Human Resources • Internet: www.statefarm.com • In over 80 years, the State Farm Insurance Companies has grown from a small farm mutual auto insurer to one of the world's largest financial institutions. State Farm provides multi-line insurance protection to millions of Policyholders throughout North America.

THE ECONOMICAL INSURANCE GROUP • 111 Westmount Road South • Waterloo, ON • N2J 4S4 • Tel: 519-570-8500 • Fax: 519-570-8389 • Contact: Human Resources • Internet: www.economicalinsurance.com • The Economical Insurance Group is a Top 10, Canadian-owned property and casualty insurer with a track record spanning over 130 years. Their full range of personal and commercial line products are tailored to rise above and beyond the needs of their customers, and their innovative technology is renowned. They have more than 2000 employees in Canada.

ZURICH NORTH AMERICA CANADA • 400 University Avenue • Toronto, ON • M5G 1S7 • Tel: 416-586-3000 • Fax: 416-586-2525 • Contact: Human Resources • Internet: www. zurichcanada.com • Zurich North America Canada is part of Zurich Financial Services Group, a global leader in the insurance-based financial services industry. Zurich focuses its activities on the key markets of North America, the United Kingdom and Continental Europe.

Career Tip

Think Internationally in Your Search for Employment
As a result of globalization, jobs are no longer defined under boundaries within a city, a country, or a continent for that matter. When looking for employment see how firms compete from a global perspective.

Investment

AGF MANAGEMENT LIMITED • P.O. Box 50, TD Bank Tower, 66 Wellington Street West • Toronto, ON • M5K 1E9 • Tel: 416-367-1900 • Fax: 416-865-4189 • Contact: Human Resources • E-mail: tiger@agf.com • Internet: www.agf.com • Founded in 1957, AGF is one of Canada's premier investment management companies with offices across Canada and subsidiaries around the world. With about $49 billion in total assets under management, AGF serves more than one million investors with offerings across the wealth continuum. AGF's products and services include a diversified family of more than 50 mutual funds, AGF Harmony tailored investment program, AGF Private Investment Management and AGF Trust GICs, loans and mortgages.

AON REED STENHOUSE INC. • 20 Bay Street, Reed Stenhouse Tower • Toronto, ON • M5J 2N9 • Tel: 416-868-5500 • Fax: 416-868-5502 • Contact: Human Resources • E-mail: aon. careers@aon.ca • Internet: www.aon.ca • Aon is the world's premier insurance brokerage, consulting services and consumer insurance underwriting organization. Aon creates value for clients by offering knowledgeable, flexible and innovative solutions, from mitigating risk to improving human resources.

NESBITT BURNS INC. • 1 First Canadian Place • Toronto, ON • M5X 1H3 • Tel: 416-359-4000 • Fax: 416-359-4311 • Contact: Human Resources • Email: ia.recruiting@bmomb.com • Internet: www.bmonesbittburns.com • BBMO Nesbitt Burns is one of North America's leading full-service investment firms; a recognized leader in personal finance. They focus on meeting the needs of individual investors through a customized approach to investing.

TD WATERHOUSE CANADA INC. • Toronto Dominion Centre • Concourse Level 1 • 55 King Street West • Toronto, ON • M5K 1A2 • Tel: 416-982-7981 • Fax: 416-944-5467 • Contact: Human Resources • Internet: www.tdwaterhouse.ca • TD Waterhouse Canada Inc. offers investment solutions for every investor through TD Waterhouse Discount Brokerage, TD Waterhouse Financial Planning, and TD Waterhouse Investment Advice. With more than 270 locations across Canada and more than one million client accounts, TD Waterhouse is a Canadian leader in wealth management. TD Wasterhouse Canada Inc. is a subsidiary of the Toronto Dominion Bank and a member of TD Bank Financial Group.

Management & Consulting

ACRODEX INC. • 11420 - 170 Street • Edmonton, AB • T5S 1L7 • Tel: 780-426-4444 • Fax: 780-426-2233 • Contact: Human Resources • Internet: www.acrodex.com • Acrodex is a full spectrum, enterprise-wide technology solution provider. They bring together the world's best technologies, processes, and solutions to help clients address critical needs at all levels of their enterprise. The five components of their solutions are: hardware, software licensing services, infrastructure services, application services, and managed services.

ARTSMARKETING SERVICES • 260 King Street East, Suite 500 • Toronto, ON • M5A 4L5 • Tel: 416-941-1041 • Fax: 416-941-8989 • Contact: Mr. Jon Shifman, Director of Administration and Personnel • Internet: www.artsmarketing.com • Artsmarketing has established a long history of outstanding results in telemarketing and telefundraising for organizations belonging to the non-profit sector. Over the course of a year, Artsmarketing employs over 3,500 full and part-time employees in offices all across North America.

BBM CANADA • 1500 Don Mills Road, 3rd Floor • Toronto, ON • M3B 3L7 • Tel: 416-445-9800 • Fax: 416-445-8644 • Contact: Human Resources Manager • E-mail: staffing@bbm.ca • Internet: www.bbm.ca • BBM Canada is a not-for-profit, broadcast research company that was jointly established in 1944 as a tripartite cooperative by the Canadian Association of Broadcasters and the Association of Canadian Advertisers. They are the leading supplier of radio and television audience ratings services to the Canadian broadcast advertising industry.

C.S.T. CONSULTANTS INC. • 240 Duncan Mill Road, Suite 600 • Toronto, ON • M3B 3P1 • Tel: 416-445-7377 • Fax: 416-445-1708 • Contact: Ms. Carla Moore, HR Manager • E-mail: hr@cst.org • Internet: www.cst.org • C.S.T. Consultants is involved in the distribution and administration of R.E.S.P.'s (Registered Education Savings Plans). The company's head office is in Don Mills, Ontario.

CARLSON MARKETING GROUP CANADA LTD. • 2845 Matheson Blvd. East • Mississauga, ON • L4W 5K2 • Tel: 905-214-8699 • Fax: 905-214-8693 • Contact: Human Resources • Internet: www.carlsoncanada.com • Carlson Marketing Group Canada is a world-leader in developing relationship marketing strategies that build stronger bonds between our clients and their customers, channel partners, and employees. We are committed to helping our clients: foster long-term relationships, influence purchasing behaviours, retain best customers, and improve their bottom lines. Carlson Marketing Group Canada began operations in 1955 and is now Canada's leading Relationship Marketing agency. We employ over 400 marketing professionals with offices in Toronto and Montreal.

CARPÉDIA INTERNATIONAL LTD. • 75 Navy Street • Oakville, ON • L6J 2Z1 • Tel: 905-337-3407 • E-mail: careers@carpedia.com • Internet: www.carpedia.com • Carpédia is an implementation-based management consulting firm that is singularly focused on providing significant and measurable improvements in revenue growth, productivity, and asset utilization without capital expenditures. The firm works with leading companies throughout North America and has conducted projects on five continents.

EDS CANADA • 33 Yonge Street, Suite 500 • Toronto, ON • M5E 1G4 • Tel: 416-814-4500 • Fax: 416-814-4600 • Internet: www.eds.com/canada • EDS Canada is a global outsourcing services company. It delivers superior returns to clients through its cost-effective, high-value information-technology and business process outsourcing services, as well as information-technology transformation services. EDS employs 7,200 employees across Canada.

ENVIRONICS RESEARCH GROUP LTD. • 33 Bloor Street East, Suite 900 • Toronto, ON • M4W 3H1 • Tel: 416-920-9010 • Fax: 416-920-3299 • Contact: Human Resources • E-mail: humanresources@environics.ca • Internet: http://erg.environics.net/ • Founded in 1970, Environics Research Group Environics has been producing reliable, qualitative and quantitative research for business and governments for more than a quarter-century. It not only includes raw numbers, but strategic answers to crucial issues and solid data, analyzed by experts with a high level of insightful interpretation.

ERNST & YOUNG • Ernst & Young Tower, 222 Bay Street, P.O. Box 251, TD Centre • Toronto, ON • M5J 1J7 • Tel: 416-864-1234 • Fax: 416-864-1174 • Contact: Human Resources • Internet: www.ey.com • Ernst & Young is one of the world's leading professional service organizations, helping companies across the globe to identify and capitalize on business opportunities. The professionals at Ernst & Young provide a broad array of services in audit, tax, corporate finance, transactions, online security, enterprise risk management, and the valuation of intangibles. They employ over 130,000 people in 140 countries around the world.

GALLUP CANADA INC. • 55 University Avenue, Suite 1805 • Toronto, ON • M5J 2H7 • Tel: 416-586-0808 • Fax: 416-586-9606 • Contact: Human Resources • Internet: www.gallup.com • Gallup has studied human nature and behavior for more than 70 years. Gallup employs many of the world's leading scientists in management, economics, psychology, and sociology. Gallup consultants help organizations boost organic growth by increasing customer engagement and maximizing employee productivity through measurement tools, coursework, and strategic advisory services. Gallup's 2,000 professionals deliver services at client organizations, through the Web, at Gallup University's campuses, and in 40 offices around the world.

GRANT THORNTON • 200 Bay Street, 19th Floor, P.O. Box 55 • Toronto, ON • M5J 2P9 • Tel: 416-360-0100 • Fax: 416-360-4949 • Internet: www.grantthornton.ca • Grant Thornton, is the sixth largest firm of chartered accountants in Canada, ranked by revenue. They have 107 offices across Canada. Grant Thornton is one of Canada's leading firms of chartered accountants and management consultants, providing the strength of advice to growing entrepreneurial businesses and not-for-profit organizations through a wide range of assurance, tax and advisory services.

HILL & KNOWLTON CANADA LTD. • 160 Bloor Street East, Suite 700 • Toronto, ON • M4W 3P7 • Tel: 416-413-4622 • Fax: 416-413-1550 • Contact: Ruth Clark, Senior Vice President, Human Resources • E-mail: ruth.clark@hillandknowlton.ca • Internet: www.hillandknowlton.ca • Hill & Knowlton Canada is the nation's leading strategic communications consultancy, with a successful track record of providing high value public relations and public affairs support to companies, agencies, government ministries and organizations. The firm is also a multi-specialist agency, offering in-depth expertise in a variety of areas and sectors such as crisis communications, public affairs, technology communications, digital communications, corporate and financial communications, health and pharmaceuticals, consumer health, Aboriginal affairs, marketing communications, and investor relations. Hill & Knowlton has eight offices in Canada and over 72 offices in more than 41 countries.

KAROM GROUP OF COMPANIES • 2384 Yonge Street, P.O. Box 1286, Station K • Toronto, ON • M4P 3E5 • Tel: 416-489-4146 • Fax: 416-489-5248 • Contact: Director of Operations • E-mail: karom@karomgroup.com • Internet: www.karomgroup.com • Karom Group of Companies is a full service marketing research company specializing in focus group, telephone, and self-administered surveys for data collection. They provide expertise in project planning, survey design, demography and sampling, tabulation, reporting and strategic analysis.

LEO BURNETT CO. LTD. • 175 Bloor Street East, North Tower • Toronto, ON • M4W 3R9 • Tel: 416-925-5997 • Fax: 416-925-3443 • Contact: Human Resources • Internet: www.leoburnett. com • Leo Burnett Co. is part of the Publicis Groupe Network providing full service across all communications media. The company employs approximately 200 people across the country.

MEDISOLUTION • 110 Cremazie Boulevard West, 12th Floor • Montréal, QC • H2P 1B9 • Tel: 514-850-5000 • Fax: 514-850-5005 • Contact: Human Resources • E-mail: careers@ medisolution.com. • Internet: www.medisolution.com • MediSolution, a subsidiary of Brascan Corporation, is a leading healthcare information technology company, providing software and services to healthcare customers across North America. MediSolution's mandate is to provide best in class technology solutions and services to ensure that healthcare providers can meet the day-to-day challenges of delivering healthcare services.

MOSAIC SALES SOLUTIONS • 2700 Matheson Blvd. East, West Tower, 2nd Floor • Mississauga, ON • L4W 4V9 • Tel: 905-238-8422 • Fax: 905-238-1998 • Contact: Human Resources • Internet: www.mosaic.com • Mosaic Sales Solutions, formerly Sales and Merchandising Group, was formed in 1986 to respond to changes in retail markets and to address the evolution of sales organizations. Mosaic Sales Solutions is a national firm representing leading organizations and employing more than 1500 full and part time people in their year round business.

NIELSEN MARKETING RESEARCH (ACNEILSON CANADA) • 160 McNabb Street • Markham, ON • L3P 4B8 • Tel: 905-475-1131 • Fax: 905-475-8357 • Contact: Human Resources

• Internet: ca.nielsen.com • ACNielsen is the world's leading marketing information company. With 21,000 employees worldwide offering services in more than 100 countries, ACNielsen provides market research, information, analysis and insights to the consumer products and service industries.

OBJEXIS CORPORATION • 1635 Sherbrooke Street West, 3rd Floor • Montreal, QC • H3H 1E2 • Tel: 514-932-3295 • Fax: 514-932-4639 • Contact: Human Resources • E-mail: jobs@ objexis.com • Internet: www.objexis.com • Objexis Corporation develops team portals for collaborative strategic management. These portals are the only ones that integrate strategic relationship, marketing and process management within one solution. Objexis Team Portals are delivered over the Internet using an ASP model supported by training, consulting and other complementary services.

OPINION SEARCH INC. • 160 Elgin Street, Suite 1800 • Ottawa, ON • K2P 2P7 • Tel: 613-230-9109 • Fax: 613-230-3793 • Contact: Recruitment Coordinator • E-mail: ottjobs@opinionsearch. com • Internet: www.opinionsearch.com • Opinion Search Inc. is one of North American's leading market research data collection agencies, providing a range of phone, site and Internet interviewing and tabulation services. With a special emphasis on telephone fieldwork, Opinion Search Inc. has developed a strong bilingual and multi-lingual team of trained interviewers, supervisors, analysts and coders.

ORGANISATION METRICS INC. • 100 Allstate Parkway, Suite 701 • Markham, ON • L3R 6H3 • Tel: 905-944-8414 • Fax: 905-944-8707 • E-mail: careers@orgmetrics.com • Internet: www.orgmetrics.com • Organization Metrics Inc. (OMI) is a Canadian company recognized internationally as a provider of custom human resource management systems. Since 1982, OMI has worked with some of North America's largest and most successful public and private organizations to ensure the development of Strategic Human Resource Management (SHRM) capabilities. The OrgMetrics suite of modules supports all aspects of human resource management, including recruitment & selection, performance management, competency assessment, learning & development, succession planning and workforce analysis.

PENTAMARK WORLDWIDE/CANADA • One Riverside Drive West • Windsor, ON • N9A 5K3 • Tel: 519-258-7584 • Fax: 519-258-4242 • Contact: Human Resources • PentaMark Worldwide/Canada is a marketing, advertising and communications company working for a major automotive company. The firm's head office is in Windsor, Ontario.

PHH ENVIRONMENTAL LIMITED • 406 - 13251 Delf Place • Richmond, BC • V6V 2A2 • Contact: Human Resources • Tel: 2604-244-8101 • Fax: 604-244-8491 • E-mail: careers@ phharcenv.com • Internet: www.phharcenv.com • PHH Environmental Limited is a full service consulting company which specializes in providing environmental health and safety services. PHH operates eleven offices including Richmond, Victoria, Prince George, Keremeos, Calgary, Edmonton, Saskatoon, Yellowknife, Cardiff (UK), and ARC Offices in Edmonton and Calgary. In Eastern Canada, PHH is affiliated with Pinchin Environmental. Their affiliation with this company provides a national presence unparalleled by any other company. With over 25 years of experience PHH is positioned to provide quality consulting and technical support for all environmental, health and safety issues.

STANTEC CONSULTING LTD. • 401 Wellington Street West, Suite 100 • Toronto, ON • M5V 1E7 • Tel: 416-596-6686 • Fax: 416-596-6680 • Contact: Human Resources • E-mail: hr@ stantec.com • Internet: www.stantec.com • Stantec, founded in 1954, provides professional design and consulting services in planning, engineering, architecture, surveying, and project management.

Merchandisers

7-ELEVEN • 632 Plains Road East • Burlington, ON • L7T 2E9 • Tel: 905-681-7299 • Contact: Human Resources • Internet: www.7-eleven.com • What started out as an ice house in Dallas, Texas back in 1927 has grown and evolved into the world's largest operator, franchisor and licensor of convenience stores. Today, 7-Eleven operates, franchises or licenses more than 7,500 7-Eleven® stores in North America. Globally, 7-Eleven operates, franchises or licenses approximately 34,200 stores in 14 countries.

BEST BUY CANADA LTD. • 8800 Glenlyon Parkway • Burnaby, BC • V5J 5K3 • Tel: 604-435-8223 • Fax: 604-412-5224 • Contact: Human Resources • E-mail: customerservice@bestbuycanada.ca • Internet: www.bestbuy.ca • Best Buy stores in Canada are a division of Burnaby, BC-based Best Buy Canada Ltd., a wholly owned subsidiary of Best Buy Co., Inc. Best Buy is Canada's newest specialty retailer of consumer electronics, personal computers and entertainment software. The Company's knowledgeable sales staff are not paid on commission and are focused on being the customer's "Smart Friend", helping them find the products and services that best fit their needs. For more information about Best Buy, including locations, visit www.BestBuy.ca

BIRKS JEWELRY • P.O. Box 210, Eaton Centre, 220 Yonge Street • Toronto, ON • M5B 2H1 • Tel: 416-979-9311 • Fax: 416-979-0919 • Contact: Human Resources Manager • Internet: www.birks.com • Birks is the sign name for stores operated by Henry Birks and Sons (1993) Inc. The company is a major retailer in the Canadian market of jewelry and giftware. Established in Canada in 1879, Birks currently has 38 outlets across the country, and employs approximately 1,000 individuals. With its head office in Montreal, candidates should apply individually to stores for employment opportunities. The address above reflects the store location at the Eaton Centre in Toronto, Ontario.

BLACK PHOTO CORPORATION • 371 Gough Road • Markham, ON • L3R 4B6 • Tel: 905-475-2777 • Fax: 905-475-8814 • Internet: www.blackphoto.com • Black Photo Corporation is a specialty photofinishing retailer with locations all across Canada. Their stores are known as Black's Camera.

CANADADRUGS.COM PARTNERSHIP • 24 Terracon Place • Winnipeg, MB • R2J 4G7 • Internet: www.canadadrugs.com • CanadaDrugs.com Partnership is a successful online retail mail-order pharmacy. Please visit their website for more information about their company.

CANADIAN TIRE CORPORATION LTD. • P.O. Box 770, Station K • Toronto, ON • M4P 2V8 • Tel: 1-800-387-8803 • Fax: 1-800-452-0770 • Internet: www.canadiantire.ca • Canadian Tire has proudly stood the test of time since our founding in 1922. What began as a small but bold entrepreneurial concept has emerged to become Canada's most-shopped retailer with more than 1,000 stores and gas bars across the enterprise. Canadian Tire is a proud Canadian family and their purpose is to serve and enrich the lives of their customers, their shareholders, their team and their communities. 48,000 Canadians work across the Canadian Tire organization from coast-to-coast in the corporation's retail, financial services, petroleum, and apparel businesses.

Surf' the Internet
As you are likely aware, there is a tremendous amount of employer and job search information on the Internet. Have a look at *Get Wired, You're Hired! The Canadian Internet Job Search Guide* for important job websites in Canada.

COTTON GINNY • 40 Samor Road • Toronto, ON • M6A 1J6 • Tel: 416-785-9686 • Fax: 905-625-9995 • Contact: Human Resources • E-mail: hr@cottonginny.ca • Internet: www. cottonginny.ca • Cotton Ginny Limited is a Canadian based, ladies retail chain with over 135 stores located in major shopping centres across Canada. They are committed to providing lifestyle, casual clothing that goes beyond weekend wear. They believe that you do not have to trade style for comfort. For more information please visit their website.

EDDIE BAUER INC. • 201 Aviva Park Drive • Vaughan, ON • L4L 9C1 • Tel: 905-851-6700 • Contact: Mr. Marcy Jensen, Human Resources Manager • Internet: www.eddiebauer.com • Eddie Bauer, Inc. is a leading international retail brand, offering casual lifestyle products for adults. Since 1920, Eddie Bauer has evolved from a single store in Seattle to a tri-channel, international company with approximately 370 stores throughout the United States and Canada.

FORZANI GROUP LTD., THE • 824 - 41 Avenue NE • Calgary, AB • T2E 3R3 • Tel: 403-717-1400 • Fax: 403-717-1491 • Contact: Human Resources • E-mail: hrcorporate@forzani.com • Internet: www.forzanigroup.com • The Forzani Group Ltd. ("FGL") is Canada's largest retailer of sporting goods, offering a comprehensive assortment of brand-name and private-label products, operating stores from coast to coast, under six corporate banners: Sport Chek , Sports Experts , Coast Mountain Sports , Sport Mart, Athletes World and National Sports. The Forzani Group is also a franchisor under the banners: Sports Experts, Intersport, RnR, Econosports and Atmosphere.

FUTURE SHOP LTD. • 8800 Glenlyon Parkway • Burnaby, BC • V5J 5K3 • Tel: 604-435-8223 • Fax: 604-412-5224 • Internet: www.futureshop.ca • With more than 130 stores across the country and the nation's premier web store, at www.futureshop.ca, Future Shop is Canada's largest, fastest-growing national retailer and e-tailer of consumer electronics. Future Shop and its 10,000 associates are committed to helping Canadians get more out of the technology they buy and offers the latest digital products along with a wide selection of brand-named televisions, computers, audio, entertainment software and hardware and appliances. For more information about Future Shop stores please visit www.futureshop.ca.

GOLF TOWN CANADA INC. • 3265 Highway 7 East, Unit 2 • Markham, ON • L3R 3P9 • Tel: 905-479-0343 • Fax: 905-479-7108 • Internet: www.golftown.com • Golf Town has grown to become Canada's largest golf retailer. Their intention is to take their customers as far beyond the conventional retail golf experience as possible. For more information on their company visit their website.

GRAND & TOY LTD. • 33 Green Belt Drive • Toronto, ON • M3C 1M1 • Tel: 416-445-7255 • Fax: 416-445-4855 • Contact: Human Resources • E-mail: careers@grandtoy.com • Internet: www.grandandtoy.com • Founded in 1882, Grand & Toy is Canada's largest commercial office products company, with 2200 associates in 26 commercial sales offices, 7 distribution centers and over 50 retail locations from coast to coast.

HARRY ROSEN INC. • 77 Bloor Street West, Suite 1600 • Toronto, ON • M5S 1M2 • Tel: 416-935-9200 • Fax: 416-515-7067 • E-mail: hrrecruitingco@harryrosen.com • Internet: www. harryrosen.com • Harry Rosen Inc. is a retailer of fine men's wear labels, including Hugo Boss, Zegna, Armani Collezioni and Versace. «Treating customers as individuals - that's the real business we're in.» They operate 16 locations in major cities across Canada.

HMV CANADA • 5401 Eglinton Avenue West, Suite 110 • Toronto, ON • M9C 5K6 • Tel: 416-620-4470 • Fax: 416-620-5064 • Contact: Human Resources Manager • Internet: www.hmv. ca • With over 75 years of music retailing history and 559 stores worldwide, HMV is the world's premier retailer of music. Throughout the entire period of its trading history, HMV had been a part of the EMI Group of companies, but in March 1998 it was sold to form a new retail concern

- the HMV Group - that also comprises the Waterstones and Dillons bookchains. Continually growing within the international retail music industry, HMV has proven itself as an innovative leader in Canada since 1986.

HUDSON'S BAY COMPANY, THE • 401 Bay Street, Suite 200 • Toronto, ON • M5H 2Y4 • Tel: 416-861-6112 • Fax: 416-861-4180 • Internet: www.hbc.com • Hudson's Bay Company, established in 1670, is Canada's oldest corporation and largest department store retailer. Through its major operating divisions, the Bay, Zellers, and Home Outfitters. Hudson's Bay Company covers the Canadian retail market across all price zones from coast to coast. The company is a major employer of more than 70,000 individuals across the country.

KATZ GROUP CANADA LTD. • 5965 Coopers Avenue • Mississauga, ON • L4Z 1R9 • Tel: 905-502-5965 • Fax: 905-502-5618 • Contact: Human Resources • Internet: www.pharmassist.ca • PharmAssist is Katz Group Canada's professional services brand and program uniting Katz Group Canada pharmacies under one nationally recognized symbol of excellence in pharmacy care. The PharmAssist program ensures consistent quality pharmacy care at over 1700 Rexall Drug Stores, Pharma Plus Drugmarts, Medicine Shoppe, Guardian and I.D.A. pharmacies.

LES DISTILLERIES CORBY LTÉE • 950 chemin des Moulins • Montreal, QC • H3C 3W5 • Tel: 514-871-9090 • Contact: Human Resources • E-mail: careers@corby.ca • Internet: www.corby. ca • Les Distilleries Corby Ltée/Corby Distilleries Ltd. is Canada's market leader in both spirits and wines. Over the past several decades Corby has branched out from it's heritage of being a Whisky producer to include dozens of Canadian and international brands, including many of the most recognized and respected in the industry.

MARK'S WORK WAREHOUSE • 1035 - 64th Avenue S.E., #30 • Calgary, AB • T2H 2J7 • Tel: 403-255-9220 • Fax: 403-255-6005 • Internet: www.marks.com • Mark's Work Warehouse provides their customers with «Clothes That Work» for their lifestyle 24 hours a day, 7 days a week. With one-stop convenience, they offer their customers exclusive private labels and Canada's best sellers in quality casual and business wear, outdoor apparel for men and women, workwear, and safety footwear.

MICHAELS OF CANADA INC. • 1650 Victoria Street East • Whitby, ON • L1N 9L4 • Tel: 905-438-1750 • Contact: Human Resources • Internet: www.michaels.com • Michaels Stores, Inc. (michaels.com) is the largest specialty retailer of arts and crafts. With more than 900 stores in the United States and Canada, the company carries a wide selection of arts and crafts merchandise. Michaels also operates specialty stores under different brand names including Aaron Brothers and Artistree manufacturing facility.

MILLWORK & BUILDING SUPPLIES LIMITED • 1279 Simcoe Street North • Oshawa, ON • L1G 4X1 • Tel: 905-728-6291 • Fax: 905-728-8589 • Contact: Ms. Jacky Jordan, Assistant Manager • Internet: www.millworkhome.com • Millwork & Building Supplies is a home centre and lumber yard in Oshawa. The retail centre offers hardware and electrical products, paint and wallpaper, and door and windows. The firm employs about 185 people.

MOUNTAIN EQUIPMENT CO-OP • 149 West 4th Avenue • Vancouver, BC • V5Y 4A6 • Tel: 604-732-3300 • Fax: 604-731-3826 • Contact: Human Resources • Email: jobs@mec.ca • Internet: www.mec.ca • MEC was conceived by a small group of Canadian climbers who wanted a place to buy gear not carried by conventional retailers: gear for mountaineering, rock climbing, ski touring, and hiking. In August 1971, these six initial members founded Mountain Equipment Co-op. Today MEC supplies outdoor equipment to over 2.6 million members worldwide, and has 12 stores across Canada.

NATIONAL GROCERS CO. LTD. • 351 Marwood Drive • Oshawa, ON • L1H 7P8 • Tel: 905-579-4955 • Fax: 905-579-5269 • Contact: Human Resources • National Grocers Co. Ltd. is the largest distributor of groceries in Canada and one of the largest in North America. National Grocers distributes to a network of company-owned retail chains in Canada, such as Loblaws.

NORTH WEST COMPANY INC. • 77 Main Street • Winnipeg, MB • R3C 2R1 • Tel: 204-943-0881 • Fax: 204-934-1696 • Contact: Human Resources • E-mail: retailcareers@northwest.ca • Internet: www.northwest.ca • The North West Company is the leading retailer in northern Canada and is quickly becoming a retailing presence in southern markets under the Giant Tiger banner. The North West Company employs 4,552 people in Canada, 736 in Alaska,and is the largest employer of Aboriginal people in Canada outside of the Federal Government. Sales and other income in 2003 totaled $782.7 million.

RED DEER CO-OP LIMITED • 5118 - 47th Avenue • Red Deer, AB • T4N 3P7 • Tel: 403-343-2667 • Fax: 403-341-5811 • Contact: Human Resources • E-mail: c.krogman@reddeercoop.com • Internet: www.reddeercoop.com • When the Red Deer Co-op was incorporated in February 1956, it originally provided Food, Hardware and Family Fashions. Over the next few years, membership increased and in 1969 the Home & Garden Centre was added. Red Deer Co-op saw continued growth with the addition of the Lacombe branch in 1979 and Deer Park Centre in 1989. The membership of Red Deer Co-op now exceeds 34,000 and this member loyalty ensures its current stability and future growth.

REGIS PICTURES AND FRAMES LTD. • 8 - 5850 Byrne Road • Burnaby, BC • V5J 3J3 • Tel: 604-327-3447 • Fax: 604-327-5223 • Regis Pictures and Frames Ltd. is a merchandiser of various styles of pictures, frames, giftware and prints. Regis Pictures & Frames has 19 stores located in major regional malls. Regis is still a privately owned and operated family business and its' success is due to the excellent management team many of whom have grown and developed along with Regis.

RONA INC. • 1170 Martin Grove Road • Toronto, ON • M9W 4X1 • Tel: 406-241-8844 • Fax: 416-241-2344 • Contact: Human Resources • Internet: www.rona.ca • RONA is the largest Canadian distributor and retailer of hardware, home renovation and gardening products. RONA operates a network of some 670 franchised, affiliated and corporate stores of various sizes and formats. With over 26,000 employees working under its family of banners across Canada and some 12 million square feet of retail space, the RONA store network generates close to $4 billion in annual sales.

SAAN STORES LTD. • 2800 Matheson Blvd. East • Mississauga, ON • L4W 4X5 • Tel: 905-219-8700 • Contact: Human Resources • Internet: www.saan.ca • SAAN Stores Ltd. is a national retail entity under the banners SAAN and The Red Apple Clearance Centre. Our stores offer a wide selection of clothing merchandise and include furnishings, housewares, general household items and confectioneries. Presently, SAAN employs approximately 3,100 full- and part-time associates in its stores, national sales office in Mississauga, and Red Apple buying office in Montreal.

SHOPPERS DRUG MART LIMITED • 243 Consumers Road • Toronto, ON • M2J 4W8 • Tel: 416-493-1220 • Fax: 416-491-1022 • Contact: Recruitment Coordinator • Internet: www.shoppersdrugmart.ca • Built on a foundation of professional expertise and personal service, the Shoppers Drug Mart/Pharmaprix organization has been meeting Canadians' health care needs for over 40 years. Shoppers Drug Mart employs many people to support their more than 1055 locations.

SOBEYS INC. • 123 Foord Street • Stellarton, NS • B0K 1S0 • Tel: 902-752-8371 • Contact: Human Resources • E-mail: hr@sobeys.com • Internet: www.sobeys.com • Sobeys Inc., headquartered in Stellarton, Nova Scotia is a leading national grocery retailer and food distributor. Founded in

Atlantic Canada in 1907, Sobeys owns or franchises more than 1,300 stores in all 10 provinces under various retail banners; including Sobeys, IGA, IGA extra, Foodland and Price Chopper. Sobeys and its franchisees employ approximately 37,000 people and collectively generate over $13.2 billion in retail sales.

SODEXO • 3350 South Service Road • Burlington, ON • L7N 3C7 • Tel: 905-632-8592 • Fax: 905-632-5619 • Internet: www.sodexhoca.com • As a leading provider of food and facilities management services in Canada, Sodexo brings the benefits of their partnership to more than 750 locations, including corporations, colleges and universities, health care organizations, private schools, and remote sites. They are working every day to improve the quality of life for the millions of people they serve.

STITCHES • 50 Dufflaw Road • Toronto, ON • M6A 2W1 • Tel: 416-789-1071 • Fax: 416-789-6969 • Contact: Human Resources • E-mail: jobs@stitchesonline.com • Internet: www. stitchesonline.com • Stitches is a national clothier with stores across the country. Their Toronto office is the head location for all of their unisex retail clothing stores.

STUDENT WORKS • 144 Main Street North, Suite 9A • Markham, ON • L3P 5T3 • Tel: 905-201-1477 • Fax: 905-201-1799 • Internet: www.studentworks.com • Student Works is an outgoing painting company that looks for hardworking result-oriented employees. They paint the interior and exterior of homes. They offer great pay and an enjoyable experience.

THE BEER STORE • 5900 Explorer Drive • Mississauga, ON • L4W 5L2 • Tel: 905-361-1005 • Fax: 905-361-4289 • Contact: Human Resources • E-mail: jobs@thebeerstore.ca • Internet: www.thebeerstore.ca • The Beer Store is the primary distribution and sales channel for beer in Ontario, operating 441 retail stores, and serving 17,500 licensed customers, 600 government-owned LCBO retail locations, 141 Retail Partners, and 82 Northern Agents. Customers can choose from more than 330 beer brands from over 75 brewers from around the world. Over 5600 people are employed in Ontario.

TLC PROMOTIONS INC. • 442 Regional Route 8 • Uxbridge, ON • L9P 1R1 • Tel: 905-852-2620 • Fax: 905-852-7720 • Contact: Recruiting • E-mail: info@tlcpromotions.ca • Internet: www.tlcpromotions.ca • TLC Promotions Inc. is a national promotions agency specializing in product demonstrations, merchandising, character visits and special events. They have positions across the country with part time flexible hours throughout the year.

TSC STORES LTD. • 1950 Oxford Street East • London, ON • N5V 2Z8 • Tel: 519-453-5270 • Fax: 519-453-6068 • Internet: www.tscstores.com • TSC Stores Ltd. is a wholly owned Canadian company with 24 retail stores in Ontario and a distribution center located in London, Ontario. They have been in the hardware, automotive and farm supply retail sector for over 40 years in Canada.

VALUE VILLAGE STORES • #200 - 3003 St. John's Street • Port Moody, BC • V3H 2C4 • Tel: 604-461-7000 • Fax: 604-461-7001 • Contact: Human Resources • Internet: www.valuevillage.ca • Value Village Stores is a privately owned retail company which sells second hand merchandise. Today they have over 200 locations worldwide. They can be reached on their employment line by calling 604-877-8298.

Understand What Skills Are Important to Employers
The exact personal skills you should possess varies with each job. Some vital skills that employers consider important are communication, leadership, adaptability, and writing skills. Do you possess any or all of these valuable traits?

WESTON PRODUCE INC. • 9625 Yonge Street • Richmond Hill, ON • L4C 5T2 • Tel: 905-883-4800 • Fax: 905-883-4330 • Contact: Human Resources • Internet: www.westonproduce.ca • Weston Produce is a grocery store, otherwise known as F & F Supermarkets. The company has an employee base of approximately 195 individuals.

WINNERS MERCHANTS INTERNATIONAL • 6715 Airport Road • Mississauga, ON • L4V 1Y2 • Tel: 905-405-8000 • Fax: 905-405-7581 • Contact: Human Resources • Internet: www.winners.ca • Winners Merchants International is Canada's leading "off-price" fashion retailer in men's, ladies', kids' wear, and giftware. They have more than 200 stores across Canada. The firm employs approximately 11,000 people across Canada under two banners, Winners and Homesense.

ZELLERS INC. • P.O. Boxm, Station A • Scarborough, ON • M1K 5C1 • Internet: www.zellers.com • Zellers is the leading national chain of discount department stores. It targets the budget-minded customer with the assurance of the lowest price. Excellent values are offered in both national and private brand merchandise and these are communicated aggressively with frequent advertising in both print and electronic media. Zellers is further distinguished by Hbc Rewards, its customer loyalty rewards program. Zellers is successful in its competitive retail segment by operating with a low expense rate. Zellers operates 350 stores across Canada, mainly in shopping malls.

Oil & Mining

AKITA DRILLING LTD. • 311 - 6th Avenue, Suite 900 • Calgary, AB • T2P 3H2 • Tel: 403-292-7979 • Fax: 403-292-7990 • Contact: Human Resources • E-mail: akitainfo@akita-drilling.com • Internet: www.akita-drilling.com • Akita Drilling Ltd. is a premium oil and gas drilling contractor with operations throughout Western Canada and the northern territories. The Company's objective is to be the industry leader in matters of equipment quality, safe and efficient drilling performance by top quality personnel, and overall customer satisfaction. In addition to conventional drilling services, the Company is active in directional, horizontal and underbalanced drilling and provides specialized drilling services to a broad range of independent and multinational oil and gas companies. Akita Drilling employs at full operations approximately 828 people operating 37 drilling rigs in all depth ranges.

BAYTEX ENERGY LIMITED • Bow Valley Square II, 205 - 5th Avenue SW, Suite 2200 • Calgary, AB • T2P 2V7 • Tel: 403-269-4282 • Fax: 403-205-3845 • Contact: Office Manager • E-mail: resumes@baytex.ab.ca • Internet: www.baytex.ab.ca • Baytex Energy is a Canadian Based income trust engaged in the development, acquisition and production of oil and natural gas in the Western Canadian Basin.

BENWELL ATKINS LTD. • 901 Great Northern Way • Vancouver, BC • V5T 1E1 • Tel: 604-872-2326 • Fax: 604-872-4235 • Contact: Human Resources • Internet: www.benwell.com • Established in 1926, Benwell Atkins has grown from a modest Vancouver-based mailing company to being one of Western Canada's most respected printing houses. Now an RR Donnelley Company, Benwell Atkins is part of North America's largest print and print communication service company. They employ more than 100 people.

BETTIS CANADA LTD. • 4112 - 91A Street NW • Edmonton, AB • T6E 5V2 • Tel: 780-450-3600 • Fax: 780-450-1400 • Contact: Personnel Administrator • E-mail: info.Bettis-Canada@EmersonProcess.com • Internet: www.bettis.com • Bettis' roots go back to 1929 when it was established as an oilfield supply house and manufacturer's representative. The company later evolved into a manufacturing organization, becoming a pioneer in the valve actuation business.

Today, Bettis is the world's leading independent manufacturer of pneumatic and hydraulic valve actuators. Bettis products are used in almost every energy related industry including on and offshore oil and gas transmission, petrochemical and petroleum refining. Other significant markets include chemical, power industry including nuclear, pulp and paper, food and beverage, pharmaceutical, textile and water systems. The company has potential in virtually any market where valves are operated automatically.

BJ SERVICES COMPANY • 1300, 801 - 6 Avenue SW • Calgary, AB • T2P 4E1 • Tel: 403-531-5151 • Fax: 403-296-1550 • Contact: Human Resources • Internet: www.bjservices.com • BJ Services Company is a leading provider of pressure pumping services worldwide. BJ also provides casing and tubular running services, process plant and pipeline services, and specialty chemical services in selected geographic markets.

CAMBIOR INC. • 1111, St-Charles Street West, East Tower, Suite 750 • Longueuil, QC • J4K 5G4 • Tel: 450-677-0040 • Fax: 450-677-3382 • Contact: Human Resources • E-mail: careers@cambior.com • Internet: www.cambior.com • Cambior is the largest gold producer in Quebec and the fifth largest in Canada, as well as the third largest producer of niobium in the world, with operating and exploration activities in Canada, the United States, Peru, Guyana, Suriname and French Guiana.

CAMECO CORPORATION • 2121 - 11th Street West • Saskatoon, SK • S7M 1J3 • Tel: 306-956-6200 • Fax: 306-956-6201 • Internet: www.cameco.com • Cameco, with its head office in Saskatoon, Saskatchewan, is the world's largest uranium supplier. The company's uranium products are used to generate electricity in nuclear energy plants around the world, providing one of the cleanest sources of energy available today. Cameco's shares trade on the Toronto and New York stock exchanges.

CHEVRON CANADA LTD. • 1500 - 1050 West Pender Street • Vancouver, BC • V6E 3T4 • Tel: 604-668-5300 • Fax: 604-668-5545 • Contact: Human Resources Division • E-mail: bccareers@chevron.com • Internet: www.chevron.ca • Chevron Canada is a British Columbia based company with retail and commercial fueling operations and lubricants distribution throughout the province. Chevron employs over 350 people, in addition to over 2,500 indirect employees in its retail and commercial networks, making it one of the major companies operating on Canada's west coast. The company is a wholly owned subsidiary of the ChevronTexaco Corporation.

ENCANA • 855 - 2nd Street, Suite 1800 • Calgary, AB • T2P 2S5 • Tel: 403-645-2000 • 403-645-3400 • Internet: www.encana.com • EnCana is the largest independent natural gas producer in North America with one of the largest proven reserves bases among independent oil and gas companies.

HALLIBURTON GROUP CANADA INC. • 645 - 7th Avenue, Suite 1600 • Calgary, AB • T2P 4G8 • Tel: 403-231-9300 • Internet: www.halliburton.com • Founded in 1919, Halliburton is one of the world's largest providers of products and services to the oil and gas industries. The company provides and integrates products and services, starting with exploration and development, moving through production, operations, maintenance, conversion and refining, to infrastructure and abandonment. Halliburton employs more than 100,000 people in nearly 70 countries working in five major operating groups: Energy Services, Drilling and Formation Evaluation, Fluids, Production Optimization, and Landmark and other Energy Services.

IMPERIAL OIL LIMITED • 237 - 4th Avenue, P.O. Box 2480, Station M • Calgary, AB • T2P 3M9 • Fax: 403-237-4017 • Contact: Human Resources Department • E-mail: campus.recruitment@esso.ca • Internet: www.imperialoil.ca • Imperial is one of Canada's largest producer of crude oil, a major producer of natural gas and a major supplier of petrochemicals. It is also the largest refiner and marketer of petroleum products sold primarily under the Esso brand, with a coast-to-coast supply network. They employ approximately 6,600 individuals across the country.

KINROSS GOLD CORP. • 40 King Street West, 52nd Floor • Toronto, ON • M5H 3Y2 • Tel: 416-365-5123 • Fax: 416-363-6622 • Contact: Human Resources Department • E-mail: info@kinross.com • Internet: www.kinross.com • Kinross Gold Corporation, a world-class gold company based in Canada, was established in 1993 and has since grown to become the third largest primary gold producer in North America by reserves. With nine mines in stable countries including the United States, Brazil, Chile and Russia, Kinross employs more than 5,000 people worldwide.

NATCO CANADA LTD. • 9423 Shephard Road S.E. • Calgary, AB • T2H 2H3 • Tel: 403-236-1850 • Fax: 403-236-0488 • Internet: www.natcogroup.com • NATCO Canada has been serving the oil & gas production, refining and distribution markets with quality process design, equipment and service, both onshore and offshore.

PARKLAND INDUSTRIES LTD. • Riverside Office Plaza • 4919 - 59th Street, Suite 236 • Red Deer, AB • T4N 6C9 • Tel: 403-357-6400 • Fax: 403-347-8795 • E-mail: hrinfo@parkland.ca • Internet: www.parkland.ca • Parkland Income Fund is an unincorporated, open-ended limited purpose mutual fund trust established under the laws of the Province of Alberta on April 30, 2002. The Fund was created to acquire the fuel marketing, convenience stores and related ancillary businesses formerly owned by Parkland Industries Ltd. The conversion to a Fund was undertaken to unlock the value of significant cash flow generated by the business and to provide an enhanced platform for growth.

PEMBINA PIPELINE CORPORATION • 700 - 9th Avenue S.W., Suite 2000 • Calgary, AB • T2P 3V4 • Tel: 403-231-7500 • Fax: 403-266-1155 • Contact: Human Resources Advisor • E-mail: careers@pembina.com • Internet: www.pembina.com • Pembina Pipeline Income Fund is a publicly traded Canadian income fund engaged, through its operating subsidiaries, in the transportation of light conventional and synthetic crude oil, condensate and natural gas liquids in Western Canada.

POTASHCORP • 122 - 1st Avenue South, Suite 500 • Saskatoon, SK • S7K 7G3 • Tel: 306-933-8500 • Fax: 306-652-2699 • Contact: Human Resources • Internet: www.potashcorp.com • PotashCorp is the world's largest integrated producer of nitrogen, phosphate and potash. As a three-nutrient company, PotashCorp is one of the world's largest producers of fertilizer products, serving global agriculture. With the most animal feed production capacity in the world, it supplies feed ingredients that help animals grow. PotashCorp is also a major industrial supplier as the world's largest producer of industrial nitrogen products and one of only two North American industrial phosphate producers. PotashCorp's products come from seven potash operations in Canada and one potassium nitrate plant in Chile; six phosphate operations in the United States and one in Brazil; and four nitrogen plants in the United States and a large complex in Trinidad.

QUÉBEC CARTIER MINING COMPANY • 24 des lies-Boulevard, Suite 201 • Port Cartier, QC • G5B 2H3 • Tel: 418-766-2000 • Fax: 418-768-2128 • Contact: Human Resources • E-mail: employment@qcmines.com • Internet: www.qcmines.com • Québec Cartier Mining Company is one of the leading producers of iron ore products in North America. The company operates an open pit mine and a crusher/concentrator facility capable of producing 18 million metric tonnes of iron ore concentrates annually at Mont-Wright in Northern Québec. The company also operates a pellet plant with an annual production capacity of some nine million metric tonnes of iron ore pellets at Port-Cartier, Québec on the North shore of the Gulf of St. Lawrence.

SHAWCOR LTD. • 25 Bethridge Road • Toronto, ON • M9W 1M7 • Tel: 416-743-7111 • Fax: 416-743-7199 • Contact: Human Resources • Internet: www.shawcor.com • ShawCor is a global energy services company specializing in products and services for the pipeline, exploration and production, and petrochemical and industrial segments of the oil and gas industry and other industrial markets. ShawCor operates through seven wholly owned business units: Bredero Shaw, Shaw Pipeline Services, Canusa-CPS, OMSCO, Guardian, DSG-Canusa and ShawFlex. Manufacturing, service facilities and sales offices, staffed by more than 5,000 employees, are located in over 20 countries around the world.

SUNCOR ENERGY INC. • Box 38, 112 - 4th Avenue SW • Calgary, AB • T2P 2V5 • Tel: 403-269-8100 • Fax: 403-269-6200 • Internet: www.suncor.com • Suncor Energy Inc. is a unique and sustainable Canadian integrated energy company dedicated to vigorous growth. The company is a world leader in oil sands development, a high-performing natural gas producer and one of the top five petroleum refiners and marketers in the country. Suncor's aggressive plans for the future are fuelled by a strong management team and energetic workforce who think creatively, set bold objectives and deliver on them. Safety is a core value in our company and an expectation of all employees.

SYNCRUDE CANADA LTD. • P.O. Bag 4023 • Fort McMurray, AB • T9H 3H5 • Tel: 780-790-6192 • Fax: 780-790-6186 • Contact: Human Resources • E-mail: info@syncrude.com • Internet: www.syncrude.com • Syncrude Canada Ltd. is the world's largest producer of crude oil from oil sands and the largest single source producer in Canada. We currently supply 15 percent of the nation's petroleum requirements.

TECK COMINCO LIMITED • 200 Burrard Street, Suite 600 • Vancouver, BC • V6C 3L9 • Tel: 604-687-1117 • Fax: 604-685-3091 • Contact: Human Resources • E-mail: hr@teckcominco.com • Internet: www.teckcominco.com • Teck Cominco Limited, based in Vancouver B.C., is a diversified mining and refining company and is a world leader in the production of metallurgical coal and zinc, in addition to being a major producer of copper and gold.

TERASEN INC. • 1111 West Georgia Street • Vancouver, BC • V6E 4M4 • Tel: 604-443-6500 • Contact: Human Resources • E-mailinfo@terasen.com • Internet: www.terasen.com • Terasen Inc. is a 100% shareholder-owned company in the businesses of energy distribution, energy transportation, and providing utility and energy products and services.

VALE INCO • 200 Bay Street, Royal Bank Plaza, Suite 1600 • Toronto, ON • M5J 2K2 • Tel: 416-361-7511 • Fax: 416-361-7781 • Internet: www.inco.com • VALE INCO is one of the world's premier mining and metals companies. It is a producer of nickel, copper, cobalt, and other precious metals. The company also manufacturers high performance alloy components such as nickel alloys, blades, rings, discs, and other forged and precision machine components for industrial applications. The company also produces sulphuric acid and liquid sulphur dioxide. INCO employs approximately 10,000 individuals and has properties, operations and markets around the world. To view and apply to employment opportunities, visit the Careers Page.

Understand that Jobs Are Won In Interviews
Jobs are won in the interview! Anticipate the questions that may be asked and plan honest, high-impact answers. Go through mock interviews to become more familiar with, and effective in, various interview situations.

Printing, Publishing & Forestry

ABITIBIBOWATER • 1155 Metcalfe Street, Suite 800 • Montreal, QC • H3B 5H2 • Tel: 514-875-2160 • Contact: Human Resources • Internet: www.abitibibowater.com • AbitibiBowater Inc. is a global leader in newprint and uncoated groundwood papers as well as a major producer of wood products. With over 15,000 employees, the company does business in approximately 70 countries.

CANFOR • 1700 West 75th Avenue, Sute 100 • Vancouver, BC • V6P 6G2 • Tel: 604-661-5241 • Fax: 604-661-5235 • Contact: Human Resources • E-mail: info@canfor.ca • Internet: www. canfor.com • Slocan has merged with Canfor. Canfor is a leading integrated forest products company based in Vancouver, British Columbia. The company is the largest producer of softwood lumber and one of the largest producers of northern softwood kraft pulp in Canada. Canfor also produces kraft paper, plywood, remanufactured lumber products, oriented strand board (OSB), hardboard paneling and a range of specialized wood products, including baled fibre and fibre mat at 34 facilities located in BC, Alberta and Quebec. Canfor employs approximately 7300 people as well as an additional 2200 contractors.

DIRECTWEST PUBLISHERS LTD. • 200 - 2550 Sandra Schmirler Way • Regina, SK • S4W 1A1 • Tel: 306-777-0333 • Fax: 306-652-6514 • Contact: Human Resources Manager • Internet: www.directwest.com • DirectWest Publishers is the publisher of SaskTel's telephone directory and Yellow Pages™ publishing agent. DirectWest brings reachs just about every Saskatchewan consumer through guaranteed delivery to homes, offices, stores and phone booths. DirectWest employs over 100 people in Saskatchewan.

DOMTAR INC. • 395 de Maisonneuve Blvd. West • Montreal, QC • H3A 1L6 • Tel: 514-848-5555 • Contact: Human Resources • Internet: www.domtar.com • Domtar is the second largest producer of uncoated free sheet in North America and the third largest in the world. It is also a leading manufacturer of printing, publishing, specialty and technical papers. Domtar manages close to 36 million acres of forest land in Canada and the United States, and is a major lumber manufacturer in eastern North America. Domtar has 11,000 employees across North America.

DUHA COLOR SERVICES • 750 Bradford Street • Winnipeg, MB • R3H 0N3 • Tel: 204-786-8961 • Fax: 204-885-3762 • Contact: Human Resources • E-mail: hr@duhagroup.com • Internet: www.duhagroup.com • Duha Color Services is a manufacturer of customized merchandising aids and colour systems, including paint strips and colour cards for paint and auto industries around the world.

DUN & BRADSTREET CANADA • 5770 Hurontario Street • Mississauga, ON • L5R 3G5 • Tel: 1-800-463-6362 • Fax: 1-800-668-7800 • Contact: Human Resources • E-mail: careers@dnb.com • Internet: www.dnb.ca • Dun & Bradstreet Canada is engaged in the provision of information processing services. The company provides consulting and market analysis services to a wide range of individual and business clientele. Dun & Bradstreet Canada employs over 400 individuals.

FRIESENS CORPORATION • One Printers Way • Altona, MB • R0G 0B0 • Tel: 204-324-6401 • Fax: 204-324-1333 • Contact: Human Resources Manager • E-mail: hr@friesens.com • Internet: www.friesens.com • Friesens Corporation is a book manufacturing company that is involved in the printing and binding of many different types of books. The firm produces books, calendars, and yearbooks. They employ over 600 individuals.

MCGRAW HILL RYERSON LTD. • 300 Water Street • Whitby, ON • L1N 9B6 • Tel: 905-430-5049 • Fax: 905-430-5227 • Contact: Ms. Nancy Pavlakovich, Human Resources • E-mail: career@mcgrawhill.ca • Internet: www.mcgrawhill.ca • McGraw Hill Ryerson Ltd. is a publishing company made up of three revenue divisions - higher education, school and trade, professional and medical. The firm has more than 1,000 Canadian produced books in print representing about 800 authors. In a year, McGraw Hill Ryerson publishes an average of 100 English language books. They employ about 290 individuals.

METROLAND PRINTING, PUBLISHING & DISTRIBUTING LTD. • 3125 Wolfedale Road • Mississauga, ON • L5C 1W1 • Tel: 905-279-0440 • Fax: 905-279-5103 • Contact: Human Resources • Internet: www.metroland.com • Metroland, Ontario's largest and most successful community newspaper publisher provides local news and advertising media/info in Canada's heartland. They currently publish 100 community newspapers with a total of 132 editions that are concentrated in southern Ontario and centered on Toronto.

MINAS BASIN PULP AND POWER COMPANY LTD. • P.O. Box 401, 53 Prince Street • Hantsport, NS • B0P 1P0 • Tel: 902-684-1313 • Fax: 902-684-1762 • Contact: Ms. Janet Thomas, Human Resources Manager • E-mail: jthomas@minas.ns.ca • Internet: www.minas.ns.ca • Minas Basin Pulp and Power Company manufactures coreboard and linerboard products from 100% recycled material. The firm employs approximately 162 individuals.

PEARSON CANADA INC. • 26 Prince Andrew Place • Toronto, ON • M3C 2T8 • Tel: 416-447-5101 • Fax: 416-447-0598 • Contact: Paula Hunter, Human Resources • Email: paula.hunter@pearsoncanada.com • Internet: www.pearsoned.ca • Pearson Canada Inc., a division of the world's leading educational and technology publisher, is owned by Pearson plc. As the largest publisher in Canada, Pearson Canada has an established reputation for producing market-leading educational products and services as well as a comprehensive range of best-selling consumer, technical and professional titles.

QUEBECOR MEDIA INC. • 612 Saint-Hacques Street • Montréal, QC • H3C 4M8 • Tel: 514-380-6110 • Fax: 514-380-1919 • Contact: Ressources humaines • Internet: www.quebecor.com • Quebecor Media is a communications company with operations in North America, Europe, Latin America and Asia. It has two operating subsidiaries, Quebecor World Inc. and Quebecor Media Inc. Quebecor World is one of the largest commercial print media services company in the world. Quebecor Media owns operating companies in numerous media-related businesses. In all, Quebecor Inc. has operations in 17 countries.

READER'S DIGEST ASSOCIATION OF CANADA LTD. • 1100 René-Lévesque Blvd. West • Montreal, QC • H3B 5H5 • Tel: 514-940-0751 • Fax: 514-940-7360 • Contact: Human Resources • E-mail: cv.ca@readersdigest.com • Internet: www.readersdigest.ca • Reader's Digest is the preeminent global leader in publishing and direct marketing of distinctive products that inform, enrich, entertain, and inspire people of all ages and all cultures, around the world.

REGAL GIFTS • 130 Bell Farm Road, Units 2 & 3 • Barrie, ON • L4M 6J4 • Internet: www.regalgreetings.com • Regal Gifts Corporation is an e-commerce, catalogue and direct marketing company operating in Canada using the Regal brand which has been part of the Canadian landscape for 8 decades. Regal Gifts re-entered the market in February of 2006, as the dominant player in the gift and gadget market for the direct selling industry in Canada.

ROGERS MEDIA, PUBLISHING • One Mount Pleasant Road • Toronto, ON • M4Y 2Y5 • Tel: 416-596-5523 • Fax: 416-596-2510 • Contact: Human Resources • E-mail: service@rmpublishing.com • Internet: www.rogersmagazines.com • Rogers Media, Publishing is Canada's largest publishing company. It owns many of Canada's best-known consumer magazines as well as the country's most respected business and professional publications.

SCHOLASTIC CANADA LTD. • 175 Hillmount Road • Markham, ON • L6C 1Z7 • Tel: 905-887-7323 • Fax: 905-887-3639 • Contact: Human Resources • E-mail: resumes@scholastic.ca • Internet: www.scholastic.ca • Scholastic Canada is one of the country's leading publishers and distributors of children's books and educational materials in both official languages. From coast to coast, Scholastic Canada employs approximately 800 Canadians, both full- and part-time.

SUNDOG PRINTING LIMITED • 1311 - 9th Avenue SW • Calgary, AB • T3C 0H9 • Tel: 403-264-8450 • Fax: 403-294-1496 • Contact: Human Resources • Internet: www.sundogprint.com • Since 1971, Sundog has grown from a small copying and instant print company to one of western Canada's leading print and pre-press facilities. They were among Canada's first printers to offer the advanced capabilities of CPC computer control on Heidelberg Speedmaster presses. A very early implementation of PostScript workflows utilizing Macintosh computers overtook previous manual pre-press methods in the late 1980's. Another Sundog first among Canadian printers was the installation of high-end Scitex electronic pre-press systems to further their role as a leader in PostScript/electronic pre-press services.

TELDON INTERNATIONAL INC. • 100 - 12751 Vulcan Way • Richmond, BC • V6C 3C8 • Tel: 604-273-4500 • Fax: 604-273-6100 • Contact: Human Resources • E-mail: jobs@teldon.com • Internet: www.teldon.com • Teldon is a leading marketer, manufacturer and distributor in the North American promotional product industry. For over 35 years, their customers have used their personalized promotional products as practical relationship-marketing tools to grow their businesses.

TELEGRAPH JOURNAL • P.O. Box 2350, 210 Crown Street • Saint John, NB • E2L 3V8 • Tel: 506-632-8888 • Fax: 506-633-6758 • Contact: Human Resources • Internet: www.telegraphjournal.com • The Saint John Telegraph Journal is Saint John's foremost daily newspaper bringing southwestern New Brunswickers local, national and global news. It is published Monday to Saturday each week. With an average daily circulation of more than 26,000 copies, and a readership of more than 55,000, the paper is growing right along with the city's economy, and is a valuable tool to both advertisers and readers in their day-to-day lives.

TEMBEC PAPER GROUP • 10 chemin Gatineau, P.O. Box 5000 • Temiscaming, QC • J0Z 3R0 • Tel: 819-627-4387 • Fax: 819-627-1178 • Contact: Human Resources • E-mail: human.resources@tembec.com • Internet: www.tembec.com • Tembec is a leading integrated Canadian forest products company principally involved in the production of wood products, market pulp and papers. With sales of over $3.5 billion dollars, the Company operates over 55 manufacturing units in the Canadian provinces of New Brunswick, Quebec, Ontario, Manitoba, Alberta and British Columbia, as well as in France, the United States and Chile. It employs approximately 8000 people.

TORONTO SUN PUBLISHING CORP., THE • 333 King Street East • Toronto, ON • M5A 3X5 • Tel: 416-947-2222 • Fax: 416-368-0374 • Contact: Human Resources • Internet: www.torontosun.com • Toronto Sun Publishing is a newspaper publishing company offering five major dailies in Canada. These newspaper dailies are operated in Toronto, Ottawa, Calgary, and Edmonton. The organization also owns community newspapers in Florida, and a commercial print press in Washington, D.C. Toronto Sun Publishing has over 2,700 employees.

TRANSCONTINENTAL DIGITAL SERVICES INC. • 1 Place Ville Marie • Montreal, QC • H3B 3N2 • Tel: 514-954-4000 • Fax: 514-954-4016 • Contact: Human Resources • Internet: www.transcontinental.com • Transcontinental Digital Services is a graphic arts company that is involved in prepress, design, photography, desktop page assembly and film output.

VANCOUVER SUN • 200 Granville Street, Suite 1 • Vancouver, BC • V6C 3N3 • Tel: 604-605-2000 • Fax: 604-605-2308 • Contact: Human Resources • Internet: www.canada.com/vancouversun • The Vancouver Sun is one of two major daily papers in British Columbia, published by Pacific Newspaper Group Inc., a CanWest company. The Vancouver Sun has been a daily newspaper since 1912, and it is published daily except Sundays and selected holidays.

WEYERHAEUSER COMPANY LIMITED • 925 West Georgia Street • Vancouver, BC • V6C 3L2 • Tel: 604-661-8000 • Internet: www.weyerhaeuser.com • Weyerhaeuser is an international forest products company whose principal businesses are the growing and harvesting of trees; the manufacture, distribution and sale of forest products, including logs, wood chips, building products, pulp, paper and packaging products; and real estate construction and development.

WILDERNESS REFORESTATION • 120 Mills Drive, P.O. Box 1400 • Wawa, ON • P0S 1K0 • Tel: 705-856-2799 • Fax: 705-856-1365 • Contact: Ms. Johanna Rowe, Personnel Manager • E-mail: jorowe@wilderness.on.ca • Internet: www.wilderness.on.ca • The Wilderness Group has been involved in the silviculture industry since 1986. Wilderness and their employees have planted more than 250 million seedlings and have thinned, sprayed, surveyed and GPS'd tens of thousands of hectares of forest. They are proud to have been involved in the regeneration of more than 150,000 hectares of clear cut forest. The Wilderness Group employs more than 700 skilled individuals at peak times of the year. They recruit from colleges and universities across the country.

Social Services

ALBERTA ALCOHOL AND DRUG ABUSE COMMISSION • 10909 Jasper Avenue, 6th Floor • Edmonton, AB • T5J 3M9 • Tel: 780-427-7935 • Fax: 780-427-1436 • Contact: Ms. Michelle Gosselin, Staffing Assistant • E-mail: hr@aadac.gov.ab.ca • Internet: www.aadac.com • As an agency of the Government of Alberta, The Alberta Alcohol and Drug Abuse Commission (AADAC) operates and funds information, prevention and treatment services to help Albertans with alcohol, other drug and gambling problems.

ALBERTA CANCER BOARD • 1220, 10405 Jasper Avenue • Edmonton, AB • T5J 3N4 • Tel: 780-643-4640 • Fax: 780-643-4556 • Contact: Human Resources • E-mail: careers@cancerboard.ab.ca • Internet: www.cancerboard.ab.ca • The Alberta Cancer Board is mandated by the government of Alberta under the Cancer Programs Act to coordinate all cancer research, prevention and treatment programs in the province of Alberta. Its services include cancer prevention and screening, patient and professional education, diagnosis and treatment, and basic and applied research. It is able to integrate research efforts with clinical practice, ensuring that Albertans benefit from the latest scientific advances in cancer treatment.

ALGOMA FAMILY SERVICES • 205 McNabb Street • Sault Ste. Marie, ON • P6B 1Y3 • Tel: 705-945-5050 • Fax: 705-945-9306 • Contact: Human Resources • E-mail: hr@algomafamilyservices.org • Internet: www.algomafamilyservices.org • Algoma Family Services is a non-profit, charitable organization providing high quality support services to individuals, children, adults, and families as part of the Algoma District system of care.

Become a Salesperson
How are you going to sell yourself to employers? Market your product (yourself) according to the needs of your intended market (potential employers). This type of sales strategy will undoubtedly lead to success!

ARBOR MEMORIAL SERVICES INC. • 2 Jane Street • Toronto, ON • M6S 4W8 • Tel: 416-763-3230 • Fax: 416-763-8714 • Contact: Human Resources • Email: hrdept@arbormemorial.com • Internet: www.arbormemorial.com • Established in 1947, Arbor Memorial Services Incorporated is a proudly Canadian company, engaged in providing interment rights, cremations, funerals, associated merchandise and services to thousands of families each year in all provinces except Newfoundland and Prince Edward Island.

BARTON PLACE LONG TERM CARE FACILITY • 914 Bathurst Street • Toronto, ON • M5R 3G5 • Tel: 416-533-9473 • Fax: 416-538-2685 • Contact: Human Resources • E-mail: kptacek@ bartonplace.ca • Barton Place Long Term Care Facility nursing home with approximately 150-300 beds, located near downtown Toronto.

BETEL HOME FOUNDATION • 212 Manchester Avenue • Selkirk, MB • R1A 0B6 • Tel: 204-482-5469 • Fax: 204-482-4651 • Contact: Human Resources • E-mail: hr@irha.mb.ca • Internet: www.betelhomefoundation.ca • Betel Home Foundation is a multi-disciplinary residential care facility established in Selkirk, Manitoba, in 1915. The facility uses a team approach to establish common goals regarding the care of residents. Betel houses 93 residents and has six wings accommodating 62 single rooms and 15 double rooms. Physician and nursing care along with occupational therapy is provided on-site. The residential facility employs approximately 100 individuals.

BETHANIA MENNONITE PERSONAL CARE HOME INC. • 1045 Concordia Avenue • Winnipeg, MB • R2K 3S7 • Tel: 204-667-0795 • Fax: 204-667-7078 • Contact: Administrator • Internet: http://bethania.mennonite.net • Bethania Mennonite Personal Care Home is a private, non-profit company founded in 1945 by the Mennonite Benevolent Society, and has been at its present location since 1970. Bethania has rooms to accommodate 140 people, and is funded from sources including the Manitoba government, fees paid by residents, and private donations. The personal care home has a total of 148 long term care beds, and employs approximately 240 individuals.

CANADA GAMES AQUATIC CENTRE • 50 Union Street • Saint John, NB • E2L 1A1 • Tel: 506-658-4715 • Fax: 506-658-4730 • Contact: Human Resources • E-mail: aquatics@nbnet.nb.ca • Internet: www.aquatics.nb.ca • The Canada Games Aquatic Centre is a recreation and programs facility in Saint John, New Brunswick. The Centre provides many swimming and fitness programs aimed towards health and wellness.

CANADIAN CANCER SOCIETY • 10 Alcorn Avenue, Suite 200 • Toronto, ON • M4T 2W6 • Tel: 416-961-7223 • Fax: 416-961-4189 • Contact: Human Resources Department • E-mail: hr@ cancer.ca • Internet: www.cancer.ca • The Canadian Cancer Society is a national, community-based organization whose mission is to eradicate cancer and to improve the quality of life of people living with cancer. Across Canada, the Society's 220,000 volunteers, supported by approximately 840 full-time staff, carry out public education programs, provide services for cancer patients and their families, support healthy public health policies and organize fundraising events.

CANADIAN INSTITUTE FOR HEALTH INFORMATION • 495 Richmond Road, Suite 600 • Ottawa, ON • K2A 4H6 • Tel: 613-241-7860 • Fax: 613-241-8120 • Contact: Human Resources • Email: careers@cihi.ca • Internet: www.cihi.ca • The Canadian Institute for Health Information (CIHI) is an independent, pan-Canadian, not-for-profit organization working to improve the health of Canadians and the health care system by providing quality health information. CIHI's mandate, as established by Canada's health ministers, is to coordinate the development and maintenance of a common approach to health information for Canada. To this end, CIHI is responsible for providing accurate and timely information that is needed to establish sound health policies, manage the Canadian health system effectively and create public awareness of factors affecting good health.

CANADIAN NATIONAL INSTITUTE FOR THE BLIND • 1929 Bayview Avenue • Toronto, ON • M4G 3E8 • Tel: 416-486-2500 • Fax: 416-480-7700 • E-mail: resumes@cnib.ca • Internet: www.cnib.ca • The Canadian National Institute for the Blind (CNIB) is a private, voluntary, not-for-profit organization providing rehabilitation and library services to blind, visually impaired and deaf-blind persons across Canada. The basic aim of CNIB is to help blind and visually impaired people find ways to lead satisfying lives. They work to achieve this goal by providing core services including counselling and referral, sight enhancement, technical aids, and career development and employment among others. Approximately 10,000 volunteers and 1,100 staff work at the CNIB.

CANCERCARE MANITOBA • 675 McDermot Avenue • Winnipeg, MB • R3V 0V9 • Tel: 204-787-2305 • Contact: Ms. Ardelle Jacques, Human Resources Co-ordinator • Internet: www.cancercare.mb.ca • CancerCare Manitoba (CCMB) is charged by an Act of the legislature of Manitoba with responsibility for cancer prevention, detection, care, research and education for the people of Manitoba. As a Centre of choice, CCMB is dedicated to enhancing the quality of life for those living with cancer and blood disorders, and to improving control of cancer for all Manitobans.

CATHOLIC CHILDREN'S AID SOCIETY FOUNDATION • 26 Maitland Street • Toronto, ON • M4Y 1C6 • Tel: 416-395-1500 • Fax: 416-395-1581 • Contact: Human Resource Services • E-mail: hrs@ccas.toronto.on.ca • Internet: www.ccas.toronto.on.ca • The Catholic Children's Aid Society Foundation provides child welfare services and family support programs to individuals throughout the community. With 10 locations in the Toronto region, the agency employs approximately 600 staff in its provision of child protection services to children and youth.

CHILDREN'S AID SOCIETY OF TORONTO • 30 Isabella Street • Toronto, ON • M4Y 1N1 • Tel: 416-924 4646 • Fax: 416-324-2400 • Internet: www.torontocas.ca • The Children's Aid Society of Toronto provides child protection services to the non-Catholic, non-Jewish population of Toronto. Front line workers investigate allegations of abuse and neglect, help families in the community and admit children into foster care if their parents are not able to care for them. Child and youth workers provide a therapeutic milieu for children in assessment and treatment placement. Volunteer activities are a major source of support to our staff and such assignments provide students with exposure to the field when making a career decision and/or applying to a professional school in the field.

CHRISTIAN HORIZONS • 4278 King Street East • Kitchener, ON • N2P 2G5 • Tel: 519-650-0966 • Fax: 519-650-8984 • Contact: Human Resources • Internet: www.christian-horizons.org • Christian Horizons is a non-denominational evangelical Christian not-for-profit organization supporting individuals with developmental disabilities across Ontario through the provision of residential and other support services. The organization covers five Districts in Ontario with over 157 locations.

COMCARE HEALTH SERVICES • 210 - 339 Wellington Road South • London, ON • N6C 4P8 • Tel: 519-432-3726 • Fax: 519-432-3731 • Contact: Human Resources Department • Internet: www.comcarehealth.ca • Comcare is a Canadian company now operating in its fourth decade, with 29 offices from coast to coast. Comcare is the premiere choice for clients in search of health care solutions. Consumers of health services in corporate or community settings can receive a comprehensive range of solutions with the help of Comcare. Interdisciplinary services include Home Support, Nursing, Physiotherapy, Occupational Therapy, Social Work and Speech Language Pathologists.

DUCKS UNLIMITED CANADA • Oak Hammock Marsh Conservation Centre, One Snow Goose Bay, P.O. Box 1160 • Stonewall, MB • R0C 2Z0 • Tel: 204-467-3000 • Fax: 204-467-9028 • Contact: Personnel • E-mail: hr@ducks.ca • Internet: www.ducks.ca • Ducks Unlimited is an international, private, non-profit conservation organization dedicated to the perpetuation and increase of North America's waterfowl resources through restoration, preservation and creation of prime breeding habitat in Canada. Development of this habitat on a multi-use concept benefits wildlife and the general environment and provides water for agriculture, domestic and recreational use. Ducks Unlimited works to foster public understanding of the value of wildlife habitat and a healthy environment.

EXTENDICARE (CANADA) INC. • 3000 Steeles Avenue East, Suite 700 • Markham, ON • L3R 9W2 • Tel: 905-470-4000 • Fax: 905-470-5588 • Contact: Director, Employment Services • E-mail: employment_canada@extendicare.com • Internet: www.extendicare.com • Extendicare operates nursing and retirement centres in Canada and the United States. In Canada, Extendicare provides home care services, health care consulting, hospital management, and development services. Extendicare Health Services employs more than 35,600 people in the United States and Canada.

FOYER VALADE INC. • 450 River Road • Winnipeg, MB • R2M 5M4 • Tel: 204-254-3332 • Fax: 204-254-0329 • Contact: Ms. Edith Alards, Human Resources • Foyer Valade is a personal care home facility established in 1976. The care home contains 115 beds and has an employee base of approximately 150 individuals. The facility is mainly French speaking, therefore staff must be at least partially fluent in the French language. There are many different types of positions that one could be involved with at Foyer Valade.

GAMMA-DYNACARE MEDICAL LABORATORIES • 115 Middair Court • Brampton, ON • L6T 5M3 • Tel: 905-790-3030 • Fax: 905-790-3055 • Contact: Human Resources • Internet: www.gamma-dynacare.ca • Gamma-Dynacare is one of the largest and most respected medical laboratories in Canada. They make a substantial contribution to the Canadian health care system. Gamma-Dynacare was formed in the mid-1990s by the merging of the operations of three prominent Ontario medical diagnostic laboratories. They have built on their many years of combined experience to become one of the largest, most innovative and most responsive providers of laboratory services, information and products in Canada.

GEORGE JEFFREY CHILDREN'S TREATMENT CENTRE • 507 Lillie Street North • Thunder Bay, ON • P7C 4Y8 • Tel: 807-623-4381 • Fax: 807-623-6626 • Contact: Ms. Carolyn Tait, Administrative Coordinator • E-mail: hr@georgejeffrey.com • Internet: www.georgejeffrey.com • Their dynamic team of clinical professionals provide paediatric therapy services to children with physical and developmental disabilities in beautiful Thunder Bay, Ontario.

GIMBEL EYE CENTRE • 4935 40 Avenue NW, Suite 450 • Calgary, AB • T3A 2N1 • Tel: 403-286-3022 • Fax: 403-286-2943 • Contact: Human Resources • E-mail: jshowell @gimbel.com • Internet: www.gimbel.com • The Gimbel Eye Centre is a progressive, sophisticated ophthalmic medical centre. They are one of the largest and busiest ophthalmic out-of-hospital facilities in Canada. The firm has a satellite centre in Edmonton. Their primary specialties are cataract and refractive ophthalmology. They have approximately 100 employees.

GOODWILL INDUSTRIES OF TORONTO • 365 Bloor Street East, Suite 1400 • Toronto, ON • M4W 3L4 • Tel: 416-362-4711 • Fax: 416-815-4790 • Contact: Human Resources • E-mail: hr@goodwill.on.ca • Internet: www.goodwill.on.ca • Goodwill Toronto is a Canadian registered charity that funds and provides a unique range of skill development opportunities and work experience to people facing employment barriers. Since 1935, Goodwill has helped communities build better futures by helping people find gainful employment. Goodwill Toronto is 90 per cent self-reliant through the sale of donated goods and other revenue-generating enterprises.

HOMEWOOD CORP. • 150 Delhi Street • Guelph, ON • N1E 6K9 • Tel: 519-824-1010 • Fax: 519-767-3535 • Contact: Human Resources • E-mail: maciann@homewood.org • Internet: www. homewoodhealth.com • The Homewood Corporation is a multi-faceted health care company providing excellence in specialized mental health and addiction programs; behavioural health services centred around an Employee Assistance Program (EAP); and senior living communities focused on retirement and nursing homes providing a continuum of care to older adults.

HURONIA REGIONAL CENTRE • 700 Memorial Avenue • Orillia, ON • L3V 6L2 • Tel: 705-326-7361 • Fax: 705-326-5269 • Contact: Human Resources • Huronia Regional Centre is a large facility that provides service and support to people with developmental disabilities. The centre employs about 1,000 individuals in total.

KENNEDY LODGE LONG TERM CARE FACILITY • 1400 Kennedy Road • Scarborough, ON • M1P 4V6 • Tel: 416-752-8282 • Fax: 416-752-0645 • Contact: Administrator • E-mail: KennedyLodge@cplodges.com • Internet: www.retirementresidencesreit.com/homes/77/ • Established in 1976 to meet the needs of aging individuals, Kennedy Lodge Long Term Care Facility, features more than 280 beds and provides skilled nursing facilities, social services, and residential care. Kennedy Lodge Nursing Home employs more than 250 individuals to work at its location in Scarborough.

KINGS REGIONAL REHABILITATION CENTRE • 1349 County Home Road, P.O. Box 128 • Waterville, NS • B0P 1V0 • Tel: 902-538-3103 • Fax: 902-538-7022 • Contact: Human Resources • E-mail: hr@krrc.ns.ca • Internet: http://krrc.nsnet.org • Located in Waterville, Nova Scotia, Kings Regional Rehabilitation Centre (KRRC) serves approximately 190 clients. Most are mentally challenged adults with developmental, emotional, behavioral, psychological and/or psychiatric problems. Clients participate in programs that target their individual needs and abilities. Individualized programs may include academic programs and social and vocational training. Clients also have access to a number of professional services including speech-language therapy, nutrition, social work, psychological services, physiotherapy, occupational therapy, nursing, psychiatry and medical services.

LES CENTRES JEUNESSE DE MONTRÉAL • 4675, rue Bélanger Est • Montréal, QC • H1T 1C2 • Tel: 514-858-3903 • Fax: 514-858-3914 • Contact: Ressources humaines • E-mail: recrutement@cjm-iu.gc.ca • Internet: www.centrejeunessedemontreal.qc.ca • Les Centres Jeunesse de Montréal is established to offer psychological services and rehabilitation to children, youth, mothers in difficulty as well as their families. Les Centres Jeunesse de Montréal operates in an urban and multi-ethnic framework. (? - can't read french)

MARITIME LIFE • 3500 Steeles Avenue East • Markham, ON • L3R 0X4 • Tel: 905-946-4050 • Fax: 905-946-3585 • Contact: Human Resources Department • Internet: www.coverme.com • Maritime Life is a life insurance company, providing quality financial protection and investment management services, tailored to customers in every market they do business in. Visit the Careers section at www.manulife.ca to view and apply to current employment opportunities.

MARYVALE ADOLESCENT AND FAMILY SERVICES • 3640 Wells Street • Windsor, ON • N9C 1T9 • Tel: 519-258-0484 • Fax: 519-258-0488 • Contact: Program Manager • E-mail: maryvale@maryvale.ca • Maryvale Adolescent and Family Services is a children's mental health centre which helps young people towards a better tomorrow. The centre is located in Windsor, Ontario.

MEDICAL LABORATORIES OF WINDSOR LIMITED • 1428 Ouellette Avenue, Suite 201 • Windsor, ON • N8X 1K4 • Tel: 519-258-1991 • Fax: 519-258-9505 • Contact: Mr. William Yee, Human Resources • Medical Laboratories of Windsor is involved in the collection and testing of medical laboratory specimens. The company employs about 85 individuals.

ONTARIO MARCH OF DIMES • 10 Overlea Blvd. • Toronto, ON • M4H 1A4 • Tel: 416-425-3463 • Fax: 416-425-8431 • Contact: Human Resources • E-mail: recruitment@marchofdimes.ca • Internet: www.marchofdimes.ca • Ontario March of Dimes is one of the largest charitable rehabilitation organizations in Ontario providing a wide range of services across the province to enhance the independence and community participation of people with physical disabilities.

PEEL CHILDREN'S CENTRE • 85A Aventura Court • Mississauga, ON • L5T 2Y6 • Tel: 905-795-3500 • Fax: 905-696-0350 • Contact: Human Resources • Internet: www.peelcc.org • Established in 1984, Peel Children's Centre is a fully accredited, community-based children's mental health centre. Located centrally within the Region of Peel, the Centre offers a comprehensive continuum of high quality, innovative services to more than 3600 children, youth and their families each year.

REENA • 927 Clarke Avenue West • Thornhill, ON • L4J 8G6 • Tel: 905-889-6484 • Fax: 905-763-1862 • Contact: Human Resources Coordinator • E-mail: hr@reena.org • Internet: www.reena.org • Reena is a non-profit social service agency dedicated to integrating individuals who have a developmental disability into the mainstream of society. Reena was established in 1973 by parents of children with developmental disabilities, as a practical alternative to institutions. They provide services to close to 1000 people who have a developmentally disability and their families.

REGIONAL RESIDENTIAL SERVICES SOCIETY • 202 Brownlow Avenue, Suite LKD1 • Dartmouth, NS • B3B 1T5 • Tel: 902-465-4022 • Fax: 902-465-3124 • Contact: Tim Perry, Human Resources Manager • E-mail: tim.perry@rrss.ns.ca • Internet: www.rrss.ns.ca • The Regional Residential Services Society (RRSS) is a non-profit agency, employing over 400 full time, part time, and casual relief staff. The agency's mission is to meet the residential needs of intellectually disabled adults from within the Metro Halifax area. Prospective employees must be able to do shift work, especially evenings, overnights and weekends.

REHABILITATION INSTITUTE OF TORONTO • 550 University Avenue • Toronto, ON • M5G 2A2 • Tel: 416-597-3422 • Fax: 416-597-6626 • Contact: Human Resources • Internet: www.torontorehab.com • The Rehabilitation Institute of Toronto (RIT) is Canada's largest provider of adult rehabilitation services and is a fully affiliated teaching hospital of the University of Toronto. They have experts on many diseases and conditions. These clinicians, researchers and other specialists are involved with our six main areas of patient care: cardiac rehab, spinal cord rehab, musculoskeletal rehab, neuro rehab, geriatric rehab, and complex continuing care (for people with complex medical conditions such as Alzheimer's disease and cerebral palsy).

SCIEX MDS HEALTH GROUP • 71 Four Valley Drive • Concord, ON • L4K 4V8 • Tel: 905-660-9005 • Fax: 905-660-2600 • Contact: Human Resources • Internet: www.sciex.com • MDS Sciex is a leading global supplier of analytical instruments and technology solutions. The company's advanced technologies play a key role in drug discovery and development in the pharmaceutical and biotechnology markets. MDS Sciex researches, designs and produces mass spectrometers and scientific instruments. MDS Sciex is the analytical instruments and the technology solutions division of MDS Inc.

Go On Informational Interviews
Even if a company is not hiring, ask an individual if you may take a few minutes of their time to talk to them about their business. You will gain a wealth of information and your enthusiasm will make a great impression as well.

SHERBROOKE COMMUNITY CENTRE • 401 Acadia Drive • Saskatoon, SK • S7H 2E7 • Tel: 306-655-3642 • Fax: 306-655-3727 • Contact: Human Resources • Email: ida.mikytyshyn@ saskatoonhealthregion.ca • Internet: www.sherbrookecommunitycentre.ca • Sherbrooke Community Centre is a long term care home that provides services for physically and mentally handicapped individuals, along with the elderly. Established in 1966, the facility has a total of 270 long term care beds, and employs approximately 500 individuals.

SKILLS SOCIETY • 203 Parkington Plaza, 10408 - 124 Street • Edmonton, AB • T5N 1R5 • Tel: 780-496-9686 • Fax: 780-482-6395 • Contact: Human Resources Manager • E-mail: jobs@ skillsedm.com • Internet: www.skillsedm.com • Skills Training and Support Services Association is a non-profit organization governed by a volunteer board of directors. Services are offered in the community and enable people with disabilities of all ages to realize their potential for growth and independence.

ST. AMANT CENTRE INC. • 440 River Road • Winnipeg, MB • R2M 3Z9 • Tel: 204-256-4301 • Fax: 204-257-4349 • Contact: Human Resources • E-mail: employment@stamant.mb.ca • Internet: www.stamant.mb.ca • A non-profit corporation, St. Amant offers a wide range of programming, services and care to support individuals with a developmental disability, acquired brain injury or autism and their families. Services include a large main residence, more than 50 community sites and homes, a research centre, a school and a daycare. Among other services, St. Amant offers an effective program for children with autism and for families who care for an individual with a developmental disability at home. Each year, St. Amant helps 1,000 Manitoba families.

ST. PAUL ABILITIES NETWORK • 4637 - 45 Avenue • St. Paul, AB • T0A 3A3 • Tel: 780-645-3441 • Fax: 780-645-1885 • Contact: Mr. Eugene McCafferty, Human Resource Manager • E-mail: hr@spanet.ab.ca • Internet: www.stpaulabilitiesnetwork.ca • St. Paul Abilities Network provides services to persons with disabilities, with in their homes and the community to assist them and their families to enjoy the highest quality of life possible.

SURREY PLACE CENTRE • 2 Surrey Place • Toronto, ON • M5S 2C2 • Tel: 416-925-5141 • Fax: 416-925-5645 • Contact: Human Resources • E-mail: hr@surreyplace.on.ca • Internet: www.surreyplace.on.ca • Surrey Place Centre is a leading community-based organization in Toronto providing complex diagnostics, counseling, service coordination, behavioural therapy and educational programs to people living with a developmental disability and their families.

THE ADDICTIONS FOUNDATION OF MANITOBA • 1031 Portage Avenue • Winnipeg, MB • R3G 0R8 • Tel: 204-944-6200 • Fax: 204-779-9165 • Contact: Human Resources • Internet: www.afm.mb.ca • The Addictions Foundation of Manitoba (AFM) is a provincial crown agency providing a broad range of services relating to alcohol, drug, and gambling problems. Substance abuse and gambling prevention, education and rehabilitation programs, and impaired driver services are available across the province through AFM. The agency also provides many youth programs in accordance with its mandate to provide counselling, education, prevention and research with regards to the problems associated with addictions.

THE ARTHRITIS SOCIETY • 393 University Avenue, Suite 1700 • Toronto, ON • M5G 1E6 • Tel: 416-979-7228 • Fax: 416-979-8366 • Contact: Human Resources • Internet: www.arthritis. ca • The mission of The Arthritis Society is to search for the underlying causes and subsequent cures for arthritis and to promote the best possible care and treatment for people with arthritis. They employ approximately 250 individuals.

TORONTO ASSOCIATION FOR COMMUNITY LIVING • 20 Spadina Road • Toronto, ON • M5R 2S7 • Tel: 416-968-0650 • Fax: 416-968-6463 • Email: hr_recruit@cltoronto.ca • Internet: www.communitylivingtoronto.ca • The Toronto Association for Community Living is a United

Way agency addressing the needs of children or adults with developmental disabilities and their families. Services provided through more than 70 program locations across Toronto include early childhood services, employment training and placement, adult residential programs, adult development centres, volunteer services and public education. The organization serves almost 6000 persons with developmental disabilities, and employs a staff of 1400 who work at various program locations.

TORONTO COMMUNITY CARE ACCESS CENTRE • 250 Dundas Street West, Suite 305 • Toronto, ON • M5T 2Z5 • Tel: 416-506-9888 • Fax: 416-506-1629 • Contact: Human Resources • E-mail: hr_recruit@toronto.ccac-ont.ca • Internet: www.toronto.ccac-ont.ca • Community Care Access Centres provide one-stop access to personal support services to help individuals live independently in their homes or assist them in making the transition to a long-term care facility.

UNIVERSAL REHABILITATION SERVICE AGENCY • 808 Manning Road NE • Calgary, AB • T2E 7N8 • Tel: 403-272-7722 • Fax: 403-273-7852 • Contact: Human Resources • E-mail: human.resources@ursa-rehab.com • Internet: www.ursa-rehab.com • Universal Rehabilitation Service Agency (URSA) is a Calgary-based, non-profit agency which was established in 1985. Their objective is to meet the needs of individuals with disabilities in community settings. "Universal" refers to an agency willing to develop and provide needed rehabilitation services not currently in existence.

VILLA PROVIDENCE SHEDIAC INC. • 403 Main Street • Shediac, NB • E4P 2B9 • Tel: 506-532-4484 • Fax: 506-532-5909 • Contact: Human Resources • • Villa Providence Shediac Inc. is a nursing home for seniors and younger persons with physical and mental illnesses.

VIPSITTERS • 154 University Avenue • Toronto, ON • M5H 3Y9 • Tel: 416-361-0000 • Fax: 905-886-1667 • Contact: Human Resources • E-mail: ask@vipsitters.com • Internet: www.vipsitters.com • vipSITTERS provides property, home care, pet care, and general property management. The firm employs approximately 200 individuals.

Telecommunications & Media

ACCESS COMMUNICATIONS CO-OPERATIVE LIMITED • 2250 Park Street • Regina, SK • S4N 7K7 • Tel: 306-569-3510 • Fax: 306-565-5395 • Contact: Human Resources • E-mail: careers@accesscomm.ca • Internet: www.accesscomm.ca • Access Communications Co-operative Limited is a community owned and operated service co-operative dedicated to providing exceptional communications and entertainment services and unique opportunities for local expression. We serve customers in 30 communities throughout the province of Saskatchewan, including Regina, Estevan, Weyburn, Yorkton, Melville and the Battlefords.

BELL ALIANT INC. • P.O. Box 1430 • Saint John, NB • E2L 4K2 • Tel: 1-877-2ALIANT • Fax: 902-429-8755 • Contact: Human Resources • Internet: www.aliant.ca • Bell Aliant provides a structure for greater focus on regional customers - leveraging the proven expertise of Aliant and Nordiq in serving geographically dispersed regions. Headquartered in Atlantic Canada, Bell Aliant is led by a dedicated, senior management team from both Bell and Aliant. Our leaders and employees are located in regional offices across the entire territory and provide customers all the benefits of a team located close to them and focused on their specific regional needs. Bell Aliant has approximately 10,000 employees.

BELL CANADA • 483 Bay Street, Suite 100 • Toronto, ON • M5G 2E1 • Tel: 416-599-3911 • Contact: Bell Staffing Solutions • Internet: www.bell.ca • Bell Canada Enterprises is Canada's largest communications company. Through our main subsidiary Bell Canada, we provide local telephone, long distance, wireless communications, Internet access, data, satellite television and other services to residential and business customers through some 26 million customer connections.

CANADA POST CORPORATION • 1 Dundas Street West, Suite 700 • Toronto, ON • M5G 2L5 • Tel: 1-888-550-6333 • Contact: Human Resources Department • Internet: www.canadapost.ca • In the 2007 fiscal period, Canada Post Corporation processed 11.8 billion pieces of mail. Each working day, Canada Post delivers an average of 37 million pieces of mail, processed through 22 major plants and many other facilities, to over 13 million addresses in Canada, and forwards mail to almost every country in the world. Canada Post is the 44th largest Canadian business in terms of revenue and is the seventh largest employer in Canada. Canada Post employs over 72,000 full and part-time employees.

CANADIAN BROADCASTING CORPORATION • P.O. Box 500, Station A • Toronto, ON • M5W 1E6 • Tel: 416-205-3311 • Internet: www.cbc.ca/jobs • 100% Canadian. As Canada's public broadcaster, CBC/Radio-Canada offers all Canadians broadcasting services that reflect and celebrate our country's diverse heritage, culture and stories. CBC/Radio-Canada reaches Canadians through eight national radio and television networks, its full-service Web sites, local/ regional stations and affiliates that bring diverse regional and cultural perspectives into the daily lives of Canadians in English, French and eight aboriginal languages. We are always looking for innovative and passionate new talent, in the areas of television, radio, and new media production and journalism. If you have relevant experience, motivation and a keen interest in the broadcasting field and are looking for a dynamic career with a high profile national employer visit our website at www.cbc.ca/jobs.

CFCN COMMUNICATIONS INC. • 80 Patina Rise SW • Calgary, AB • T3H 2W4 • Tel: 403-240-5712 • Fax: 403-246-8879 • Internet: www.cfcn.ca • CFCN Communications is engaged in the field of television broadcasting in Calgary. A subsidiary of Maclean Hunter Limited, this company was established in 1962, and has approximately 216 employees. Interested candidates should include a resume tape for related positions (i.e. reporter, photographer, etc.). As a mid market TV station, they have very little requirement for entry-level candidates as almost all of their positions would require three to five years of small market television experience.

CGI • 1130 Sherbrooke Street West, 5th Floor • Montreal, QC • H3A 2M8 • Tel: 514-841-3200 • Fax: 514-841-3299 • Contact: Human Resources • Internet: www.cgi.com • Founded in 1976, CGI is the largest Canadian independent information technology (IT) services firm and the fifth largest in North America. CGI and its affiliated companies employ approximately 25,000 professionals. CGI provides end-to-end IT and business process services to clients worldwide, utilizing a highly customized, cost efficient delivery model.

EXFO • 2260 Argentia Road • Mississauga, ON • L5N 6H7 • Tel: 905-821-2600 • Fax: 905-821-2055 • Contact: HR Specialist • E-mail: hrtoronto@exfo.com • Internet: www.exfo. com • Founded in Quebec City in 1985, EXFO is a recognized expert in the global optical communications industry through the design and manufacture of advanced and innovative test and measurement solutions.

Do a Little Bit Each Day
If you are searching for employment, don't try to cram your day full of tasks. If you set aside a little bit of time each day you can accomplish a lot. Spread out the workload, but make sure to keep at it!

GLENTEL INC. • 8501 Commerce Court • Burnaby, BC • V5A 4N3 • Tel: 604-415-6500 • Fax: 604-415-6565 • Contact: Human Resources • Internet: www.glentel.com • Glentel is a leading provider in wireless business communications in Canada. The company offers the full range of wireless services across Canada: from paging and cellular, to two-way radio and wireless data, and now satellite communications. Glentel was founded in 1963 with the goal of providing wireless communications capabilities to all Canadians.

MEMOTEC COMMUNICATIONS INC. • 7755 Henri Bourassa Boulevard West • Saint Laurent, QC • H4S 1P7 • Tel: 514-738-4781 • Fax: 514-738-4436 • Contact: Human Resources • Email: poh-kin.ng@memotec.com • Internet: www.memotec.com • Memotec Inc. is an industry-leading provider of next-generation solutions for telecommunications service providers, mobile network operators and corporate customers. With over 30 years of experience, Memotec has developed a comprehensive range of multi-service platforms capable of optimizing communications networks.

MTS ALLSTREAM INC. • P.O. Box 6666, 333 Main Street • Winnipeg, MB • R3C 3V6 • Tel: 204-941-7267 • Fax: 204-772-4847 • Contact: Mr. Ken Larence, Human Resources • Internet: www.mts.mb.ca • MTS allstream is Canada's third-largest communications provider, with 6000 dedicated employees focused on delivering outstanding value to its customers. Seamlessly blending innovative solutions and world-class technology, MTS connects its customers to the world. MTS serves enterprise and residential customers in Manitoba with a full suite of services ranging from wireline voice and high-speed data services, to next-generation wireless services, to MTS TV, through its MTS (Manitoba) division.

NELVANA LIMITED • 42 Pardee Avenue • Toronto, ON • M6K 1X8 • Tel: 416- 535-0935 • Fax: 416-530-2832 • Internet: www.nelvana.com • Nelvana, a Corus Entertainment company, is one of the world's leading international producers and distributors of children's animation and related consumer products. For more than 30 years, they have produced over 100 major television series, specials and movies, which are available in over 150 countries around the world. Along with creating great shows, they work with their partners to develop merchandise, publishing, music, interactive and home video products that add to children's lives.

NORTHWESTEL INC. • 301 Lambert Street, P.O. Box 2727 • Whitehorse, YK • Y1A 4Y4 • Tel: 867-668-5300 • Fax: 867-766-2530 • Contact: Human Resources • E-mail: careers@nwtel. ca • Internet: www.nwtel.ca • Established over 50 years ago, Northwestel delivers a broad range of telecommunications solutions to a population of 110,000 northern Canadians in 96 communities scattered throughout the Yukon, the Northwest Territories, Nunavut, and northern British Columbia.

PELMOREX INC. • 2655 Bristol Circle • Oakville, ON • L6H 7W1 • Fax: 905-829-1332 • Contact: Human Resources • E-mail: hr@pelmorex.com • Internet: www.theweathernetwork. com • Pelmorex is the parent company that owns and operates the broadcasting licence for The Weather Network and its French sister station, MétéoMédia. The two networks are Canada's only English and French specialty channels devoted to Canada's favourite topic of conversation -- the weather! Pelmorex Inc. offers a full range of weather-related products, services and multimedia applications to a number of consumer and commercial clients.

REUTERS INFORMATION SERVICES (CANADA) LTD. • Standard Life Centre, 121 King Street West, Suite 2000 • Toronto, ON • M5H 3T9 • Tel: 416-941-8000 • Contact: Human Resources • Internet: www.reuters.com • Reuters is a global information company providing indispensable information tailored for professionals in the financial services, media and corporate markets. Their information is trusted and drives decision making across the globe. They have a reputation for speed, accuracy and freedom from bias.

ROGERS • 333 Bloor Street East • Toronto, ON • M4W 1G9 • Tel: 416-935-1100 • Fax: 416-935-3330 • Contact: Human Resources • Internet: www.rogers.com • Rogers Communications (TSX: RCI; NYSE: RG) is a diversified Canadian communications and media company engaged in four primary lines of business. Rogers Wireless is Canada's largest wireless voice and data communications services provider and the country's only carrier operating on the world standard GSM/GPRS/EDGE technology platform; Rogers Cable is Canada's largest cable television provider offering cable television, high-speed Internet access, voice over cable telephony services and video retailing; Rogers Media is Canada's premier collection of category leading media assets with businesses in radio, television broadcasting, television shopping, publishing and sports entertainment; and Rogers Telecom is a national provider of telephony, data networking, and broadband Internet connectivity, to small, medium and large businesses across the country

SASKTEL • 2121 Saskatchewan Drive, Main Floor • Regina, SK • S4P 3Y2 • Tel: 306-777-2029 • Fax: 306-359-0653 • Internet: www.sasktel.com • SaskTel is the leading full service communications provider in Saskatchewan, offering competitive voice, data, dial-up and high speed internet, entertainment and multimedia services, security, web hosting, text and messaging services, and cellular and wireless data services over its digital networks. The SaskTel serving area within Saskatchewan links 13 cities with 535 smaller communities and their surrounding rural areas, including 49,000 farms. All told, SaskTel serves more than 425,000 business and residential customers. SaskTel and its wholly-owned subsidiaries have a workforce of 5,200 full-time, part-time and temporary employees.

SHOPPING CHANNEL, THE • 59 Ambassador Drive • Mississauga, ON • L5T 2P9 • Tel: 888-2020-888 • Fax: 905-362-7712 • Contact: Human Resources • Internet: www. theshoppingchannel.com • The Shopping Channel is a 24-hour, seven day per week broadcast retailer available on a variety of cable channels as well as Star Choice, ExpressVu and Look TV satellite throughout Canada. They carry both common, brand-name items; as well as unique items new to the market that cannot be found anywhere else. These products range from fashions to jewellery to household appliances. The Shopping Channel is 100% Canadian and employs over 500 people.

TELEBEC S.E.C. • 7151 Jean-Talon Street East, 7th Floor • Anjou, QC • H1M 3N8 • Tel: 514-493-5565 • Fax: 514-493-5377 • Email: emplois@telebec.com • Internet: www.telebec.com • Québec's leading regional telecommunications company, Télébec, its subsidiaries, and nearly 800 employees provide a complete range of integrated and innovative telecommunications services to more than half the province. Télébec's 180,000 customers are located in 300 municipalities across Québec. This vast territory of 750,000 square kilometres is bounded to the north by the James Bay territory, to the south by Venise-en-Québec, near the U.S. border, to the west by Ville-Marie in Abitibi-Témiscamingue, and to the east by the Îles-de-la-Madeleine.

TELESAT • 1601 Telesat Court • Glouchester, ON • K1B 5P4 • Tel: 613-748-0123 • Fax: 613-748-8712 • Contact: Human Resources • E-mail: info@telesat.ca • Internet: www.telesat.ca • Created in 1969, Telesat launched the world's first commercial geostationary satellite in 1972. Today, the company is one of the world's top satellite operators, providing telecommunications and broadcasting services throughout the Americas with one of the most modern fleets in the world. With more than thirty-five years of engineering and technical experience, Telesat is a diversified, end-to-end satellite services company, with a well-established history of innovation and success.

TELUS CORPORATION • 10020 - 100 Street N.W., 30th Floor • Edmonton, AB • T5J 0N5 • Tel: 780-498-7311 • Fax: 708-493-7399 • Contact: Human Resources • Internet: www.telus.com • Telus Corporation is one of Canada's leading providers of data, Internet Protocol (IP), voice and wireless communications services. They provide and integrate a full range of communications products and services that connect Canadians to the world.

VIACOM OUTDOOR CANADA • 377 Horner Avenue • Toronto, ON • M8W 1Z6 • Tel: 416-255-1392 • Fax: 416-255-2063 • Contact: Director, Human Resources • E-mail: eniven@ viacomoutdoor.ca • Internet: www.viacomoutdoor.ca • Viacom Outdoor Canada is an out-of-home advertising company and our primary function is to sell advertising space. They also have their own print production facilities.

YTV CANADA INC. • 64 Jefferson Avenue, Unit 18 • Toronto, ON • M6J 3H3 • Tel: 416-534-1191 • Fax: 416-534-8465 • Contact: Human Resources • Internet: www.ytv.com • YTV Canada is a specialty network which acquires, produces and delivers award-winning Canadian and international programming for children and their families.

Transportation

AIR CANADA • P.O. Box 14000 • Ville St. Laurent, QC • H4Y 1H4 • Tel: 514-422-6635 • Fax: 514-422-7997 • Contact: Human Resources • Internet: www.aircanada.ca/careers • Air Canada is Canada's largest full-service airline and the largest provider of scheduled passenger services in the Canadian market, the Canada-U.S. transborder market and in the international market to and from Canada. Together with its regional affiliate Jazz, Air Canada serves over 32 million customers annually and provides direct passenger service to over 170 destinations on five continents. As it celebrates its 70th anniversary, Air Canada is the 14th largest commercial airline in the world, with approximately 23,000 fulltime equivalent employees.

ATLAS VAN LINES (CANADA) LTD. • 485 North Service Road East • Oakville, ON • L6J 5M7 • Tel: 905-844-0701 • Fax: 905-844-7326 • Contact: Human Resources • Internet: www.atlasvanlines. ca • • As a member of the 800 agent strong Atlas World Group, Atlas Van Lines (Canada) Ltd. is part of the third largest transportation company. In addition to their "transportation arm", Atlas World Group also holds a majority ownership position in a U.S. based, third party relocation company. With their North American network and our International Division's global affiliates, they are able to provide comprehensive door to door service anywhere in the world. They are headquartered in Oakville, ON with more than 120 full time staff members.

BEARSKIN LAKE AIR SERVICE LTD. • 1475 West Walsh Street • Thunder Bay, ON • P7E 4X6 • Tel: 807-577-1141 • Fax: 807-474-2610 • Contact: Human Resources • Internet: www. bearskinairlines.com • Bearskin Airlines offers scheduled, charter and freight services in Northern Ontario. With operation bases in both Sioux Loout and Thunder Bay, they are committed to providing excellent customer service and ensuring safe and comfortable air travel. They employ over 200 employees throughout Northern Ontario and Manitoba. In addition to the two bases, Bearskin employs passenger service agents at various counters in airports around Northern Ontario and Manitoba.

BRITISH COLUMBIA FERRY SERVICES INC. • 1112 Fort Street • Victoria, BC • V8V 4V2 • Tel: 250-381-3431 • Fax: • Contact: Human Resources • Internet: www.bcferries.com • With 38 ships, 25 routes and 47 ports of call, BC Ferries provides a vital transportation link for the coastal communities of "Super, Natural" British Columbia. They employ approximately 4,500 people.

 Career ✓ Tip

Visit a Human Resources Centre of Canada
Human Resource Centres of Canada provide employment counselling and placement, job training, labour market information, services to employers, and Unemployment Insurance administration.

BRITISH COLUMBIA TRANSIT • 520 Gorge Road East, P.O. Box 610 • Victoria, BC • V8W 2P3 • Tel: 250-385-2551 • Fax: 250-995-5664 • Contact: Human Resources Department • E-mail: employment_services@bctransit.com • Internet: www.bctransit.com • BC transit is the provincial crown agency charged with coordinating the delivery of public transportation throughout British Columbia (outside the Greater Vancouver Regional District). BC Transit manages and operates the Victoria Regional Transit System, and plans, funds, manages, markets, and contracts for transit systems in 50 British Columbia local governments in the Municipal Systems Program.

CHALLENGER MOTOR FREIGHT INC. • 300 Maple Grove Road • Cambridge, ON • N3E 1B7 • Tel: 800-265-6358 • Fax: 519-653-9058 • Contact: Human Resources Manager • E-mail: resumes@challenger.com • Internet: www.challenger.com • Since its inception in 1975, Challenger Motor Freight Inc. has provided customers with truckload, flatbed and logistics services. Their reputation throughout the transportation industry can be attributed to their impressive record of customer satisfaction, safe and knowledgeable drivers, late model, well maintained equipment, and technological applications.

COAST MOUNTAIN BUS COMPANY LTD. • C650 - 13401 108th Avenue • Surrey, BC • V3T 5T4 • Tel: 604-953-3000 • Internet: www.coastmountainbus.com • Formerly known as BC Transit, Coast Mountain Bus Company Ltd. is an operating subsidiary of the Greater Vancouver Transportation Authority (TransLink) that serves more than 2 million people throughout British Columbia by bus and seabus in the Lower Mainland. The corporation's conventional transit systems, and community transit service, in Greater Vancouver carry 600,000 passengers per day. Coast Mountain Bus Company Ltd. employs more than 5200 individuals including temporary and casual employees.

COUGAR HELICOPTERS INC. • 40 Craig Dobbins' Way, St. John's International Airport • St. John's, NL • A1A 4Y3 • Tel: 709-758-4800 • Fax: 708-758-4850 • Contact: Human Resources • E-mail: hr@cougar.ca • Internet: www.cougar.ca • Cougar Helicopters Inc. is a helicopter charter service that provides support services for transferring crews and personnel to and from oil rigs, forest fire patrol, aerial photography, power line patrol, executive charter, emergency medical service, search and rescue, herbicide spraying, helideck inspections, and third party maintenance.

DISCOUNT CAR AND TRUCK RENTALS • 720 Arrow Road • North York, ON • M9M 2M1 • Tel: 416-744-0123 • Fax: 416-744-9829 • Contact: Human Resources • E-mail: hr@disountcar. com • Internet: www.discountcar.com • Discount Car & Truck Rentals is Canadian owned and operated. Our founders, Herb and Rhoda Singer, opened Discount's first location in 1980, in Hamilton, Ontario. • Since its inception, Discount has grown dramatically, now boasting over 300 locations from coast to coast, comprised of both corporate and franchised operations. Internationally, their presence can be felt in Australia, where they are rapidly expanding.

HELIJET INTERNATIONAL INC. • 5911 Airport Road South, Vancouver Int'l Airport • Richmond, BC • V7B 1B5 • Tel: 604-273-4688 • Fax: 604-273-5301 • Contact: Karen Sabourin, Director Human Resources • E-mail: ksabourin@helijet.com • Internet: www.helijet.com • For over 20 years, Helijet has flown passengers above South Western British Columbia and the Pacific Northwest on Sikorsky S76 helicopters and an 18-passenger Beech 1900D Turboprop aircraft. They offer daily scheduled services from downtown Vancouver, Vancouver International, Victoria Harbour, Victoria Airport, Campbell River, Whistler, and Seattle. The firm employs over 100 people in different capacities at all different locations.

HOUSEHOLD MOVERS & SHIPPERS LIMITED • 19 Clyde Avenue • St. John's, NL • A1B 4R8 • Tel: 709-747-4222 • Fax: 709-368-2619 • Contact: Human Resources • E-mail: householdmovers@nfld.net • Internet: www.householdmovers.ca • Household Movers and Shippers is a privately owned household goods transportation company which is an agent for

North American Van Lines. With branches throughout the Maritimes, the company employs 25 permanent full time individuals, which increases during seasonal times to 200 full and part time staff.

KELRON LOGISTICS • 1355 Meyerside Dr. • Mississauga, ON • L5T 1C9 • Tel: 905-795-9136 • Fax: 905-795-8406 • Contact: Human Resources • E-mail: toronto@kelron.com • Internet: www. kelron.com • Kelron provides a complete range of logistics services throughout North America including transportation, warehousing and distribution, and logistics planning.

LAIDLAW INC. • 3221 North Service Road, P.O. Box 5028 • Burlington, ON • L7R 3Y8 • Tel: 905-336-1800 • Fax: 905-336-8177 • Internet: www.laidlaw.ca • Laidlaw Inc.'s 60,000 employees provide high quality, cost-effective transportation management services to municipalities, businesses, industries and individuals. Operating from 900 locations throughout Canada and the U.S., Laidlaw is the largest service company in school bus transportation and health care transportation.

MARINE ATLANTIC INC. • 10 Fort William Place, Suite 802 • St. John's, NL • A1C 1K4 • Tel: 709-772-8957 • Fax: 709-772-8956 • Contact: Human Resources • Internet: www.marine-atlantic.ca • Marine Atlantic is a Canadian Federal Crown Corporation that provides a vital marine transportation link across the Cabot Strait between Newfoundland and Labrador and mainland Canada. Marine Atlantic Inc. employs approximately 1,200 people based at its three port locations: Port aux Basques and Argentia in Newfoundland and Labrador, and North Sydney in Nova Scotia.

MSM TRANSPORTATION INC. • 124 Commercial Road • Bolton, ON • L7E 1K4 • Tel: 800-667-1475 • Fax: 800-268-0405 • Contact: Mr. John Wheeler, Director of Operations • E-mail: jwheeler@shipmsm.com • Internet: www.shipmsm.com • MSM is an expedited, satellite tracked, over the road carrier. Founded in 1989, MSM offers customers a powerful and comprehensive distribution system between Canada and the United States.

SASKATCHEWAN TRANSPORTATION COMPANY • 2041 Hamilton Street • Regina, SK • S4P 2E2 • Tel: 306-787-3347 • Fax: 306-787-1633 • Contact: Human Resources • E-mail: careers@stcbus.com • Internet: www.stcbus.com • Saskatchewan Transportation Company (STC) was established in 1946 to act as a common carrier providing passenger service and parcel express service throughout the province. It is a provincial coach company which provides affordable, accessible bus passenger and freight service to 276 communities in Saskatchewan.

SIGNATURE VACATIONS INC. • 1685 Tech Avenue • Mississauga, ON • L4W 0A7 • Tel: 416-967-1510 • Fax: 416-969-2698 • Contact: Human Resources • Internet: www.signaturevacations. com • Signature Vacations has been helping plan vacations since 1972. As Canada's leading tour operator, their products include sundestinations, domestic charters and European summer programs.

SMIT • 2285 Commissioner Street, P.O. Box 3650 • Vancouver, BC • V5L 1A8 • Tel: 604-255-8881 • Fax: 604-255-9322 • Contact: Human Resources • E-mail: company.vancouver@smit. com • Internet: www.smit.com • Rivtow Marine Ltd. is a tug boat company. Their company's head office is in Vancouver, British Columbia.

SOUTHERN RAILWAY OF BRITISH COLUMBIA LTD. • 2102 River Drive • New Westminster, BC • V3M 6S3 • Tel: 604-527-6342 • Fax: 604-526-0914 • Contact: W. Carrey, Director of Human Resources • E-mail: bcarrey@sryraillink.com • Internet: www.sryraillink.com • Southern Railway of British Columbia provides movement of freight cars to customer sidings. They also are involved in locomotive and RR car repair. The firm employs about 160 people in total.

THOMAS COOK NORTH AMERICA • 130 Merton Street • Toronto, ON • M4S 1A4 • Tel: 416-485-1700 • Fax: 416-485-1805 • Contact: Human Resources • E-mail: resume@ thomascookgroup.ca • Internet: www.thomascook.com • Thomas Cook North America, a billion+ dollar travel company, is headquartered in Toronto, Canada. They are comprised of market leading tour operators, wholesalers, and travel agencies located in Canada and the United States.

THOMPSON'S MOVING AND STORAGE • 3 Freeman Street, P.O. Box 639 • Middleton, NS • B0S 1P0 • Tel: 902-825-3929 • Fax: 902-825-6261 • Contact: Human Resources • Internet: www.thompsonsmoving.ca • Thompson's Moving and Storage is engaged in the business of moving services for individuals and businesses in Nova Scotia.

TIPPET-RICHARDSON LTD. • 25 Metropolitan Road • Toronto, ON • M1R 2T5 • Tel: 416-291-1200 • Fax: 416-291-2601 • Contact: Human Resources • Internet: www.tippet-richardson.com • Tippet-Richardson was founded in 1927, with its primary goal to provide high quality residential and commercial moving services in the Toronto area. The two founding partners were Basil Tippet and C.A. Richardson.

UPS CANADA LTD. • 6285 Northam Drive, Suite 400 • Mississauga, ON • L4V 1X5 • Tel: 800-742-5877 • Fax: 905-660-8515 • Contact: Human Resources • Internet: www.ups.com/canada • Founded in 1907 as a messenger company in the United States, UPS has grown into a $42.6 billion corporation by clearly focusing on the goal of enabling commerce around the globe. Today UPS, or United Parcel Service Inc., is a global company with one of the most recognized and admired brands in the world. As the largest express carrier and package delivery company in the world, we are also a leading provider of specialized transportation, logistics, capital, and e-commerce services. Every day, we manage the flow of goods, funds, and information in more than 200 countries and territories worldwide.

VANCOUVER INTERNATIONAL AIRPORT • P.O. Box 23750 Airport Postal Outlet • Richmond, BC • V7B 1Y7 • Tel: 604-207-7077 • Fax: 604-232-6008 • Contact: Human Resources • Internet: www.yvr.ca • Vancouver International Airport provides transportation facilities and services to airlines travelling in and out of Vancouver. The airport employs approximately 300 individuals in total.

VIA RAIL CANADA INC. • 3, Place Ville-Marie • Montreal, QC • H3B 2C9 • Tel: 514-871-6000 • Fax: 514-871-6105 • Contact: Human Resources • Internet: www.viarail.ca • VIA Rail Canada Inc. is Canada's national passenger rail company, dedicated to providing safe and efficient intercity and transcontinental rail services. VIA operates more than 460 trains weekly and employs approximately 3,000 people. VIA Rail covers the country from coast to coast, serving more than 450 communities.

WESTJET AIRLINES LTD. • 5055 - 11th Street NE • Calgary, AB • T2E 8N4 • Tel: 403-444-2600 • Fax: 403-444-2301 • Contact: Human Resources • Internet: www.westjet.com • Westjet Airlines is the leading low-fare airline that people want to work with, customers want to fly with and shareholders want to invest with. The company employs approximately 1,200 people.

WESTSHORE TERMINALS LTD. • 1 Roberts Bank Road • Delta, BC • V4M 4G5 • Tel: 604-946-4491 • Fax: 604-946-1388 • Contact: Human Resources • Internet: www.westshore.com • Located in Vancouver, Westshore Terminals is Canada's leading coal export facility and the largest dry bulk terminal on the west coast of the Americas. It has been an essential link in the coal chain between mines, rail and end user for more than 35 years. Shipments regularly go to about 24 countries and bring $2 billion or more of wealth each year to Canada.

YANKE GROUP OF COMPANIES • 2815 Lorne Avenue • Saskatoon, SK • S7J 0S5 • Tel: 306-955-4221 • Fax: 306-955-5663 • Contact: Human Resources Manager • E-mail: human_resources@yanke.ca • Internet: www.yanke.ca • Yanke Group of Companies is a Saskatchewan based transportation company, which is committed to being a community and industry leader providing unequalled transportation solutions across North America. Yanke has 8 terminals across Canada, and operates 6 different business units that provide a "one-stop" source of transportation solutions.

PART II

DIRECTORIES OF RESOURCES

Recruiters

Recruiters

WHAT IS A RECRUITER?

Among other names, recruiters are also known as headhunters, executive search firms, placement firms, or employment agencies. Basically a recruiter is a consultant or a company engaged in the business of bringing together employers and job seekers. The employment agency can efficiently provide a large selection of qualified candidates to a busy employer. As a result, the employer pays the search firm a fee for their services.

You as an employee should NOT have to pay a recruiting firm to list you on their roster. The recruiter's client is the employer, while you are more or less the raw material in the placement process.

Different agencies may focus only on specific segments, such as temporary, contract, part time, or permanent employment. Others specialize in certain industries or just on higher end positions. Many others pride themselves on being generalists. It is important to contact the proper recruiter for the type of industry or position you wish to enter.

HOW CAN A RECRUITER HELP YOU?

Since recruiters have access, on average, to about 15% of all available jobs, they are a necessary part of your well-rounded work search. Your objective is to make a recruiting company interested in your skills and qualifications. The most common method of contact is to phone or e-mail a relevant recruiter, spark their interest, send them your resumé and then follow-up. Getting referred by a friend or colleague the recruiter knows and likes can make a world of difference.

As with anyone you do business with, try to do some research on the agencies you choose to deal with. Are they legitimate? Do they treat candidates (job applicants) well? Have they been successful in placing people like you before? The more you know upfront, the fewer problems you a likely to have down the road. Talk to others who have used recruiters in the past to find out what kind of experience to expect.

The following list is only a sampling of some of the larger recruiting firms across the country. We have compiled this list directly from the firms themselves, or in some cases from the Internet with contact verification afterward. Both permanent and temporary recruiters are listed. For additional employment agencies in your area check your local phone book – or head to your closest library for a copy of **The Directory of Executive Recruiters** from Kennedy Publications.

500 STAFFING SERVICES INC., THE • 465 Morden Road, 2nd Floor • Oakville, ON • L6K 3W6 • Tel: 905-845-0045 • Fax: 905-845-2100 • E-mail: fretz@the500.com or hague@the500.com • Internet: www.the500.com • Contact: Bill Fretz • The 500 is one of Canada's leading organizations providing full-time and temporary staffing solutions to companies across Canada. Established in 1953, The 500 is well positioned to assist both the job seeker and client organization in two distinct areas: Executive & Professional Search and Temporary Staffing.

30 Duke Street
Suite 901
Kitchener, ON N2H 3W5
Tel: 519-568-8300
Fax: 519-568-8165
Toll Free: 1-866-261-8300
Contact: Wendy Best
best@the500.com

341 Talbot Street
Suite 217
London, ON N6A 2R5
Tel: 519-457-0400
Fax: 519-457-3393
Toll Free: 1-866-863-9868
Contact: Carole Alain
alain@the500.com

4300 Village Centre Court
Suite 100
Mississauga, ON L4Z 1S2
Tel: 905-361-1486
Fax: 905-361-1596
Contact: Robert Pole
poole@the500.com

465 Morden Road
2nd Floor
Oakville, ON L6K 3W6
Tel: 905-845-0045
Fax: 905-845-2100
Toll Free: 1-888-500-9675
Contact: Bill Fretz
fretz@the500.com

275 Slater Street
Suite 203
Ottawa, ON K1P 5H9
Tel: 613-237-2888
Fax: 613-327-2070
Toll Free: 1-866-307-9675
Contact: Joanne Prud'Homme
prudhomme@the500.com

595 Burrard Street
Suite 433
Vancouver, BC V7X 1J1
Tel: 604-685-1400
Fax: 604-685-1425
Toll Free: 1-866-685-1400
Contact: Joan Page
temp@the500.com
perm@the500.com

1070 Douglas Street
Suite 660
Victoria, BC V8W 2C4
Tel: 250-412-0841
Fax: 250-412-0857
Toll Free: 1-866-412-0841
Contact: Norma McCrea
victoria@the500.com

3333 Boulevard de la Côte Vertu
Bureau 202
Ville St-Laurent, QC H4R 2N1
Tel: 514-338-3800
Fax: 514-866-6180
Toll Free: 1-888-465-9675
Contact: Carol-Anne Scanlon
scanlon@the500.com

A. R. BEADLE & ASSOCIATES LTD. • #98 - 5900 Ferry Road • Delta, BC • V4K 5C3 • Tel: 604-952-0702 Toll Free: 1-888-330-6714 • E-mail: info@arbeadle.com • Internet: www.arbeadle.com • A. R. Beadle & Associates Ltd. is a management consulting firm specializing in processes aimed at increasing organizational and team effectiveness. They provide quality services to their clients by providing strategic human resource planning, training, and consulting. Their philosophy is to respect and adhere to the values of their clients. Their job is to enhance their clients' organizational culture.

A.E. HARRISON & PARTNERS INC. • 4 Robert Speck Pkwy., Suite 1500 • Mississauga, ON • L4Z 1S1 • Tel: 905-615-1577 • E-mail: mail@aeharrison.com • Internet: www.aeharrison.com • Contact: Rick Harrison, President • A.E. Harrison and Partners is a professional search company which was founded in1968 by Al Harrison. The company is now managed by his son, Rick Harrison. They are a retainer based search company that specializes in the recruitment of sales, marketing and general management executives for leading companies in most industry sectors. They take great pride in their ability to find the right executive for every search.

A.W. FRASER & ASSOCIATES • 1060-1055 Hastings Street West • Vancouver, BC • V6E 2E9 • Tel: 604-685-4700 • E-mail: info@awfraser.com • Internet: www.awfraser.com • A.W. Fraser & Associates offers a full range of psychological and human resource services to enhance individual and organizational effectiveness. The A. W. Fraser & Associates' practice began in Edmonton in 1963. For almost 40 years, the consultants and psychologists have provided human resource consulting services to over 1,000 organizations across Canada and the United States, the United Kingdom, and Western Europe. They are members of a national partnership, covering Canada from Vancouver to Montreal.

2660-10303 Jasper Ave. NW	1060-1055 Hastings Street West	280-600 6 Ave. SW
Edmonton, AB	Vancouver, BC	Calgary, AB
T5J 3N6	V6E 2E9	T2P 0S5
Tel: 780-428-8578	Tel: 604-685-4700	Tel: 403-264-4480

ABANE & ASSOCIATES • 16715 - 12 Yonge Street, Suite 269 • Newmarket, ON • L3X 1X4 • Tel: 905-836-9764 • Fax: 905-836-1259 • E-mail: info@abane-associates.com • Internet: www. abane-associates.com • Abane & Associates are committed to continually seeking new and better ways to provide quality recruitment solutions to their clients. They achieve this by referring only the best-suited candidates according to their clients' requirements and by applying their unique selection system developed to meet each company's specific needs. Abane & Associates help fill employment opportunities as accountants, analysts, business managers, call centre representatives, engineers, technical writers and more.

ABCO DESIGNS INC. • 4700 de la Savane, Suite 215 • Montreal, QC • H4P 1T7 • Tel: 514-731-9479 • Fax: 514-341-5641 • Toll Free: 800-563-3939 • E-mail: info@abcoinc.ca • Internet: www.abcoinc.ca • Abco's clients can vouch for the value of dealing with a firm that has built practical expertise, since 1957, in the area of engineering support staff. Your specific needs will be appreciated and all your personnel will be tailor-selected to suit your exacting requirements.

Commerce Court West	Calgary
Toronto, ON	Tel: 403-538-0058
M5L 1J3	Toll Free: 800-563-3939
Tel: 416-777-9778	
Fax: 416-777-9663	

ABEL PLACEMENT CONSULTANTS INC. • 7030 Woodbine Avenue, Suite 100 • Markham, ON • L3R 6G2 • Tel: 905-513-1515 • Fax: 905-513-2769 • E-mail: info@abelplacement.com • Internet: www.abelplacement.com • Abel Placement Consultants Inc. is a well-established placement firm that is committed to providing superior value-added service to their clients and candidates alike, thereby becoming one of the most respected and effective recruitment/ search firms for permanent placements in the Greater Toronto Area. Located in Markham, Abel Placement Consultants provides permanent search and placement services for Executives and General Management, Accounting Management, Administration, Office Support, Sales Representative, Information Technology and support Staff, Engineers, Construction Management, and Architectural Staff.

ABL • 777 Guelph Line, Suite 212 • Burlington, ON • L7R 3N2 • Tel: 905-631-7050 • Fax: 905-631-7088 E-mail: pjf@ablemployment.com • Internet: www.ablemployment.com • ABL is a local company that specializes in industrial and warehouse positions throughout Burlington, Oakville, Hamilton, Milton, Mississauga, West Toronto and now, the London area. Their focus is on long-term temporary and temp-to-hire opportunities. ABL is an independently owned, corporately financed company. This means that both their customers and temporary employees enjoy the personal service of a locally owned and operated company and the financial security and resources of a large network of companies. ABL's President is PJ Ferguson. PJ has been in the staffing industry since 1987 and she has a keen understanding of what employees and client companies need in this market.

ABOUT STAFFING LTD. • 110, 707 - 10 Avenue S.W. • Calgary, AB • T2R 0B3 • Tel: 403-508-1000 • Email: info@aboutstaffing.com• Internet: www.aboutstaffing.com • About Staffing provides professional permanent and temporary placement services. They are a multi-million dollar, registered trademarked company, with a new license office recently opened in Edmonton. Their vision for the future is to sell licenses to operate across North America.

1506, 10250-101 Street
Edmonton, AB
T5J 3P4
Tel: 780-409-8100

ABSOLUTE RECRUITMENT • 90 Burnhamthorpe Road West, Suite 1202 • Mississauga, ON • L5B 3C3 • Tel: 905-275-3033 • Fax: 905-275-8233 • Email: resumes@absoluterecruitment. com• Internet: www.absoluterecruitment.com • They want your experience with us to be a professional and enjoyable one. They promise to learn your company profile and customize their recruiting practices to ensure they find you the ideal recruit. Whether it is an entire sales force you need or a temporary receptionist to cover a vacation, they will staff it quickly and well. They are drive to achieve RESULTS – they won't waste your time or theirs. They are sure you will find that they break the trend in agencies, recruitment firms and professional search groups.

390 Bay Street, 3rd Floor
Toronto, ON
M5H 2Y2
Tel: 416-644-1600
Fax: 416-644-1604

650 West Georgia Street, Suite 1620
Vancouver, BC
V6B 4N7
Tel: 604-678-3030
Fax: 604-678-3031

ACADEMY PLACEMENT SERVICES • 303 Dunlop Street West • Barrie, ON • L4N 1C1 • Tel: 705-739-4004 • Fax: 705-720-6557 • E-mail: info@academyplacement.com • Internet: www. academyplacement.com • Academy Placement Services is a Canadian owned company who knows how to get the job done. When you enlist their services, they ensure that only qualified candidates are referred for your consideration, and consistent high levels of personalized services are maintained.

ACCESS CAREER SOLUTIONS INC. • 2 County Court Blvd., Suite 302 • Brampton, ON • L6W 3W8 • Tel: 905-866-6616 • Fax: 905-866-6683 • E-mail: info@accesscareers.com • Internet: www.accesscareers.com • Contact: Linda Ford, President or Lori Robinson, Vice President • Access Career Solutions provide their clients with a wide range of Human Resource Services. While Recruitment, Selection and Executive Search is their main focus, they also provide other services including training, outplacement and career transition counselling and HR Strategic Planning. Access Career Solutions helps companies achieve their hiring objectives by providing them with 'Access' to the most qualified candidates.

ACCESS CORPORATE TECHNOLOGIES • 620-1600 Carling Avenue • Ottawa, ON K1P 1G3 • Tel: 613-236-6114 • Fax: 613-236-5552 • E-mail: careers@accesscorp.ca • Internet: www. accesscorp.ca • Access, we are focused on customer service. Our knowledge and experience within different work environments allows us to understand our client base in all phases of a project including business planning, information processing and roll-out. Access is a 100% Canadian-owned company, offering quality, administrative and professional services to businesses in the National Capital Region since 1996. ACCESS Corporate Technologies has a strong background in information technology, information systems, marketing, business administration, strategic planning and business management.

ACCOUNTEMPS INC. • 181 Bay St., Suite 820, P.O. Box 824 • Toronto, ON • M5J 2T3 Tel: 416-365-9140 • Fax: 416-350-3573 • E-mail: toronto@accountemps.com • Internet: www. accountemps.com • Accountemps, a division of Robert Half International Inc. (RHI), is the world's first and largest staffing service specializing in the temporary placement of accounting and financial professionals. With offices throughout the United States, Canada and Europe, they specialize in accounting, bookkeeping, finance, data entry, credit and collections, and payroll. The firm has offices across Canada in Calgary, Mississauga, Montreal, North York and Ottawa.

888 3rd St. S.W.
Suite 4200
Calgary, AB
T2P 5C5
Tel: 403-269-5387
Fax: 403-264-0934

10180-101 St.
Suite 1280
Edmonton, AB
T5J 3S4
Tel: 780-423-1466
Fax: 780-423-1581

1055 Dunsmuir St.
Suite 724
Vancouver, BC
V7X 1L4
Tel: 604-685-4253
Fax: 604-687-7533

15127 100th Ave.
Suite 302
Surrey, BC
V3R 0N9
Tel: 604-581-4254
Fax: 604-581-4225

201 Portage Ave.
Suite 2400
Winnipeg, WB
R3B 3K6
Tel: 204-957-5400
Fax: 204-957-5385

1 Robert Speck Parkway
Suite 940
Mississauga, ON
L4Z 3M3
Tel: 905-273-6524
Fax: 905-273-6217

5515 North Service Rd.
Suite 302
Burlington, ON
L7L 6G4
Tel: 905-319-9384
Fax: 905-319-2095

80 King St. S.
Suite 206
Waterloo, ON
N2J 1P5
Tel: 519-884-5016
Fax: 519-884-4632

175 Commerce Valley Dr. W.
Suite 300
Thornhill, ON
L3T 7P6
Tel: 905-709-8009
Fax: 905-709-3664

5140 Yonge St.
Suite 1500
North York, ON
M2N 6L7
Tel: 416-226-4570
Fax: 416-226-4498

360 Albert Street
Constitution Square Suite 520
Ottawa, ON
K1R 7X7
Tel: 613-236-4253
Fax: 613-236-2159

P.O. Box 824, 181 Bay St.
Suite 820
Toronto, ON
M5J 2T3
Tel: 416-365-9140
Fax: 416-350-3573

1 Place ville Marie
Suite 2330
Montreal, QC
H3B 3M5
Tel: 514-875-6585
Fax: 514-875-8066

1111 Saint Charles
Suite 650
Longueuil, QC
J4K 5G4
Tel: 450-679-3774
Fax: 450-679-8443

755 St. Jean Boulevard
Suite 404
Pointe-Claire, QC
H9R 5M9
Tel: 514-694-9609
Fax: 514-694-3460

ACCU-STAFF RESOURCE STAFFING SYSTEMS LTD. • 7755 Tecumseh Road East, • Windsor, ON • N8T 1G3 • Tel: 519-974-8888 • Fax: 519-974-6167 Toll Free: 1-888-283-1391• E-mail: corporate@accustaff.com • Internet: www.accu-staff.com • Accu-Staff Resource Systems Ltd. Is a full-service employement agency which originated in Windsor, Ontario in 1990 and now has locations in Detroit, Kingsville and throughout the GTA (Greater Toronto Area). Independently owned and operated, Accu-Staff has the capacity to offer both their clients and candidates all the emenities characteristic of a large agency, yet the ability to customize and adapt according to client-specific needs.

ACTION MANUTENTION LASALLE INC. • 2222-A, avenue Dollard   Lasalle, QC H8N 1S6 • Tel: 514-363-1531 • Fax: 514-363-3930 • E-mail: e.cayer@actionmanutentionlasalle.com • Internet: www.actionmanutentionlasalle.com • Action Manutention Lasalle inc. is an agency with a mission to provide experienced, reliable and qualified warehousing, handling and truck drivers field personnel.

ACTION PERSONNEL INC. • 280 Albert St., Suite 200   Ottawa, ON • K1P 5G8 • Tel: 613-238-8511 • Fax: 613-230-8380 • E-mail: info@actionpersonnel.ca • Internet: www.actionpersonnel. ca • Since 1977, Action Personnel of Ottawa-Hull Ltd. has provided many area firms, large and small, with quality personnel. With their experienced, professional staff, they have earned an excellent reputation based on quality personnel and superior service. Now, more than ever, it makes good business sense to take advantage of Action's skill and expertise for all your placement and temporary staffing needs.

ADAPT INC. • 1060 Croissant Augusta   Mascouche, QC • J7K 4H1 • Tel: 450-474-4999 • Fax: 450-474-4446 • Internet: www.adapt.qc.ca • Adapt Inc is issued from a senior executive search and recruitment firm (PAC) who holds over 15 years of experience. Attribute fairly to all standards and enquirements of confidentiality and quality which entitles an excellent reputation. This association allows ADAPT of a wider network involving every market segments.

ADDMORE PERSONNEL • 5799 Yonge St., Suite 510   Toronto, ON • M2M 3V3 • Tel: 416-229-6868 • Fax: 416-229-0297 • E-mail: hylton@addmorepersonnel.com • Internet: www. addmorepersonnel.com • Contact: Hylton Maizels • Addmore Personnel Inc. is Canada's premier job recruitment firm specializing in SAP and other leading ERP, CRM and SCM applications.
Suite 510, 5799 Yonge St.
Toronto, ON
M2M 3V3
Tel: 416-229-6868
Fax: 416-229-0757

ADECCO CANADA • 109 King St. E. • Toronto, ON • M5C 1G6 • Tel: 416-646-3322 • Toll Free 1-866-646-3322 • Fax: 416-368-4199 • Internet: www.adecco.ca • Adecco serves thousands of clients every day, including small, medium and large corporations, in a large variety of business sectors. The company employs 11,000 temporary employees daily, making Adecco the largest Recruitment Solutions and HR Consulting Services company in Canada. Over 60 offices are located across Canada. They arrived here by fostering better opportunities for people, and by finding the right fit. Visit their website for a complete list of their locations.

4664 Lougheed Hwy.	19916 - 64th Ave.	150-5890 No. 3 Rd.
Suite 140	Suite 104	Richmond, BC
Burnaby, BC	Langley, BC	V6X 3P7
V5C 5T5	V2Y 1A2	Tel: 604-273-8761
Tel: 604-421-3005	Tel: 604-514-5567	Fax: 604-270-4298
Fax: 604-421-3088	Fax: 604-514-5574	

ADECCO CANADA continued

505 Burrard St.
Suite 1650, Bentall 1
Vancouver, BC
V7X 1M4
Tel: 604-669-1203
Fax: 604-682-3078

1844 Scarth St.
Regina, SK
S4P 2G3
Tel: 306-359-9720
Fax: 306-359-9722
Toll Free: 1-888-359-9720

566 Byrne Dr.
Unit A
Barrie, ON
L4N 9P6
Tel: 705-728-5757
Fax: 705-728-6898

134 Dalhousie St.
Brantford, ON
N3T 2J3
Tel: 519-756-1793
Fax: 519-756-7427

43 Cork St. E.
Guelph, ON
N1H 2W8
Tel: 519-763-9689
Fax: 519-763-6494

920 Princess St.
101A
Kingston, ON
K7L 1H1
Tel: 613-541-1100
Fax: 613-541-1643

8500 Leslie St.
Suite 530
Markham, ON
L3T 7M8
Tel: 905-474-9555
Fax: 905-474-1860

707, 7th Avenue S.W.
Suite 120
Calgary, AB
T2P 3H6
Tel: 403-237-7296
Fax: 403-233-2537

135 - 21st St. E.
Suite 200
Saskatoon, SK
S7K 0B4
Tel: 306-975-7170
Fax: 306-975-1021

345 College St.
Belleville, ON
K8N 5S7
Tel: 613-967-9995
Fax: 613-967-2693

51 King St. W.
Brockville, ON
K6V 3P8
Tel: 613-498-1717
Fax: 613-498-3377

211 Centennial Pkwy. N.
Unit 3
Hamilton, ON
L8E 1H8
Tel: 905-561-9992
Fax: 905-561-9993
Toll Free: 1-877-599-5222

73 King St. W.
Kitchener, ON
N2G 1A7
Tel: 519-741-5559
Fax: 519-741-5578

4557 Hurontario Rd.
Unit B-4B
Mississauga, ON
L4Z 3M2
Tel: 905-272-4344
Fax: 905-896-4907

10279 Jasper Ave.
Edmonton, AB
T5J 1X9
Tel: 780-428-1266
Fax: 780-426-0031
Toll Free: 1-888-819-3222

228 Notre Daame Ave.
Winnipeg, MB
R3B 1N7
Tel: 204-956-6464
Fax: 204-956-4590
Toll Free: 1-877-222-8562

21 Nelson St. W.
Brampton, ON
L6X 4B6
Tel: 905-796-1550
Fax: 905-796-1544

5000 New St.
Burlington, ON
L7L 1V1
Tel: 905-634-4445
Fax: 905-634-0011

329 March Rd.
Suite 228
Kanata, ON
K2K 2E1
Tel: 613-599-3151
Fax: 613-599-3162

562 Wellington St.
Main Floor
London, ON
N6A 3R5
Tel: 519-667-7774
Fax: 519-667-7017
Toll Free: 1-888-823-3226

6435 Erin Mills Pkwy.
Unit C-05
Mississauga, ON
L5N 4H4
Tel: 905-567-6800
Fax: 905-567-0046

ADECCO CANADA continued

The Tannery Mall
465 Davis Dr., Suite 104
Newmarket, ON
L3Y 2P1
Tel: 905-836-0132
Fax: 905-836-9576
Toll Free: 1-866-836-0132

245 King St. W.
Unit 12
Oshawa, ON
L1J 2J7
Tel: 905-436-6202
Fax: 905-576-4698

1550 Kingston Rd.
Suite 20
Pickering, ON
L1V 1C3
Tel: 905-831-7359
Fax: 905-831-4922

105 Adelaide St. W.
Suite 101
Toronto, ON
M5H 1P9
Tel: 416-214-2244
Fax: 416-214-9181
Toll Free: 1-888-805-5921

56B Quinte St.
Trenton, ON
K8V 3S9
Tel: 613-965-5927
Fax: 613-965-6881

75 St-Luc Boulevard W.
Alma, QC
G8B 6W7
Tel: 418-662-5587
Fax: 418-662-2117

3246 Jean Béraud
Laval, QC
H7T 2S4
Tel: 450-682-8700
Fax: 450-682-7606

700 Forval Dr.
Suite 111
Oakville, ON
L6K 3V3
Tel: 905-842-5173
Fax: 905-842-6468

204-2277 Riverside Dr.
Ottawa, ON
K1H 7X6
Tel: 613-230-7777
Fax: 613-230-3411

55 Town Centre Court
Suite 106
Scarborough, ON
M1P 4X4
Tel: 416-296-0822
Fax: 416-296-0829

145 King St. W.
Suite 102
Toronto, ON
M5H 1J8
Tel: 416-226-1516
Fax: 416-226-5711
Toll Free: 1-877-746-7790

1600 Steeles Ave. W.
Unit 31
Vaughan, ON
L4K 4M2
Tel: 905-695-0202
Fax: 905-695-0212
Toll Free: 1-866-695-0202

345 the Saguueneens W.
Office 040
Chicoutimi, QC
G7H 6K9
Tel: 418-549-8787
Fax: 418-549-7022

370 chemin Chambly
Bureau 110
Longueill, QC
J4H 3Z6
Tel: 450-674-8787
Fax: 450-674-3126

229 Broadway
Unit 5
Orangeville, ON
L9W 1K4
Tel: 519-942-9149
Fax: 519-942-1496
Toll Free: 1-888-942-9149

126 York St.
Suite 308
Ottawa, ON
K1N 5T5
Tel: 613-244-0241
Fax: 613-244-7385

163 Main St. W.
Shelburne, ON
L0N 1S0
Tel: 519-925-9004
Fax: 519-925-9006
Toll Free: 1-888-491-9004

671 The Queensway
Toronto, ON
M8Y 1K8
Tel: 416-640-1883
Fax: 416-640-1884

325 Tecumseth Rd. W.
Windsor, ON
N8X 1G3
Tel: 519-977-5363
Fax: 519-977-5368

740 Principale Rd.
Suite 105
Granby, QC
J2G 2Y4
Tel: 450-375-8788
Fax: 450-375-5888

600 boul. De Maisonneve
Montréal, QC
H3A 3J2
Tel: 514-847-1105
Fax: 514-847-1557

ADECCO CANADA continued

6068 rue Sherbrooke est
Suite A
Montréal, QC
H1N 1C1
Tel: 514-256-6776
Fax: 514-256-5750

635 Grand Allée est
Québec, QC
G1R 2K4
Tel: 418-523-9922
Fax: 418-523-8697
Fax: 514-426-4352

65 Belvédére nord
Bureau 300
Sherbrooke, QC
J1H 4A7
Tel: 819-346-9922
Fax: 819-346-1567

39 King St.
Level 3
Saint John, NB
E2L 4W3
Tel: 506-638-0020
Fax: 506-638-0027
Toll Free: 1-866-423-3226

Place Bonaventure
800 De la Gauchetiere W.
Bureau 584
Montréal, QC
H5A 1K6
Tel: 514-847-1175
Fax: 514-287-0481

824, Ste.-Croix
St-Laurent, QC
H4L 3Y3
Tel: 514-333-5551
Fax: 514-333-1325

195 rue Sainte-Marie
Terrebonne, QC
J6W 3E2
Tel: 450-961-9449
Fax: 450-961-9883
Toll Free: 1-877-777-5134

Park Lane Terrances, Box 233
5657 Spring Garden Rd.
Suite 402
Halifax, NS
B3J 3R4
Tel: 902-423-3344
Fax: 902-420-0039
Toll Free: 1-888-874-0875

1000 boul. St-Jean
Bureau 100
Pointe Claire, QC
H9R 5P1
Tel: 514-426-2234

430 avenue Sainte-Anne
Sainte-Hyacinthe, QC
J2S 5G2
Tel: 450-771-1553
Fax: 450-771-4949

ADVOCATE PLACEMENT LTD. • 1200 Bay St., Suite 200 • Toronto, ON • M5R 2A5 • Tel: 416-927-9222 Fax: 416-927-8772 • E-mail: resume@advocateplacement.com • Internet: www.advocateplacement.com • Advocate Placement Ltd. (APL) is a niche company specializing in diverse recruiting solutions for lawyers and legal professionals in law firms, companies, associations, and government.

AEK & ASSOCIATES • 55 Harbtheir Square, Suite 3116 • Toronto, ON • M4J 2L1 • Tel: 416-359-0219 • E-mail: actuarial@aekassociates.com • Internet: www.aekassociates.com • A.E.K. & Associates founded in 1986, is a client-centered search consulting practice, specializing in the recruitment and evaluation of actuarial and executive talent on a global basis. They conduct both contingent and retained searches for clients and function as an introducing intermediary between organizations requiring specialized professionals, and candidates with the appropriate achievement records.

AEROTEK • 350 Burnhamthorpe Rd. W., 7th/8th Floors • Mississauga, ON • L5B 3J1 • Tel: 905-283-1200 • Toll Free: 800-850-1393 • Internet: www.aerotekcanada.com • With hundreds of locations throughout Canada and the United States, their professionally trained recruiters and salespeople are dedicated to serving you in nearly every major industry. Aerotek's good name thrives by continually placing qualified personnel at all skill levels and expertise. Their over 20 year history in dealing fairly and personally with clients and job seekers is what has made us a leader in the marketplace. They know first hand that expertise is critical for finding the perfect fit and a successful placement.

AEROTEK continued

40 Hine Road, Suite 120	4510 Rhodes Dr.	7326 10th St. N.E.
Ottawa, ON	Unit 735	Suite 105
K2K 2M5	Windsor, ON	Calgary, AB
Tel: 613-254-5000	N8W 5K5	T2E 8W1
Fax: 613-254-5090	Tel: 519-256-3655	Tel: 403-516-3650
Toll Free: 800-759-3855	Fax: 519-256-5696	Fax: 403-516-3690
		Toll Free: 1-866-870-9330
10088-102 Avenue	13575 Commerce Pkwy.	9800 Boulevard Cavendish
Suite 2501, TD Tower	Suite 150	Bureau 120
Edmonton, AB	Richmond, BC	Montreal, QC
T5J 2Z1	V6V 2L1	H4M 2V9
Tel: 780-577-1850	Tel: 604-244-1007	Tel: 514-798-6450
Fax: 780-577-1800	Fax: 604-244-7001	Fax: 514-798-6480
		Toll Free: 1-800-811-5444

AES RECRUITMENT • 120 Carleton St., Suite 301 • Toronto, ON • M5A 4K2 • Tel: 416-924-1818 • Fax: 416-924-1030 • E-mail: mscott@aescompany.com • Internet: www.aescompany.com • Whether it's through advertising, job fair booths or recruitment brochures, AES has the experience and expertise to develop the creative that will effectively project your company's image and generate the response you're looking for.

AFFORDABLE PERSONNEL SERVICES INC. • 1750 Steeles Ave. W., Suite 219 • Concord, ON • L4K 2L7 • Tel: 905-761-0415 • Fax: 905-761-0413 • E-mail: info@affordablepersonnel.com • Internet: www.affordablepersonnel.com • Affordable Personnel Services Inc., prefers to create partnerships with their clients and applicants. They look forward to being involved in and solving their customer's peak production demands, staffing and training needs. Their applicants and employee's are treated with fairness, honesty & respect. They adhere to all Ontario Human Rights, Employment Standards, and the Acsess Code of Ethics.

AGRINET MANAGEMENT, TRAINING AND EMPLOYMENT SERVICES LTD. • #203, 4711 - 51 Avenue • Red Deer, AB • T4N 6H8 • Tel: 403-347-7877 • Fax: 403-347-7890 • E-mail: info@agrinet-mte.com • Internet: www.agrinet-mte.com • As a Red Deer based corporate, networking association of agricultural professionals, their mandate is to provide industry leading management, training and employment services to the agricultural community. They want to help farmers and agricultural businesses become more competitive in this ever changing world. If you need a new employee or are looking for a job, just call us. If there is a field of agriculture that you would like a career in, but need training, they can help with that too. AGRINET was started in 1995 with the idea that farmers and ag businesses required information, employees and training services specific to the agricultural industry. Their projects and ideas have expanded rapidly.

AIM PERSONNEL SERVICES • Suite 126-130 Albert St. • Ottawa, ON • K1P 5G4 • Tel: 613-230-6991 • Fax: 613-230-7183 • E-mail: info@aim-personnel.com • Internet: www.aimpersonnel.ca • AIM Personnel Services Inc. is a full service Staffing Organization established in 1988 to provide engineering, information technology and administrative personnel to the public and private sectors in Canada, the United States and abroad. Personnel are provided either for temporary or contract assignments or permanent employment.

AIMCO STAFFING SOLUTIONS • 700 Dundas St. E., Suite #10 • Mississauga, ON • L4Y 3Y5 • Tel: 905-896-3181 • Fax: 905-896-2589 • E-mail: mississauga@aimco.ca • Internet: www.aimco.ca • Established in 1984, Aimco Staffing Solutions has grown to become one of the largest

Canadian owned suppliers of staffing solutions. Aimco was created to provide local industry with professional temporary industrial personnel. However, today they provide their clients with a wide range of services on a temporary or permanent basis. They specialize in light industrial and skilled labtheir, driver placement, office and administrative personnel, call centre personnel, finance and accounting, and payroll services.

2100 Ellesmere Rd.	700 Dundas St. E.	284 Queen St. E.
Unit 108	Suite 10	Suite 123
Scarborough, ON	Mississauga, ON	Brampton, ON
M1H 3H7	L4Y 3Y5	L6V 1C2
Tel: 416-439-4106	Tel: 905-896-3181	Tel: 905-454-4972
Fax: 416-439-7597	Fax: 905-896-2589	Fax: 905-454-8333
scarborough@aimco.ca	mississauga@aimco.ca	brampton@aimco.ca

871 Equestrian Ct.
Unit 4
Oakville, ON
L6L 6L7
Tel: 905-825-8788
Fax: 905-825-0375
oakville@aimco.ca

AJILON CANADA • Waterpark Place, 10 Bay St., 7th Floor • Toronto, ON • M5J 2R8 • Tel: 416-367-2020 • Fax: 416-366-2804 • E-mail: toronto@ajilon.com • Internet: www.ajilon. ca • For over twenty-five years in Canada, Ajilon Consulting has been a premier provider of Information Technology (IT) solutions, addressing their clients' critical business needs through the appropriate use and implementation of technology. Please take the time to explore their website and discover how their expertise can meet all of the technical requirements of your organization.

5 Donald St.	10 Bay St.	155 Queen St.
Suite 200	7th Floor	Suite 1206
Winnipeg, MB	Toronto, ON	Ottawa, ON
R3L 2T4	M5J 2R8	K1P 6L1
Tel: 204-942-6699	Tel: 416-367-2020	Tel: 613-786-3106
Fax: 204-942-8833	Fax: 416-366-2804	Fax: 613-567-3341
Toll Free: 888-942-6699	Toll Free: 800-842-5907	Toll Free: 888-817-4632
winnipeg@ajilon.com	international@ajilon.com	ottawa@ajilon.com
1155 University	P.O. Box 8505	1959 Upper Water St.
Suite 1410	St. Johns, NF	Suite 1700
Montreal, QC	A1B 3N9	Halifax, NS
H3B 3A7	Tel: 709-754-4240	B3J 3N2
Tel: 514-875-9520	Fax: 709-722-1871	Tel: 902-421-2025
Fax: 514-875-9241	stjohns@ajilon.com	Fax: 902-422-8686
montreal@ajilon.com		halifax@ajilon.com
550-805 8th Ave. S.W.	543 Granville St.	1290 Broad Street
Calgary, AB	Suite 701	Suite 201
T2P 1H7	Vancouver, BC	Victoria, BC
Tel: 403-233-7233	V6C 1X8	V8W 2A5
Fax: 403-233-7343	Tel: 604-689-8717	Tel: 250-382-3722
Toll Free: 888-595-4164	Fax: 604-629-1182	Fax: 250-382-3724
calgary@ajilon.com	Toll Free: 888-238-5908	victoria@ajilon.com
	vancouver@ajilon.com	

AJILON CANADA continued

1914 Hamilton Street	355 Rue St-Catherine W.
Suite 300	Suite 601
Regina, SK	Montreal, QC
S4P 3N6	H3B 1A5
Tel: 306-757-3119	Tel: 514-982-4225
Fax: 306-757-3732	Fax: 514-848-6238
Toll Free: 888-757-3119	msc_hr@ajilongsc.com
regina@ajilon.com	

AJJA INFORMATION TECHNOLOGY CONSULTANTS INC. • 785 Carling Ave., Suite 800 • Ottawa, ON • K1S 5H4 • Tel: 613-563-2552 • Fax: 613-563-3438 • E-mail: consulting@ajja. com • Internet: www.ajja.com • Ranked in March 2004 by Branham in the top 250 Technology Companies in Canada, AJJA has a team of over 270 professionals delivering technology solutions for federal government departments and high technology companies in the National Capital Region. Their consultants provide expertise in project management, business analysis, technology architecture, customized development and quality assurance expertise for IT applications.

ALAN DAVIS AND ASSOCIATES INC. • 538 Main Rd. • Hudson, QC • J0P 1J0 • Tel: 450-458-3535 • Fax: 450-458-3530 • E-mail: cvmail@alandavis.com • Internet: www.alandavis.com • Contact: Alan Davis, President • Alan Davis & Associates Inc., is an Executive and Professional Search Firm providing highly innovative solutions for positions which are difficult to fill. They offer solutions for the short and long term. They proactively recruit, and manage relationships with external candidates to fill the gaps in your succession plan. They have a proven search methodology which is visible to you. They offer fixed fees, and you, the client can hire as many candidates as you want from a search without incurring additional expense. They provide a range of professional services to an impressive list of long-standing clients, many of whom are world leaders in their respective industries. They enjoy a reputation for excellence in the field of recruiting, selection, interview training, coaching, and consulting.

ALCEA TECHNOLOGIES INC. • 1355 Bank St., Suite 401 • Ottawa, ON • K1H 8K7 • Tel: 613-563-9595 • Fax: 613-563-9494 • E-mail: info@alceatech.com • Internet: www.alceatech. com • Incorporated in 1997, Alcea was created by a group of individuals whom shared the same vision of an Information Technology (IT) company. Their vision was a company that delivers a broad base of information technology solutions that meets the needs of both the clients and of the technology professionals working to deliver them. Each founding member of Alcea brought their own individual IT experiences to the table, thus making Alcea's strengths diverse. These strength cover numerous technical fields including database management, quality assurance, programming, and Internet technologies, among many.

One Executive Pl.
1816 Crowchild Trail N.W.
Suite 700
Calgary, AB
T2M 3Y7
Tel: 403-313-5906
Fax: 403-220-1389

ALDONNA BARRY PERSONNEL & MANAGEMENT CONSULTANTS INC. • R.R. 3, Stn. Main • Caledon East, ON • L0N 1E0 • Tel: 905-584-4242 • Fax: 905-584-5357 • E-mail: welcomecentre@ABPhireandinspire.com • Internet: www.abphireandinspire.com • Contact: Aldonna Kaulius-Barry, President • Aldonna Barry Personnel & Management Consultants Inc.

has been recruiting professionally for over two decades, providing top quality personnel to a wide variety of business types and sizes, including: corporate, manufacturing, family business, multi-national enterprises, sales & service and distribution.

ALICIA RAE CAREER CENTRE INC. • 352 Donald St., Suite 702A • Winnipeg, MB • R3B 2H8 • Tel: 204-943-1947 • E-mail: info@aliciarae.com • Internet: www.aliciarae.com • Alicia Rae Career Centre Inc. is a licensed employment agency personally managed by Alicia Rae, a Certified Human Resources Professional, with over twenty years of challenging experiences handling multi-tasks project management in the multi-cultural and international public sector, manufacturing employment, placement and outplacement services.

ALL STAFF INC. • 717 Richmond St., Suite 210 • London, ON • N6A 1S2 • Tel: 519-432-7772 • Fax: 519-432-1066• Toll Free: 1-866-878-WORK(9675) • E-mail: jobs@allstaff.com • Internet: www.allstaff.ca • With years in the personal services industry they've developed the best approach to help job seekers and potential employers find the perfect match. Their amiable staff and one-on-one approach makes finding a job a better experience, and they are a free service to all candidates seeking employment.

260 Holiday Inn Dr.
Building A, Unit 9
Cambridge, ON
N3C 4E8
Tel: 519-654-9675
Fax: 519-654-2219
Toll Free: 1-877-659-WORK(9675)
info@allstaff.ca

ALLEMBY MANAGEMENT GROUP INC. • North York Square, 45 Sheppard Avenue East, Suite 900 • Toronto, ON • M2N 5W9 • Tel: 416-783-1881 • Fax: 416-783-0831 • E-mail: info@allemby.com • Internet: www.allemby.com • Contact: Melissa Schafer, President • At Allemby Management Group Inc., their expert consultants have over nineteen years of experience in the Executive Search field. They can handle all your executive recruiting needs. Their consultants have expertise in recruiting business professionals within several industries. AMGI has an excellent track record of success. They have a reputation for building teams that stay in place and contribute to the long-term growth of your organization. They are committed to conducting each executive search to the complete satisfaction of their clients.

ALLEN PERSONNEL SERVICES • 362 Dufferin Ave. • London, ON • N6B 1Z4 • Tel: 519-672-7040 • Fax: 519-672-7044 • E-mail: london@allenpersonnel.com • Internet: www.allenpersonnel.com • Contact: Cindy McPherson, Branch Manager • Since 1970, Allen Personnel has grown and expanded. Today they're one of the most extensive human resource suppliers in southwestern Ontario, offering quality search services in Manufacturing, Transportation, Distribution, Processing, Fabricating, Assembly, Warehousing, Services, Government, Education, Medical, Research and Development and Financial Services.

ALLIANCE PERSONNEL GROUP, THE • 2892 Portland Drive • Oakville, ON • L6H 5W8 • Tel: 905-829-1444 or 1-800-661-6718 • Fax: 905-829-9664 • E-mail: info@thealliancegroup.ca • Internet: www.thealliancegroup.ca • The Alliance Group is one of Canada's foremost providers of logistics personnel. Through The Alliance Group you can count on receiving the most comprehensive and responsive staffing services available. As logistics staffing specialists, The Alliance Group provides highly qualified permanent contract and temporary contract personnel to a broad range of industries. By offering a full complement of human resource services, we bring a singular focus to your personnel requirements, allowing you to concentrate on your core competencies.

ALTIS HUMAN RESOURCES • 330 Bay St., Suite 1400 • Toronto, ON • M5H 2S8 • Tel: 416-214-9280 • Fax: 416-214-9479 • E-mail: jobs@altishr.com • Internet: www.altishr.com • Altis Human Resources is among Canada's fastest growing contracting and recruiting firms. Since its inception in 1989, Altis HR has experienced an average growth of over 100% per annum. Altis HR offers both business solutions and business opportunities. It provides the employer with the most qualified resource at the best price and the candidate with the best possible position at the best rate in the areas of administration and accounting placement.

Suite 375	102 Bank St.	905 West Pender St.
33 City Center Dr.	Suite 302	Suite 405
Mississauga, ON	Ottawa, ON	Vancouver, BC
L5B 2N5	K1P 5N4	V6C 1L6
Tel: 905-279-9229	Tel: 613-230-5350	Tel: 604-408-8862
Fax: 905-279-1693	Fax: 613-230-1623	Fax: 604-408-8875

ALUMNI NETWORK RECRUITMENT CORPORATION • Oakville, ON • Tel: 905-465-2547 • E-mail: karen@alumni-network.com • Internet: www.alumni-network.com • Alumni-Network Recruitment Corporation is a full service professional search and recruitment firm, specializing in ERP, E-Commerce and Engineering. They have client coverage internationally and have individual applicant inventories by country including Canada, United States, Asia Pacific, Australia, Europe, Russia, South Africa, the Middle East and more. To this end they work directly with other ERP, E-Commerce and Engineering Trading Partners globally.

ANCIA PERSONNEL • 8032, avenue des églises, bureau 226 • Charny, QC • Q6X 1X7 • Tel: 418-832-6600 • Fax: 418-832-6511 • E-mail: ancia.personnel@videotron.net • Internet: www. ancia.qc.ca • Founded in 1996, ANCIA specializes on the level of the search for frameworks, the placement of personnel and the organizational development in the most neuralgic sectors of the organizations. They offer a complete and exclusive range of solutions to measure, in perfect conformity with the requirements and the respective objectives of the candidates and the employers.

ANGUS EMPLOYMENT LIMITED • 1100 Burloak Dr., 4th Floor-• Burlington, ON • L7L 6B2 • Tel: 905-319-0773 • Fax: 905-336-9445 • E-mail: resumes@angusemployment.com • Internet: www.angusemployment.com • Angus has had 39 very successful years in the placement business. They are a permanent placement firm, recruiting individuals in all professional occupations, ranging from entry-level to senior management. Their areas of specialty include management, sales and marketing, information systems, clerical and administrative, accounting and finance, engineering and technical, hi tech and emerging technologies and eCommerce specialists.

ANGUS ONE PROFESSIONAL RECRUITMENT LTD. • 1800 - 777 Hornby St. • Vancouver, BC • V6Z 1S4 • Tel: 604-682-8367 • Fax: 604-682-4664 • Toll Free: 1-888-682-8367 • E-mail: info@ angusone.com • Internet: www.angusone.com • Founded in 1986, Angus One Professional Recruitment & Templine is a proud BC owned & operated employment agency serving the professional recruitment needs of Greater Vancouver & the entire Lower Mainland business community. Angus One represents many of British Columbia's most exciting organizations & candidates.

ANNE WHITTEN BILINGUAL HUMAN RESOURCES INC. • 123 Edward Street, Suite 705 • Toronto, ON • M5G 1E2 • Tel: 416-595-5974 • Fax: 416-598-5127 • E-mail: info@annewhitten. com • Internet: www.annewhitten.com • Contact: Anne Whitten • Toronto's premiere placement firm specializing in English/French bilingual jobs, employment and recruiting. Since 1974, Anne Whitten Bilingual Human Resources Inc. has successfully brought together demanding employers and job candidates. They handle permanent, contract, and temporary positions in Toronto, Ontario and across Canada.

ANIIWIN EMPLOYMENT SOLUTIONS • 105 - 260 St. Mary Ave. • Winnipeg, MB • R3C 0M6 • Tel: 204-925-2790 • Fax: 204-943-0023 • E-mail: work@anokiiwin.com • Internet: www. anokiiwin.com/work • Anokiiwin Employment Solutions, an Aboriginal owned and operated, nationally licensed, award-winning employment agency, offers high quality, professional services to private and public sectors employers seeking employees and individuals seeking employment.

ANT & BEE CORPORATION • 123 John St. • Toronto, ON • M5V 2E2 • Tel: 416-646-2811 • Fax: 416-847-0108 • E-mail: inquiries@antandbee.com • Internet: www.antandbee.com/applicants. html • Ant & Bee Corporation, located in Toronto, Ontario, is an Information Technology (IT) consulting company, specializing in providing IT project solutions, including outstheircing, project consulting, pay rolling, and permanent and contract employment staffing services, for private and public sector clients across North America.

APEX SEARCH INC. • 45 Sheppard Ave E., Suite 900 • North York, ON • M2N 5W9 • Tel: 416-226-2828 • E-mail: resume@apexsearch.com • Internet: www.apexsearch.com • Contact: Karen Agulnik or Joanne Crossman • Apex Search specializes in the location and placement of highly talented IT professionals in both permanent and contract positions. Since 1994, they have been bringing companies and IT professionals together in successful working relationships.

API ADPEOPLE INC. • 40 Holly Street, Suite 203 • Toronto, ON • M4S 3C3 • Tel: 416-486-1220 • E-mail: general@api-adpeople.com • Internet: www.api-adpeople.com • Api Adpeople Inc. is the perfect definition of a market-driven idea – a creative resource of communications professionals available to you by the htheir (on site or off).

APPLE ONE EMPLOYMENT SERVICES • 3331 Bloor St. W. • Etobicoke, ON • M8X 1E7 • Tel: 416-236-4000 • Fax: 416-921-9627 • Internet: www.appleone.ca • Founded in 1964, and built on a policy of helping quality individuals like yourself achieve your employment goals, AppleOne has grown to become the single largest privately owned employment service in North America. Offering full-service career assistance and numerous special benefits, AppleOne can help you with everything from temporary projects to full-time (permanent placement) positions. And, with over 200 offices located throughout Canada and the United States, you'll always find an AppleOne close to the places where you live and work! If you are moving to a new location, chances are there's already an AppleOne in place, ready to serve you.

4603 Kingsway Suite 405 Burnaby, BC Tel: 604-678-8028	21 Commerce Park Dr. Barrie, ON Tel: 705-735-1707	295 Queen St. East Brampton, ON East Unit 38 Tel: 905-453-8000
1035 Brant Street Unit #4 Burlington, ON Tel: 905-631-3333 40 Sheppard Ave. West North York, ON Tel: 416-225-2000	33 City Centre Dr., Ste. 16 Mississauga, ON L5B 2N5 Tel: 905-277-2770 233 Cross Avenue, Unit 1 Oakville, ON Tel: 905-339-3333	17480 Yonge St. Unit C007 Newmarket, ON Tel: 905-868-8608 1794 Liverpool Rd. Unit 21 Pickering, ON Tel: 905-831-3400
9555 Yonge St. Richmond Hill, ON Tel: 905-787-9911	2206 Eglinton Ave. E. Scarborough, ON M1K 5G8 Tel: 416-750-4718	

APPLIED TECHNOLOGY SOLUTIONS • 55 York St., Suite 1100 • Toronto, ON • M5J 1R7 • Tel: 416-369-0008 • Fax: 416-369-0199 • E-mail: resumes@atsglobal.com • Internet: www. atsglobal.com • Established in 1992, ATS (Applied Technology Solutions Inc.) is a dynamic IT solutions and staffing firm dedicated to providing cost-effective professional services and resources to the Canadian and US job markets. ATS helps both companies looking to recruit the industry's top candidates as well as technology professionals in search of new employment opportunities in the high tech sector.

AQUENT CANADA • 77 Bloor St. West, Suite 1405 • Toronto, ON • M5S 1M2 • Tel: 416-323-0600 • Fax: 416-323-9866 • E-mail: questions@aquent.com • Internet: www.aquent.ca • Aquent is a professional services firm that specializes in helping companies all over the world, across a variety of industries, make use of people, processes, and technology more effectively than ever before. Since its founding in 1986, Aquent's pioneering approach to staffing, consulting, and outstheircing keeps the company a step ahead. Among its many industry-leading innovations, Aquent was the first company in the United States to offer comprehensive benefits to temporary employees, including a company-matching 401(k) plan. In addition, Aquent was the first in the field to offer an unconditional 110% money-back guarantee to clients, and the first to create a Web site featuring thousands of portfolios created by prequalified talent.

815 Hornby St., Suite 606	1350, rue Sherbrooke Ouest
Vancouver, BC	Bureau 320
V6Z 2E6	Montreal, QC
Tel: 604-669-5600	H3G 1J1
Fax: 604-669-5665	Tel: 514-289-9009
	Fax: 514-289-1003

ARLYN PERSONNEL AGENCIES LTD. • 1160 - 625 Howe Street • Vancouver, BC • V6C 2T6 • Tel: 604-681-4432 • Fax: 604-681-4418 • E-mail: info@arlynreid.net • Internet: www. arlynreid.net • Arlyn Personnel has remained a leader in successful temporary and permanent placements for more than ten years in the areas of legal secretarial, accounting, general clerical and secretarial

ARMOR PERSONNEL • 8 Nelson St. W., Suite 104A • Brampton, ON • L6X 4J2 • Tel: 905-459-1617 • Fax: 905-459-1704 • E-mail: brampton@armorpersonnel.com • Internet: www. armorpersonnel.com • Armor is a Professional Employment Organization providing opportunities for strategic partnerships for their clients, vendors, community, candidates, associates and internal staff.

36 Bessemer Court	8 Nelson St. W.	75 Waitline Ave.
Units 1, 2	Suite 104A	Suite 110
Vaughan, ON	Brampton, ON	Mississauga, ON
L4K 3C9	L6X 4J2	L4Z 3E5
Tel: 905-660-7888	Tel: 905-454-3333	Tel: 905-566-4591
Fax: 905-660-0874	Fax: 905-459-0132	Fax: 905-566-9783

6755 Mississauga Rd.
Suite 104
Mississauga, ON
L5N 7Y2
Tel: 905-567-6855
Fax: 905-567-6857

ARMSTRONG DAY INTERNATIONAL • 1800-360 Main Street • Winnipeg, MB • R3C 3Z3 • Tel: 204-940-3900 • Fax: 204-940-3901 • Toll Free: 1-866-940-3950 • Internet: www. armstrongday.com • Contact: Paul Croteau • Armstrong Day International provides high-quality executive recruitment services customized to better meet their clients needs.

ARTEMP • 294 Albert Street, Suite 104 • Ottawa, ON • K1P 6E6 • Tel: 613-232-9767 • Fax: 613-232-7050 • E-mail: info@artemp.ca • Internet: www.artemp.ca • Since 1987, ARTEMP has been the Ottawa region's single most successful provider of creative personnel to both public and private sectors.

ASA STAFFING PARTNERS • 700 - 177 Lombard • Winnipeg, MB • R3B 0W5 • Tel: 204-943-0002 • Fax: 204-957-0762 • E-mail: aallard@mts.net • Internet: www.asastaffingpartners.com • ASA Staffing Partners is an incorporated company with memberships in the Human Resource Management Association of Manitoba, and the Winnipeg Chamber of Commerce. They provide contract and direct hire recruitment services to clients and strategically allianced recruitment firms in Canada, Bermuda and the Caribbean. Their candidate focus is on individuals in the professions, accounting and management, legal and administrative fields.

ASHLAR-STONE MANAGEMENT CONSULTANTS INC. • 50 Burnhamthorpe Rd. W., Suite 401 • Mississauga, ON • L5B 3C2 • Tel: 905-615-0900 • Fax: 905-615-0917 • E-mail: cntc6@ ashlar-stone.com • Internet: www.ashlar-stone.com • Contact: Stuart Moore • Ashlar-Stone Management Consultants Inc.® is a small, responsive retainer-based executive search firm providing high quality service for senior and middle management requirements within most industry sectors, primarily within Canada and the USA. Since 1990 the Company has established a reputation for consistency in recruiting exceptional candidates for particularly demanding assignments. Unlike most retainer-based executive search firms, one senior consultant manages every detail of the assignment; from client contact though market research, screening, recruiting and interviewing, short-list presentation, reference-checking and contract negotiation. While much more demanding in time, this close relationship with both client and candidate, together with the resulting first-hand knowledge of the market provides the notable difference in fit.

ASL CONSULTING • Woodbine Place, Suite 550, 135 Queens Plate Drive • Toronto, ON • M9W 6V1 • Tel: 416-740-6996 • Fax: 416-740-4203 • E-mail: info@aslconsulting.com • Internet: www.aslconsulting.com • Since 1989 ASL has been developing, selling, implementing and supporting its Human Resources Management System (HRMS) Suite of best-of-breed applications for organizations of all sizes. HRMS Solutions to Integrate the Enterprise. Their strengths are rooted in their group-based approach, which facilitates managerial and technical excellence as well as innovation in products and services. They are committed to complete client satisfaction and to becoming a global leader in the provision of Human Resources Information Technology solutions. Their clients value their approach and commitment to excellence and range in size from small and mid-sized companies to Fortune 500 corporations.

ASSET COMPUTER PERSONNEL • 48 Yonge St., Suite 500 • Toronto, ON • M5E 1G6 • Tel: 416-777-1717 • Fax: 416-777-0647 • E-mail: asset@asset.ca, resume@asset.ca • Internet: www. asset.ca • In business since 1985, Asset Computer Personnel has become a leading supplier of contract and full-time Information Technology people in Canada. In fact, more than 7,000 people (1,000 in the 12 months ending December 2000) have found meaningful employment through Asset since their inception.

ASSOCIATION RESOURCE CENTRE • 151 Bloor Street West, Suite 800 • Toronto, ON • M5S 1S4 • Tel: 416-926-8780 • Fax: 416-926-1225 • E-mail: info@associationconsultants.com • Internet: www.associationconsultants.com • The Association Resource Centre (ARC) is a full service management consulting and executive search firm specifically tailored to the needs of associations and charities. They are based in Toronto, but they have experience working with clients around the globe.

1568 Merivale Rd.
Suite 120
Ottawa, ON
K2G 5Y7
Tel: 613-825-8480
Fax: 613-825-1263

142-757 West Hastings St.
Suite 505
Vancouver, BC
V6C 1A1
Tel: 604-215-4452

ASTON MANAGEMENT GROUP INC. • 120 Eglinton Ave. E., Suite 1100 • Toronto, ON • M4P 1E2 • Tel: 416-932-8008 • Fax: 416-932-3754 • E-mail: aston@astonmanagement. com • Internet: www.astonmanagement.com • Contact: Marc Aston • They have experience throughout North America, as well as alliances with other recruiters locally and nationally.

ATS RELIANCE TECHNICAL GROUP • 200 Yorkland Blvd., Suite 600 • Toronto, ON • M2J 5C1 • Tel: 416-482-8002 • Fax: 416-482-1210 • E-mail: ats@atsrecruitment.com • Internet: www. atsrecruitment.com • Since 1975, ATS Reliance Technical Group has been a leading supplier of recruitment solutions to the Manufacturing, Engineering and Consulting Industries. Through their network of offices across Canada and the United States and their 120,000-plus candidate database, ATS Reliance is also able to draw upon the support of their associate companies within the Vedior Group (the 3rd largest staffing service in the World) and their 2,242 offices in 30 countries. ATS Reliance has the capability to identify skilled professionals locally, nationally and internationally to meet the staffing and placement needs of their clientele.

3027 Harvester Rd.
Suite 212
Burlington, ON
L7N 3G7
Tel: 905-333-9632
Fax: 905-333-9326

730-10655 Southport Rd. SW
Suite 730
Calgary, AB
T2W 4Y1
Tel: 403-261-4600
Fax: 403-265-2909

171 Queens Ave.
Suite 601
London, ON
N6A 5J7
Tel: 519-679-2886
Fax: 519-679-1483

260 Holiday Inn Drive
Unit 32, Building C
Cambridge, ON
N1R 1S3
Tel: 519-658-5535
Fax: 519-658-5530

1501 West Broadway
Suite 300
Vancouver, BC
V6J 4Z6
Tel: 604-915-9333
Fax: 604-915-9339

10117 Jasper Ave.
Suite 607
Edmonton, AB
T5J 1W3
Tel: 780-462-1815
Fax: 780-461-9968

150 Consumers Rd.
Suite 308
North York, ON
M2J 1P9
Tel: 416-498-9494
Fax: 416-498-0594

78 Walker Dr.
Brampton, ON
L6T 4H6
Tel: 905-458-1607
Fax: 905-458-5597

ATTICUS RESOURCES INC. • Suite 1800, 250 - 6th Avenue S.W. BowValley Sq. IV • Calgary, AB • T2P 3H7 • Tel: 403-237-8484 • E-mail: dtaylor@atticusresources.com • Internet: www. atticusresources.com • Atticus Resources is a Calgary based search firm with operations focused in the information technology sector. They have been successfully providing solutions to hiring managers in the Calgary market since 1995. Their focus is to allow you to spend your time focusing on what you do best by doing what they do best.

AUSTIN PARK MANAGEMENT GROUP INC. • 164 Eglinton Ave. E., Suite 103 • Toronto, ON • M4P 1G4 • Tel: 416-488-9565 • Fax: 416-488-9601 • E-mail: austin@austinpark.com • Internet: www.austinpark.com • Austin Park Management Group Inc. has been a successful leader in the placement of permanent and contract Information Technology professionals, throughout Canada and the United States, since 1985. Since their inception they have built and maintained excellent long-term relationships with their clients. They now serve a wide range of industries including, but not limited to, Technology, Manufacturing, Finance, Healthcare, Government and Media, many of which are Fortune 100 companies.

AVALON EMPLOYMENT INC. • P.O. Box 2574, Stn C • St. John's, NF • A1C 6K1 • Tel: 709-579-4866 • Fax: 709-579-4892 • E-mail: aei@avalonemploy.com • Internet: www.avalonemploy.com • Contact: Joan Holloway • The A.E.I. team provides job search assistance and support to adults with barriers to employment in the St. John's, Conception Bay South, and surrounding areas. They remain involved with all parties to ensure that the job placements are running smoothly. Their staff can help you find the right employee for positions within your company.

AYRSHIRE GROUP, THE • 67 Yonge St., Suite 808 • Toronto, ON • M5E 1J8 • Tel: 416-364-6388 • Fax: 416-364-5302 • E-mail: resume@ayrshiregroup.com • Internet: www.ayrshiregroup.com • The mission of The AYRSHIRE GROUP is to refer top-quality Staff to the Financial Services Industry in the Greater Toronto Area. To assist their Clients to compete in today's sophisticated and competitive markets, they represent Candidates who possess a balance of education, industry related ctheirses, experience, flexibility and commitment. The AYRSHIRE GROUP provides recruitment expertise to their Financial Services Client companies and Career Counseling and professional opportunities to their Candidates.

B P FLOATER STAFFING INC. • Sloane Square, Suite 401, 5920 - 1A St. S.W. • Calgary, AB • T2H 0G3 • Tel: 403-252-1987 • Fax: 403-252-2847 • E-mail: floaters@floaterstaffing.com • Internet: www.floaterstaffing.com • Contact: Barbara Premdas • Since 1983, Calgary-based and independently owned Floater Staffing has provided custom solutions for all your human resource requirements. Floater Staffing fills office, industrial, technical, professional, and hospitality positions with qualified candidates. Their mission is to partner with their customers to provide the right people for the right positions, while empowering employees and job candidates with opportunity and choice.

B.C. HEALTH SERVICES LTD. (BCHS) • Suite 410-2608 Granville Street • Vancouver, BC • V6H 3V3 • Tel: 604 488-0600 • Fax: 604 488-0665 • E-mail: ikandal@bchs.bc.ca • Internet: www.bchs.bc.ca • Contact: Ingrid Kandal, Chief Operating Officer • B.C. Health Services Ltd. (BCHS) was incorporated in British Columbia in 1989. Since then they have satisfied hundreds of Canadian clients whose priority is to achieve maximum value from restrictive budgets. Whether your organization is in the public sector, or from private industry, they can show you many ways to reduce your costs while adding value, flexibility, and efficiency.

BALL LANGE & ASSOCIATES INC. • Unit B1, 285 Weber Street North • Waterloo, ON • N2J 3H8 • Tel: 519-747-2727 • Fax: 519-747-0728 • E-mail: waterloo@balltraining.com • Internet: www.balltraining.com • Contact: Fred Lange, President • Since 1984, Ball Lange & Associates Inc. has achieved a breadth of experience encompassing a highly diverse client group. Their professionals reflect this expertise in assessment, service delivery and tangible results. All of their programs and services are tailored to the individual needs of each client. They work with their clients to create the appropriate service program that will achieve the desired work life goals. They are not satisfied until their client sees results. That is why Ball Lange & Associates Inc. has a solid reputation for producing professional and measurable outcomes. Each client receives excellent service at competitive fees that deliver maximum value to the organization.

BALL LANGE & ASSOCIATES INC. continued

450 Speedvale Ave. W.
Suite 104
Guelph, ON
N1H 7Y6
Tel: 519-763-2120
Fax: 519-763-1292

BANKSIDE CHASE CORPORATION • 80 Bloor St. West, Suite 1200 • Toronto, ON • M5S 2V1 • Tel: 416-640-1900 • Fax: 416-640-1901 • E-mail: administrator@banksidechase.com • Internet: www.banksidechase.com • Bankside Chase has a domestic and international reputation for providing suitable placements for top quality IT professionals.
25 Mary St., Suite 307
Waterloo, ON
N2J 1G1
Tel: 416-640-1900

BARBARA PERSONNEL INC. • 350 rue Sparks, Suite 601 • Ottawa, ON • K1R 7S8 • Tel: 613-236-9689 • Fax: 613-236-7524 • E-mail: jdurocher@barbarapersonnel.com • Internet: www.barbarapersonnel.com • Barbara Personnel is widely recognized as the firm of choice in providing challenging assignments for everyone. Whether you want to re-enter the workforce or remain active in retirement, or again you are young and wish to acquire work experience? Barbara Personnel can assist you at every stage of your professional career.

BARBARA SHORE & ASSOCIATES • 1155, rue University, Suite 1414 • Montreal, QC • H3B 3A7 • Tel: 514-878-3443 • Fax: 514-878-2473 • E-mail: bshore@shoreassoc.com • Internet: www.shoreassoc.com • Contact: Barbara Shore • Barbara Shore & Associates specializes in recruiting professionals, managers and executives for their clients. Barbara Shore & Associates' strong team has several years of experience filling positions across numerous industries, including telecommunications, information technology, pharmaceuticals, manufacturing, consulting and professional services.

BARRETT ROSE & LEE INC. • 6 Adelaide St. E., Suite 400 • Toronto, ON • M5C 1H6 • Tel: 905-678-3222 • Toll Free: 1-888-678-3228 • E-mail: sbyrd@barrettrose.com • Internet: www. barrettrose.com • Barrett Rose & Lee is focused on senior/middle level management and professional individuals in the disciplines of Management Information Systems, Professional Sales & Marketing and, Finance & Administration. Their industrial emphasis tends to be new economy companies such as software & hardware technology vendors and, business services. They market organizations within the Golden Horseshoe directly and utilize their affiliates to complete assignments throughout Canada and North America.

BAUSCHKE & ASSOCIATES LTD. • 1615 St. Mary's Rd., Suite 100 • Winnipeg, MB • R2M 3W8 • Tel: 204-949-1890 • Fax: 1-888-441-6777 • E-mail: form • Internet: www.bauschke. com • Bauschke & Associates is a full service consulting firm. Its exposure to a wide spectrum of business challenges in many industries, both in the U.S.A. and Canada provides considerable depth and expertise in providing advisory services. These credentials, coupled with their acute awareness of the complex challenges facing management today, enable us to provide superior objective advice.

BCGI BARON CONSULTING GROUP INC. • Hudson's Bay Centre, 2 Bloor Street East, Suite 2306 • Toronto, ON • M4W 1A8 • Tel: 416-979-2404 • Fax: 416-979-1567 • E-mail: carol@bcgi. ca • Internet: www.bcgi.ca • The team of Search Consultants and Research Associates at BCGI are dedicated to planning and executing senior level searches, with particular expertise in the financial services, accounting, real estate and construction sectors. BCGI consultants commit to an exclusive partnership with each client, employing industry best practices, performance based fee structure, and a team-based approach to achieving superior results.

BDK GLOBAL SEARCH INC. • 1115 Sherbrooke St. W., Suite 1401 • Montréal, QC • H3A 1H3 • Tel: 514-281-9999 • E-mail: montreal@krecklo.com • Internet: www.bdkglobal.com • Contact: Brian D. Krecklo, President • Considered an innovator in the retained search industry, BDK Global Search Inc., "BDKGlobal", has carved out a niche specializing in CIO, executive IT management, and senior IT specialist searches for publicly-held, as well as, venture-backed and private equity companies. BDKGlobal, through its managing director, began as an information technology search company in 1978 with the vision to grow vertically and become the recognized leader in Information Systems and Technology retained executive search, leadership assessment, executive coaching and interim management.

BEDFORD CONSULTING GROUP INC., THE • 145 Adelaide St. W., Suite 400 • Toronto, ON • M5H 4E5 • Tel: 416-963-9000 • Fax: 416-963-9998 • E-mail: search@bedfordgroup. com • Internet: www.bedfordgroup.com • Bedford Group is a Toronto-based executive search firm with international search capability for clients ranging from multi-nationals to early stage companies. As the Toronto office of TRANSEARCH, they have over 56 offices in 36 countries to serve their clients globally. Focussing on six sectors, they have deep knowledge and insight in the following areas: technology, health sciences, natural resources/heavy industry, consumer products/retail/media, manufacturing/supply chain and financial services.

132 Reynolds St.
Oakville, ON
L6J 3K5
Tel: 905-338-7008
Fax: 905-338-0662

BEECHEY MANAGEMENT RESOURCES • 5109 Lampman Avenue • Burlington, ON • L7L 6L1 • Tel: 905-331-8182 • Fax: 905-331-9027 • E-mail: lynn@beechey.org • Internet: www. beechey.org • Lynn Beechey, a Certified Personnel Consultant, is a recruitment professional with over 15 years of business experience. Beechey Management Resources proviceds a unique and specialized recruitment service. The reputable companies that they choose to work with offer strong opportunities for career growth, and rely on the services of their company to help build their teams. Beechey Management Resources is a member of the Association of Canadian Search Employment and Stadding Services (ACSESS).

BESTARD AGRICULTURAL PLACEMENTS • Box 519 • Grand Bend, ON • N0M 1T0 • Tel: 519-780-5403 • E-mail: egraham@bestardagplacements.com • Internet: www.bestard.on.ca • Contact: Elaine Graham • Bestard Agricultural Placements (BAP) searches for candidates for the Agri-business industry- in feed, crop, animal health, seed, banking, credit, fertilizer, crop protection, advertising agencies, retail and equipment sectors of agriculture. They search for candidates across Canada, (including the bilingual parts of Eastern Ontario and Quebec) United States and Internationally. Most positions filled are Canadian and Northern U.S.A. in nature.

BEVERTEC CST INC. • 5935 Airport Rd., Suite 400 • Mississauga, ON • L4V 1W5 • Tel: 416-695-7525 • Fax: 416-695-7526 • E-mail: info@bevertec.com • Internet: www.bevertec.com • Established in 1981, Bevertec CST Inc. is based in Toronto, Ontario, serving clients in Canada, the US, South America and Asia. They develop and implement innovative software solutions for the financial services, manufacturing, communications and transportation sectors, and for federal, provincial and municipal government agencies.

BEYONDTECH SOLUTIONS INC. • #243-4299 Canada Way • Bur, BC • V5R 5W2 • Fax: 604-433-0627 • E-mail: info@beyond-tech.com • Internet: www.beyond-tech.com • They are a provider if contract and permanent recruitment services to clients across industry sectors. At BeyondTech Solutions, they believe in making recruitment simple for employers and job seekers. With their convenient staffing options, you can exercise knowledge and freedom in choosing your career or personnel solutions.

BILINGUAL SOURCE / SOURCE BILINGUE • 30 St. Clair Ave. W., Suite 302 • Toronto, ON • M4V 3A1 • Tel: 416-515-8880 • Fax: 416-515-8324 • E-mail: info@bilingualsource.com • Internet: www.bilingualsource.com • Bilingual Sourcee is a full service staffing company, with a sole focus on the French/English marketplace. Since its inception, in 1984, Bilingual Source has focussed on ethics, quality, and customer service, believing that they have two customers to serve: their client companies and the many candidates that they represent. They provide bilingual professionals at all skill levels, to corporate clients in the Greater Toronto Area, for permanent and contract positions.

BILINGUAL TARGET • 45 St. Clair Avenue W., Suite 200 • Toronto, ON • M4V 1K6 • Tel: 416-920-9622 • Fax: 416-920-1601 • E-mail: contact@bilingualjobs.ca • Internet: www.bilingualjobs.ca • Contact: Pat A. Giannone • Established in 1986, Bilingual Target has been providing specialized Bilingual (English/French) placement services to the Greater Toronto Area.

BIRCH & ASSOCIÉS • 1405 Transcanada, Suite 110 • Dorval, QC • H9P 2V9 • Tel: 514-685-9900 • Fax: 514-685-5855 • E-mail: info@birch.ca • Internet: www.birch.ca • Birch & Associates was the product of a market need matched with the far-reaching network of the Birch partners. The impeccable reputation of the partners has allowed the firm to grow from a basement operation into one of the premier executive search firms in Canada. Continuously tracking marketplace trends, they offer insight into various industries form both a client and candidate perspective.

BLACKSHIRE RECRUITING SERVICES INC. • 713 Columbia St., Suite 103 • New Westminster, BC • V3M 1B2 • Tel: 604-517-3550 • E-mail: resumes@blackshire.com • Internet: www.blackshire.com • Blackshire Recruiting Services recruits for technical careers in Vancouver in the following sectors: software and development, systems engineering, computer systems, consulting, systems integration, hardware development, technology and data processing.

BOWEN • 525 - 7 Avenue SW, Suite 101 • Calgary, AB • T2P 3V5 • Tel: 403-262-1156 • Fax: 403-537-6952 • E-mail: info@bowenworks.ca • Internet: www.bowenworks.ca • BOWEN's focus is on building meaningful relationships with its clients and candidates, delivering a more-than-lip-service commitment to unparalleled and proactive service, and emphasizing a culture and work environment that cultivates passion, balance and philanthropy as corporate values. As a leader in the industry, they are extremely proud to be in a position to boast that many of their clients have been with us since the early days of their existence. Their focus is on simply being "better".

BOWER NG STAFF SYSTEMS INC. • 1205 - 750 West Pender Street • Vancouver, BC • V6C 2T8 • Tel: 604-688-8282 • Fax: 604-669-9088 • E-mail: careers@staffsystems.ca • Internet: www.staffsystems.ca • Contact: Allison MacInnes, Business Manager • Bower NG Staff Systems, a full service recruitment company, was founded in 1991. Serving a client base from large corporations to small companies, Jamesie Bower, President/Owner, and her Associates at Staff Systems are committed to sharing their vision and values to their clients and applicants.

BOYDEN GLOBAL EXECUTIVE SEARCH • Suite 1060, SunLife Tower West 144 - 4th Avenue SW • Calgary, AB • T2P 3N4 • Tel: 403-237-6603 • Fax: 403-237-5551 • E-mail: info@boyden. ca • Internet: www.boyden.com • Boyden seeks to add value to the search process through the knowledge and experience of trained consultants, the resources of their global firm and their commitment to becoming trusted advisers to their clients. They view the relationship with their clients as a true partnership—they work side by side with their clients to identify and resolve issues related to finding the most qualified candidates.

401 Bay Street
Suite 2420
Toronto, ON
M5H 2Y4
Tel: 416-640-1300
Fax: 416-979-8418

BP FLOATER STAFFING INC. • Sloane Square - Suite 401, 5920 - 1A Street SW • Calgary, AB • T2H 0G3 Tel: 403-252-1987 • Fax: 403-252-2847 • E-mail: floaters@floaterstaffing.com • Internet: www.floaterstaffing.com • Since 1983, Calgary-based and independently owned Floater Staffing has provided custom solutions for all your human resource requirements. Floater Staffing fills office, industrial, technical, professional, and hospitality positions with qualified candidates. Their mission is to partner with their customers to provide the right people for the right positions, while empowering employees and job candidates with opportunity and choice.

BRAINHUNTER • 2 Sheppard Ave. E., Suite 700 • Toronto, ON • M2N 5Y7 • Tel: 416-225-9900 • Fax: 416-225-9104• E-mail: protec@protecstaff.com • Internet: www.protecstaff.com • Brainhunter is dedicated to helping employers and job seekers make best-fit connections. They are a one-stop shop specializing in providing high-growth sectors with pre-screened, top-tier contract and permanent hires.

1545 Carling Ave.	1155, boul. Rene-Levesque	Deerfoot Atria, 6815-8th St. NE
Suite 600	Bureau 2500	Suite 125
Ottawa, ON	Montreal, QC	Calgary, AB
K1Z 8P9	H3B 2K4	T2E 7H7
Tel: 613-789-7000	Tel: 514-842-8888	Tel: 403-266-6110
Fax: 613-722-8756	Fax: 514-842-6235	Fax: 416-733-5474
Toll Free: 1-877-761-9436		
1155, boul. Rene-Levesque	Deerfoot Atria, 6815-8th St. NE	100 Park Royal
Bureau 2500	Suite 125	Suite 200
Montreal, QC	Calgary, AB	West Vancouver, BC
H3B 2K4	T2E 7H7	V7T 1A2
Tel: 514-842-8888	Tel: 403-266-6110	Toll Free: 1-866-508-1122
Fax: 514-842-6235	Fax: 416-733-5474	
Toll Free: 1-877-842-9988	Toll Free: 1-877-999-1344	

BRAY, LAROUCHE ET ASSOCIÉS INC. • 2000, rue Peel, Bureau 5050 • Montréal, QC • H3A 2W5 • Tel: 514-845-2114 • Fax: 514-845-3808 • E-mail: candidat@braylarouche.com • Internet: www.braylarouche.com • Contact: Nancy Boulay • Consultants in human resources since 1991, Bray, Larouche and Associates specializes in recruiting administrative support staff on either a permanent or temporary basis.

BRETHET, BARNUM & ASSOCIATES INC. • 703 Evans Avenue, Suite 300 • Etobicoke, ON • M9C 5E9 • Tel: 416-621-4900 • Toll Free: 1-888-284-8465 • Internet: www.brethetbarnum.com • Contact: Anne Brethet • Brethet, Barnum and Associates was founded in 1980 by 2 partners from the Pharmaceutical Industry. They are Industry Experts, working exclusively in Health Care. They are well established with an extensive knowledge of the industry, and have developed relationships with literally thousands of industry professionals.

BRIDGE INFORMATION TECHNOLOGY INC. • 916 West Broadway St., Suite 369 • Vancouver, BC • V5Z 1K7 • Tel: 604-739-4383 • Fax: 604-736-7453 • E-mail: info@bridge-infotech.com • Internet: www.bridge-infotech.com • Contact: Ben Lamprecht • Bridge Information Technology assists companies to find software engineers, developers, project managers, business analysts, network administrators, and technical writers for contract consulting assignments. They also find permanent staff.

BROCK PLACEMENT GROUP INC. • 300-1370 Don Mills Road • Toronto, ON • M3B 3N7 • Tel: 416-642-3992 • Toll Free: 1-800-543-7325 • E-mail: resume@brockplacement.com • Internet: www.brockplacement.com • Brock Placement Group Inc. is a successful national search firm specializing in the permanent placement of sales, marketing, and management professionals.

BRUCE R. DUNCAN & ASSOCIATES • 8 King Street East, Suite 1005 • Toronto, ON • M5C 1B5 • Tel: 416-361-1451 • Fax: 416-361-1225 • E-mail: staff@bruceduncan.com • Internet: www.bruceduncan.com • Bruce R. Duncan & Associates offers placement services in the areas of accounting and finance, brokerage, sales and marketing, management, administration and technical. Visit their website for more information.

BRUNEL ENERGY CANADA INC. • 815-8 Avenue S.W., Suite 860 • Calgary, AB • T2P 3P2 • Tel: 403-539 5009 • Fax: 403-294 9594 • E-mail: resumes@brunelenergy.ca • Internet: www. brunelenergy.net • Brunel Energy is the division, which provides specialised knowledge to the international oil and gas, petrochemical, power generating, and the general construction industries. The parent company, Brunel International NV, is publicly listed on the Amsterdam stock exchange and has over 100 operating offices in different countries. Globally, Brunel Energy operates out of 14 25 countries which consist of: the Netherlands, the United Kingdom, Kazakhstan, United States of America, Canada, France, Russia, United Arab Emirates, Qatar, Angola, Libya, Nigeria, Chad, Cameroon, Singapore, Malaysia, Indonesia, Thailand, Australia, China, Korea, Norway, Vietnam, India and Philipines.

BRYAN, JASON AND ASSOCIATES INC. • 111 Richmond Street West, Suite 1200 • Toronto, ON • M5H 2G4 • Tel: 416-867-9295 • Fax: 416-867-3067 • E-mail: careers@bryan-jason.ca • Internet: www.bryan-jason.ca • Founded in 1992, Bryan, Jason and Associates is a leading search and recruitment firm whose objective is to find candidates who are well qualified and can meet specific challenges facing a company at its particular stage of development. The firm is currently composed of a group of seasoned professional consultants who have a broad range of business knowledge and over 50 years of combined placement experience.

BURKE & ASSOCIATES INC. • Suite 1304, Maritime Centre, 1505 Barrington Street • Halifax, NS • B3J 3K5 • Tel: 902-425-5216 • Fax: 902-425-6049 • E-mail: recruit@burke-assoc.com • Internet: www3.burke-assoc.com/home.html • Burke & Associates, they begin the recruitment process by performing an in-depth analysis of their client's recruitment requirements. By learning as much as they can about the organization, they are able to select the best possible candidate for the position. By matching the unique requirements of the company with individuals who possess the right combination of skills, core competencies and personal qualities, they help you find the appropriate employer.

BURKE GROUP, THE • 50 William Street • St. Catharines, ON • L2R 5J2 • Tel: 905-641-3070 • Fax: 905-641-0478 • Toll Free: 1-888-896-3618 • E-mail: tbg@theburkegroup.com • Internet: www.theburkegroup.com • The Burke Group was founded in 1979 and has since become a leader in the human resources market. The Burke Group is a Canadian company, committed to providing the best in human resources services. Burke professionals know the market and understand the distinctive characteristics of business and industry in both unionized and non-unionized environments within the private and public sectors.

BUSINESS FIT • 8 Brule Gardens, 2nd Floor • Toronto, ON • M6S 4J2 • Tel: 416-362-2000 • Fax: 416-362-8000 • E-mail: info@businessfit.com • Internet: www.businessfit.com • Business Fit supports the work of the Career Foundation, a non-profit organization, whose mission is to link the resources of private sector companies, labtheir, education and government to help all members of the community make the transition into employment. Revenue from Business Fit helps facilitate the re-employment of adults and new Canadians. They specialize in Information Technology, Manufacturing, Accounting/ Finance, Sales/ Marketing, Admin/ Operations, Customer Service and Management.

BUXTON CONSULTING LTD. • 11830 - 223rd St. • Maple Ridge, BC • V2X 5Y1 • Tel: 604-463-4312 • Fax: 604-463-2413 • E-mail: admin@buxtonconsulting.bc.ca • Internet: www.buxtonconsulting.bc.ca • Contact: Wendy Buxton • Buxton Consulting was founded in October 1987 and is a privately owned limited company. The owner Bruce Buxton has a Master's Degree in Social Work and is an Accredited Rehabilitation Professional (ARP). Buxton Consulting is a private company that specializes in providing career planning; vocational and rehabilitation assessments; employment marketing and placement; occupational and lifestyle counselling; as well as conducting training seminars and workshops for corporate and public sector organizations.

206-2540 Shaughnessy St.	3-2316 McCallum Rd.	#4 45780 Yale Rd.
Port Coquitlam, BC	Abbotsford, BC	Chilliwack, BC
Tel: 604-941-4555	V2S 3P4	V2P 2N4
Fax: 604-941-4673	Tel: 604-504-5419	Tel: 604-792-2807
	Fax: 604-504-4439	Fax: 604-792-2816
7311 James St.		
Unit C		
Mission, BC		
V2V 3V5		
Tel: 604-820-4140		
Fax: 604-820-4141		

C. SCOTT & ASSOCIATES INC. • 130 King St. West, P.O. Box 427, Suite 1800 •Toronto, ON • M5X 1E3 • Tel: 416-214-9822 • Fax: 416-214-9820 • E-mail: info@cscottinc.com • Internet: www.cscottinc.com • Scott & Associates Inc. specializes in the recruitment, selection, and placement of information technology professionals for the financial services sector. They have collectively over 15 years of recruitment expertise. Their clients, who are leaders in the financial services sector include Schedule A and Schedule B Banks, brokerage houses, mutual fund companies and consulting firms. Their success stems from their ability to develop strong partnerships with their candidates and clients alike. They have built a respectful reputation with these individuals by providing personalized and professional service as well as expertise in the technical placement industry.

C.C.T. INC. • 119 - 2550 Argentia Road •Mississauga, ON • L5N 5R1 • Tel: 905-858-1481 • Fax: 1-800-546-4483 • Internet: www.cctinc.org • CCT Inc. was established in 1993. Their Associates are placed with many of southern Ontario's leading manufacturing companies. CCT Inc. specializes in providing Engineering and Technical Personnel to manufacturing companies in Southern Ontario. They can provide personnel on contract or permanent placement to meet project demands, overload work, specialty work, or additional staff requirements.

202-3425 Harvester Rd.	151 York St.	151 Frobisher Drive
Burlington, ON	London, ON	Suite E218
L7N 3N1	N6A 1A8	Waterloo, ON
Tel: 905-631-9709	Tel: 519-858-8369	N2V 2C9
		Tel: 519-743-4894

C.J. STAFFORD & ASSOCIATES • 2323 Yonge Street, Suite 501 •Toronto, ON • M4P 2C9 • Tel: 416-484-1960 • Fax: 416-484-0626 • E-mail: cjstaff@cjstafford.com • Internet: www.cjstafford. com • Contact: Chris Stafford • C.J. Stafford and Associates, established in 1981, provides executive search, recruitment, and project staffing services for clients in mining, engineering and construction industries. Through dedication and commitment the company has become recognised as a leader in these sectors, across Canada and internationally.

C.L.A. PERSONNEL • 424C Queen St. • Ottawa, ON • K1R 5A8 • Tel: 613-567-0045 • Fax: 613-567-0049 • E-mail: ejoanisse@clapersonnel.ca • Internet: www.clapersonnel.ca • Contact: Eric Joanisse • C.L.A. Personnel has been in the personnel placement business since 1988. From the very beginning, C.L.A. Personnel has been recognised for its efficiency, its professionalism, and its dynamism. Throughout the years, they have emphasised on providing efficient and human services to their employees and clients. C.L.A. Personnel 's team of professional consultants who have over 65 collective years of personnel-related experience, have an excellent understanding of the public and private sector markets, enabling them to respond accurately to their client's needs.

C.W. CLASEN RECRUITING SERVICES • 3030 Lincoln Ave., Suite 211 • Coquitlam, BC • V3B 6B4 • Tel: 604-942-1314 • E-mail: colinc@clasenrcruiting.com • Internet: www.clasenrecruiting. com • Contact: Colin Clasen • C.W. Clasen Recruiting Services assists forest industry companies with recruiting, management, technical and professional employees. Candidates must have education and/or experience directly related to the forest industry. They specialize in all areas of the industry including woodlands, manufacturing and sales, sawmills, plywood/composite board plants, and pulpmills.

CABINET-CONSEIL PCR • 353 rue St-Nicolas, Bureau 307 • Montréal, QC • H2Y 2P1 • Tel: 514-843-6664 • Fax: 514-843-9300 • E-mail: cv@ccpcr.com • Internet: www.ccpcr.com • Cabinet-Conseil PCR offers executive search and recruitment services to clients seeking exceptional candidates. PCR presents its clients with executives and professionals that would otherwise be unavailable through traditional channels.

CADMAN CONSULTING GROUP INC., THE • 500 Park Place, 666 Burrard St. • Vancouver, BC • V6C 3P6 • Tel: 604-689-4345 • Fax: 604-676-2458 • E-mail: info@cadman.ca • Internet: www.cadman.ca • The Cadman Consulting Group Inc. is a Vancouver based leading provider of Information Technology Consultants. Since 1994, The Cadman Group has specialized in providing IT professionals for contract and full-time engagements throughout the lower mainland. Over the years of operation, they have worked with many companies both in the public and private sectors providing highly skilled IT Resources.

CALDWELL PARTNERS INTERNATIONAL, THE • 165 Avenue Rd. • Toronto, ON • M5R 3S4 • Tel: 416-920-7702 • Fax: 416-922-8646 • E-mail: leaders@caldwell.ca • Internet: www. caldwell.ca • The Caldwell Partners International has been Canada's leader in executive search since 1970. Their clients are business and public organizations who retain them to carry out searches to fill their need for leaders, financial heads, and senior professionals.

850, 1095 West Pender St.	360 Main Street, Suite 2110	1 Place Ville Marie, Suite 1611
Vancouver, BC	Winnipeg, MB	Montreal, QC
V6E 2M6	R3C 3Z3	H3B 2B6
Tel: 604-669-3550	Tel: 204-943-8870	Tel: 514-908-2954
Fax: 604-669-5095	Fax: 204-943-8925	Fax: 514-908-2953
vancouver@caldwell.ca	winnipeg@caldwell.ca	montreal@caldwell.ca
5657 Spring Garden Rd.	505 Third St.	421 Gilmtheir St.
Suite 500	Suite 800	Ottawa, ON
Halifax, NS	Calgary, AB	K2P 0R5
B3J 3R4	T2P 3E6	Tel: 613-745-1771
Tel: 902-429-5909	Tel: 403-265-8780	Fax: 613-231-5866
Fax: 902-429-5606	Fax: 403-263-6508	leaders@caldwell.ca
halifax@caldwell.ca	calgary@caldwell.ca	

CALIAN • 2 Beaverbrook Road • Ottawa, ON • K2K 1L1 • Tel: 613-599-8600 • Fax: 613-599-8650 • E-mail: info@calian.com • Internet: www.calian.com • Founded in 1982, Calian has emerged as a leader in the technology services industry. Their customers are many and varied, and include organizations in both the public and private sectors. With annual revenues in excess of $170 million (CDN) and a staff of over 2200, Calian ranks among the largest professional services companies in Canada.

123 Slater St., Suite 150	1 City Centre Drive
Ottawa, ON	Suite 700
K1P 5H2	Mississauga, ON
Tel: 613-238-2600	L5B 1M2
Fax: 613-233-2166	Tel: 905-848-2818
Toll Free: 1-866-233-4133	Fax: 905-848-4944
	Toll Free: 1-888-922-5426

CAMBRIDGE MANAGEMENT PLANNING INC. • 2323 Yonge St., Suite 203 • Toronto, ON • M4P 2C9 • Tel: 416-484-8408 • Fax: 416-484-0151 • E-mail: mail@cambridgemgmt.com • Internet: www.cambridgemgmt.com • Incorporated in 1976, Cambridge Management Planning was established as an Executive Search firm, specializing in senior management recruitment requirements of manufacturing businesses. Their services have grown and diversified to include executive search, co-management/interim, career management, and management consulting. Over the years, Cambridge widened its client base to a broader spectrum of industry including healthcare, pharmaceuticals, food service, financial services, consumer products and packaging, aerospace, technology and engineering.

CAMPBELL, EDGAR INC. • 4388 - 49th St. • Delta, BC • V4K 2S7 • Tel: 604-946-8535 • Fax: 604-946-2384 • E-mail: info@retailcareers.com • Internet: www.retailcareers.com • Contact: Elaine Hay, President • With offices located in Western Canada, Campbell, Edgar Inc. is the largest recruitment firm in Canada that is dedicated to the retail industry. Their commitment to clients and their commitment to candidates is unparalleled within the recruitment industry.

CAMPBELL, EDGAR INC. continued
#1-9059 Shaugnessy St.
Vancouver, BC
V6P 6R9
Tel: 604-321-8515
Fax: 604-321-8541
Toll Free: 888-367-3131

CANADIAN EXECUTIVE CONSULTANTS INC. • 1111 Finch Ave. W., Suite 400 • North York, ON • M3J 2E5 • Tel: 416-665-7577 • Fax: 416-665-8509 • E-mail: info@cdnexec.com • Internet: www.cdnexec.com • Canadian Executive Consultants is a professional management consulting firm specializing in the human resources field. They offer professional services including personnel recruitment, mergers and acquisitions, attitude surveys, assessment centres, leadership training, vocational assessment, outplacement counselling, organizational development, employee assistance programs, performance appraisals, job analysis, and resume preparation.

CANADIAN MEDICAL PLACEMENT SERVICE • 148 York St. • London, ON • N6A 1A9 • Tel: 519-672-0777 • Fax: 519-672-0830 • E-mail: info@cmps.ca • Internet: www.cmps.ca • The Canadian Medical Placement Service specializes in the placement of permanent or Locum: Family Practitioners, Physio/Physical Therapists, General Surgeons, Occupational Therapists, Obstetrics/Gynecology, Specialty Nurses, Pediatricians, Psychiatrists, Internal Medicine, Radiologists, Anesthesiologists, Otolaryngologists, and other specialties.

CANMED CONSULTANTS INC. • 659 Mississauga Cres. • Mississauga, ON • L5H 1Z9 • Tel: 905-274-0707 • Fax: 905-274-0067 • E-mail: resume@canmed.com • Internet: www.canmed. com • CanMed Consultants is a recruiting firm that works in the recruitment for pharmaceuticals and related industries including hospitals, clinics and physicians. Their areas of specialty include placement of hospital executives, and contract personnel. They recruit for the following sectors including pharmaceutical, biotechnology and biologicals, hospital products, medical devices and diagnostics, hospitals and medical centres, and government.

CANPRO EXECUTIVE SEARCH • 7321 Victoria Park Ave. • Markham, ON • L3R 2Z8 • Tel: 905-475-3115 • Fax: 905-475-2849 • Internet: www.canpro.com • Contact: Art Boyle, President • Canpro is an executive search firm that specializes in the areas of administration (finance, human resources), operations (manufacturing management, logistics, distribution), sales & marketing (sales management, marketing management), and technical work (engineering, R & D).

CAN-TECH SERVICES • 45 Baldwin St. • Whitby, ON • L1M 1A2 • Tel: 905-655-8441 • Fax: 905-655-8443 • E-mail: pgeissler@cantechservices.com • Internet: www.cantechservices.com • Can-Tech Services is an agency that supplies personnel to the Aeronautical Industry as well as related technical fields. Some of these related fields have included automotive, marine, computer, and manufacturing industries. Since 1974 Can-Tech Services has provided the best human resources available, through both permanent placement and on a contract basis.

5929 Trans-Canada
Suite 270
St. Laurent, QC
Postal: H4T 1Z6
Tel: 514-744-2121
Fax: 514-744-1616

CAPITAL EXECUTIVE LTD. • Suite 1010, 441 5th Ave. S.W. • Calgary, AB • T2P 2V1 • Tel: 403-266-2020 • Fax: 403-237-7929 • E-mail: alison@capitalexecutive.com • Internet: www. capitalexecutive.com • Contact: Alison Goodchild • Capital Executive is a highly successful recruitment agency that has been placing quality professionals in the Calgary market place since 1983. The success behind Alison Goodchild, Tanya Ring and their associates lie in the strong belief of quality and integrity of service to both the company hiring and the professional seeking employment. Capital Executive Ltd. has set high standards of professionalism that have earned us the reputation of being a leader in their industry. Their long-term success in placing permanent and contract professionals in oil and gas accounting can be attributed to their sincere effort to make the best possible match between client and candidate. They base their business on building solid relationships with all parties through an extensive process of getting to know and understand the needs and desires of both their clients and their candidates.

CARE 4 YOU PLACEMENT AGENCY • 1112 Finch Avenue West, Unit 18 • Toronto, ON • M3J 3J5 • Tel: 416-635-2888 • Fax: 416-635-0858 • E-mail: contact@care4you.ca • Internet: www.care4you.ca • Since 2001, Care 4 You Placement Agency has been dedicated to matching the perfect candidate to the right job. Our superior customer service has proven itself through thousands of satisfied employees and employers.

CAREER ADVANCEMENT EMPLOYMENT SERVICES INC. • 522 Burlington Ave., Suite 200 • Burlington, ON • L7S 1R8 • Tel: 905-681-8240 • Fax: 905-639-4601 • E-mail: info@ careeradvancement.on.ca • Internet: www.careeradvancement.on.ca • Since 1997 Career Advancement Employment Services Inc. has built their reputation by successfully exceeding the recruiting requirements of a wide range of company clientele and employment candidates in the manufacturing, environmental, and consulting industries.

CAREER SERVICES OF BROCKVILLE • 89 Hubbell St. • Brockville, ON • K6V 4K6 • Tel: 613-342-5775 • Fax: 613-342-1733 • E-mail: info@careerservices.ca • Internet: www.careerservices. ca • Contact: Cynthia Sparring • Career Services, founded in 1972, is a unique non-profit business which combines a vocational service to adults with disabilities with an industrial service to customers in the area. Although each side of the agency contributes to the other, their priority is serving clients with barriers to employment and assisting people in finding and maintaining work opportunities in the community.

Employment & Education Centre
P.O. Box 191
105 Strowger Blvd.
Brockville, ON
K6V 5V2
Tel: 613-498-2111
Fax: 613-498-21163

CARTEL INC. • 100 King St.W., One, First Canadian Place, Suite 2680 • Toronto, ON • M5X 1A4 • Tel: 416-359-9000 • Fax: 416-359-9500 • E-mail: info@cartelinc.com • Internet: www. cartelinc.com • Contact: Marsha Meyers, President • Since 1975 Cartel has been supplying professional personnel services to corporations and law firms throughout Toronto. Their consultants have the experience and ability to provide solutions to both your temporary and permanent requirements.

CATALYST CAREER STRATEGIES INC. • 3080 Yonge Street, Suite 6000 • Toronto, ON • M4N 3N1 • Tel: 647-227-3377 • E-mail: info@catalystcareers.com • Internet: www.catalystcareers. com • Catalyst Career Strategies Inc. is a Toronto-based specialty consulting firm which takes pride in providing top quality strategic career guidance to executives and professionals. Clients include corporate executives, partners of professional firms, lawyers, accountants, engineers, business owners, consultants, scientists, professors, politicians, writers, etc.

CBM PROJECTS INC. • 9705 Horton Road SW, Suite 206B • Calgary, AB • T2V 2X5 • Tel: 403-270-3444 • Fax: 403-225-2924 • E-mail: mbyrne@cbmprojects.com • Internet: www. cbmprojects.com • Contact: Myles Byrne, Manager-Operations • At CBM Projects, they understand your project needs. Their team has the depth and knowledge necessary to ensure your company receives the right professional(s) for your job. They work closely with you from project feasibility through to completion. They'll help you to control costs, resources and time by providing guidance and support through all the phases of your project, so you receive maximum performance with minimal project risk. Their experience and reputation for quality ensure the highest level of professionalism for both client and contractor.

CCT INC. • 119-2550 Argentia Road • Mississauga, ON • L5N 5R1 • Tel: 905-858-1481 • Fax: 1-800-546-4483 • Internet: www.cctinc.org • CCT Inc. specializes in providing Engineering and Technical Personnel to manufacturing companies in Southern Ontario. They can provide personnel on contract or permanent placement to meet project demands, overload work, specialty work, or additional staff requirements. They have become the sole supplier of engineering and technical personnel for many of their clients.

151 York Street	151 Frobisher Drive	202-3425 Harvester Road
London, ON	Suite E218	Burlington, ON
N6A 1A8	Waterloo, ON	L7N 3N1
Tel: 519-858-8369	N2V 2C9	Tel: 905-631-9709
Fax: 1-800-546-4483	Tel: 519-743-4894	Fax: 1-800-546-4483

CDI CORP. • Professional Services, 710 Dorval Dr., Suite 220 • Oakville, ON • L6K 3V7 • Tel: 905-338-3100 • Fax: 905-338-3425 • E-mail: oakville@cdicorp.com • Internet: www. cdicorp.com • CDI Corp. (NYSE: CDI) is a provider of engineering and information technology outstheircing solutions and professional staffing. With more than 50 years in the industry and an extensive network of offices, recruiters and technical professionals, CDI helps Fortune 1000 clients in targeted vertical markets improve profitability and efficiency by allowing them to focus on their core competencies. Operating divisions include CDI Business Solutions, a global leader in providing managed solutions in major industries; CDI AndersElite Limited, a professional staffing and services firm focusing on the construction and engineering markets in the United Kingdom; Management Recruiters International, Inc. (MRI) the world's largest executive search and recruitment organization with more than 1000 franchised offices worldwide; and, Todays Staffing, Inc. which provides temporary and permanent placement services for the administrative, legal and financial staffing markets.

CDI Professional Services	CDI Professional Services	Asset Computer Personnel
Process & Industrial	736 8th Ave. S.W.	48 Yonge St.
710 Dorval Dr., Suite 220	Calgary, AB	Suite 500
Oakville, ON	T2P 1H4	Toronto, ON
L6K 3V7	Tel: 403-266-1009	M5E 1G6
Tel: 905-338-3100	Fax: 403-264-1961	Tel: 416-777-1717
Fax: 905-338-3425		Fax: 416-777-0647

CENERA • 1100-1015 - 4th Ave. S.W. • Calgary, AB • T2R 1J4 • Tel: 403-290-0466 • Fax: 403-294-0513 • E-mail: form • Internet: www.career-partners.com • Cenera is a Calgary, Alberta based integrated Human Resource and Business Consulting firm providing integrated strategies, practical solutions and measurable results to clients in a variety of areas. When possible, they integrate their services to benefit clients' needs, offering expertise in human resource consulting, business consulting, privacy, training and development, coaching, career transition, contract HR staffing and search.

CEO INC. EMPLOYMENT SOLUTIONS • 133 Church St. N. • Cambridge, ON • N3H 1V8 • Tel: 519-650-1600 • Fax: 519-650-1615 • E-mail: krogers@ceoemp.com • Contact: Kim Rogers, Director of Services • Internet: www.ceoemp.com • CEO Inc. - Employment Solutions is a private firm operating in the Waterloo Region for over 20 years. Their goal is to get the right people in the right jobs with the partnership of local businesses and organizations. CEO offers three basic themes of service; assessment, training and placement services. Their mandate is to help adults re-enter the work force by becoming a part of the working class in their community. In November of 2004, a new division opened in Hamilton where it provides like services. CEO Inc. works in partnership with Rehabilitation Specialists, Case Managers and the business community. They build partnerships with businesses to deliver training that develops excellence and encourages life-long learning. CEO Inc. provides employment counseling and training that is professional, progressive and reflective of local labour market demands.

CHACRA, BELLIVEAU & ASSOCIATES INC. • 625, President-Kennedy Avenue, Suite 1005 • Montréal, QC • H3A 1K2 • Tel: 514-931-8801 • Fax: 514-931-1940 • E-mail: info@chacra.com • Internet: www.chacra.com • Contact: Contact: Steven Chacra • Chacra, Belliveau & Associates are staffing specialists dedicated to exclusively to the recruitment and placement of information systems and information technologies personnel in both permanent and contract positions.

CHAD MANAGEMENT GROUP • 21 St. Clair Ave. E., Suite 1000 • Toronto, ON • M4T 1L9 • Tel: 416-968-1000 • Fax: 416-968-7754 • E-mail: jobs@chadman.com • Internet: www. chadman.com • Contact: Rick Chad • One of Canada's leading executive recruiting and consulting agencies whose senior associates have over 40 years of combined experience. The majority of their search is with marketing design organizations in a number of different functional areas. Chad Management Group specializes in marketing, including direct marketing, as well as promotion, finance, advertising, sales and systems.

CHALLENGE COMMUNITY VOCATIONAL ALTERNATIVES • 1148 - 1st Avenue • Whitehorse, YK • Y1A 1A6 • Tel: 867-668-4421 • Fax: 867-667-4337 • E-mail: rick.goodfellow@. ccva.ca • Internet: www.ccva.ca • Challenge is a non-profit organization that has been assisting people with disabilities in ever-increasing capacities, and numbers, since 1976. In 1988 Challenge adopted a supported employment model of vocational training for adults with disabilities. Our mandate is to assist people with disabilities to become active in their community, by learning real job skills and entering the job market.

CHAPMAN AND ASSOCIATES • One Bentall Centre, Suite 480, 505 Burrard St. • Vancouver, BC • V7X 1M3 • Tel: 604-682-7764 • Fax: 604-682-8746 • E-mail: resumes@chapmanassoc.com • Internet: www.chapmanassoc.com • For over 50 years Chapman & Associates have enjoyed the privilege of working closely with company owners and executive teams to plan, acquire and manage their most valuable assets... people. From evaluating existing talent and structure, to aligning those skills with the objectives of the business plan, their clients are better prepared to anticipate future personnel needs, be more selective with candidates, and be more effective in retaining high performance people.

CHASE CONSULTANTS INC. • 151 City Centre Dr., Suite 400 • Mississauga, ON • L5B 1M7 • Tel: 905-566-9448 • Fax: 905-566-9606 • E-mail: information@chaseconsultants.com • Internet: www.chaseconsultants.com • Contact: Michelle Pearson • Chase Consultants offers recruiting and consulting services to many types of companies. They provide personality profiles for career planning to assist firms in identifying candidates. The firm specialists in the fields of sales and marketing.

CHEMPHARM ASSOCIATES • 106 Danforth Avenue, Suite 300 • Toronto, ON • M4K 1N1 • Tel: 647-435-0010 • Fax: 647-435-0011 • E-mail: info@chempharmassociates.ca • Internet: www.chempharmassociates.ca • ChemPharm Associates, Inc. is Canada's Premier Executive Search Firm specializing only in the Chemical and Pharmaceutical disciplines. Whereas other search firms recruit for all positions in many different industries, ChemPharm Associates Inc. provides clients with only Chemical and Pharmaceutical industry specialists.

CHERYL CRAIG CAREERS • 110 Burloak Dr., Suite 300 • Burlington, ON • L7L 6B2 • Tel: 905-332-1600 • Fax: 905-332-7993 • E-mail: info@cherylcraigcareers.com • Internet: www.cherylcraigcareers.com • Cheryl Craig Careers, a privately owned Canadian company has been practicing relationship building with a philosophy of "finding out what the customer needs", since 1981. Cheryl Craig Career's team of personnel specialists have over five decades of industry experience and offer broad expertise in all facets of temporary, alternative and permanent staffing solutions.

CHISHOLM & PARTNERS INTERNATIONAL INC. • BCE Place Canada Trust Tower, 161 Bay St., Suite 2600 • Toronto, ON • M5J 2S1 • Tel: 416-777-6800 • Fax: 416-777-6777 • E-mail: info@chisintl.com • Internet: www.chisintl.com • Chisholm & Partners International Inc. was founded to carry on the tradition of service excellence that clients have come to expect from their Principals for over 15 years. Committed to an uncompromised level of service, Chisholm & Partners tailors each search to meet the needs of their clients in a timely manner. Every search is carefully planned and executed to identify and attract the best candidates available in today's professional arena.

CHOICE OFFICE PERSONNEL • Edmonton City Centre, 10025 102A Ave, Suite 1102 • Edmonton, AB • T5J 2Z2 • Tel: 780-424-6816 • Fax: 780-425-7426 • E-mail: team@choice.ab.ca • Internet: www.choice.ab.ca • Incorporated in 1985, Choice Office Personnel Ltd. is proud to be Edmonton owned and operated. For 20 years they have been providing quality staff and service to the Edmonton business community in both the public and private sectors.

CITÉ LINK PERSONNEL INC. • 92 Lakeshore Rd. E., Suite 209 • Mississauga, ON • L5G 4S2 • Tel: 905-891-5989 • Fax: 905-271-8547 • E-mail: valerie@citelinkpersonnel.com • Internet: www.citelinkpersonnel.com • Contact: Valérie Cité, Owner • At Cité Link Personnel Inc, their intention is to provide professional and reliable permanent placement services to medium, large and international companies whose focus is on achieving long-term human resource goals.

CLASSIC CONSULTING GROUP INC. • 607, 706 - 7th Ave. S.W. • Calgary, AB • T2P 0Z1 • Tel: 403-233-8388 • Fax: 403-233-8755 • E-mail: classic@classicconsulting.com • Internet: www.classicconsulting.com • Contact: Karen McGrath • Classic Consulting Group Inc. has been providing clients and candidates with market-leading recruiting services since 1989. While their primary focus is on the energy sector, they also believe in keeping in tune with Calgary's diversifying marketplace. As a result, they are able to address the needs of employers and candidates in a wide range of industries, including not only the energy sector, but also transportation, marketing, distribution and financial services to name a few. They take pride in providing the most up-to-date information on market conditions. Whether it is insight into the latest hiring and salary trends or the availability of career opportunities for select candidates, Classic Consulting should be your firm of choice.

COAPE STAFFING NETWORK • 400 Fifth Ave, S.W. • Calgary, AB • T2P 0L6 • Tel: 403-509-0100 • Fax: 403-509-0114 • E-mail: calgary@coapestaffing.com • Internet: www.coapestaffing.com • As part of the largest independent employment services in North America they have million dollar contracts with companies like Boeing, AT&T and Ford. In fact, they provide services to many Fortune 100 companies. The "Silicon Forest" has become the hub of IS/IT employment and they have alliances with the big leaders, such as Microsoft, RealNetworks, Sierra, Nth Dimension, Amazon.com, Starbucks, MicroEncoder, SpaceLabs, Applied Micro Systems, etc.

885 Dunsmuir St.	10235-101St., Oxford Tower
Suite 370	Suite 516
Vancouver, BC	Edmonton, AB
V6C 1N5	T5J 3G1
Tel: 604-687-2226	Tel: 780-424-1088
Fax: 604-687-2251	Fax: 780-421-0055
vancouver@coapstafffing.com	edmonton@coapstaffing.com

COE & COMPANY INTERNATIONAL INC. • 700 Bow Valley Square II, 205 - 5th Avenue SW • Calgary, AB • T2P 2V7 • Tel: 403-232-8833 • Fax: 403-237-0165 • E-mail: coe@coeandcompany.com • Internet: www.coeandcompany.com • Coe & Company International Inc./EMA Partners International Inc. is a Calgary based executive search management consulting firm. Their specialized search and human resource services are provided across Canada and internationally. They have a premier list of clients, focused primarily in the energy, advanced technology, telecommunications, consumer products and manufacturing industries.

COLES ASSOCIATES • 6 Prince St., P.O. BOX 695 • Charlottetown, PE • C1A 7L3 • Tel: 902-368-2300 • Fax: 902-566-3768 • E-mail: hcoles@caltech.ca • Internet: www.colesassociates.com • Since 1959, Coles Associates has delivered quality Architectural, Engineering, and Project Mangement solutions to a diverse local, national, and international clientele. Their dedicated professional and technical personnel are familiar with the demands placed on organizations in today's dynamic business environment. Their collaborative work process links clients to each project team. Their clients are offered access to secure project work suites via the World Wide Web to actively participate with project teams and to enable optimal sharing of common resources.

COLINTEX PLACEMENTS • Toronto, ON • Tel: 416-449-3100 • Fax: 647-723-0385 • E-mail: colin@colintex.com • Internet: www.colintex.com • Contact: Colin Lewis, President • Colintex Placements are recruitment specialists in the Textile and Fashion Industries with over 25 years of experience. From wholesale to retail, Colintex Placements matches qualified candidates with the right employers. They find personnel at all levels from store managers and area managers, and patternmakers and designers, all the way up to senior positions.

COMPUFORCE INC. • Hanover Place, Suite 1220, 101 - 6th Avenue S.W. • Calgary, AB • T2P 3P4 • Tel: 403-233-7871 • Fax: 403-205-4460 • E-mail: general@compuforceinc.com • Internet: www.compuforceinc.com • For over fifteen years, CompuForce has been responding to client needs for information technology professionals with "IT Staffing Solutions" that deliver superior value in service excellence. Their success in matching professional resources to client requirements is a direct result of extensive industry experience, current technical knowledge, proactive management skills and an understanding of people. They care about our valued customers and our team of systems professionals and work hard to ensure total satisfaction in quality people, products and services.

COMPUTER HORIZONS ISG • 5045 Orbitor Dr., Bldg. 7 Suite 200• Mississauga, ON • L4W 4Y4 • Tel: 905-602-6085 • Fax: 905-602-0425 • E-mail: toronto@isgjobs.com • Internet: www. isgjobs.com • Contact: Kevin Golden, Manager, Recruitment Services • Computer Horizons Canada is a wholly-owned subsidiary of Computer Horizons Corp., founded in 1969 and headquartered in Mountain Lakes, New Jersey. They are a publicly held global organization with over 30 offices worldwide, including Canada, the United States, and the United Kingdom. Their Canadian presence includes offices in Calgary, Toronto, Ottawa, Edmonton, Winnipeg, Vancouver and Montreal. They also have a Solutions Outstheircing Center located in Montreal. Since inception, their staffing focus has been exclusively on IT positions, allowing Computer Horizons Canada to become one of the largest, most respected IT staffing firms in the country today. They have forged long-standing relationships as a nationally preferred supplier to industry leaders in market verticals such as Finance, Insurance, Retail, Pharmaceutical, Government, and Systems Integration.

805-8th Avenue S.W.
Suite 900
Calgary, AB
T2P 1H7
Tel: 403-265-3380
Fax: 403-265-3301

1770 Woodward Drive
Suite 101
Ottawa, ON
K2C 0P8
Tel: 613-228-0010
Fax: 613-228-9022

650 Boul. De Maisonneuve
Ouest
Suite 830
Montreal, QC
H3A 3T2
Tel: 514-840-6198

10020-101A Ave.
Phipps McKinnon Bldg.
Edmonton, AB
T5J 3G2
Tel: 780-409-8500
Fax: 780-428-0064

28 Bret Bay
Winnipeg, MB
R2G 2C4
Tel: 204-256-2121
Fax: 204-256-5317

989 Nelson St.
Suite 1214
Vancouver, BC
V6Z 2S1
Tel: 604-681-7463

COMTECH INTERNATIONAL DESIGN GROUP INC. • 3200 Deziel Drive, Suite 411 • Windsor, ON • N8W 5K8 • Tel: 519-944-6335 • E-mail: info@teamcomtech.com • Internet: www.teamcomtech.com • Contact: Lou Tortola • Comtech is an industry leader in the provision of Contract Engineering & Technology Staffing solutions for Fortune 500 Corporations. With offices in Canada & the United States, Comtech specializes in providing contract technical resources in engineering, information technology, facilities/architectural design and technical application training.

2 Robert Speck Parkway
Suite 750
Mississauga, ON
L4Z 1H8
Tel: 1-888-467-1848

675 Cochrane Dr.
East Tower, 6th Floor
Markham, ON
L3R 0B8
Tel: 1-888-467-1848

CONCEPT II EMPLOYMENT SERVICE • 236 St. George St., Suite 412 • Moncton, NB • E1C 1W1 • Tel: 506-388-9675 • Fax: 506-388-9674 • E-mail: info@concept2employment. com • Internet: www.concept2employment.com • Concept II Employment Service is a 100% locally owned and operated staffing and recruiting company established in 1997. Their goals are simple: provide the best service possible; be ethical in their approach to business; provide gainful employment for local workers; support local business; give back to the community.

CONESTOGA PERSONNEL RESOURCES • 421 Greenbro Drive • Kitchener, ON • N2M 4K1 • Tel: 519-570-1226 • Fax: 519-570-9530 • E-mail: info@ConestogaPersonnel.com • Internet: www.conestogapersonnel.com • Contact: Garry Logel, President/Recruiter • Conestoga

Personnel Resources Inc. is a professional placement and personnel search facility. They are dedicated to providing organizations with the best service possible to meet their recruitment needs. Conestoga's particular skill is in providing permanent and contract placements. They also provide temporary to permanent placements.

CONROY ROSS PARTNERS LIMITED • 1650 Canadian Western Bank Place, 10303 Jasper Avenue • Edmonton, AB • T5J 3N6 • Tel: 780-432-5490 • Fax: 780-432-5936 • E-mail: mail@ conroyross.com • Internet: www.conroypartners.com • Conroy Ross Partners Limited is an executive search and management consulting companies in western Canada. Established in 1994, the firm's partners and associates enjoy extensive trusting relationships in all sectors of the dynamic and robust western Canadian economy.

830 Bow Valley Square 3
255 - 5th Avenue SW
Calgary, AB
T2P 3G6
Tel: 403-261-8080
Fax: 403-261-8085
mail@conroyross.com

CONSTRUCTION JOB CENTRE • #3636 E. 4th Ave. • Vancouver, BC • V5M 1M3 • Tel: 604-294-3766 • Fax: 604-298-9326 • E-mail: info@construction-jobs.ca • Internet: www. construction-jobs.ca • Contact: Marlene Derksen • Assisting construction employers with their human resource recruitment needs and helping people secure a career in construction. The Construction Job Centre recruitment service registers people who are seeking employment in the construction sector, from entry level to experienced construction workers or professionals.

CONSULPRO EXECUTIVE SEARCH • Tel: 514-932-9523 • E-mail: info@consulpro.com • Internet: www.consulpro.com • Contact: Ed Kaluzny • Consulpro is a Montreal based search firm that recruits computer and engineering professionals.

CORE CAREER STRATEGIES INC. • 555 Burnhamthorpe Rd., Suite 219 • Toronto, ON • M9C 2Y3 • Tel: 416-445-7855 • Fax: 416-445-7853 • E-mail: info@corecareer.com • Internet: www. corecareer.com • The Core Group has provided expert leadership and direction to the executive recruiting and career transition fields since 1968. The organization, augmented by an established international business network, has successfully provided these services to clients, large and small, in the public and private business sectors in Canada, the United States, Europe and Asia.

CORPORATE RECRUITERS LTD. • 1140 West Pender St., Suite 490 • Vancouver, BC • V6E 4G1 • Tel: 604-687-5993 • E-mail: careers@corporate.bc.ca • Internet: www.corporate.bc.ca • Corporate Recruiters Ltd. is celebrating it's 21st anniversary as Western Canada's leading High-Tech recruitment specialist! Since 1980, they have been recognized as the premier resource for permanent and contract technical, management, support and sales professionals.

CORTEX HR INC. • 434 Rushton Rd. • Toronto, ON • M6C 2Y3 • Toll Free: 1-877-6CORTEX • Fax: 416-485-0027 • E-mail: info@cortexhr.com • Internet: www.cortexhr.com • Cortex HR Inc. utilizes the combined expertise of Ph.D. level life scientists and human resource professionals to effectively execute human resource consulting services to meet the immediate and long term needs within the hi-tech, biotechnology and pharmaceutical industries.

COUNSEL NETWORK, THE • 736 Granville St., Suite 1010 • Vancouver, BC • V6Z 1G3 • Tel: 604-643-1755 • Fax: 604-575-9156 • E-mail: dal@headhunt.com • Internet: www.headhunt. com • Contact: Dal Bhathal • The Counsel Network is an innovative and unique consulting firm specializing exclusively in the provision of lawyer recruitment and career services. The Counsel

Network has offices in Vancouver British Columbia, Seattle, Washington and Calgary, Alberta and maintains formal and informal affiliations with select legal recruitment and consulting firms in other parts of Canada, the USA, the United Kingdom, Asia and Australia. They can be reached toll free at 1-800-COUNSEL.

1600 West Tower	141 Adelaide St. W.
144, 4th Ave., S.W.	Suite 350
Calgary, AB	Toronto, ON
T2P 3N4	M5J 2S1
Tel: 403-264-3838	Tel: 416-360-1080
Fax: 403-264-3819	snash@headhunt.com-
ssereda@headhunt.com	

CREATIVE FINANCIAL STAFFING • 1200 Bay St., Suite 1004 • Toronto, ON • M5R 2A5 • Tel: 416-596-7075 • Fax: 416-596-1456 • E-mail: cfstor@cfstoronto.com • Internet: www. cfstaffing.com • Creative Financial Staffing (CFS) is an interim and direct-hire financial placement company committed to providing the best service to our clients and candidates and to working in a partnership with them to accomplish all of our combined goals. From CFOs to Accounting Clerks, CFS can provide our clients with quality staff who have a high level of professionalism, integrity and skill.

1000-1177 West Hastings St.
Vancouver, BC
V6E 4T5
Tel: 604-669-9525
Fax: 604-669-5357
seanfanning@cfstaffing.ca

CREATIVE FORCE NETWORK LTD. • 150 Eglinton Ave. E., Suite 303 • Toronto, ON • M4P 1E8 • Tel: 416-932-3830 • Fax: 416-932-3506 • E-mail: info@creativeforcenetwork.com • Internet: www.creativeforcenetwork.com • Creative Force Network are agents for creative professionals that have been handpicked from the print and interactive industry. With 20 years experience in the creative industry, Creative Force Network has become an indispensable resource for companies who need on-call creative services and talented people looking for new career opportunities.

CREATIVE PERSONNEL INC. • 2200 Yonge St., Suite 1302, Toronto, ON • M4S 2C6 • Tel: 416-222-4431 • Fax: 416-222-7738 • E-mail: creative@creative-personnel.com • Internet: www.creative-personnel.com • Creative Personnel's mandate is to foster a long-term mutually beneficial relationship with its clients and applicants. Creative Personnel's ultimate objective is to service the immediate, short and long term employment needs of its clients and applicants in an ethical and cost effective manner to ensure the workforce of today becomes the future of tomorrow. "People Creating Futures!"

1134, rue Ste-Catherine Ouest
Suite 406
Montréal, QC
H3B 1H4
Tel: 514-904-1624
Fax: 514-904-1621

CROMARK INTERNATIONAL • Box 878 • Erin, ON • N0B 1T0 • Tel: 416-657-2886 • Fax: 416-410-4424 • E-mail: info@cromark.com • Internet: www.cromark.com • Contact: Clive Crowe, President • Cromark International Inc. has its roots assisting employers and qualified candidates to arrive at effective employment related solutions in the automotive and related industry recruiting business for over 25 years. Clients have ranged from Manufacturers, Importers, Dealers, Vehicle & Equipment Leasing, Financial Institutions , Automotive Aftermarket, Distribution & Logistic and Transportation companies.

CRUISE SERVICES INTERNATIONAL • 601 Dundas Street West, Box 24070 • Whitby, ON • L1N 8X8 • Tel: 905-430-0361 • Fax: 905-430-4610 • E-mail: info@cruisedreamjob.com or resumes@cruisedreamjob.com • Internet: www.cruisedreamjob.com • Cruise Services International is a Canadian Recruiting Agency that assists dedicated and motivated individuals from all over the world in securing shipboard positions on board luxury cruise lines.

DA SILVA & ASSOCIATES INC. • 1 Yorkdale Rd, Suite 202 • Toronto, ON • M6A 3Λ1 • Tel: 416-489-1600 • Fax: 416-489-1640 • E-mail: mail@dasilva.net • Internet: www.dasilva.net • Over 20 years of experience and outstanding customer service. DaSilva and Associates is the complete solution for all your recruiting needs.

DANILUCK & ASSOCIATES INTERNATIONAL • 10160-116th St., Suite 705 • Edmonton, AB • T5K 1V9 • Tel: 780-448-1717 • Fax: 780-669-9681 • E-mail: search@daniluck.com • Internet: www.daniluck.com • Daniluck and Associates International is a human resources consulting firm specializing in executive search on a regional, national, and international basis since the mid-1970s.

DARE HUMAN RESOURCES CORP. • 275 Slater Street, 9th Floor • Ottawa, ON • K1P 5H9 • Tel: 613-238-3273 • Fax: 613-238-9532 • E-mail: ottawa@darehr.com • Internet: www.darehr.com • The professionals at Dare Human Resources Corporation deliver a complete suite of Integrated Human Capital Management (HCM) Services to meet the needs of their many public and private sector clients. DareHR clients reap the rewards of their personal service approach and deep experience in Permanent Recruitment, Executive Search, Flexible Staffing, IT Contracting and their full range of HR Consulting and Business Growth Solutions.

275 Slater St.	800 Rene Levesque Ave. W.	300-1055 West Hastings St.
Suite 1750	Suite 2450	Vancouver, BC
Ottawa, ON	Montreal, QC	V6E 2E9
K1P 5H9	H3B 4V7	Toll Free: 1-877-346-7823
Tel: 613-238-3273	Toll Free: 1-877-346-7823	
Fax: 613-238-9532		

1 Dundas St. W., Suite 2500
Toronto, ON
M6G 1Z3
Tel: 416-979-4605
Fax: 416-979-4607
toronto@darehr.com

DATALIST • 55 Eglinton Ave. E., Suite 605 • Toronto, ON • M4P 1G8 • Tel: 416-483-7424 • Fax: 416-483-7676 • E-mail: info@datalist.com • Internet: www.datalist.com • Datalist is a full service IT staffing company, locating skilled contract and full time professionals for Canada's leading employers. Their experience now extends deep into every major IT-intensive industry, including banking and insurance, manufacturing, retail, telecom, professional services, public sector, research-based organizations and technology vendors.

DAVID ALPIN RECRUITING • 2300 Oxford Tower, 10235 - 101 St. • Edmonton, AB • T5J 3G1 • Tel: 780-428-6663 • Fax: 780-421-4680 • Internet: www.aplin.com • Contact: David Aplin, President • David Aplin Recruiting, incorporated in 1975, has developed into a true success story. Today, they are one of Canada's largest and most successful recruiting firms, finding the strongest talent for top tier organizations. They have successfully placed over 5,000 great people with over 1,000 great companies. Some of their clients have been hiring from us for more than 20 years, and over 80% of their business is with repeat customers! While their major focus is Canada, they regularly place people around the world.

3850 Scotia Centre	602 One Lombard Place	650 West Georgia St.
700 2nd St. S.W.	Winnipeg, MB	Suite 1400
Calgary, AB	R3B 0X3	P.O. Box 11518
T2P 2W2	Tel: 204-235-0000	Vancouver, BC
Tel: 403-261- 9000	Fax: 204-235-0002	V6B 4N7
Fax: 403-266-7195		Tel: 604-648-2799
		Fax: 604-648-2787
1791 Barrington St.	350 Sparks Street	123 Front St. W.
Suite 1630	Suite 910	Suite 905
Halifax, NS	Ottawa, ON	Toronto, ON
B3J 3L1	K1R 7S8	M5J 2M2
Tel: 902-461-1616	Tel: 613-288-2211	Tel: 416-367-9700
Fax: 902-435-6300	Fax: 613-288-0213	Fax: 416-367-1577
354 Notre-Dame Ouest	2300 Oxford Tower	Sussex Centre
Suite 200	10235-101 St.	90 Burnhamthorpe Rd. W.
Montreal, QC	Edmonton, AB	Suite 1504
H2Y 1T9	T5J 3G1	Mississauga, ON
Tel: 514-284-7444	Tel: 780-428-6663	L5B 3C3
Fax: 514-284-9290	Fax: 780-421-4680	Tel: 905-566-9700
		Fax: 905-566-9982

DAVID WARWICK KENNEDY & ASSOCIATES • Suite 500, 666 Burrard St. • Vancouver, BC • V6C 3P6 Tel: 604-685-9494 • Fax: 604-535-3044 • E-mail: david@dwksearch.com • Internet: www.dwksearch.com • The firm was founded in 1984 and since then has assisted over 40 different organisations in recruiting top executive , managerial and professional talent.

DDP CONSULTING GROUP • P.O. Box 28609, RPO WH • Burnaby, BC • V5C 6J4 • Tel: 604-294-9193 • Fax: 604-294-9155 • E-mail: ddp_info@ddp.ca • Internet: www.ddp.ca • DDP Consulting Group is a company specializing in development, management, technical support and other services designed to assist people make computers work for them. Their team consists of 25 people, composed of consultants, marketing and administrative people. DDP Consulting Group is based in Vancouver, B.C. and provides services to the Pacific Northwest, including the Yukon Territory.

DESCHENEAUX RECRUITMENT SERVICES LTD. • #503 - 570 Granville Street • Vancouver, BC • V6C 3P1 • Tel: 604-669-9787 • E-mail: info@insuranceheadhunters.com • Internet: www. insuranceheadhunters.com • They've been bringing talent and opportunity together for over 25 years. Recruiting exclusively for the insurance industry with placements both locally and nationally. Maintaining utmost integrity and confidentiality.

DESIGN GROUP STAFFING SERVICES INC. • 333 Seymour Street, Suite 1210 • Vancouver, BC • V6B 5A6 • Tel: 604-683-6400 • Fax: 604-669-3540 • E-mail: vancouver@dg.ca • Internet: www.dg.ca • Since 1976, Design Group Staffing Inc. has been providing Canadian and

International business with contract, temporary, leased and full-time technical, professional and management personnel. With offices coast to coast, we understand industry challenges that are unique to each region. We are the largest agency of our kind in Western Canada and are one of the top technical recruiting firms in the nation. We combine advanced technology with highly experienced trained consultants to ensure your needs are understood and that each assignment is completed to your satisfaction. Our comprehensive database enables us to track and maintain contact with over 100,000 contract personnel across Canada.

10012 Jasper Avenue	800 - 5 Ave. S.W. , Suite 1500	2010 Winston Park Dr.
Edmonton, AB	Calgary, AB	Suite 101
T5J 1R2	T2E 2R2	Oakville, ON
Tel: 780-428-1505	Tel: 403-233-2788	L6H 5R7
Fax: 780-428-7095	Fax: 403-266-5203	Tel: 905-829-4848
edmonton@dg.ca	calgary@dg.ca	Fax: 905-829-8888
		toronto@dg.ca

647 Bedford Hwy, Suite 101	Second Floor, 4915 – 54th Street
Halifax, NS	Red Deer, AB
B3M 0A5	T4N 2G7
Tel: 902-442-0398	Tel: 403-309-0757
Fax: 902-442-0399	Fax: 403-309-0852
halifax@dg.ca	reddeer@dg.ca

DESTINATIONS • 1207 Douglas St., Suite 400 • Victoria, BC • V8W 2E7 • Tel: 250-382-3303 • Fax: 250-383-4142 • E-mail: info@destinations.ca • Internet: www.destinations.ca • Founded in 1995, Destinations is one of the largest employment placement services in British Columbia. They find qualified job candidates for prospective employers - to the benefit of both parties. The result is effective staffing solutions for employers and helping capable people find meaningful work. They have 26 offices located throughout the province.

764 Fort Street	204, 4190 Lougheed Hwy.	303, 909 Island Hwy.
Victoria, BC	Burnaby, BC	Campbell River, BC
V8W 1H2	V5C 6AB	V9W 2C2
Tel: 250-388-0858	Tel: 604-451-4593	Tel: 250-286-4231
Fax: 250-388-0814	Fax: 604-451-4596	Fax: 250-830-1414
211, 2270 Cliffe Avenue	104, 80 Station Street	305, 155 Skinner St.
Courtenay, BC	Duncan, BC	Nanaimo, BC
V9N 2L4	V9L 1M4	V9R 5E8
Tel: 250-334-9823	Tel: 250-701-0885	Tel: 250-741-8824
Fax: 250-334-9824	Fax: 250-701-0883	Fax: 250-741-8825
2nd Floor	6, 120 Alberni Hwy.	101, 7337 - 137 St.
1500 Marine Drive	Parksville, BC	Surrey, BC
North Vancouver, BC	V9P 2H4	V3W 1A4
V7P 1T7	Tel: 250-951-2235	Tel: 604-598-2306
Tel: 604-904-9945	Fax: 250-951-2245	Fax: 604-598-2307
Fax: 604-904-9965		

DEVONWOOD PARTNERS • 2 Bloor St. W., Suite 700 • Toronto, ON • M4W 3R1 • Tel: 416-944-9000 • Fax: 905-821-7006 • E-mail: resumes@devonwood.com • Internet: www. devonwood.com • Devonwood Partners is a recruiting and consulting firm that specializes exclusively in the life insurance industry. It is the largest of its kind in Canada. Their clients are life insurance companies, reinsurance companies, benefits consultants, actuarial consulting firms, insurance software companies and insurance agencies in the Southern Ontario area. They handle a variety of recruiting assignments where a background in life insurance is an asset or a requirement, including management positions, underwriting, marketing, claims, finance, actuarial, administration, service and business systems analysis.

DGA CAREERS • Hanover Place, Suite 225, 101 - 6th Avenue SW • Calgary, AB • T2P 3P4 • Tel: 403-262-8383 • Fax: 403-263-8336 • E-mail: info@dgacareers.com • Internet: www.dgacareers.com • DGA Careers, originally Donald Givelos & Associates Inc., is the definitive recruiting firm for the Canadian Property-Casualty Insurance and Finance Industry. For over 20 years, they have maintained a reputation for being referral-based recruiters who excel in their ability to be proactive and forward thinking. Their Recruiters are located in Toronto and Calgary allowing complete coverage of the immediate GTA, as well as the rest of Ontario, in addition to Eastern and Western Canada. Their services include permanent and contract placements in claims, underwriting, customer service and finance, from junior to executive levels. Their clients include major insurers, insurance brerage firms, independent adjusting firms and government agencies, as well as companies in finance and insurance-related industries.

503-110 Yonge St.
Toronto, ON
M5C 1T4
Tel: 416-868-6711
Toll Free: 1-877-868-6711
Fax: 416-868-6329

DIAL SOLUTIONS • 1700, 246 Stewart Green S.W. • Calgary, AB • T3H 3C8 • Tel: 403-265-6544 • Fax: 403-264-9086 • E-mail: joanne@dialsolutionsgroup.com • Internet: http://dialsolutionsgroup.com • Contact: Joanne Dial, Operations • Dial Solutions Group was started in 1996 with one man, one desk and a deep desire to help people be more successful in the workplace. They originally offered only search services to clients in Calgary and Western Canada. They successfully placed positions ranging from executive to entry level in Sales, Accounting, Operations Management, Administration, IT and more. Within a short period of time they had successfully placed everything from truck drivers to V.P.s with clients from Winnipeg to Victoria. They even did some limited work with clients in Seattle, Portland and Chicago.

DION MANAGEMENT EXECUTIVE SEARCH • 1, Place Ville-Marie, Bureau 2821 • Montreal, QC • H3B 4R4 • Tel: 514-861-3331 • Internet: www.dion-management.com • Dion Management is a firm specialized in executive search and management consulting offering highly professional and confidential services of identification and selection of executives and specialized managers. Founded in 1990, Dion Management has acquired an enviable reputation among many leaders in the business community. Dion Management professionals have acquired expertise and experience from serving mid-sized and large businesses throughout Canada and abroad. Their professional ethics and neutrality ensure to their clients the most objective opinions and advice.

120 Adelaide St. W.	885, West Georgia St.
Suite 2500	Suite 1500
Toronto, ON	Vancouver, BC
M5H 1T1	V6C 3E8
Tel: 416-867-1176	Tel: 604-683-7330

DIRECT STAFFING SOLUTIONS INCORPORATED • 2425 Eglinton Avenue East, Unit 3 • Scarborough, ON • M1K 5G8 • Tel: 416-759-1500 • Fax: 416-759-8300 • E-mail: jbumpas@on.aibn.com • Internet: www.directstaffingsolutions.com • Contact: John Bumpas, President

• DSS Inc. is a professional supplier of temporary help dedicated to the provision of superior customer service and satisfaction. Whether the assignment is a temporary or long term position, every placement made by DSS Inc. is professionally screened with either a thorough background or proven track record. They closely monitor their applicants for attendance, attitude, commitment and desire to work. It is very common for a DSS Inc, representative to make sight visits to ensure their services are at a superior level of satisfaction. Their main focus at DSS Inc. is to build a professional relationship with their clients, and to enctheirage them to utilize the expertise of their staff to advise you in selecting a suitable solution for all of your staffing needs.

DIVERSIFIED STAFFING SERVICES LTD. • 805 - 5th Avenue S.W. • Calgary, AB • T2P 0N6 • Tel: 403-237-5577 • Fax: 403-269-1428 • E-mail: dsscal@diversifiedstaffing.com • Internet: www.diversifiedstaffing.com • Contact: Ed Murphy, General Manager • Diversified Staffing Group was started by two Canadians, born and raised in Calgary. Today, although they are still very involved, Diversified Staffing Group is 20% employee owned. The company began operations in the fall of 1978 with a staff of five, all of whom had experience in the temporary service industry. The Diversified Staffing Group now employs 110 people, operating from their centrally located head office in Calgary and their branch offices in Edmonton, Banff, Red Deer and Toronto.

10405 Jasper Ave.	Shop C	4957, 49 St.
Main Floor	208 Caribou St.	Red Deer, AB
Edmonton, AB	Banff, AB	T4N 1S8
T5J 3N4	T1L 1A7	Tel: 403-343-8161
Tel: 780-429-9058	Tel: 403-760-6288	Fax: 403-343-3899
Fax: 780-425-7419	Fax: 403-760-6206	

DONALD L. HART & ASSOCIATES • 3 Church Street, Suite 604 • Toronto, ON • M5E 1M2 • Tel: 416-862 7104 • Fax: 416-862 7139 • E-mail: info@dlhart.com • Internet: www.dlhart.com • Established in 1981, Donald L. Hart & Associates specializes in recruiting information technology professionals with the desired credentials. They place candidates to meet the employment needs presented to us in the following areas: general management, sales management, technical management, sales and marketing, and hands on technical development.

DRAKE INTERNATIONAL CANADA • 2323 Bloor St. W., Suite 218A, Toronto, ON • M6S 4W1 • Tel: 416-762-4414 • Fax: 416-763 0823 • E-mail: torontowest@na.drakeintl.com • Internet: www.drakeintl.com • Now in its fifth decade, Drake operates in 12 countries, each year interviewing more than 100,000 candidates. Drake also places tens of thousands of people in permanent and temporary employment and trains in excess of 140,000 students annually. The company has approximately 20,000 registered contractors and casual workers and employs about 2,500 internal staff worldwide. Check their website for a list of all their locations.

1111 West Hastings St.	535 West 10th Ave.	4536 Willington Ave.
Suite 520	Suite 200	Powell River, BC
Vancouver, BC	Vancouver, BC	V8A 2M8
V6E 2J3	V5Z 1K9	Tel: 604-485-2508
Tel: 604-601-2800	Tel: 604-877-0690	Fax: 604-485-2566
Fax: 604-682-8523	Fax: 604-876-9875	
707-7th Ave. S.W.	13222 118 Avenue	221 Portage Ave.
Suite 140	Edmonton, AB	Winnipeg, MB
Calgary, AB	T5L 4N4	R3B 2A6
T2P 3H6	Tel: 780-414-6341	Tel: 204-947-0077
Tel: 403-266-8791	Fax: 780-488-1678	Fax: 204-947-5678
Fax: 403-262-1045		

DRAKE INTERNATIONAL CANADA

2025 Corydon Ave.
Suite 116
Winnipeg, MB
R3P 0N5
Tel: 204-452-8600
Fax: 204-477-1645

226 Pitt St.
Cornwall, ON
K6J 3P6
Tel: 613-938-4777
Fax: 613-938-0147

201 Queen Ave.
London, ON
N6A 1J1
Tel: 519-433-3151
Fax: 519-673-3770

340 Albert St.
Suite 1300
Ottawa, ON
K1R 7Y6
Tel: 613-237-3370
Fax: 613-237-2901

600 boul. Rene Levesque W.
Unit 002
Montreal, QC
H3B 1N4
Tel: 514-395-9595
Fax: 514-395-9922

1819 Granville St.
Suite 100
Halifax. NS
B3J 3R1
Tel: 902-429-2490
Fax: 902-429-2408

170 North Front St.
Unit 4A
Belleville, ON
K8N 5H5
Tel: 613-966-7283
Fax: 613-966-0421

25 Main St. W.
Suite 1610
Hamilton, ON
L8P 1H1
Tel: 905-528-9855
Fax: 905-528-0014

165 Dundas St. W.
Mississauga, ON
L5B 2N6
Tel: 905-279-9000
Fax: 905-279-1915

79 Wellington St. W.
Suite 2400
Toronto, ON
M5K 1H6
Tel: 416-216-1000
Fax: 416-216-1109

320 St-Joseph Est.
Bureau RC-105
Quebec City, QC
G1K 8G5
Tel: 418-529-9371
Fax: 418-529-9364

102 King St. W.
Brockville, ON
K6V 3P9
Tel: 613-342-2653
Fax: 613-342-7089

370 King St. W.
Kingston, ON
K7K 2Y2
Tel: 613-542-3790
Fax: 613-542-6335

710 Dorval Dr.
Suite 514
Oakville, ON
L6K 3V7
Tel: 905-337-9898

2323 Bloor St. W.
Suite 218
Toronto, ON
M6S 4W1
Tel: 416-762-4414
Fax: 416-763-0823

805 Main St.
Moncton, NB
E1C 1G1
Tel: 506-862-1808
Fax: 506-862-1893

DRAKKAR HUMAN RESOURCES • 1137 Derry Road East • Mississauga, ON • L5T 1P3 • Tel: 905-795-1397 • Fax: 905-795-1391 • E-mail: dvance@drakkar.ca • Internet: www.drakkar.ca • Drakkar was founded in 1991 by Michel Blaquière and Denis Deschamps. In the early years, the company specialized in the placement of industrial workers in the transportation, distribution and logistics sectors.

1200 Ave. McGill College
Bureau 2220
Montréal, QC
H3B 4G7
Tel: 514-871-0300
Fax: 514-871-0916

8746 Cote-de-Liesse
Saint-Laurent, QC
H4T 1H2
Tel: 514-733-6655
Fax: 514-733-2828

766 Rene-Levesque
Boulevard West
Quebec, QC
G1S 1T2
Tel: 1-800-667-1988

DRIVER CARRIER PLACEMENT DEPOT • 83 Galaxy Blvd., Suite 1 • Toronto, ON • M9W 5X6 • Tel: 416-249-2373 • Fax: 416-249-3039 • E-mail: info@fordrivers.com • Internet: www. fordrivers.com/DCPD/dcpd.html • Driver Carrier Placement Depot was established to meet truck driver recruitment and training challenges, facing the for-hire and private motor carrier industry throughout North America. Professional drivers can register with them to find their most desired driving job. This enables them to carefully recruit the safety conscious, AZ & DZ licensed professional drivers required for a truck fleet of any size. They can be reached toll free at 1-800-810-0205.

DYNAMIC EMPLOYMENT SOLUTIONS INC. • 197 County Court Blvd., Suite 300 • Brampton, ON • L6W 4P6 • Tel: 905-796-0210 • Fax: 905-796-5251 • E-mail: steveh@ dynamicemployment.com • Internet: www.dynamicemployment.com • Dynamic Employment Solutions Inc. is a targeted and focused recruiting team providing employment solutions for both the applicants and clients. In eight years of business, they have diversified into a successful search firm assisting their clients with all levels of recruiting & Human Resource consulting. Dynamics goal is to successfully match superior candidates with quality customers by understanding each party's needs to ensure a winning match. Dynamic prides itself in the growth they have achieved through client and applicant referrals and networking.

EAGLE PROFESSIONAL RESOURCES INC. • 67 Yonge St., Suite 200 • Toronto, ON • M5E 1J8 • Tel: 416-861-1492 • Fax: 416-861-8401 • E-mail: hr@eagleonline.com • Internet: www. eagleonline.com • Contact: Paul Cameron • Eagle Professional Resources Inc. is a truly Canadian staffing service company providing the best Hi-Tech professionals to meet today's technology challenges. Founded in 1996, Eagle has expanded significantly from 3 to 10 offices across the country. Over the last nine years, Eagle has grown from $10 million in annual revenue and ten employees, to the current 2005 revenues of $87 million with ninety employees. Throughout its nine year history, Eagle has achieved recognition through numerous accreditations, most notably as one of Canada's 50 Best Managed Companies for the last six years running and currently ranking 11th on the Branham Group's list of the Top 25 Canadian IT Services Companies and 42nd on their list of the Top 250 Canadian Technology Companies. Today, Eagle is one of Canada's largest and most successful technology staffing companies and a leader within the staffing industry. The company has earned a solid international reputation for quality and value by meeting the Hi-Tech staffing needs of clients around the world.

736 6th Ave. S.W. Suite 850 Calgary, AB T2P 3T7 Tel: 403-205-3770 Fax: 403-205-3774	1 Place Ville Marie Suite 2821 Montreal, PQ H3B 4R4 Tel: 514-396-6594 Fax: 514-396-6596	700 West Georgia St. Suite 1410 Vancouver, BC V7Y 1A1 Tel: 604-899-1130 Fax: 604-899-1150
170 Laurier Ave. W. Suite 902 Ottawa, ON K1P 5V5 Tel: 613-234-1810 Fax: 613-234-0797	Purdy's Wharf, Tower II 1969 Upper Water St. Halifax, NS B3J 3R7 Tel: 902-491-4275 Fax: 902-429-5018	10117 Jasper Ave. Suite 810 Edmonton, AB T5J 1W8 Tel: 780-423-6700 Fax: 780-423-6704
167 Lombard Ave. Suite 909 Winnipeg, MB R3B 0V3 Tel: 204-284-2059 Fax: 204-942-1225	1914 Hamilton St. Suite 300 Regina, SK S4P 3N6 Tel: 306-352-3310 Fax: 306-352-4110	201-1290 Broad St. Victoria, BC V8W 2A5 Tel: 250-414-7456 Fax: 250-383-2978

EASTMAN EMPLOYMENT SERVICES • 395 Main St., Box 730 • Steinbach, MB • R5G 1Z4 • Tel: 204-326-4099 • Fax: 204-326-5481 • E-mail: eesinfo@mts.net • Contact: Brenda Andrews • Eastman Employment Services assists individuals with disabilities (physical, social, developmental), mental health issues and/or other barriers to employment in developing the skills, abilities and contacts they need to obtain and maintain meaningful paid employment in their community. EES is committed to providing services to unemployed or underemployed Manitobans who are interested in seeking employment in Southeast Manitoba. Eastman Employment Services assists individuals with employment search plans, job search techniques, vocational assessments, pre-employment skills workshops, resume workshops, and access to computer/internet to update or create your own resume or search for job opportunities.

EBY'S BUSINESS SERVICES • 1994 Comox Ave. • Comox, BC • V9M 3M7 • Tel: 250-339-2261 • Fax: 250-339-5855 • E-mail: james@ebys.com • Internet: www.ebys.com • Eby's Business Services is a progressive Vancouver Island company that provides a wide variety of business services. They offer complete services in income tax preparation, personnel placement, resume creation, computer training, business support, domain hosting, internet web page development, office rental and other related services.

EDMONTON & CAPITOL PERSONNEL SERVICES • 9526 Jasper Avenue NW • Edmonton, AB • T5H 3V3 • Tel: 780-426-3585 • Fax: 780-425-7792 • E-mail: service@edmontonpersonnel. com • Internet: www.edmontonpersonnel.com • Edmonton & Capitol Personnel Services is Edmonton's finest stheirce of temporary and general labtheir personnel. Founded in 1975 to offer industrial support to companies in and around the Edmonton vicinity. Since that time they have become a full service agency specializing in construction, distribution, transportation and oilfield / shutdown personnel throughout Western Canada.

EHL CORPORATION - MEDICAL SERVICES • 300, 3665 Kingsway • Vancouver, BC • V5R 5W2 • Tel: 604-504-3800 • Fax: 604-504-3906 • E-mail: info@e-h-l.com • Internet: www.e-h-l.com • EHL is a healthcare solutions company delivering comprehensive business management solutions services, software solutions, and e-health solutions. E H L is focused on providing healthcare business related solutions to governments, hospitals, healthcare organizations and physicians throughout Canada, USA and International destinations. The primary functions of E H L are in the areas of management consulting, training and industry research.

ÉLAN DATA MAKERS • Scotia Place, Suite 1140, 10060 Jasper Avenue • Edmonton, AB • T5J 3R8 • Tel: 780-428-8798 • E-mail: elanedm@elandatamakers.com • Internet: www.elandatamakers. com • Established in 1972, élan Data Makers has become Western Canada's largest data entry service bureau by providing quality data capture services from their ftheir branch locations to customers in Ontario, Manitoba, Alberta, British Columbia and more recently Washington DC, New York, Chicago and Alaska. élan offers a wide range of services including large scale scanning, data entry and optical character recognition solutions, imaging and indexing services, report generation, database management, temporary and permanent placement services and project administration.

788 Beatty St.	910 7th Ave. SW	755 Hillside Ave.
Suite 307	Suite 1020	Suite 100
Vancouver, BC	Calgary, AB	Victoria, BC
V6B 2M1	T2P 3N8	V8T 5B3
Tel: 604-688-8521	Tel: 403-290-1661	Tel: 250-383-2226
Fax: 604-669-0171	Fax 403-263-5038	Fax 250-383-8018

EMPIRE STAFFING SERVICES, INC. • 83 Kennedy Road South, Suite 12 • Brampton, ON • L6W 3P3 • Tel: 905-459-1429 • Fax: 905-549-1897 • E-mail: ccampbell@empirestaffing.ca • Internet: www.empirestaffing.ca • Contact: Cassandra Campbell, President • Empire Staffing Services consist of a team of professional providing quality support to business throughout the greater Toronto and Peel region in the staffing services industry.

EMPLOYMENT ACTION • 1268 5th Aven, Suite 300 • Prince George, BC • V2L 3L2 • Tel: 250-564-8044 • Fax: 250-564-8864 • Internet: www.employment-action.bc.ca • Contact: Lorna Dittmar • Employment Action offers Employment Assistance Services specifically for injured workers and people with disabilities - any injury or disability that is a barrier to employment or a threat to continued employment.

EMPLOYMENT NETWORK CANADA INC. • 2932 Victoria Ave. • Regina, SK • S4T 1K7 • Tel: 306-585-7244 • Fax: 306-584-3544 • E-mail: linda@employmentnetwork.ca • Internet: www.employmentnetwork.ca • Contact: Linda Langelier, CHRP (Human Resources Consultant/ Owner) • Since 1996 the staff of Employment Network has provided "service with a difference" to Employers and Candidates within Saskatchewan and beyond. They have built their reputation on knowledge, honesty and personalized service. Whether you are loing for a job or loing to hire, they want to give you the best they have to offer.

EMPLOYMENT SOLUTION, THE • 40 Holly St., Suite 500 • Toronto, ON • M4S 3C3 • Tel: 416-482-2420 • Fax: 416-482-9282 • Internet: www.tes.net • The Employment Solution has maintained a dedication to quality, a sense of urgency and an entrepreneurial spirit for over 30 years. They provide a creative and resourceful approach to professional staffing challenges in the fields of Engineering, Information Technology, Senior Management and Professional Office Services.

1155 René-Lévesque Blvd.
Suite 2500
Montreal, QC
H3B 2K4
Tel: 514-866-2493
Fax: 514-866-6488

1 City Centre Dr., Suite 705
Mississauga, ON
L5B 1M2
Tel: 905-272-4296
Fax: 905-272-1068

3430 South Service Rd.
Burlington, ON
L7N 3T9
Tel: 905-639-2600
Fax: 905-639-4998

301 Moodie Dr.
Suite 410
Nepean, ON
K2H 9C4
Tel: 613-828-7887
Fax: 613-828-2729

400, 5th Ave. S.W.
Suite 300
Calgary, AB
T2P 0L6
Tel: 403-538-4788
Fax: 403-538-4789

1200 West 73rd Ave.
Suite 1100
Vancouver, BC
V6P 6G5
Tel: 604-707-9018
Fax: 604-707-9021

1969 Upper Water St.
22nd Floor , Penthouse Suite
Halifax, NS
B3J 3R7
Tel: 902-491-4494
Fax: 902-444-4784

ENGLISH TEACHERS OVERSEAS • 1330 Burrard Street, Suite 813 • Vancouver, BC • V6Z 2B8 • Tel: 604-689-3677 • Fax: 604-682-2905 • E-mail: eto@direct.ca • English Teachers Overseas recruits qualified teachers for jobs in Asia, specifically Japan, Korea, and China. They offer teacher placements, info services and E.S.L. referrals.

EVEREST MANAGEMENT NETWORK INC. • 390 Bay Street, Suite 2410 • Toronto, ON • M5H 2Y2 • Tel: 416-363-9798 • Fax: 416-363-3930 • E-mail: info@everestmanagement.com • Internet: www.everestmanagement.com • Contact: Matthew Standish • Everest Management Network Inc. is a team of professionals possessing diverse academic and business backgrounds dedicated to excellence, integrity and client satisfaction. Founded in 1990, Everest has grown rapidly into a successful search practice providing services for clients ranging from entrepreneurial (ventures) to multinational corporations.

EXCEL HUMAN RESOURCES • 102 Bank St., Suite 300 • Ottawa, ON • K1P 5N4 • Tel: 613-230-5393 • Fax: 613-230-1623 • E-mail: excel@excelhr.com • Internet: www.excelhr.com • Excel Human Resources is a contract and permanent placement firm involved in recruiting technology professionals in Ontario. They specialize in presenting the most highly skilled individuals, within the areas of business systems and software engineering to corporate and government clients.

EXECUTIVE ASSISTANCE INC. • 25 Adelaide Street East, Suite 1711, Victoria Tower • Toronto, ON • M5C 1Y7 • Tel: 416-368-8700 • Fax: 416-368-0555 • E-mail: team@execassistance.com • Internet: www.execassistance.com • Executive Assistance Inc.'s objective has been to provide exceptional service to many clients amongst a vast array of industries across Canada. As a leader in the recruiting field they pride themselves on bringing a disciplined and comprehensive approach to the staffing requirements of their corporate clients. National in scope, but singular in focus, their innovative company is dedicated to helping you to achieve your specific human resources needs with the help of one of their skilled and knowledgeable consultants.

EXECUTIVE SOLUTIONS • 840 - 7th Avenue SW, Suite 1220 • Calgary, AB • T2P 3G2 • Tel: 403-269-6979 • Fax: 403-269-6629 • E-mail: info@executivesolutions.ca • Internet: www.executivesolutions.ca • They are a locally owned, dynamic company specializing in all facets of office staffing solutions. Executive Solutions operates as a team in the true sense of the word. When you call their office to place a job order or to register - you will be working with the Executive Solutions team.

EXECUTRADE CONSULTANTS LTD. • 9917 - 112 Street • Edmonton, AB • T5K 1L6 • Tel: 780-944-1122 • Fax: 780-482-3037 • E-mail: executrade@executrade.com • Internet: www.executrade.com • Contact: Contact: Richard Stoppler • Their team has the expertise and the flexibility to handle short-term, long-term or career placements from general office support to the highest levels of management. Their divisions are: executive and management; human resources; accounting; secretarial and administrative; information technology; engineering and technical; sales and marketing; and payroll services.

Sun Life Plaza, West Tower
144 - 4 Avenue SW
Suite 1600
Calgary, AB
T2P 3N4
Tel: 403-252-5835
Fax: 403-695-1795

EXPRESS PERSONNEL SERVICES • 220 Laurier Ave. W., Suite 560 • Ottawa, ON • K1P 5Z9 • Tel: 613-233-5988 • Fax: 613-233-4651 • E-mail: jobs.ottawaon@expresspersonnel.com • Internet: www.expresspersonnel.com • Express Professional Staffing provides both contract staffing and professional placement services. Express's recruiters are professionals who have firsthand knowledge of the industries they serve, and have the ability to analyze employment skills and match those skills with the particular requirements of a prospective employer.

EXPRESS PERSONNEL SERVICES continued

201 County Court Blvd.
Suite 103
Brampton, ON
L6W 4L2
Tel: 905-874-9824

440 Elizabeth St.
Suite 300
Burlington, ON
L7R 2M1
Tel: 905-639-7117

318 Guelph St.
Unit 1A
Georgetown, ON
L7G 3B4
Tel: 905-877-1466

45 Speedvale Ave. E.
Suite 100
Guelph, ON
N1H 1J2
Tel: 519-821-4275

151 York Blvd.
Main Level
Hamilton, ON
L8R 3M2
Tel: 905-528-7744

50 Queen St. N.
Suite 704
Kitchener, ON
N2H 6P4
Tel: 519-578-9030

150 Dufferin Ave.
Suite 100
London, ON
N6A 5N6
Tel: 519-672-7620

75 Dundas St. N.
Unit 6C
Cambridge, ON
N1R 6G5
Tel: 519-624-0131

2825 Lauzon Parkway
Unit 118
Windsor, ON
N8T 3H5
Tel: 519-251-1115

115 Curtis St.
St. Thomas, ON
N5P 1J4
Tel: 519-631-9495

347 Christina St. North
Sarnia ON
N7T 5V6
Tel: 519-336-7962
Fax: 519-336-4769

1100 Finch Ave. W.
Suite 518
Toronto, ON
M3J 2T2
Tel: 416-590-9948

2885 Lauzon Parkway
Suite 118
Windsor, ON
N8T 3H5
Tel: 519-251-1115

3800 Steeles Ave. W.
Suite 202
Woodbridge, ON
L4L 4G9
Tel: 905-264-7130

FELDMAN GRAY & ASSOCIATES • 45 St. Clair Ave. West, Suite 700 • Toronto, ON • M4V 1K0 • Tel: 416-515 7600 • Fax: 416-515-7595 • E-mail: general@feldman-gray.com • Internet: www.feldman-gray.com • Since their founding in 1991, the professionals at Feldman Gray have been serving business and institutional clients, large and small.

FINANCE DEPARTMENT LIMITED, THE • 1 City Centre Drive, Suite 610 • Mississauga, ON • L5B 1M2 • Tel: 905-897-5630 • Fax: 905-897-5636 • E-mail: info@tfdl.com • Internet: www. tfdl.com • The Finance Department is a very dynamic and agile firm that specializes in the strategic placement of accounting professionals. Their candidates carry accounting designations (including CA, CGA and CMA) and are experienced in a wide range of business sectors. Their employment backgrounds range from Financial Analyst to CFO and their level of experience ranges from recent graduates to seasoned veterans. Their strict qualification guidelines and selection process ensures that their clients get the best person, every time.

FINNEY-TAYLOR PERSONNEL LTD. • 602 11th Ave. SW, Sun Rise Square, Suite 200 • Calgary, AB • T2R 1J8 • Tel: 403-264-4001 • Fax: 403-264-4057 • E-mail: mailbox@finney-taylor.com • Internet: www.finney-taylor.com • Contact: David Skode • They are an Information Technology Staffing Solutions provider that assists clients in meeting their staffing demands. With over 365 clients and over 20,000 registered IT professionals Finney Taylor is Alberta's premier IT restheircing management firm. Their clients are companies that need mid to senior level IT professionals and they include over 50 of Canada's biggest firms.

FORBES & GUNN CONSULTANTS LTD. • 1168 Hamilton St., Suite 505 • Vancouver, BC • V6B 2S2 • Tel: 604-484-4715 • E-mail: jobs@forbes-gunn.com • Internet: www.forbes-gunn. com • Forbes & Gunn is a leading recruitment and consulting firm that specializes exclusively in Information Systems professionals and management. Providing their clients with proven, skilled and capable IT professionals since 1991, their reputation has been built on integrity and the ability to satisfy not only their clients' IT personnel needs but also satisfy their talented candidates' career goals.

FOREST PEOPLE • 800 - 1100 Melville Street • Vancouver, BC • V6E 4A6 • Tel: 604-669-5635 • Fax: 604-684-4972 • E-mail: people@forestpeople.com • Internet: www.forestpeople.com • Forest People is Canada's largest forest industry personnel recruiting firm. Serving all sectors of the industry, they recruit executive, operational management, professional and technical personnel for a large group of industry companies and firms serving the industry. Their clients include companies across Canada and internationally.

FRIDAY PERSONNEL SERVICES LTD. • 703 - 6th Avenue S.W., Suite 120 • Calgary, AB • T2P 0T9 • Tel: 403-233-0499 • Fax: 403-444-0086 • E-mail: friday@friday.ab.ca • Internet: www. friday.ab.ca • Friday Personnel Services provides both permanent and temporary office staff for Calgary. They specialize in the areas of word processing, spreadsheets, presentation software, databases, office administration, accounting, secretarial/reception, and records management.

FROMM & ASSOCIATES • 65 Queen Street West, Suite 500 • Toronto, ON • M5H 2M5 • Tel: 416-368-0050 • Fax: 416-368-2858 • E-mail: admin@fromm.net • Internet: www.fromm.net • Fromm & Associates is a leading provider of accounting and financial staffing services in the Greater Toronto Area. As a specialized boutique firm they offer a highly personalized, results-driven service. Their consultants' combined years of recruiting experience is well over 50 years. They represent their clients and candidates with the highest level of professional integrity and pride themselves on the speed and effectiveness with which they execute the placement process. Their client list includes some of the most recognized names in the business community, and their bank of candidates currently exceeds 20,000.

FRONTLINE RESOURCES • Unit 50 Hamlyn Road Plaza, Suite 408 • St. John's, NF • A1E 5X7 • Tel: 709-738-5627 • Fax: 709-738-5628 • E-mail: frontline@thezone.net • Internet: www. frontline.nf.net • Frontline Resources offers a number of services in the construction industry, including recruiting.

FULCRUM SEARCH SCIENCE INC. • 85 Richmond Street West, Suite 702 • Toronto, ON • M5H 2C9 • Tel: 416-847-4990 • E-mail: info@fulcrumsearchscience.com • Internet: www. fulcrumsearchscience.com • Contact: Bruce McAlpine, President • Fulcrum Search Science Inc. is an executive search and human capital management firm serving the Canadian business community since 1971. In the past 33 years they have completed over 2,000 searches on behalf of their clients, and have watched with pride as leaders they have placed have grown into the top positions within their organizations. At the same time, they have taken a leadership role within their industry, having continuous representation at the national level of their industry associations for over 20 years. Their Founder is a past President of the Association of Professional Placement Agencies and Consultants (APPAC), and an hontheirary life member of the Association of Canadian Search, Employment and Staffing Services (ACSESS), the national voice of the recruiting and staffing industries in Canada.

FULLER LANDAU • 1010 De La Gauchetiere St. W., Suite 200 • Montreal, QC • H3B 2N2 • Tel: 514-875-2865 • Fax: 514-866-0247 • E-mail: info.mtl@fullerlandau.com • Internet: www. fullerlandau.com • Fuller Landau, Chartered Accountants and Business Advisors, has more than fifty years of experience working with mid-market, entrepreneurial-driven companies. The people on their team unite some of the most enlightened and experienced business minds.

Each client team is led by one of their partners from either their Montreal or Toronto offices, and is carefully cast to ensure the collective knowledge is synergistic for you and your business.

151 Bloor St. W.
12th Floor
Toronto, ON
M5S 1S4
Tel: 416-645-6500
Fax: 416-645-6501
info.tor@fullerlandau.com

FUSION RECRUITMENT GROUP • 777 Hornby St., Suite 2088 • Vancouver, BC • V6Z 1S4 • Tel: 604-678-5627 • Fax: 604-669-6047 • E-mail: info@fusion-recruitment.com • Internet: www.fusion-recruitment.com • Fusion Recruitment Group is a professional services company specializing in the recruitment of business development, sales, marketing, and management categories. In short, they identify, recruit, and retain sales and marketing professionals which meet your needs and corporate objectives. By doing so, they assist individuals maximize their career potential and offer options with career development and new opportunities.

FUTURE EXECUTIVE PERSONNEL LTD. • 425 University Ave., Suite 800 • Toronto, ON • M5G 1T6 • Tel: 416-850-9747 • Fax: 416-979-3030 • E-mail: staff@futureexec.com • Internet: www. fepsearchgroup.com • Since 1975, they have been one of North America's premier search firms with a track record of successful placements for top tier companies. Thousands of professionals turn to us to maximize their career opportunities.

GALLANT SEARCH GROUP • 431 Boler Rd., P.O. Box 20086 • London, ON • N6K 2K0 • Tel: 1-888-663-1070 • Fax: 1-888-663-1074 • E-mail: gallant@automotivecareers.com • Internet: www.automotivecareers.com • Gallant Search Group has over twenty years experience servicing the Automotive and related industries. They have the strength to recruit talent for your specific employment needs. Management is their main area of expertise, although they recruit for Engineering, Human Resources, Quality, Materials, Purchasing and Sales as well.

GALLOWAY & ASSOCIATES • 633 Bay Street, Suite 1414 • Toronto, ON • M5G 2G4 • Tel: 416-969-8989 • Fax: 416-969-9498 • E-mail: glenn@gallowaysearch.com • Internet: www. gallowaysearch.com • Galloway and Associates has gained an enviable reputation for quality of service and dedication to client satisfaction. Their area of specialization is in the recruitment and selection of executive level professionals. As an endorsement of their success, they have been retained by several leading companies to help with staffing of important positions.

GAUTHIER CONSULTANTS • 1010 Sherbrooke St. W., Suite 1800 • Montreal, QC • H3A 2R7 • Tel: 514-528-9089 • E-mail: info@gauthier.com • Internet: www.gauthier.com • For 15 years, Gauthier Conseils have specialized in recruitment of mid-and senior-management personnel. Main sectors of activity include administration, finance, accounting, engineering, technical (IT), production, marketing, sales, and human resources.

GEORGIAN STAFFING SERVICES • 50 Hume St. • Collingwood, ON • L9Y 1V2 • Tel: 705-444-1645 • Fax: Fax:705-443-4026 • E-mail: gsvws@georgionstaffing.on.ca • Internet: www. georgianstaffing.on.ca • Georgian Staffing Services provides temporary, permanent, and outplacement services. A division of Tracks, they provide assistance to businesses in the Georgian Triangle area.

GERALD WALSH ASSOCIATES INC. • 2020 - 1801 Hollis Street • Halifax, NS • B3J 3N4 • Tel: 902-421-1676 • Fax: 902-491-1300 • E-mail: apply@geraldwalsh.com • Internet: www. geraldwalsh.com • Founded in 1990, Gerald Walsh Recruitment Services Inc. is one of Atlantic

Canada's leading executive recruitment and human resources firms. They focus on placing middle-to-senior level managers and professionals in a variety of disciplines including finance, accounting, human resources, marketing, communications, production, sales, office services, information technology and engineering.

GILLESPIE PERSONNEL LTD. • 630 – 20 Avenue NW • Calgary, AB • T2M 1C8 • Tel: 403-250-1750 • Fax: 403-250-2190 • E-mail: info@gillespiepersonnel.com • Internet: www. gillespiepersonnel.com • Contact: Gayle Gillespie • Gillespie Personnel Ltd. provides staffing services. They are committed to providing these services in an ethical and cost effective manner. Gayle Gillespie has been providing these human resource services since 1979 where she worked as the manager of the automated services division of Keyword Office Technologies Ltd. In 1991, Gayle purchased the division, and incorporated as Gillespie Personnel Ltd. The cornerstone of Gillespie is their dedication to quality, attention to detail and unparalleled customer service.

GILMORE STAFFING SOLUTIONS • 1200 Bay St., Suite 502 • Toronto, ON • M5R 2A5 • Tel: 416-928-1368 • Fax: 416-928-3432 • E-mail: mail@gilmorestaffing.com • Internet: www. gilmorestaffing.com • Gilmore Staffing Solutions, since its start-up in 1985, has earned its reputation as the leading Toronto search firm specializing in top-quality management and office professionals.

GLEN ABBEY EXECUTIVE SEARCH INC. • 122 Milne Place • Rockwood, ON • N0B 2K0 • Tel: 519-856-1520 • Fax: 519-856-1619 • E-mail: art@execuprolink.com • Internet: www. execuprolink.com • With more than 20 years of senior level search experience, one of the prime objectives of Glen Abbey Executive Search is to match high calibre candidates with high profile and reputable clients by carrying out a comprehensive value-added interview and screening process.

GLOBAL CONSULTING GROUP INC. • 195 Main St. N. • Markham, ON • L3P 1Y4 • Tel: 905-472-9677 • Fax: 905-472-9671 • E-mail: infoweb@globalrecruit.com • Internet: www. globalrecruit.com • Finding the best people in today's competitive marketplace can be a full-time job. Maintaining your momentum and focus are crucial to a successful hire. At Global Consulting Group (GCG), they find the right people for your team while you strive to ensure that your business is a success. Their expertise is targeted at the mid to senior level in a wide variety of industries. Their searches include Executive Management, Information Technology, Engineering, Operations, Marketing, Sales, Scientific and Biotech Research.

GLOBAL HOSPITALITY • 4170, avenue Marlowe • Montreal, QC • H4A 3M2 • Tel: 514-488-4842 • E-mail: montrealmail@globalhospitality.com • Internet: www.globalhospitality.com • Global Hospitality is an executive search firm serving the hospitality industry exclusively. With international offices and a professional and experienced staff in the specialized needs of the hospitality profession, Global provides world-wide, industry-wide reach in finding and recruiting "star" candidates for all key positions. The company has earned an extraordinary reputation for successful placement of corporate-level executives, property-level management and culinary staff in hotels, resorts, spas, clubs, casinos, restaurants, convention facilities, food service companies, cruise ships and all other facets of the travel and theme attraction industries.

2430 Meadowpine Blvd.
Suite 107
Mississauga, ON
L5N 6S2
Tel: 905-814-5701
Fax: 905-814-5702
torontomail@globalhospitality.com

GLOBAL HUMAN RESOURCE CENTRE INC. • 185 Brock St. N. • Whitby, ON • L1N 4H3 • Tel: 905-666-2858 • Fax: 905-427-6623? • E-mail: generalinquiries@ghrc.ca • Internet: www. ghrc.ca • In 1991, Global Human Resource Centre was formed out of the merging of two other personnel companies founded in 1977. A dynamic company, Global has done business in Ontario and other provinces, servicing many multi-national corporations, as well as large cross-sections of local industry. They began their business by servicing the Greater Toronto Area, but they quickly expanded their servicing range to other Ontario centres, as their clients' needs increased.

777 Warden Avenue	159 King Street	1 William Street S.
Suite 217	Suite 103	Suite 5
Scarborough, ON	Peterborough, ON	Lindsay, ON
M1L 4C3	K9J 2R8	K9V 3A3
Tel: 416-285-6858	Tel: 705-745-6858	Tel: 705-878-3633

GLOBAL PERSONNEL • 40 Eglinton Ave. E., Suite 204 • Toronto, ON • M4P 3A2 • Tel: 416-482-5115 • Fax: 416-482-8998 • E-mail: resumes@globalpersonnel.com • Internet: www. globalpersonnel.com • Since 1992, Global Personnel has provided timely employment solutions for Fortune 1000 employers primarily in the Greater Toronto area. At the same time, they have provided challenging and rewarding permanent career opportunities and exciting assignments for qualified temporary and contract employees. They offer a wide range of expertise, from IT to sales and customer services.

GOLDBECK RECRUITING INC. • 475 West Georgia Street, Suite 510 • Vancouver, BC • V6B 4M9 • Tel: 604-684-1428 • Fax: 604-684-1429 • E-mail: contact@goldbeck.com • Internet: www.goldbeck.com • Contact: Henry E. Goldbeck, President • Goldbeck Recruiting Inc. is an executive recruiting and headhunting agency based in Vancouver, BC. Goldbeck's recruiters specialize in the recruitment and placement of Sales, Marketing and Operations professionals in Commercial, Industrial, Financial, Information Technology (IT), Telecommunications and Wireless industries throughout North America and China. Goldbeck Recruiting is the leading recruiting and headhunting agency headquarters in Vancouver since 1997.

GRAND RIVER PERSONNEL LTD. • 842 Victoria St. N., Unit #16 • Kitchener, ON • N2B 3C1 • Tel: 519-576-0920 • Fax: 519-576-0099 • E-mail: recruit@grandriverpersonnel.ca • Internet: www.grandriverpersonnel.ca • Contact: Linda Dancey, President and Owner • Grand River Personnel (GRP) is a locally owned and operated placement and corporate training service located in Kitchener, Ontario. Their mission is to provide professional quality and service to the business and candidate communities. Their main function is to recruit for local businesses who are searching for candidates to accept temporary, contract and full-time positions. Their service is completely free of charge to all candidates. Corporate training and development is also offered through their certified professional trainer, Linda Dancey.

GRASSLANDS GROUP INC. • # 5, 244 - 1st Avenue N.E. • Swift Current, SK • S9H 2B4 • Tel: 306-778-0570 • Fax: 306-778-6403 • E-mail: info@grasslandsgroup.ca • Internet: www.grasslandsgroup.ca • Contact: Blair Clark, Senior Partner • Grasslands Group Inc. is an employment services dompany that has provided human resource services and products to thousands of employers and has placed over 1,500 workers across the prairie provinces of Western Canada since 1993. Their corporate Head Office is in Swift Current, Saskatchewan. They are dedicated to the continued growth and diversity of the western Canadian economy.

GRH INC. • 250 Grande Allée Ouest, Bureau 801 • Québec, QC • G1K 3G9 • Tel: 418-648-8414 • Fax: 418-648-9814 • E-mail: grh@grh.ca • Internet: www.grh.ca • Fondée en 1989, GRH inc. est une firme de consultants en gestion des resstheirces humaines établie à Québec et Montréal.

Une des principales activités de GRH inc. consiste en la recherche et la sélection de cadres, de professionnels et de techniciens.

1, Place Ville-Marie	320, rue St-Germain
Suite 2821	Suite 502
Montréal, QC	Rimouski, QC
H3B 4R4	G5L 1C2
Tel: 514-874-9106	Tel: 418-723-6269
Fax: 514-866-2115	Fax: 418-722-9058

GRIFFIN SPROSTON • 55 Bloor St. W., Suite 228, Manulife Ctr • Toronto, ON • M4W 1A5 • Tel: 416-922-7777 • Fax: 416-922-3061 • E-mail: info@griffinsproston.com • Internet: www. griffinsproston.com • Contact: Dana Wright • Serving clients since 1973 on a boutique basis, Griffin Sproston stands out as one of the few Toronto-based firms that has survived and succeeded through a multitude of changing and changeable economic and business conditions.

GROUP FOUR MANAGEMENT CONSULTANTS INC. • 126 Hazelton Avenue • Toronto, ON • M5R 2E5 • Tel: 416-961-4555 • Fax: 416-961-3223 • E-mail: michael@groupfour.net • Internet: www.groupfour.net • With over 30 year combined experience in the Legal Recruiting Industry, Group Four Management have always been proven leaders within the law, management consulting, pharmaceutical, investment and financial elite.

GROUPE PERSPECTIVE • 425 Boulevard de Maisonneuve Ouest, Suite 1008• Montréal, QC • H3A 3G5• Tel: 514-499-0089 • Fax: 514-844-7938 • E-mail: info@perspectivetravail. com • Internet: www.perspectivetravail.com • Groupe Perspective has been in the business of recruitment since 1977. The company started as an agency for temporary and permanent job placement under the name of Perspective Travail. In 1983, the founding owner, Mr. Jacques Plante, launched a new partner company, R. Jacques Plante & associés, which specialized in headhunting executives and professionals.

1135 Grande Allée Ouest
Suite 300
Quebec City, QC
G1S 1E7
Tel: 418-681-4700
Fax: 418-681-4190

GSA SEARCH CONSULTANTS INC. • 200 Waterfront Dr., Suite 100 • Bedford, NS • B4A 4J4 • Tel: 902-492-1053 • Fax: 902-422-6675 • E-mail: jobs@gsa-search.com • Internet: www. gsa-search.com • GSA Search Consultants (formally Gosine Sulley & Associates), merged with Noramtec Consultants in 2000. GSA builds on the strengths of Noramtec's over 37 years of experience in Engineering and IT recruitment. With offices across the country and into the USA, the GSA Search Consultants' team have the networks, industry experience and connections it takes to offer a wealth of career opportunities and resources. GSA Search Consultants offer flexible staffing solutions to premier organizations on contract, contract-to-hire or a full-time basis. Their mission to deliver superior candidates as quickly and cost-effectively as possible is backed by a sterling record of successful placements.

19 Heritage Dr.	10506 Jasper Ave.	180 René Lévesque Blvd. E.
P.O. Box 331	Suite 1006	Suite 112
Bath, ON	Edmonton, AB	Montreal, QC
K0H 1G0	T5J 2W9	H2X 1N5

GSA SEARCH CONSULTANTS INC. continued

6 Gurdwara Rd.	1382 Main St.
Suite 200	North Vancouver, BC
Nepean, ON	V7J 1C6
K2E 8A3	

GSI INTERNATIONAL CONSULTING GROUP • 1620 Scott Street, Unit 22 • Ottawa, ON • K1Y 4S7 • Tel: 613-782-2361 • Fax: 613-782-2920 • E-mail: info@gsigroup.com • Internet: www.gsigroup.com • For over a decade, GSI group, a privately owned Canadian company, has been an innovative leader in staffing solutions, outstheircing and consulting services for Canada's technology sector. GSI group holds multiple Government Vendor of Record agreements, and is also a preferred staffing and consulting services provider to several large private sector clients. Their customers include Federal, Provincial and Municipal Governments, as well as clients within the telecommunication, banking, insurance, retail and manufacturing sectors.

55 University Ave.
Suite 1601
Toronto, ON
M5J 2H7
Tel: 416-777-2525
Fax: 416-777-2547

HALLMARK PERSONNEL LIMITED • 700 Dorval Dr., Suite 503 • Oakville, ON • L6K 3V3 • Tel: 905-842-3753 • Fax: 905-842-3680 • E-mail: hallmark@globalserve.net • Internet: www.globalserve.net/~hallmark/ • Hallmark Personnel Limited is a professional search firm which specializes in the recruitment of technical, engineering, materials, production, logistics and administration personnel at all levels. Established in 1971, they are actively involved in a variety of industries such as automotive, metal fabrication and consumer products.

HARRINGTON STAFFING SERVICES AND INFORMATICS RESOURCES • 300-30 Metcalfe St. • Ottawa, ON • K1P 5L4 • Tel: 613-236-4600 • Fax: 613-236-2192 • E-mail: it@harringtonhr.com • Internet: www.harringtonhr.com • Contact: Garry Harrington • Harrington has been a leading human resource firm in the National Capital Region since 1975 operating as Harrington Informatics Resources and Harrington Staffing Services. As a Canadian-owned company, Harrington is dedicated to serving the needs of this region's employees and employers as well as strategic alliances with firms in the U.S.

HAYS SPECIALIST RECRUITMENT CANADA INC. • 6 Adelaide St. E., Suite 600 • Toronto, ON • M5C 1H6 • Tel: 416-367-4297 • Fax: 416-203-1923 • E-mail: recruit@hays.ca • Internet: www.hays.ca • Hays Personnel Services Canada Inc. is a wholly owned subsidiary of Hays plc, which has been at the forefront of recruitment for over thirty-five years and which boasts annual revenues of over £1.3 billion. With the corporate head office located in the United Kingdom, Hays Personnel is the largest specialist recruitment consultancy in the world. With 603 specialist business units and over 4600 employees, the company has over 300 offices worldwide. There are over 270 offices in the UK and Ireland alone.

5775 Yonge Street	201 City Centre Drive	1050 West Pender Street
Suite 1802	Suite 701	Suite 2150
North York, ON	Mississauga, ON	Vancouver, BC
M2M 4J1	L5B 2T4	V6E 3S7
Tel: 416-223-4297	Tel: 905-848-4297	Tel: 604-648-4297
Fax: 416-223-4232	Fax: 905-566 8877	Fax: 604-648-0588

HAYS SPECIALIST RECRUITMENT CANADA INC. continued

22 Frederick St.	45 O'Connor St.	630 6th Avenue S.W.
Suite 1010	Suite 320	Suite 660
Kitchener, ON	Ottawa, ON	Calgary, AB
N2N 6M6	K1P 1A4	T2P 0S8
Tel: 519-772-1000	Tel: 613-288-4297	Tel: 403-269-4297
Fax: 519-772-1007	Fax: 613-288-4298	Fax: 403-705-3399
10180 101 Street	150 Dufferin St.	
11th Floor, Suite 1100	Suite 702	
Edmonton, AB	London, ON	
T5J 3S4	N2H 6M6	
Tel: 780-469-4297	Tel: 519-850-4297	
Fax: 780-485-0429	Fax: 519-850-1991	

HCR PERSONNEL SOLUTIONS INC. • 17705 Leslie Street, Suite 102 • Newmarket, ON • L3Y 3E3 • Tel: 905-954-0210 • Fax: 905-954-0214 • E-mail: info@hcrpsi.com • Internet: www. hcr.ca • At HCR, it's all about you, their employees! You'll always be treated with respect and fairness. HCR began operations in 1996 and today is one of the leading staffing companies in the Greater Toronto Area. They provide jobs in the industrial sector, working with large manufacturing organizations. Because of their established reputation, HCR is able to offer qualified candidates exciting job opportunities with world-class companies. Rest assured, providing safe and healthy work environments is always their priority.

Four Seasons Place	310 Main St. E.
2nd Floor	Suite 205
Toronto, ON	Milton, ON
M9B 6E7	L9T 1P4
Tel: 416-622-1427	Tel: 905-876-4661
Fax: 416-622-7258	Fax: 905-876-4090

HEAD2HEAD.COM INC. • 31 Davisville Ave. • Toronto, ON • M4S 2Y9 • Tel: 416-440-0097 • Fax: 416-440-0188 • E-mail: info@head2head.ca • Internet: www.head2head.ca • Head2Head is a brave new concept in the world of recruiting. They don't fill job openings but they find the people who do. In other words, they recruit talented staffing specialists that organizations can hire or use on contract to help with their in-house recruitment efforts.

HEC GROUP • 69 John Street South, Suite 400 • Hamilton, ON • L8N 2B9 • Tel: 905-527-7761 • Fax: 905-527-9937 • E-mail: hec@hec-group.com • Internet: http://hec-group.com • Originally founded in 1976 as a local recruiting firm, the HEC Group has evolved into an international presence with an extensive network of affiliates throughout North America. They specialize in the areas of manufacturing, engineering, high tech, information technology networking, sales and marketing, accounting, administration, and human resources.

HELPFAST PERSONNEL INC. • 2200 Dundas St. W., Suite 400 • Mississauga, ON • L4X 2V3 • Tel: 905-625-2220 • Fax: 905-625-9949 • E-mail: ellen@helpfastworks.com • Internet: www. helpfastworks.com • Helpfast is recognized as the premiere employment service in the Toronto area. They specialize, but are not limited to, opportunities in the transportation, distribution and logistics industries. Whether you're interested in temporary, temp-to-perm or straight permanent placement, they have regular employment opportunities available.

HENRY HILL & ASSOCIATES INC. • 2000 Argentia Road, Meadowvale Corporate Centre, Plaza 4, Suite 480 • Mississauga, ON • L5N 1W1 • Tel: 905-814-1114 • Fax: 905-814-1110 • E-mail: l.beaton@hhai.ca • Internet: www.henryhillassociates.com • Henry Hill & Associates Inc. (HHAI) is a nationally recognized search company dedicated to providing human resource solutions in a prompt, efficient and professional manner. HHAI was established in 1996 with a health care focus. Since then, communication, advertising, commercial, retail and consumer product manufacturers, distributors and suppliers have also enlisted their services.

HERRMANN GROUP LIMITED, THE • 60 Bloor St. W., Suite 1100 • Toronto, ON • M4W 3B8 • Tel: 416-922-4242 • Fax: 416-922-4366 • E-mail: info@herrmanngroup.com • Internet: www. herrmanngroup.com • Contact: Gerlinde Herrmann, President • The Herrmann Group, founded in 1985, is a generalist executive search and management consulting firm with experience throughout America. This search firm recruits for the following industries: consumer packaged goods, insurance, entertainment, waste management, information technology, financial services, manufacturing and crown corporations. The firm has clients in both Canada and the United States.

HESS ASSOCIATES EXECUTIVE SEARCH • 1500 Don Mills Rd., Suite 712 • Toronto, ON • M3B 3K4 • Tel: 416-447-3355 • Fax: 416-447-3595 • E-mail: HR@hessjobs.com • Internet: www.hessjobs.com • Since 1976, Hess Associates has been recruiting contract and permanent Information Technology, Biotechnology, Genomics, Proteomics, Pharmaceutical, and Bioinformatics professionals. Headquartered in Toronto, Canada, Hess Associates make placements across Canada, the United States and internationally through an affiliated network of independent search firms.

HIGH-ROAD PERSONNEL OF BURLINGTON • 562 Maple Ave. • Burlington, ON • L7S 1M6 • Tel: 905-632-5870 • Fax: 905-632-5454 • E-mail: info@highroadpersonnel.com • Internet: www.highroadpersonnel.com • High-Road Personnel of Burlington has over 30 years experience as human resource specialists in Halton Region. Because they are a Canadian company independently owned and operated by a local resident, all decisions concerning your account/ file can be made at the highest level without delay and with a single phone call to one office. This independence allows High-Road Personnel of Burlington to offer the flexibility today's business community requires in an ever-changing market.

HIRE VISION RECRUITMENT STRATEGIES INC. • 84 Yorkville Ave., 3rd Floor • Toronto, ON • M5R 1B9 • Tel: 416-927-7272 • Fax: 416-927-7474 • E-mail: information@hirevision.com • Internet: www.hirevision.com • Hire Vision is made up of a group of dedicated professionals with over 50 years of combined experience in human resources staffing and management. In partnering with clients, they understand corporate culture and the valuable differences inherent within individual companies and customize their recruiting strategy to each specific need. Commitment, outstanding service and optimum client satisfaction are the cornerstones of their business, which are achieved through superior communication and front-line services.

HOLLOWAY SCHULZ & PARTNERS • 1188 West Georgia St., Suite 1500 • Vancouver, BC • V6E 4A2 • Tel: 604-688-9595 • Fax: 604-688-3608 • E-mail: info@recruiters.com • Internet: www.recruiters.com • A great business starts with great people - people who are committed to the organization's vision, are focused on results, and deliver outstanding customer satisfaction. With over 30 years of professional recruitment experience, Holloway Schulz & Partners offers an extensive resource network to be able to identify and attract these high calibre candidates to your company.

HOSPITALITY PERSONNEL • 8 Appledale Rd. • Toronto, ON • M9B 5G4 • Tel: 416-207-9543 • Fax: 416-207-0264 • E-mail: info@hpeople.com • Internet: www.hpeople.com • Contact: David Chun, President • Since 1986, Hospitality Personnel have been matching candidates with employers in the hospitality industry. The staff they help to find include dishwashers, kitchen prep, prep cos, grill cos, sous chefs, porters, cashiers, bussers, waitstaff, bartenders, maitre'd and managers. Hospitality Personnel currently supplies well over 200 locations in Greater Toronto area with unbeatable quality.

HRCONNECTIONS • 1200 Eglington Ave. E., Suite 808 • Toronto, ON • M3C 1H9 • Tel: 416-444-4060 • Fax: 416-285-8969 • E-mail: info@hrconnects.com • Internet: www.hrconnects.com • HRConnections is your complete resource for human resource management and recruitment services. They cater to organizations in various industries. From start-ups to Fortune 1000, they have provided custom-tailored solutions that fit their clients specific HR needs. Outstheircing your HR requirements to HRConnections will allow you to focus on and grow your own business, as only you know how.

HT SEARCH COMPANY LTD. • 12 York St., 4th Floor • Ottawa, ON • K1N 5S6 • Tel: 613-226-9900 • Fax: 613-727-9248 • E-mail: info@htsearch.com • Internet: www.htsearch.com • HT Search has been a leader in Human Capital Management since 1995. HT Search is a preferred supplier to many of North America's leading private and public organizations. They provide recruiting and HR services for organizations across North America, including executive search, interim management and mergers and acquisitions services.

1 Yonge St.	1555 Blvd. de l'Avenir
Suite 1801	Suite 206
Toronto, ON	Laval, QC
M5E 1W7	H7S 2N5
	Tel: 450-667-8800
	Fax: 450-667-8100

HUMANRESOURCES.COM • P.O. Box 12530, 415 The Westway • Toronto, ON • M9R 4C7 • Tel: 416-240-9398 • Fax: 416-240-0789 • E-mail: info@HumanResources.ca • Internet: www.humanresources.ca • HumanResources.com is the stheirce for information, products and services that are related to the human resources field of activity. They cater to human resources professionals, recruiters, career seekers, people on the job, as well as executives. They are committed to providing an environment that cultivates knowledge, insight, and personal development.

HUNT PERSONNEL • 357 Bay Street, Suite 301 • Toronto, ON • M5H 2T7 • Tel: 416-860-0016 • Fax: 416-860-0029 • E-mail: toronto@hunt.ca • Internet: www.hunt.ca • Hunt Personnel / Temporarily Yours has built a reputation as a highly respected, successful career placement agency providing guaranteed temporary and permanent employment services, human resources outstheircing and consulting services.

789 Pender St. W.	170 Elveden House	25 Main St. W.
Suite 760	717-7th Avenue S.W.	Suite 600
Vancouver, BC	Calgary, AB	Hamilton, ON
V6C 1H2	T2P 0Z3	L4K 4N3
Tel: 604-688-2555	Tel: 403-269-6786	Tel: 905-540-4868
Fax: 604-688-6437	Fax: 403-237-9016	Fax: 905-540-9313
50 Burnhamthorpe Rd. W.	6 Lansing Sq., Suite 214	220 Laurier Ave. W.
Suite 204	North York, ON	Suite 300
Mississauga, ON	M2J 1T5	Ottawa, ON
L5B 3C2	Tel: 416-730-1700	K1P 5Z9
Tel: 905-273-3221		Tel: 613-238-8801
Fax: 905-273-6487		Fax: 613-238-5586

HUNT PERSONNEL continued

3300 Highway 7
Suite 809
Vaughan, ON
L4K 4N3
Tel: 416-730-1700
Fax: 416-492-4722

6 Lansing Sq.
Suite 214
Willowdale, ON
M2J 1T5
Tel: 416-492-8500
Fax: 416-492-4722

230, rue Brock
Suite 235
Drummondville, QC
J2C 1M3
Tel: 819-850-1555
Fax: 819-477-4145

515 boul de la Concord W.
Suite 215
Laval, QC
H7N 5L9
Tel: 450-669-1115
Fax: 450-669-6311

450, rue St-Charles W.
Suite 201
Longueuil, QC
J4H 1G4
Tel: 450-463-4224
Fax: 450-463-2288

666 rue Sherbroe O.
Suite 1801
Montreal, QC
H3A 1E7
Tel: 514-842-4691
Fax: 514-842-2997

935 Décarie Blvd.
St. Laurent, QC
H4L 3M3
Tel: 514-744-8400
Fax: 514-744-2264

6020, Jean-Talon Est
bureau 430
Ville St Léonard, QC
H1S 3B1
Tel: 514-253-4444
Fax: 514-253-1819

HUNTECH CONSULTANTS INC. • P.O. Box 36, 5160 Yonge St., Suite 1005 • North York, ON • M2N 6L9 • Tel: 416-730-9188 • Fax: 416-730-9185 • E-mail: careers@huntech.com • Internet: www.huntech.com • They are a national Technology/Executive Search practice leader, one of the pioneering and most established Engineering/Management Search firms with a strict focus on Advanced Technology covering Software, Silicon and Electronics Engineering/Multimedia and Wireless sectors coast to coast since April 1982.

HURON SERVICES GROUP LIMITED • 418 North Service Rd. E., Suite 3C • Oakville, ON • L6H 5R2 • Tel: 905-845-4075 • Fax: 905-845-4802 • E-mail: info@hurongroup.ca • Internet: www. hurongroup.ca • Huron Services partners with their corporate clients and the employees they hire, facilitating a win-win process that benefits all parties. Working with each other as a team, they present an opportunity to meet both the human resources requirements of companies as well as the need for employment and a career path for employees.

3777 Lakeshore Blvd. W.
Toronto, ON
M8W 1R1
Tel: 416-252-6324
Fax: 416-252-6456

IAN MARTIN LIMITED • 465 Morden Rd., 2nd Floor • Oakville, ON • L6K 3W6 • Tel: 905-815-1600 • Fax: 905-815-1624 • E-mail: gamble@ianmartin.com • Internet: www.iml.com • Contact: Loree Gamble • With over 40 years of industry-related experience and numerous branch offices strategically located throughout Canada and the U.S., Ian Martin has become a vital staffing resource for over 1000 of North America's leading public and private companies.

IAN MARTIN LIMITED continued

433-595 Burrard St.
P.O. BOX 49140
Vancouver, BC
V7X 1J1
Tel: 604-637-1400
Fax: 604-685-1425
rpage@ianmartin.com

138-4th Ave. S.E.
Suite 700
Calgary, AB
T2G 4Z6
Tel: 403-262-2600
Fax: 403-262-2670
king@ianmartin.com

11523 100 Ave.
Suite 205
Edmonton, AB
T5K 0J8
Tel: 780-420-1005
Fax: 780-420-1040
leanneb@ianmartin.com

34 Stone Church Rd. W.
Suite 201
Ancaster, ON
L9K 1P4
Tel: 905-304-7383
Fax: 905-304-5450
youngson@ianmartin.con

411 Legget Rd.
Suite 501
Kanata, ON
K2K 3C9
Tel: 613-271-0155
Fax: 613-271-9504
oconnor@ianmartin.com

30 Duke St.
Suite 901
Kitchener, ON
N2H 3W5
Tel: 519-568-8300
Fax: 519-568-8165
coulis@ianmartin.com

1940 Oxford St. E.
Unit 7
London, ON
N5V 4L8
Tel: 519-457-3420
Fax: 519-457-3419
kirkland@ianmartin.com

465 Morden Rd.
2nd Floor
Oakville, ON
L6K 3W6
Tel: 905-815-1600
Fax: 905-845-2100
recruit@ianmartin.com

275 Slater St.
Suite 203
Ottawa, ON
K1P 5H9
Tel: 613-237-0155
Fax: 613-237-2070
oconnor@ianmartin.com

940 Brock Rd. S.
Unit 3
Pickering, ON
L1W 2A1
Tel: 905-831-3535
Fax: 905-831-9596
abel@ianmartin.com

111 Grangeway Ave.
Suite 500
Scarborough, ON
M1H 3E9
Tel: 416-439-6400
Fax: 416-439-6922
nicholas@ianmartin.com

55 Main St., Unit 1
P.O. BOX 426
Tiverton, ON
N0G 2T0
Tel: 519-368-6014
Fax: 519-368-6017
abbott@ianmartin.com

3333 Boul. de la Cote Vertu
Bureau 202
Ville St-Laurent, QC
H4R 2N1
Tel: 514-338-3800
Fax: 514-866-9675
hehn@ianmartin.com

580 Main St.
Suite B203
St. John, NB
E2K 1J5
Tel: 506-696-9040
Fax: 506-635-7880
mcgrath@ianmartin.com

IDEAL PERSONNEL • 55 City Centre Drive, Suite 501 • Mississauga, ON • L5B 1M3 • Tel: 905-279-8050 • Fax: 905-279-0901 • E-mail: ideal@idealpersonnel.com • Internet: www. idealpersonnel.com • They are Mississauga's oldest established staffing and recruitment firm, having been in business since 1965. With their long term staffing specialists they offer over 70 years of combined expertise in successfully matching companies to 'Ideal' candidates in a wide variety of areas including but not limited to administration, reception, customer care, finance/accounting, marketing, logistics, operations, human resources, health & safety, payroll and benefits in both management and support positions on a permanent, contract and temporary basis. Their talent pool includes candidates from the pharmaceutical, food, chemical, management consulting, health care, consumer products and entertainment industry some of whom are bilingual (English/French, English/Spanish and English/German).

IMATICS INC. • P.O. Box 3037, Station C • Ottawa, ON • K1Y 4J3 • Tel: 613-860-2662 • Fax: 613-860-1915 • E-mail: info@imatics.com • Internet: www.imatics.com • Contact: Rob Bros, General Manager • They maintain a multi-disciplinary staff of experienced professionals, both permanent and contract, including web site developers, web application developers, multimedia developers, information architects, usability and accessibility analysts, database administrators, system administrators, program and project managers. All of their people are trained specifically for web and other digital media projects.

IMPACT STAFFING INC. • 1 Hanna St. W. • Windsor, ON • N8X 1C7 • Tel: 519-972-8932 • Fax: 519-972-8128 • E-mail: staff@impact-staffing.com • Internet: www.impact-staffing.com • Contact: Rita Olivito • Impact Staffing works with client HR departments to facilitate recruitment, screening, and hiring of employees when they require personnel on a full time or temporary basis for office and manufacturing sectors. Candidates register at no charge. They are interviewed, tested, and their references are checked before placed on their system. Subsequently, they are matched with a client's specific requirements. Positions of specialization include insurance brers, automotive engineers, general clerical fields, and computerized accounting, administrative and clerical, accounting and finance, engineering and manufacturing, information systems, human resources, health and safety, sales and marketing, production and skilled trades.

IN TRANSIT PERSONNEL INC. • 6200 Dixie Rd., Units 112/114 • Mississauga, ON • L5T 2E1 • Tel: 905-564-9424 • Fax: 905-564-8970 • E-mail: info@in-transit.com • Internet: www.in-transit.com • In Transit Personnel is the leading supplier of personnel for the transportation industry in the Greater Toronto Area. They are a single stheirce provider of personnel services including both contract and permanent placement. In addition, In Transit offers safety training, software skills evaluation and training and payroll services. They provide experienced drivers for city and local highway transportation, certified forklift and reach operators, light industrial personnel for order picking, loading, assembly, administrative staff for junior, intermediate and senior positions in customer service, dispatch, distribution and operations.

INDUSTRIAL TEMPORARY SOLUTIONS INC. • 720 Guelph Line, Suite 302 • Burlington, ON • L7R 4E2 • Tel: 905-333-2692 • Fax: 905-333-0912 • E-mail: burlington@itsjobs.ca • Internet: www.itsjobs.ca • Industrial Temporary Solutions Inc. (ITS) employs Internal Team Members, with direct hands on experience, to better meet the requirements of their clients. They are committed to ensuring quality service to their customers, while maintaining competitive pricing. ITS personally inspects each job site and facility to ensure the safety of their most valued asset, their employees.

1150 Eglinton Ave. E.	3961 61st Ave. S.E.	7403 Progress Way
Suite 205	Calgary, AB	Delta, BC
Mississauga, ON	T2C 1Z4	V4G 1E7
L4W 2M6	Tel: 403-236-2960	Tel: 604-628-6109
Tel: 905-361-9675	Fax: 403-236-3681	Fax: 778-785-6061
Fax: 905-361-9673	calgary@itsjobs.ca	vancouver@itsjobs.ca
mississauga@itsjobs.ca		

INFORMATION TECHNOLOGY RECRUITING LTD. (I.T.R. LIMITED) • 200 Consumers Rd., Suite 100 • Willowdale, ON • M2J 4R4 • Tel: 416-502-3400 • Fax: 416-502-9666 • E-mail: resumes@itrlimited.com • Internet: www.itrlimited.com • I.T.R.'s goal is to develop lasting and mutually beneficial business relations with their clients and the candidates they serve. As a full service recruiting organization I.T.R. acknowledges that they attend to two sets of clients, hiring corporations and I.T. professionals. They recognize the value of their customers and they understand the importance of good service to their candidates.

INNOVATIVE MANAGEMENT SOLUTIONS GROUP • 1881 Yonge St., Suite 708 • Toronto, ON • M4S 3C4 • Tel: 416-515-2939 • Fax: 416-515-2938 • E-mail: careers@imsgroup.net • Internet: www.imsgroup.net • IMS specializes in contingency search and recruitment for both contract and permanent positions in the Information Processing, Biotechnology, Engineering and Sales, Promotion and Marketing arenas. They specialize specifically in MIS management, systems and application programming, office automation, technical support, hardware/sofware sales, database administration, LAN-WAN implementation & support, consulting and marketing.

INSURANCE OVERLOAD SYSTEMS INC. • 130 Adelaide St. W., Suite 2105 • Toronto, ON • M5H 3P5 • Tel: 416-861-1952 • Fax: 416-861-9977 • E-mail: dan_canfield@insuranceoverload. com • Internet: www.insuranceoverload.com • Founded in 1983, Insurance Overload Systems has grown to be the largest insurance-specific staffing business in North America, serving 58 cities throughout the U.S. and Canada. The officers and managers of IOS are career insurance personnel. They come from the insurance industry, and they lead the industry in staffing services due to extraordinary concentration on their Quality Screening Verification (QSV) system. No one in insurance recruiting and temporary personnel goes farther, invests more, or does it better than IOS.

INTEGRA I.T. PARTNERS INC. • 40 Eglinton Ave. E., Suite 304 • Toronto, ON • M4P 3A2 • Tel: 416-487-3301 • Fax: 416-440-4025 • E-mail: recruiting@integra.ca • Internet: www.integrait. com • Contact: Robyn Keenan • Integra I.T. Partners specializes in the recruitment and selection of information technology professionals, on a permanent and contract basis. Individuals must have a minimum of 1 to 2 years hands-on experience. This firm works in all areas of industry.

INTEGRITY TECHNOLOGY CONSULTANTS • 703 Evans Ave., Suite 202 • Toronto, ON • M9C 5E9 • Tel: 416-747-5959 • Fax: 416-747-8786 • E-mail: services@integritycanada.com • Internet: www.integritycanada.com • Integrity Technology Consultants, based in Toronto, works with IT managers and departments to meet their short- and long-term staffing needs, by finding, qualifying and placing IT professionals in contract and permanent positions, and assembling and overseeing specialized project teams.

INTELLIGENT MINDS SEARCH CONSULTANTS INC. • 19 Redner Lane, R.R. #1 • Carrying Place, ON • K0K 1L0 • Tel: 613-961-1555 • Fax: 613-961-1222 • E-mail: webmaster@intelminds.com • Internet: www.intelminds.com • Intelligent Minds is in the business of helping IT organizations operate more productively and profitably through a full spectrum of specialized staffing and project implementation products and services. They specialize in the areas of E-Commerce, Web Development, Online Content Management, Network integration and solutions, Oracle and Oracle Financials implementation and Custom Application Development for vertical markets including telecommunications, healthcare, financial services, insurance, and energy. They deliver qualified consultants and project managers for both contract and ongoing requirements across all science and technology disciplines.

INTERCOM SEARCH INC. • 56 The Esplanade, Suite 208 • Toronto, ON • M5E 1A7 • Tel: 416-364-5338 • Fax: 416-574-0935 • Internet: www.intercomjobs.ca • E-mail: harry@intercomjobs.ca • Contact: Harry Teitelbaum, President • At InterCom they specialize in Marketing and Marcom. These umbrellas capture professionals that are in the Advertising and Marketing industries. Their Clients work in a variety of categories including financial services, telco, packaged goods, automotive but are all loing to staff either their account management staff or brand managers.

INTERSEARCH CANADA • 2 St. Clair Avenue East, Suite 800 • Toronto, ON • M4T 2T5 • Tel: 416-488-4111 • E-mail: cmf@intersearchcanada.com • Internet: www.intersearch-canada.com • InterSearch Canada is a partnership of Canadian executive search firms who joined forces seven years ago. Their objective in forming InterSearch Canada was to lever the strengths and capabilities of their five businesses in order to provide their clients with a broad reaching national search capability.

700 West Georgia St.
Suite 700
Vancouver, BC
V7Y 1A1
Tel: 778-371-8728
Fax: 604-683-6345

IQ PARTNERS INC. • 99 Spadina Ave., Suite 650 • Toronto, ON • M5V 3P8 • Tel: 416-599-4700 • E-mail: info@IQPartners.com • Internet: www.iqpartners.com • IQ Partners is one of Canada's leading integrated HR Services firms. They help their clients build, manage and maintain world-class sales, marketing, management and production teams; and they specialize in smart people.

ISOTEC MANAGEMENT INC. • 200 Adelaide Street West, Suite 101 • Toronto, ON • M5H 1W7 • Tel: 416-868-0100 • Fax: 416-868-6292 • E-mail: info@isotecmgt.com • Internet: www. isotecmgt.com • ISOTEC Management Inc. exists to provide professional, results-oriented recruitment solutions to clients with information technology (IT) recruitment needs. Their web site provides information and assistance for professionals loing for employment in Canada, the United States and the rest of the world.

J.G. FLYNN & ASSOCIATES INC. • 885 West Georgia St., Suite 1500 • Vancouver, BC • V6C 3E8 • Tel: 604-689-7202 • Fax: 604-689-2676 • E-mail: recruit@jgflynn.com • Internet: www. jgflynn.com • Contact: Jerry Flynn • Established in 1983, J.G. Flynn & Associates (JGF & A) is an independent, Vancouver-based executive recruitment firm with affiliated offices in Beijing, Shanghai, Guangzhou, Hong Kong, Kuala Lumpur, Singapore and Bangkok. They are known for their ability to research any industry thoroughly in order to ferret out the best candidates having the specific expertise and experience that their clients require.

J.P. ANDERSON & ASSOCIATES INC. • 241 Amberly Blvd. • Ancaster, ON • L9G 3Y4 • Tel: 905-648-4583 • Fax: 905-542-3981 • E-mail: careers@jpanderson.com • Internet: www. jpanderson.com/recruiter.html • Contact: Jeff Anderson • J.P. Anderson & Associates Inc. is a part of a Canadian co-operative search group that is in partnership with six other well established recruitment firms. Collectively, they cover a large segment of business employment needs and requirements and therefore present more opportunities for applicants in search of a new career. They specialize in the areas of logistics, engineering, and operations management.

JACOBSEN SECRETARIAL SERVICES • 9483 152A Street • Surrey, BC • V3R 9B8 • Tel: 604-930-9386 • Fax: 604-930-9386 • E-mail: mailbox@jacobsensecretarial.com • Internet: www.jacobsensecretarial.com • Jacobsen Secretarial Services is proud to be a member of the Association of Canadian Search, Employment and Staffing Services. ACSESS has a membership of over 260 staffing agencies across Canada, representing over 700 offices. ACSESS member companies pledge to uphold the Associations Code of Ethics & Standards. This code has been developed to protect and promote the professionalism and integrity of the industry, something that they at Jacobsen Secretarial Services have always endeavored to incorporate into their business practices.

JAN HOWARD ASSOCIATES • Toronto Eaton Centre, Box 515, 220 Yonge St., Suite 115 • Toronto, ON • M5B 2H1 • Tel: 416-598-1775 • Fax: 416-598-0363 • E-mail: janhoward@ sympatico.ca • Contact: Jan Howard • They place applicants in temporary and permanent positions. Areas the firm specializes in include secretarial jobs, administration, reception, bilingual (French and English) work, accounting, data entry, along with engineering and computer work.

JENEREAUX & ASSOCIATES • 1 Yorkdale Rd., Suite 202 • North York, ON • M6A 3A1 • Tel: 416-780-1961 • Fax: 416-489-1640 • E-mail: mail@jenereaux.com • Internet: www.jenereaux.com • Contact: Catherine Jenereaux, Director • Jenereaux & Associates offers specialized recruiting up to Executive level in a number of fields including: Engineering, Materials/Logistics/Purchasing, Production, Finance/Accounting, Human Resources, Operations, IT, Healthcare Professionals and Sales and Marketing. They also have a division that recruits administrative support staff.

JOANNE STARR CONSULTANTS LTD. • 287 Richmond Street East, Suite 103 • Toronto, ON • M5A 1P2 • Tel: 416-360-1855 • Fax: 416-360-1884 • E-mail: resumes@jostarr.com • Internet: www.jostarr.com • Joanne Starr Consultants is a personnel recruiting agency specializing in the Insurance Industry. They are dedicated to identifying and placing the highest quality candidates available with their clients which include both Companies and Brokers.

JROSS RETAIL RECRUITERS • 1681 Chestnut St., Suite 400 • Vancouver, BC • V6J 4M6 • Tel: 604-268-6202 • Fax: 604-676-2799 • Internet: www.jrossrecruiters.com • With extensive hospitality and retail industry operations and search experience, they recruit for positiions in the executive suite, store/property operations positions and key head office support positions coast to coast.

45 Sheppard Ave. E.	508 – 24 Avenue
Suite 900	Suite 300
North York, ON	Calgary, AB
M2N 5W9	T2S 0K4
Tel: 416-742-9200	Tel: 403-670-9101
Fax: 416-849-0619	Fax: 403-451-1905

JSG GROUP • 178 Main St., Suite 400 • Unionville, ON • L3R 2G9 • Tel: 905-477-3625 • E-mail: rick@jsggroup.com • Internet: www.jsggroup.com • JSG Group's goal is to recruit only the very best managers and executives to assist their clients in growing more profitable businesses. They will deliver timely and cost effective results and leverage their clients' position in the marketplace by providing a level of service which exceeds expectations.

JUST CRUIS'N RECRUITMENT INC. • Box 462 - 1755 Robson Street • Vancouver, BC • V6G 3B7 • Tel: 604-542-5568 • E-mail: resumes@cruiseshipemployment.ca • Internet: www. shipboardemployment.com • There are many employment opportunities within the cruise industry. As a shipboard employee, you will have the opportunity to work with a team from more than 107 different countries around the world. Cruise lines seeks highly motivated, energetic, outgoing, friendly and professional employees with a positive attitude. Many of the staff aboard have been with the company for many years showing stability, care and commitment. Just Cruis'n Recruitment Inc.is an Official Hiring Partner for Royal Caribbean International and Celebrity Cruises Inc. and they are based in beautiful Vancouver, British Columbia.

KCI CAREERS INC. • 36 Toronto St., Suite 850 • Toronto, ON • M5C 2C5 • Tel: 416-366-9166 • Fax: 416-366-0269 • E-mail: info@kcicareers.com • Internet: www.kcicareers.com •

KCI Careers builds teams of highly experienced business professionals who place ethics and integrity first. Service, enthusiasm and professionalism combined with genuine concern and a keen awareness make the ideal consultant.

KEITH BAGG GROUP, THE • 85 Richmond St. W., Suite 700 • Toronto, ON • M5H 2C9 • Tel: 416-863-1800 • Internet: www.bagg.com • The Keith Bagg Group is one of the most respected names in the staffing industry. Over the ctheirse of their 32+ year history, they have worked hard to influence the way that their industry works and to help build their image as a socially responsible, highly regarded and dedicated staffing services provider. They provide solutions for clients across many industries, including: Financial Services, Government, Manufacturing, Market Research, Transportation, Logistics, Engineering, Hospitality, Education, Consumer Goods - and many more. They work with candidates across a broad range of specialties, including Accounting, Administrative, Financial, Human Resources, Information Technology, Logistics, Marketing, Operations, Production and Sales.

30 Eglinton Ave. W.	2900 Steeles Ave. E.
Suite 812	Suite 218
Mississauga, ON	Thornhill, ON
L5R 3E7	L3T 4X1
Tel: 905-890-1023	Tel: 905-709-3917

KELLY SCIENTIFIC RESOURCES • 505 Burrard St., Suite 410 • Vancouver, BC • V7X 1M3 • Tel: 604-669-1236 • Fax: 604-689-0939 • E-mail: ksr7177@kellyservices.com • Internet: www. kellyscientific.com • Since founding in 1995 as Kelly's scientific business unit, Kelly Scientific Resources (KSR) has emerged as the leading scientific and clinical trials staffing company in the world today. On average they employ over 400 clinical trials professionals and 4,500 scientists in temporary, contract and full-time positions - from more than 100 locations in North America, Europe and the Pacific Rim.

77 City Centre Dr.	1111 Boul Dr. Frederik Philips
Suite 104	Bureau 110
Mississauga, ON	Ville St-Laurent, QC
L5B 1M5	H4M 2X6
Tel: 905-949-0428	Tel: 514-388-9779

KELLY SERVICES • 1 University Ave., Suite 500 • Toronto, ON • M5J 2P1 • Tel: 416-368-1058 • Fax: 416-368-3987 • Internet: www.kellyservices.ca • Kelly Services, Inc. is a Fortune 500 company headquartered in Troy, Mich., offering staffing solutions that include temporary staffing services, staff leasing, outstheircing, vendor on-site and full-time placement. Kelly owns and operates nearly 2,600 offices in 29 countries and territories. Kelly provides employment to more than 700,000 employees annually, with skills including office services, accounting, engineering, information technology, law, science, marketing, light industrial, education, health care and home care.

240 Graham Ave.	1945 Hamilton St.	300 Consilium Place
Suite 100	Suite 9	Suite G100
Winnipeg, MB	Regina, SK	Scarborough, ON
R3C 0J7	S4P 2C7	M1H 3G2
Tel: 204-944-1114	Tel: 306-359-7449	Tel: 416-290-6790
Fax: 204-943-1737	Fax: 306-525-6071	Fax: 416-290-6604
7211@kellyservices.com	7920@kellyservices.com	7695@kellyservices.com

KELLY SERVICES continued

101 Frederick St.
Scott Tower
Kitchener, ON
N2H 6R2
Tel: 519-578-9640
Fax: 519-570-4249
7650@kellyservices.com

33 Bloor St. E.
Suite 800
Toronto, ON
M4W 3H1
Tel: 416-967-6356
Fax: 416-967-6737
767E@kellyservices.com

10025 Jasper Ave.
Suite 100
Edmonton, AB
T5J 2B8
Tel: 780-421-7777
Fax: 780-426-5355
7021@kellyservices.com

505 Burrard St.
Suite 410
Vancouver, BC
V7X 1M3
Tel: 604-669-1236
Fax: 604-669-1270
7111@kellyservices.com

90 King St.
Suite L 140
Saint John, NB
E2L 1G4
Tel: 506-658-0285
Fax: 506-653-9310
7413@kellyservices.com

1809 Barrington St.
Main Floor, Suite B101
Halifax, NS
B3J 3K8
Tel: 902-425-8770
Fax: 902-466-7990
7311@kellyservices.com

KEN MURPHY & ASSOCIATES • 5112 Prince St. • Halifax, NS • B3J 1L3 • Tel: 902-425-4495 • Fax: 902-425-6691 • E-mail: info@kma.ns.ca • Internet: www.kma.ns.ca • Kenneth Murphy and Associates provides recruitment services for mid to senior managers across Eastern Canada. KMA was formed in 1992 offering a special focus on the information technology industry. It has evolved into a well-respected firm that currently conducts searches for its clients in a variety of market sectors. Search capabilities range across Canada from a Halifax operations base. KMA continually attracts new clients drawn to the firm's impressive track record in sales, marketing and finance.

KEY EXECUTIVE CONSULTANTS • 605 Liverpool Rd. • Pickering, ON • L1W 1R1 • Tel: 905-831-6788 • E-mail: admin@keyexecutive.com • Internet: www.keyexecutive.com • Key Executive Consultants have been in business since 1989. They are specialists in the recruitment and placement of manufacturing, operations, engineering, information systems, sales and financial management professionals. Key Executive Consultants has an extensive client base and a solid track record.

KITCHENER EXECUTIVE CONSULTANTS • 1601 River Rd. E., Suite 201 • Kitchener, ON • N2A 3Y4 • Tel: 519-894-3030 • Fax: 519-594-5196 • E-mail: info@kitchenerexecutive.com • Internet: www.kitchenerexecutive.com • This site provides an employment data bank for persons conducting a job search in the United States and Canada. Jobs in various employment categories can be quickly searched and accessed. Their easy to use job index will allow you to quickly locate prospective employment opportunities. Kitchener Executive Consultants specializes in the search and placement of individuals for manufacturing companies. Engineering, quality assurance, materials, human resources, accounting, finance, design, tooling, production, information systems and general management are some of the positions that their clients regularly require.

KORN/FERRY INTERNATIONAL • BCE Place, Bay Wellington Tower, Box 763, 181 Bay St., Suite 3320 • Toronto, ON • M5J 2T3 • Tel: 416-365-1841 • Internet: www.kornferry.com • For 35 years, Korn/Ferry International has been a leader in executive recruitment, conducting over 100,000 senior-level searches for clients worldwide. Today, Korn/Ferry is the premier provider of executive human capital solutions, with services ranging from corporate governance and CEO recruitment to executive search, middle-management recruitment and Leadership Development Solutions (LDS). LDS includes strategic management assessment, executive coaching and development, and supporting IT platforms.

KORN/FERRY INTERNATIONAL continued

1055 Dunsmuir St.	630, Rene-Levesque Blvd. W.	Gulf Canada Square
Suite 3300	Suite 3125	401-9th Avenue SW
P.O. Box 49206	Montreal, QC	Suite 910
Vancouver, BC	H3B 1S6	Calgary, AB
V7X 1K8	Tel: 514-397-9655	T2P 3C5
Tel: 604-684-1834		Tel: 403-269-3277

LA GENS INC. • 1650 Michelin St. • Laval, QC • H7L 4R3 • Tel: 514-288-0909 • Fax: 514-288-0909 • E-mail: info@lagens.qc.ca • Internet: www.lagens.qc.ca • La Gens builds the bridge between the employer looking for a candidate and a candidate loing for work. Their approach allows the rapid recruitment of personnel from the best candidates available in the market. They are the ultimate choice in placement services with their recognized methods.

LABOR TEK PERSONNEL SERVICES LTD. • 1370 Triole • Ottawa, ON • K1B 3M4 • Tel: 613-741-1128 • Fax: 613-741-1130 • E-mail: industrial@labortek.com • Internet: www.labortek. com • Labor Tek marries a broad range of professional, skilled trade and labor personnel on a contract, full or part time basis, to clients who are seeking specific, matching talents. They ensure their employees are experienced, properly trained, committed, safe workers; then they support the process through constant follow up and improvement, through consultation with the parties involved. They firmly believe themselves to be second to none when it comes to satisfying both their employee, and their corporate, partners.

1891 Merivale Rd.
Ottawa, ON
K2G 1E5
Tel: 613-688-0807
Fax: 613-688-1378

LABOUR FORCE PERSONNEL • 8 Appledale Rd. • Toronto, ON • M9B 5G4 • Tel: 416-207-9543 • Fax: 416-207-0264 • E-mail: info@hpeople.com • Internet: www.hpeople.com • Contact: David Chun, President • Labour Force Personnel supplies skilled industrial staff such as forklift operators, production welders, machine operators, electrical assemblers, industrial electricians, machinists, millwrights as well as unskilled labtheir including warehouse staff, cleaners, painters, shipper/receivers, driver's helpers and construction labtheirers.

LAKELAND PERSONNEL & SECURITY • 400 Scott St., 2nd Floor • Fort Frances, ON • P9A 1H2 • Tel: 807-274-2108 • Fax: 807-274-3560 • E-mail: todd@lakelandpersonnel.ca Internet: www.lakelandpersonnel.ca • Contact: Marlyce Huitikka, Roslyn Broman or Todd Hamilton • Lakeland Personnel & Security offers permanent and temporary staffing in areas of security and investigation services, business and office services, as well as in marketing services.

LANNICK ASSOCIATES • 20 Queen St. W., Suite 3402 • Toronto, ON • M5H 3R3 • Tel: 416-340-1500 • Fax: 416-340-1344 • E-mail: lannick@lannick.com • Internet: www.lannick. com • Lannick Associates is an executive search firm that works exclusively with accounting professionals and executives in the Greater Toronto Area with a particular emphasis on Chartered Accountants. They work in virtually every industry sector and have assisted companies of every kind and size, from Schedule I banks to bio-tech start-ups.

1 City Centre Drive	255 Albert St.	5160 Yonge St.
Suite 600	Suite 500	Suite 1850
Mississauga, ON	Ottawa, ON	North York, ON
L5B 1M2	K1P 6A9	M2N 6L9
Tel: 905-804-0600	Tel: 613-566-7048	Tel: 416-646-5200
Fax: 905-804-9594	Fax: 613-566-7049	Fax: 416-646-5428

LEADS EMPLOYMENT SERVICES LONDON INC. • 171 Queens Ave., Suite 410 • London, ON • N6A 5J7 • Tel: 519-439-0352 • Fax: 519-439-7502 • E-mail: info@leadslondon • Internet: www.leadsservices.com • Leads Employment Services London Inc., is a not-for-profit employment and skills development agency for persons with physical, mental, developmental and learning disabilities and/or barriers to employment, directed by a Volunteer Board of Directors. Leads began in February 1986. They have served over 5000 clients and successfully secured over 4500 placements in the job market at minimum wage or better.

The Gain Centre, Kenwick Mall
51 Front St. E.
Strathroy, ON
N7G 1Y5
Tel: 519-245-3900
Fax; 519-245-5065

LEAPJOB • 4 Robert Speck Parkway, Suite 1500 • Mississauga, ON • L4Z 1S1 • Tel: 905-281-3090 • E-mail: info@leapjob.com • Internet: www.leapjob.com • LEAPJob is a human resources consulting firm specialized in recruitment and selection process improvement. They are committed to helping their clients' to attract, hire and retain the right talent. In any business people make the difference. It is their driving passion and mission to deliver well thought out business processes, systems and tools that align people for the desired results. They believe that hiring and retaining great people drive great results.

LECOURS, WOLFSON LIMITED • 116 Spadina Ave., Suite 700 • Toronto, ON • M5V 2K6 • Tel: 416-703-5482 • Fax: 416-703-5486 • E-mail: careers@lecourswolfson.com • Internet: www.lecourswolfson.com • Lecours Wolfson is North America's leading recruiter of Hospitality Executives, Managers and Chefs serving all industry sectors including Hotels & Resorts, Restaurant Operations, Contract Catering and other related businesses.

LEGAL PERSONNEL CONSULTANTS INC. • 20 Adelaide St. E., Suite 920 • Toronto, ON • M5C 2T6 • Tel: 416-955-9035 • Fax: 416-955-9204 • E-mail: resumes@legalpersonnel.net • Internet: www.legalpersonnel.net • Legal Personnel Consultants is a specialized service that matches the employment needs of the Legal Office with those of highly skilled Legal Personnel.

LEVEL A INC. • 277 George St. N., Suite 212 • Peterborough, ON • K9J 3G9 • Tel: 705-749-1919 • Fax: 705-749-5494 • E-mail: info@levela.net • Internet: www.levela.net • Contact: Kathy Pyle, President and Owner • Level A Inc. is a full-service personnel agency committed to qualifying and placing effective temporary and permanent placements. Level A candidates are talented individuals with experience in general office, clerical and data entry work, intermediate to senior administration, as well as financial and technical areas such as IT and AutoCAD.

245 Division St.	141 Dunlop St. E.
Cobourg, ON	Barrie, ON
K9A 3P8	L4M 1A6
Tel: 905-373-4676	Tel: 866-680-4676
Fax: 905-377-0495	Fax: 705-719-9118

LEWIS COMPANIES INC. • 131 Bloor St. W., Suite 5-03 Commercial • Toronto, ON • M5S 1R1 • Tel: 416-929-1506 • Fax: 416-929-8470 • E-mail: info@lewiscos.com • Internet: www.lewiscos.com • Lewis Companies Inc.'s search activity focuses on senior management positions in all industry sectors and functional areas. Recruiting is carried out directly by the firm's partners who conduct each project in a disciplined yet flexible manner. The firm is focused on improving efficiency through high-quality executive search solutions.

LIFE AFTER LAW • 2 St. Clair Ave. E., Suite 800 • Toronto, ON • M4T 2T5 • Tel: 416-789-1444 • Fax: 416-789-4114 • E-mail: info@lifeafterlaw.com • Internet: www.lifeafterlaw.com • Canada's only recruitment and placement firm dedicated to placing highly skilled legal professionals in careers outside the traditional practice of law.

355 Burrard St.
Suite 1000
Vancouver, BC
V6C 2G8
Tel: 866-227-1444
Fax: 866-467-4114

LINE 1000 PLACEMENT SERVICES • 1355 Bank St., Suite 1 • Ottawa, ON • K1H 8K7 • Tel: 613-526-1000 • Fax: 613-731-3510 • E-mail: placement@line1000.ca • Internet: www. line1000.ca • Line 1000 Placement Services, Inc. is a community based non-profit employment placement agency that has provided individualized assistance to disabled and disadvantaged people within the Ottawa-Carleton area. Areas of specialties include: marketing placement, career counselling, provision of individualized job search support, development and delivery of specialized career and employment workshops. On a fee-for-service basis, Line 1000 can provide transitional counselling, interview and résumé consultation, job search workshops, and placement services. There are free workshops available for disabled employment seekers. (TTY: 613-731-1621)

LINK RESOURCE PARTNERS • 4120 Yonge St., Suite 308 • Toronto, ON • M2P 2B8 • Tel: 416-224-5465 • Fax: 416-224-5450 • E-mail: resume@linksearch.com • Internet: www. linksearch.com • Link Resource Partners is Canada's leader in providing corporate finance and investment banking services to entrepreneurial and small cap businesses. Their clients include start-up companies, small cap listed companies, and small to medium sized businesses. They help their clients secure financing, implement mergers and acquisitions, and sell divisions of their businesses.

LINTEX COMPUTER GROUP INC. • 1280 Finch Ave. W., Suite 312 • Toronto, ON • M3J 3K6 • Tel: 416-663-0900 • Fax: 416-663-7315 • E-mail: jobs@lintexgroup.com • Internet: www. lintexgroup.com • Contact: Jas Mann, President & CEO • Serving the I.T. community since 1981, they specialize in placing I.T. professionals on contract assignments and permanent positions in Ontario.

341 Talbot St.
Suite 214
London, ON
Tel: 519-432-0078
Fax: 519-668-0784

LOCK & ASSOCIATES • 1040 West Georgia St., Suite 1770 • Vancouver, BC • V6E 4H1 • Tel: 604-669-8806 • Fax: 604-669-5385 • E-mail: info@lock-associates.com • Internet: www.lock-associates.com • Contact: Andrew Jones • Lock & Associates is a recruiter that specializes in the field of sales and marketing and management.

2600 West Tower	10180 101 Street NW	405 The West Mall
144 4th Avenue SW	Suite 1000, Manulife Place	Suite 910
Calgary, AB	Edmonton, AB	Toronto, ON
T2P 3N4	T5J 3S4	M9C 5J1
Tel: 403-234-8500	Tel: 780-429-9044	Tel: 416-626-8383
Fax: 403-234-8503	Fax: 780-424-1806	Fax: 416-626-6609

LOCK & ASSOCIATES continued

410 - 22nd St. E.	TD Centre, 201 Portage Ave.	1800 McGill College Ave.
Suite 810	Suite 1106	Suite 2605
Saskatoon, SK	Winnipeg, MB	Montreal, QC
S7K 5T6	R3B 3K6	H3A 3J6
Tel: 306-244-2000	Tel: 204-987-3744	Tel: 514-866-2121
Fax: 306-244-0087	Fax: 204-987-3745	Fax: 514-866-5257
1969 Upper Water St.	633 Main St.	100 Queen St.
Suite 2200	Suite 650	Suite 330
Halifax, NS	Moncton, NB	Ottawa, ON
B3J 3R7	E1C 9X9	K1P 1J9
Tel: 902-491-4491	Tel: 506-389-7835	Tel: 613-751-4450
Fax: 902-429-4327	Fax: 506-389-7801	Fax: 613-233-1663

Bureau de la colline
3187 Chemin Ste-Foy
Quebec, QC
G1X 1R3
Tel: 418-653-8288
Fax: 418-653-9848

LONDON EXECUTIVE CONSULTANTS • 380 Wellington St., Suite 1420 • London, ON • N6A 5B5 • Tel: 519-434-9167 • Fax: 519-434-6318 • E-mail: info@londonexecutive.com • Internet: www.londonexecutive.com • London Executive Consultants and their affiliate branches have serviced the human resource requirements of the manufacturing community in many disciplines for the past 20 years. Specializing in engineering/technical, information systems, general/plant management, materials/purchasing, manufacturing/production, human resources, accounting/finance, sales/marketing, quality/engineering.

LOUISE ROBINSON PLACEMENT SERVICES • RR #2 • Keene, ON • K0L 2G0 • Tel: 705-295-4607 • Fax: 705-295-6100 • E-mail: lrps@recruitersnet.com • Internet: www.recruitersnet.com • Contact: Louise Robinson • For over 20 years L. Robinson Placement Services (LRPS) has specialized recruiting Manufacturing and Engineering Professionals for Canada's leading Food and Pharmaceutical Firms.

LOVELL & ASSOCIATES INC. • 4 Upload Rd. • Toronto, ON • M8X 2A9 • Tel: 416-620-4155 ext. 221 • Fax: 415-620-9474 • E-mail: andree@lovellinc.ca • Internet: www.lovellinc.ca • Lovell & Associates Inc. has been providing permanent search solutions since 1988. There are multiple search associates to serve their clients needs. Their client base is typically but not restricted to Ontario. They recruit for all levels of salaried positions and their searches typically span finance, sales & marketing, human resources, management, engineering, manufacturing, R&D, chemical, pharmaceutical and information technology. Their specialty is customizing effective recruiting programs that seek out and evaluate the most qualified candidates to match their client's needs.

LSM CONSULTING • 67 Yonge St. • Toronto, ON • M5E 1J8 • Tel: 416-361-7033 • Fax: 416-361-0728 • E-mail: info@LSMconsulting.com • Internet: www.lsmconsulting.com • LSM Consulting specializes in executive recruiting for senior and mid-management positions. They have developed a diversified executive recruiting practice. They focus their activity in the areas of sales, marketing, finance, general management, technology, engineering, and not-for-profit. They have recruited for CEO's, CFO's, VP's, Directors, Engineers, Project Managers, Sales and Marketing Professionals. Their collective industry expertise further extends to consulting, aerospace, mining, utilities, consumer products and services, telecommunications, financial services, public services, pharmaceutical, and information services.

LUSSIER EXECUTIVE SEARCH INC. • 1235 Bay St., Suite 1000 • Toronto, ON • M5R 3K4 • Tel: 416-860-6236 • E-mail: helene@lussiersearch.ca • Internet: www.lussiersearch.ca • LUSSIER Executive Search Inc. is a registered Ontario Corporation, incorporated under the laws of Ontario in February 1997. The firm specializes in the search and recruitment of risk management, finance and accounting professionals who are experts in their fields.

LYNN DOYLE & ASSOCIATES • 1235 Bay St., Suite 1000 • Toronto, ON • M5R 3K4 • Tel: 416-578-4300 • Fax: 416-515-1273 • E-mail: info@lynndoyleassoc.com • Internet: www. lynndoyleassoc.com • Contact: Lynn Doyle • Lynn Doyle is a respected executive search specialist with sixteen years of proven recruitment experience. For the past decade she has focused on marketing and communications as well as sales and merchandising.

LYNWOOD SMITH INC. • 33 Hazelton Ave., Suite 200 • Toronto, ON • M5R 2E3 • Tel: 416-962-1500 • E-mail: info@lynwoodsmith.com • Internet: www.lynwoodsmith.com • Lynwood Smith provides research and recruitment services primarily in the areas of sales and marketing; high technology; and finance and investment. They work on behalf of client companies to meet their individual staffing requirements from administrative support to senior management levels.

LYNX CAREER CONSULTANTS INC. • 4283 Village Centre Crt. • Mississauga, ON • L4Z 1S2 • Tel: 905-897-5969 • E-mail: opportunities@lynxcareers.com • Lynx Career Consultants Inc. is an employment agency that primarily focuses on permanent career opportunities throughout the Ontario region. The client base represents a wide scope of industries, ranging from sales and service, manufacturing, distribution, retail, engineering, telecommunications, high tech and finance.

M E R MCDANIEL EXECUTIVE RECRUITERS • 1661 Portage Ave., Suite 705 • Winnipeg, MB • R3J 3T7 • Tel: 204-953-3939 • Fax: 204-953-3933 • E-mail: mcdaniel@justcareers.com • Internet: www.justcareers.com • Contact: Chad McDaniel, President • M.E.R. is the premier executive search firm in the CRM, direct marketing and BPO (business process outstheircing).

M.I.S. CONSULTANTS • 55 Eglinton Ave. E., Suite 701 • Toronto, ON • M4P 1G8 • Tel: 416-489-4334 • Fax: 416-489-0918 • E-mail: jobs@misconsultants.ca • Internet: http:// misconsultants.ca • Established in 1978, MIS Consultants has been a leading Toronto resource to the Information Technology industry. IT Contracting, Consulting and Permanent Placement. Their highly specialized recruiters are as conversant with Mainframe to Mid Range technologies as they are with 3 tier Relational Database Development - Data Warehousing cm, Technologies, Object Oriented Methodologies and Architectures, Multi-Networked Environments, Case Tool software and E-Commerce development and implementation.

M.J. JANSEEN & ASSOCIATES INC. • 170 Robert Speck Parkway, Suite 202 • Mississauga, ON • L4Z 3G1 • Tel: 905-272-1335 • Internet: www.mjjanssen.com • M.J. Janssen & Associates Inc. is a leading search firm offering recruitment expertise in all disciplines within a diverse cross section of industries. Over the past fifteen years they have provided ambitious professionals with rewarding careers in a wide spectrum of fields across Canada. Well known for their specialty in recruitment in supply chain management, they have been making significant contributions by putting teams together with an emphasis on business process improvements/change management and e-commerce in the new economy. Focusing on their candidates they have added tremendous value to their interviewing process with their career planning.

MACK O'SULLIVAN SEARCH INC. • 2300 Yonge St., Suite 401, P.O. Box 2427 • Toronto, ON • M4P 1E4 • Tel: 416-481-2992 • Fax: 416-481-3424 • E-mail: resumes@osullivansearch.com • Internet: www.osullivansearch.com • Contact: General Attention • Mack O'Sullivan Services is an employment agency which screens and tests applicants to try and match them with the needs of their clients. Areas of specialization include management, human resources, underwriting, claims, business analysts, sales and marketing, accounting and finance, customer service representatives, administration, property managers/land development, leasing executives, property administrators, site administrators, project management, systems support, accounting store operations and various levels of franchise-related positions, such as: franchise administrators, leasing administrators, store managers, and customer service representatives.

MADISON MACARTHUR INC. • 33 Madison Ave. • Toronto, ON • M5R 2S2 • Tel: 416-920-0092 • Fax: 416-920-0099 • E-mail: info@mmsearch.com • Internet: www.macarthursearch.com • Madison MacArthur delivers professional services to the communications, marketing, advertising, financial services, manufacturing, e-commerce and internet related business sectors. As one of Toronto's most highly respected executive recruiting firms, they work with their clients to strategically enhance their workforce. Their broad range of expertise, commitment to ethical business standards, and ability to provide premiere talent quickly and cost-effectively ensures a positive experience for both clients and candidates alike.

MAIZIS & MILLER CONSULTANTS • 5405 Eglinton Ave. W., Suite 109 • Etobice, ON • M9C 5K6 • Tel: 416-620-5111 • Fax: 416-620-5216 • E-mail: inquire@maizisandmiller.com • Internet: www.maizisandmiller.com • Maizis & Miller Consultants was founded in 1988 as a division of Centennial Personnel. Their certified Staffing Specialists offer diverse backgrounds which facilitates a broad understanding of a variety of positions and industries to better assist both their clients and candidates in the placement process. Their reputation for excellence has been earned by providing outstanding service to their clients and candidates who represent various levels of responsibility from many different industries.

MANAGEMENT SOLUTIONS CONSULTING INC. • 190 Robert Speck Parkway, Suite 107 • Mississauga, ON • L4Z 3K3 • Tel: 905-276-7856 • Fax: 905-897-8385 • E-mail: info@msci.net • Internet: www.msci.net • Contact: Ken Lachine, President • Management Solutions is a recruiter that focuses on the computer and medical industry. They are a professional search firm specializing in the areas of information technology consulting, human resources consulting, executive job searches, and contracting services.

MANDRAKE MANAGEMENT CONSULTANTS LTD. • 55 St. Clair Ave. W., Suite 401 • Toronto, ON • M4V 2Y7 • Tel: 416-922-5400 • Fax: 416-922-1356 • E-mail: info@mandrake.ca • Internet: www.mandrake.ca • Mandrake is one of Canada's foremost executive search and consulting firms. As a strategic partner to some of the world's leading businesses, their primary goal is to enhance organizations by identifying and attracting outstanding leadership executives. They excel at brering mergers and acquisitions, forging strategic alliances, and developing organization structures for long-term results. They offer clients a complete range of recruitment, selection, and hiring services through their subsidiary company, wwwork!com. In addition, they provide a full range of outplacement, executive coaching and performance improvement services through their sister company, NEXCareer.

2000 Mansfield St.
Suite 1610
Montréal, QC
H3A 3A4
Tel: 514-878-4224
Fax: 514-878-4222
nlebeau@mandrake.ca

400 3rd Ave. S.W.
Suite 1400
Calgary AB
T2P 4H2
Tel: 416-922-5600 x208
daigneault@mandrake.ca

MANPOWER • 200 University Ave, Suite 110 • Toronto, ON • M5H 3C6 • Tel: 416-977-7748 • Fax: 416-977-0947 • Internet: www.manpower.ca • Manpower is the largest staffing and training organization in the world. Manpower has been in business since 1948. There are over 2,500 offices in 48 countries. They provide job placement (permanent, contract and temporary) in office, call centre, industrial, technical, IT, skilled trades, and professional jobs. Visit their Internet site for office locations.

320-9940 Lougheed Hwy.	1380 Burrard St.	#360, 7347th Ave S.W.
Burnaby, BC	Suite 210	Calgary, AB
V3J 7T8	Vancouver, BC	T2P 3P8
Tel: 604-444-3339	V6Z 2H3	Tel: 403-269-6936
Fax: 604-444-3307	Tel: 604-682-1651	Fax: 403-265-4063
	Fax: 604-669-5397	
201 City Centre Drive	4950 Yonge St.	55 Metcalfe
Suite 101	Suite 700	Suite 800
Mississauga, ON	North York, ON	Ottawa, ON
L5B 2T4	M2N 6K1	K1P 6L5
Tel: 905-276-2000	Tel: 416-225-5599	Tel: 613-237-9070
Fax: 905-276-2596	Fax: 416-225-9096	Fax: 613-563-9735

MARBERG LIMITED • 390 Bay St., Suite 601 • Toronto, ON • M5H 2Y2 • Tel: 416-363-6442 • Fax: 416-363-7966 • E-mail: jobs@marberg.com • Internet: www.marberg.com • Since 1980 Marberg has provided quality permanent and temporary personnel to Toronto's financial, legal, bilingual, insurance, medical and government communities. Their team of specialists is dedicated to excellence, with a commitment to exceeding the performance expectations of their clients and candidates.

MARK STAFFING SOLUTIONS INC. • 734 – 7th Avenue S.W., Suite 730 • Calgary, AB • T2P 3P8 • Tel: 403-263-5120 • Fax: 403-266-5691 • E-mail: info@markstaffing.com • Internet: www.markstaffing.com • Contact: Bev Hughes • Mark Staffing Solutions is committed to offering creative, flexible and quality staffing solutions that exceed an organization's human resource objectives. Specialized services include temporary and full-time placement of office support and light industrial staff payrolling, planned staffing consultation, reception/customer service training, and instructor-led computer training.

MAXIM GROUP INC. • 734 - 7 Ave S.W., Suite 602 • Calgary, AB • T2P 3P8 • Tel: 403-263-1200 • Fax: 403-263-1211 • E-mail: calgary.jobs@webmaxim.com • Internet: www.maxim.ca • Maxim Group Inc. is an Alberta based organization with a diverse foundation of service offerings. Founded in 1989, Maxim has proven itself as an industry leader based on firm business ethics and integrity. Using a combination of high tech recruiting methods and old fashioned 'stick-to-it-ness' Maxim has earned an enviable position as recruiter of choice for many organizations. Maxim operates with several divisions, namely 'Maxim Engineering Technical', 'Power Dynamics', 'Maxim Group IT Consulting', 'Maxim Design Studios', EZ-referral.com. Ultimately, the work of each division, evolves around people and the work they do, especially in the Engineering and Information Technology industries.

10250 101st	1130 W. Pender St.	390 Bay St.
Suite 1040	Suite 1101	Suite 700
Edmonton, AB	Vancouver, BC	Toronto, ON
T5J 3P4	V6E 4A4	M5H 2Y2
Tel: 780-990-1300	Tel: 604-488-1500	Tel: 416-703-2255
Fax: 780-990-1302	Fax: 604-488-1510	Fax: 416-703-6600
edmonton.jobs@maxim.ca	vancouver.jobs@maxim.ca	toronto.jobs@maxim.ca

MAYFAIR PERSONNEL NORTHERN LTD. • 9804 - 100 Avenue, Suite 305 • Grande Prairie, AB • T8V 0T8 • Tel: 780-539-5090 • Fax: 780-539-7089 • E-mail: mayfair@telusplanet.net • Contact: Irene Hamilton • Mayfair Personnel is a full service employment agency that places temporary and permanent office, sales, and technical personnel. There is no charge to register for employment. They also own a Computer and Business Training Centre.

MCDONALD-GREEN PERSONNEL INC. • 215 Holiday Inn Dr. • Cambridge, ON • N3C 3T2 • Tel: 519-654-9388 • Fax: 519-654-9362 • E-mail: info@mcdonaldgreen.com • Internet: www.mcdonaldgreen.com • Contact: Helen Jowett, President, CEO • McDonald-Green Personnel offers temporary and permanent employment opportunities in various skilled trades. Opportunities include general labour, administration, millwrights, welders, machinists, engineers, apprenticeships, and technical and executive positions.

140-355 Elmira Rd.
Guelph, ON
N1K 1S5
Tel: 519-824-6781
Fax: 519-824-7205

MCINTYRE MANAGEMENT RESOURCES • Box 10043, 27 Legend Court • Ancaster, ON • L9K 1P3 • Tel: 905-574-6765 • Fax: 905-574-5025 • E-mail: jobs@mcintyrejobs.com • Internet: www.mcintyremgmt.com • McIntyre Management Resources is involved in the areas of information technology, engineering, high technology, accounting, manufacturing and human resources.

MCKINNON MANAGEMENT GROUP INC. • 5160 Yonge St., Suite 700 • Toronto, ON • M2N 6L9 • Tel: 416-250-6763 • Fax: 416-250-6916 • E-mail: Information info@mckinnon.com • Internet: www.mckinnon.com • McKinnon Management Group Inc. is an executive recruitment firm combining over 50 years of search experience. Many of their consultants have direct experience in the industries that they service. Their intimate knowledge of industry issues and challenges provides a more meaningful communication with their customers and ultimately, produces a better match between employer and candidate. They have completed searches across North America at all management and executive levels. They represent many of North America's largest and most progressive companies.

MCNEILL NAKAMOTO RECRUITMENT GROUP • 1250 Homer St., Suite 305 • Vancouver, BC • V6B 1C6 • Tel: 604-662-8967 • Fax: 604-662-8927 • E-mail: jobs@peoplebuzz.com • Internet: www.peoplebuzz.com • McNeill Nakamoto was created as a boutique style recruitment firm with a vision to provide the highest quality of recruitment service by personalizing all aspects of the recruitment process for its clients and applicants. The McNeill Nakamoto team can assist in staffing for a diverse range of positions including accounting, administrative (including entry level), customer service & call centre, financial services, human resources, information technology, management/professional, marketing & sales, real estate/property management and transportation/logistics.

MEDA LIMITED • 1575 Lauzon Rd. • Windsor, ON • N8S 3N4 • Tel: 519-944-7221 • Fax: 519-944-6862 • E-mail: meda@medagroup.com • Internet: www.medagroup.com • Contact: Richard Rosenthal, Executive Vice President • MEDA Limited was established in 1970 by Melvyn (Mel) and Carole Lawn. Their company is strategically located central to the primary automotive, heavy construction and manufacturing industries of North America. MEDA Limited provides consistently high quality contract technical services and engineering support to the North American automotive industry.

MEDA LIMITED continued

2916 South Sheridan Way
Suite 100
Oakville, ON
L6J 7J8
Tel: 905-829-4929
Fax: 905-829-2437

MEDHUNTERS • 180 Dundas St. W., Suite 2403 • Toronto, ON • M5G 1Z8 • Tel: 416-977-5777 • Fax: 416-977-2869 • E-mail: info@medhunters.com • Internet: www.medhunters.com • MedHunters is a leader in the provision of recruitment services for health care employers and health care professionals. The firm recruits, promotes and maintains an extensive database of medical and health care professionals. MedHunters is the sister company of Helen Ziegler & Associates (HZA), the largest international health care recruitment company in North America.

MERIDIA RECRUITMENT SERVICES INC. • Cornwallis House 6th Floor, 5475 Spring Garden Rd. • Halifax, NS • B3J 3T2 • Tel: 902-421-1330 • Fax: 902-425-1108 • E-mail: info@robertsonsurrette.com • Internet: www.meridia.ca • As a member of the Robertson Surrette Group, Meridia draws on over 25 years experience in recruiting for Atlantic Canadian organizations. Robertson Surrette began as a single company in 1975. Today, they are Robertson Surrette; a group of 30 passionate individuals working throughout Atlantic Canada offering the full continuum of integrating human resource consulting services.

77 Vaughan Harvey Blvd.	10 Fort William Place	133 Prince William St.
Suite 101	Suite 101	Harbour Center
Moncton, NB	St. John's, NF	Saint John, NB
E1C 0K2	A1C 1K4	E2L 2B5
Tel: 506-855-8169	Tel: 709-722-6890	Tel: 506-847-0359
Fax: 506-854-8464	Fax: 709-722-8685	Fax: 506-652-1562

2 Appledore Lane
Charlotte, PEI
C1B 2P9
Tel: 902-940-2181
Fax: 902-569-3837

MERIDIAN MANAGEMENT SERVICES • 1000 Roundelay Dr. • Oshawa, ON • L1J 7R9 • Tel: 905-242-5865 • Fax: 905-435-0436 • E-mail: info@meridiansearch.ca • Internet: www.meridiansearch.ca • At Meridian Management Services they are dedicated to fulfilling the staffing needs of their client companies by providing the highly skilled and professional personnel who are leaders in the printing/packaging industry. Through innovation and customer focus, they will become the clear choice for both Employers and Job-seekers alike in their endeavour to realize working goals.

MERIT VENDOR PERSONNEL INC. • 64 Charles St. E. • Toronto, ON • M4Y 1T1 • Tel: 416-392-9226 • Fax: 416-928-2298 • E-mail: jobs@meritvp.com • Internet: www.meritvp.com • Merit Vendor Personnel is one of Canada's leading recruiting agencies, specializing in the Software Vendor marketplace. Their clients offer application solutions, data warehousing, object oriented tools, internet/intranet product and services, implementation and training services, project leadership and project management. Their focus is to work with the clients to address their requirements for pre-sales technical support, sales, marketing, management, and all post sales positions.

MINDSCOPE STAFFING SOFTWARE • 100 Wingold Ave., Suite 1 • Toronto, ON • M6B 4K7 • Tel: 416-780-9804 • Fax: 416-780-9318 • Internet: www.mindscope.com • One On One, now known as Mindscope Staffing Software, initially started as the Canadian distributor of a Swedish computer based training software. By 1999, the product focus became increasingly centered on applicant tracking and candidate testing software programs, primarily geared towards the staffing industry. Their current staffing software product mindSCOPE has been designed to focus on facilitating the requirements of Staffing agencies, contingency search firms, executive search firms and temporary placement agencies. They currently operate offices in Toronto and Los Angeles.

MIS CONSULTANTS • 55 Eglinton Ave. East, Suite 701 • Toronto, ON • M4P 1G8 • Tel: 416-489-4334 • Fax: 416-489-0918 • E-mail: jobs@misconsultants.ca • Internet: http://misconsultants.ca • Established in 1978, MIS Consultants is a leading Toronto recruiter in the Information Technology industry. I.T. Contracting, Consulting and Permanent Placement is their specialty.

MORRIS GROUP INTERNATIONAL • 2 Bloor St. W., Suite 1730 • Toronto, ON • M4W 3E2 • Tel: 416-440-8434 • Fax: 416-440-0484 • E-mail: bmorris@morrisgroup.ca • Internet: www.morrisgroup.ca • When a client engages us, they make a professional and personal commitment to achieve a timely and definitive solution to their client's executive needs. These days, identifying and recruiting the right-fit candidate for the job is only half the job; helping their clients retain that person is the other half. It's a task that requires diplomacy, fairness and strong negotiation skills – as well as coaching and mentoring. All of which, they have built in their years of experience – both as search professionals and as clients of search professionals.

MOXON PERSONNEL LTD. • 1185 West Georgia Street, Suite 905 • Vancouver, BC • V6E 4E6 • Tel: 604-688-5100 • Fax: 604-688-0342 • E-mail: moxon@telus.net • Internet: www.moxonpersonnel.com • Contact: Ben Moxon • Moxon Personnel is the leading accounting placement agency in British Columbia. Founded in 1988, they pride themselves on their ability to match your skills and objectives with the recruitment needs of their clients. Providing permanent, temporary and contract employment, they place qualified accounting personnel in a variety of positions including CFOs, VP finance, chicf accountants, controllers (all levels), accounting managers, public practice, senior accountants, accounting clerks, accounts payable, accounts receivable, junior & intermediate accountants, bookkeepers, credit and payroll.

MPA EXECUTIVE SEARCH INC. • 7900, boul. Taschereau Ouest, Bureau A-204 • Brossard, QC • J4X 1C2 • Tel: 514-875-3996 • Fax: 450-465-9215 • E-mail: courrier@m-p-a.qc.ca • Internet: www.m-p-a.qc.ca • MPA Executive Search inc. is a firm with recognized expertise in locating intermediate-and executive-level personnel. Their work involves locating high-calibre candidates recognized for their professional activities and the quality of their work. Most of them are already pursuing brilliant careers in dynamic environments, but may see the appeal of a new challenge. They communicate with them personally, under conditions of strict confidentiality.

MULTEC CANADA LTD. • 200 Ronson Dr., Suite 200 • Toronto, ON • M9W 5Z9 • Tel: 416-244-2402 • Fax: 416-244-6883 • E-mail: toronto@brunelmultec.ca • Internet: www.multec.ca • Brunel Multec Canada offers professionals a seamless and effortless job search experience. From start-up companies to multinational corporations, they are the recruitment partner of choice for a wide variety of staffing assignments. They are in daily contact with the top 10% of employers in their niche markets. They often represent the "hidden job opportunities" not advertised or made public by employers. They are an equal opportunity employer and promote the highest level of ethics in conjunction with A.C.S.E.S.S, their industry association.

MULTEC CANADA LTD. continued

380 Wellington St.	2000 Rue Peel	555 Kingston Rd.
Suite 206	Suite 680	Ajax, ON
London, ON	Montreal, QC	L1S 6M1
N6A 5B5	H3A 2W5	Tel: 905-426-5822
Tel: 519-439-7479	Tel: 514-396-7890	Fax: 905-426-3774
Fax: 519-439-0108	Fax: 514-396-7144	ajax@brunelmultec.ca
london@brunelmultec.ca	montreal@brunelmultec.ca	

N.A.P. EXECUTIVE SERVICES (CANADA) INC. • 3101 Bathurst St., Suite 300 • Toronto, ON • M6A 2A6 • Tel: 416-949-8896 • E-mail: toronto@fashion-career.com • Internet: www.fashion-career.com • N.A.P. has been proudly servicing the apparel, textiles and retail industries for over twenty-five years. To better serve you, they maintain offices in Toronto and Montreal and work with strategic partners in every fashion center in Canada.

1230 Dr. Penfield
Suite 904
Montreal, QC
H3G 1B5
Tel: 514-592-8896

NATIONAL EXECUTIVE • 3200 Dufferin St., Suite 305 • North York, ON • M6A 3B2 • Tel: 416-258-0300 • Fax: 416-256-0035 • E-mail: resume@national-executive.com • Internet: www.national-executive.com • Contact: Don Cormier • National Executive is a well established firm that has been in business since 1984; specializing in the recruitment and placement of Engineering, Information Technology, and Computer professionals. Permanent and contract personnel is available.

NETWORK CORPORATE SEARCH PERSONNEL INC., THE • 505 - 8th Avenue SW, Suite 310 • Calgary, AB • T2P 1G2 • Tel: 403-262-6630 • Fax: 403-262-5150 • E-mail: info@networksearch.net • Internet: www.networksearch.net • Contact: Pat Ridell • The Network Corporate Search Personnel Inc. is a search firm that specializes in the recruitment & placement of professionals primarily for permanent positions. The Company was established in 1990 when Pat Riddell of Corporate Search & Kim McKay from The Network Personnel merged to form the diverse company it is today.

NEVIAN CONSULTING & PLACEMENT SERVICES INC. • The Madison Centre, 4950 Yonge Street, Suite 2200 • Toronto, ON • M2N 6K1 • Tel: 416-805-9636 • E-mail: sales@nevian.com • Internet: www.nevian.com • They are Toronto's reliable choice for bilingual recruiting services. They specialize in the placement of bilingual professionals for all occupations where French / English employees are needed.

NEW MEDIA LINKS • 30 Duncan St., Suite 203 • Toronto, ON • M5V 2C3 • Tel: 416-977-0124 • Fax: 416-640-1045• E-mail: info@newmedialinks.com • Internet: www.newmedialinks.com • New Media Links represents clients and candidates in the strategic, creative and technical sectors of interactive communications and technology.

NEWFOUNDLAND PERSONNEL INC. • P.O. Box 1840, Station C, 3 Queen St., 2nd Floor • St. John's, NF • A1C 5R2 • Tel: 709-579-3400 • Fax: 709-579-0464 • E-mail: info@nfpersonnel.com • Internet: www.nfpersonnel.com • Newfoundland Personnel Inc. is the province's premiere staffing service established in 1983. They offer temporary and full time placement.

NEXSTAF INC. • 116 Spadina Ave., Suite 300 • Toronto, ON • M5V 2K6 • Tel: 416-203-1711 • Fax: 416-203-1577 • E-mail: resumes@nexstaf.com • Internet: www.nexstaf.com • Nexstaf was formed by the same ownership group that created one of Canada's largest and best known, IT recruiting companies. Rooted in ethics and professionalism, they aspire to earn the loyalty of all their stakeholders. Nexstaf works diligently to build relationships, not simply fill positions. While achieving this standard is more difficult, it ensures more satisfied employees, and ultimately, greater value to their clients.

5045 Orbitor Dr.
Building 7, Suite 200
Mississsauga, ON
L4W 4Y4

NICEJOB.CA • 1 place Ville Marie, bureau 2821 • Montréal, QC • H3B 4R4 • Tel: 514-448-5295 • Fax: 514-582-0227 • E-mail: info@nicejob.ca • Internet: www.nicejob.ca • Nicejob.ca is a young team who has been working in the recruitment and high technology universe for many years They believe that recruitment via Internet will simplify the life of candidates as well as recruiters. They know that, for the moment, Internet has not fulfilled all the expectations of candidates and recruiters and that unsatisfaction elements remain numerous. They are convinced that the future of online recruitment relies on efficiency and ethics.

NOVA STAFFING INC. • 1550 Enterprise Road, Suite 302 • Mississauga, ON • L4W 4P4 • Tel: 905-795-9779 • Fax: 905-795-9449 • E-mail: info@novastaffinginc.com • Internet: www. novastaffinginc.com • Nova Staffing was founded in July 2000 as a supplier of temporary and permanent help. Their service area includes Mississauga, Brampton, Etobicoke, Downsview and Rexdale with their head office centrally located in Mississauga.

OASIS SEARCH GROUP INC. • 67 Mowat Ave., Suite 242 • Toronto, ON • M6K 3E3 • Tel: 416-690-2551 • Fax: 416-690-2551 • E-mail: stuart@oasissearchgroup.com • Internet: www. oasissearchgroup.com • Oasis Search Group Inc. is a unique executive recruitment-consulting agency, specializing in marketing, category management, customer marketing, sales and sales management, in both the retail and foodservice sectors for the CPG Industry. Their firm's philosophy in search is to provide the highest quality service to their corporate clients and candidates through a professional, innovative and ethical approach.

OEM SEARCH INTERNATIONAL • 380 Wellington Street, Suite 1420 • London, ON • N6A 5B5 • Tel: 519-434-9167 • Fax: 519-434-6318 • E-mail: info@oemsearch.com • Internet: www.oemsearch.com • OEM Search International is the parent company of Toronto Executive Consultants, OEM Search International and Kitchener Executive Consultants. A partnership with OEM Search International means national and international reach through their membership in the National Personnel Associates - a worldwide recruiting network. They have serviced the human resource requirements of the manufacturing community since 1976 in the disciplines of engineering/technical, information systems, general/plant management, materials/purchasing, manufacturing/production, human resources, accounting/finance, Sales/marketing and quality engineering.

OFFICETEAM • 1055 Dunsmuir Street, Suite 724 • Vancouver, BC • V7X 1L4 • Tel: 604-687-8367 • Fax: 604-687-7533 • E-mail: vancouver.bc@officeteam.com • Internet: www.officeteam. com • OfficeTeam is the world's largest specialized temporary staffing service for administrative professionals. OfficeTeam has the resources, experience, and expertise to coordinate the match between employer and administrative specialist. OfficeTeam provides support throughout an organization, including administrative assistants, specialized assistants, executive assistants, customer service representatives, office managers, receptionists, data entry specialists and word processors.

5140 Yonge St.
Suite 1500
North York, ON
M2N 6L7
Tel: 416-226-1051
Fax: 416-226-4498
north.york@officeteam.com

181 Bay St.
Suite 820
Toronto, ON
M5J 2T3
Tel: 416-350-2010
Fax: 416-350-3573
toronto@officeteam.com

175 Commerce Valley Dr. W.
Suite 300
Thornhill, ON
L3T 7P6
Tel: 905-771-8272
Fax: 905-709-3664
markham@officeteam.com

1 Robert Speck Pkwy
Suite 940
Mississauga, ON
L4Z 3M3
Tel: 905-306-8326
Fax: 905-273-6217
mississauga@officeteam.com

360 Albert St.
Constitution Sq., Suite 520
Ottawa, ON
K1R 7X7
Tel: 613-234-0159
Fax: 613-236-2159
ottawa@officeteam.com

1111 Saint Charles
Suite 650
Longueuil, QC
J4K 5G4
Tel: 450-679-7528
Fax: 450-679-8443
rive.sud@officeteam.com

888 3rd St. S.W.
Suite 4200
Calgary, AB
T2P 5C5
Tel: 403-263-7266
Fax: 403-264-0934
calgary@officeteam.com

10180 - 101 Street
Suite 1280
Edmonton, AB
T5J 3S4
Tel: 780-429-1750
Fax: 780-423-1581
edmonton@officeteam.com

15127 100th Avenue
Suite 302
Surrey, BC
V3R 0N9
Tel: 604-581-8361
Fax: 604-581-4225
fraser.valley@officeteam.com

5515 North Service Rd.
Suite 302
Burlington, ON
L7L 6G4
Tel: 905-331-0456
Fax: 905-319-2095
burlington@officeteam.com

201 Portage Ave.
Suite 2400
Winnipeg, MB
R3B 3K6
Tel: 204-947-9670
Fax: 204-957-5385
winnipeg@officeteam.com

1, Place Ville Marie
Suite 2330
Montreal, QC
H3B 3M5
Tel: 514-875-1859
Fax: 514-875-8066
montreal@officeteam.com

80 King St. S.
Suite 206
Waterloo, ON
N2J 1P5
Tel: 519-884-3520
Fax: 519-884-4632
waterloo@officeteam.com

175 Commerce Valley Dr. W.
Suite 300
Thornhill, ON
L3T 7P6
Tel: 905-771-8272
Fax: 905-709-3664
markham@officeteam.com

OPTIMUM PERSONNEL LTÉE • 3073 boul. des Sources • Dorval, QC • H9B 1Z6 • Tel: 514-683-1057 • Fax: 514-683-1858 • E-mail: info@optimumpersonnel.com • Internet: www.optimumpersonnel.com • Optimum Personnel is an employment agency providing permanent and temporary job placements. They specialize in areas such as accounting, finance, marketing, sales, human resources, information management, credit management, secretarial, receptionist, order desk, word processing and purchasing.

OPTIONS PERSONNEL INC. • 80 Bloor St. W., Suite 1003 • Toronto, ON • M5S 2V1 • Tel: 416-926-8820 • Fax: 416-926-1977 • E-mail: options@optionspersonnel.com • Internet: www.optionspersonnel.com • Founded in 1991, Options Personnel's team of experienced, educated professionals is committed to serving your needs. They have a very distinct culture, which has been paramount to their success. At any given time, multiple staff members work in conjunction to provide the best possible service. They are committed to understanding, anticipating and fulfilling their clients' needs in a professional and ethical manner.

OSBORNE GROUP, THE • 190Attwell Dr., Suite 120 • Toronto, ON • M9W 6H8 • Tel: 416-498-1550 • Fax: 416-498-1029 • E-mail: toronto@osborne-group.com • Internet: www.osborne-group.com • The The Osborne Group was founded in 1993 to provide clients with the focused, functional expertise they need to quickly meet their management challenges during periods of rapid growth, transition and decline. They work with their clients to provide management solutions that exceed expectations and build strong, performance-based successful companies or the future.

New Look Business Centre	3553 31st N.W.	1080 Beaver Hall Hill
1275 West 6th Ave.	Suite 550	Suite 2
Vancouver, BC	Calgary, AB	Montreal, QC
V6H 1A6	T2L 2K7	H2Z 1S8
Tel: 604-688-4960	Tel: 403-264-8195	Tel: 514-989-2213
Fax: 604-738-8883		Fax: 514-989-0240
17008 90th Avenue	1188 Wellington St.	
Suite 210	Suite 201	
Edmonton, AB	Ottawa, ON	
T5T 1L6	K1Y 2Z5	
Tel: 780-451-4698	Tel: 613-722-0479	
	Fax: 613-248-5005	

OVER 55 (LONDON) INC. • 78 Riverside Dr. • London, ON • N6H 1B4 • Tel: 519-680-1464 • Fax: 519-680-1012 • E-mail: over55@bellnet.ca • Internet: www.over55london.ca • Contact: Emilie Dudley-Jones • Over 55 (London) Inc. is a non-profit agency that was started in 1985 to connect mature, experienced, and capable men and women with London area employers. Over the past 19 years, thousands of skilled Over 55 (London) Inc. members have been successfully linked with home owners, seeking maintenance and home care services, and local firms requiring skilled, dependable, and motivated workers.

PACIFIC FIRST SYSTEMS • BCE Place, 161 Bay St., 27th Floor • Toronto, ON • M5J 2S1 • Tel: 416-350-2050 • E-mail: mail@pacificfirst.com • Internet: www.pacificfirst.com • Founded in 1986, Pacific First Systems is a global leader in Information Technology recruitment and placement of contract and permanent/full-time professionals. They supply quality candidates with all levels of qualifications, for a wide range of positions up to the President level. They currently have offices in the United States of America and Canada. Their firm's headquarters are conveniently located in downtown Toronto.

PAL PERSONNEL SERVICES • 200 Consumers Rd., Suite 300 • Willowdale, ON • M2J 4R4 • Tel: 416-497-8200 • Fax: 416-497-8352 • E-mail: toronto@pal.stivers.com • Internet: www.pal.stivers.com • Pal Personnel Services was established in Toronto in 1977. They are a division of Stivers Temporary Personnel, Inc., the oldest national temporary personnel service in the U.S.A. They are a one-stop staffing company specializing in temporary office help.

37 Main Street St. N.
Suite 203
Markham, ON
L3P 1X3
Tel: 905-472-4222

PARTNERVISION CONSULTING GROUP INC. • 101 King St., Mezzanine Floor (M7) • St. Catherines, ON • L2R 3H6 • Tel: 905-641-4480 • E-mail: info@partnervision.net • Internet: www. partnervision.net • Contact: Lynn Lefebvre • Established in 1991 by Lynn Lefebvre, Partnervision is located in downtown Toronto. As their name emphasizes, their focus is on understanding your vision, business framework and, within that context, provide the leadership and human solutions to drive your organization forward or change the leverage of staff effectiveness.

PATTY SHAPIRO & ASSOCIATES • 555 Chabanel R-17 • Montreal, QC • H2N 2H7 • Tel: 514-389-5627 • Fax: 514-389-9969 • Internet: www.pattyshapiro.com • Since 1992, Patty Shapiro and Associates Inc. has offered clients a wide range of specialized services. The company is a leader in personnel recruitment, management training and development, fashion forecasting, computerized garment design courses, CAD (computer-assisted design) training using Lectra, PAD and Gerber software for pattern, grading and marking, as well as Web site design.

PD BUREAU • 330 Bay St., Suite 1304 • Toronto, ON • M5H 2S8 • Tel: 416-364-1226 • Fax: 416-364-1204 • E-mail: info@pdbureau.com • Internet: www.pdbureau.com • PD Bureau is a specialist in administrative staffing. Established in 1969 and located in the heart of the financial district of Toronto on Bay Street, PD has been playing a pivotal role in the provision of clerical and administrative staff in Toronto for over thirty years. They specialize in temporary placements as well as having a solid and successful record in permanent placements. In fact many of their staff are offered permanent or contract positions after only a short time on a "temporary" assignment.

PEAPELL & ASSOCIATES • 5251 Duke St., Suite 1206 • Halifax, NS • B3J 1P3 • Tel: 902-421-1523 • Fax: 902-425-8559 • E-mail: resumes@peapell.ca • Internet: www.peapell.ca • Contact: Jill Peapell • Peapell & Associates (a division of Jill Peapell Personnel Consultants Ltd.), a Nova Scotian owned company, is a full-service human resource consulting firm which has been operating since 1989. The company provides a full range of human resource services, including Recruitment Services, Candidate Assessment & Evaluation and General Human Resources Consulting. The company operates a temporary placement division under the business name Supertemp, which is the largest independent temporary placement agency in Nova Scotia.

PEGASUS CONSULTING • 55 Eglintion Ave. E., Suite 208 • Toronto, ON • M4P 1G8 • Tel: 416-488-7007 • Fax: 416-488-7337 • E-mail: resume@pegsoft.com • Internet: www.pegsoft. com • Pegasus is a privately held corporation, founded in 1987 to meet a growing market need for qualified professionals with specialized IT skills, by John Goldsmith, the present Chairmen and founding partner. Their management team has over 25 years of business experience each in a variety of national and international industries.

PEOPLE BANK, THE • 220 Yonge St., P.O. Box 603, Suite 204 • Toronto, ON • M5B 2H1 • Tel: 416-340-1004 • Fax: 416-340-0447 • E-mail: toroffice@thepeoplebank.com • Internet: www.thepeoplebank.com • For over 29 years, they have fostered many successful working relationships by bringing thousands of employers and potential candidates together. So whether you're looking to land your dream job, or your organization needs to fill a vacancy, they have the resources you need, to help you find the right fit.

715 Portage Ave.	10 Kingsbridge Garden Circle	130 Slater St.
Winnipeg, MB	Ground Floor, Suite 103	Suite 100
R3G 0M8	Mississauga, ON	Ottawa, ON
Tel: 204-772-5040	L5R 3K6	K1P 6E2
Fax: 204-772-5747	Tel: 905-890-0093	Tel: 613-234-8118
	Fax: 905 890-0094	Fax: 613-234-7365

PEOPLE BANK, THE continued

362 Dufferin Ave.
London, ON
N6B 1Z4
Tel: 519-672-7040
Fax: 519-672-7044

35 Wellington St. N.
2nd Floor
Woodstock, ON
N4S 3H4
Tel: 519-533-6038
Fax: 519-533-6252

3100 Steeles Ave. E.
Suite 401
Markham, ON
L3R 8T3
Tel: 905-470-3111
Fax: 905-470-5822

1255 Carre Philips
Bureau 801
Montreal, QC
H3B 3G1
Tel: 514-875-2122
Fax: 514-875-2232

1820 Hollis St.
Suite 400
Halifax, NS
B3J 1W4
Tel: 902-442-3955
Fax: 902-442-3956

261 Tillson Ave.
Tillsonburg, ON
N4G 5X2
Tel: 519-842-9555
Fax: 519-842-9596

PEOPLE WEB INC., THE • 54 Muriel Avenue • Toronto, ON • M4J 2X9 • Tel: 416-602-3837 • Fax: 416-774-2475 • E-mail: mail@peopleweb.ca • Internet: www.thepeopleweb.ca • The PeopleWeb Inc. is a technology recruiting organization, headed by experienced technology professionals. The management team at The PeopleWeb Inc. have been involved in the technology industry in Canada since 1985, and in the Technology placement industry since 1995. The PeopleWeb was founded in December, 1997, with the intention of building an organization that respected the needs of the applicants, as well as our clients. The Interlocking "C"s in our logo was designed to show the connection, or "Perfect fit" between Candidates and Clients.

PEP HUMAN RESOURCES CONSULTING SERVICES • 58 Eighth Concession Rd. • Burford, ON • N0E 1A0 • Tel: 519-537-3709 • Fax: 519-290-1111 • E-mail: peptalk@execulink.com • Internet: http://consultpep.com • They offer a variety of HR Services that can make your business more successful. Whether it is recruiting the right person to fill that key position, handling your sensitive outplacement needs, or any other of their services, you have their personal guarantee of satisfaction. The PEP difference is simple. Start by caring about each person that they work with, combine that with over 40 years of experience and a unique ability to quickly understand the culture of your business. The result...excellence in every assignment they take on.

PERFORMANCE SYSTEMS INC. • 8119-188A Street • Edmonton, AB • T5T 5A8 • Tel: 780-481-0588 • Fax: 780-444-5018 • E-mail: human.resources@performancesystems.ca • Internet: www.performancesystems.ca • Contact: Steve Knight, President • Performance Systems Inc. is an information technology resources provider. They focus on providing skilled IT individuals or a full complement of staff tailored to a client's needs. Their goal is to find the best solution for IT staffing requirements.

PERMANENT SEARCH GROUP • 4310 Sherwoodtowne Blvd., Suite 304 • Mississauga, ON • L4Z 4C4 • Tel: 905-276-2006 • Fax: 905-276-0258 • E-mail: jobs@permanentsearch.com • Internet: http://permanentsearch.com • Permanent Search Group invests in both clients and candidates to ensure mutual success. They foster long-term partnerships, procuring information that facilitates a suitable match. After 18 years in strategic recruitment, they've forged numerous relationships in diverse sectors around Toronto and throughout Canada.

PERM-A-TEM INC. • 45 Place Charles Lemoyne, Suite 100 • Longueuil, QC • J4K 5G5 • Tel: 450-651-7001 • Fax: 450-651-7007 • E-mail: info@perm-a-tem.com • Internet: www.perm-a-tem.com • Perm-A-Tem Inc. is a professional personnel service firm. Their one stop HR shop provides innovative human capital solutions to hundreds of engineering, technology, and technical firms across North America.

PERSONNEL BY ELSIE • 3837 Wyandotte St. E. • Windsor, ON • N8Y 1G4 • Tel: 519-944-0669 • Fax: 519-944-4902 • E-mail: pbe@personnelbyelsie.com • Internet: www.jobswindsor.com • Personnel by Elsie, established in 1992, is a full service employment agency. Their Windsor and Leamington offices provide temporary or permanent employees to many types of businesses in many skill levels. They are locally owned and operated and have the advantage of on-site owner representation.

21 Princess St.
Leamington, ON
N8H 2X8
Tel: 519-324-9305
Fax: 519-324-9307

PERSONNEL MANAGEMENT GROUP • P.O. Box 48071, RPO Lakewood • Winnipeg, MB • R2J 4A3 • Tel: 204-982-1100 • E-mail: yvonne@pmg.mb.ca • Internet: www.pmg.mb.ca • Contact: Yvonne Baert, Director & Technical Recruiter • Personnel Management Group is a recruiting company that specializes in providing permanent and contract personnel to the following industries: information technology & bio-sciences, transportation, logistics & supply chaing management, engineering, manufacturing, construction, skilled trades & quality assurance, account, administration and human resources. With over 25 years experience in the Manitoba market, they have the knowledge and resources to assist you whether you are an employer or a candidate for employment. They have earned their solid reputation and loyal clientele by providing accurate, honest information to both parties. They work thoroughly and quickly to ensure their clients find the best candidates.

PERSONNEL OPPORTUNITIES LTD. • 70 Yorkville Ave., Suite 8 • Toronto, ON • M5R 1B9 • Tel: 416-515-2073 • Fax: 416-515-8351 • E-mail: info@personnelopportunities.com • Internet: www.personnelopportunities.com • Contact: Linda Toster • Personnel Opportunities Ltd. provides contract, temporary and permanent personnel services. The range of applicants they place covers a broad spectrum: all office support staff, customer service, sales, computer specialists, financial/accounting personnel, as well as supervisory and management positions, both unilingual and bilingual.

PERSONNEL SEARCH LTD. • 883 Main St. • Moncton, NB • E1C 1G5 • Tel: 506-857-2156 • Fax: 506-857-9172 • E-mail: pscareer@nbnet.nb.ca • Internet: www.personnel-search.com • Since they made their first match in the Maritimes in 1978, their goal has been to achieve the perfect combination of a candidate's aspirations and an employer's expectations. This results in their clients and their candidates experiencing the employment success they deserve. Personnel Search Ltd. is a recruiter which specializes in many areas including accounting and finance, engineering, medicine, hospitality, hi-tech, sales and marketing.

PETER SHENFIELD & ASSOCIATES INC. • 507 Douglas Avenue • Toronto, ON • M5M 1H6 • Tel: 416-783-6390 • Fax: 416-783-8931 • E-mail: info@petershenfieldandassociates.com • Internet: www.petershenfieldandassociates.com • Their mission at Peter Shenfield & Associates Inc. is to help you in any way they can to successfully recruit the right people you need to grow your business, and help candiates find the right employer to fit their skills and experience.

PETRO STAFF INTERNATIONAL • 40 Sunpark Plaza S.E., Suite 208 • Calgary, AB • T2X 3X7 • Tel: 403-266-8988 • Fax: 403-262-1310 • E-mail: resumes@Petro-Staff.com • Internet: www. petro-staff.com • Established in 1983, Petro Staff International has long been one of Canada's pioneering global search and placement companies for the oil and gas, mining, finance, information systems, information technology, business development and medical industries. With their head office located in Calgary, Alberta, Petro Staff International is ideally located for sourcing and recruiting top quality personnel in the Canadian and American markets. Their team of dedicated and experienced staff provides expatriate recruitment and full training services to companies locally, nationally, within North America, Europe, the Middle East, South East Asia and South America.

PHASE V SEARCH • 1524 Summerhill Ave. • Montreal, QC • H3H 1B9 • Tel: 1-800-590-6991 • E-mail: info@phaseVsearch.com • Internet: www.phasevsearch.com • Phase V Search is a team of specialized headhunters that recruits executives, professionals and scientists for the biotech industry and related fields.

PIVOTAL INTEGRATED HR SOLUTIONS • 100 Milverton Dr., Suite 801 • Mississauga, ON • L5R 4H1 • Tel: 905-890-8558 • Fax: 905-507-9718 • E-mail: info@pivotalsolutions.com • Internet: www.itecc.com • Pivotal Integrated HR Solutions has over 24 years of combined experience and is a leading provider of broad-based HR services to small and mid-sized organizations. The firm partners with hundreds of companies to provide HR consulting, staffing, payroll and full-scale business process outsourcing.

PLACEMENT GROUP • 1027 Pandora Avenue • Victoria, BC • V8V 3P6 • Tel: 250-413-3111 • Fax: 250-413-3122 • E-mail: victoria@pgstaff.com • Internet: www.pgstaff.com • Placement Group is an ISO 9001:2000 certified, full service agency and is a division of Design Group Staffing Inc., a Canadian owned and operated company. They constantly seek innovative ways of improving the quality of their service and understand the individual needs and objectives of their customers. With leading edge technology and an experienced team of consultants, they provide their customers with access to highly qualified candidates and the certainty that their individual requirements will be met with the utmost professionalism and integrity.

333 Seymour St.	Main Floor	222 – 58th Ave. S.W.
Suite 1210	736 6th Ave. SW	Suite 111
Vancouver, BC	Calgary, AB	Calgary, AB
V6B 5A6	T2P 3T7	T2H 2S3
Tel: 604-689-7717	Tel: 403-777-9000	Tel: 403-301-5305
Fax: 604-683-6440	Fax: 403-777-9007	Fax: 403-301-5329
vancouver@pgstaff.com	calgary@pgstaff.com	calgary@pgstaff.com
Suite 201	4915 - 54th Street	
10080 Jasper Avenue	Second Floor	
Edmonton, AB	Red Deer, AB	
T5J 1V9	T4N 2G7	
Tel: 780-421-7702	Tel: 403-309-0757	
Fax: 780-426-3427	Fax: 403-309-0852	
edmonton@pgstaff.com	reddeer@pgstaff.com	

PLANET PERSONNEL AGENCY INC. • 55 Yonge St., Suite 603 • Toronto, ON • M5E 1J4 • Tel: 416-363-9888 • Fax: 416-363-9899 • E-mail: planet@planet4it.com • Internet: www.planet4it.com/planetweb.nsf • Canadian owned and operated, Planet Personnel Agency Inc. is a professional contract and permanent placement agency exclusive to the Information Technology industry, representing superior candidates with a comprehensive range of technology experience.

PMJ & ASSOCIATES • 15 Toronto St., Suite 602 • Toronto, ON • M5C 2E3 • Tel: 416-364-9997 • Fax: 416-364-8735 • E-mail: info@pmjpersonnel.com • Internet: www.pmjpersonnel.com • Contact: Allen Funk / Miriam Frankel • PMJ & Associates is a fully qualified, highly professional organization with over 25 years experience in the recruitment and search field. At PMJ they are a team of knowledgeable consultants who care about making the right match for you, on a permanent/temporary/contract basis in the specialized areas of accounting, finance, taxation, credit, insurance, bilingual services and information technology.

POMMEN GROUP • 33 Blackfoot Rd., Suite 800 • Sherwood Park, AB • T8A 4W5 • Tel: 780-497-8877 • Fax: 780-416-9091 • E-mail: dpommen@pommen.com • Internet: www.pommen.com • With significant experience at government and business levels and many contacts in business, municipal, health, educational, provincial government and the business community, this firm is well positioned to undertake a broad range of assignments. They practice the code of ethics and professional standards of Rotary International, CLGM, CAMA, ICMA, CHRP, ASQ and Alberta Certified Peer Health and Safety Auditor. The consulting company has evolved since 1990 serving over 300 clients in Western Canada and the territorial regions.

PORTAGE PERSONNEL LTÉE • 5 rue Laval, Bureau 201 • Hull, QC • J8X 3G6 • Tel: 819-770-6918 • Fax: 819-777-8367 • E-mail: info@portagepersonnel.ca • Internet: www.portagepersonnel.ca • Every employment opportunity they provide is unique. You'll face new goals, new objectives and a variety of challenges. They're committed to helping you meet these opportunities with confidence. That's why they profile your work experience, training, references and personal interests. For you, it means more rewarding and challenging work. For their customers, the result is better productivity. They offer opportunities in clerical, secretarial, receptionists, word processing, data entry operators, desktop publishing and administrative/executive assistants.

POSITIONWATCH • 60 Bloor St. W., Suite 1400 • Toronto, ON • M4W 3B8 • Tel: 416-962-9262 • E-mail: info@positionwatch.com • Internet: www.positionwatch.com • Positionwatch is one of Canada's premier Information Technology and high-tech job boards. Launched in 1995, Positionwatch is a pioneer of the online recruitment industry, bringing together skilled IT professionals and top employers since the early days of the Internet revolution. Today, despite significant fall-offs in successful Web-based business, Positionwatch is still going strong, providing employers and job seekers alike with value and functionality to make their connections faster and easier.

POSITIVE PEOPLE PLACEMENT INC. • 802 Main St., Suite 202 • Canmore, AB • T1W 2B7 • Tel: 403-678-0782 • Fax: 403-678-0785 • E-mail: info@positivepeopleplacement.com • Internet: www.positivepeopleplacement.com • Positive People Placement is a dynamic, growing company. They are the leading provider of recruitment services in the Bow Valley. They attribute their success to their responsiveness and focus on customer service. They offer the following services across a variety of industries: temporary work, permanent recruitment, temp-to-hire options, resume screening & candidate interviewing & selection, payroll services and HR consulting.

PRIME MANAGEMENT GROUP INC. • 365 Queens Ave. • London, ON • N6B 1X5 • Tel: 519-672-7710 • Fax: 519-672-5155 • E-mail: jobs2@pmg.on.ca • Internet: www.pmg.on.ca • Contact: Jay McKillop, Senior Recruitment Specialist • Prime Management Group is an Executive Search and Recruitment firm specializing in the placement of professionals for both management and non-management positions in many fields including: systems/technology, manufacturing, heath care, sales, retail, human resources, accounting and finance, engineering, administration and earth sciences.

PRIME SOURCE MANAGEMENT INC. • 95 Wellington St. W., Suite 1711 • Toronto, ON • M5J 2N7 • Tel: 416-362-6222 • Fax: 416-362-4506 • E-mail: hr@primesourcemgmt.com • Internet: www.primesourcemgmt.com • Whether you are an employer seeking high-caliber talent or a professional looking for your next career move, Prime Source is the partner you can count on to find that perfect fit. Their 20+ year track record is one of a trusted and efficient partner successfully uniting highly skilled, highly trained specialists with exciting assignments.

PRIME STAFFING SERVICES • 10335 - 95 Street • Edmonton, AB • T5H 2B6 • Tel: 780-424-3663 • Fax: 780-425-7572 • E-mail: info@primestaffing.ca • Internet: www.primestaffing.ca • Prime Staffing Services specializes in the recruiting of skilled labour for the construction and oilfield industry in Alberta.

PRINTLINK • 466 Speers Rd., Suite 314 • Oakville, ON • L6K 3W9 • Tel: 905-842-2600 • Fax: 800-856-8501 • E-mail: cdnjobs@printlink.com • Internet: www.printlink.com • PrintLink is North America's leading professional placement firm specializing in the graphic communications industry. Their managers offer discreet, confidential permanent placement for all printing, publishing, packaging and document management positions. Their objective is to make introductions that result in productive long-term employer/employee relationships.

PRIOR RESOURCE GROUP INC., THE • 50 Queen St. N., Suite 120 • Kitchener, ON • N2H 6P4 • Tel: 519-570-1100 • Fax: 519-579-2330 • E-mail: kitchener@priorresource.com • Internet: www.priorresource.com • Contact: Janice McVey • For more than 30 years, Prior Resource Group has offered innovative staffing solutions for executive, professional, technology, administrative, industrial and skilled trades positions to leading corporations in the Kitchener, Waterloo, Guelph and Cambridge areas.

485 Silvercreek Pkwy. N.	480 Hespeler Rd.	515 Park Rd. N.
Unit 9	Unit 9	Main Level
Guelph, ON	Cambridge, ON	Brantford, ON
N1H 7K5	N1R 7R9	N3R 7K8
Tel: 519-824-2428	Tel: 519-624-6800	Tel: 519-750-0063
Fax: 519-824-4540	Fax: 519-624-4300	Fax: 519-750-0779

PRIORITY PERSONNEL INC. • 281 Queen St. • Fredericton, NB • E3B 1A9 • Tel: 506-459-6668 • Fax: 506-459-5224 • E-mail: ppi@prioritypersonnel.nb.ca • Internet: www.hiredesk.net/clients/priority • Priority Personnel Inc. is an independent New Brunswick company. They have established a proven track record for providing high quality, cost effective services to businesses throughout the Province. Experienced professionals deliver a wide range of employment services.

PROAXIA • 5600, Boul. des Rossignols, Suite 103 • Laval, QC • H7G 5Z1 • Tel: 450-624-0304 • Fax: 450-624-0302 • E-mail: info@proaxia.com • Internet: www.proaxia.com • With the Proaxia's wide network of contacts within the I.T. industry, they can play a pro-active role for your career management. The Proaxia advantage includes their professional and confidential methods as well as their guarantee, unique in the industry.

2975, rue Hochelaga
Montreal, QC
H1W 1G1
Tel: 514-788-5750
Fax: 514-788-5760

PROBANK SERVICES • 6-2400 Dundas St. W., Suite 305 • Mississauga, ON • L5K 2R8 • Tel: 905-238-5648 • E-mail: info@probankservices.com • Internet: www.probankservices.com • Since its inception, Probank has provided employers with an effective means of streamlining their operation's resources and has assisted job seekers in their journey to find meaningful employment. As dedicated professionals, they offer you the best of both worlds -- service excellence and cost efficiency. Their motto, "Pay for Results - Not Time" is your guarantee of their commitment and integrity.

PROCOM SERVICES • 2323 Yonge St., Suite 400 • Toronto, ON • M4P 2C9 • Tel: 416-483-0766 • Fax: 416-483-8102 • E-mail: info@procom.ca • Internet: www.procom.ca • Procom is a leading provider of professional IT services to businesses and governments in North America. Privately held, Procom was launched 1978 by President Frank McCrea and is dedicated to consistently achieving superior client results by adapting to their unique needs. This dedication is matched by a rigorous approach to standardization that has resulted in ISO 9001-2000 certification for Procom's industry-leading processes. They specialize in virtually all industries, such as telecommunications, banking and financial, insurance, manufacturing, government and software development.

300 March Rd.	607 8th Ave. S.W.	1350 rue Sherbrooke Ouest
Suite 600	Suite 760	Bureau 1500
Kanata, ON	Calgary, AB	Montreal, QC
K2K 2E2	T2P 0A7	H3G 1J1
Tel: 613-270-9339	Tel: 403-571-7241	Tel: 514-731-7224
Fax: 613-270-9449	Fax: 403-571-7195	Fax: 514-731-7244
871 Victoria St. N.	1995 rue Frank-Carrel	289 Dufferin Ave.
Suite 226	Bureau 219	Suite 400
Kitchener, ON	Quebec, QC	London, ON
N2B 3S4	G1N 4H9	N6B 1Z1
Tel: 519-885-4331	Tel: 418-682-2097	Tel: 519-640-5326
Fax: 519-885-5308	Fax: 418-780-1963	Fax: 519-640-5704
10180 – 101 St.	1040 West Georgia St.	1959 Upper Water St.
Suite 1000	Suite 1750	Suite 1700
Edmonton, AB	Vancouver, BC	Halifax, NS
T5J 3S4	V6C 2G8	B3J 3N2
Tel: 780-489-8878	Tel: 604-633-1676	Tel: 902-482-1115
Fax: 780-489-8823	Fax: 604-669-5715	Fax: 902-482-1116

PROFILE PERSONNEL CONSULTANTS • 65 Queen St. W., Suite 1504 • Toronto, ON • M5H 2M5 • Tel: 416-363-1488 • Fax: 416-363-9125 • E-mail: profile@profileconsultants.com • Internet: www.profileconsultants.com • Profile Personnel specializes in highly qualified Permanent, Temporary and Contract office support, administrative, accounting and management positions. Their clients include well known national and global corporations located in downtown Toronto, Mississauga, Brampton, Scarborough and Markham. These companies have worked with Profile on a long term basis, with many new clients and candidates referred to us from their extensive network of contacts including Banking, Brerage, Financial, Mutual Funds, Accounting, High-Tech and Software, Management Consulting, Food and Beverage, Government, Insurance, Pharmaceutical, Professional and Non-Profit Associations, Media, Communications, Publishing, Manufacturing and Distribution.

PROFILE SEARCH SOLUTIONS • 2901 Bayview Ave., P.O. Box 91136 • North York, ON • M2K 2Y6 • Tel: 416-609-8070 • E-mail: resume@profilesearchsolutions.com • Internet: www. profilesearchsolutions.com • They at Profile Search Solutions pride themselves in offering a personalized consultative-approach to providing their candidates and clients valued results. They build long-term relationships with their customers. When working with you, they do not speculate and are very detailed in finding the best opportunity for your business and career. Over the years, many high-profile organizations have depended upon their service to play an important role in their future success.

PROHAD PERSONNEL • 8455 Boulevard Decarie, Suite 200 • Montreal, QC • H4P 2J2 • Tel: 514-286-1159 • Fax: 514-286-1169 • E-mail: info@prohad.com • Internet: www.prohad. com • Founded in 2000, Prohad Personnel Inc. is a human ressource agency specializing in the recruiting and hiring of skilled and competent employees. Their mission is to support your business in its search for reliable workers.

PROTEMPS • 4283 Village Centre Court, Suite 200 • Mississauga, ON • L4Z 1V3 • Tel: 905-270-0022 • Fax: 905-270-4222 • E-mail: mississauga@protempscanada.com • Internet: www. protempscanada.com • ProTemps is a full service personnel placement agency founded and incorporated in 1985, with more than 20 years of service specializing in staffing solutions for office and general labour needs. ProTemps offers services in temporary, contract and permanent recruitments.

824-5th Ave. S.W.	101 10011-109 Street	14 Nelson St. W.
Calgary, AB	Edmonton, AB	Suite 3
T2P 0N3	T5J 3S8	Brampton, ON
Tel: 403-264-9000	Tel: 780-425-9000	L6X 1B7
Fax: 403-261-4766	Fax: 780-426-3413	Tel: 905-451-8100
		Fax: 905-451-9586

PULSEHR INC. • 548 Aberfoyle Circle • Ottawa, ON • K2K 3R2 • Tel: 613-231-6308 • Fax: 613-231-2900 • E-mail: info@pulsehr.com • Internet: www.pulsehr.com • PulseHR Inc. is a privately-owned healthcare recruiting agency based in Ottawa, Ontario, Canada. They introduced their operation in August 2002 as an employment service for medical, nursing, healthcare and biotechnology professionals in North America and worldwide, with the focus on Canada and the United States.

QUALITY PERSONNEL INC. • 45 Bramalea Rd., Suite 205 • Brampton, ON • L6T 2W4 • Tel: 905-792-0088 • Fax: 905-792-7115 • E-mail: resume@qualitycareer.com • Internet: www. qualitycareer.com • Quality Personnel is a human resources firm providing permanent, contract and temporary staffing services to companies and organizations in the Greater Toronto Area, including Brampton, Mississauga, Etobice and North York. They provide access to employment opportunities including professional, administrative, technical, skilled labour, general labour and IT positions.

QUANTUM MANAGEMENT SERVICES LTD. • 55 University Ave., Suite 950 • Toronto, ON • M5J 2H7 • Tel: 416-366-3660 • Fax: 416-366-4363 • E-mail: toronto@quantum-qtr. com • Internet: www.quantum-qtr.com • Quantum is involved in the recruitment of all levels of permanent and temporary positions. They specialize in the areas of office support, and management professionals. Quantum also works in the recruitment of information systems and data processing professionals through a special division called Quantum EDP Division.

275 Slater St.	2000 McGill College Ave.	1 Holiday Rd., West Tower
Suite 500	Suite 1800	Suite 400
Ottawa, ON	Montreal, QC	Pointe-Claire, QC
K1P 5H9	H3A 3H3	H9R 5N3
Tel: 613-237-8888	Tel: 514-842-5555	Tel: 514-694-9994
Fax: 613-230-7711	Fax: 514-849-8846	Fax: 514-694-0269

QUANTUM TECHNOLOGY RECRUITING INC. • 2000 av McGill College, Bureau 1800 • Montréal, QC • H3A 3H3 • Tel: 514-842-5555 • Fax: 514-849-8846 • E-mail: montreal@ quantum-qtr.com • Internet: www.quantum-qtr.com • In today's fast-evolving, technology-driven markets, achieving synergy among people, skill sets and objectives has never been more crucial. Quantum makes it happen. They combine vision, expertise and experience with entrepreneurial spirit to solve the most complex staffing challenges quickly, efficiently and professionally.

55 University Avenue	275 Slater St.
Suite 950	Suite 500
Toronto, ON	Ottawa, ON
M5J 2H7	K1P 5H9
Tel: 416-366-3660	Tel: 613-237-8888
Fax: 416-366-4363	Fax: 613-230-7711

QUESTUS RECRUITMENT CORP. • 1015 - 4th St. S.W., Suite 1060 • Calgary, AB • T2R 1J4 • Tel: 403-232-1333 • Fax: 403-263-4893 • E-mail: mail@questus.ca • Internet: www.questus. ca • Contact: Morgan Arndt, President • Questus Recruitment is widely respected as one of Western Canada's leading specialists in the recruitment of sales, management, I.T. and technical professionals for career opportunities in the following sectors: business to business, information technology, telecommunications, consumer packaged goods, medical/pharmaceutical, industrial/technical, retail management, finance/accounting/legal, human resources and office administration.

QUINTAL & ASSOCIATES • 354 Notre-Dame St. W., Suite 200 • Montreal, QC • H2Y 1T9 • Tel: 514-284-7444 • Fax: 514-284-9290 • E-mail: administration@quintal.ca • Internet: www. quintal.ca • The company was founded in 1991 by Yves Quintal with the clear objective of offering integrated services related to human resources issues. Unlike traditional recruiting agencies and "head-hunters", they offer: Organisational Development services, Selection & Recruitment services, Customized training programs, Career Transition services and, through their affiliated company Gen-X Human Capital Inc., Contract Representation services.

RAY & BERNDSTON / ROBERTSON-SURRETTE • Cornwallis House 6th Floor, 5475 Spring Garden Rd. • Halifax, NS • B3J 3T2 • Tel: 902-421-1330 • Fax: 902-425-1108 • E-mail: halifax@ rayberndston.ca • Internet: www.rayberndtson.ca • Ray & Berndtson/Robertson Surrette was created in year 2000 as a result of a merger of two of Canada's leading executive search firms. Founded in 1975, the Halifax office has strategically developed into one of the largest executive search practices in Atlantic Canada. They are a search firm that specializes in finding leaders - people whose performance will have a marked affect on an organization. With a focus on finding the very best, Ray & Berndtson/Robertson Surrette conduct exhaustive and pervasive searches on a retainer basis. In addition to Executive Search, they also provide selection and other search-related consulting services.

1050 West Pender St.	29 Beechwood Ave.	Royal Bank Plaza
Suite 710	Suite 200	200 Bay St.
Vancouver, BC	Ottawa, ON	Suite 3150, South Tower
V6E 3S7	K1M 1M2	Toronto, ON
Tel: 604-685-0261	Tel: 613-749-9909	M5J 2J3
Fax: 604-684-7988	Fax: 613-749-9599	Tel: 416-366-1990
		Fax: 416-366-7353
1250 W. Rene Levesque	250 – 6th Ave. S.W.	Baine Johnston Centre
Suite 3925	Suite 1600	10 Fort William Place
Montreal, QC	Calgary, AB	Suite 101
H3B 4W8	T2P 3H7	St. John's, NF
Tel: 514-937-1000	Tel: 403-410-6700	A1C 1K4
Fax: 514-937-1264	Fax: 403-410-7523	Tel: 709-722-6890
		Fax: 709-722-8685

RCM TECHNOLOGIES • 6620 Kitimat Rd. • Mississauga, ON • L5N 2B8 • Tel: 905-821-1616 • Fax: 905-821-1613 • Internet: www.rcmt.ca • RCM Technologies is a leading provider of IT Business Solutions and Professional Engineering Services to over 1,000 clients in the commercial and government sectors. RCM partners with clients to define, implement, and manage a broad range of technologies across multiple platforms, systems, and networks. Their broad geographic presence ensures that a proven and reliable tactical and strategic capability is available and deployable virtually everywhere in North America.

895 Brock Road S.
Pickering, ON
L1W 3C1
Tel: 905-837-8333
Fax: 905-837-8248

REACHING E-QUALITY EMPLOYMENT SERVICES • 1200 Portage Ave., Suite 305 • Winnipeg, MB • R3G 0T5 • Tel: 204-947-1609 • Fax: 204-947-2932 • E-mail: info@re-es.org • Internet: www.re-es.org • Reaching E-Quality Employment Services (REES) is a non-profit organization with charitable status. REES offers a wide range of services both to job seekers and employers hiring workers with disabilities. REES offers assistance in career exploration, resume development and cover letter writing as well as interview, job search and employment maintenance skills.

RECAREER.COM • 3500 Dufferin St., Suite 401 • Toronto, ON • M3K 1N2 • Tel: 416-630-7771 • Fax: 416-631-8144 • E-mail: info@recareer.com • Internet: www.recareer.com • Founded in 1999, Recareer was established to offer superior service for staffing in the GTA region. Since their inception, they have grown to offer their services all across Canada. At Recareer qualified recruiters have been on board since their beginning. Recareer is a boutique generalist staffing firm. Their focus ranges from warehouse personnel to sales executives.

RECRU SCIENCE INC. • 32 St-Charles W., Suite 370 • Longueuil, QC • J4H 1C6 • Tel: 450-463-0903 • Fax: 450-463-0324 • E-mail: info@recruscience.com • Internet: www.recruscience.com • Recru Science Inc. was founded in 1997 to create a recruitment platform for the scientific community and the Canadian science based industry. Their mission is to provide their customers with quality service by identifying their professional needs and by screening their candidates accordingly. Their consultants are well trained with in-depth technical knowledge to verify scientific information while respecting each recruitment assignment.

RENAISSANCE PERSONNEL INC. • 300 Grand Ave. W. • Chatham, ON • N7L 1C1 • Tel: 519-351-1957 • Fax: 519-351-5254 • E-mail: chatham@renaperson.com • Internet: www.renaperson.com • Renaissance is a retained by reputable companies throughout Ontario/Canada to offer a wide range of career opportunities.

3200 Deziel Dr.
Suite 217
Windsor, ON
N8W 5K8
Tel: 519-944-1066
Fax: 519-944-2075
windsor@renaperson.com

390 Commissioners Rd. W.
Suite 201
London, ON
N6J 1Y3
Tel: 519-472-8822
Fax: 519-472-0199
london@renaperson.com

RENARD HOSPITALITY SEARCH CONSULTANTS • 121 Richmond St. W., Suite 500 • Toronto, ON • M5H 2K1 • Tel: 416-364-8325 • Fax: 416-364-4924 • E-mail: consultants@renardinternational.com • Internet: www.renardinternational.com • Over the last thirty years, Renard Hospitality has provided services for most major hotel corporations, independent hotel groups, some of the top international restaurant companies, many industrial and commercial multinationals, and government agencies. Renard Hospitality has dedicated itself to becoming one of the leading human resource search firms exclusively serving the hospitality industry worldwide. Their extensive database includes candidates and employment opportunities in such areas as culinary, industrial catering, senior management, food and beverage management, cruiseships, casino and many more. Renard Hospitality does charge a fee to be listed in their database.

REQUEST PERSONNEL SERVICES INC. • 350 Rutherford Rd. S., Plaza 2, Suite 100 • Brampton, ON • L6W 4N6 • Tel: 905-459-3110 • Fax: 905-459-3103 • E-mail: jobs@requestpersonnel. com • Internet: www.requestpersonnel.com • Request Personnel Services Inc. is a full-service temporary and permanent placement firm offering a range of staffing solutions to employers and job seekers.

RESOURCE PROFESSIONALS INC. • 736 - 6th Ave. S.W., Suite 1020 • Calgary, AB • T2P 3T7 • Tel: 403-269-3044 • Fax: 403-264-8509 • E-mail: rpi@resourceprof.com • Internet: www. resourceprof.com • Resource Professionals Inc. has access to the best available professional people for positions within a wide range of disciplines. Such expertise includes senior and middle management; system specialists, engineers, geologists, geophysicists, technologists, and technicians. They are also experts in the areas of finance, marketing, accounting, law and human resources; and people with specific expertise such as international experience or language abilities.

RIS RESOURCE INFORMATION SYSTEMS INC. • 150 York St., Suite 1910 • Toronto, ON • M5H 3S5 • Tel: 416-360-1430 • Fax: 416-360-1431 • Internet: www.riscan.com • RIS Resource Information Systems Inc. is a Canadian information systems consulting firm. Started in 1979, RIS has grown to become a prominent information technology consulting company, with over 300 staff in Calgary, Regina and Toronto. Their experience is in the areas of application development, application maintenance, contract and consulting services.

Eau Claire II	1821 Scarth St.	10665 Jasper Ave. N.W.
Penthouse Suite 1700	2nd Floor	Suite 1150
521-3rd Avenue S.W.	Regina, SK	Edmonton, AB
Calgary, AB	S4P 2G9	T5J 3S9
T2P 3T3	Tel: 306-359-0668	Tel: 780-421-8003
Tel: 403-263-2272	Fax: 306-757-1865	Fax: 780-421-8065
Fax: 403-266-4281		

ROAN INTERNATIONAL INC. • 2155 Dunwin Dr., Unit 4 • Mississauga, ON • L5L 4M1 • Tel: 905-820-3511 • Fax: 905-820-0679 • E-mail: info@roan.ca • Internet: www.roan.ca • Roan specializes in recruiting engineering and technical personnel. They recruit personnel locally and internationally to fill either temporary assignments or permanent positions. They have placed thousands of highly skilled candidates with leading corporations in the industries they serve.

ROBERT HALF FINANCE & ACCOUNTING • 1 Place Ville Marie, Suite 2330 • Montreal, QC • H3B 3M5 • Tel: 514-875-8585 • Fax: 514-875-8066 • E-mail: montreal@roberthalffinance.com • Internet: www.roberthalffinance.com • Founded in 1948, Robert Half Finance & Accounting, a division of Robert Half International Inc., is the world's first and largest specialized financial recruiting service. Robert Half Finance & Accounting's recruiting managers have backgrounds in the industry, which affords them a unique advantage in working with clients and candidates. Robert Half Finance & Accounting helps clients locate qualified financial professionals for a variety of positions.

ROBERT HALF FINANCE & ACCOUNTING continued

15127 100th Avenue
Suite 302
Surrey, BC
V3R 0N9
Tel: 604-581-6636
Fax: 604-581-4225

10180-101 Street
Suite 1280
Edmonton, AB
T5J 3S4
Tel: 780-424-4220
Fax: 780-423-1581

1 Robert Speck Pkwy
Suite 940
Mississauga, ON
L4Z 3M3
Tel: 905-273-4229
Fax: 905-273-6217

181 Bay St.
Suite 820
Toronto, ON
M5J 2T3
Tel: 416-350-2330
Fax: 416-350-3573

1, Place ville Marie
Suite 2330
Montreal, QC
H3B 3M5
Tel: 514-875-8585
Fax: 514-875-8066

1055 Dunsmuir St.
Suite 724
Vancouver, BC
V7X 1L4
Tel: 604-688-7572
Fax: 604-687-7533

201 Portage Ave.
Suite 2400
Winnipeg, MB
R3B 3K6
Tel: 204-957-7110
Fax: 204-957-5385

5140 Yonge St.
Suite 1500
North York, ON
M2N 6L7
Tel: 416-226-2538
Fax: 416-226-4498

360 Albert St.
Suite 520
Ottawa, ON
K1R 7X7
Tel: 613-236-4253
Fax: 613-236-2159

755 St. Jean Boulevard
Suite 404
Pointe-Claire, QC
H9R 5M9
Tel: 514-694-9609
Fax: 514-694-3460

888 3rd St. S.W.
Suite 4200
Calgary, AB
T2P 5C5
Tel: 403-237-9363
Fax: 403-264-0934

5515 North Service Rd.
Suite 302
Burlington, ON
L7L 6G4
Tel: 905-319-7779
Fax: 905-319-2095

175 Commerce Valley Dr. W.
Suite 300
Thornhill, ON
L3T 7P6
Tel: 905-709-2458
Fax: 905-709-3664

80 King St. S.
Suite 206
Waterloo, ON
N2J 1P5
Tel: 519-884-4701
Fax: 519-884-4632

ROBERT HALF TECHNOLOGY • 5140 Yonge St., Suite 1500 • North York, ON • M2N 6L7 • Tel: 416-227-0581 • Fax: 416-226-4498 • E-mail: northyork@roberthalftechnology.com • Internet: www.roberthalftechnology.com • Robert Half Technology offers flexible staffing solutions to premier organizations worldwide that require technical expertise on demand. Projects range from complex e-business and web development initiatives to enterprise wide application development and technical system support. The technology professionals they deploy, on either a contract, contract-to-hire or full-time basis, include software developers, project managers, database specialists, networking and internetworking specialists, and help desk support professionals.

1055 Dunsmuir St.
Suite 724
Vancouver, BC
V7X 1L4
Tel: 604-688-5256
Fax: 604-687-7533

888 3rd St. S.W.
Suite 4200
Calgary, AB
T2P 5C5
Tel: 403-237-7500
Fax: 403-264-0934

10180-101 Street
Suite 1280
Edmonton, AB
T5J 3S4
Tel: 780-426-6642
Fax: 780-423-1581

ROBERT HALF TECHNOLOGY continued

1 Robert Speck Pkwy	360 Albert St.	175 Commerce Valley Dr. W.
Suite 940	Suite 520	Suite 300
Mississauga, ON	Ottawa, ON	Thornhill, ON
L4Z 3M3	K1R 7X7	L3T 7P6
Tel: 905-273-4092	Tel: 613-236-7442	Tel: 905-763-2851
Fax: 905-273-6217	Fax: 613-236-8301	Fax: 905-709-3664

P.O. Box 824
181 Bay St., Suite 820
Toronto, ON
M5J 2T3
Tel: 416-350-8143
Fax: 416-350-3573

ROBERT L. HOLMES PROFESSIONAL PLACEMENT SERVICES INC. • 264-266 Water St. N. • Cambridge, ON • N1R 3C2 • Tel: 519-621-4373 • Fax: 519-621-4084 • E-mail: careers@ robertlholmes.com • Internet: www.robertlholmes.com • Robert L. Holmes Professional Placement Services Inc. has been serving the manufacturing sector of Ontario since 1986. They are in the business of, and not limited to, providing clients in the plastic, rubber and metal industries with the best candidates to meet their diverse recruiting needs.

ROBERT W. HORT & ASSOCIATES • 620 Wilson Ave., Suite 230 • Toronto, ON • M3K 1Z3 • Tel: 416-636-3933 • Fax: 416-636-8113 • E-mail: info@canadausemployment.com • Internet: www.canadausemployment.com • RWH & Associates® specializes in finding suitable employment in Canada and the United States for professionals in all fields of employment, graduating students and numerous other qualified employment seeking individuals wishing to emigrate (or relocate) to (or within) Canada and the United States. They can be reached Toll Free in North America: 1-800-600-4091.

ROBERTSON HUMAN ASSET MANAGEMENT INC. • 1455 Lakeshore Rd., Suite 204 South • Burlington, ON • L7S 2J1 • Tel: 905-333-9188 • Fax: 905-333-9148 • E-mail: reception@ robertsonhumanasset.com • Internet: www.robertsonhumanasset.com • Robertson specializes in helping organizations and individuals maximize their human assets in four distinct ways: professional recruitment, psychometric profiling, training and development, coaching and consulting. Robertson's Associates include skilled Nurses, Sales professionals, Managers, Trainers and Human Resource consultants. They specialize in the Healthcare, Information Technology, Pharmaceutical, Medical, Dental, Surgical, and manufacturing industries. Each Associate brings work experience, professional designation and a unique skill set to their team.

ROD TURPIN & ASSOCIATES • 10308 - 121 Street • Edmonton, AB • T5N 1K8 • Tel: 780-944-1650 • Fax: 780-452- 2576 • E-mail: adam@rtastaffing.com • Internet: www.rtastaffing.com • As staffing specialists for clients in the engineering, construction, fabrication and natural resources sectors, Rod Turpin & Associates provides recruiting and selection services for permanent employment, professional and technical specialists on a contract hire basis, staff planning for engineering and construction projects, and labour market information to client companies.

ROEVIN TECHNICAL PEOPLE • 6860 Century Avenue, Suite 2002 • Mississauga, ON • L5N 2W5 • Tel: 905-826-4155 • Fax: 905-826-5336 • E-mail: resumes@roevin.ca • Internet: www. roevin.ca • The Roevin Group, founded over 30 years ago, is one of the largest suppliers of skilled technical and professional manpower and currently comprises 7 offices in Canada linked via a sophisticated computer network, as well as 18 offices in the UK, one in the USA, and one in Norway. As a wholly owned subsidiary of Adecco, the world's largest employment business and a public company, Roevin operates at the highest standards of professionalism within their industry.

10115 – 100A St. N.W.	2912 Memorial Dr. S.E.	9816 Hardin St.
Suite 200	Suite 303	Suite 104B
Edmonton, AB	Calgary, AB	Fort McMurray, AB
T6J 2W2	T2A 6R1	T9H 4K3
Tel: 780-420-6232	Tel: 403-264-3283	Tel: 780-714-6554
Fax: 780-423-3679	calgary@roevin.ca	Fax: 780-714-6443
edmonton@roevin.ca		ftmc@roevin.ca

265 North Front St.	39 King St.
Suite 103	Level 3
Sarnia, ON	Saint John, NB
N7T 7X1	E2L 4W3
Tel: 519-383-6630	Tel: 506-638-0020 x27
Fax: 519-383-6631	dcybulski@roevin.ca
sarnia@roevin.ca	

ROSSI & ASSOCIATES INC. • 1400-1500 West Georgia St. • Vancouver, BC • V6G 2Z6 • Tel: 604-683-3755 • Fax: 604-683-3721 • E-mail: resumes@rossipeople.com • Internet: www.rossipeople.com • The owner absorbed all of the lessons from her sales experience and education and carried them forward as a foundation for Rossi & Associates in 1980. She added formal training in Job Descriptions, Organizational Planning, and Compensation. In the twenty-three years since that time she has developed the only recruitment practice in Western Canada dedicated to business to business sales executives.

ROSTIE & ASSOCIATES INC. • Waterpark Place, Suite 1205, 20 Bay St., 11th Floor • Toronto, ON • M5J 2N8 • Tel: 416-777-0780 • Fax: 416-777-0451 • E-mail: rostie@rostie.com • Internet: www.rostie.com • Rostie & Associates Inc. was formed in Toronto and incorporated in Boston, to service the recruitment demand for highly skilled professionals, as companies positioned themselves to succeed in a new global IT environment. For the North American hi-tech marketplace their staffing professionals provide expertise in recruiting for progressive careers in the computer industry.

RUSSELL REYNOLDS ASSOCIATES • Scotia Plaza, 40 King Street West, Suite 3410 • Toronto, ON • M5H 3Y2 • Tel: 416-364-3355 • Fax: 416-364-5174 • E-mail: pcantor@russellreynolds. com • Internet: www.russellreynolds.com • Founded in 1969, Russell Reynolds Associates is a global executive recruitment and management assessment firm that delivers solutions to organizational challenges through the recruitment of exceptional leaders. Based in 33 wholly owned offices, their associates work in more than 40 practice areas to provide specialized industry and functional expertise to clients in major markets around the world.

RUTHERFORD INTERNATIONAL ESG • 200 Bay St., Royal Bank Plaza, North Tower, Suite 1650 • Toronto, ON • M5J 2J2 • Tel: 416-250-6300 • E-mail: info@rutherfordinternational. com • Internet: www.rutherfordinternational.com • Rutherford International ESG is an integrated executive resources firm providing advice on a broad range of management-based human affairs. They possess a keen interest in issues related to executive leadership, corporate governance, organizational effectiveness, staffing, compensation design and the measurement of performance. Their core competency is to assist clients to identify, evaluate, attract, apply and retain superior board, executive and management talent.

RUTHERFORD INTERNATIONAL ESG continued

144 4th Ave. S.W.
Sun Life Plaza, Suite 1600
Calgary, AB
T2P 3N4
Tel: 403-698-8266

S. TANNER & ASSOCIATES INC. • P.O. Box 91 • Mount Forest, ON • N0G 2L0 • Tel: 519-323-1474 • E-mail: resume@tannerinc.net • Internet: www.tannerinc.net • S. Tanner & Associates Inc. is a professional search firm specializing in the recruitment of high caliber personnel to satisfy the most demanding of staffing requirements in the key areas of engineering, operations management and logistics.

S.I. SYSTEMS LTD. • 1015 4 St. S.W., Suite 330 • Calgary, AB • T2R 1J4 • Tel: 403-450-5174 • Fax: 403-450-5175 • E-mail: info@sisystems.com • Internet: www.sisystems.com • Contact: Joanne Shaver • S.i. Systems is a national supplier of contract I.T. professionals to businesses across Canada with offices in Calgary, Edmonton, Ottawa and Vancouver. Working with a growing database of over 29,035 active I.T. contractors across Canada, S.i. Systems consistently provide the best person for each new contract requirement.

4170 Still Creek Dr.	1290 Broad St.	10130 103 St.
Suite 160	Suite 201	Suite 1350
Burnaby, BC	Victoria, BC	Edmonton, AB
V5C 6C6	V8W 2A5	T5J 3N9
Tel: 604-669-1387	Tel: 250-414-7455	Tel: 780-424-3999
Fax: 604-669-2576	Fax: 250-383-2978	Fax: 780-426-0626
71 Bank St.	90 Eglinton Ave. E.	
4th Floor	Suite 970	
Ottawa, ON	Toronto, ON	
K1P 5N2	M4P 2Y3	
Tel: 613-786-3290	Tel: 416-485-8001	
Fax: 613-786-3291	Fax: 416-485-1711	

SAFETY FIRST TRAINING • 6760 Davand Dr., Unit 3 • Mississauga, ON • L5T 2L9 • Tel: 905-672-3600 • Fax: 905-672-3335 • E-mail: info@safetyfirsttraining.ca • Internet: www.staffing-training.com • Safety First Training specializes in Work Place Health and Safety, Transportation Safety and Compliance. Safety First Training and Support Services today have assisted and provide ongoing services to over 310 companies. Their clients are from all industries, transportation, construction, distribution and manufacturing sector.

SALES SEARCH • 17 Goodwill Ave. • Toronto, ON • M3H 1V5 • Tel: 416-636-3660 • Fax: 416-638-9997 • E-mail: info@salessearch-toronto.com • Internet: www.salessearch-toronto.com • Sales Search is a recruiting and search firm which acts on behalf of their client companies to search for employee candidates and submit the most appropriate for potential hire by their clients.

SAPPHIRE TECHNOLOGIES• 60 Bloor St. W., Suite 1400 • Toronto, ON • M4W 3B8 • Tel: 416-962-9262 • Fax: 416-962-4489 • Internet: www.sapphireca.com • Sapphire Technologies Canada Limited (formerly CNC Global Limited) is the country's leading provider of IT staffing services. They help organizations achieve their goals through improved access to their most important resource - talent. They also help candidates and consultants create rewarding careers.

Since 1981, they have worked with organizations across North America to create highly successful solutions for full-time recruitment, contract staffing, payroll management and contact centre staffing. As part of the Vedior network, they also provide access to global expertise in specialty staffing, vendor management, recruitment advertising, employer branding, HR communications and Recruitment Process Augmentation.

609 Granville St.
Suite 630
Vancouver, BC
V7Y 1G5
Tel: 604-687-5919
Fax: 604-687-5397

1027 Pandora Ave.
Victoria, BC
V8V 3P6
Tel: 250-383-4004
Fax: 1-866-815-3422

Energy Plaza
311-6th Avenue SW
Suite 1275
Calgary, AB
T2P 3H2
Tel: 403-263-4501
Fax: 403-263-4502

10088 102 Ave.
Suite 801
Edmonton, AB
T5J 2Z1
Tel: 780-497-7750
Fax: 780-497-7760

177 Lombard Avenue
Suite 701
Winnipeg, MB
R3B 0W5
Tel: 204-942-1208
Fax: 204-204-0251

675 Queen St. W.
Kitchener, ON
N2M 1A1
Tel: 519-579-9727
Fax: 519-579-5482

1600 Carling Ave.
Suite 410
Ottawa, ON
K1Z 1G3
Tel: 613-727-1411
Fax: 613-727-1412

1 West Pearce St.
Suite 307
Richmond Hill, ON
L4B 3K3
Tel: 905-882-1044
Fax: 905-882-1230

1001 de Maisonneuve West
Suite 1510
Montreal, QC
H3A 3C8
Tel: 514-845-5775
Fax: 514-845-0774

1809 Barrington St.
Suite 708
Halifax, NS
B3J 3K8
Tel: 902-444-7750
Fax: 1-888-333-9190

SEARCH ASSOCIATES INC. • 113 Front St. E. • Toronto, ON • M5A 4S5 • Tel: 416-363-4040 • Fax: 416-363-4616 • E-mail: info@searchassociatesinc.com • Internet: www.searchassociatesinc. com • Search Associates Inc. is a human resources management company specializing in the field of Information Technology. Search Associates Inc. provides recruiting services to client companies and to job seekers matching positions with people.

SEARCH WEST INC. • 595 Howe St., Suite 1125 • Vancouver, BC • V6C 2T5 • Tel: 604-684-4237 • Fax: 604-684-4240 • E-mail: careers@searchwest.ca • Internet: www.searchwest.ca • Their motto is bringing people and opportunities together and since 1990 they have been successful in matching hundreds of Sales and Marketing professionals with exciting and rewarding career opportunities. Some of the industries they recruit for include: Telecommunications, Executive & Management, High Tech & IT, Medical & Pharmaceutical, Business & Professional Services, Consumer Products, Dental, Veterinary, Financial Services, Utilities & Natural Resources, Education & Human Resources, Retail Management, Sports Entertainment, Advertising/Media, Not-For-Profit, Industrial and Transportation and Logistics.

SELECTION GROUP, THE • 701 Evans Ave., Suite 705 • M9C 1A3 • Tel: 416-236-3635 • Fax: 416-236-5395 • E-mail: jobs@theselectiongroup.com • Internet: www.theselectiongroup. com • Contact: Susan M. Strickland • They are a Staffing Service specializing in the recruitment and placement of professional and office support staff at a variety of levels and in a multitude of disciplines. Their Recruitment Specialists offer in-depth interviewing, screening, reference checking, and skill testing (ability/aptitude) for all candidates. They are a community-based company proudly serving clients and candidates in the west end of Toronto including Mississauga, Etobicoke, Brampton, Oakville, North York, Woodbridge, and Concord since 1991.

SIMON A. BULL & ASSOCIATES • P.O. Box 20046, Cambridge Centre • Cambridge, ON • N1R 8C8 • Tel: 519-622-9000 • Fax: 519-740-3439 • E-mail: careers@simonbull.com • Internet: www.simonbull.com • Contact: Simon A. Bull • Simon A. Bull & Associates are recruiting specialists in the automotive industry. They offer careers in automotive parts manufacturing.

SIMPSON ASSOCIATES • 139 Parkside Dr. • Port Moody, BC • V3H 4K5 • Tel: 604-461-6101 • Toll Free: 1-800-419-7473 • E-mail: info@djsimpson.com • Internet: www.djsimpson.com • Simpson Associates, now in its 20th year of operation, is a technically specialized management consulting firm based in Mississauga, Ontario. Their specific focus on operations restructuring is supported with a broad range of resident expertise in the areas of psychometric assessment, mission profiling and executive coaching. Over the years, they have had the opportunity of working with a wide range of well established companies in the manufacturing, engineering, retail, high tech and service sectors.

SLATE PERSONNEL LTD. • 10621 100 Ave. N.W., Suite 303 • Edmonton, AB • T5J 0B3 • Tel: 780-424-7528 • Fax: 780-426-7528 • E-mail: resumes@slatepersonnel.com • Internet: www. slatepersonnel.com • Contact: Margaret Slate • Slate Personnel has been matching employees to employers since 1964. With over 35 years of experience and labour market knowledge, Slate is one of today's leading agencies servicing Edmonton and surrounding areas with temporary, permanent and contract placements. Slate's professional recruiters are experienced in providing temporary, permanent and contract placement services for a variety of occupations, including accounting, secretarial and administration, call centre associates, computer/IT specialists, credit/collections, engineering, human resources, legal, sales/marketing, technicians/technologists, warehouse and inventory.

SOLUTIONS • 225 Pitt St. • Cornwall, ON • K6J 3P8 • Tel: 613-936-2728 • Fax: 613-936-6685 • E-mail: clientservices@wehire4U.ca • Internet: www.solutions.on.ca • Solutions can provide qualified staff ranging from professionals to general labourers. They actively recruit for industries, institutions, government and businesses throughout the area. Traditional contract staffing, recruitment of full time staff, Corporate Staffing Services (long-term contract or employee leasing), job search training and resume preparation are provided to the Cornwall and area community.

SOS PERSONNEL (SARNIA) INC. • 189 Wellington St., Unit 2 • Sarnia, ON • N2T 1G6 • Tel: 519-336-6620 • Fax: 519-336-7531 • E-mail: sos@slicc.net • Internet: www.sospersonnelinc. com • SOS Personnel (Sarnia) Inc. provide permanent, temporary and contract work. They have a strong 40 year history serving the industries of Sarnia and area, providing a solid cash base which allows comfort in growth of payroll and related expenses, including benefits for employees.

SPHERION • 4 Cedar Pointe, Unit D • Barrie, ON • L4N 5R7 • Tel: 705-735-1106 • Internet: www.spherion.com • As a pioneer in the temporary staffing industry, Spherion has screened and placed millions of individuals in flexible and full-time jobs that have ranged from administrative and industrial positions to a host of professions that include accounting, finance, sales, marketing, manufacturing, engineering, law, human resources and technology.

SPHERION continued

5951 No 3 Road
Suite 628
Richmond, BC
V6X 2E3
Tel: 604-273-5474

700 - 6 Ave. S.W.
Suite 110
Calgary, AB
T2P 1H4
Tel: 403-266-1082

2 County Court Blvd.
Suite 432
Brampton, ON
L6W 3W8
Tel: 905-450-2224

235 King St. E.
Main Floor
Kitchener, ON
N2G 4N5
Tel: 519-742-5400

5450 Explorer Dr.
Suite 102
Mississauga, ON
L4W 5N1
Tel: 905-361-1550

2100 Ellesmere Rd.
Suite 103
Scarborough, ON
M1H 3B7
Tel: 416-431-6077

4950 Yonge St.
Suite 1010
Toronto, ON
M2N 6K1
Tel: 416-250-1500

77 Vaughan Harvey Blvd.
Suite 102
Moncton, NB
E1C 0K2
Tel: 506-383-6060

1090 West Georgia St.
Suite 950
Vancouver, BC
V6E 3V7
Tel: 604-688-9556

10104 103 Ave.
Suite 101
Edmonton, AB
T5J 0H8
Tel: 780-426-6666

350 Rutherford Rd. S., Plaza II
Suite 110
Brampton, ON
L6W 4N6
Tel: 905-452-7110

171 Queens Ave.
Suite 300
London, ON
N6A 5J7
Tel: 519-673-5574

419 King St.
Suite 601
Oshawa, ON
L1J 2K5
Tel: 905-579-2911

655 Bay St.
Suite 113
Toronto, ON
M5G 2K4
Tel: 416-596-3434

111 Consumers Dr.
Whitby, ON
L1N 5Z5
Tel: 905-430-4258

1791 Barrington St.
Suite 1130
Halifax, NS
B3J 3K9
Tel: 902-422-9675

730 View St.
Suite 420
Victoria, BC
V8W 3Y7
Tel: 250-383-1389

275 Notre Dame Ave.
Winnipeg, MB
R3B 1P1
Tel: 204-943-5211

3060 Mainway Dr.
Suite 201
Burlington, ON
L7W 1A2
Tel: 905-331-1530

77 City Centre Dr.
Suite 601
Mississauga, ON
L4Z 1S1
Tel: 905-896-1055

440 Laurier Ave. W.
Suite 120
Ottawa, ON
K1R 7X6
Tel: 613-782-2333

2 Bloor St. W.
Suite 1505
Toronto, ON
M4W 3E2
Tel: 416-944-3434

625, av. President-Kennedy
Bureau 300
Montreal, QC
H3A 1K2
Tel: 514-874-8014

SPI CONSULTANTS • 1455 Youville Dr., Suite 209 • Ottawa, ON • K1K 4H4 • Tel: 613-590-1503 • Fax: 613-824-3593 • E-mail: general@spi.ca • Internet: www.spi.ca • SPI Consultants has built a reputation for quality service since 1983. As their company has grown and increased its reach, they have maintained a commitment to high performance and unsurpassed industry knowledge. They offer candidates and clients personal service, confidentiality, and the most ethical standards in the industry.

ST. ARMOUR & ASSOCIATES • 302 The East Mall, Suite 103 • Etobicoke, ON • M9B 6C7 • Tel: 416-626-6151 • Fax: 416-620-7189 • E-mail: careers@st-amour.com • Internet: www. st-amour.com • Contact: Jeff Courey • St. Armour & Associates is involved in the recruiting of sales, marketing and technical personnel. Industry areas specialized in include pharmaceutical, medical and surgical, chemical, industrial, commercial, and consumer packaged goods.

666 Sherbrooke St. W.
Suite 2000
Montreal, PQ
H3A 1E7
Tel: 514-288-7400
Tel: 514-288-6745
info@st-amour.com

STAFFWORKS LTD. • 1235 Bay Street, Suite 905 • Toronto, ON • M5R 3K4 • Tel: 416-927-7575 • Fax: 416-927-7806 • E-mail: info@staffworkscanada.com • Internet: www.staffworkscanada. com • Contact: Loni Attrell, Recruitment Manager • At Staffworks, partnering with their clients means understanding the challenges and market conditions they face every day. It means actively listening and responding with business solutions that work. It is their commitment and consistent attention to detail that earns us the trust and respect of their customers, day in and day out.

STARDOT CONSULTING INC. • 633 - 6th Ave. S.W., Suite 720 • Calgary, AB • T2P 2Y5 • Tel: 403-264-3897 • Fax: 403-264-3901 • E-mail: stardotassociates@stardot.ca • Internet: www. stardot.ca • StarDot was founded in Calgary in 1994 with a mission to provide high quality resource personnel to clients on a permanent, contract or Flow-Through engagements. StarDot has shown continuous growth through strategic expansions in a variety of industries including, but not exclusively, Oil & Gas, Transportation, Education, Municipal and Provincial Governments, Real Estate and Finance.

STELLAR PERSONNEL PLACEMENT • 2417 Main St.., P.O. Box 219, Lambeth Station • London, ON • N6P 1P9 • Tel: 519-652-2540 • Fax: 519-652-5683 • E-mail: stellar@stellarplacement. com • Internet: www.stellarplacement.com • Stellar Personnel Placement began in 1994 as a small driver supply agency. Since that time they have grown significantly and are now a recognized leader in personnel placement for many diverse clients and companies throughout Southwestern Ontario.

STEPHEN LARAMEE & ASSOCIATES INC. • 2810 Matheson Blvd., 2nd Floor • Toronto, ON • L4W 4X7 • Tel: 1-877-897-1474 • Fax: 905-371-9283 • E-mail: slaramee@on.aibn.com • Internet: www.larameeassociates.com • Contact: Stephen Laramee • Stephen Laramee & Associates offers permanent positions from junior to senior managers in manufacturing and service related fields. They have provided over 25 years of recruiting for clients across Canada and are particularly focused in Automotive, Textile, Plastics, Apparel, Printing, Piping, Consumer Products, Sporting Goods and Corporate Retail.

STEVENS RESOURCE GROUP INC. • 496 Adelaide Street • Woodstock, ON • N4S 4B4 • Tel: 519-421-9556 • Fax: 519-421-0237 • E-mail: corporate@stevensresourcegroup.com • Internet: www.srgstaffing.com • Since 1990, Stevens Resource Group Inc. has earned a solid reputation for providing superior human resource solutions. Stevens Resource Group Inc. provides knowledge and expertise in a variety of human resource functions, including temporary staffing, professional search and recruitment as well as behavioural and technical employee assessments.

325 West Street
Suite 203A
Brantford, ON
N3R 6B7
Tel: 519-751-7707
Fax: 519-751-2373

386 Cambria Street
Suite 202
Stratford, ON
N5A 1J4
Tel: 519-273-7000
Fax: 519-273-9395

1240 Commissioners Rd. W.
Suite 200
London, ON
N6E 1W4
Tel: 519-668-7702
Fax: 519-668-6859

19 Baldwin St.
Tillsonburg, ON
N4G 2K3
Tel: 519-842-7003
Fax: 519-842-4887

225 Main St. E.
Suite 11
Milton, ON
L9T 1N9
Tel: 905-878-7789

569 Dundas St.
Woodstock, ON
N4S 1C6
Tel: 519-421-7000
Fax: 519-421-3839
Fax: 905-878-8312

200 Metcalfe St. E.
Strathroy, ON
N7G 1P8
Tel: 519-245-7727
Fax: 519-245-4432

200 Hespeller Rd.
Cambridge, ON
N1R 3H3
Tel: 519-620-2797
Fax: 519-624-8537

526 Fredrick St.
Kitchener, ON
N2B 3R1
Tel: 519-772-1770
Fax: 519-772-0963

1717 2nd Ave. E.
Suite 208
Owen Sound, ON
N4K 6V4
Tel: 519-371-3585
Fax: 519-376-1992

STEVENSON & WHITE • 2301 Carling Ave., Suite 100 • Ottawa, ON • K2B 7G3 • Tel: 613-225-5417 • Fax: 613-225-0913 • E-mail: info@stevensonandwhite.com • Internet: www. stevensonandwhite.com • Anne Stevenson and Trevor White, the two founding partners of Stevenson & White, have over 20 years combined recruiting experience in the Ottawa market place. They are well respected for their knowledge and expertise in the financial recruiting area. Customers know that by selecting Stevenson & White as their recruiting company of choice, they are selecting a firm with a proven track record of success.

STOAKLEY-DUDLEY CONSULTANTS LTD. • 6547 Mississauga Rd. N., Unit A • Mississauga, ON • L5N 1A6 • Tel: 905-821-3455 • Fax: 905-821-3467 • E-mail: stoakley@stoakley. com • Internet: www.stoakley.com • Contact: Ernie Stoakley • Since 1977, Stoakley-Dudley Consultants have established an incredibly solid reputation for finding top quality candidates for job opportunities, especially in the high technology arena. They are dedicated to providing the highest level of recruiting services with integrity, speed, and effectiveness.

STRATEGIC RESOURCE CONSULTANTS INC. • 480 University Ave., Suite 1403 • Toronto, ON • M5G 1V2 • Tel: 416-977-6462 • Fax: 416-977-5719 • E-mail: info@srcpro.com • Internet: www.srcpro.com • Strategic Resource Consultants Inc (SRC) is an Ontario Corporation with its main office in Unionville. SRC conducts its recruitment business primarily in the financial services Industry with emphasis on Insurance Professionals. SRC understands that organizations are facing many challenges, one of which is to secure the right Human Capital to compete. They are committed to providing their clients with employees who best match their needs. Their candidates must also have a genuine interest in partnering their expertise with employers in a mutually beneficial arrangement.

STRATUM EXECUTIVE SEARCH GROUP • 1614 Dundas St. E., Suite 202 • Whitby, ON • L1N 8Y8 • Tel: 905-720-0660 • Fax: 905-720-2924 • E-mail: info@stratumesg.com • Internet: www. stratumesg.com • Stratum Executive Search Group, is an executive search firm dedicated to working with you, the client, to recruit and develop the one differentiator that exists in today's hyper-competitive marketplace, your people - the individuals that build, shape and determine the results of your organization.

SUMMIT SEARCH GROUP • 602 – 12th Avenue S.W., Suite 640 • Calgary, AB • T2R 1J3 • Tel: 403-303-2727 • Fax: 403-303-2728 • E-mail: brucep@summitsearchgroup.com • Internet: www.summitsearchgroup.com • Established in 2000, Summit Search Group is a Calgary-based recruitment firm that specializes in the permanent placement of sales, management and accounting professionals. Their clients benefit from over 50 years of combined recruiting experience.

1150 Manulife Place
10180 – 101 Street
Edmonton, AB
T5J 3S9
Tel: 780-497-7667

SUPERTEMP • Peapell & Associates, 5251 Duke St., Suite 1206 • Halifax, NS • B3J 1P6 • Tel: 902-421-1523 • Fax: 902-425-8559 • E-mail: resumes@supertemp.ca • Internet: www. supertemp.ca • Supertemp is Atlantic Canada's choice for temporary staffing. Founded in 1989, Supertemp is the largest independent placement service in Atlantic Canada.

SYSTEM DEVELOPMENT GUILD INC. • 701 West Georgia St., Suite 1500 • Vancouver, BC • V7Y 1A1 • Tel: 604-683-2658 • Fax: 604-682-0997 • E-mail: info@sdgworld.com • Resume: resume@sdgworld.com • Internet: www.sdgworld.com • System Development Guild is a Vancouver based IT consulting agency that provides training, mentoring, consulting and recruiting in object technology. They offer the best in high quality, professional and services.

SYSTEMATIX INFORMATION TECHNOLOGY CONSULTANTS • 41 Britain St., Suite 301 • Toronto, ON • M5A 1R7 • Tel: 416-595-5331 • Fax: 416-595-1525 • E-mail: scitor@systematix. ab.ca • Internet: www.systematix.com • Contact: Jean Gagne • Established in 1975, Systematix has steadily grown to become one of the largest information technology consulting firms in Canada. From their network of eight regional offices, their team of over 600 consultants works together with their clients to implement leading-edge solutions and harness the power of information technologies - today and for the future.

Box 51 Lower Concourse	Southcentre Executive Tower	2600, boul. Laurier
2016 Sherwood Dr.	404, 11012 Macleod Trail S.E.	Tour de la Cité
Sherwood Park, AB	Calgary, AB	Suite 990
T8A 3X3	T2J 6A5	Quebec, QC
Tel: 780-416-4337	Tel: 403-237-8990	G1V 4W2
Fax: 780-416-1429	Fax: 403-233-0036	Tel: 418-681-0151
		Fax: 418-681-4061
141 Laurier Ave. W.	1 Place Ville Marie	601 West Broadway
Suite 366	Suite 1601	Suite 400
Ottawa, ON	Montréal, QC	Vancouver, BC
K1P 5J3	H3B 2B6	V5Z 4C2
Tel: 613-567-8939	Tel: 514-393-1313	Tel: 604-872-0038
Fax: 613-567-1916	Fax: 514-393-8997	Fax: 604-872-0089

SYSTEMS ON TIME INC. (SYSTEGRA) • 20 Holly St., Suite 202 • Toronto, ON • M4S 3B1 • Tel: 416-657-4359 • Fax: 416-485-2252 • E-mail: info@systegra.ca • Internet: www.systegra. ca • Since 1996, Systems OnTime has been supplying clients with IT resources, and candidates with challenging and satisfying employment. They take pride in their ability to provide excellent, technically qualified individuals, both contract and permanent, who will meet your needs. Since all their recruiters have a technical background and were once programmers, or are still involved technically, they can understand your needs from a systems perspective. Their Areas of Service include, but are not limited to: placing permanent and contract IT professionals; developing and implementing complete systems solutions for small and large businesses; and maintaining and enhancing existing systems.

TALENTWORKS INC. • 5525 Artillery Place • Halifax, NS • B3J 1J2 • Tel: 902-491-7600 • Fax: 902-491-7610 • E-mail: info@talentworks.biz • Internet: www.talentworks.biz • Talentworks is an Atlantic Canadian Search and Recruitment firm. They are dedicated to bringing talented people together with companies. They understand that changing demographics and a shrinking workforce require active, innovative strategies to find the best candidates. Their areas of expertise include positions within manufacturing, law and information technology. Their team, technology, network, experience and exceptional service to businesses and individuals will bring you results.

TAPSCOTT ASSOCIATES • 133 King St. E., 3rd Floor • Toronto, ON • M5C 1G6 • Tel: 416-367-7300 • Fax: 416-367-7333 • E-mail: wkt@tapscott.com • Internet: www.tapscott.com • Tapscott Associates is a consulting practice specializing in executive search and information systems development.

TAYLOR, LOW & ASSOCIATES INC. • 1200 Sheppard Ave. E., Suite 406 • Toronto, ON • M2K 2S5 • Tel: 416-494-3315 • Fax: 416-491-5301 • E-mail: kathy@taylorlow.com • Internet: www. taylorlow.com • Contact: Kathy Low • Through the use of innovative search services, Taylor, Low & Associates keeps abreast of transitions within the information technology recruitment arena. Since 1987, Taylor, Low has provided both full-time and contract personnel to many of the world's leading corporations. To ensure the best possible fit, they provide personalized services to all their Business, SAP, AS/400, networking and client-server clients. These include in-depth individual interviews, screens and reference checks to qualify potential candidate's necessary abilities and attitudes, always keeping in mind corporate fit.

TDS PERSONNEL LTD. • 1240 Bay St., Suite 805 • Toronto, ON • M5R 2A7 • Tel: 416-923-4397 • Fax: 416-923-9100 • E-mail: tds@tdspersonnel.com • Internet: www.tdspersonnel.com • Contact: Sandra Title • Established in 1975, TDS is a private Canadian-owned and operated company that services the personnel needs of businesses in the Greater Toronto Area. They are a full service employment agency offering temporary, contract and permanent employment. Industry areas they specialize in include finance, law, advertising, customer service, and computers.

TECHAID INC. • 5165 ch. Queen-Mary, Bureau 401 • Montréal, QC • H3W 1X7 • Tel: 514-482-6790 • Fax: 514-482-0324 • E-mail: info@techaid.ca • Internet: www.techaid.ca • Techaid Inc. recruits technical personnel for temporary and permanent employment. They specialize in the areas of information technology, engineering, manufacturing, architecture, sales and purchasing.

TECHHI CONSULTANTS LTD. • 100 King St. W., Suite 3700 • Toronto, ON • M5X 1C9 • Tel: 416-644-8529 • E-mail: contact@techhi.com • Internet: www.techhi.com • TechHi Consultants Limited is a recruitment firm specializing in the hi tech arena. Visit their website for a list of consultants to obtain more information.

TECHHI CONSULTANTS LTD continued

1 Place Ville Marie	5 Cherry Blossom Rd.
Suite 2001	Suite 2
Montreal, QC	Cambridge, ON
H2B 2C4	N3H 4R7
Tel: 514-940-1780	Tel: 519-201-1020
Fax: 514-866-2115	Fax: 519-201-1070

TECHNICAL CAREER CONNECTION INC. • 13300 Tecumseh Rd. E., Suite 382 • Tecumseh, ON • N8N 4R8 • Tel: 519-979-6026 • Fax: 519-979-6507 • E-mail: career@mnsi.net • Internet: www.technicalcareerconnection.com • Technical Career Connection Inc. is your professional career connection for manufacturing, technical and administrative positions in Windsor and Essex County. They specialize in permanent placement.

TECHNICAL RESOURCE NETWORK • 2906 West Broadway St., Suite 212 • Vancouver, BC • V6K 2G8 • Tel: 604-739-1711 • Fax: 604-739-1710 • E-mail: jobs@VanJobs.com • Internet: www. trnvancouver.com • The Technical Resource Network is a technology placement service firm. Their areas of expertise are engineering research and development for data/telecommunications manufacturers, senior sales and systems engineering, and premier personnel for high tech companies.

TECHNICAL SKILLS CONSULTING INC. • 90 Sumach St., Suite 312 • Toronto, ON • M5A 4R4 • Tel: 416-586-7971 • Fax: 416-927-8446 • E-mail: tscinc@tscinc.on.ca • Internet: www.tscinc.on.ca • Technical Skills Consulting is closely connected with a broad spectrum of Canadian industry. Their search process includes the identification and attraction of a wide range of qualified candidates. They then provide a thorough and professional assessment of those candidates who are identified for review. Their task is to identify and evaluate those candidates that best meet the needs of their clients.

TECHNIX INC. • 100 Esgore Dr. • North York, ON • M5M 3S2 • Tel: 416-250-9195 • Fax: Fax: 416-485-7964 • E-mail: tnixon@technix.ca • Internet: www.technix.ca • Contact: Ted Nixon, President • TechNix is a full service Toronto-based executive recruitment firm dedicated to helping advanced technology vendors find top-notch sales and marketing specialists. Since 1990, they have matched talent with clients' needs for numerous vendors, service providers, and consultants. TechNix serves clients based in Canadian, North American, or international environments and focus on mid to senior level recruits.

TEMPS 4U CORP. • 1200 Bay St., Suite 502 • Toronto, ON • M5R 2A5 • Tel: 416-928-1368 • Fax: 416-928-3432 • E-mail: mail@temps4u.com • Internet: www.temps4u.com • Temps 4U Corp. specializes in the placement of office support for temporary positions.

THE ADMINISTRATIVE EDGE INC. • 74 Simcoe St. S., Suite 301 • Oshawa, ON • L1H 4G6 • Tel: 905-436-5818 • Fax: 905-436-6291 • E-mail: admin@adminedge.com • Internet: www. adminedge.com • The mission of The Administrative Edge Inc. is to contribute to the success of their customers through a level of service designed to be responsive to their distinctive requirements and standards. This will be achieved through partnerships with their customers, their employees, and their business associates for a shared sense of accomplishment and reward. Their 27 years combined experience in the Durham Region has been focused on association management, data management, business function planning and support services for human resources. Their background qualifies us to effectively assist businesses in all these varied aspects, saving your company time and money.

THE ASSOCIATES GROUP OF COMPANIES • 222 Somerset St. W., Suite 700 • Ottawa, ON • K2P 2G3 • Tel: 613-567-0222 • Fax: 613-567-6441 • E-mail: associates@theassociatesgroup. com • Internet: www.theassociatesgroup.com • The Associates Group have been providing quality consulting services and workforce solutions to their clients in the National Capital Region since 1988. They have a proven track record in building and nurturing long-term relationships with clients and candidates, and by effectively matching the best candidates with suitable positions, ensuring success for their clients and their candidates.

THE CREATIVE GROUP • 181 Bay St., Suite 820 • Toronto, ON • M5J 2T3 • Tel: 416-365-2010 • Fax: 416-350-3573 • E-mail: toronto@creativegroup.com • Internet: www.creativegroup. com • The Creative Group, a division of specialized staffing leader Robert Half International Inc. focuses on placing freelance professionals in the creative, advertising, marketing, web and public relations fields.

THE HOUSTON PERSONNEL GROUP • 28 Queen Elizabeth Way, Suite 100 • Winnipeg, MB • R3L 2R1 • Tel: 204-947-6751 • Fax: 204-944-0177 • E-mail: mhouston@houstongrp.com • Internet: www.houstongrp.com • Contact: Marilyn Houston, General Manager • The Houston Personnel Group is Winnipeg's largest, full-service, privately owned recruiting firm. It offers executive, sales, accounting/finance, human resource and information technology recruiting, as well as administrative and industrial temporary placements.

THE NORAMTEC GROUP • 200 Waterfront Dr., Suite 100 • Bedford, NS • B4A 4J4 • Tel: 902-492-1053 • Fax: 902-422-6675 • E-mail: cfraser@gsa-search.com • Internet: www.noramtec. com • The Noramtec Group has been established since 1964 and is a leading contract technical services company providing highly skilled engineers, designers, drafters and field personnel for project assignments to clients throughout North America. Through their eight offices in Canada and the United States, Noramtec furnishes specialized services to a wide range of consulting, manufacturing, utility and government clientele. Noramtec Consultants Inc. has provided project management personnel, senior design specialists, engineers, stress analysts, computer system analysts and support engineering personnel including planners, procurement personnel and estimators. They have experience in recruiting for and staffing of large projects involving 30-60 persons as well as small assignments requiring particularly specialized personnel.

2055 Peel St. Suite 625 Montreal, QC H3A 1V4 Tel: 514-861-6678 Fax: 514-861-0307	1400 Clyde Ave. Suite 217 Nepean, ON K2G 3J2 Tel: 613-727-3997 Fax: 613-727-5116	505 Consumers Rd. Suite 511 Toronto, ON M2J 4V8 Tel: 416-644-4949 Fax: 416-644-4948
10601 Southport Rd. S.W. Suite 204, Southland Crt. Calgary, AB T2H 3M6 Tel: 403-256-2514 Fax: 403-201-3311	1334 Main St. North Vancouver, BC V7J 1C3 Tel: 604-983-3551 Fax: 604-983-3552	10368-82 Ave. Suite 302 Edmonton, AB T6E 4E7 Tel: 780-409-9429 Fax: 780-409-8410
187 Ontario St. Suite 7 Stratford, ON N5A 3H3 Tel: 519-271-6122 Fax: 519-273-5465	4145 North Service Rd. Suite 200 Burlington, ON L7L 6A3 Tel: 905-315-5040 Fax: 905-315-5041	

THE PERSONNEL DEPARTMENT • 595 Howe St., Suite 1205 • Vancouver, BC • V6C 2T5 • Tel: 604-685-3530 • Fax: 604-689-5981 • E-mail: info@goodstaff.com • Internet: www. goodstaff.com • The Personnel Department provides staffing services locally, nationally and internationally for both permanent and temporary employment. The Personnel Department has job opportunities globally using CareerMachine technology and through offices in Vancouver, BC; Calgary and Edmonton, Alberta; Salem, Portland and Beaverton, Oregon; Salt Lake City, Utah; Boise, Idaho; lahoma City, lahoma and Sydney, NSW, Australia and associates across Canada, the USA and Australia.

255 5th Ave. S.W.	10250, 101 Street
Suite 269	Suite 1806
Calgary, AB	Edmonton, AB
T2P 3G6	T5J 3P4
Tel: 403-266-7030	Tel: 780-421-1811
Fax: 403-265-8388	Fax: 780-421-1814
calgary@goodstaff.com	edmonton@goodstaff.com

THE PLACEMENT GROUP • 10080 Jasper Ave., Suite 201 • Edmonton, AB • T5J 1V9 • Tel: 780-421-7702 • Fax: 403-426-3427 • E-mail: info@pgstaff.com • Internet: www.pgstaff.com • Placement Group specializes in supplying well qualified and dependable temporary, contract and permanent employees. They cover all aspects of business from receptionists and executive assistants, through to executives and senior level administrators; warehouse personnel through to warehouse managers. They provide a full range of recruitment and employee management services that can save you time, money and headaches. Their specialists can quickly identify and select the personnel you need to keep your company fully functioning and expanding.

333 Seymour St.	1027 Pandora Ave.	222 – 58th Ave. S.W.
Suite 1210	Victoria, BC	Suite 111
Vancouver, BC	V8V 3P6	Calgary, AB
V6B 5A6	Tel: 250-413-3111	T2H 2S3
Tel: 604-689-7717	Fax: 250-413-3122	Tel: 403-301-5305
Fax: 604-683-6440		Fax: 403-301-5329
Main Floor	4915 – 54th St.	
736-6 Avenue S.W.	2nd Floor	
Calgary, AB	Red Deer, AB	
T2P3T7	T4N 2G7	
Tel: 403-777-9000	Tel: 403-309-0757	
Fax: 403-777-9007	Fax: 403-309-0852	

THE POLLACK GROUP • 225 Metcalfe St., Suite 702 • Ottawa, ON • K2P 1P9 • Tel: 613-238-2233 • Fax: 613-238-4407 • E-mail: pollack.group@pollackgroup.com • Internet: www. pollackgroup.com • Contact: Paul Pollack • The Pollack Group was founded in 1973 and is a Canadian owned and operated full service staffing firm. Their reputation and expertise are in both the public and private sectors. Permanent, Contract, Temporary, and Temp to Perm Services are staffing options that provide their clients with contemporary and cost-effective business strategies to assist them with their staffing requirements.

THE STONEWOOD GROUP • 100 Schneider Rd., Suite 3 • Ottawa, ON • K2K 1Y2 • Tel: 613-592-4145 • Fax: 613-963-1155 • E-mail: info@stonewoodgroup.com • Internet: www. stonewoodgroup.com • Since 1981, Stonewood Group has assisted organizations find, assess and develop their exceptional leaders. The StoneWood Group research team boasts more than

70 years of accumulated experience and is supported by uniquely interactive and exhaustive electronic tools built from years of networking, and world class sources of executive management information. Their leadership development approach and tools are second to none and geared specifically to their target markets.

330 Bay St.
Suite 1100
Toronto, ON
M5H 2S8
Tel: 416-365-9494
Fax: 416-365-7081

TODAYS STAFFING LTD. • 360 Main Street, Suite 160 • Winnipeg, MB • R3C 3Z3 • Tel: 204-956-5600 • Fax: 204-947-9672 • E-mail: consultant8335@todays.com • With a network of more than 70 offices, Todays provides administrative, legal, finance & accounting personnel to businesses throughout the United States and Canada. They maintain a workforce of skilled employees in word processing, secretarial, administrative, data processing, accounting, legal, office communications, and general clerical categories. Services include temporary, temporary-to-hire, and direct hire placements and on-site managed staffing programs.

10 Stanley Avenue	450 Speedvale Ave. W.	22 Frederick St.
Suite 4A	Suite 103	Suite 100
Brantford, ON	Guelph, ON	Kitchener, ON
N3S 7N4	N1H 7Y6	N2H 6M6
Tel: 519-758-1511	Tel: 519-763-7775	Tel: 519-742-5875
Fax: 519-758-8153	Fax: 519-763-2369	Fax: 519-742-7354
33 City Centre Dr.	48 Yonge St.	
Suite 601	Suite 500	
Mississauga, ON	Toronto, ON	
L5B 2N5	M5E 1G6	
Tel: 905-848-5900	Tel: 416-360-7700	
Fax: 905-848-8828	Fax: 416-360-7524	

TORONTO EXECUTIVE CONSULTANTS • 20 Bay St., Suite 1205 • Toronto, ON • M5J 2N8 • Tel: 416-366-6120 • Fax: 416-366-6117 • Internet: www.torontoexecutive.com • Toronto Executive Consultants specializes in search and placement of individuals for manufacturing companies. Engineering, Quality Assurance, Materials, Human Resources, Accounting, Finance, Design, Tooling, Production, Information Technology and General Management are some of the positions that their clients regularly require.

TRAFALGAR PERSONNEL LTD. • Miller Mews at 323 Church St., Unit 17 • Oakville, ON • L6J 1P2 • Tel: 905-849-6520 • Fax: 905-849-6921 • Internet: www.trafalgarpersonnel.com • E-mail: info@trafalgarpersonnel.com • Contact: Marna Martin • Trafalgar Personnel specializes in home care giving for children, elders, and those with special needs. Positions may involve live in or live out care, full time or part time work, and occasional or temporary care. All applicants must be interviewed.

TREBOR PERSONNEL INC. • 1090 Dundas St. E., Suite 203 • Mississauga, ON • L4Y 2B8 • Tel: 905-566-0922 • Fax: 905-566-0925 • E-mail: mississauga@tpipersonnel.com • Internet: http://trebor.packetworks.net • Established in January, 1985, Trebor Personnel Inc. (TPI) is one of the largest suppliers of industrial help and drivers in Southern Ontario and more recently has become very significant in the technical and office environments. TPI has nine offices that supply personnel from Belleville in the east to Kitchener in the west. The company's "temporary to permanent" program allows a client to try the individual before he is hired.

1680 Jane St.
Suite 202
Toronto, ON
M9N 2S2
Tel: 416-244-5693
Fax: 416-244-3659

2312 Eglington Ave. E.
Suite 201
Scarborough, ON
M1K 2M2
Tel: 416-750-4291
Fax: 416-750-4292

16 George St. North
Brampton, ON
L6X 1R2
Tel: 905-457-1326
Fax: 905-457-8213

276 King St. W.
Suite 305
Kitchener, ON
N2G 1B6
Tel: 519-894-1337
Fax: 519-894-5364

1395 Main St. E.
Hamilton, ON
L8K 1B9
Tel: 905-549-6259
Fax: 905-549-9763

TRILLIUM TALENT RESOURCE INC. • 244 Water St. N. • Cambridge, ON • N1R 3C1 • Tel: 519-620-9683 • Fax: 519-620-9686 • E-mail: kathuria@trilliumhr.com • Internet: www.trilliumhr.com • The Trillium Talent Resource (TTR) Group is a fifteen-year old international and domestic Executive Search and Management consulting firm with offices in Toronto and Cambridge, Ontario, Birmingham, Alabama, New Delhi, India and Manila, Philippines. The firm focuses on two distinct business sectors - (a) Healthcare and (b) The General Industry. They can be reached toll free at 1-800-335-9668.

99 Sheppard Ave. W.
Toronto, ON
M2N 1M4
Tel: 416-497-2624
Fax: 416-497-8491

7455 – 132 Street
Suite 206
Surrey, BC
Tel: 604-598-2881
Fax: 604-598-1891

7930 Bowness Rd. N.W.
Suite 306
Calgary, AB
Tel: 403-202-5892
Fax: 403-202-5980

TRISER CORP. • 610 Ford Dr., Suite 254 • Oakville, ON • L6J 7W4 • E-mail: webinquiry@triser.com • Internet: www.triser.com • Triser Corp. is an organization of systems professionals that have extensive experience in various market sectors, dealing at all levels within the industry. They provide a wide range of technical and industry knowledge to their clients. They are able to offer their clients value added services that include capacity planning and performance analysis, project management, system management, technical sessions for staff, and education and employee training in specific methodologies and tools.

TRS STAFFING SOLUTIONS, INC. • 340 Midpark Way S.E., Suite 105 • Calgary, AB • T2X 1P1 • Tel: 403-571-4775 • Fax: 403-571-4795 • E-mail: info-CN@trsstaffing.com • Internet: www.trsstaffing.com • Established in 1984, TRS Staffing has extensive experience in recruiting for engineering, management, construction, design, and maintenance positions throughout a broad spectrum of industries. Through their streamlined processes, they successfully identify, screen, and mobilize candidates who meet job requirements.

TSI GROUP • 2630 Skymark Ave., Suite 700 • Mississauga, ON • L4W 5A4 • Tel: 905-629-3701 • Fax: 905-629-0799 • E-mail: tsi@tsigroup.com • Internet: www.tsigroup.com • TSI has become the Human Resource partner for many major firms in supply chain management. As an expert in its field, TSI provides a full range of Recruiting solutions to businesses across North America. The firm's competitive advantage lies in its ability to effectively source the right professionals for corporate and third party logistics, all sectors of transportation, and IT for the logistics industry.

TUNDRA SITE SERVICES • 10302 - 121 Street • Edmonton, AB • T5N 1K8 • Tel: 780-944-1650 • Fax: 780-452-2576 • E-mail: adam@tundrasiteservices.com • Internet: www.tundrasiteservices. com • Tundra Site Services provides a full range of skilled trades personnel for facilities and plant maintenance, shutdowns, plant operations and industrial construction projects in Alberta and northern Canada. They specialize in construction managers, construction specialists, estimators, field procurement specialists, inspectors, planners and schedulers, plant operators, safety coordinators, site administrators, site supervisors, carpenters, electricians, engineers, heavy duty mechanics, instrumentation technicians, machinists, millwrights, pipefitters, and welders.

URENTIA INC. • 4400, Lasalle Blvd. • Verdun, QC • H4G 2A8 • Tel: 514-396-0011 • Fax: 514-396-0012 • E-mail: info@urentia.com • Internet: www.urentia.com • Urentia provides a full range of consulting services in Information Technology, Information System service solutions and now in the healthcare sector. They have worked with hundreds of the most competent Technology-based professionals and their clients have greatly benefited from their technical expertise.

VALLEY STENO PERSONNEL AGENCY & SECRETARIAL SERVICES • 2469 Pauline St., Suite 101 • Abbotsford, BC • V2S 3S1 • Tel: 604-859-6511 • Fax: 604-852-8099 • E-mail: info@ valleypersonnel.com • Internet: www.valleypersonnel.bc.ca • Valley Personnel was founded in 1976 and is locally owned. Their years of experience enable them to react quickly to the marketplace and your needs whether you are a business with staffing needs or you are loing for temporary or permanent work. They cover the Fraser Valley, which includes Abbotsford, Chilliwack, Mission and Aldergrove areas.

VERRIEZ GROUP INC., THE • 252 Pall Mall St., Suite 203 • N6A 5P6 • Tel: 519-673-3463 • Fax: 519-673-4748 • E-mail: verriez@verriez.com; paul@verriez.com • Internet: www.verriez. com • Contact: Paul Verriez • The Verriez Group was started in 1985 and has grown to become one of the leading boutique executive search firms in Ontario and the only retained search firm in Southwestern Ontario that is an AESC member.

36 Toronto St.
Suite 850
Toronto, ON
M5C 2C5
Tel: 647-288-3662
Fax: 519-673-4748

VOLT HUMAN RESOURCES • 10 Kelfield St., Suite 100 • Toronto, ON • M9W 5A2 • Tel: 877-287-6139 • Fax: 416-306-1449 • E-mail: torontotechjobs@volt.com • Internet: www.volt.com • Volt Human Resources provides technical, scientific and IT personnel for more than 60 of the largest companies in North America, including Hewlett-Packard, John Deere, Rockwell, Boeing and Microsoft.

1155, rue Metcalfe
Bureau 55
Montreal, QC
H3B 2V6
Tel: 800-253-9605
Fax: 416-306-1449
montreal@volt.com

W5 RESOURCES, INC. • 100 Allstate Parkway, Suite 302 • Markham, ON • L3R 6H3 • Tel: 905-940-0255 • Fax: 905-940-0258 • E-mail: info@w5.net • Internet: www.w5.net • W5 Resources, Inc. is a Canadian Information Technology Consulting company located in Markham, Ontario. With a resource database of more than 15,000 full time and contract I.S. Professionals, W5 provides resources to their clients during times of resource or skill shortages.

WELLINGTON PARTNERS INTERNATIONAL INC. • 508 Riverbend Dr., Suite 302 • Kitchener, ON • N2K 3S2 • Tel: 519-744-2444 • Fax: 519-744-0913 • E-mail: info@wellingtonpartners.com • Internet: www.wellingtonpartners.com • Established in 1991 with the objective to provide outstanding service to clients in automotive, manufacturing, and plastics in North America, the staff at Wellington Partners has a well developed network of industry contacts in these industry sectors.

90 Kimberly Ave.
Bracebridge, ON
P1L 2A4
Tel: 705-646-3200
Fax: 519-744-0913

WESTERN HR CONSULTING LTD. • 7058B Farrell Rd. S.E. • Calgary, AB • T2H 0T2 • Tel: 403-215-2150 • E-mail: careers@westernhr.com • Internet: www.westernhr.com • Their success as a company is based on focus and dedication. Western HR Consulting Ltd. has been a recruitment specialist for the food and beverage, and consumer goods industries in Western Canada, for over ten years.

WILLIAM LEE & ASSOCIATES, INC. • 885 West Georgia St., Suite 1500 • Vancouver, BC • V6C 3E8 • Tel: 604-689-7893 • Fax: 604-689-7882 • E-mail: info@WLEE.com • Internet: www.wlee.com • Contact: William Lee • William Lee & Associates, Inc. is an executive search firm specializing in the field of Information Technology.

WILSON EXECUTIVE SEARCH • 5945 Spring Garden Road • Halifax, Nova Scotia • B3H 1Y4 • Tel: (902) 423-1657• Fax: (902) 423-0277 • Email: Inquiries@WilsonExecutiveSearch.com • Internet: http://wilsonexecutivesearch.com • Wilson Executive Search exists to help solve one of the greatest challenges facing your business today - finding and keeping the best talent. They help you target, attract and keep the best and the brightest people. Clients appreciate their unique and innovative approaches to finding the right people, and they know that the right people will deliver the competitive edge needed to drive superior business results. Over the last two decades, their motto, "The best are not seeking, they are sought," has proven itself. Over 85 per cent of their executive search assignments are completed with candidates that they were previously aware of, or who they directly sourced. They've got great contacts and an extensive database.

WOLF GUGLER & ASSOCIATES • 1370 Don Mills Rd., Suite 300 • Toronto, ON • M3B 3N7 • Tel: 1-888-848-3006 • E-mail: wolf@wolfgugler.com • Internet: www.wolfgugler.com • Wolf Gugler & Associates Limited offers a comprehensive range of retainer-based executive search services to locate specialized people for retailers and their suppliers. These services are augmented by the capability to assess talent through the use of management appraisals. Offices in the United States and Canada.

WOOD WEST & PARTNERS INC. • 1281 West Georgia St., Suite 312 • Vancouver, BC • V6E 3J7 • Tel: 604-682-3141 • Fax: 604-688-5749 • E-mail: search@wood-west.com • Internet: www.wood-west.com • Contact: Ron Wood • Wood West recruits achievers for quality clients in engineering, the sciences and construction. Their services are focused at the executive, management and specialist levels, for permanent and for contract positions.

WORLD PERSONNEL SERVICES INC. • Atrium on Bay, 20 Dundas St. W., Suite 1531, P.O. Box 62 • Toronto, ON • M5G 2C2 • Tel: 1-877-UWORLD2 • Fax: 416-596-9632 • E-mail: iam@ worldpersonnel.com • Internet: www.worldpersonnel.com • World Personnel Services Inc. has extensive information systems recruiting experience. They have over 21 years experience as an information technology recruiter.

WWWORK!COM • 55 St. Clair Ave. W., Suite 402 • Toronto, ON • M4V 2Y7 • Tel: 416-922-3800 • Fax: 416-922-5643 • E-mail: info@wwwork.com • Internet: www.wwwork.com • wwwork!com is a proven provider of organizational staffing solutions and recruitment services. Their experienced search professionals provide best-in-class recruitment, selection and hiring services to organizations that have "targeted" hiring requirements. Each of wwwork!com's consultants has direct operating experience in their service target markets and areas of expertise.

255 Albert St.	155 Rene-Levesque Boul. W.	70 Dalhousie St.
Suite 600	Suite 2500	Suite 100
Ottawa, ON	Montreal, QC	Quebec City, QC
K1P 6A9	H3B 2K4	G1K 4B2
Tel: 613-686-4302 x615	Tel: 514-315-8660	Tel: 418-649-0767
Fax: 866-563-9675	Fax: 866-563-9675	Fax: 418-649-1518

YOUR ADVANTAGE STAFFING CONSULTANTS INC. • 426 Queen St. W. • Cambridge, ON • N3C 1H1 • Tel: 519-651-2120 • Fax: 519-651-2780 • Internet: www.yasci.com • Contact: Lori VanOpstal • Your Advantage Staffing Consultants Inc. began operations in 1997 with the mandate of becoming one of the best recruiting companies that will not only meet but also exceed the staffing needs of the Transportation Industry. They do this by employing the best staff, utilizing the best resources and consistently being aware of the changing needs and trends of the industry. They can be reached toll-free at 1-888-213-3375.

ZSA LEGAL RECRUITMENT • 200 University Ave., Suite 1000 • Toronto, ON • M5H 3C6 • Tel: 416-368-2051 • Fax: 416-368-5699 • E-mail: info@zsa.ca • Internet: www.zsa.ca • ZSA Legal Recruitment is Canada's leading and only national legal recruitment firm. With offices in Vancouver, Calgary, Edmonton, Toronto, Ottawa and Montreal, they are uniquely positioned to serve the legal recruitment needs across Canada.

250, 6th Ave. S.W.	1055 West Hastings St.	1470 rue Peel
Suite 1800	Suite 300	Bureau 725
Calgary, AB	Vancouver, BC	Montréal, QC
T2P 3H7	V6E 2E9	H3A 1T1
Tel: 403-205-3444	Tel: 604-681-0706	Tel: 514-228-2880
Fax: 403-205-3428	Fax: 604-681-0566	Fax: 514-228-2889
10180 - 101 St.	116 Lisgar St.	1969 Upper Water St.
Suite 1150	Suite 101	Purdy's Tower II, Suite 2200
Edmonton, AB	Ottawa, ON	Halifax, NS
T5J 3S4	K2P 0C2	B3J 3R7
Tel: 780-702-1000	Tel: 613-232-8828	Tel: 902-474-5192
Fax: 780-701-5022	Fax: 613-232-8887	Fax: 1-866-368-5699

PART II

DIRECTORIES OF RESOURCES

Industry and Professional Associations

Industry Associations

WHAT ARE INDUSTRY AND PROFESSIONAL ASSOCIATIONS?

Sometimes known as trade associations, each one is a group that is dedicated to promoting a specific sector, industry or occupation. For instance, if you want to work in the oil and gas exploration industry, you might consider joining the Canadian Association of Petroleum Producers. If you happen to be in sales, there's the Canadian Professional Sales Association. There are literally thousands of different associations for almost any type of industry or occupation.

HOW CAN THEY HELP YOU IN YOUR JOB SEARCH?

Associations are a wonderful way to learn more about your occupation. By joining one, or by attending their meetings, you will gain insight into your field's latest trends. More importantly you can get to know individuals who are already employed in your area. You never know when someone will know someone else who's hiring.

Many associations have regular guest speakers and post employment opportunities on their website. Quite a few publish trade magazines that may be helpful. Not to mention the conferences and trade shows they sponsor – where companies you might be targeting display their booths and are open to discussions.

The following is a list of selected trade associations categorized by industry. This index is merely a representative sampling. The publication, **Directory of Associations in Canada** (IHS/Micromedia Limited), lists over 20,000 trade associations (as well as local chapters). This is an invaluable resource. Ask for it at your local library, in hard copy, or possibly free on the library's database.

Accounting & Legal

CANADIAN BAR ASSOCIATION • 500 - 865 Carling Avenue • Ottawa, ON • K1S 5S8 • Tel: 613-237-2925 • Fax: 613-237-0185 • E-mail: info@cba.org • Internet: www.cba.org • The Canadian Bar Association (CBA) is the essential ally and advocate of all members of the legal profession; it is the voice for all members of the profession and its primary purpose is to serve its members; it is the premier provider of personal and professional development and support to all members of the legal profession; it promotes fair justice systems, facilitates effective law reform, promotes equality in the legal profession and is devoted to the elimination of discrimination. The CBA is a leading edge organization committed to enhancing the professional and commercial interests of a diverse membership and to protecting the independence of the judiciary and the Bar.

CANADIAN ENVIRONMENTAL LAW ASSOCIATION • 130 Spadina Avenue, Suite 301 • Toronto, ON • M5V 2L4 • Tel: 416-960-2284 • Fax: 416-960-9392 • E-mail: millers@lao.on.ca • Internet: www.cela.ca • The Canadian Environmental Law Association (CELA) is a non-profit, public interest organization established in 1970 to use existing laws to protect the environment and to advocate environmental law reforms. It is also a free legal advisory clinic for the public, and will act at hearings and in courts on behalf of citizens or citizens' groups who are otherwise unable to afford legal assistance.

CANADIAN INSTITUTE OF CHARTERED ACCOUNTANTS • 227 Wellington Street West • Toronto, ON • M5V 3H2 • Tel: 416-977-3222 • Fax: 416-977-8585 • Internet: www.cica.ca • The Canadian Institute of Chartered Accountants, together with the provincial, territorial and Bermuda Institutes/Ordre of Chartered Accountants, represents a membership of approximately 72,000 CAs and 10,000 students in Canada and Bermuda. The CICA conducts research into current business issues and supports the setting of accounting, auditing and assurance standards for business, not-for-profit organizations and government.

CERTIFIED GENERAL ACCOUNTANTS' ASSOCIATION OF CANADA • 800 - 1188 West Georgia Street • Vancouver, BC • V6E 4A2 • Tel: 604-669-3555 • Fax: 604-689-5845 • E-mail: public@cga-canada.org • Internet: www.cga-canada.org • The Certified General Accountants Association of Canada is a national self-regulating association of approximately 68,000 Certified General Accountants and students. CGAs work in Canada and elsewhere throughout the world; students are enrolled in the CGA program of professional studies in Canada, Bermuda, the Caribbean, Hong Kong and the People's Republic of China.

CERTIFIED MANAGEMENT ACCOUNTANTS CANADA • Mississauga Executive Centre • One Robert Speck Parkway, Suite 1400 • Mississauga, ON • L4Z 3M3 • Tel: 905-949-4200 • E-mail: info@cma-canada.org • Internet: www.cma-canada.org • Certified Management Accountants (CMA) Canada grants a professional designation in management accounting and regulates its members under the authorization of provincial legislation. CMA Canada, a self-regulating body, maintains the highest standards, practices and professional conduct in management accounting to protect the public interest.

FEDERATION OF LAW SOCIETIES OF CANADA • Constitution Square 360 Albert Street, Suite 1700 • Ottawa, ON • K1R 7X7 • Tel: 613-236-7272 • Fax: 613-236-7233 • E-mail: info@flsc.ca • Internet: www.flsc.ca • The Federation is the coordinating body of the 14 law societies in Canada who have the overall responsibility to regulate the legal profession in Canada comprised of 95,000 lawyers in Canada and 3,500 notaries in Quebec.

Aerospace & High Technology

AEROSPACE INDUSTRIES ASSOCIATION OF CANADA • 60 Queen Street, Suite 1200 • Ottawa, ON • K1P 5Y7 • Tel: 613-232-4297 • Fax: 613-232-1142 • E-mail: info@aiac.ca • Internet: www.aiac.ca • The Aerospace Industries Association of Canada (AIAC) is a member-driven, not-for-profit national trade association that promotes and facilitates Canadian competitiveness in the global market for aerospace goods and services. It is the collective voice of Canada's leading aerospace manufacturers and service providers — an effective advocate on a broad range of public policy issues that have a direct impact on aerospace companies in Canada. Through its network of member companies, its productive relationships with federal government departments and agencies, and its globe-spanning international contacts, AIAC responds quickly and effectively to capitalize on sector opportunities, and to combat threats to sector competitiveness.

AIR TRANSPORT ASSOCIATION OF CANADA • 255 Albert Street, Suite 1100 • Ottawa, ON • K1P 6A9 • Tel: 613-233-7727 • Fax: 613-230-8648 • E-mail: atac@atac.ca • Internet: www.atac.ca • The mission of the Air Transport Association of Canada is to support their members in the pursuit of a safe, world-leading and competitive Canadian air transport industry.

ASSOCIATION OF PROFESSIONAL COMPUTER CONSULTANTS • 2323 Yonge Street, Suite 400 • Toronto, ON • M4P 2C9 • Tel: 416-545-5275 • E-mail: information@apcconline.com • Internet: www.apcconline.com • The Association of Professional Computer Consultants (APCC) is a national, not-for-profit organization which promotes the interests of independent IT consultant. The association provides its members with relevant seminars and networking events; offers a valuable group insurance plan; and makes availablean online members directory, an email newsletter, and an online resource library.

CANADIAN ADVANCED TECHNOLOGY ALLIANCE • 388 Albert St. • Ottawa, ON • K1R 5B2 • Tel: 613-236-6550 • Fax: 613-236-8189 • E-mail: info@cata.ca • Internet: www.cata. ca • CATAAlliance is Canada's leading, most influential and entrepreneurial technology alliance. It is committed to growing the global competitiveness of its members, 80% of which are currently active exporters. With offices across the country, they are focused on the foundation for commercialization, market research, networking, events, access to other associations, and professional development, across the nation.

CANADIAN AERONAUTICS AND SPACE INSTITUTE, THE • 350 Terry Fox Drive, Suite 104 • Kanata, ON • K2K 2W5 • Tel: 613-591-8787 • Fax: 613-591-7291 • E-mail: casi@casi. ca • Internet: www.casi.ca • The Canadian Aeronautics and Space Institute (CASI) is a non-profit scientific and technical organization devoted to the advancement of the art, science and engineering relating to aeronautics, astronautics, and associated technologies and their applications. The Institute consists of Branches across Canada, specialist Sections, and constituent Societies which cater to related technologies.

CANADIAN ASSOCIATION OF INTERNET PROVIDERS • 388 Albert Street 2nd FL • Ottawa, ON • K1R 5B2 • Tel: 613-232-6550 • Fax: 613-236-8189 • E-mail: info@cata.ca • Internet: www. cata.ca/Communities/caip • The Canadian Association of Internet Providers (CAIP) represents a large and ever-growing group of service providers across the country. CAIP's Mission is to foster the growth of a healthy and competitive Internet service industry in Canada through collective and cooperative action on Canadian and international issues of mutual interest.

CANADIAN CHEMICAL PRODUCERS' ASSOCIATION • 350 Sparks Street, Suite 805 • Ottawa, ON • K1R 7S8 • Tel: 613-237-6215 • Fax: 613-237-4061 • E-mail: glaurin@ccpa.ca • Internet: www.ccpa.ca • The Canadian Chemical Producers' Association (CCPA) represents over 70 member-companies and Responsible Care Partners with more than 200 basic chemical and resin manufacturing sites across Canada. Together, these companies generate revenues of more than $24 billion annually.

CANADIAN COUNCIL OF TECHNICIANS AND TECHNOLOGISTS • 295 - 1101 Prince of Wales Drive • Ottawa, ON • K2C 3W7 • Tel: 613-238-8123 • Fax: 613-238-8822 • E-mail: ccttadm@cctt.ca • Internet: www.cctt.ca • Canada is a world leader in the application of new technology, and technicians and technologists are key elements in Canada's success. Keeping Canada at the top is the business of the Canadian Council of Technicians and Technologists (CCTT), and we do this by ensuring that our technicians and technologists maintain high standards of excellence. That is CCTT's commitment to Canada, and our significance to our members. The more than 49,000 members of CCTT's provincial associations use CCTT as their national advocate on issues such as pan-Canadian standards, national and international mobility, and national accreditation of technology programs.

CANADIAN ASSOCIATION OF DEFENCE AND SECURITY INDUSTRIES (CADSI) • 130 Slater Street, Suite 1250 • Ottawa, ON • K1P 6E2 • Tel: 613-235-5337 • Fax: 613-235-0784 • E-mail: cadsi@defenceandsecurity.ca • Internet: www.defenceandsecurity.ca • The Canadian Association of Defence and Security Industries (CADSI) is a not-for-profit national business association that represents the Canadian defence and security industries. Our mission is to foster an environment for member firms to thrive in the domestic and international defence and security marketplaces, thereby contributing to Canada's defence and security goals. CADSI currently represents approximately 500 member companies.

CANADIAN INFORMATION PROCESSING SOCIETY • 5090 Explorer Drive, Suite 801 • Mississauga, ON • L4W 4T9 • Tel: 905-602-1370 • Fax: 905-602-7884 • E-mail: info@cips.ca • Internet: www.cips.ca • Founded in 1958, The Canadian Information Processing Society (CIPS) represents more than 6,000 Information Technology (IT) professionals in 25 sections across Canada. They provide leadership in information systems and technologies by developing and promoting quality standards and practices, research, certification, and professional development while safeguarding the public interest.

CHEMICAL INSTITUTE OF CANADA, THE • 130 Slater Street, Suite 550 • Ottawa, ON • K1P 6E2 • Tel: 613-232-6252 • Fax: 613-232-5862 • E-mail: info@cheminst.ca • Internet: www.chemist.ca • The Chemical Institute of Canada is an umbrella organization for three Constituent Societies: the Canadian Society for Chemistry (CSC), the Canadian Society for Chemical Engineering (CSChE) and the Canadian Society for Chemical Technology (CSCT). The purpose of the Institute is to promote common scientific and technical interests and to provide service to all its members.

INFORMATION TECHNOLOGY ASSOCIATION OF CANADA • 5090 Explorer Drive, Suite 801 • Mississauga, ON • L4W 4T9 • Tel: 905-602-8345 • Fax: 905-602-8346 • E-mail: jgrosse@itac.ca • Internet: www.itac.ca • The Information Technology Association of Canada (ITAC) is the voice of the Canadian information technology industry. Together with its affiliated organizations across the country, the association represents 1300 companies in the information and communications technology (ICT) industry in all sectors including the production of hardware, microelectronics, software and electronic content and the delivery of ICT services.

INTERACTIVE MULTIMEDIA ARTS & TECHNOLOGIES ASSOCIATION • 4th Floor, 439 King Street W. • Toronto, ON • M5V 1K4 • Tel: 416-644-8685 • E-mail: imat@imat.ca • Internet: www.imat.ca • The Interactive Multimedia and Arts and Technologies Association (IMAT), Canada's largest, and fastest growing, non-profit, member-supported business association is dedicated to fostering growth and convergence between all partners in the new media cluster to strengthen the development, growth and recognition of Ontario's world-class digital-media industry. IMAT provides industry research, professional development, marketing, promotion and international trade opportunities for the New Media industry.

SOCIETY OF GRAPHIC DESIGNERS OF CANADA • ArtsCourt, 2 Daly Avenue • Ottawa, ON • K1N 6E2 • Tel: 613-567-5400 • Fax: 613-564-4428 • E-mail: info@gdc.net • Internet: www.gdc.net • The Society of Graphic Designers of Canada (GDC) is Canada's graphic design association. They are a member-based organization of design professionals, educators and students.

Biotechnology & Pharmaceutical

BIOTECANADA • 130 Albert Street, Suite 420 • Ottawa, ON • K1P 5G4 • Tel: 613-230-5585 • Fax: 613-563-8850 • E-mail: info@biotech.ca • Internet: www.biotech.ca • Biotechnology is broadly defined as the use of living organisms (plants, animals and micro organisms) to develop and improve products. BIOTECanada represents Canadian health care, agricultural, food, research and other organizations that are involved in biotechnology. BIOTECanada also offers a range of services to its members.

CANADA'S RESEARCH BASED PHARMACEUTICAL COMPANIES • 55 Metcalfe Street, Suite 1220 • Ottawa, ON • K1P 6L5 • Tel: 613-236-0455 • Fax: 613-236-6756 • E-mail: info@canadapharma.org • Internet: www.canadapharma.org • Canada's Research-based Pharmaceutical Companies is the national association representing over 22,000 Canadians who work for more than 50 research-based pharmaceutical companies in Canada.

CANADIAN ASSOCIATION OF PHARMACY STUDENTS & INTERNS • 17 Houde Drive. • Winnipeg, Manitoba • R3V 1C4 • Tel: 613-523-7877 • Fax: 613-523-0445 • E-mail: n/a • Internet: www.capsi.ca • The Canadian Association of Pharmacy Students (CAPSI) is a national organization unifying pharmacy students and interns across Canada. The mission of CAPSI and Interns is to provide its members with opportunities to strengthen their commitment to professionalism.

CANADIAN GENERIC PHARMACEUTICAL ASSOCIATION • 4120 Yonge Street, Suite 409 • Toronto, ON • M2P 2B8 • Tel: 416-223-2333 • Fax: 416-223-2425 • E-mail: info@canadiangenerics. ca • Internet: www.canadiangenerics.ca • The Canadian Generic Pharmaceutical Association (CGPA) represents the Canadian-based pharmaceutical industry: a dynamic group of companies which specialize in the production of high quality, affordable generic drugs, fine chemicals and new chemical entities. The industry plays a vital role in Canada's health care system by providing safe, proven alternatives to more expensive brand name prescription drugs. In addition, our companies are increasingly exporting their products and expanding their presence throughout the world.

CANADIAN PHARMACISTS ASSOCIATION • 1785 Alta Vista Drive • Ottawa, ON • K1G 3Y6 • Tel: 613-523-7877 • Fax: 613-523-0445 • E-mail: info@pharmacists.ca • Internet: www.cdnpharm.ca • The Canadian Pharmacists Association (CPhA) is the national voluntary organization of pharmacists committed to providing leadership for the profession. Their vision is to establish the pharmacist as the health professional whose practice, based on unique knowledge and skills about drug therapy, ensures optimal patient outcomes. CPhA achieves its vision by serving its members through advocacy, facilitation, provision of knowledge, participation in partnerships, research and innovation, education and health promotion.

CANADIAN SOCIETY OF HOSPITAL PHARMACISTS • 30 Concourse Gate, Unit 3 • Ottawa, ON • K2E 7V7 • Tel: 613-736-9733 • Fax: 613-736-5660 • Internet: www.cshp.ca • The Canadian Society of Hospital Pharmacists is the national voluntary organization of pharmacists who share an interest in pharmacy practice in hospitals and related health care settings.

FOOD BIOTECHNOLOGY COMMUNICATIONS NETWORK • 1 Stone Road, West • Guelph, ON • N1G 4Y2 • Tel: 519-826-3440 • Fax: 519-826-3441 • Internet: www.foodbiotech.org • The Food Biotechnology Communications Network (FBCN) is becoming Canada's leading information source for balanced, science-based facts about food biotechnology and its impact on our food system. FBCN offers a range of services including information referrals, a monthly fax newsletter, a regional network of experts, a website and issues management activities.

Business Services

ADVANCING CANADIAN ENTREPRENEURSHIP INC. • 100 Adelaide Street W., Suite 1302 • Toronto, ON • M5H 1S3 • Tel: 416-304-1566 • Fax: 416-864-0514 • Internet: www.acecanada. ca • ACE is a national, not-for-profit organization that is igniting young Canadians to create brighter futures for themselves and their communities. Working in partnerships with business and higher education. ACE organizes and motivates teams of university and college students who practice and teach others the principles and values of entrepreneurship and market economics. ACE currently delivers two programs on over 50 university and college campuses across Canada with the involvement of over 2000 student leaders and student entrepreneurs.

ASSOCIATION OF ADMINISTRATIVE ASSISTANTS • 97 - 1042 Falgarwood Drive • Oakville, ON • L6H 2P3 • Tel: 416-760-6907 • Fax: 416-324-0696 • E-mail: toronto-membership@aaa. ca • Internet: www.aaa.ca • The Association of Administrative Assistants is a charted, non-profit Canadian organization founded in April 1951. The Association's mission is to assist members in the continuing development of administrative skill, underlying knowledge and professional growth, thus enhancing employment opportunities and contributions to both work place and community.

ASSOCIATION OF CANADIAN SEARCH, EMPLOYMENT & STAFFING SERVICES • 6835 Century Avenue, 2nd Floor • Mississauga, ON • L5N 2L2 • Tel: 905-826-6869 • Fax: 905-826-4873 • E-mail: acsess@acsess.org • Internet: www.acsess.org • The Association of Canadian Search, Employment & Staffing Services (ACSESS) is a single voice for the employment, recruitment and staffing services in Canada. It promotes advancement and growth of the industry. The association is also proud to introduce a Canadian industry program, which has been designed to offer educational components that will confirm an individual staffing professional's comprehensive industry based knowledge. ACSESS also assumes a leadership role in ensuring that industry members are aware of legislation and regulatory changes which may (drastically) affect their business and responsibilities as employers.

ASSOCIATION OF INTERNATIONAL CUSTOMS AND BORDER AGENCIES • P.O. Box 40166, 2515 Bank Street • Ottawa, ON • K1V 0W8 • Tel: 613-822-6969 • Fax: 613-822-2889 • Internet: www.aicba.org • The Association of International Customs and Border Agencies (AICBA) is an association of corporations, proprietorships, and partnerships that are carriers of international freight, customs brokers, or international bridge or tunnel operators. AICBA's purpose is to secure public support in Canada and the United States of America, to make representations to governments, and to co-ordinate activities with other organizations.

CANADIAN ASSOCIATION OF IMPORTERS AND EXPORTERS • 160 Eglinton Avenue East Suite 300 • Toronto, ON • M4P 3B5 • Tel: 416-595-5333 • Fax: 416-595-8226 • E-mail: info@iecanada.com • Internet: www.importers.ca • The Canadian Association of Importers and Exporters (CAIE) is a private, non-profit organization, which has been servicing Canada's trade community since 1932. For more than 60 years, this Association has been the recognized voice of the importing community in Canada and internationally.

CANADIAN FEDERATION OF INDEPENDENT BUSINESS • 4141 Yonge Street, Suite 401 • Willowdale, ON • M2P 2A6 • Tel: 416-222-8022 • Fax: 416-222-7593 • E-mail: cfib@cfib.ca • Internet: www.cfib.ca • Since 1971 the Canadian Federation of Independent Business (CFIB) has been giving small firms a big voice in the public arena. If you own and operate your own business and are looking for ways to help it prosper, then CFIB can be of service. They have offices across the country. Best known for high-profile actions with governments on policies like tax, labour laws and public sector spending, they have also achieved many behind-the-scenes changes that have meant real dollars-and-cents benefits to all firms.

CANADIAN FINANCE & LEASING ASSOCIATION • 15 Toronto Street, Suite 301 • Toronto, ON • M5C 2E3 • Tel: 416-860-1133 • Fax: 416-860-1140 • E-mail: info@cfla-acfl.ca • Internet: www.cfla-acfl.ca • The Canadian Finance & Leasing Association (CFLA) represents the asset-based financing, equipment and vehicle leasing industry in Canada. With over $92.3 billion of financing in place with Canadian businesses and consumers, the asset-based financing industry is the largest provider of debt financing in this country after the traditional lenders (banks and credit unions).

CANADIAN FRANCHISE ASSOCIATION • 5399 Eglinton Avenue West, Suite 116 • Toronto, ON • M9C 5K6 • Tel: 416-695-2896 • Fax: 416-695-1950 • E-mail: info@cfa.ca • Internet: www. cfa.ca • The Canadian Franchise Association (CFA) represents over 350 franchise companies and the professionals who support this way of doing business. They are a national trade association of franchisors including Canada's leading franchise systems, all committed to achieving excellence in franchising. Their membership represents a diverse cross-section of franchisors in Canada, ranging from very large established systems to smaller regional concepts.

CANADIAN INDUSTRIAL RELATIONS ASSOCIATION • Université Laval • Ste-Foy, QC • G1K 7P4 • Tel: 418-656-2468 • Fax: 418-656-3175 • E-mail: acri-cira@rlt.ulaval.ca • Internet: www.cira-acri.ca • The Canadian Industrial Relations Association (CIRA) is a national network promoting discussion, research and education in the field of work and industrial relations. CIRA is open to any individual interested in industrial relations, work and employment, including union-management relations, labour law, human resources management, unionism, etc.

CANADIAN MANUFACTURERS & EXPORTERS • 6725 Airport Road Suite 200 • Mississauga ON • L4V 1V2 • Tel: 905-672-3466 • Fax: 905-672-1764 • Internet: www.cme-mec.ca • Canadian Manufacturers & Exporters (CME), known as the Alliance of Manufacturers & Exporters Canada until October, 2000, was formed through the merger in 1996 of the Canadian Manufacturers Association (CMA) and the Canadian Exporters Association (CEA). For more than 130 years, CME has successfully represented the interests of Canadian business, keeping members on the competitive edge of world-class manufacturing and trade. With strong divisions in every province, CME is a truly national association and the undisputed champion of business issues in Canada. Their mission is to continuously improve the competitiveness of Canadian industry and to expand export business.

CANADIAN OFFICE PRODUCTS ASSOCIATION • 135 Queens Plate Drive, Suite 525 • Toronto, ON • M9W 6V1 • Tel: 416-740-1363 • Fax: 416-740-1981 • E-mail: info@copa. ca • Internet: www.copa.ca • The Canadian Office Products Associaton (COPA) is an industry association representing the interests of Canada's office products retailers and manufacturers. They provide their members with programs and services that assist them in their day-to-day business, offering not only educational and networking opportunities, but also significant discounts on business expenditures that positively affect the bottom line.

CANADIAN PAYROLL ASSOCIATION • 250 Bloor Street East, Suite 1600 • Toronto, ON • M4W 1E6 • Tel: 416-487- 3380 • Fax: 416-487- 3384 • Internet: www.payroll.ca • The Canadian Payroll Association (CPA), founded in 1978 is the national association representing the payroll community in Canada. The CPA is influential, affecting payroll practices in hundreds of thousands of small, medium and large employers, and payroll service and software providers. Their mission is to provide leadership through advocacy and education to enable payroll practitioners to enhance operations, meet new legislative requirements and utilize emerging technologies.

CANADIAN PUBLIC RELATIONS SOCIETY, THE • 4195 Dundas Street West, Suite 346 • Toronto, ON • M8X 1Y4 • Tel: 416-239-7034 • Fax: 416-239-1076 • E-mail: admin@cprs.ca • Internet: www.cprs.ca • The Canadian Public Relations Society (CPRS) is an organization of men and women who practice public relations in Canada and abroad. Members work to maintain the highest standards and to share a uniquely Canadian experience in public relations. Today, CPRS is a federation of 16 Member Societies based in major cities or organized province-wide. All Member Societies adhere to the constitution of the National and Member Society.

CANADIAN REAL ESTATE ASSOCIATION • 200 Catherine Street, 6th Floor • Ottawa, ON • K2P 2K9 • Tel: 613-237-7111 • Fax: 613-234-2567 • E-mail: info@crea.ca • Internet: http://crea. ca • The Canadian Real Estate Association (CREA) is one of Canada's largest single-industry trade associations, representing more than 92,000 real estate brokers/agents and salepeople working through more than 100 real estate boards and 10 provincial association.

CANADIAN SOCIETY OF CUSTOMS BROKERS, THE • 320, 55 Murray Street, Suite 320 • Ottawa, ON • K1N 5M3 • Tel: 613-562-3543 • Fax: 613-562-3548 • E-mail: cscb@cscb.ca • Internet: www.cscb.ca • The Canadian Society of Customs Brokers' (CSCB) primary task is to represent the interests of members to government departments and agencies, and to work with both government and the trade community to ensure the health of the industry. They actively seek and achieve improvements their members look for in government policies and procedures. They provide advice and guidance to Canadian and international regulators on new policy directions. They develop strong partnerships throughout the industry to create effective business solutions for the future.

CANADIAN YOUTH BUSINESS FOUNDATION • 100 Adelaide Street West, Suite 1410 • Toronto, ON • M5H 1S3 • Tel: 1-866-646-2922 ext. 2108 • Fax: 1-877-408-3234 • E-mail: form • Internet: www.cybf.ca • The Canadian Youth Business Foundation's mission is to provide start-up financing, mentoring and educational resources that empower young canadians 18-34 to start and grow businesses which contribute to sustainable economic development in communities across Canada.

HUMAN RESOURCES PROFESSIONALS ASSOCIATION • 2 Bloor Street West, Suite 1902 • Toronto, ON • M4W 3E2 • Tel: 416-923-2324 • Fax: 416-923-7264 • E-mail: info@hrpao. org • Internet: www.hrpao.org • The Human Resources Professionals Association of Ontario (HRPAO) is the professional association for human resource management in Ontario. A growing association, HRPAO is moving forward strategically to meet the needs of the profession and business community for leading-edge human resource management. With over 16,000 members in chapters across the province, HRPAO connects professionals to an unmatched range of HR information resources, events, professional development and networking opportunities. As the voice of HR experience and expertise in Ontario, the association administers the Certified Human Resource Professional (CHRP) designation.

INTERNATIONAL PERSONNEL MANAGEMENT ASSOCIATION - CANADA • 14868 41 Avenue • Edmonton, AB • T6H 5N7 • Tel: 780-433-0234 • Fax: 780-433-0295 • E-mail: info@ipma-aigp.ca • Internet: www.ipma-aigp.ca • The International Personnel Management Association (IPMA) is a national human resource association with international connections to IPMA-HR in the United States and chapters worldwide. We are a non-profit organization, run by a dedicated team of volunteers. Our mission is to promote excellence in the practice of human resources management.

THE CANADIAN COURIER & LOGISTICS ASSOCIATION • 91 Rylander Boulevard, Unit 7, Suite 266 • Toronto, ON • M1B 5M5 • Tel: 905-837-1302 • Fax: 905-837-1758 • Internet: www.canadiancourier.org • The Canadian Courier & Logistics Association (CCLA) is a non-profit organization, whose mission is to represent and advance the interests of couriers and time sensitive logistics service providers operating in Canada.

Diversified

CANADIAN CO-OPERATIVE ASSOCIATION • 275 Bank Street, Suite 400 • Ottawa, ON • K2P 2L6 • Tel: 613-238-6711 • Fax: 613-567-0658 • E-mail: info@coopscanada.coop • Internet: www.coopscanada.coop The Canadian Co-operative Association (CCA) -is a national umbrella organization representing co-operatives and credit unions. They are a not-for-profit co-operative owned by their members. Their mission is to promote the growth and development of the co-operative sector for the economic and social betterment of communities and people in Canada and internationally.

Education

ASSOCIATION OF CANADIAN COMMUNITY COLLEGES • 1223 Michael Street North, Suite 200 • Ottawa, ON • K1J 7T2 • Tel: 613-746-2222 • Fax: 613-746-6721 • Internet: www. accc.ca • The Association of Canadian Community Colleges (ACCC) is the national, voluntary membership organization created in 1972 to represent colleges and institutes to government, business and industry, both in Canada and internationally.

ASSOCIATION OF UNIVERSITIES AND COLLEGES OF CANADA • 350 Albert Street, Suite 600 • Ottawa, ON • K1R 1B1 • Tel: 613-563-1236 • Fax: 613-563-9745 • E-mail: info@aucc.ca • Internet: www.aucc.ca The Association of Universities and Colleges of Canada is the voice of Canada's universities. They represent 92 Canadian public and private not-for-profit universities and university-degree level colleges. Since 1911, they have provided strong and effective representation for our members, in Canada and abroad. Their mandate is to facilitate the development of public policy on higher education and to encourage cooperation among universities and governments, industry, communities, and institutions in other countries.

CANADIAN ASSOCIATION OF SCHOOL ADMINISTRATORS • 1123 Glenashton Drive • Oakville, ON • L6H 5M1 • Tel: 905-845-2345 • Fax: 905-845-2044 • Internet: www.casa-acas.ca • The Canadian Association of School Administrators (CASA) is the national voice for senior educational leaders. The organization is a federation of the professional associations representing the senior administrators in Canadian provinces and territories. Associate members include professors of educational administration, graduate students in educational administration, and individual administrators.

CANADIAN BUREAU FOR INTERNATIONAL EDUCATION • 220 Laurier Avenue West, Suite 1550 • Ottawa, ON • K1P 5Z9 • Tel: 613-237-4820 • Fax: 613-237-1073 • E-mail: info@cbie.ca • Internet: www.cbie.ca • The Canadian Bureau for International Education (CBIE) is an umbrella non-governmental organization comprised of 200 colleges, universities, schools, school boards, educational organizations and businesses across Canada. Nationally, CBIE engages in policy development, research, advocacy and public information. CBIE is both a leader in shaping Canada's international education agenda and a highly recognized provider of professional development programs for Canada's international educators. CBIE manages vital services for foreign students in Canada.

CANADIAN COUNSELLING ASSOCIATION • 16 Concourse Gate, Suite 600 • Ottawa, ON • K2E 7S8 • Tel: 613-237-1099 • Fax: 613-237-9786 • E-mail: info@ccacc.ca • Internet: www.ccacc.ca • The Canadian Counselling Association is a national and bilingual organization dedicated to the enhancement of the counselling profession in Canada.

CANADIAN EDUCATION ASSOCIATION • 317 Adelaide Street West, Suite 300 • Toronto, ON • M5V 1P9 • Tel: 416-591-6300 • Fax: 416-591-5345 • E-mail: info@cea-ace.ca • Internet: www.cea-ace.ca • The Canadian Education Association is the network for leaders in education. Leaders depend on them to look at the latest trends and to connect them with the most innovative ideas and important research focussing not only on Canada but internationally as well.

CANADIAN FOUNDATION FOR ECONOMIC EDUCATION • 110 Eglinton Avenue West, Suite 201 • Toronto, ON • M4R 1A3 • Tel: 416-968-2236 • Fax: 416-968-0488 • E-mail: info@cfee.org • Internet: www.cfee.org • The Canadian Foundation for Economic Education was established in 1974 as a nationwide, non-profit, non-partisan organization. They work to promote and assist the enhanced economic capability of Canadians — that is, to increase the extent to which Canadians assume their economic roles, and make economic decisions, with competence and confidence. The Foundation produces resources, both teaching kits and student materials, on the economy, economics, and entrepreneurship in all formats — print, video, and CD-ROM in both official languages.

CANADIAN LIBRARY ASSOCIATION • 328 Frank Street • Ottawa, ON • K2P 0X8 • Tel: 613-232-9625 • Fax: 613-563-9895 • E-mail: info@cla.ca • Internet: www.cla.ca • The Canadian Library Association (CLA) membership consists of a diverse group of individuals and organizations involved or interested in library or information sciences. A large proportion of CLA Members work in college, university, public, special (corporate, non-profit and government) and school libraries. Others sit on the boards of public libraries, work for companies that provide goods and services to libraries, or are students in graduate level or community college programs. Membership categories of the Canadian Library Association include: Personal, Institutional, Associate and Trustee.

CANADIAN TEACHERS' FEDERATION • 2490 Don Reid Drive • Ottawa, ON • K1H 1E1 • Tel: 613-232-1505 • Fax: 613-232-1886 • E-mail: info@ctf-fce.ca • Internet: www.ctf-fce.ca • As the national bilingual umbrella organization for teachers in this country, the Canadian Teachers' Federation (CTF) has 14 provincial and territorial Member organizations representing 220,000 teachers across Canada. CTF is a powerful voice for the profession and provides much needed support to its Member organizations and teachers at a time when many governments have moved ahead with very regressive education agendas. CTF's major areas of concern include: defending public education; promoting the teaching profession; providing support to Member organizations and teachers across Canada; addressing societal issues that affect the health and well-being of children and youth in Canada and abroad; and providing assistance and support to teacher colleagues in developing countries.

Energy

CANADIAN ELECTRICITY ASSOCIATION • 350 Sparks Street, Suite 907 • Ottawa, ON • K1R 7S8 • Tel: 613-230-9263 • Fax: 613-230-9326 • E-mail: info@canelect.ca • Internet: www. canelect.ca • Founded in 1891, the Canadian Electricity Association (CEA) is the national forum and voice of the evolving electricity business in Canada. The Association contributes to the regional, national and international success of its members through the delivery of quality value-added services.

CANADIAN ENERGY RESEARCH INSTITUTE • 3512 - 33rd Street NW, Suite 150 • Calgary, AB • T2L 2A6 • Tel: 403-282-1231 • Fax: 403-284-4181 • Internet: www.ceri.ca • The Canadian Energy Research Institute (CERI) is an independent, non-profit research institute committed to excellence in the analysis of energy economics and related environmental policy issues in the producing, transportation, and consuming sectors.

CANADIAN INSTITUTE OF ENERGY • 987 Devon Road • North Vancouver, BC • V7R 1V8 • Tel: 604-290-0880 • Fax: 604-922-2002 • E-mail: info@cienergy.org • Internet: www.cienergy. org • The Canadian Institute of Energy (CIE) is a broadly based, non-profit organization open to those involved in all aspects of the energy industry. CIE's objectives are to provide a Canadian perspective on energy technology, business and policy, nationally and internationally, for those affected professionally or personally by energy issues; to encourage energy research, education and dissemination of topical information; and to provide an unbiased forum for discussion and debate of energy-related issues.

CANADIAN NUCLEAR ASSOCIATION • 130 Albert Street, Suite 1610 • Ottawa, ON • K1P 5G4 • Tel: 613-237-4262 • Fax: 613-237-0989 • Internet: www.cna.ca • The Canadian Nuclear Association (CNA) is a non-profit organization established in 1960 to represent the nuclear industry in Canada and promote the development and growth of nuclear technologies for peaceful purposes. Nuclear energy in Canada generates over 15% of Canada's electricity and almost half of Ontario's without polluting the air. It directly employs over 21,000 people and another 10,000 indirectly in industry, government and other organizations involved in the nuclear field including uranium milling, mining and processing, developers and operators of nuclear power plants and facilities, electrical utilities, nuclear medicine to aerospace and automotive research, manufacturing, engineering, consulting and educational institutions.

ENERGY COUNCIL OF CANADA • 350 Sparks Street, Suite 608 • Ottawa, ON • K1R 7S8 • Tel: 613-232-8239 • Fax: 613-232-1079 • E-mail: brigitte.dignard@energy.ca • Internet: www.

energy.ca • The Energy Council of Canada (ECC) is the Canadian Member Committee of the World Energy Council. With over 75 members from Canada's energy sector, they are a non-profit organization dedicated to enhancing the effectiveness of our national energy policy. The ECC also provides consumers with the information to incorporate greener options.

Engineering & Architectural

ASSOCIATION OF CONSULTING ENGINEERS OF CANADA • 130 Albert Street, Suite 616 • Ottawa, ON • K1P 5G4 • Tel: 613-236-0569 • Fax: 613-236-6193 • E-mail: info@acec. ca • Internet: www.acec.ca • Founded in 1925, the Association of Consulting Engineers of Canada (ACEC) is the national association of consulting firms that provide engineering and other technology-based intellectual services to the build and natural environment. Member companies offer professional engineering services world wide to private sector and government clients. ACEC's mission is to promote and safeguard the business and professional interests of the Canadian consulting engineering industry in Canada and abroad.

CANADIAN SOCIETY FOR PROFESSIONAL ENGINEERS, THE • 4950 Yonge Street, Suite 502 • Toronto, ON • M2N 6K1 • Tel: 416-223-9961 • E-mail: info@cspe.ca • Internet: www. cspe.ca • The Canadian Society for Professional Engineers is a non-regulatory, non-profit, federal corporation. CSPE has been restructured into an umbrella organization for provincial and territorial P.Eng. advocacy societies, to provide member services and advance advocacy for Canada's professional engineers.

CANADIAN SOCIETY OF LANDSCAPE ARCHITECTS • P.O. Box 13594 • Ottawa, ON • K2K 1X6 • Tel: 613-622-5520 • Fax: 613-622-5870 • E-mail: franpauze@csla.ca • Internet: www. aapc.ca • The CSLA represents over 1300 landscape architects and acts as a communication tool to increase public awareness and promote the profession.

INTERIOR DESIGNERS OF CANADA • 220 - 6 Adelaide Street East • Toronto, ON • M5C 1H6 • Tel: 416-594-9310 • Fax: 416-921-3660 • E-mail: info@interiordesigncanada.org • Internet: www.interiordesigncanadaorg • The Interior Designers of Canada has served the industry in advancing the profession through high standards of education, professional development, professional responsibility and communication.With the support of its seven provincial association members, IDC provides a forum for the unified voice of Canadian interior designers, so that the profession continues to grow and receive recognition and respect, locally, nationally and internationally, from government, industry and the public sector.

ROYAL ARCHITECTURAL INSTITUTE OF CANADA, THE • 330-55 rue Murray Street • Ottawa, ON • K1N 5M3 • Tel: 613-241-3600 • Fax: 613-241-5750 • E-mail: info@raic.org • Internet: www.raic.org • The Royal Architectural Institute of Canada (RAIC), established in 1907, is a voluntary national association representing more than 3,600 architects, and faculty and graduates of accredited Canadian Schools of Architecture from every region of the country. RAIC is the voice for architecture and its practice in Canada. It provides the national framework for the development and recognition of architectural excellence.

Entertainment & Leisure

ALLIANCE OF CANADIAN CINEMA, TELEVISION AND RADIO ARTISTS • 625 Church Street • Toronto, ON • M4Y 2G1 • Tel: 416-489-1311 • Fax: 416-489-8076 • E-mail: national@ actra.ca • Internet: www.actra.com • ACTRA is a national organization of 21,000 Canadian performers working in the English-language recorded media: Film, Television, Video and all other recorded media. The Mission of ACTRA - and its predecessors - has always been to negotiate, safeguard and promote the professional rights of their Members. Interpreting this in its broadest sense, ACTRA also strives to increase work opportunities for their Members and to pursue performer-friendly public policies at the municipal, provincial and federal levels.

CANADIAN ACADEMY OF RECORDING ARTS & SCIENCE • 345 Adelaide Street West, 2nd Floor • Toronto, ON • M5V 1R5 • Tel: 416-485-3135 • Fax: 416-485-4978 • E-mail: info@ carasonline.ca • Internet: www.carasonline.ca • The Canadian Academy of Recording Arts & Science is established to administer the Juno Awards annually, which recognizes and celebrates excellence of achievement in recorded music.

CANADIAN MARINE MANUFACTURERS ASSOCIATION • 243 North Service Road West, Suite 106 • Oakville, ON • L6M 3E5 • Tel: 905-845-4999 • Fax: 905-845-1701 • Internet: www. cmma.ca • Email: cmma_info@cmma.ca • The Canadian Marine Manufacturers Association (CMMA) is the Canadian recreational marine industry association which represents the interests of those companies who manufacture and distribute recreational boating products in Canada. CMMA members come from all provinces and include companies supplying boats, motors, trailers and other products and services to Canada's recreational boating market. The CMMA currently has 80 members.

CANADIAN PARKS & RECREATION ASSOCIATION • 2197 Riverside Drive, Suite 404 • Ottawa, ON • K1H 7X3 • Tel: 613-523-5315 • Fax: 613-523-1182 • E-mail: cpra@cpra.ca • Internet: www.cpra.ca • The Canadian Parks and Recreation Association is a national voluntary-sector organization dedicated to realizing the full potential of parks and recreation services as a major contributor to community health and vibrancy. Our members are parks and recreation professionals represented in over 2,600 communities in Canada.

CANADIAN SPECIAL EVENTS SOCIETY • 7950 Suncrest Drive • Burnaby, BC • V5J 3N5 • Tel: 604-438-3687 • Fax:604-320-1938 • E-mail: bc@cses.ca • Internet: www.cses.ca • The Canadian Special Events Society (CSES) is a non-profit organization that represents the interests of the Special Events Industry in Canada.

MUSIC INDUSTRIES ASSOCIATION OF CANADA • 505 Consumers Road Suite 807 • Toronto, ON • M2J 4V8 • Tel: 416-490-1871 • Fax: 416-490-0369 • E-mail: info@miac.net • Internet: www.miac.net • The Music Industries Association of Canada (MIAC) is a national, non-profit, trade association representing Canadian manufacturers, distributors and retailers of musical instruments and accessories, keyboards, sound reinforcement products and published music.

PROFESSIONAL ASSOCIATION OF CANADIAN THEATRES • 215 Spadina Avenue, Suite 210 • Toronto, ON • M5T 2C7 • Tel: 416-595-6455 • Fax: 416-595-6450 • E-mail: info@pact. ca • Internet: www.pact.ca • The Professional Association of Canadian Theatres is a member-driven organization of professional Canadian theatres which serves as the collective voice of its members. For the betterment of Canada theatres, PACT provides leadership, national representation and a variety of programs and practical assistance to member companies.

Financial Institutions

CANADIAN BANKERS ASSOCIATION • Commerce Court West, 199 Bay Street, 30th Floor, Box 348 • Toronto, ON • M5L 1G2 • Tel: 416-362-6092 • Fax: 416-362-7705 • E-mail: inform@cba.ca • Internet: www.cba.ca • Established in 1891, the CBA works on behalf of 54 domestic chartered banks, foreign bank subsidiaries and foreign bank branches operating in Canada to advocate for efficient and effective public policies governing banks and to promote an understanding of the banking industry and its importance to Canadians and the Canadian economy.

CANADIAN CHAMBER OF COMMERCE • 360 Albert Street Suite 420 • Ottawa, ON • K1R 7X7 • Tel: 613-238-4000 • Fax: 613-238-7643 • E-mail: info@chamber.ca • Internet: www.chamber.ca • The Canadian Chamber of Commerce seeks to create a business climate of competitiveness, profitability, and job creation for businesses of all sizes in all sectors across Canada. They are the national and international voice for Canadian business.

CSI GLOBAL EDUCATION INC. • 200 Wellington Street West, 15th Floor • Toronto, ON • M5V 3C7 • Tel: 1-866-866-2601 • Fax: 1-866-866-2660 • E-mail: icb.info@csi.ca • Internet: www.csi. ca • CSI has been setting the standard for life-long education for financial professionals for more than 30 years. Having trained over 700,000 global professionals, our focus on leading educational and ethical standards means that our graduates have met the highest level of proficiency and certification, also to ensure that our graduates are the most current in every financial sector.

Food Manufacturers & Wholesalers

AGRICULTURAL INSTITUTE OF CANADA, THE • 280 Albert Street, Suite 900 • Ottawa, ON • K1P 5G8 • Tel: 613-232-9459 • Fax: 613-594-5190 • E-mail: office@aic.ca • Internet: www.aic.ca • The Agricultural Institute of Canada (AIC) represents individuals and organizations involved in Canadian Agriculture, food, environment and health, providing them opportunities for involvement in AIC activities, connection to a broad network of credible members and a voice for their views on food sufficiency, environment and food safety.

CANADA GRAINS COUNCIL • 220 Portage Avenue, Suite 1215 • Winnipeg, MB • R3C 0A5 • Tel: 204-925-2130 • Fax: 204-925-2132 • E-mail: office@canadagrainscouncil.ca • Internet: www.canadagrainscouncil.ca • The Canada Grains Council is an organization of companies and associations from the grain industry formed in 1969 to co-ordinate efforts to increase the sales and use of Canadian grains in domestic and world markets.

CANADIAN FEDERATION OF AGRICULTURE, THE • 75 Albert Street, Suite 1101 • Ottawa, ON • K1P 5E7 • Tel: 613-236-3633 • Fax: 613-236-5749 • E-mail: info@cfa-fca.ca • Internet: www.cfa-fca.ca • The Canadian Federation of Agriculture (CFA) was formed in 1935 to answer the need for a unified voice to speak on behalf of Canadian farmers. It continues today as a farmer-funded, national umbrella organization representing provincial general farm organizations and national commodity groups. Through its members, it represents over 200,000 Canadian farm families from coast to coast.

CANADIAN INSTITUTE OF FOOD SCIENCE & TECHNOLOGY • 3-1750 The Queensway, Suite 1311 • Toronto, ON • M9C 5H5 • Tel: 905-271-8338 • Fax: 905-271-8344 • E-mail: cifst@cifst.ca • Internet: www.cifst.ca • Founded in 1951, the Canadian Institute of Food Science & Technology (CIFST) is the national association for food industry professionals. Its membership of more than 1,200 is comprised of scientists and technologists in industry, government and academia who are committed to advancing food science and technology.

CANADIAN PRODUCE MARKETING ASSOCIATION • 162 Cleopatra Drive • Ottawa, ON • K2G 5X2 • Tel: 613-226-4187 • Fax: 613-226-2984 • E-mail: question@cpma.ca • Internet: www.cpma.ca • The Canadian Produce Marketing Association (CPMA) is a not-for-profit organization representing companies that are active in the marketing of fresh fruits and vegetables in Canada from the farm gate to the dinner plate. CPMA members include major grower/shippers/packers, importer/exporters, carriers, brokers, wholesalers, retailers, fresh cuts and foodservice distributors, integrating all segments of the fresh produce industry. The CPMA also represents 670 members who are responsible for 90% of fresh fruit and vegetable sales in Canada.

DIETITIANS OF CANADA • 480 University Avenue, Suite 604 • Toronto, ON • M5G 1V2 • Tel: 416-596-0857 • Fax: 416-596-0603 • Internet: www.dietitians.ca • E-mail: centralinfo@ dietitians.ca Dietitians of Canada (DC) is the nation-wide voice of dietitians - the most trusted source of information on food and nutrition for Canadians. DC brings the knowledge and skills of its members together to influence decisions that affect food, nutrition and health. Formerly the Canadian Dietetic Association (1935-96), DC has set the standard for education of dietitians and professional dietetic practice.

FOOD BEVERAGE CANADA • 17914 - 105 Avenue, Suite 201 • Edmonton, AB • T5S 2H5 • Tel: 780-486-9679 • Fax: 780-484-0985 • Internet: www.foodbeveragecanada.com • Food Beverage Canada Association is an industry association committed to the development of export strategies and programs that will strengthen and increase its members' share of global food and beverage markets. The programs FBC offers are designed to be focused, relevant, user-friendly, and result oriented.

FOOD PROCESSORS OF CANADA • 350 Sparks Street • Ottawa, ON • K1R 7S8 • Tel: 613-722-1000 • Fax: 613-722-1404 • E-mail: fpc@foodprocessors.ca • Internet: http://foodnet. fic.ca • Food Processors of Canada (FPC) is an internationally respected business association serving food industry executives on matters concerning trade, commerce and manufacturing. The members of FPC own or manage food processing companies in Canada. They add value to inputs sourced from around the world and service markets in 80 countries.

Government

CANADIAN INSTITUTE OF STRATEGIC STUDIES • 165 University Ave. • Toronto, ON • M5H 3B8 • Tel: 416-322-8128 • Fax: 416-322-8129 • E-mail: info@ciss.ca • Internet: www. ciss.ca • Established in 1976, the Canadian Institute of Strategic Studies (CISS) has gained wide recognition as the nation's foremost source of independent and balanced information and research on a broad range of issues affecting Canada. It satisfies a need for a body of informed opinion on defence and security issues and stimulates greater public awareness of national and international developments.

FEDERATION OF CANADIAN MUNICIPALITIES • 24 Clarence Street • Ottawa, ON • K1N 5P3 • Tel: 613-241-5221 • Fax: 613-241-7440 • Internet: www.fcm.ca • The Federation of Canadian Municipalities (FCM) has been the national voice of municipal government since 1901. FCM is dedicated to improving the quality of life in all communities by promoting strong, effective and accountable municipal government.

Hospitality

CANADIAN RESTAURANT & FOODSERVICES ASSOCIATION • 316 Bloor Street West • Toronto, ON • M5S 1W5 • Tel: 416-923-8416 • Fax: 416-923-1450 • E-mail: info@crfa.ca • Internet: www.crfa.ca • The Canadian Restaurant and Foodservices Association is the largest hospitality association in Canada. Since its founding in 1944, CRFA has grown to represent more than 25,000 members. Members include restaurants, bars, hotels, caterers, institutions, educators and foodservice suppliers. CRFA's mission is to create a favourable business environment and deliver tangible value to our members in all sectors of Canada's foodservice industry.

HOTEL & RESTAURANT SUPPLIERS ASSOCIATION INC. • 9300 Henri Bourassa Blvd West, suite 230 • Saint-Laurent, QC • H4S 1L5 • Tel: 514-334-5161 • Fax: 514-334-1279 • E-mail: info@afhr.com • Internet: www.afhr.com • The Hotel and Restaurant Suppliers Association (HRSA) is the resource centre for suppliers in the hotel, restaurant and institutional sectors.

The Association wishes to ensure exposure for its members and to establish business relations between buyers and product and service suppliers in the industry.

HOTEL ASSOCIATION OF CANADA • 130 Albert Street, Suite 1206 • Ottawa, ON • K1P 5G4 • Tel: 613-237-7149 • Fax: 613-237-8928 • E-mail: info@hotelassociation.ca • Internet: www.hotelassociation.ca • Founded in 1913, the Hotel Association of Canada is the national organization representing the accommodation industry in Canada. Their membership encompasses the provincial and territorial hotel associations, the corporate hotel chains, independent hotels, motels and resorts and the many suppliers to the hotel industry.

Hospitals & Medical

CANADIAN ASSOCIATION OF OCCUPATIONAL THERAPISTS • CTTC Building, 1125 Colonel By Drive, Suite 3400 • Ottawa, ON • K1S 5R1 • Tel: 613-523-2268 • Fax: 613-523-2552 • E-mail: sdokuchie@caot.ca • Internet: www.caot.ca • The Canadian Association of Occupational Therapists provides services, products, events and networking opportunities to assist occupational therapists achieve excellence in their professional practice. In addition CAOT provides national leadership to actively develop and promote the client-centred profession of occupational therapy in Canada and internationally.

CANADIAN ASSOCIATION ON GERONTOLOGY • 222 College St. Suite 106 • Toronto, ON • M5T 3J1 • Tel: 416-978-7977 • Fax: 416-978-4771 • E-mail: contact@cagacg.ca • Internet: www.cagacg.ca • The Canadian Association on Gerontology (CAG) is a national, multidisciplinary association established to provide leadership in matter relating to the aging population in Canada. Through its many activities, CAG helps to foster research, education, and policy aimed at improving the quality of life of the elderly in Canada.

CANADIAN CENTRE FOR OCCUPATIONAL HEALTH AND SAFETY • 135 Hunter Street East • Hamilton, ON • L8N 1M5 • Tel: 905-570-8094 • Fax: 905-572-2206 • E-mail: clientservices@ccohs.ca • Internet: www.ccohs.ca • The Canadian Centre for Occupational Health and Safety (CCOHS) is a Canadian federal government agency based in Hamilton, Ontario, which serves to support the vision of eliminating all Canadian work-related illnesses and injuries.

CANADIAN CHIROPRACTIC ASSOCIATION, THE • 600 - 30 St. Patrick Street • Toronto, ON • M5T 3A3 • Tel: 416-781-5656 • Fax: 416-781-0923 • E-mail: ccachiro@ccachiro.org • Internet: www.ccachiro.org • The Canadian Chiropractic Association is a national, voluntary organization representing Canada's licensed chiropractors. The CCA is committed to enhancing the health of Canadians by supporting clinical excellence, chiropractic research and inter-disciplinary collaboration. There are approximately 6,000 chiropractors in Canada of whom 85 per cent are members of the association.

CANADIAN DENTAL ASSOCIATION • 1815 Alta Vista Drive • Ottawa, ON • K1G 3Y6 • Tel: 613-523-1770 • E-mail: reception@cda-adc.ca • Internet: www.cda-adc.ca • The Canadian Dental Association (CDA) is the authoritative national voice of dentistry dedicated to advancement and leadership of a unified profession and to the promotion of optimal oral health, an essential component of general health.

CANADIAN HEALTHCARE ASSOCIATION • 17 York Street • Ottawa, ON • K1N 9J6 • Tel: 613-241-8005 • Fax: 613-241-5055 • E-mail: info@cha.ca • Internet: www.cha.ca • The Canadian Healthcare Association (CHA) is the federation of provincial and territorial hospital and health organizations across Canada. Through their members, CHA represents a broad continuum of care, including acute care, home and community care, long term care, public health, mental health, palliative care, addiction services, children, youth and family services, housing services, and professional and licensing bodies.

CANADIAN MEDICAL ASSOCIATION • 1867 Alta Vista Drive • Ottawa, ON • K1G 3Y6 • Tel: 1-888-855-2555 • Fax: 613-236-8864 • E-mail: cmamsc@cma.ca • Internet: www.cma.ca • The Canadian Medical Association (CMA) is the national voice of physicians in Canada. Their mission is to serve and unite the physicians of Canada and be the national advocate, in partnership with the people of Canada for the highest standards of health and health care.

CANADIAN NURSES ASSOCIATION • 50 Driveway • Ottawa, ON • K2P 1E2 • Tel: 613-237-2133 • Fax: 613-237-3520 • E-mail: info@cna-aiic.ca • Internet: www.cna-aiic.ca • The Canadian Nurses Association (CNA) is a federation of 11 provincial and territorial registered nurses associations representing more than 133,714 Canadian registered nurses. CNA is the national professional voice of Registered Nurses,supporting them in their practice and advocating for health public policy and a quality, publicly funded, not-for-profit health system.

CANADIAN PHYSIOTHERAPY ASSOCIATION • 2345 Yonge Street; Suite 410 • Toronto, ON • M4P 2E5 • Tel: 416-932-1888 • Fax: 416-932-9708 • E-mail: information@physiotherapy.ca • Internet: www.physiotherapy.ca • The Canadian Physiotherapy Association (CPA) is the national professional association representing almost 10,000 members distributed throughout all provinces and territories. CPA's mission is to provide leadership and direction to the physiotherapy profession, foster excellence in practice, education and research, and promote high standards of health in Canada.

CANADIAN PSYCHOLOGICAL ASSOCIATION • 141 Laurier Avenue West, Suite 702 • Ottawa, ON • K1P 5J3 • Tel: 613-237-2144 • Fax: 613-237-1674 • E-mail: cpa@cpa.ca • Internet: www.cpa.ca • The Canadian Psychological Association was organized in 1939 and incorporated under the Canada Corporations Act, Part II, in May 1950. Its objectives are to improve the health and welfare of all Canadians; to promote excellence and innovation in psychological research, education, and practice; to promote the advancement, development, dissemination, and application of psychological knowledge; and to provide high-quality services to members.

CANADIAN SOCIETY FOR INTERNATONAL HEALTH • One Nicholas Street, Suite 1105 • Ottawa, ON • K1N 7B7 • Tel: 613-241-5785 • Fax: 613-241-3845 • E-mail: csih@csih.org • Internet: www.csih.org • The Canadian Society for International Health (CSIH) is a national non-governmental organization with members committed to the promotion of international health and development. CSIH members offer a solid network of experts and experience with the Canadian government, international agencies, non-governmental organizations and academia to promote a collective agenda.

CANADIAN SOCIETY OF MICROBIOLOGISTS • 305-1750 Courtwood Crescent • Ottawa, ON • K2C 2B5 • Tel: 613-225-8889 • Fax: 613-225-9621 • E-mail: info@csm-scm.org • Internet: www.csm-scm.org • The Canadian Society of Microbiologists seeks to advance microbiology in all its aspects and to facilitate the interchange of ideas between microbiologists. The membership includes honorary, emeritus, ordinary, student and sustaining members.

CANADIAN VETERINARY MEDICAL ASSOCIATION • 339 Booth Street • Ottawa, ON • K1R 7K1 • Tel: 613-236-1162 • Fax: 613-236-9681 • E-mail: admin@cvma-acmv.org • Internet: http://canadianveterinarians.net • The Canadian Veterinary Medical Association (CVMA) is the national body serving and representing the interests of the veterinary profession in Canada. The association is committed to excellence within the profession and to the well-being of animals.

COLLEGE OF FAMILY PHYSICIANS OF CANADA, THE • 2630 Skymark Avenue • Mississauga, ON • L4W 5A4 • Tel: 905-629-0900 • Fax: 905-629-0893 • Internet: www.cfpc.ca • The College of Family Physicians of Canada is a national voluntary organization of family physicians that makes continuing medical education of its members mandatory. The College strives to improve the health of Canadians by promoting high standards of medical education and care in family practice, by contributing to public understanding of healthful living, by supporting ready access to family physician services, and by encouraging research and disseminating knowledge about family medicine.

MEDICAL COUNCIL OF CANADA • P.O. Box 8234, Stn. T, 2283 St. Laurent Blvd., Suite 100 • Ottawa, ON • K1G 3H7 • Tel: 613-521-6012 • Fax: 613-521-9417 • E-mail: MCC_Admin@mcc. ca • Internet: www.mcc.ca • The Medical Council of Canada (MCC) is committed to ensuring the highest level of medical care for Canadians through excellence in evaluation of physicians. The license to practice medicine in Canada is granted by each provincial and territorial medical licensing authority, under respective Medical Acts and upon meeting specific regulated conditions. In 1912, the Medical Council of Canada was constituted by the Canada Medical Act in order to facilitate portability and reciprocity between the different provinces.

OPTICIANS ASSOCIATION OF CANADA • 83 Garry Street, Suite 2706 • Winnipeg, MB • R3C 4J9 • Tel: 204-982-6060 • Fax: 204-947-2519 • E-mail: canada@opticians.ca • Internet: www.opticians.ca • The Opticians Association of Canada is a non profit organization which was ultimately incorporated in 1990. The OAC represents approximately 6000 opticians. The objective and purpose of the Association are to represent the common interest of dispensing opticians in Canada. The Association strives to ensure high quality products and services are provided in Canada by its opticians and to promote the highest standard of education for those opticians. In addition, the Association is mandated to review legislation affecting the eye care industry and to seek changes where deemed necessary.

Insurance

CANADIAN ASSOCIATION OF INSURANCE AND FINANCIAL ADVISORS (ADVOCIS) • 390 Queens Quay West, Ste. 209 • Toronto, ON • M5V 3A2 • Tel: 416-444-5251or 1-800-563-5822 • Fax: 416-444-8031 • E-mail: info@advocis.ca • Internet: www.advocis.ca • Advocis is the brand name of The Financial Advisors Association of Canada. In September 2002, members of the Canadian Association of Insurance and Financial Advisors (CAIFA) and the Canadian Association of Financial Planners (CAFP) voted in favour of merging their two groups to create Advocis, Canada's largest association of professional financial advisors, representing approximately 12,000 members in 49 Chapters across the country.

INSURANCE BROKERS ASSOCIATION OF CANADA • 1230-155 University Avenue • Toronto, ON • M5H 3B7 • Tel: 416-367-1831 • Fax: 416-367-3687 • E-mail: ibac@ibac.ca • Internet: www.ibac.ca • The Insurance Brokers Association of Canada (IBAC) is a federation of 11 provincial/regional associations, representing about 30,000 property and casualty (P&C) insurance brokers in Canada.

INSURANCE INSTITUTE OF CANADA • 18 King Street East 16th Floor • Toronto, ON • M5C 1C4 • Tel: 416-362-8586 • Fax: 416-362-8081 • E-mail: IIOmail@insuranceinstitute.ca • Internet: www.insuranceinstitute.ca • The Insurance Institute is the professional education arm of the general insurance industry in Canada. It is a not-for-profit association of 35,000 individual members employed in the general insurance business with insurance reinsurance companies, brokerages, agencies, adjusting firms and employers of risk managers. This number includes some 20,000 active students and 15,000 graduates of institute programs.

LIFE INSURANCE INSTITUTE OF CANADA • 1243 Islington Avenue, Suite 505 • Toronto, ON • M8X 1Y9 • Tel: 416-234-5661 • Fax: 416-233-5031 • E-mail: liic@loma.org • Internet: www.liic.ca • The Life Insurance Institute of Canada (LIIC), A LOMA Institute, is a non-profit association representing a major portion of Canada's life and health insurance industry, in business to serve the educational and professional development needs of their membership and their employees.

Investment

ADVOCIS, THE FINANCIAL ADVISORS ASSOCIATION OF CANADA • 390 Queens Quay West, Suite 209 • Toronto, ON • M5V 3A2 • Tel: 416-444-5251 or 1-800-563-5822 • E-mail: info@advocis.ca • Internet: www.advocis.ca • Today, Advocis, The Financial Advisors Association of Canada, is the oldest and largest voluntary professional membership association of financial advisors in Canada. We are the home and the voice of Canada's financial advisors. Through its predecessor associations Advocis proudly continues a century of uninterrupted history of serving Canadian financial advisors, their clients, and the nation.

CANADIAN INSTITUTE OF PLANNERS • 116 Albert Street, Suite 801 • Ottawa, ON • K1P 5G3 • Tel: 613-237-7526 • Fax: 613-237-7045 • E-mail: general@cip-icu.ca • Internet: www. cip-icu.ca • The Canadian Institute of Planners (CIP) has been dedicated to the advancement of responsible planning throughout Canada since 1919. In its capacity as the national professional institute and certification body for the planning profession in Canada.

CANADIAN SECURITIES INSTITUTE • 200 Wellington Street West, 15th Floor • Toronto, ON • M5V 3C7 • Tel: 1-866-866-2601 • Fax: 1-866-866-2660 • E-mail: customer_support@csi.ca • Internet: www.csi.ca • The Canadian Securities Institute (CSI) is Canada's leader in investment learning. Created in 1970, CSI has launched and enchanced the careers of more than 500,000 financial professionals through our courses and programs.

CREDIT INSTITUTE OF CANADA • 219 Dufferin Street Suite 216C • Toronto, ON • M6K 3J1 Tel: 416-572-2615 • Fax: 416-572-2619 • E-mail: generalinformation@creditedu.org • Internet: www.creditedu.org • The Credit Institute of Canada is a not-for-profit Educational and Membership Association of Credit Professionals. Their goal is to educate and continuously develop Credit Professionals for their personal development and for the benefit of the Canadian Businesses that employ them. The Credit Institute of Canada has been recognized for the knowledge and expertise in Credit Management for almost 75 years.

INVESTMENT DEALERS ASSOCIATION OF CANADA • 121 King Street West, Suite 1600 • Toronto, ON • M5H 3T9 • Tel: 416-364-6133 • Fax: 416-364-0753 • E-mail: secretary@ida. ca • Internet: www.ida.ca • The Investment Dealers Association of Canada, the national self-regulatory organization and trade association for the Canadian securities industry, represents more than 200 Member firms across the country.

INVESTMENT FUNDS INSTITUTE OF CANADA, THE • 11 King Street West, 4th Floor • Toronto, ON • M5H 4C7 • Tel: 416-363-2150 • Fax: 416-861-9937 • Internet: www.ific.ca • The Investment Funds Institute of Canada (IFIC) is the national association of the Canadian mutual fund industry. IFIC is dedicated to enhancing the integrity and growth of the industry with a consistently high level of service in a cooperative forum to allow Members to work together to enhance their industry.

TREASURY MANAGEMENT ASSOCIATION OF CANADA • 8 King St. E., Suite 1010 • Toronto, ON • M5C 1B5 • Tel: 416-367-8500 • Fax: 416-367-3240 • E-mail: info@tmac.ca • Internet: www.tmac.ca • The Treasury Management Association of Canada (TMAC) is a federation of 14 regional associations of professional treasury managers. TMAC offers educational and networking opportunities to treasury and financial professionals in all sectors of the Canadian economy

Management & Consulting

ASSOCIATION OF CANADIAN ADVERTISERS INC. • 95 St. Clair Avenue West Suite 1103 • Toronto, ON • M4V 1N6 • Tel: 1-800-565-0109 or 416-964-3805 • Fax: 416-964-0771 • E-mail: cpagnoud@ACAweb.ca • Internet: www.aca-online.com • The Association of Canadian Advertisers Incorporated (ACA) is a national, not-for-profit association exclusively dedicated to serving the interests of companies that market and advertise their products and services in Canada. Founded in 1914 and incorporated in 1917, membership in the ACA is restricted to advertisers only. Unlike most industry associations, the ACA does not represent just one industry. It cuts across all products and service sectors, and speaks on behalf of over 200 companies and divisions who collectively account for estimated annual sales of $350 billion.

ASSOCIATION OF CANADIAN LANDS SURVEYORS • 900 Dynes Road, Suite 100E • Ottawa, ON • K2C 3L6 • Tel: 613-723-9200 • Fax: 613-723-5558 • E-mail: admin@acls-aatc.ca • Internet: www.acls-aatc.ca • The Association of Canada Lands Surveyors (ACLS) is a federally enacted professional Association. The ACLS has members located across Canada who have expertise in surveying, photogrammetry, remote sensing, geodesy, hydrography and land information systems.

CANADIAN INSTITUTE OF MANAGEMENT • 15 Collier Street, Lower Level • Barrie, ON • L4M 1G5 • Tel: 705-725-8926 • Fax: 705-725-8196 • E-mail: office@cim.ca • Internet: www.cim.ca • The Canadian Institute of Management (CIM) is Canada's senior management association. As a non-profit organization, the Institute was established in 1942 and is dedicated to enhancing managerial skills and professional development. Currently, there are 17 branches coast-to-coast with the National Office in Barrie.

CANADIAN MANAGEMENT CENTRE • 150 York Street, 5th Floor • Toronto, ON • M5H 3S5 • Tel: 1-877-CMC-2519 • Fax: 416-313-4985 • E-mail: cmcinfo@cmctraining.org • Internet: www.cmctraining.org • Canadian Management Centre (CMC) is the Canadian affiliate of the American Management Association (AMA), the world's largest membership-based training and business solutions organization. This connection allows them to offer a global network of world-renowned practitioners, powerful partnerships and international resources.

INSTITUTE OF COMMUNICATION AGENCIES • 2300 Yonge Street, Suite 3002 • Toronto, ON • M4P 1E4 • Tel: 416-482-1396 • Fax: 416-482-1856 • E-mail: ica@icacanada.ca • Internet: www.ica-ad.com • The Institute of Communication Agencies, formerly the Institute of Communications and Advertising, founded in 1905, represents Canada's communications and advertising agencies. ICA promotes higher standards and best practices, and serves as the largest source of information, advice and training for Canada's communication and advertising industry, whose economic impact is worth $14.5 billion annually.

INSTITUTE OF PUBLIC ADMINISTRATION OF CANADA • 1075 Bay Street, Suite 401 • Toronto, ON • M5S 2B1 • Tel: 416-924-8787 • Fax: 416-924-4992 • E-mail: form • Internet: www.ipaciapc.ca • The Institute of Public Administration of Canada (IPAC), founded in 1947, is a dynamic association of public servants, academics, and others interested in public administration.

PURCHASING MANAGEMENT ASSOCIATION OF CANADA • 777 Bay Street, Suite 2701, P.O. Box 112 • Toronto, ON • M5G 2C8 • Tel: 416-977-7111 • Fax: 416-977-8886 • E-mail: info@pmac.ca • Internet: www.pmac.ca • The Purchasing Management Association of Canada (PMAC) is the leading professional association in Canada for supply chain management professionals. The Association has more than 40,000 members and program participants working in all sectors of the Canadian economy, including retail, manufacturing, transportation, distribution, government, natural resources and service sectors.

Manufacturing

AUTOMOTIVE INDUSTRIES ASSOCIATION OF CANADA • 1272 Wellington Street West • Ottawa, ON • K1Y 3A7 • Tel: 1-800-808-2920 • Fax: 613-728-6021 • Internet: www.aiacanada. com • E-mail: info.aia@aiacanada.com • The Automotive Industries Association of Canada (AIA) is a national trade association representing the automotive aftermarket industry. AIA is the voice and the resource for the automotive aftermarket industry in Canada. Its mandate is to promote, educate and represent members in all areas that impact the growth and prosperity of the industry. AIA represents suppliers, distributors, wholesalers, and retailers.

AUTOMOTIVE PARTS MANUFACTURERS' ASSOCIATION • 10 Four Seasons Place, Suite 801 • Toronto, ON • M9B 6H7 • Tel: 416-620-4220 • Fax: 416-620-9730 • E-mail: info@apma. ca • Internet: www.apma.ca • Automotive Parts Manufacturers' Association (APMA) is Canada's national association representing OEM producers of parts, equipment, tools, supplies and services for the worldwide automotive industry. APMA's fundamental objective is to promote the automotive parts manufacturing industry both domestically and internationally. The Association provides important representation to both the Federal and Provincial Governments and also creates and executes global marketing initiatives in order to develop international trade and business opportunities for the membership.

CANADIAN AUTOMOBILE ASSOCIATION • 2525 Carling Avenue • Ottawa, ON • K2B 7Z2 • Tel: 613-820-1890 • Internet: www.caa.ca • The Canadian Automobile Association (CAA) is a federation of nine automotive clubs serving about 4.9 million members through 140 offices across Canada. CAA provides a wide range of member services and works to improve traveling and motoring conditions at home and around the world.

CANADIAN CONSTRUCTION ASSOCIATION • 75 Albert Street, Suite 400 • Ottawa, ON • K1P 5E7 • Tel: 613-236-9455 • Fax: 613-236-9526 • E-mail: cca@cca-acc.com • Internet: www. cca-acc.com • The Canadian Construction Association is the voice of Canada's largest industry. Representing interests of the non-residential sector of an industry that employs close to 1.1 million Canadian men and women, and that produces $140 billion in goods and services, CAA is uniquely positioned to speak to the federal government on a wide range of issues.

CANADIAN DIE CASTERS ASSOCIATION • 3-247 Barr Street • Renfrew, ON • K7V 1J6 • Tel: 1-866-809-7032 • Fax: 1-613-432-6840 • E-mail: info@diecasters.ca • Internet: www.diecasters. ca • Incorporated in 1978, the Canadian Die Casters Association is a national trade association representing Canadian metal casters, suppliers, and associates.

CANADIAN FOUNDRY ASSOCIATION • 1 Nicholas Street, Suite 1500 • Ottawa, ON • K1N 7B7 • Tel: 613-789-4894 • Fax: 613-789-5957 • E-mail: judy@foundryassociation.ca • Internet: www.foundryassociation.ca • The Canadian Foundry Association (CFA) is the national voice for the foundry industry in Canada. The Association assists and represents its members, to deal with government on industry specific issues, as well as other areas of common interest. CFA gathers information and initiates crucial programs to assist members in strengthening their competitive position, thus ensuring a strong Canadian foundry industry. The CFA membership is comprised of major metal casters operating over 50 plants throughout Canada and represents approximately 80% of production and sales in the Canadian foundry industry.

CANADIAN INSTITUTE OF PLUMBING AND HEATING • 295 The West Mall, Suite 330 • Toronto, ON • M9C 4Z4 • Tel: 416-695-0447 • Fax: 416-695-0450 • E-mail: rcp@ciph.com • Internet: www.ciph.com • The Canadian Institute of Plumbing & Heating is a not for profit trade association founded in Montreal in 1933. They are the Manufacturers, Wholesaler Distributors, Master Distributors, Manufacturers' Agents and allied companies who manufacture and distribute plumbing, hydronic heating, industrial, waterworks and other mechanical products.

CANADA MASONRY CENTRE • 360 Superior Blvd. • Mississauga, ON • L5T 2N7 • Tel: 905-564-6622 • Fax: 905-564-5744 • E-mail: form • Internet: www.canadamasonrycentre.com • The Canadian Masonry Centre ensures the advancement of masonry technology, skills development and the use of masonry products in construction across Canada. The Canadian Masonry Centre ensures the advancement of masonry technology, skills development and the use of masonry products in construction across Canada. The Canada Masonry Centre (CMC) is the administrative home of: Canadian Masonry Contractors' Association (CMCA), Ontario Masonry Contractors' Association (OMCA), Metropolitan Industrial & Commercial Masonry Contractors Inc. (MICMCI), Canada Masonry Design Centre (CMDC), Ontario Masonry Training Centre (OMTC), and Masonry Industry Employers Council of Ontario (MIECO). The Canada Masonry Centre provides managerial, technical, accounting & financial, promotional & marketing, and other services to these organizations serving the masonry industry in Canada.

CANADIAN PLASTICS INDUSTRY ASSOCIATION • 5925 Airport Road, Suite 712 • Mississauga, ON • L4W 1T1 • Tel: 905-678-7748 • Fax: 905-678-0774 • E-mail: info@cpia.ca • Internet: www.cpia.ca • The Canadian Plastics Industry Association is an industry organization designed to deliver core services and value to members of the Canadian plastics community. They are a hands-on, proactive association that can reach right across the country through their four regional offices, as well as their national office located in Mississauga, Ontario.

CANADIAN STEEL PRODUCERS ASSOCIATION • 350 Sparks Street, Suite 906 • Ottawa, ON • K1R 7S8 • Tel: 613-238-6049 • Fax: 613-238-1832 • Internet: www.canadiansteel.ca • The Canadian Steel Producers Association (CSPA) is the national voice for Canada's $12.6 billion steel sales industry. The member companies of the CSPA produce over 15 million metric tons of steel per year from 13 facilities in five provinces. Basic steel production supports about 150,000 direct and indirect jobs across Canada, and contributes about $9 billion every year in purchased goods and services in communities across Canada.

CANADIAN TOOLING & MACHINING ASSOCIATION • 140 McGovern Drive, Unit 3 • Cambridge, ON • N3H 4R7 • Tel: 519-653-7265 • Fax: 519-653-6764 • E-mail: info@ctma.com • Internet: www.ctma.com • The Canadian Tooling & Machining Association (CTMA) was established in 1963 by combining various trade associations to produce one strong organization to represent the "Tooling Industry".

FOOD AND CONSUMER PRODUCTS MANUFACTURERS OF CANADA • 885 Don Mills Road, Suite 301 • Toronto, ON • M3C 1V9 • Tel: 416-510-8024 • Fax: 416-510-8043 • E-mail: info@fcpmc.com • Internet: www.fcpmc.com • Food & Consumer Products of Canada (FCPC) is the largest industry association in Canada representing the food and consumer products industry. Our member companies make and market retailer and national brands sold through grocery, drug, convenience, mass merchandise and foodservice distribution channels.

Oil & Mining

CANADIAN ASSOCIATION OF PETROLEUM PRODUCERS • 350 7th Ave. S.W., Suite 2100, Calgary, AB • T2P 3N9 • Tel: 403-267-1100 • Fax: 403-261-4622 • E-mail: communication@capp.ca • Internet: www.capp.ca • The Canadian Association of Petroleum Producers (CAPP) is the voice of the upstream oil and natural gas industry in Canada. CAPP represents 150 member companies who explore for, develop and produce more than 95 per cent of Canada's natural gas, crude oil, oil sands and elemental sulphur.

CANADIAN DIAMOND DRILLING ASSOCIATION • 437-101 Worthington Street East • North Bay, ON • P1B 1G5 • Tel: 705-476-6992 • Fax: 705-476-9494 • E-mail: office@cdda.ca • Internet: www.canadiandrilling.com • The Canadian Diamond Drilling Association has it's finger on the pulse of the industry. It represents and deals with government departments and agencies to keep you abreast of the latest regulatory changes affecting your industry lobby governments.

CANADIAN GAS ASSOCIATION • 350 Sparks Street, Suite 809 • Ottawa, ON • K1R 7S8 • Tel: 613-748-0057 • Fax: 613-748-9078 • E-mail: info@cga.ca • Internet: www.cga.ca • Founded in 1907, the Canadian Gas Association (CGA) is the voice of Canada's natural gas delivery industry. The Association is made up of over 125 companies, organizations and individuals who are involved in the delivery of natural gas in Canada and the United States. CGA members are typically local gas distribution companies from coast to coast, transmission companies, related equipment manufacturers, and other service providers.

CANADIAN INSTITUTE OF MINING, METALLURGY & PETROLEUM • Suite 855, 3400 de Maisonneuve Blvd. W. • Montréal, QC • H3Z 3B8 • Tel: 514-939-2710 • Fax: 514-939-2714 • E-mail: cim@cim.org • Internet: www.cim.org • Founded in 1898, the Canadian Institute of Mining, Metallurgy and Petroleum is the leading technical society of professionals in the Canadian minerals, metals, materials and energy industries. With over 12,000 national members, CIM strives to be the association of choice for professionals in the minerals industries.

CANADIAN PETROLEUM PRODUCTS INSTITUTE • 275 Slater Avenue, Suite 1000 • Ottawa, ON • K1P 5H9 • Tel: 613-232-3709 • Fax: 613-236-4280 • Internet: www.cppi.ca • The Canadian Petroleum Products Institute (CPPI) represents the petroleum refining and marketing industry in dealing with governments, media and interest groups on matters of common interest in public policy and industry reputation. Since its creation in 1989, the Institute has represented the views of its membership on business, environmental, and health and safety issues.

MINING ASSOCIATION OF CANADA • 350 Sparks Street, Suite 1105 • Ottawa, ON • K1R 7S8 • Tel: 613-233-9391 • Fax: 613-233-8897 • Internet: www.mining.ca • The Mining Association of Canada is a national organization of the Canadian mining industry. It comprises companies engaged in mineral exploration, mining, smelting, refining and semi-fabrication. Member companies account for the majority of Canada's output of metals and major industrial minerals

PETROLEUM SERVICES ASSOCIATION OF CANADA • 800 - 6th Avenue SW, Suite 1150 • Calgary, AB • T2P 3G3 • Tel: 403-264-4195 • Fax: 403-263-7174 • E-mail: info@psac.ca • Internet: www.psac.ca • The Petroleum Services Association of Canada is the national trade association representing the service, supply and manufacturing sectors within the upstream petroleum industry. PSAC represents a diverse range of over 270 member companies, employing more than 68,000 people and contracting almost exclusively to oil and gas exploration and production companies. PSAC member companies represent over 80 per cent of the business volume generated in the petroleum services industry.

Printing, Publishing & Forestry

ASSOCIATION OF CANADIAN PUBLISHERS • 174 Spadina Ave, Suite 306 • Toronto, ON • M5T 2C2 • Tel: 416-487-6116 • Fax: 416-487-8815 • E-mail: admin@canbook.org • Internet: www.publishers.ca • The Association of Canadian Publishers (ACP) represents approximately 140 Canadian-owned and controlled book publishers from across the country. The ACP assists Canadian-owned publishers in promoting the excellence of Canadian books, in bringing more Canadian books to more readers in Canada and in expanding domestic and international market share.

CANADIAN FOREST SERVICE • Natural Resources Canada, 580 Booth Street, 8th Floor • Ottawa, ON • K1A 0E4 • Tel: 613-947-7341 • Fax: 613-947-7397 • E-mail: cfs-scf@nrcan.gc.ca

• Internet: www.nrcan-rncan.gc.ca • The Canadian Forest Service (CFS) is a science-based policy organization within Natural Resources Canada. The CFS promotes the responsible and sustainable development of Canada's forests and competitiveness of the Canadian forest sector.

CANADIAN FORESTRY ASSOCIATION • 1027 Pembroke St. E. • Pembroke, ON • K8A 3M4 • Tel: 613-732-2917 • Fax: 613-732-3386 • E-mail: cfa@canadianforestry.com • Internet: www.canadianforestry.com • Founded in 1900, the CFA is Canada's oldest conservation organization. For over 100 years it has advocated the protection and wise use of Canada's forest, water and wildlife resources through public awareness and education programs. By promoting sustainable forest development, management and conservation, the CFA helps shape the future of Canada's forest and nurtures our economic and environmental health.

CANADIAN INSTITUTE OF FORESTRY • P.O. Box 430, 6905 Hwy. 17 • West Mattawa, ON • P0H 1V0 • Tel: 705-744-1715 ext. 585 • Fax: 705-744-1716 • E-mail: admin@cif-ifc.org • Internet: www.cif-ifc.org • The Canadian Institute of Forestry/Institut forestier du Canada (CIF/IFC) has been the national voice of forest practitioners since 1908. Their mission is to advance the stewardship of Canada's forest resources, provide national leadership in forestry, promote competence among forestry professionals, and foster public awareness of Canadian and international forestry issues.

MAGAZINES CANADA • 425 Adelaide Street West, Suite 700 • Toronto, ON • M5V 3C1 • Tel: 416-504-0274 • Fax: 416-504-0437 • E-mail: info@magazinescanada.ca • Internet: www.cmpa.ca • Magazines Canada is Canada's leading professional magazine industry association, representing over 300 of the country's consumer titles. The member-driven, not-for-profit organization strives to serve Canadian magazines of all scope and size through ongoing advocacy and special initiatives.

CANADIAN NEWSPAPER ASSOCIATION • 890 Yonge Street, Suite 200 • Toronto, ON • M4W 3P4 • Tel: 416-923-3567 • Fax: 416-923-7206 • E-mail: info@cna-acj.ca • Internet: www.cna-acj.ca • The Canadian Newspaper Association (CNA) is a non-profit organization, representing Canadian daily newspapers (English and French) with circulations ranging from 3,500 to more than 500,000 per day.

CANADIAN PRINTING INDUSTRIES ASSOCIATION • 151 Rue Slater, Suite 1110 • Ottawa, ON • K1P 5H3 • Tel: 613-236-7208 • Fax: 613-232-1334 • E-mail: belliott@cpia-aci.ca • Internet: www.cpia-aci.ca • The Canadian Printing Industries Association (CPIA) is the national voice of the pre-press, press and allied printing industries in Canada. Since 1939, the Association has served as the collective body to represent the interests of its member firms for policy formation, regulation and legislation.

CANADIAN PUBLISHERS' COUNCIL • 250 Merton Street, Suite 203 • Toronto, ON • M4S 1B1 • Tel: 416-322-7011 • Fax: 416-322-6999 • E-mail: pubadmin@pubcouncil.ca • Internet: www.pubcouncil.ca • The Canadian Publishers' Council, as Canada's main English language book publishing trade association was founded in 1910 and represents the interests of publishing companies that publish books and other media for elementary and secondary schools, colleges and universities, professional and reference markets, the retail and library sectors.

CANADIAN WOOD COUNCIL • 99 Bank Street, Suite 400 • Ottawa, ON • K1P 6B9 • Tel: 613-747-5544 • Fax: 613-747-6264 • Internet: www.cwc.ca • E-mail: info@cwc.ca . • The Canadian Wood Council (CWC) is the national association representing manufacturers of Canadian wood products used in construction. The Canadian Wood Council's mission is to enable the selling of Canadian wood products through programs and services focused on creating market access and demand.

EDITORS' ASSOCIATION OF CANADA • 502 - 27 Carlton Street • Toronto, ON • M5B 1L2 • Tel: 416-975-1379 • Fax: 416-975-1637 • E-mail: info@editors.ca • Internet: www.editors.ca • The Editors' Association of Canada (EAC) promotes professional editing as key in producing effective communication. Its 1,700 plus members, salaried and freelance, work with individuals in the corporate, technical, government, non-profit and publishing sectors.

FOREST PRODUCTS ASSOCIATION OF CANADA • 99 Bank Street, Suite 410 • Ottawa, ON • K1P 6B9 • Tel: 613-563-1441 • Fax: 613-563-4720 • E-mail: ottawa@fpac.ca • Internet: www. fpac.ca • The Forest Products Association of Canada (FPAC) is the voice of Canada's wood, pulp, and paper producers nationally and internationally in government, trade, and environmental affairs. Their organization represents the largest Canadian producers of forest products and are responsible for 75% of the working forests in Canada.

Retail

CANADIAN APPAREL FEDERATION • 504 - 124 O'Connor Street • Ottawa, ON • K1P 5M9 • Tel: 613-231-3220 • Fax: 613-231-2305 • E-mail: info@apparel.ca • Internet: www.apparel.ca • The Canadian Apparel Federation is the national industry association for the apparel industry. It represents the industry in consultations with the federal government on trade, legislative, and regulatory matters. Services to members include newsletters, trade and customs information, marketing services, reference materials and marketing information.

CANADIAN FEDERATION OF INDEPENDENT GROCERS • 2235 Sheppard Avenue East, Suite 902 • Willowdale, ON • M2J 5B5 • Tel: 416-492-2311 • Fax: 416-492-2347 • E-mail: info@ cfig.ca • Internet: www.cfig.ca • The Canadian Federation of Independent Grocers (CFIG) is a non-profit trade association founded in 1962 with the purpose of furthering the unique interests of Canada's independently owned and franchised supermarkets.

CANADIAN PROFESSIONAL SALES ASSOCIATION • 310 Front Street West Suite 800 • Toronto, ON • M5V 3B5 • Tel: 416-408-2685 • Fax: 416-408-2684 • Internet: www.cpsa.com • The Canadian Professional Sales Association (CPSA) is a national association comprised of more than 30,000 sales and marketing professionals located in communities of all sizes in every part of Canada.

RETAIL COUNCIL OF CANADA • 1255 Bay Street, Suite 800 • Toronto, ON • M5R 2A9 • Tel: 416-922-6678 • Fax: 416-922-8011 • Internet: www.retailcouncil.org • Founded in 1963, Retail Council of Canada is the Voice of Retail. RCC is a not-for-profit, industry-funded association representing more than 40,000 store fronts of all retail formats across Canada, including department, specialty, discount, and independent stores, and online merchants.

RETAIL MERCHANTS ASSOCIATION OF CANADA INC. • 10 Milner Business Court. Suite 401 • Scarborough, ON • M1B 3C6 • Tel: 905-764-0893 • Fax: 905-764-8312 • E-mail: info@ rmacanada.com • Internet: www.rmacanada.com • The Retail Merchants' Association of Canada (Ontario) Inc., the RMA, is an Ontario based non-profit organization serving the retailer since 1948. With an experienced staff and management team, RMA has the capacity to provide retailers the answers they seek in today's competitive market.

TEXTILES HUMAN RESOURCES COUNCIL • 500 - 222 Somerset Street West • Ottawa, ON • K2P 2G3 • Tel: 613-230-7217 • Fax: 613-230-1270 • E-mail: info@thrc-crhit.org • Internet: www.thrc-crhit.org • The Textiles Human Resources Council (THRC) is a non-profit industry partnership that was created in 1994. THRC's mandate is to help industry develop training and education solutions that respond to both established and emerging needs. Its membership includes the majority of textile companies in Canada as well as textile-related organizations and associations.

Social Services

BIG BROTHERS AND SISTERS OF CANADA • 3228 South Service Road, Suite 113E • Burlington, ON • L7N 3H8 • Tel: 905-639-0461 • Fax: 905-639-0124 • E-mail: pcampanaro@ bbbsc.ca • Internet: www.bigbrothersbigsisters.ca • Big Brothers Big Sisters of Canada (BBBSC) is the leading child and youth serving organization providing mentoring programs across the country. Providing support to more than 1000 Canadian communities, our over 150 local agencies offer the service that the organization was founded on one-to-one matching. Men and women (age 18 or older) give of their time to become a mentor to a youngster who can greatly benefit from having an adult role model to look up to.

CANADIAN ASSOCIATION OF SOCIAL WORKERS • 383 Parkdale Avenue, Suite 402 • Ottawa, ON • K1Y 4R4 • Tel: 613-729-6668 • Fax: 613-729-9608 • E-mail: casw@casw-acts. ca • Internet: www.casw-acts.ca • Founded in 1926 to monitor employment conditions and to establish standards of practice within the profession, the Canadian Association of Social Workers (CASW) has evolved into a national voice on behalf of some 15,000 members. CASW promotes social justice and well-being for all Canadian residents.

CANADIAN COUNCIL FOR INTERNATIONAL CO-OPERATION • 1 Nicholas Street, Suite 300 • Ottawa, ON • K1N 7B7 • Tel: 613-241-7007 • Fax: 613-241-5302 • E-mail: info@ccic. ca • Internet: www.ccic.ca • The Canadian Council for International Co-operation is a coalition of Canadian voluntary sector organizations working globally to achieve sustainable human development. CCIC seeks to end global poverty, and to promote social justice and human dignity for all.

CANADIAN ENVIRONMENTAL NETWORK • 300 - 945 Wellington Street • Ottawa, ON • K1Y 2X5 • Tel: 613-728-9810 • Fax: 613-728-2963 • E-mail: info@cen-rce.org • Internet: www. cen-rce.org • The Canadian Environmental Network is set up to support, facilitate and advance the work of its member groups to protect the Earth and promote ecologically sound ways of life.

CANADIAN HOME CARE ASSOCIATION • 17 York Street, Suite 401 • Ottawa, ON • K1N 9J6 • Tel: 613-569-1585 • Fax: 613-569-1604 • Internet: www.cdnhomecare.ca • E-mail: chca@ cdnhomecare.ca • The Canadian Home Care Association is a national not-for-profit membership organization representing over 600 home care stakeholders across Canada. Their members include representatives from publicly funded home care programs, federal government, provincial and territorial governments, not-for-profit and proprietary service providers, consumers, equipment suppliers, pharmaceutical manufacturers, researchers, educators and others with an interest in home care.

CANADIAN MENTAL HEALTH ASSOCIATION • 595 Montreal Road, Suite 303 • Ottawa, ON • K1K 4L2 • Tel: 416-484-7750 • Fax: 416-484-4617 • E-mail: info@cmha.ca • Internet: www.cmha.ca • The Canadian Mental Health Association (CMHA) exists to promote the mental health of all people and to serve mental health consumers, their families and friends. Founded in 1918, it is one of the oldest voluntary organizations in Canada. Each year, CMHA provides direct service to more than 100,000 Canadians through the combined efforts of more than 10,000 volunteers and staff in locally run organizations in all provinces and territories, and branches in more than 135 communities.

FAMILY RESOURCE PROGRAMS CANADA (FRP CANADA) • 707 - 331 Cooper Street • Ottawa, ON • K2P 0G5 • Tel: 613-237-7667 • Fax: 613-237-8515 • E-mail: info@frp.ca • Internet: www.frp.ca • FRP Canada is a national association providing innovative leadership to advance social policy, research, resource development and training for those who enhance the capacity of families to raise their children.

Telecommunications & Media

CANADIAN ASSOCIATION OF BROADCASTERS • 350 Sparks St., Suite 306, Box 627, Stn. B • Ottawa, ON • K1P 5S2 • Tel: 613-233-4035 • Fax: 613-233-6961 • E-mail: cab@cab-acr. ca • Internet: www.cab-acr.ca • The Canadian Association of Broadcasters is the national voice of Canada's private broadcasters, representing the vast majority of Canadian programming services, including private radio and television stations, networks, and specialty, pay and pay-per-view services.

CANADIAN ASSOCIATION OF JOURNALISTS • Algonquin College, 1385 Woodroffe Avenue, B224 • Ottawa, ON • K2G 1V8 • Tel: 613-526-8061 • Fax: 613-521-3904 • E-mail: canadianjour@ magma.ca • Internet: http://eagle.ca/caj/ • The Canadian Association of Journalists is a national non-profit public interest advocacy and professional development organization serving Canadian journalists from all media, including print, radio, television and online. It is the only group of its kind in Canada. Founded in 1978, and counting more than 1,500 active members across the country, the CAJ is run by a volunteer board of professional journalists.

CANADIAN FILM AND TELEVISION PRODUCTION ASSOCIATION • 151 Slater Street, Suite 902 • Ottawa, ON • K1P 5H3 • Tel: 613-233-1444 • Fax: 613-233-0073 • E-mail: ottawa@ cftpa.ca • Internet: www.cftpa.ca • The Canadian Film and Television Production Association's is a non-profit, trade association representing almost 400 Canadian production companies involved in television, film and interactive media.

CANADIAN WIRELESS TELECOMMUNICATIONS ASSOCIATION • 130 Albert Street, Suite 1110 • Ottawa, ON • K1P 5G4 • Tel: 613-233-4888 • Fax: 613-233-2032 • E-mail: info@cwta. ca • Internet: www.cwta.ca • The Canadian Wireless Telecommunications Association (CWTA) is the authority on wireless issues, developments and trends in Canada. It represents cellular, PCS, messaging, mobile radio, fixed wireless and mobile satellite carriers as well as companies that develop and produce products and services for the industry.

Transportation

ASSOCIATION OF CANADIAN TRAVEL AGENTS • 350 Sparks Street, Suite 510 • Ottawa, ON • K1R 7S8 • Tel: 613-237-3657 or 1-866-725-ACTA (2282) • Fax: 613-237-7052 • E-mail: actacam@acta.travel • Internet: www.acta.ca • Established in 1977, the Association of Canadian Travel Agencies (ACTA), is a national trade association representing the retail travel sector of Canada's tourism industry. ACTA is an industry-led, non profit, membership based organization. Our members include retail travel agencies and suppliers such as tour operators, travel wholesalers, airlines, hotels, destination marketing organizations, cruise and rail lines, and automobile rental companies. We represent the interests of Canadian travellers through approximately 3,000 members employing 14,000 travel professionals.

CANADIAN BUS ASSOCIATION • 451 Daly Avenue • Ottawa, ON • K1N 6H6 • Tel: 613-238-1800 • Fax: 613-241-4936 • Internet: www.buscanada.ca • The mandate of the Canadian Bus Association is to act as the national voice of the Canadian bus industry. It also acts as a national forum for the discussion of bus related issues and the establishment of positions in relation to industry-wide areas of concern.

CANADIAN INSTITUTE OF TRAFFIC AND TRANSPORTATION • 10 King Street East, Suite 400 • Toronto, ON • M5C 1C3 • Tel: 416-363-5696 • Fax: 416-363-5698 • E-mail: info@citt.ca • Internet: www.citt.ca • Since 1958, the C.I.T.T. (Canadian Institute of Traffic and Transportation) has been helping individuals on the path to success in logistics. In the face of an ever changing future, the C.I.T.T. has continued to provide the stability of a time-honoured history, the proven reputation for competence, and the ability to meet the challenges of today and tomorrow.

CANADIAN INSTITUTE OF TRAVEL COUNSELLORS, THE • 505 Consumers Road, Suite 406 • Toronto, ON • M2J 4V8 • Tel: 416-484-4450 • Fax: 416-484-4140 • E-mail: info@citc.ca • Internet: www.citc.ca • The Canadian Institute of Travel Counsellors is a national, non-profit organization, incorporated in 1968 to raise the level of professionalism within the travel industry by offering a wide range of education programs.

CANADIAN TRUCKING ALLIANCE • 324 Somerset Street West • Ottawa, ON • K2P 0J9 • Tel: 613-236-9426 • Fax: 613-563-2701 • E-mail: info@cantruck.ca • Internet: www.cantruck. com • The Canadian Trucking Alliance is a federation of provincial trucking associations. We represent a broad cross-section of the trucking industry—some 4,500 carriers, owner-operators and industry suppliers.

INTERNATIONAL AIR TRANSPORT ASSOCIATION • 800 Place Victoria, P.O. Box 113 • Montréal, QC • H4Z 1M1 • Tel: 514-874-0202 • Fax: 514-874-9632 • Internet: www.iata.org • IATA is an international trade body, created some 60 years ago by a group of airlines. Today, IATA represents some 240 airlines comprising 94% of scheduled international air traffic. The organization also represents leads and serves the airline industry in general.

RAILWAY ASSOCIATION OF CANADA • 99 Bank Street, Suite 1401 • Ottawa, ON • K1P 6B9 • Tel: 613-567-8591 • Fax: 613-567-6726 • E-mail: rac@railcan.ca • Internet: www.railcan. ca • The Railway Association of Canada (RAC), situated in the nation's capital, represents some 60 member freight, tourist, commuter, and intercity Canadian railways, playing a major role in promoting the safety, viability, and growth of the railway industry within Canada.

TRANSPORTATION ASSOCIATION OF CANADA • 2323 St. Laurent Boulevard • Ottawa, ON • K1G 4J8 • Tel: 613-736-1350 • Fax: 613-736-1395 • E-mail: secretariat@tac-atc.ca • Internet: www.tac-atc.ca • The Transportation Association of Canada is a national association with a mission to promote the provision of safe, efficient, effective and environmentally and financially sustainable transportation services in support of Canada's social and economic goals.

PART II

DIRECTORIES OF RESOURCES

Career Resources on the Internet

Career Resources on the Internet

BC WorkInfoNET
www.workinfonet.bc.ca

BC WorkInfoNET is a comprehensive and helpful website providing information in several areas including education and learning, career planning, employment and the labour market. It aims to collect and research websites containing any and all information that can be categorized into three main topics: Career Planning, Learning, and Employment.

Need to Register: No
Submit Resume: No
Job Board/Listing: Yes
Free to Job Seeker: Yes

Contact:
ASPECT
975 Alston Street
Victoria, BC V9A 3S5
Tel: 250-382-9675
info@aspect.bc.ca

Canadian Careers
www.canadiancareers.com

Online since 1996, CanadianCareers.com is a website with ample career and employment information, nicely divided into three main sections - Explore Career Options, Market Yourself, and Finding Work. Explore Career Options invites you to try some fun and interesting online skills tests that match occupations with skills, interests and values, and lets you learn more about labour market trends and education and training. Market Yourself focuses on resume preparation, cover letter writing, electronic job applications, interviews, and salary expectations. Finding Work emphasizes the importance of networking, job searching on industry specific job boards, volunteering, self-employment, internships and researching. Tips for discussing salary expectations and searching for employment as a job seeker with a disability is also covered in this area of the website.

Need to Register: No
Submit Resume: No
Job Board/Listing: No
Free to Job Seeker: Yes

Contact:
questions@canadiancareers.com

Career Bookmarks - Toronto Public Library
http://careerbookmarks.tpl.toronto.on.ca

The Toronto Public Library staff use their expertise in finding, selecting and organizing information to develop and maintain a site which brings together Internet and library resources in an impressive, well-organized manner. Information has been organized according to the career planning and job search process and users are encouraged to develop their own 'filebox' or customized report with stored information they have gathered during their visit. Career Bookmarks also includes an online tutorial and research guide.

Need to Register: No
Submit Resume: No
Job Board/Listing: No
Free to Job Seeker: Yes

Contact:
cbmmail@tpl.toronto.on.ca

CareerOwl

www.careerowl.ca

Started by professors and in operation since 1999, CareerOwl has signed up top alumni and students of major universities, colleges and technical schools all across this great land. More than 101,000 of Canada's best and brightest are registered CareerOwl users. CareerOwl is a sophisticated search tool. Jobseekers are invited to fill out an extensive profile allowing employers to search for the specific skills, education and talents.

Need to Register: Yes
Submit Resume: Yes
Job Board/Listing: Yes
Free to Job Seeker: Yes

Contact:
CareerOwl Institute
6018 Crown Street
Vancouver, BC V6N 2B8
Tel: 1-877-695-7678

LMIworks.nl.ca

www.lmiworks.nl.ca

lmiworks.nl.ca is a powerful labour market information tool that provides one-stop access to the latest and most complete set of employment and career information resources available in the Newfoundland and Labrador.

Need to Register: No
Submit Resume: No
Job Board/Listing: No
Free to Job Seeker: Yes

Contact:
Labour Market Development Division
Department of Human Resources, Labour
and Employment
Government of Newfoundland and
Labrador
P.O. Box 8700
St. John's, NF A1B 4J6
Tel: 709-729-5184
Toll Free: 1-800-563-6600
Fax: 709-729-1129
labourmarket@gov.nl.ca

Manitoba WorkinfoNET

www.mb.workinfonet.ca

Manitoba WorkinfoNET's newly re-designed and re-launched English, French and Youth sites continue to work as a gateway to relevant information on different aspects of the labour market. But now with the new design, Manitobans can quickly find the information they are looking for in three easy to understand categories. They are: Employment, Career Planning and Learning. Manitoba WorkinfoNET has also added a local job search tool, provided the ability to search by user groups and added an Aboriginal site to their network.

Need to Register: No
Submit Resume: No
Job Board/Listing: Yes
Free to Job Seeker: Yes

Contact:
Manitoba WorkinfoNET
P.O. Box 2521
Winnipeg, MB R3C 4A7
Tel: 204-231-5543
admin@mbwin.org

NWT WorkInfoNET

www.northwin.ca

If you are a job seeker, an employer, small business or career professional, NorthWIN is your gateway to Nunavut and Northwest Territories online career and work information. NorthWIN is a dynamic partnership of government, business, community and non-profit organizations, whose mission is to establish and maintain an electronic information network. It ensures that all Northerners have access to reliable and timely labour market information, career services, training programs, and other supports.

Need to Register: Yes
Submit Resume: Yes
Job Board/Listing: Yes
Free to Job Seeker: Yes

Contact:
northwin@theedge.ca

Ontario WorkInfoNET

www.onwin.ca

Formed as a non-profit corporation in January 1998, Ontario WorkInfoNet (OnWIN) is a bilingual website that provides links to over 2,000 websites specializing in Ontario-based employment and career information. The main categories created to help you zero in on the exact resources and information you need are Jobs, Work and Recruiting, Occupations and Careers, Learning, Education and Training, Labour Market Information, Self- Employment, Workplace Issues, and Financial Help.

Need to Register: No
Submit Resume: No
Job Board/Listing: Yes
Free to Job Seeker: Yes

Contact:
Ontario WorkInfoNet
Algoma University College
NW 307E 1520 Queen Street East
Sault Ste. Marie, ON P6A 2G4
Tel: 705.949.2301 x3145
info@onwin.ca

P.E.I. WorkinfoNET

www.gov.pe.ca/infopei/index.php3?number=846

Prince Edward Island WorkinfoNET, in partnership with Holland College, the Province of P.E.I., the University of P.E.I., and the Government of Canada, is dedicated to making the task of career planning and job seeking easier for residents of Prince Edward Island. Its aim is to create a one-stop site to career and labour market information in P.E.I. Information on P.E.I. WorkinfoNET is accessible through a series of categories and subcategories divided to help you find resources and links quickly and easily.

Need to Register: No
Submit Resume: No
Job Board/Listing: No
Free to Job Seeker: Yes

SaskNetWork

www.sasknetwork.gov.sk.ca

SaskNetWork provides career, employment and labour market information at your fingertips. If you need help planning your career, searching for work, looking for qualified employees or finding education and training information in Saskatchewan then this is your starting point. The SaskNetWork website is about helping people connect to the resources they need in the areas of jobs, work, education and training, career planning, self-employment, labour market information, financial help and the workplace.

Need to Register: No
Submit Resume: Yes
Job Board/Listing: Yes
Free to Job Seeker: Yes

Contact:
hotline@gov.sk.ca

The Job Bus

www.jobbus.com

The Job Bus was built after a growing number of Internet users mentioned having problems finding employment online in Canada. They have strived to find sites to suit everyone's interests. From agriculture workers to X-ray technicians, this site has information for those looking for either high-tech or non-computer jobs. Their extensive job links section will help you find the employment pages of companies, personnel agencies, and government in Canada.

Need to Register: No
Submit Resume: No
Job Board/Listing: No
Free to Job Seeker: Yes

Contact:
webmaster@jobbus.com

YukonWorkinfoNET

www.yuwin.ca

Yukon WorkinfoNET (YUWIN) was designed to provide provincial, territorial and national labour market and career information. YUWIN is committed to providing Yukon job seekers, employers, students, career practitioners, teachers, parents, and counsellors with easy access to information on education and training, careers, employment, workplace issues and labour market related information that reflects the diversity of the Yukon's population. This includes First Nations communities, people with disabilities, new Canadians, private business, industry sectors, educational groups and government.

Need to Register: No
Submit Resume: No
Job Board/Listing: Yes
Free to Job Seeker: Yes

Contact:
YuWIN - Yukon WorkinfoNET
Box 2799
Whitehorse, YK Y1A 5K4
Tel: 867-393-3874
grant@yuwin.ca

Check out our other guide, *Get Wired, You're Hired!* to gain more insight about online career searching and to learn about additional resources available on the Internet.

PART II
DIRECTORIES OF RESOURCES
Trade Directories

Trade Directories

There are many directories that can help you in your job search. We have listed below some of the more popular titles. Most of these directories are quite expensive to purchase, however, the larger libraries or career centres should have them available. Make sure to use them in your job search. All of these books contain a wealth of information to help you network and contact firms and organization across the country.

AIAC GUIDE TO CANADA'S AEROSPACE INDUSTRY

Canada is a world leader in the design and production of regional aircraft, business jets, commercial helicopters, small gas turbine engines, landing gear and flight simulation systems. Canadian firms are integral elements of the global aerospace supply chain. They provide aircraft structures, systems, components and materials, and a wide range of specialized products and services. The companies showcased in this guide offer globally competitive, innovative solutions, and a highly skilled workforce. This guide is your window on Canada's world-class aerospace capabilities. (Aerospace Industries Association of Canada • Suite 1200, 60 Queen Stree t• Ottawa, ON • K1P 5Y7 • Tel: 613-232-4297 • Fax: 613-232-1142 • E-mail: info@aiac.ca • Internet: www.aiac.ca)

ASSOCIATIONS CANADA

Associations Canada covers regional, national, and international organizations including industry, commercial and professional associations, registered charities, special interest and common interest organizations. (Micromedia ProQuest • 20 Victoria St. • Toronto, ON • M5C 2N8 • Tel: 1-800-387-2689 • E-mail: info@proquest.com• Internet: www. proquest.com)

BLUE BOOK OF CANADIAN BUSINESS

The Blue Book of Canadian Business, a hard cover printed book, is released each year in September. It contains all of the corporate profiles presented on their website and 2,750 of the largest companies listed in their website's subscriber database. (Canadian Business Resource • 1400 Bayly Street, OM2, Unit 5 • Pickering, ON • L1W 3R2 • Tel: 905-428-8926 • Toll Free:: 1-888-422-4742 • E-mail: info@bluebook.ca • Internet: www.cbr.ca)

BODYSHOP

Bodyshop magazine services the Canadian autobody and repair market. Readers are kept informed of the latest technical information, business management issues, new product ideas, shop profiles and other timely industry insights. (Business Information Group l 12 Concorde Place, Suite 800 • Toronto, ON • M3C 4J2 • Tel: 416-442-5600, ext. 3542 or Toll Free: 1-800-268-7742 • Fax: 416-442-2291 • E-mail: vfraser@bodyshopbiz.com • Internet: www.bodyshopbiz.com)

BROADCASTER DIRECTORY

Broadcaster Directory is Canada's most comprehensive information source for companies in the communications industry. You will have instant access to address and contact information for: radio stations, television stations, cable companies, video production, post-production, equipment manufacturers and distributors, advertising and government agencies, and associations and consultants. (Business Information Group • 12 Concorde Place, Suite 800 • Toronto, ON • M3C 4J2 • Tel: 416-510-6871 or Toll Free: 1-800-268-7742 • Fax: 416-510-5134 • E-mail: jcook@broadcastermagazine.com • Internet: www.broadcastermagazine.com)

CANADIAN ALMANAC & DIRECTORY

Canada's best-selling national sourcebook since 1847, the Canadian Almanac & Directory contains ten directories in one - giving you all the facts and figures you will ever need about Canada. No other single source provides users with the quality and depth of up-to-date information for all types of research. This national directory and guide gives you access to statistics, images, and over 45,000 names and addresses for everything from Airlines to Zoos - updated every year. (Micromedia ProQuest • 20 Victoria St. • Toronto, ON • M5C 2N8 • Tel: 1-800-387-2689 • E-mail: info@proquest.com • Internet: www.proquest.com)

CANADIAN BUSINESS DIRECTORY

The Canadian Business Directory provides information on over 2 million businesses in Canada, organized by category and industry-specific franchise/brand/specialty classification. (International Press Publications Inc. • 90 Nolan Court, Suite 21 • Markham, ON • L3R 4L9 • Tel: 905-946-9588 • Fax: 905-946-9590 • Internet: www.ippbooks.com)

CANADIAN BUSINESS FRANCHISE DIRECTORY

Canada's number-one selling directory, Canadian Business Franchise Directory is one of the most innovative and comprehensive guides in the world. Along with articles by leaders within Canada's franchise industry, the directory features listings of over 1,000 franchise systems operating within the country. Canadian Business Franchise Directory also includes helpful information about support services for both franchisors and franchisees, ranging from financial institutions, accountants and lawyers, to global franchising organizations and franchising publications. (Kenilworth Group of Companies • 15 Wertheim Court, Suite 710 • Richmond Hill, ON • L4B 3H7 • Tel: 905-771-7333 • Toll Free: 1-800-409-8688 • Fax: 905-771-7336 • E-mail: info@kenilworth.com • Internet: www.cgb.ca)

CANADIAN DENTAL DIRECTORY

The Canadian Dental Directory is the largest, most comprehensive, and most accurate database of over 16,000 Canadian dentists and dental facilities of its kind. Each listing is alphabetized with complete contact information. Whether your focus is local or national, the Canadian Dental Directory is the only place you need to look for full coverage of all dental information across Canada. (Business Information Group • 12 Concorde Place, Suite 800 • Don Mills, ON • M3C 4J2 • Tel: 416-442-2122 or Toll Free: 1-800-668-2374 • Fax: 416-442-2191 • Internet: www.businessinformationgroup.ca)

CANADIAN DIRECTORY OF SHOPPING CENTRES

The Canadian Directory of Shopping Centres provides you with information on shopping centres and mixed-use centres with at least 25,000 square feet of gross leasable area and three or more CRU's. (Monday Report on Retailers, Rogers Media Inc. • One Mount Pleasant

Rd., 7th Floor • Toronto, ON • M4Y 2Y5 • Tel: 416-764-1469 • Fax: 416-764-1469 • E-mail: mary.tommasone@mondayreport.rogers.com • Internet: www.mondayreport.ca)

CANADIAN ENVIRONMENTAL DIRECTORY
The Canadian Environmental Directory is Canada's most-complete and only national listing of environmental associations and organizations, governmental regulators and Purchasing Groups, Product and Service Companies, special libraries and more. (Micromedia ProQuest • 20 Victoria St. • Toronto, ON • M5C 2N8 • Tel: 1-800-387-2689 • E-mail: info@proquest.com • Internet: www.proquest.com)

CANADIAN EXPORTERS CATALOGUE
The Canadian Exporters Catalogue fulfills its commitment to help Canadian companies market themselves cost-effectively on a global scale by providing qualified foreign buyers with information about Canadian products and services. The Catalogue is an invaluable reference tool for consular trade officials. As such, copies of the Catalogue are sent to all Canadian trade missions, embassies and consulate offices worldwide in a total of over 128 host countries. (International Publishing & Development • 8080 19th Avenue • Burnaby, BC • V3N 1G3 • Tel: 604-523-0093 • Fax: 604-523-0090 • E-mail: ipd@worldexport.com • Internet: www.worldexport.com)

CANADIAN GROCER
Canadian Grocer magazine has been the voice of the grocery industry since 1886 and is Canada's only national grocery publication. Our readership of 19,000 consists of store/grocery/produce managers in a wide range of food outlets such as grocery/club/mass and convenience stores. Retailers count on Canadian Grocer to keep them informed about the grocery industry both here and abroad and we are the most requested magazine in the industry. (Canada Grocer • 1 Mount Pleasant Rd., 7th Floor • Toronto, ON • M4Y 2Y5 • Tel: 1-800-268-9119 • Fax: 416-764-1523 • Internet: www.bizlink.com/cangrocer.htm)

CANADIAN KEY BUSINESS DIRECTORY
Continually researched and completely updated annually, the D&B Canadian Key Business Directory is an important source of information on the top 2% of Canada's businesses. It provides more than 20,000 listings of the largest companies in Canada and over 60,000 key contact names. (D&B Canada • 5770 Hurontario Street, 9th Floor • Mississauga, ON • L5A 4G4 • Toll Free: 1-800-267-2990 • Internet: www.dnb.ca)

CANADIAN MEDICAL DIRECTORY
MDSelect is the premier medical and physician directory in Canada. With more than 60,000 doctors listed, it is the most complete medical directory and available in print, CD ROM or Web-based formats. (MDSelect • 12 Concorde Place, Suite 800 • Toronto, ON • M3C 4J2 • Tel: 416-442-2010 • Toll Free: 1-800-408-9431 • E-mail: sales@scottinfo.com • Internet: www.mdselect.com)

Use Business Directories
Learn as much as you can about companies, their products or services, missions, and future plans, etc. This information will better equip you to correspond with firms and give you the upper hand in a job interview.

CANADIAN MINES HANDBOOK

The Canadian Mines Handbook is the world's foremost annual reference guide to the exploration and development activities of publicly-owned Canadian mining companies. Over 2,400 companies, mines advanced projects, smelters and refineries are profiled in the Handbook's pages. (Southam Mining Group • 12 Concorde Place, Suite 800 • Toronto, ON • M3C 4J2 • Tel: 416-442-2122 • Fax: 416-442-2191 • E-mail: northernminer2@ northernminer.com • Internet: www.northernminer.com)

CANADIAN PHARMACISTS DIRECTORY

The Canadian Pharmacists Directory (CPD) is the most valuable resource for accurate etailed information on Canada's pharmaceutical community. Reach any of the over 7,000 pharmacists nationwide or locate major pharmaceutical players across Canada.Each listing is alphabetized with complete contact information. Whether your focus is local or national, the Canadian Pharmacists Directory is the only resource you need for full coverage of Canada's pharmaceutical industry. (Business Information Group • 12 Concorde Place, Suite 800 • Toronto, ON • M3C 4J2 • Tel: 416-442-2122 • Toll Free: 1-800-668-2374 • Fax: 416-442-2191 • Internet: www.businessinformationgroup.ca)

CANADIAN PLASTICS DIRECTORY AND BUYERS' GUIDE

The Canadian Plastics Directory is your guide to Canada's plastics industry. With over 3,200 companies listed, the Buyers' Guide is your established reference source for finding contacts, products, and services across Canada. (Business Information Group • 12 Concorde Place, Suite 800 • Toronto, ON • M3C 4J2 • Tel: 416-442-2122 • Toll Free: 1-800-668-2374 • Fax: 416-442-2191 • Internet: www.businessinformationgroup.ca)

CANADIAN SPACE GUIDE, THE

AERO JOBS and SPACE JOBS provide a direct employment advertising channel to professionals in the aeronautics and space industries. Their industry specific approach provides the greatest efficiency for employers to find the people they need. Job Seekers in the space and aeronautics industries now have one single location they can use to find employment directly related to their fields. (SPACE JOBS Inc. • 126 York Street, Suite 4 • Ottawa, ON • K1N 5T5 • Tel: 1-888-366-6337 • E-mail: info@spacejobs.com • Internet: www.spacejobs.com)

CANADIAN TRADE INDEX, THE

The Canadian Trade Index (CTI) was first published in the year 1900 by the Alliance of Manufacturers and Exporters Canada (formerly the Canadian Manufacturers Association). The Canadian Trade Index provides detailed information regarding over 30,000 Canadian companies, including Manufacturers, Active Exporters, Distributors of products in Canada, and Service companies for manufactured products. CTI features nearly 100,000 product listings under 20,000 headings. They can be reached toll free at 1-877-463-6284. (Canadian Trade Index, c/o MacRAE's Blue Book Ltd. • 2085 Hurontario Street, Suite 208 • Mississauga, ON • L5A 4G1 • Tel: 905-290-1818 • Toll Free: 1-877-463-6284 • Fax: 905-290-1760 • E-mail: owenmediainfo@owen-media.com • Internet: www.ctidirectory.com)

CANADIAN TRANSPORTATION & LOGISTICS BUYERS' GUIDE

Stay informed about new carrier services and logistics resources with Canadian Transportation & Logistics Buyers' Guide. The guide gives you access to all the essential contacts and services you require in the transportation industry such as: air and marine cargo, rail and motor Carriers, Products and services, and logistics resources. (Business Information Group • 12 Concorde Place, Suite 800 • Toronto, ON • M3C 4J2 • Tel: 416-442-2122 or Toll Free: 1-800-668-2374 • Fax: 416-442-2191 • Internet: www.businessinformationgroup.ca)

CANADIAN WOMEN'S BUSINESS NETWORK

The Canadian Women's Business Network is a web site listing hundreds of useful links and resources to guide women in their business initiatives. (Canadian Women's Business Network • 3019 Hammond Bay Rd. • Nanaimo, BC • V9T 1E1 • Tel: 250-751-2133 • E-mail: admin@cdnbizwomen.com • Internet: www.cdnbizwomen.com)

CHEMICAL DIRECTORY

Whether you buy or sell chemicals, the 2008 Canadian Chemical Directory will put the industry at your fingertips. The latest edition of the Canadian Chemical Directory lists 570 chemical suppliers, 750 principal companies, more than 3,330 chemical products and 3,800 trade names. Feedstocks, chemicals, minerals, metals, resins, and drugs all in one volume. (Camford Information Services • Tel: 416-291-3215 • E-mail: jpiccione@camfordinfo.com • Internet: www.camfordinfo.com)

CONTACT TORONTO

Contact Toronto is a directory that profiles the 4,000 largest organizations and more than 17,000 executives in the Greater Toronto Area. (The Toronto Board of Trade • 1 First Canadian Place, P.O. Box 60 • Toronto, ON • M5X 1C1 • Tel: 416-366-6811 • Fax: 416-366-8406 • E-mail: publications@bot.com • Internet: www.bot.com)

DIRECTORY OF CHARTERED ACCOUNTANT FIRMS – CA SOURCE

The Canadian Institute of Chartered Accountants provides an online directory of CA Firms by firm name, location, firm size, industries served and/or services offered. (The Canadian Institute of Chartered Accountants • 277 Wellington Street West • Toronto, ON • M5V 3H2 • Tel: 416-204-3341 or 416-204-3368 • Fax: 416-977-8585 • E-mail: casource@cica.ca • Internet: www.casource.com)

DIRECTORY OF RESTAURANTS AND FAST FOOD CHAINS IN CANADA

The Directory of Restaurant & Fast Food Chains in Canada provides you with information on chains with three or more locations in Canada and includes restaurants with plans to expand. (Monday Report on Retailers, Rogers Media Inc. • One Mount Pleasant Rd., 7th Floor • Toronto, ON • M4Y 2Y5 • Tel: 416-764-1469 • Fax: 416-764-1711 • E-mail: mary.tommasone@mondayreport.rogers.com • Internet: www.mondayreport.ca)

DIRECTORY OF RETAIL CHAINS IN CANADA

The Directory of Retail Chains in Canada provides you with information on chains with 3 or more locations in Canada and includes stores with plans to expand. (Monday Report on Retailers, Rogers Media Inc. • One Mount Pleasant Rd., 7th Floor • Toronto, ON • M4Y 2Y5 • Tel: 416-764-1469 • Fax: 416-764-1711 • E-mail: mary.tommasone@mondayreport.rogers.com • Internet: www.mondayreport.ca)

FINANCIAL POST 500 - FP 500 DATABASE, THE

Financial Services Canada provides the full spectrum of the finance industry in Canada: accounting firms, associations, banks and depository institutions, non-depository institutions, financial planning and investment management firms, insurance companies, law firms, and government offices. (Micromedia ProQuest • 20 Victoria Street • Toronto, ON • M5C 2N8 • Tel: 1-800-387-2689 • E-mail: info@proquest.com • Internet: www. proquest.com)

FINANCIAL POST CORPORATE SURVEYS

The FP Corporate Survey database combines the contents of The Financial Post Survey of Mines and Energy Resources and FP's Survey of Industrials. The database provides detailed corporate and investment information on all companies publicly traded in Canada, as well as information on close to 8,000 subsidiaries and affiliates. Data is prepared and verified by The Financial Post's team of financial analysts. (FPinfomart.ca, CanWest Interactive Inc. • 1450 Don Mills Rd. • Toronto, ON • M3B 2X7 • Tel: 416-442-2121 • Fax: 416-442-2968 • E-mail: helpdesk@canwest.com • Internet: www.fpinfomart.ca)

FINANCIAL SERVICES CANADA

Financial Services Canada provides the full spectrum of the finance industry in Canada: accounting firms, associations, banks and depository institutions, non-depository institutions, financial planning and investment management firms, insurance companies, law firms, and government offices. (Micromedia ProQuest • 20 Victoria Street • Toronto, ON • M5C 2N8 • Tel: 1-800-387-2689 • E-mail: info@proquest.com • Internet: www. proquest.com)

FRASERS CANADIAN TRADE DIRECTORY

Frasers is a comprehensive directory and search tool, providing information on Canadian industrial wholesalers, manufacturers, distributors and their products and services. In addition, we list international companies that supply goods and services to the Canadian marketplace. (Frasers Canadian Trade Directory • One Mount Pleasant Road, 7th Floor • Toronto, ON • M4Y 2Y5 • Tel: 1-888-297-7195 • Fax: 416-764-1710 • E-mail: frasers@ rmpublishing.com • Internet: www.frasers.com)

GUIDE TO CANADIAN MANUFACTURERS

A three volume set with more than 50,000 manufacturers listed. Volume I encompasses the Western Region, Volume II the Central Region, and Volume III the Eastern Region. (D&B Canada Canada • 5770 Hurontario Street, 9th Floor • Mississauga, ON • L5R 3G5 • Tel: 1-800-463-6362 • Fax: 1-800-668-7800 • E-mail: cic@dnb.com • Internet: www. dnb.ca)

INDUSTRIAL SOURCEBOOK

Canada's directory of industrial products and services, the Industrial Sourcebook, provides users with an organized easy-to-follow format to search and locate the products and/or services they need. (CLB Media Inc. • 240 Edward Street • Aurora, ON • L4G 3S9 • Tel: 905-727-0077 • Fax: 905-727-0017 • E-mail: jantoniadis@clbmedia.ca• Internet: www. industrialsourcebook.com)

JOBBER NEWS ANNUAL MARKETING GUIDE

Jobber News Annual Marketing Guide is Canada's most comprehensive guide to who's who and who does what in the Canadian automotive aftermarket. Gain instant access to: Industry associations, manufacturers, product listings index, engine rebuilders buyers' guide, warehouse distributors, service providers and more. All listings include company name, address, phone and fax number, contact name, website and e-mail (if available). (Business Information Group • 12 Concorde Place, Suite 800 • Toronto, ON • M3C 4J2 • Tel: 416-442-2122 or Toll Free: 1-800-668-2374 • Fax: 416-442-2191 • Internet: www. businessinformationgroup.ca)

MULTIMEDIATOR COMPANY DIRECTORY

The MultiMediator is an extensive directory of links to Canadian multimedia developers. Links to over 1,487 Canadian companies involved with the development of CD-ROMs, websites and kiosks are included and organized by company name and province. (MultiMediator • 689 Queen Street West, Suite 198 • Toronto, ON • M6J 1E6 • Tel: 416-352-5471 • E-mail: webmaster@multimediator.com • Internet: www.multimediator.com)

NATIONAL DIRECTORY OF MAGAZINES, THE

A comprehensive presentation of U.S. and Canadian magazines with expanded international coverage. (Oxbridge Communications Inc. • 186 Fifth Ave., Suite 302 • New York, NY • 10010 • Tel: 1-800-955-0231 • Fax: 212-633-2938 • E-mail: info@oxbridge. com • Internet: www.oxbridge.com)

PROFESSIONAL, TRADE AND INTERNATIONAL ASSOCIATIONS DIRECTORY

Trade and professional associations are authoritative sources for a wealth of information. Use this 200-page directory to find business opportunities, qualified leads, mailing lists, market size. Flush out a business plan, track an industry, get a job, access foreign markets! (The Toronto Board of Trade • 1 First Canadian Place, P.O. Box 60 • Toronto, ON • M5X 1C1 • Tel: 416-366-6811 • Fax: 416-366-8406 • E-mail: publications@bot.com • Internet: www.bot.com)

PULP & PAPER CANADA ANNUAL DIRECTORY

This Directory is Canada's best resource for information about the Canadian pulp and paper industry. The directory is comprehensively organized in three distinct sections: Pulp, Paper & Board Manufacturing Sector, Supply Sector, and Support Sector. (Business Information Group • 12 Concorde Place, Suite 800 • Toronto, ON • M3C 4J2 • Tel: 416-442-2122 • Toll Free: 1-800-668-2374 • Fax: 416-442-2191 • Internet: www.businessinformationgroup. ca)

SCOTT'S GREATER TORONTO BUSINESS DIRECTORY

The information in the Scott's Greater Toronto Business Directory is so detailed and immense that the Directory is split into three convenient volumes: The Metro Edition, The Boundary Edition, and The Southwestern Edition. Each volume includes information on manufacturers, distributors, wholesalers, contractors, service companies and more. (Scott's Directories • 12 Concorde Place, Suite 800 • Don Mills, ON • M3C 4J2 • Tel: 416-442-2122 • Toll Free 1-800-668-2374 • Fax: 416-510-6870 • E-mail: sales@scottsinfo.com • Internet: www.scottsinfo.com)

SCOTT'S ATLANTIC INDUSTRIAL

The entrepreneurial spirit is alive and well in Atlantic Canada. Reach over 7,200 manufacturers, wholesalers, distributors, and manufacturers' agents located throughout the Maritime provinces with the most current and complete company profiles available. (Scott's Directories • 12 Concorde Place, Suite 800 • Don Mills, ON • M3C 4J2 • Tel: 416-442-2122 • Toll Free 1-800-668-2374 • Fax: 416-510-6870 • E-mail: sales@scottsinfo.com • Internet: www.scottsinfo.com)

SCOTT'S CANADIAN BUSINESS DIRECTORY AND DATABASE

Scott's Directories and scottsinfo.com contain more than 115,000 companies and 210,000 executive contacts. Scott's is the best source for mailing lists and information on Canadian manufacturers, distributors and business service providers. (Scott's Directories • 12 Concorde Place, Suite 800 • Don Mills, ON • M3C 4J2 • Tel: 416-442-2122 • Toll Free 1-800-668-2374 • Fax: 416-510-6870 • E-mail: sales@scottsinfo.com • Internet: www. scottsinfo.com)

SCOTT'S DIRECTORY OF CANADIAN ASSOCIATIONS

The Scott's Directory of Canadian Associations is the most powerful fact-finder to consumer, trade, business and professional organizations. (Scott's Directories • 12 Concorde Place, Suite 800 • Don Mills, ON • M3C 4J2 • Tel: 416-442-2122 • Toll Free 1-800-668-2374 • Fax: 416-510-6870 • E-mail: sales@scottsinfo.com • Internet: www.scottsinfo.com)

SCOTT'S GREATER MONTREAL & LAVAL BUSINESS

Are you doing business in the industrial heartland of Québec? Then Scott's new Greater Montréal Business Directory will be an invaluable tool, covering the Communauté Urbaine de Montréal as well as Laval. Reach over 23,100 manufacturers, manufacturers' agents, contractors, distributors, service companies, transportation firms, legal firms, computer firms, wholesalers, financial companies, retail head offices, and more! (Scott's Directories • 12 Concorde Place, Suite 800 • Don Mills, ON • M3C 4J2 • Tel: 416-442-2122 • Toll Free 1-800-668-2374 • Fax: 416-510-6870 • E-mail: sales@scottsinfo.com • Internet: www. scottsinfo.com)

SCOTT'S ONTARIO MANUFACTURERS

Reach Canada's Industrial heartland with Scott's Ontario Manufacturers Directory. There are over 26,500 manufacturers and 59,000 executives listed. (Scott's Directories • 12 Concorde Place, Suite 800 • Don Mills, ON • M3C 4J2 • Tel: 416-442-2122 • Toll Free 1-800-668-2374 • Fax: 416-510-6870 • E-mail: sales@scottsinfo.com • Internet: www. scottsinfo.com)

SCOTT'S QUÉBEC INDUSTRIAL

There's a gold mine of business in the Scott's Québec Industrial Directory. You'll find essential details on more than 24,000 Québec manufacturers, Wholesales, Distributors and Manufactures' Agents. (Scott's Directories • 12 Concorde Place, Suite 800 • Don Mills, ON • M3C 4J2 • Tel: 416-442-2122 • Toll Free 1-800-668-2374 • Fax: 416-510-6870 • E-mail: sales@scottsinfo.com • Internet: www.scottsinfo.com)

SCOTT'S WESTERN INDUSTRIAL

From British Columbia to Manitoba, if you're going to do business in Western Canada, you have to know who your best prospects are. Scott's Western Industrial Directory can put you in touch with over 22,100 Western manufacturers, wholesalers, distributors, and manufacturers' agents and over 39,000 Executives contacts. (Scott's Directories • 12 Concorde Place, Suite 800 • Don Mills, ON • M3C 4J2 • Tel: 416-442-2122 • Toll Free 1-800-668-2374 • Fax: 416-510-6870 • E-mail: sales@scottsinfo.com • Internet: www. scottsinfo.com)

TECHNO-CONNECT

The Techno-Connect product database offers detailed information on IT specialty companies, showcasing 7,000 products in more than 100 different product categories. It is a powerful internet-based growth tool available for companies or individuals seeking to identify information technology products for their business needs. (CATAAlliance • 388 Albert Street • Ottawa, ON • K1R 5B2 • Tel: 613-236-6550 • Fax: 613-236-8189 • E-mail: technoconnect@cata.ca • Internet: http://www1.cata.ca/technoconnect)

 Career Tip

Don't Give Up!
If your resumé is not getting you any interviews, consider rewriting it or asking people you know and trust to review it. Don't allow rejections to deflate your self-confidence and your sense of self-worth!

PART II

DIRECTORIES OF RESOURCES
Sector Councils

Sector Councils

WHAT IS A SECTOR COUNCIL?

Sector Councils are alliances of representatives from business, labour, education, and other professional groups within an industry or group of related industries. They generally address a wide range of issues involving things like human resource development, technological change, quality standards, and labour planning.

HOW CAN A SECTOR COUNCIL HELP YOU?

Sector Councils are active in many areas relating to employment. We have provided an overview of some of these areas along with profiles on some prominent Sector Councils that have provided us with their information. You can visit www.councils. org for more information.

Sector Council Activities Related to Employment:

Apprenticeship – a training approach that combines practical on-the-job training with theoretical in-school instruction.

Career Awareness – to assist individuals, a number of Sector Councils have developed career awareness programs or products on the occupations in their sectors.

Job Banks – a number of Sector Councils have established job banks to permit the matching of those seeking work with those seeking workers.

Labour Forecasting – Councils often supply the government with labour statistics, employment prospects over the next few years, and data regarding which communities in Canada need specific types of workers.

Occupational Certification – with certification, an employer knows the potential of the new employee, and consequently the pay at point of hire is more likely to reflect the individual's knowledge and skills. Sector Councils have developed quite a variety of certification strategies.

Occupational Standards – the work of the Sector Councils in occupational standards has put Canada on the cutting edge in terms of improving its training programs to meet industry requirements, and in many cases to meet international industry requirements.

Youth Initiatives – many of the Sector Councils have been active partners with Human Resources and Skills Development Canada in the creation and delivery of projects across Canada to help young people gain experience in the workplace, to obtain on-the-job training, or simply to have a greater awareness of career options.

ABORIGINAL HUMAN RESOURCE COUNCIL
708-2nd Avenue North • Saskatoon, SK • S7K 2E1
Tel: 306-956-5360 or 1-866-711-5091 • Fax: 306-956-5361
E-mail: contact.us@aboriginalhr.ca • Internet: www.aboriginalhr.ca
The Aboriginal Human Resource Council of Canada (AHRC) is a public-private partnership established in 1998 with the mission to increase Aboriginal people's participation in Canada labour markets. The Council's partnership model encourages a collaborative relationship with provinces, the private sector, organized labour, education and Aboriginal leadership. Its partnership framework brings together social, financial, human and knowledge capital and uses these resources to better connect supply and demand dimensions of the labour market. Through its partnership models the Council is achieving considerable success accelerating Aboriginal skills and learning as well as connecting employers with potential workers.

CANADIAN APPRENTICESHIP FORUM / FORUM CANADIEN SUR L'APPRENTISSAGE
116 Albert Street, Suite 812 • Ottawa, ON • K1P 5G3
Tel: 613-235-4004 • Fax: 613-235-7117
E-mail: info@caf-fca.org • Internet: www.caf-fca.org
The Canadian Apprenticeship Forum / Forum canadien sur l'apprentissage is a diverse, not-for-profit organization that brings together the key participants who make up the Canadian apprenticeship community. This dynamic partnership works within the Canadian labour market to promote apprenticeship as an effective training and education system that contributes to the development of a skilled labour force.

CANADIAN AQUACULTURE INDUSTRY ALLIANCE
116 Albert Street, Suite 705 • Ottawa, ON • K1P 5G3
Tel: 613-239-0612 • Fax: 613-239-0619
E-mail: ruth.salmon@aquaculture.ca • Internet: www.aquaculture.ca
The Canadian Aquaculture Industry Alliance (CAIA) is a national industry association, headquartered in Ottawa, that represents the interests of Canadian aquaculture operators, feed companies and suppliers, as well as provincial finfish and shellfish aquaculture associations. The Aquaculture Career and Training Directory is a comprehensive, electronically searchable directory of education-based career and training opportunities currently offered within post-secondary institutions in Canada, including aquaculture technology, research and development, business and business management, environmental and social sciences. This directory is intended to be used by those interested in pursuing or advancing a career in aquaculture operations and development, and by employers seeking program information pertaining to improving their own and their employee's skills and capabilities. Sample occupational areas within this Sector Council are: Aquaculture Technician, Veterinarian, Water Quality Technician, Fish Health Technician, and Broodstock Technician.

ENGINEERS CANADA
180 Elgin Street, Suite 1100 •Ottawa, ON •K2P 2K3
Tel: 613-232-2474 •Fax: 613-230-5759
Email: info@engineerscanada.ca •Internet: www.engineerscanada.ca
Engineers Canada is the national organization of the 12 provincial and territorial associations that regulate the practice of engineering in Canada and license the country's more than 160,000 professional engineers. Engineers Canada is the national body of professional engineers who enable the evolution of Canada's future by delivering national programs that ensure the highest standards of engineering education, professional qualifications and professional practice. Sample occupational areas within this Sector Council are: Civil Engineering, Electrical/Electronics Engineering, Mechanical Engineering, Manufacturing/ Industrial Engineering, and Chemical Engineering.

CANADIAN COUNCIL OF TECHNICIANS AND TECHNOLOGISTS
295 – 1101 Prince of Wales Drive • Ottawa, ON • K2C 3W7
Tel: 613-238-8123 • Fax: 613-238-8822
E-mail: ccttadm@cctt.ca • Internet: www.cctt.ca
Canada is a world leader in the application of new technology, and technicians and technologists are key elements in Canada's success. Keeping Canada at the top is the business of the Canadian Council of Technicians and Technologists (CCTT), and we do this by ensuring that our technicians and technologists maintain high standards of excellence. That is CCTT's commitment to Canada, and our significance to our members. Sample occupational areas within this Sector Council are: Construction, Information Technology, Chemical, Electronics, and Forestry.

CANADIAN EQUIPMENT INDUSTRY TRAINING COMMITTEE
4531 Southclark Place • Ottawa, ON • K1T 3V2
Tel: 613-822-8861 • Fax: 613-822-8862
E-mail: nleu@caed.org • Internet: www.caed.org/ceitc/index.html
The Careers in the Canadian Equipment Industry page for the Canadian Association of Equipment Distributors turns the spotlight on this growing industry and focuses on its place in today's labour market. It provides profiles on service technician jobs, parts management jobs, and customer service jobs in its "Getting a Great Start" section and provides profiles of equipment specialists currently working in the field in its "Real Time Experiences" section. Sample occupational areas within this Sector Council are: Apprentice Mechanic, Parts Person, Accounts Receivable, Reception, and Administrative Assistant.

CANADIAN PLASTICS SECTOR COUNCIL
200 Colonnade Road, Unit 1 • Ottawa, ON • K2E 7M1
Tel: 613-231-4470 • Fax: 613-231-3775
E-mail: info@cpsc-ccsp.ca • Internet: www.cpsc-ccsp.ca
The Canadian Plastics processing industry employs over 160,000 people across Canada in different types of plastics manufacturing plants and has outgrown all other forms of manufacturing by more than double for the past decade. The CPSC's Career Website is designed to provide individuals with information on the industry in general and the career opportunities it has to offer. This website has been designed to attract potential job entrants into the industry and consequently help to reduce the lack of skilled workers in the industry. Sample occupational areas within this Sector Council are: Processing Operator - Injection Moulding, Line Operator - Injection Moulding, Machine Setup - Injection Moulding, Blow Machine Operator - Blow Moulding, and Setup Operator - Blow Moulding, Plastics Fabricator, Mechanical Engineer.

CANADIAN STEEL TRADE AND EMPLOYMENT CONGRESS
234 Eglinton Avenue East, Suite 501 • Toronto, ON • M4P 1K7
Tel: 416-480-1797 • Fax: 416-480-2986
E-mail: general@cstec.ca • Internet: www.cstec.ca
The Canadian Steel Trade and Employment Congress (CSTEC) is a joint venture between the United Steel Workers of America (USWA) and Canada's steel producing companies. CSTEC provides a range of services to employers and employed and unemployed workers both inside and outside the steel industry. Under the New Entrant Services click on Career Information to access information on skilled trades, steel making production, academic and skill requirements, overview of the steel industry, workplace and education opportunities and current employment opportunities. CSTEC also provides training services that address the common training needs of the current workforce and entry-level services that assist in the recruitment and pre-employment training of new entrants. CSTEC's Action (Job Placement) Centres located in Toronto, Hamilton, Sault Ste. Marie and Quebec assist unemployed individuals with interviewing skills, training, job counselling and more.

CANADIAN TECHNOLOGY HUMAN RESOURCES BOARD

1071 Ambleside Drive, Suite 818 • Ottawa, ON • K2B 6V4
Tel: 613-862-9061 • Fax: 613-233-3812
E-mail: : info@cthrb.ca • Internet: www.cthrb.ca
The Canadian Technology Human Resources Board (CTHRB) represents industry, educational, and individual stakeholders in the Engineering Applied Science technology sector. Its mission will be considered a success when Canadian organizations competing globally have access to a unique competitive advantage. CTHRB believes that it is extremely important to continue to encourage young people, women, minority groups, workers in transition and newcomers to Canada, to consider careers in technology.

CANADIAN TOURISM HUMAN RESOURCE COUNCIL

151 Slater Street, Suite 608 • Ottawa, ON • K1P 5H3
Tel: 613-231-6949l Fax: 613-231-6853
E-mail: info@cthrc.ca • Internet: www.cthrc.ca
The Canadian Tourism Human Resource Council (CTHRC) is a national non-profit organization that promotes and enhances professionalism in the Canadian tourism industry. The Council's strength lies in its network of partners. The CTHRC brings together tourism businesses, labour unions, provincial, territorial and national associations, education/training providers and government to address the tourism industry's human resource needs. They have a career planning section on their website. Other resources include occupational standards, professional certification programs, and training, including online training (see emerit.ca for more information on these resources). Sample occupational areas within this Sector Council are: Food & Beverage Server, Front Desk Agent, Housekeeping Room Attendant, Cook, and Reservations Sales Agent, Food and Beverage Manager, Event Manager / Event Co-ordinator.

CULTURAL HUMAN RESOURCES COUNCIL

17 York Street, Suite 201 • Ottawa, ON • K1N 9J6
Tel: 613-562-1535 • Fax: 613-562-2982
E-mail: info@culturalhrc.ca • Internet: www.culturalhrc.ca
Are you interested in a career in the arts? Or trying to further your career in the arts? The Cultural Human Resources Council (CHRC) is a national arts service organization dedicated to strengthening Canada's Cultural workforce. The CHRC hosts Canada's premier online job board for artists and cultural workers, produces career development tools, publishes research, and manages youth internship programs. The Youth Internship Program (YIP), offered through CHRC in partnership with Human Resources Development Canada and the Department of Canadian Heritage, offers 6-12 month paid internships in exciting and diverse cultural organizations and disciplines. Our job board, www.cultureworks.ca, is an online recruitment tool for employers and job seekers in Canada's cultural sector that offers assistance to students, graduates and professionals wishing to pursue a career in the cultural sector.

FORUM FOR INTERNATIONAL TRADE TRAINING

116 Lisgar Street, Suite 300 • Ottawa, ON • K2P 0C2
Tel: 613-230-3553 or Toll Free: 1-800-561-FITT (3488) • Fax: 613-230-6808
E-mail: info@fitt.ca • Internet: www.fitt.ca
The Forum for International Trade Training (FITT), Canada's centre for international trade training and certification, is a national, not-for-profit organization that develops and delivers international trade training programs and services, establishes country-wide standards and certification, and generally ensures continuing professional development in the practice of international trade. FITT programs are delivered across Canada through community colleges, universities, private organizations and on-line. Links to help you make your online job search more efficient are included on the site. Internship resources and a two-part guide to careers in International Business Trade is also available on this page.

INSTALLATION, MAINTENANCE & REPAIR SECTOR COUNCIL AND TRADE ASSOCIATION

5800 Explorer Drive, Suite 200 • Mississauga, ON • L4W 5K9
Tel: 905-602-8877 or 1-866-602-8877 • Fax: 905-602-5686
E-mail: info@imrsectorcouncil.ca • Internet: www.imrsectorcouncil.ca
The Installation, Maintenance and Repair Sector Council (IMR) is led by dedicated champions from industry, education and the workforce who collectively address the human resources challenges in the consumer electronics and appliance installation, maintenance and repair service industry. Visit their website for more information. Sample occupational areas within this Sector Council are: Appliance Installation and Repair Technican, Customer Electronic Installation Maintenance, and Repair Service Technician.

MOTOR CARRIER PASSENGER COUNCIL OF CANADA

306 - 9555 Yonge Street • Richmond Hill, ON • L4C 9M5
Tel: 905-884-7782l Fax: 905-884-8335
E-mail: info@buscouncil.ca • Internet: www.buscouncil.ca
Learn about career choices in Canada's bus industry. The Motor Carrier Passenger Council of Canada (MCPCC) are a nationally recognized resource, working with the private sector, labour and government to strengthen the industries image, profitability, and vitality. We'd like you to think about putting you career in gear – and joining the 80,000 men and women in Canada who drive and maintain buses. Leading edge technology, including integrated electronics, voice and satellites, create a dynamic new environment. Sample occupational areas with this Sector Council are: Bus Operator, Mechanic, Customer Service, and Office/Clerical.

NATIONAL SEAFOOD SECTOR COUNCIL

130 Albert Street, Suite 910 • Ottawa, ON •K1P 5G4
Tel: 613-782-2391 • Fax: 613-782-2386
E-mail: info@nssc.ca • Internet: www.nssc.ca
The National Seafood Sector Council (NSSC) is a unique partnership, bringing together employers, employees, unions, associations, regulatory agencies and training centres to work toward one common goal: a strong and prosperous seafood processing industry created by a well trained and productive workforce. The NSSC is a non-profit, industry driven organization. Established in 1995, the NSSC works on behalf of the entire seafood processing industry to provide up-to-date training programs and information services.

PETROLEUM HUMAN RESOURCES COUNCIL OF CANADA

1538 - 25 Avenue North East • Calgary, AB • T2E 8Y3
Tel: (403) 537-1230 or Toll free: 1-866-537-1230 • Fax: 403-537-1232
E-mail: info@petrohrsc.ca • Internet: www.petrohrsc.ca
The Petroleum Human Resources Council of Canada (Petroleum HR Council) is a national, collaborative forum that addresses human resource issues within the upstream petroleum industry. The organization is supported by 11 oil and gas national and regional organizations, including one union, and represents the key sectors of the upstream petroleum industry in Canada: exploration, development, production, service industries, pipeline transmission, gas processing, and mining, extracting and upgrading heavy oil and bitumen. Sample occupational areas within this Sector Council are: Engineer, Geologist, Floorhand (Drilling), Seismic Worker, and Service Assistant (Coiled Tubing, Cementing, Fracturing). Visit their website for more important information.

INFORMATION AND COMMUNICATIONS TECHNOLOGY COUNCIL
116 Lisgar Street Suite 300 • Ottawa, ON • K2P 0C2
Tel: 613-237-8551 • Fax: 613-230-3490
E-mail: info@ictc-ctic.cal • Internet: www.ictc-ctic.ca
The Information and Communications Technology Council which was formerly known as the Software Human Resource Council, is a not-for-profit sector council. ICTC is a catalyst for change, pushing for innovations that will provide skills definitions, labour market intelligence, career awareness and professional development for the Canadian ICT industry, educators and governments. A new initiative by the Information and Communications Technology Council (ICTC) aims to improve the attraction of women to the Canadian ICT Industry. By seeking out products and business opportunities that assist in developing tomorrow's workforce can improve Canada's position as a leader in the global marketplace.

THE CANADIAN AVIATION MAINTENANCE COUNCIL
955 Green Valley Crescent, Suite 155 • Ottawa, ON • K2C 3V4
Tel: 613-727-8272 or Toll Free: 1-800-448-9715 • Fax: 613-727-7018
E-mail: cgalvis@camc.ca • Internet: www.camc.ca
The Canadian Aviation Maintenance Council (CAMC) provides a wealth of information on the aviation industry. Everything from types of aviation careers, high schools in Canada that offer the youth aviation technology program, and CAMC accredited training centres are provided on this site. Click on the Careers section link from their homepage to view all this information. Sample occupational areas within this Sector Council are: Aircraft Maintenance Technician, Aircraft Structures Technician and Structures Assembler, Avionics Technician / Electrical Electronic Assembler, Gas Turbine Technician, Aviation Stores Personnel, and Aircraft Interior Technician.

THE LOGISTICS INSTITUTE
160 John Street, Suite 200 • Toronto, ON • M5V 2E5
Tel: 416-363-3005 or Toll Free: 1-877-363-3005 • Fax: 416-363-5598
E-mail: loginfo@loginstitute.ca • Internet: www.loginstitute.ca
The particular focus of the Logistics Institute is on building the professional skills of Logistics practitioners in Canada and worldwide. The mandate of the Logistics Institute is to coordinate efforts among stakeholders in order to: Define Logistics career opportunities for the global economy; Sustain Logistics human resource development; Develop comprehensive training in Logistics; and Establish a logistics profession. The Logistics Institute is pleased to make life-long learning easier which, also provides open access to online training resources.

WOOD MANUFACTURING COUNCIL
130 Albert Street, Suite 1016 • Ottawa, ON • K1P 5G4
Tel: 613-567-5511 • Fax: 613-567-5411
E-mail: wmc@wmc-cfb.ca • Internet: www.wmc-cfb.ca
The Wood Manufacturing Council represents the Human Resource needs of Canada's advanced wood products manufacturing sector. This covers such products as wood windows and doors, wood kitchen cabinets, wood furniture, pre-fabricated wooden buildings, and other millwork products. Their mandate is to plan, develop and implement human resources strategies to support the sector and its workforce. This includes developing career information for job seekers at a variety of levels. Sample occupational areas within this Sector Council are: Cabinet & Furniture Manufacturer, Wood Machinist, Product Design & Development, Quality Control Manager, and Computer Draftsperson. The WMC is pleased to launch www.careersinwood.ca as its latest tool to provide awareness to Canadians seeking information on careers in the advanced wood processing sector.

INDEXES

Firms and Organizations Index

Recruiters Index

Industry and Professional Associations Index

Career Resources on the Internet Index

Trade Directories Index

Firms and Organizations

Recruiters Index

Industry and Professional Associations Index

Career Resources on the Internet

Trade Directories Index

Books by Sentor Media

The Canadian Summer Job Directory
4th Edition
ISBN 978-1-896324-33-3 $19.95

Get Wired, You're Hired! The Canadian
Internet Job Search Guide, 4th Edition
ISBN 978-1-896324-31-9 $29.95

The Canadian Hidden Job Market Directory
7th Edition
ISBN 978-1-896324-32-6 $29.95

Guide to Professional Programs in Canada
2nd Edition
ISBN 978-1-896324-35-7 $34.95

Hire Power
2nd Edition
ISBN 978-1-896324-38-8 $24.95

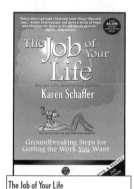

The Job of Your Life
2nd Edition
ISBN 978-1-896324-37-1 $23.95

Best Canadian Résumés
ISBN 978-1-896324-27-4 $28.95

Ten Ways to Straight A's
ISBN 978-1-896324-36-3 $28.95

Available online at:
www.CareerBookstore.ca

SENTOR MEDIA INC.

388 Richmond St. W., Suite 1120 Toronto, ON M5V 3P1
Tel: 416-971-5090 Fax: 416-971-5857 Email: orders@sentormedia.com